LITERACY

MAJOR THEMES IN EDUCATION
Other titles in this series

Exmouth

7 Day

University of Plymouth Library

Subject to status this item may be renewed
via your Voyager account

http://voyager.plymouth.ac.uk

Exeter tel: (01392) 475049
Exmouth tel: (01395) 255331
Plymouth tel: (01752) 232323

LITERACY

Major Themes in Education

Edited by David Wray

Volume I

Literacy: its Nature and its Teaching

RoutledgeFalmer
Taylor & Francis Group

LONDON AND NEW YORK

First published 2004
by RoutledgeFalmer
2 Park Square, Milton Park, Abingdon, Oxfordshire OX14 4RN

Simultaneously published in the USA and Canada
by RoutledgeFalmer
270 Madison Avenue, New York, NY 10016

RoutledgeFalmer is an imprint of the Taylor & Francis Group

Editorial Matter and Selection © 2004 David Wray; individual
owners retain copyright in their own material

Typeset in Times by Wearset Ltd, Boldon, Tyne and Wear
Printed and bound in Great Britain by MPG Books Ltd, Bodmin

British Library Cataloguing in Publication Data
A catalogue record for this book is available from the British Library

Library of Congress Cataloging in Publication Data
A catalog record for this book has been requested

ISBN 0-415-27708-6 (Set)
ISBN 0-415-27709-4 (Volume I)

Publisher's note
References within each chapter are as they appear in the original
complete work.

CONTENTS

CONTENTS

CONTENTS

CONTENTS

CONTENTS

VOLUME III   WRITING: PROCESSES AND TEACHING

CONTENTS

CONTENTS

VOLUME IV   NEW LITERACIES: THE IMPACT OF TECHNOLOGY

CONTENTS

CONTENTS

ACKNOWLEDGEMENTS

The publishers would like to thank the following for permission to reprint their material:

Wadsworth for permission to reprint K. Au, 'An expanded definition of literacy', in *Literacy Instruction in Multi-Cultural Settings*, Fort Worth, TX, 1993, pp. 20–34. © 1993. Reprinted with permission of Wadsworth, a division of Thomson Learning: www.Thomsonrights.com. Fax 800 730–2215.

Routledge for permission to reprint A. Webster, M. Beveridge and M. Reed, 'Rethinking the meaning of literacy', in *Managing the Literacy Curriculum*, London, 1996, pp. 5–32.

Routledge for permission to reprint C. Lankshear, 'Understanding literacy', in *Literacy, Schooling and Revolution*, Lewes: Falmer, 1987, pp. 37–77.

Routledge for permission to reprint Frances Christie, 'Learning the literacies of primary and secondary schooling', in Christie, F. and Mission, R. (eds), *Literacy and Schooling*, London, 1998, pp. 47–73.

The University of Chicago Press for permission to reprint Michael Pressley, Joan Rankin and Linda Yokoi, 'A survey of instructional practices of primary teachers nominated as effective in promoting literacy', in *Elementary School Journal* 4 (1996): 363–384.

Trentham Books for permission to reprint Jane Medwell, David Wray, Louise Poulson, and Richard Fox, 'The characteristics of effective teachers of literacy', in *Education 3 to 13* 27(1) (1999): 46–52.

Cambridge University Press for permission to reprint Shirley Brice Heath, 'What no bedtime story means: narrative skills at home and school', in *Language in Society* 11 (1982): 49–76. Copyright © Cambridge University Press.

Taylor & Francis for permission to reprint P. W. Hannon and P. Cuckle, 'Involving parents in the teaching of reading: a study of current school practice', in *Educational Research* 26(1) (1984): 7–13, http://www.tandf.co.uk.

ACKNOWLEDGEMENTS

American Psychological Association for permission to reprint Jenny Hewison and J. Tizard, 'Parental involvement and reading attainment', in *British Journal of Educational Psychology* 50 (1980): 209–215. Copyright © 1980 by the American Psychological Association. Reprinted with permission.

Taylor & Francis for permission to reprint Peter Hannon, 'Rhetoric and research in family literacy', *British Educational Research Journal* 26(1) (1999): 121–138, http://www.tandf.co.uk.

Blackwell Publishing Ltd for permission to reprint Jo Weinberger, 'A longitudinal study of children's early literacy experiences at home and later literacy development at home and school', in *Journal of Research in Reading* 19(1) (1996): 14–24.

The International Reading Association for permission to reprint Susan B. Neuman and Kathy Roskos, 'Literacy objects as cultural tools: effects on children's literacy behaviors in play', in *Reading Research Quarterly* 27 (1992): 203–225.

Elsevier for permission to reprint Elfrieda H. Hiebert and Jacqueline M. Papierz, 'The emergent literacy construct and kindergarten and readiness books of basal reading series', in *Early Childhood Research Quarterly* 5(3) (1990): 317–334.

Elsevier for permission to reprint Lesley Mandel Morrow, 'Preparing the classroom environment to promote literacy during play', in *Early Childhood Research Quarterly* 5 (1990): 537–554.

The International Reading Association for permission to reprint Susan B. Neuman and Kathleen Roskos 'Literacy knowledge in practice: contexts of participation for young writers and readers', *Reading Research Quarterly* 32 (1997): 10–32.

Barbara K. Gunn, Deborah C. Simmons and Edward J. Kameenui for permission to reprint Barbara K. Gunn, Deborah C. Simmons and Edward J. Kameenui, 'Emergent literacy: synthesis of the research', university of Oregon/NCITE, 1995, Source:http://idea.uoregon.edu/-ncite/documents/techrep/tech19.html.

Blackwell Publishing Ltd for permission to reprint Ros Fisher, Maureen Lewis and Bernie Davis, 'Progress and performance in National Literacy Strategy classrooms', in *Journal of Research in Reading* 23(3) (2000): 256–266.

National Center on Adult Literacy, Graduate School of Education/University of Pennylvania, Philadelphia, PA, USA for permission to reprint Larry Mikulecky, Peggy Albers and Michele Peers, 'Literacy transfer: a review of the literature', in NCAL Technical Report TR94–05, 1994.

Harvard Education Publishing Group for permission to reprint Bernado M. Ferdman, 'Literacy and cultural identity', in *Harvard Educational Review* 60(2) (1990): 181–204. Copyright © 1990 by the President and Fellows of Harvard College. All rights reserved.

Australian Literacy Educators' Association for permission to reprint Pam Gilbert, '(Sub)versions: using sexist language practices to explore critical literacy', in *The Australian Journal of Language and Literacy* 16(4) (1993): 323–331.

United Kingdom Reading Association for permission to reprint Jennifer O'Brien, 'Show mum you love her: taking a new look at junk mail', in *Reading* 28(1) (1994): 43–46.

Australian Literacy Educators' Association for permission to reprint Barbara Comber, 'Classroom explorations in critical literacy', in *The Australian Journal of Language and Literacy* 16(1) (1993): 73–83.

Disclaimer

Chronological table of reprinted chapters and articles

Date	Author	Chapter/article	Reference	Vol.	Chap.
1967	K. Goodman	Reading: a psycholinguistic guessing game	*Journal of the Reading Specialist* 6(4): 33–43	II	23
1970	John Downing	Children's concepts of language in learning to read	*Educational Research* 12: 106–112	II	28
1975	Donald H. Graves	An examination of the writing processes of seven year old children	*Research in the Teaching of English* 9: 227–241	III	42
1978	James Britton	The composing process and the functions of writing	Cooper, C. R. and Odell, L. (eds) *Research on Composing* Urbana, IL: NCTE, 13–28	III	43
1979	Brian Cambourne	How important is theory to the reading teacher?	*Australian Journal of Reading* 2(2): 78–90	II	24
1980	Jenny Hewison and J. Tizard	Parental involvement and reading attainment	*British Journal of Educational Psychology* 50: 209–215	I	9
1981	Linda Flower and John R. Hayes	A cognitive process theory of writing	*College Composition and Communication* (December) 32: 365–387	III	44
1982	Shirley Brice Heath	What no bedtime story means: narrative skills at home and school	*Language in Society* 11: 49–76	I	7
1982	J. Richard Gentry	An analysis of developmental spelling in *GNYS AT WRK*	*The Reading Teacher* 36(2): 192–200	III	54
1982	George Hillocks, Jr.	The interaction of instruction, teacher comment, and revision in teaching the composing process	*Research in the Teaching of English* 16(3): 261–278	III	45
1983	Sheridan Blau	Invisible writing: investigating cognitive processes in composition	*College Composition and Communication* 34(3): 297–312	III	46
1983	J. Emig	Non-magical thinking: presenting writing developmentally in schools	Goswami, D. and Butler, M. (eds) *The Web of Meaning: Essays on Writing, Teaching, Learning and Thinking* Upper Montclair, NJ: Boynton/Cook, 135–144	III	47

Date	Author	Chapter/article	Reference	Vol.	Chap.
1983	Ann Hume	Research on the composing process	Review of Educational Research 53(2): 201–216	III	50
1983	Shirley A. Wagoner	Comprehension monitoring: what it is and what we know about it	Reading Research Quarterly 18: 328–346	II	38
1984	P. W. Hannon and P. Cuckle	Involving parents in the teaching of reading: a study of current school practice	Educational Research 26(1): 7–13	I	8
1984	Annemarie Palincsar and Ann L. Brown	Reciprocal teaching of comprehension-fostering and comprehension-monitoring activities	Cognition and Instruction 1(2): 117–175	II	39
1986	Colette Daiute	Physical and cognitive factors in revising: insights from studies with computers	Research in the Teaching of English 20(2): 141–159	IV	84
1986	Keith E. Stanovich	Matthew effects in reading: some consequences of individual differences in the acquisition of literacy	Reading Research Quarterly 21(4): 360–406	II	29
1987	Jill Fitzgerald	Research on revision in writing	Review of Educational Research 57(4): 481–506	III	51
1987	C. Lankshear	Understanding literacy	Literacy, Schooling and Revolution Lewes: Falmer, 37–77	I	3
1987	P. David Pearson and Janice A. Dole	Explicit comprehension instruction: a review of research and a new conceptualization of instruction	The Elementary School Journal 88(2): 151–165	II	40
1987	Peter Smagorinsky	Graves revisited: a look at the methods and conclusions of the New Hampshire study	Written Communication 4(4): 331–342	III	55
1988	Judith A. Bowey and Rinu K. Patel	Metalinguistic ability and early reading achievement	Applied Psycholinguistics 9: 367–383	II	27

Date	Author	Chapter/article	Reference	Vol.	Chap.
1990	Lesley Mandel Morrow	Preparing the classroom environment to promote literacy during play	*Early Childhood Research Quarterly* 5: 537–554	I	14
1991	Marilyn Jager Adams	Why not phonics *and* whole language?	Ellis, W. (ed.) *All Language and the Creation of Literacy* Baltimore, MD: Orton Dyslexia Society, 40–53	II	31
1991	Myra Barrs	Genre theory: what's it all about?	*Language Matters* 1: 9–16	III	57
1991	Marilyn Cochran-Smith	Word processing and writing in elementary classrooms: a critical review of related literature	*Review of Education Research* 61(1): 107–155	IV	83
1991	Janice Dole, Gerald G. Duffy, Laura R. Roehler and P. David Pearson	Moving from the old to the new: research on reading comprehension instruction	*Review of Educational Research* 61(2): 239–264	II	41
1991	Tom Nicholson	Do children read words better in context or in lists? a classic study revisited	*Journal of Educational Psychology* 83(4): 444–450	II	25
1992	Yola Center, Kevin Wheldall and Louella Freeman	Evaluating the effectiveness of reading recovery: a critique	*Educational Psychology* 12(3–4): 263–274	II	32
1992	Susan B. Neuman and Kathy Roskos	Literacy objects as cultural tools: effects on children's literacy behaviors in play	*Reading Research Quarterly* 27: 203–225	I	12
1993	K. Au	An expanded definition of literacy	*Literacy Instruction in Multi-Cultural Settings* Fort Worth, TX: Harcourt, Brace, Jovanovitch, 20–34	I	1

Year	Author	Title	Source	Vol	Page
1993	Robert L. Bangert-Drowns	The word processor as an instructional tool: a meta-analysis of word processing in writing instruction	*Review of Educational Research* 63(1): 69–93	IV	82
1993	Daniel Chandler	Writing strategies and writers' tools	*English Today* 9(2): 32–38	III	48
1993	Barbara Comber	Classroom explorations in critical literacy	*The Australian Journal of Language and Literacy* 16(1): 73–83	I	22
1993	Pam Gilbert	(Sub)versions: using sexist language practices to explore critical literacy	*The Australian Journal of Language and Literacy* 16(4): 323–331	I	20
1993	James R. Martin	Genre and literacy: modeling context in educational linguistics	*Annual Review of Applied Linguistics* 13: 141–172	III	58
1993	David Wray	What do children think about writing?	*Educational Review* 45(1): 67–77	III	49
1994	Lynne Anderson-Inman, Mark A. Horney, Der-Thanq Chen and Larry Lewin	Hypertext literacy: observations from the ElectroText project	*Language Arts* 71: 279–287	IV	70
1994	Marilyn L. Chapman	The emergence of genres: some findings from an examination of first-grade writing	*Written Communication* 11(3): 348–380	III	59
1994	Steve Graham and Karen Harris	The effects of whole language on children's writing: a review of the literature	*Educational Psychologist* 29(4): 187–192	III	62
1994	Gunther Kress and Peter Knapp	Genre in a social theory of language	*English in Education* 26(2): 4–15	III	60
1994	Jane Medwell	Contexts for writing: the social construction of classroom writing	Wray, D. and Medwell, J. (eds) *Teaching Primary English: The State of the Art* London: Routledge	III	63
1994	Larry Mikulecky, Peggy Albers and Michele Peers	Literacy transfer: a review of the literature	National Center on Adult Literacy, University of Pennsylvania, Technical Report TR94-05 http://www.literacyonline.org/products/ncal/pdf/TR9405.pdf	I	18

Year	Author	Title	Publication	Section	No.
1996	David J. Ayersman	Reviewing the research on hypermedia-based learning	Journal of Research on Computing in Education 28(4): 500–525	IV	71
1996	Johan Davidson, Jonathan Elcock and Peter Noyes	A preliminary study of the effect of computer-assisted practice on reading attainment	Journal of Research in Reading 19(2): 102–110	IV	79
1996	Marilyn E. Greenlee-Moore and Lawrence L. Smith	Interactive computer software: the effects on young children's reading achievement	Reading Psychology 17: 43-64	IV	81
1996	Jane Medwell	Talking books and reading	Reading 30(1): 41–49	IV	75
1996	Michael Pressley, Joan Rankin and Linda Yokoi	A survey of instructional practices of primary teachers nominated as effective in promoting literacy	Elementary School Journal 96(4): 363–384	I	5
1996	A. Webster, M. Beveridge and M. Reed	Rethinking the meaning of literacy	Managing the Literacy Curriculum London: Routledge, 5–32	I	2
1996	Jo Weinberger	A longitudinal study of children's early literacy experiences at home and later literacy development at home and school	Journal of Research in Reading 19(1): 14–24	I	11
1997	Bertram C. Bruce	Literacy technologies: what stance should we take?	Journal of Literacy Research 29(2): 289–309	IV	67
1997	Charles K. Kinzer and Donald J. Leu, Jr.	The challenge of change: exploring literacy and learning in electronic environments	Language Arts 74: 126–136	IV	68
1997	Susan B. Neuman and Kathleen Roskos	Literacy knowledge in practice: contexts of participation for young writers and readers	Reading Research Quarterly 32(1): 10–32	I	15
1997	Keith J. Topping	Family electronic literacy: home–school links through computers	Reading 31(2): 12–21	IV	66
1997	David Wray and Maureen Lewis	Teaching factual writing: purpose and structure	The Australian Journal of Language and Literacy 20(2): 43–52	III	65

Date	Author	Chapter/article	Reference	Vol.	Chap.
1998	Frances Christie	Learning the literacies of primary and secondary schooling	Christie, F. and Misson, R. (eds) *Literacy and Schooling* London: Routledge, 47–73	I	4
1998	Barbara R. Foorman, David J. Francis, Jack M. Fletcher, Christopher Schatschneider and Paras Mehta	The role of instruction in learning to read: preventing reading failure in at-risk children	*Journal of Educational Psychology* 90(1): 37–55	II	35
1999	Maureen Carroll	Dancing on the keyboard: a theoretical basis for the use of computers in the classroom	*Reading Online* (November). Available: http://www.readingonline.org/articles/art_index.asp?HREF=carroll/index.html	IV	78
1999	Karin L. Dahl, Patricia L. Scharer, Lora L. Lawson and Patricia R. Grogan	Phonics instruction and student achievement in whole language first-grade classrooms	*Reading Research Quarterly* 34(3): 312–341	II	36
1999	Peter Hannon	Rhetoric and research in family literacy	*British Educational Research Journal* 26(1): 121–138	I	10
1999	Donald J. Leu, Jr., Rachel A. Karchmer and Deborah Diadiun Leu	The Miss Rumphius Effect: envisionings for literacy and learning that transform the Internet	*The Reading Teacher*: 636–642	IV	73
1999	Jane Medwell, David Wray, Louise Poulson and Richard Fox	The characteristics of effective teachers of literacy	*Education 3 to 13* 27(1): 46–52	I	6

2000	Ros Fisher, Maureen Lewis and Bernie Davis	Progress and performance in National Literacy Strategy classrooms	*Journal of Research in Reading* 23(3): 256–266	I	17
2000	Linda D. Labbo and Melanie R. Kuhn	Weaving chains of affect and cognition: a young child's understanding of CD-ROM talking books	*Journal of Literacy Research* 32(2): 187–210	IV	74
2000	Donald J. Leu, Jr.	Our children's future: changing the focus of literacy and literacy instruction	*The Reading Teacher* (February): 424–429	IV	72
2000	Jennifer Rennie	Teaching reading: oral reading practices as a pedagogical tool in the primary school	*The Australian Journal of Language and Literacy* 23(3): 197–211	II	37
2001	Melanie Kuhn	Taking computers out of the corner: making technology work in the classroom	*Reading Online* 4(9). Available: http://www.readingonline.org/electronic /elec_index.asp?HREF=/electronic/kuhn/index.html	IV	77

INTRODUCTION TO VOLUME I
Literacy: its nature and its teaching

Debates in literacy

The chapters in these volumes have been chosen to try to exemplify some of the major debates in the area of literacy, its development and teaching. Many of these chapters have themselves been seminal in changing general perceptions of aspects of literacy and its teaching. Subsequent volumes cover some very specific issues, such as the teaching of reading, and the development of ability in writing. In the present volume, the focus is on literacy in general, and the controversies that have emerged in its study.

This volume is structured around six, central 'major themes' in thinking about literacy and its teaching.

Theme 1: defining literacy

Perhaps unsurprisingly, given its obvious complexity, there has been considerable debate about the very nature of literacy. Such debate is not merely semantic: how one defines literacy influences and determines how one teaches it.

A common-sense definition of literacy may simply be that it consists of activities involving print. The emphasis here is on the physical actions associated with literate behaviour. Of course, literacy does involve some physical actions such as the use of one's eyes and hands, but this is a comparatively minor aspect of the process. The processes which take place inside the head are clearly much more crucial.

In our everyday use of language, we commonly use the term 'literate' in similar ways to 'educated' or 'cultured'. We might say things such as 'These children come from highly literate home backgrounds', or 'This man is extremely literate. He seems to have read everything.' The term here means more than simply reading and writing, but has implications of some kind of quality.

This usage stems from the historical development of literacy. We are so accustomed nowadays to literacy being a more or less universal phenomenon that it is difficult to appreciate that, for hundreds of years, it was not. Before the invention of the printing press, literacy was very much the preserve of an elite. Reading and writing were not skills possessed by the majority of the population, but were concentrated in certain groups. Religious groups used them to preserve and embellish sacred works. Other written materials, because they were painstaking to produce, were scarce and expensive and therefore the preserve of those with sufficient resources.

The effect of the introduction of printing was to make the elitist view of literacy increasingly untenable. The more people had reading and writing available to them, the more they came to involve themselves in it, and in the end rely upon it. The spread of literacy made for a more complex society which, in turn, demanded greater mastery of literacy. Universal literacy became essential for the effective functioning of society.

One of the chief motivating forces behind universal education was the need for literate workers. The 'three Rs' were given the central position in education that they have occupied ever since. In more recent times the degree of literacy in a country has come to be a measure of the civilisation of that country. Revolutions in countries such as Russia, China and Cuba have had the spread of literacy as one of their chief aims. Literacy is no longer elitist but universal. Modern society needs people with sufficient command of literacy to act as good and useful citizens.

The idea that a person needs to be literate in order to be a good citizen is subject to the very powerful criticism that it sees literacy as an essentially passive thing. If individuals are thought of as existing to serve society's needs and to fit in with its demands, literacy can be seen as one device for controlling them. The mechanisms of social control in modern society depend upon literacy. Propaganda, rules, regulations, publicity of various forms all use print and depend upon the population's ability to decipher that print.

Literacy, however, can be defined as involving much more than this passive approach. One definition of literacy claims that it involves having mastery over the process by which culturally significant information is coded. If this is accepted, it implies that the literate person, far from being controlled by the manifestations of literacy, is, in fact, in control of them. This involves having some autonomy in the process of using literacy, and having the ability to make choices. Propaganda and publicity rely for their effect upon recipients' lack of autonomy, and their sometimes overpowering influence upon the choices made.

So far, we have discussed the abilities which are involved in literacy, but have said little about what might be termed the affective side of literacy. This is certainly an issue for debate. Should we apply the term 'literate' to people who can do all the things associated with literacy, but decide they do not wish to? It has long been argued that the term 'educated' implies not just a mastery of knowledge and skills but also the acceptance of a set of values, these values implying a belief that being educated is a worthwhile thing to be. Applying the same argument to literacy, it might be seen to imply a belief in the value of being literate. It would be difficult to conceive of anyone who valued literacy yet did not choose to use it.

The issue is of greater importance than a mere debating point. It is very common indeed to find products of our educational system who are quite able to use literacy when they need to, but who do not choose to very often. Many children are reluctant readers for whom reading holds no interest whatsoever, and who will scarcely ever voluntarily read a book, especially a work of fiction. Most teachers will recognise children like this in their own classes, and it would be an unusual teacher who did not feel some sense of having failed with these children.

Theme 2: teacher effectiveness in literacy teaching

One major factor in raising standards must be the quality of the teaching of literacy which children experience, particularly during the primary phase of schooling. High-quality literacy teaching demands high-quality literacy teachers and any education system must attempt to maximise the expertise of teachers in teaching literacy. In order to direct improvements in the selection, training and professional development of teachers of literacy most profitably, a great deal can be learned from studies of those teachers identified as effective in the teaching of literacy. Such thinking has led to major research projects in both the United Kingdom and the USA and articles describing these are included here.

Theme 3: family literacy

It was surprisingly recently that deliberate attention began to be paid to the positive role that parents might play in the development of their children's literacy. Studies have explored the ways in which involving parents can enhance the development of children's literacy, particularly reading, but a growing trend in thinking in this area has been to explore and target the development of parents' own literacy. Literate parents produce literate children, the argument goes, so improving parental literacy will have the effect of improving that of their children. This contention has, however, itself been exposed as rather simplistic by Peter Hannon, one of the most significant UK researchers in this area.

Theme 4: emergent literacy

The late 1980s saw the beginning of a major refocusing on the nature and development of literacy. This came about through a number of studies of the literacy of very young children. The dominant view previously had been that mastery of literacy was bound up with physical and mental maturation and that before a certain maturation level it was actually not possible to teach children to read and write in any meaningful way. 'Readiness' had to be awaited, and prior to this being reached, children should only be taught 'pre-reading' or 'pre-writing' skills.

This view was made untenable by several studies of very young children engaged in obviously literate activities well before the age at which they were supposed to achieve readiness. A new, emergent literacy perspective became widely accepted, which held that young children, being immersed from birth in heavily literate environments, very quickly began to try to make sense of these environments, which in turn involved responding to and using the print all around them.

As this new concept has matured it has begun to stimulate studies of the ways in which teachers can deliberately use literate environments to promote emergent literacy in children. Teachers are certainly no longer advised to simply wait until 'readiness' appears, but instead actively to encourage play with literacy from a very early age.

Theme 5: teaching literacy

The teaching of literacy, naturally, accounts for more research studies than any other aspect of education. Most of the issues connected with this are covered in other, more specific, volumes. One key issue which is raised here, however, is that of transfer of learning. As literacy is so basic a skill, it has, naturally, usually been taught in specific lessons and with specific focal points. The United Kingdom National Literacy Strategy is only the most recent attempt to systematise this. Literacy, however, is of much wider importance than as a set of discrete skills: it is also the key medium for learning in virtually every area of educational endeavour. There has often been an assumption that learners only needed to be taught to read and write, and they would themselves then be able to apply these skills in a range of wider learning contexts. Research into the difficulties involved in transferring learning has consistently suggested that this assumption is false. Transfer of literacy skills to learning in other areas cannot be assumed – it must, therefore, be taught.

Theme 6: critical literacy

The newest 'kid on the block' in terms of ideas in literacy is that of critical literacy. Ideas about literacy as a mechanism of social control have been developed, largely by Australian researchers and theorists, into a more general approach to teaching literacy as a tool for having influence upon the world. Critical literacy means being alert to the ways in which texts position readers, and being able to combat this positioning if it is appropriate. The development of pedagogies to further critical approaches to texts is probably the next major task for literacy researchers and teachers during the next few years.

1

AN EXPANDED DEFINITION OF LITERACY

K. Au

Source: *Literacy Instruction in Multi-Cultural Settings* (1993) Fort Worth, TX: Harcourt, Brace, Jovanovitch, 20–34

A definition of literacy

> Literacy is defined as: The ability and the willingness to use reading and writing to construct meaning from printed text, in ways which meet the requirements of a particular social context.

Consider the various parts of this definition and their relationship to instruction in multicultural settings.

Willingness to use literacy

First, the definition addresses one's willingness, as well as one's ability, to use literacy. This feature is important, because students of diverse backgrounds may have the ability to use literacy but be unwilling to do so. This situation is illustrated in the following example. A teacher asks her third grade students to complete a textbook exercise that requires them to write a friendly letter. On this exercise, students show little ability to compose letters. A few days later, the teacher announces that she has arranged for everyone in the class to have a pen pal. Now, with a real audience for their writing, the students show a great deal of letter-writing ability. The teacher sees that students have a sense of the information their pen pals will find interesting, and that they know how to write a greeting and a closing for their letters.

As a comparison of these two letter-writing activities reveals, students' literacy ability might appear very different depending on the nature of the literacy activity. The textbook exercise shows the old familiar pattern of teaching literacy as a set of skills in isolation, apart from useful communication. Having students write to pen pals is an example of a new, more beneficial pattern based on teaching literacy in a meaningful context, with an authentic purpose for communication. While instruction centered on meaningful, rewarding activities is beneficial to all students, it may be critical to the success of students of diverse backgrounds. The reasons for this situation are addressed in work by D'Amato (1988), to be discussed in chapters 3 and 7.

Much depends on the teacher's ability to provide opportunities for literacy learning that students find meaningful and interesting. Students' willingness is an important factor in their demonstrating existing literacy skills and learning new ones. Literacy is not just a matter of skill or cognitive strategies, it is also a matter of will or feelings and emotions (Winograd and Paris, 1988).

Reading and writing

Second, the definition of literacy mentions both reading and writing. You are probably familiar with the idea that literacy involves both reading and writing, although traditionally reading has received much more attention in the elementary school. Reading and writing are both processes of composing meaning from text (Pearson and Tierney, 1984). In the case of reading, the text is already present, while in the case of writing, the text must be created.

One of the implications for literacy instruction is that teachers will want to give an equal emphasis to reading and writing, and to look at ways that instruction of one can strengthen learning of the other. For example, if students read biographies, they might be inspired to write biographies of their own.

Although not mentioned in our definition, speaking and listening, the other language arts, also have a crucial role in students' literacy development. Students may read aloud or listen to someone else read aloud. Or they may discuss their ideas about the same text, whether a newspaper editorial or a new novel. When students write, they may meet with the teacher or a peer to talk about their drafts and to get ideas for revision.

The ability to read and write well in standard American English is certainly a goal for all students. However, teachers should be aware of allowing students of diverse backgrounds to use strengths in their home languages as the basis for becoming proficient in reading and writing in English. For example, as shown in chapters 8 and 9, students might read a standard English text but discuss their ideas in their home languages, such as Hawaiian Creole English or Spanish. During the discussion the teacher models the use of standard English to express the same ideas and encourages students to use these new terms and structures.

8

Constructing meaning

Third, in our definition of literacy, reading and writing are used to construct meaning. This view is consistent with research which suggests that meaning does not reside in the text, but in the interaction among the reader, the text, and the social context (Wixson, Peters, Weber, and Roeber, 1987). A text may be compared to a blueprint, and the reader's job is to interpret and fill in the gaps in order to create meaning (Collins, Brown, and Larkin, 1980). Similarly, with writing, the writer's job is to create a text. Viewing reading and writing as constructive, creative processes takes us away from a mechanistic, skill-by-skill approach to literacy instruction.

Viewing reading and writing as constructive processes also reminds us of the importance of the background knowledge that students bring to the task. Readers' background knowledge strongly influences their interpretation of a text (Anderson and Pearson, 1984). In multicultural classrooms, teachers may find that students arrive at what appear to be unusual interpretations of a particular text. These varying interpretations may result, not from careless reading, but from differences in the background knowledge or cultural schemata students bring to the reading task.

The influence of cultural schemata on text interpretation is illustrated in a study conducted by Steffensen, Joag-dev, and Anderson (1979). The subjects were adults residing in a university community; half were from the United States, while half were from India. The subjects read two letters, one describing a wedding in the United States and one a wedding in India. Subjects recalled more information from the letter describing an event in their own country, and were able to make more culturally appropriate inferences about that text. When it came to the letter describing an event in another country, subjects made more interpretations that a native of that country would regard as inappropriate.

For example, the letter about the Indian wedding described the two events for guests that followed the wedding. Indian subjects were aware of the two events, a feast and a reception, while American subjects collapsed the two into a single event. The letter about the American wedding stated that the bride was going to wear her grandmother's wedding dress. American subjects recognized the connection to family tradition shown by the wearing of an heirloom dress. In contrast, one Indian subject described the gown as "too old and out of fashion," because in Indian weddings, the bride's wearing of a fashionable new sari is an indication of the financial status of her family. Clearly, American and Indian subjects interpreted the letters in terms of different cultural schemata or frameworks of knowledge.

The effects of different cultural schemata upon reading comprehension are also shown in a study conducted by Reynolds, Taylor, Steffensen,

9

Shirey, and Anderson (1982). They asked eighth grade students to read a letter that included the following passage:

> Classes went at their usual slow pace through the morning, so at noon I was really ready for lunch. I got in line behind Bubba. As usual the line was moving pretty slow and we were all getting pretty restless. For a little action Bubba turned around and said, "Hey Sam! What you doin' man? You so ugly that when the doctor delivered you he slapped your face!" Everyone laughed, but they laughed even harder when I shot back, "Oh yeah? Well, you so ugly the doctor turned around and slapped your momma!" It got even wilder when Bubba said, 'Well man, at least my daddy ain't no girlscout!" We really go into it then. After a while more people got involved – 4, 5, then 6. It was a riot! People helping out anyone who seemed to be getting the worst of the deal. All of sudden Mr. Reynolds the gym teacher came over to try to quiet things down.
>
> (p. 358)

What do you think the passage describes? From the perspective of most readers from mainstream backgrounds, the passage appears to be about a fight or physical aggression in a school cafeteria. That is the way the passage was interpreted by the European American students in the study. However, the African American students in the study recognized that the passage described an instance of **sounding**, a form of ritual insult and verbal play practiced mainly by teenage boys in many African American communities.

These studies suggest that teachers need to encourage students to explain their interpretations of text so that the reasons behind their interpretations become evident. In some cases, the cultural schemata of students from diverse backgrounds may give them insights about a text that the teacher and other students do not have.

Printed text

Fourth, our definition of literacy ties literacy to a **printed text** (Snow, 1983), which distinguishes the way we are using the word *literacy* from the way it is often used as a synonym for knowledge, as in "cultural literacy" or "computer literacy." Literacy in our definition refers to a person's ability to work with printed text, that is, to read and write. However, there are times when a person is not reading or writing text but seems to be using a form of literacy. Think about a situation in which students are discussing a story read aloud by the teacher. Students have not done any of the reading themselves, but they are using their ability to interpret a text.

10

Is this literacy? Or consider a situation in which two students are working together to compose a story. One of the students is coming up with new ideas, while the other is writing the words down on paper. Is the student who is generating the ideas showing literacy?

We would suggest that these situations both involve literacy, even though students are not reading the text themselves, and one of the students is not putting words down on paper. The teacher's reading aloud of literature and collaborative writing are both excellent occasions for literacy learning. However, students also need to be involved in reading on their own and writing on their own. This is important if they are to develop the skills of fluent, independent reading, and of fluent, independent writing.

At the same time, teachers should be aware that school literacy activities, which usually emphasize individual performance, differ significantly from literacy activities in the community and workplace. In settings outside of school, literacy is often carried out in a collaborative manner. For example, Fingeret (1983, cited in Guthrie and Greaney [1990]) shows that neighborhood literacy may involve individuals in the joint reading of income tax forms, bank statements, bills, and other materials. It is likely that children also collaborate to use literacy in settings outside of school, although there is little research on this topic.

Social context

Finally, our definition of literacy states that reading and writing are used in ways appropriate to the requirements of a particular **social context**. A social context is any of the situations someone may experience in settings such as the school, home, neighborhood, workplace, shopping mall, or elsewhere, whether alone or with other people. When someone reads or writes, those acts of literacy are taking place in some social context. The reading of a newspaper at home, while surrounded by family members, is an example of literacy taking place in a particular social context. Taking notes at the library on information needed for a term paper is another example of literacy in a particular social context. Still another example is seen when two first graders read a book together in the classroom library corner.

The idea of social context is especially important when it comes to the literacy instruction of students of diverse backgrounds. The social contexts of the home and community often prepare students of diverse backgrounds to learn in ways quite different from those expected by the school, as explained in chapters 6 and 7. Also, as discussed later in this chapter, students of diverse backgrounds often experience literacy in social contexts vastly different from those typically found in schools. Culturally responsive instruction, as defined in chapter 1, involves changing the social context of instruction so that lessons can be more effective for students of diverse backgrounds. The teacher's goal is to enable students of diverse backgrounds to use literacy successfully in mainstream social contexts, as well as in the contexts of their homes and communities.

Meeting requirements

What does it mean for literacy to **meet the requirements** of a particular social context? Many social contexts in a society such as the United States call for the use of literacy. Literacy is required to read street signs, to look up phone numbers in the telephone directory, and to complete the application for a driver's license. To accomplish each of these tasks successfully, the individual must possess certain knowledge and skills or be prepared to seek help from others.

To read most newspaper articles easily, one must be able to comprehend text written at a tenth- to eleventh-grade level (Wheat, Lindberg, and Naumann, 1977). Taking notes requires the ability to identify relevant points and write them down in just a few words. To read a book together, first graders must know how to handle books (hold them right side up, turn pages), to track print, and to appreciate illustrations.

The requirements for literacy may vary even when the printed text remains constant. For example, I may read a novel for my own enjoyment, without reflecting much about it. But if the same novel were assigned reading for an English course, I would probably read it in a different manner. I might link what I am reading to points discussed in class, compare and contrast the novel with others read as part of the same course, and jot down questions that come to mind.

There is not just one way to read or just one way to write. The literate person is one who can read or write in ways that meet the requirements of the various social contexts in his or her worlds. For example, a parent reading a storybook to a child will read aloud with expression, saying every word. At the office, the same adult might scan a memo quickly and silently, perhaps just to find out about the time and location of a meeting.

We may judge different forms of reading and writing to be appropriate or inappropriate, on the basis of the requirements of the social context. Our expectations and sense of what is appropriate may even cause us to overlook certain types of literacy entirely. In a study of an elementary school in an African American neighborhood in Philadelphia, Gilmore (1983) discovered that students used literacy in certain ways that teachers did not acknowledge. For example, students often wrote notes to one another, but teachers did not see the composing of these notes as writing. Similarly, teachers did not recognize the spelling and decoding skills girls showed when they participated in "doin' steps," a distinctive type of street rhyme. Gilmore concludes that, because only officially sanctioned activities count as literacy in school, teachers are often unaware of the full range of literacy skills students of diverse backgrounds may possess. Gilmore's research highlights the role that power relationships between teachers and students, reflecting those in the larger society, may play in endorsing some forms of literacy while dismissing others.

As Gilmore suggests, even within the school itself there may be different literacies associated with the different worlds of teachers and students. Discussing this idea in a more general way, Erickson (1984) writes that

> ... the notion of literacy, as knowledge and skill taught and learned in school, is not separable from the concrete circumstances of its uses inside and outside school, nor is it easily separable from the situation of its acquisition in the school as a social form and as a way of life. The school can be seen as an arena of political negotiation that embodies individual and group interests and ideologies. It is reasonable to expect that various kinds of literacies might represent a variety of interests and be embedded in a variety of belief systems.
>
> (p. 525)

Teachers need to be aware that literacy may take many forms. While teachers will want to acquaint all students with mainstream forms of literacy, they will want to be aware that other forms of literacy may also be significant in the lives of students of diverse backgrounds.

Community differences in literacy

Teachers working in multicultural setting will find it especially important to understand how literacy may vary depending on the social contexts of students' homes and communities. The manner in which literacy may vary from community to community is illustrated in research conducted by Shirley Brice Heath (1983). She describes the nature of literacy in two communities, Trackton and Roadville, only a few miles from one another in the Piedmont Carolinas. Both are working-class communities. Trackton is an African American community. It was once a farming area but residents now work in the textile mills. Roadville is a European American community where families have worked in the textile mills for four generations. As Heath shows, each community has its own literate traditions.

Literacy in Trackton

Trackton homes often contain newspapers, advertisements, church materials, homework, and school notices. Besides the Bible there are likely to be no books except those from the school or church. Trackton parents do not buy either special toys or books for their children. They do not create reading and writing tasks for their children or consciously demonstrate reading and writing for them. Yet children develop literacy skills in their encounters with the environment. They learn to identify labels on soups, cereals, and other items and to read price tags. Preschoolers have a sense of the print in newspapers and know, for example, that the print in a headline at the top of the page is bigger than the print in the story beneath it.

Literacy events in Trackton tend to involve a process of social negotiation and to be public and group-oriented. Talk is an integral part of literacy events. Authority does not reside in the printed text but in the meanings that are negotiated as the text is discussed in terms of the group's experiences. One example involes the reading of the evening newspaper. Obituaries are read and discussed in terms of possible connections to the deceased, his or her relatives, place of birth, church, or school. There is active discussion about the individual and those who are likely to have known him or her.

Another example involves circulars or letters informing people of recreational, medical, educational, and other services that have become available. One day Lillie Mae received a letter about a day-care program and decided she wanted to enroll her two-year old son. Lillie Mae initiated a discussion by standing on her front porch and reading aloud the first paragraph of the letter. Neighbors on their porches and in their yards joined in the conversation, which lasted for almost an hour. They discussed specific points, such as how Lillie Mae might obtain a copy of her son's birth certificate, and shared their knowledge about day-care programs. Lillie Mae drew relationships between the text and the experiences shared by the group and came to a final synthesis of meaning, which she checked with some members of the group.

In Trackton the generally accepted procedure is for reading materials to be interpreted as part of a group process, rather than individually. Heath notes:

> In general, reading alone, unless one is old and very religious, marks an individual as someone who cannot make it socially.
>
> (p. 191)

Writing follows similar patterns. Women write down phone numbers and addresses, appointments, and the dates of school holidays; some write notes to the school and to local merchants; and a few write letters to relatives. Men appear to do less writing, except perhaps in connection with tax preparation and church activities. The preparation of written materials such as church bulletins and schedules is negotiated during meetings and no individual takes sole responsibility for any writing tasks. In short, community literacy activities in Trackton tend to be public, social events in which members of the group work together to synthesize information from the text with their collective experiences.

14

Literacy in Roadville

Different patterns are seen in Roadville. Homes have an abundance of reading materials, including magazines, newspapers, advertisements, church circulars, and children's books. Parents read books to their children at bedtime, and children are allowed to participate actively in this event, for example by making the sounds of the animals or by responding to questions such as "What is it?" and "Who is it?" This pattern shifts as children reach the age of three or so, when adults begin to encourage them just to sit quietly and listen. As children near the age for entering kindergarten, parents give them workbooks and assist them in writing their names, coloring within the lines, matching shapes and letters, and so on. Parents convey to children that these are things they need to know before they go to school.

In Sunday school as well as at home, children are taught to listen passively and respond to questions with the right answers. Answers to questions that come from books are assumed to have just one correct answer, because authority and meaning are believed to reside in the written word, not in the individual's experiences and interpretation.

Reading is much talked about in Roadville, but few people do much reading or take action based upon the reading they have done. For example, Jay Turner praises reading and subscribes to three magazines, but he spends his evenings watching television. Women clip recipes and ideas for home decorating that they save with the intention of reading over "someday." The use of patterns for dressmaking is the one area in which women rely upon and follow written instructions.

Women write letters to family members to keep in touch and share news about friends and relatives. Because those exchanging letters know each other so well, letters take the form of "conversations written down." (p. 213) Women also send greeting cards and thank-you notes, and children are taught to write thank-you notes. When greeting cards, notes, and letters are received, they are shared orally, especially among women and children. For example, a mother may read a letter aloud to her children, or a child may be informed that he or she has received a birthday card in the mail. Roadville residents also write notes, for example, to explain a child's absence from school, to remind children of their chores, or to outline the plan for a church meeting. Men write checks and make notes for preparing income tax forms, but they write lists and notes much less frequently than women.

Heath's research in Trackton and Roadville shows how literacy is carried out differently in different communities. There are fewer reading

Each community has its own literate traditions.

materials in Trackton but a more collaborative, interpretive approach to literacy. Reading has a higher value in Roadville, in terms of people's statements but not necessarily their actions. Parents in Trackton and Roadville have different beliefs about how their children will learn to read and write. However, as Heath discovered, neither community's literacy concepts and practices matches well with the concepts and practices of school literacy. This issue is pursued in chapter 5, which discusses Heath's work further.

The point is that Heath's research shows how literacy in the home and community is very much a part of people's culture. Different cultures or subcultures, such as those of Trackton and Roadville, incorporate different beliefs about literacy and have different customary uses for literacy.

Practical implications

Teachers need to be aware that when students from diverse backgrounds participate in school literacy activities, they are in essence being socialized into the literacy practices of a different culture, the culture of the school. Furthermore, the culture of the school tends to be primarily a reflection of mainstream culture. As shown in chapter 1, in classrooms with students of diverse backgrounds, there are many possibilities for mismatches between the culture of the school and the culture of the home. In school literacy instruction we should seek to develop students' ability to read and write through approaches that do not threaten their cultural identity or violate their cultural values.

Ferdman (1991) writes:

> In the context of literacy education, the issue has to do with what is experienced by the student as "owned" and what is experienced as "not owned" by his or her group. To which texts and to which writing tasks does the student engage in a relation of "us" or "ours" and to which as "they" or "theirs"?
>
> (pp. 107–8)

On the one hand, when students perceive reading and writing tasks and materials to reaffirm their cultural identity, they are likely to become more deeply involved and to construct their own personal meanings. On the other hand, when students feel that school literacy tasks and materials deny or devalue their cultural identity, they are likely to show indifference or resistance.

Redefining school literacy

As part of putting new patterns of literacy instruction in place in schools, we need to consider how school literacy may be redefined to affirm the cultural identities of students of diverse backgrounds. Several possible steps toward redefining school literacy appear promising.

Types of texts

First, school literacy can be redefined in terms of the types of texts students read. In the past, students were often taught to read using texts that reflected only mainstream culture. Such ethnocentric texts served to affirm the cultural identity only of students from mainstream backgrounds. Today the texts students read should include many works of literature reflecting the varying perspectives of authors from diverse backgrounds, such as *Roll of Thunder, Hear My Cry* by Mildred Taylor (1976) and *Dragonwings* by Laurence Yep (1975). Reading multicultural literature is one way for students of diverse backgrounds to affirm their own cultural identity and to develop an appreciation for the cultural heritage of others (Martinez and Nash, 1990), as discussed further in chapter 11.

Instruction centered on meaning

Another step toward redefining school literacy involves changing the nature of instructional activities. In the past, reading and writing activities often centered on the learning of low-level skills, such as decoding, spelling, grammar, and literal comprehension (associated with transmission models of instruction, to be discussed in chapter 3). Reading and writing were treated as mechanistic processes instead of active, constructive processes. Today instruction should center on students' efforts to make meaning from text, whether in reading or in writing, and skills should be taught in the context of this meaning-making (in keeping with constructivist models of instruction, discussed in chapter 3). The basis for meaning-making is students' prior experience and knowledge. As a primary means of instruction, the teacher seeks to involve students in a dynamic process of discussion about texts, whether written by the students themselves or by others, in which students draw upon their background experience and knowledge. This approach to instruction is also discussed in more detail in chapter 3.

School literacy may be redefined through:
    Types of texts;
    Instruction centered on meaning;
    Writing based on students' experiences;
    Culturally responsive instruction;
    Critical literacy.

Here is an example of a text and instructional activities that show school literacy redefined to affirm the cultural identities of students from diverse backgrounds. Students read *Family Pictures* by Carmen Lomas Garza (1990), which describes scenes from the author's childhood growing up in a Mexican American community in Texas. The cultural schemata some Mexican American students in the class may bring to this text enables them to make many connections to their own lives, and to appreciate nuances and details that elude students from other backgrounds. Differences in comprehending and appreciating the text can and should be discussed among the students and teacher. Certainly, students of all backgrounds can benefit from trying to understand the author's childhood experiences and comparing and contrasting them with their own. Students may then draw and write about family pictures of their own, as the class continues its discussion of family and community customs, activities, and values.

Writing based on students' experiences

Still another step in redefining school literacy is to make central the writing students do about their own experiences and from their own perspectives. This is consistent with the principles of the process approach to writing and the writers' workshop (Graves, 1983). Students should be allowed to choose the topics they want to write about and the forms or genres in which their ideas can most effectively be presented.

Nancie Atwell (1987) gives the example of a Vietnamese student who was struggling to write about a dream of her mother's. Her first drafts were in prose. While Atwell respected the student's rights as an author, she did not take a laissez-faire attitude; she provided the student with guidance and offered options. Atwell suggested the student try poetry, but she did not force the issue. Eventually the student did decide to frame her thoughts as a poem, and both teacher and student were pleased with the results.

Writing about their own experiences and from their own perspectives provides students with the opportunity to gain a better understanding of their own lives. The pieces written by students of diverse backgrounds are multicultural texts from which other students and the teacher may learn.

Teachers may be surprised by students' choices but should be prepared to reflect upon whether their students do not have some insight they lack. The following example illustrates the situation of a teacher who failed to accept other perspectives. As part of a unit on explorers, a Native Hawaiian student in the ninth grade chose to write about the Polynesian voyagers who first discovered and settled the Hawaiian Islands, instead of about the first contact with the islands made by a European, the British explorer James Cook. Through his reading, the student learned that at several periods between about 900 and 1400 A.D., Polynesians made the voyage back and forth between Hawaii and the Marquesan Islands and Tahiti, using sophisticated skills of non-instrument navigation. As a Polynesian, he felt a sense of pride in the accomplishments of these explorers. When the student turned in his paper, his teacher accused him of "rewriting history" and gave him a failing grade. The student's research was accurate, but the teacher evidently saw his job as that of reinforcing a mainstream perspective on history and so failed to appreciate and learn from the understandings the student introduced. The student and his family correctly perceived this incident as a example of how schools typically honor the accomplishments of some groups but ignore the accomplishments of others. In keeping with the theory of structural inequality, as discussed in chapter 1, this is an example of how schools serve to maintain the power relations between dominant and subordinate groups.

Culturally responsive instruction

School literacy may also be redefined through culturally responsive instruction. School literacy activities can be adjusted to follow the form of activities familiar to students in the home and community. For example, as discussed in chapter 1, students may work on reading and writing activities collaboratively, rather than individually, to build on strengths gained through home experiences with sibling caretaking. Or classroom discussions may take a culturally responsive form, rather than following mainstream rules for discussion. For example, with Native Hawaiian children, teachers find it effective to conduct literature discussions following the interactional rules for talk story, a Hawaiian community speech event (Au, 1980). These and other adaptations, and the subject of culturally responsive instruction, will be covered in detail in chapters 6 and 7.

As part of culturally responsive instruction, teachers may explore with their classes the ways in which students and their families use literacy at home and in the community. Students and their families may use literacy in sophisticated ways which are not necessarily familiar to teachers from mainstream backgrounds. Knowledge of these uses of literacy may give teachers ideas about how classroom literacy activities may be adapted to relate to the literacy skills students already have or may want to have. In any event, teachers will have increased their knowledge of their students' lives. For example, teachers may not be aware of the degree of responsibility students from diverse backgrounds have in their households, particularly if both parents must work at one or more jobs (Delgado-Gaitan and Trueba, 1991).

Trueba (1984) describes some of the home literacy activities of Alma, a 12-year-old Mexican American girl. Alma's younger sister, Carmen, had Down syndrome and attended a special school. Each day Carmen's teacher wrote a brief report on Carmen's progress in a diary. So that her mother would be able to understand the report, Alma translated the teacher's message from English to Spanish. Her mother then dictated a reply in Spanish, which Alma translated and wrote down in English. With her mother's permission, Alma opened mail written in English and explained its contents in Spanish. Alma and her sisters assisted her parents with filling out forms and documents, although they often made mistakes in these tasks.

A teacher familiar with Alma's responsibilities at home might introduce some classroom literacy activities to strengthen the skills Alma and other students could use to assist family members with forms and documents. Skills of document literacy, such as reading bills and completing applications, often receive scant attention in the elementary grades but could be immediately useful to students like Alma.

Critical literacy

Still another step is to expand our views of school literacy to include a critical reading of the world and the word, in the sense intended by Paulo Freire (1985), a Brazilian educator noted for his work in using education and literacy to help members of subordinate or oppressed groups to achieve freedom. Freire proposes that reading involves a constant movement between the reading of words and the "reading" of reality. Reading entails a critical perception of the world and the transformation of the world through practical action. This type of literacy is called **critical literacy**. Henry Giroux (1988) and other proponents of critical literacy challenge the view that students' acquisition of literacy in school is simply the process of mastering the technical skills of literacy and of learning the mainstream academic knowledge represented in works such as the "great books." Developing a critical literacy in schools is a way of helping students understand the nature of inequalities in society, how some groups are privileged over others, and to empower students to work toward positive changes in their own lives and in society.

Critical literacy requires not just that teachers accept students' experiences but that they help students of diverse backgrounds understand their own experiences, as well as the experiences of others, in terms of the dynamics of the larger society. According to Giroux (1987):

> At issue here is understanding that student experience has to be understood as part of an interlocking web of power relations in which some groups of students are often privileged over others. But if we are to view this insight in an important way, we must understand that it is imperative for teachers to critically examine the cultural backgrounds and social formations out of which their students

produce the categories they use to give meaning to the world. For teachers are not merely dealing with students who have individual interests, they are dealing primarily with individuals whose stories, memories, narratives, and readings of the world are inextricably related to wider social and cultural formations and categories. The issue here is not merely one of relevance but one of power.

(p. 177)

Redefining school literacy should involve all of the steps described above, to the degree that the teacher feels ready and able to attempt them. Each of these steps takes us forward toward new patterns and away from old patterns that have often blocked the school literacy success of students from diverse backgrounds.

Summary

An expanded definition of literacy goes beyond skills to include people's willingness to use literacy, the connections between reading and writing, the dynamic process of constructing meaning (including the role of cultural schemata), and the importance of printed text. Social context is a particularly important concept for teachers to consider, both in terms of understanding literacy and of understanding how typical school literacy lessons might need to be adjusted to be more beneficial for students of diverse backgrounds. Patterns of literacy use and beliefs about literacy may differ from community to community, as shown in the examples of Trackton and Roadville. Literacy practices are very much a part of culture. For the benefit of students of diverse backgrounds, school literacy should be redefined to highlight the study of multicultural literature, instructional practices that involve an active process of meaning-making, writing instruction that makes students' background experiences central, culturally responsive instruction, and the development of critical literacy.

References

Anderson, R.C., and P.D. Pearson (1984). "A Schema-Theoretic View of Basic Processes in Reading Comprehension." In P.D. Pearson, ed. *Handbook of Reading Research*. New York: Longman.

Atwell, N. (1987). *In the Middle: Writing, Reading, and Learning with Adolescents*. Portsmouth, NH: Boynton/Cook.

Au, K.H. (1980). "Participation Structures in a Reading Lesson with Hawaiian Children: Analysis of a Culturally Appropriate Instructional Event." *Anthropology and Education Quarterly*, 11(2), pp. 91–115.

Collins, A., J.S. Brown, and J.M. Larkin (1980). "Inference in Text Understanding." In R.J. Spiro, B.C. Bruce, and W.F. Brewer, eds. *Theoretical Issues in Reading Comprehension*. Hillsdale, NJ: Erlbaum.

D'Amato, J. (1988). " 'Acting:' Hawaiian Children's Resistance to Teachers." *Elementary School Journal*, 88(5), pp. 529–44.

Delgado-Gaitan, C., and H.T. Trueba (1991). *Crossing Cultural Borders: Education for Immigrant Families in America*. London: Falmer Press.

Erickson, F. (1984). "School Literacy, Reasoning, and Civility: An Anthropologist's Perspective." *Review of Educational Research*, 54(4), pp. 525–46.

Ferdman, B.M. (1991). "Becoming Literate in a Multiethnic Society." In E.M. Jennings and A.C. Purves, eds. *Literate Systems and Individual Lives: Perspectives on Literacy and Schooling*. Albany, NY:

Fingeret, A. (1983). "Social Network: A New Perspective on Independence and Illiterate Adults." *Adult Education Quarterly*, 33(3), pp. 133–46.

Freire, P. (1985). "Reading the World and Reading the Word: An Interview with Paulo Freire." *Language Arts*, 62(1), pp. 15–21.

Garza, C.L. (1990). *Family Pictures*. San Francisco: Children's Book Press.

Gilmore, P. (1983). "Spelling 'Mississippi': Recontextualizing a literacy-related speech event." *Anthropology & Education Quarterly*, 14(4), pp. 235–55.

Giroux, H.A. (1987). "Critical Literacy and Student Experience: Donald Graves' Approach to Literacy." *Language Arts*, 64(2), pp. 175–81.

Graves, D. (1983). *Writing: Teachers and Children at Work*. Exeter, NH: Heinemann.

Guthrie, J.T., and V. Greaney (1990). "Literacy Acts." In R. Barr, M.L. Kamil, P.B. Mosenthal, and P.D. Pearson, eds. *Handbook of Reading Research*, Vol. II. New York: Longman, pp. 68–96.

Heath, S.B. (1983). *Ways with Words: Language, Life, and Work in Communities and Classrooms*. Cambridge, MA: Cambridge University Press.

Martinez, M., and M.F. Nash (1990). "Book-alogues: Talking About Children's Literature." *Language Arts*, 67(6), pp. 599–606.

Pearson, P.D., and R. Tierney (1984). "On Becoming a Thoughtful Reader: Learning to Read Like a Writer." In A. Purves and O. Niles, eds. *Becoming Readers in a Complex Society*. Chicago: National Society for the Study of Education.

Reynolds, R.E., M.A. Taylor, M.S. Steffensen, L.L. Shirey, and R.C. Anderson (1982). "Cultural Schemata and Reading Comprehension." *Reading Research Quarterly*, 17, pp. 353–66.

Snow, C.E. (1983). "Literacy and Language: Relationships During the Preschool Years." *Harvard Educational Review*, 53, pp. 165–89.

Steffensen, M.S., C. Joag-dev, and R.C. Anderson (1979). "A Cross-Cultural Perspective on Reading Comprehension." *Reading Research Quarterly*, 15(1), pp. 10–29.

Taylor, M. (1976). *Roll of Thunder, Hear My Cry*. New York: Dial.

Trueba, H.T. (1984). "The Forms, Functions, and Values of Literacy: Reading for Survival in a Barrio as a Student." *NABE Journal*, 9(1), pp. 21–40.

Wheat, T., M. Lindberg, and M. Nauman (1977). "An Exploratory Investigation of Newspaper Readability." *Illinois Reading Council Journal*, 5, 4–7.

Winograd, P., and S.G. Paris (1988). "A Cognitive and Motivational Agenda for Reading Instruction." *Educational Leadership*, 46(4), pp. 30–36.

Wixson, K.K., C.W. Peters, E.M. Weber, and E.D. Roeber (1987). "New Directions in Statewide Reading Assessment," *The Reading Teacher*, 40(8), pp. 749–54.

Yep, L. (1975). *Dragonwings*. New York: Harper and Row.

2

RETHINKING THE MEANING OF LITERACY

A. Webster, M. Beveridge and M. Reed

Source: *Managing the Literacy Curriculum* (1996) London: Routledge, 5–32

> Everything should be made as simple as possible, but not simpler.
>
> Albert Einstein

No-one seriously questions the need for all children to become literate. In most modern, schooled societies, children are surrounded by examples of written language and literate ways of thinking from birth. Most children enter school at four or five with considerable awareness of the significance of literacy for coping with everyday life. Children are usually orientated to explore what print can do, to realize its power.

Children of all ages come to the classroom with a richness of experience of story and song, and will have shared something of their family's myriad of mundane reasons for using print, such as paying bills, filling in coupons, choosing items from catalogues and writing shopping lists. However, the differences between children in terms of their various experiences of family literacy, their dialogues around stories, access to books, libraries and other print-related resources, are more important to the teacher as indicators of differences in experience and opportunity, than as indicators of ability.

The question of how to develop every child's emergent understanding of the purposes and practices of storymaking and other forms of writing and representation, is a central one for education, especially in the early years. Schools introduce children to very specific ways of using print, and in so doing, stimulate new ways of thinking and provblem-solving. In the course of this book we shall be arguing that a key challenge for all teachers concerns how to provide and sustain learning experiences and teaching contexts which enable all children to share the power of literacy, its scope and application.

If pupils spend far more time than previously, particularly when not at school, engaged with other forms of media to which print is secondary, such as video games and films, teachers have to find ways of utilizing these interests, making links and demonstrating the powerful functions and limitations of different media forms in ways which inform and elaborate pupils' choices. If literacy *per se* is to become an 'amplifier of human capabilities', as Pumfrey (1990) suggests, then the school's particular role is to find the most effective opportunities for all children to be so 'enlarged'.

Debates about literacy have a tendency to be conducted at a high level of generality around a number of common themes. These often include the notion that children read and write less well now than in the recent past. This is the 'standards are falling' complaint. There is also an influential 'progressive' view that many children have been impeded and alienated by the 'meaningless' ways in which reading and writing have been taught. This is often contrasted with an opposing belief that literacy has suffered because of the abandonment of 'traditional' classroom methods. A further, perhaps less dominant, theme concerns the changing demands on children's literacy in an increasingly technological society.

The arguments which centre around these themes are important, if only because they are part of an educational and political climate through which any new approaches, including our own, will be interpreted.

Evidence of falling standards

We begin by examining the evidence concerning falling standards of literacy and how schools might interpret it. Evidence of falling standards has to take account of differences in bench marks, as well as the motives of those presenting the data. Even so, important questions are raised for teachers and for children, in relation to where the problem is located and who should take responsibility for it. One of the arguments which we shall put forward concerning the fall in standards complaint, is that evidence is collected and presented to answer questions which are least likely to inform what teachers do in the classroom. Put bluntly, the wrong questions are being addressed in a debate which is staged frequently without, or in contradiction of, informed perspectives or clear research (Reed et al., 1995).

A number of studies in the last twenty-five years have highlighted an apparent decline in reading achievements across particular age groups, such as the NFER study *The Trend of Reading Standards* (Start and Wells, 1972). Closely following this publication, a committee of inquiry was set up under the chairmanship of Sir Alan Bullock. Its brief was to consider all aspects of the teaching of English in schools, including reading, writing, spelling and oracy. The Bullock enquiry encountered difficulties in finding an acceptable definition of literacy upon which everyone agreed, an issue to which we shall be returning in due course. It also had problems interpreting results from different tests carried out in different areas to arrive at an estimate of national trends. Notwithstanding these serious question marks over the status of the evidence available, the 'Bullock Report' did allege a general decline in reading performance from the age of seven years onwards, relative to children in the same age groups in previous decades.

Bullock ascribed the causes of reading failure to factors in the child's home background ('where conversation is limited and books unknown', DES, 1975, para 18.5); to children's 'limited natural abilities'; to the displacement of reading by watching television; and to badly trained teachers and poorly organized remedial teaching. 'The Bullock Report' suggested that 'literacy is a corporate responsibility' in which every teacher shares. It made 333 specific recommendations to schools, many of which were accepted at the time, but few acted upon. Our own research gives a clear indication that, despite the 'Bullock Report's' call for 'language across the curriculum', literacy currently seems to belong nowhere, certainly not in the whole-school policies envisaged.

Perhaps the most important source of information about standards of pupil achievement, drawn on for example, in the 'Three Wise Men' Report on primary schools (Alexander et al., 1992) is the data collected by the Assessment of Performance Unit. From 1975 onwards the APU began to devise methods of monitoring the attainments of school children and to identify the incidence of underachievement. The APU undertook five annual surveys between 1978 and 1984, which involved some 2 per cent of 10-year-olds nationally in English, maths and science testing, whilst a second phase of testing in English took place in 1988. In fact, the APU data showed that on the measures devised for testing reading and writing, national standards appeared to have shifted very little overall in this age group.

Evidence of a decline in reading standards amongst 7-year-olds was at the heart of the controversy which arose when the results of tests administered in the 1980s by nine anonymous Local Education Authorities were published by Turner (1990). In his view, changes in methods of teaching reading account for pupil failure in recent years. He argues the traditional case, that reading is not a natural activity, but a set of gradually acquired component skills which must be taught. Consequently, declining standards can be blamed on teachers moving away from more traditional, skill-based approaches involving reading schemes and 'phonics', in favour of informal 'apprenticeship' models and the use of 'real books'.

As we shall illustrate later, the most important problem with this view is that, if one actually studies real classrooms with real children and teachers, an exclusive reliance on new, more fashionable methods and an absence of traditional approaches is not characteristic. The real problem with the teaching of literacy lies in aspects of its management and organization, not simply its method.

In support of this view is the recent report drawn up by HMI entitled *The Teaching and Learning of Reading in Primary Schools 1991* (DES, 1992). From the visits made to 120 schools, HMI surmised that general standards of teaching and learning of reading have either improved or remained the same, certainly not declined. The HMI report did point out some worrying inconsistencies in the way pupils were taught and between the achievements of pupils in broadly similar schools. HMI also high-lighted many of the factors which appear to contribute to high pupil progress. These include clear policies on literacy and effective leadership by the head teacher, managing the work to match pupil needs, classroom organization factors, use of resources and the skills of the teacher.

HMI suggests that the great majority of teachers use a variety of approaches to teach reading, including 'real books', 'phonics', and reading schemes. In other words, HMI proposes that 'within-school' factors, such as class management, account for much of the difference between high and low achieving pupils. Over-reliance on one method of teaching to the exclusion of others is neither significant nor typical.

Perhaps this HMI view is not a surprising one. Since HMI is directed to evaluate the quality of educational provision, it is likely that our attention will be drawn to the difference good teaching makes, in contrast to the damage wider social inequalities may wreak. However, teachers who sustain high-quality opportunities with a variety of well-chosen and care-fully managed methods of teaching do bring about considerable achieve-ments for pupils, particularly in areas of social deprivation.

Other evidence on reading standards is more equivocal. In the autumn of 1990 the government commissioned a survey of the evidence on reading standards of 7-year-olds held by LEAs. This survey, carried out by the National Foundation for Educational Research, considered information from ninety-five LEAs out of a total of 116 in England and Wales. In only twenty-six of the LEA returns was it possible to make a judgement about changes in standards. In three instances no change was indicated, one showed no consistent pattern at all, whilst three other LEAs reported a rise. Of the nineteen where a decline could be interpreted, this mainly occurred in the 1980s and often was offset by a more recent rise. The NFER report concluded that it was impossible to make an accurate judge-ment from these data regarding the national trends in reading standards for 7-year-olds.

More recently, results from the first administration of National Curricu-lum assessments in 1991 show that 61 per cent of Year 2 pupils attained level 2 in English, with 17 per cent at level 3. Since this was the first run of National Curriculum assessments, with teachers new to the procedures, many local variations in resources and training, and the possibility of wide discrepancies in how statements of attainment are interpreted, it is difficult to draw any firm conclusions from these results.

Had the current English Orders remained in place long enough for data from further cohorts of children to be considered against these initial baselines, it might have been possible to make comparisons. The new Statutory Orders for English which change the level requirements, particularly at the entry level of KS1, mean that any data gained from 1996 onwards will not be directly comparable with the data collected so far.

Of course, one consequence of implementing the National Curriculum, particularly in English, is an inescapable pressure on schools to follow the content of the programmes of study, whatever principles are compromised in the process. As the English Orders continue to dictate rather than describe effective practice, there is a danger that literacy will be considered as a basic, isolable subject on the curriculum, taken care of by English specialists.

Literacy health warnings

How should teachers respond to this range of data and what is its significance? We suggest a number of health warnings should be appended to any particular interpretation of literacy figures, drawing attention to unproven assumptions and speculative conclusions.

What all of this evidence of attempts to standardize a measure of literacy illustrates, is the difficulty of arriving at a valid national picture. It is particularly important to remember that, despite the widespread use of tests in schools, these differ in scope, content and focus, and are carried out at different points in time on different age groups and samples. Such test data cannot easily be summarized. We are left with no cumulative picture of the direction in which standards may be moving, or if they are moving at all. If, like most European railways, reading tests followed a standard gauge, then we might be able to assess performance by different rolling stock over the same track. Given that the gauge is actually as variable as those of toy trains in High Streets shops, the resulting measurements do not lead to useful comparisons.

Furthermore, existing large-scale survey data provide no explanation for any differences observed. Links which have been intimated between changes in reading standards and the adoption of new teaching methods by schools are based on assumption, not evidence.

Inevitably, individuals with political ends in view will select the research evidence which suits their immediate purpose, hoping that others will not query the basis of their argument. This way of discussing the issues suggests that educators are ill-advised to enter the political debate on falling standards. Nevertheless we would emphasize that:

1   There is no consistent evidence of a general decline in reading stand-
    ards;
2   General descriptions of teaching methods have not been shown to
    account for any differences in children's reading test performance;
3   Teachers will not find strategies for more effective teaching of literacy
    in simplistic philosophies like 'back to basics'.

There is one important question which remains. Independently of whether
standards are rising or falling, we need to know better how to prepare all
pupils to cope with increasing demands on literacy as they move through
the school system and encounter a world in which they will have to
compete for work. This issue cannot be dealt with retrospectively by
looking back at children's failure to achieve. We must pose this question
prospectively, breaking the current discourse on standards with an equally
common-sense assertion that quality of education starts from now and
progresses for each and every pupil. How schools can begin to address
more effective literacy teaching for the future is the substance of the chapters which follow in this book.

However, we should emphasize that we are not, as this book makes clear,
complacent about the development and use of literacy by pupils. Our view is
that in the midst of heated arguments about falling standards, important
issues about educational process in relation to literacy are being ignored.

Models of reading and writing

Over the last fifty years, models of reading or writing processes have fallen
in and out of favour. They are usually adopted because they reflect the
particular concerns of people with influence at the time. They, in turn, are
influenced by the political climate, research culture and prevailing educational values. Some models of reading and writing concentrate on the per-
ceptual/cognitive acts – what might be going on when a person is actually
scanning and encoding the printed word, identifying and defining letters,
words or larger units and sequences of text. Other models are concerned
with some of the consequences for individuals of learning to read and
write – how this may change problem-solving, reasoning, the organization
of information, and conceptual growth.

It is sometimes forgotten in the desire for certainty that our models of
reading or writing are based on incomplete knowledge. Of course, even
complete knowledge would still be expressed in terms of models, analogies, theories or rules. However, in the case of reading or writing, the
available models rely on very limited data. It is also tempting to believe
that models of reading – the mental processes involved as individuals exercise their literate skills – can be turned into, or reduced to, programmes
and stages for the teaching of literacy.[2]

However, as we shall see, modelling the cognitive processes involved in skilled reading or writing is not the same as modelling how children learn to become literate. We wish to stress that, in our view, children's learning proceeds in relation to the opportunities and practices in which literacy is engaged.

In some circumstances, models can help us to understand more and to reveal underlying principles at work. However, there is a danger that issues may be vastly over-simplified and our understanding misdirected. In this book we propose that existing models of literacy have not been very helpful as far as informing and enhancing teaching and learning processes. This is not surprising, since the models evolved have been encouraged by the political climate to focus on rapid, quantitative measurements of normal readers or readers with disabilities.

However, the decade or more during which children learn to read at home and in school, encompasses a vast array of potential and actual encounters with literacy. All of these encounters could be incorporated in a more complete model of the literacy acquisition process. In fact, the processes of identifying, categorizing and studying these experiences has already begun where they can be seen specifically in psycho-linguistic

---

a)   ... it is the total pattern or schema or gestalt of the word that young pupil and mature reader alike first observe – mature readers, of course, may take in two or three word wholes in a perceptual span or unit.

Schonell, 1945, p. 13

b)   Reading, then is a process of transfer. We have, as it were, to recognise (on British Railways, for instance) that the sound of a whistle has a visual alternative – the waving of a green flag: by both of these the train guard may say to the engine driver 'proceed'.

Wilkinson, 1971, p. 198

c)   We make predictions about what we are about to read in order to comprehend, and we make hypotheses about what a particular word or passage is likely to be in order to learn.

Smith, 1978, p. 98

d)   Access to print, demonstrations of written language use, and opportunities to use written language represent a continuum ... where the meanings of literacy and literate acts are cooperatively explored within an interactive environment ... in which children can construct, realistically, images of themselves as genuine users of written language.

Wray et al, 1989, p. 72

Figure 1 Examples of different models of reading since 1945[1]

29

terms, such as in the early developmental stages (Bryant and Bradley, 1985; Goswami and Bryant, 1990).

Some of what happens in early literacy development is essentially the re-encoding of aspects of language into the relevant rules of the printed word, for example, through grapheme-phoneme (sign-sound) correspondences. And, perhaps not surprisingly, performance on relevant language tasks predicts success in this aspect of the reading acquisition process (Goswami and Bryant, 1990). However, school requires that literacy becomes a tool for thought. It is this process, which inevitably involves identifying factors in teaching and learning contexts, which is the focus of this book. How, if at all, does this happen in school? How do teachers understand the strategic role of literacy and how can we develop and test descriptions of practice which help them to do so?

Standard models of literacy

Standard models of literacy have usually been categorized according to whether they focus on features of the text, or alternatively, on features brought to the text by the reader or writer, in the form of language and experience. The term 'bottom-up' has been used to refer to those approaches which are concerned with identifying the significant units on the page which readers attend to and analyse, in order to decode the message. Text-based analyses, by definition, are highly focused and exclude many factors and influences which most teachers consider important to reading. In fairness, these models derive from the experimental work of researchers whose concern lies not with teaching, but with describing the nature of the perception, analysis, storage and retrieval of linguistic information.

In contrast, 'top-down' models suggest that reading is guided by decisions which draw on the structure of stories and other text genres, and general knowledge of the world. Top-down models should be, in principle, closely aligned with the theme of this book in that they tend not to isolate literacy from other aspects of the child's learning. However, it is one thing for a theory to be consistent with good practice and another to express clearly the nature of the connections and its practical applications. All these theories specify reading and writing, not as special activities, but as natural extensions of the possibilities of language. Also, such 'whole language' theories postulate that reading should be acquired like spoken language, by immature users being surrounded by more mature users, who support the young child's active and emerging mastery of the system. An appropriate way of referring to this is as a form of 'apprenticeship', a term popularized in the writing of Waterland (1988).

Reading as a natural language activity

The view that reading and writing are natural extensions of children's language use, drawing heavily on what children know about language and have experienced in the world, is one which most teachers are in accord with. In the 1970s, Goodman made famous the dictum that 'reading is a psycholinguistic guessing game' (Goodman, 1972). At the heart of Goodman's theorizing is the belief that reading, like spoken language, draws on the natural capacity of children to make sense of any language system to which they are exposed. Children approach reading expecting to find particular things and, as naturally curious problem-solvers, make hypotheses about the written word from their existing knowledge of the properties of spoken language. The reader is said to bring meaning to print, rather than derive meaning from it.

Goodman drew attention to the miscues (the deviations from the specific wording of the text being read) that children make when reading, revealing something of the active processes of reconstruction which go on in the reader's mind as use is made of sentence context, pictures and knowledge of stories to search for meaning. According to Goodman, readers who make mistakes are not guessing at random. Proficient readers have developed their sampling and prediction procedures to the point where they use the least number of clues necessary, given the redundancy of information available. The reading process goes awry because the poor reader is less proficient in sampling the text and putting forward hypotheses that accurately predict the unfolding of meaning.

In fact, the strength of the reader is indicated by whether miscues preserve the sense of a sentence, whether errors are self-corrected, and whether any substitutions made are of an appropriate grammatical class to fit the syntax given. Goodman talks of a continuous cycle of prediction, sampling the text for cues, confirming and disconfirming, as the child asks questions of print which are actively checked out and give rise to new questions. In his view, fluent readers have learned to make 'guesses that are right the first time' (Goodman, 1967, p. 127).

Top-down theorists such as Goodman believe that fluent readers are much more sensitive than poor readers to the information provided by the context, and that this facilitates ongoing word recognition. This view prompted Smith (1973), another well-known proponent of top-down models, to argue that reading is not primarily a visual process. In other words, the meaning derived by the reader arises from the brain behind the eye, as the reader utilizes only as much information in the text as is required for understanding. On this basis, Smith argued vehemently against the use of structured approaches in teaching reading, such as phonics, since these distract children and fragment a process that must remain 'whole'. He believed that fluent reading is too rapid for letter-by-letter decoding, whilst the spelling-to-sound correspondences of English are too inconsistent to be anything other than confusing to learners. In Smith's opinion, 'Learning to read is not a matter of mastering rules' (Smith, 1973, p. 184) and teachers can only proceed by supporting children in the business of reading for meaning.

These approaches to literacy have had a powerful impact on certain areas of some teachers' practice, although as we shall see later, teachers have not generally endorsed all that these theorists have said. Rather than emphasizing rules for decoding print, many teachers are convinced of the value of exposing children to stimulating and interesting texts, stressing enjoyment and meaning-making in both reading and writing. Assisting children through apprenticeship is often perceived as part of a holistic policy to foster children's development through a language experience approach.

Problems with 'natural language' models

We can draw attention to a number of ways in which top-down models of reading are now thought to be less than fully accurate. Assumptions are made about the nature of spoken (or signed) language and problem-solving applied to reading, which need to be questioned. One of the defining features of any human language is its creative potential, its capacity to generate an infinite number of novel combinations of meaning and effect. On the other hand, the morphology of a language which describes the word forms which people use in sentences, is relatively stable. It is at the level of the word that we find the greatest predictability, whilst language itself is essentially unpredictable. This is borne out by work on speech comprehension which shows that listeners only guess at meaning and use contextual cues when the speech signal is degraded. Speech comprehension is very largely controlled by the sound signals of the spoken word and is not driven by top-down processing (Tyler and Marslen-Wilson, 1982). What theorists such as Goodman and Smith have tried to suggest reverses these priorities by claiming that good readers, in parallel with spoken language users, are more driven by context, rather than by code.

A number of studies have shown that good readers do not rely solely on hypothesis testing and prediction when reading, nor do they rely on experience or contextual cues to meaning. For fluent readers the visual processing of text is automatic and very rapid, leaving thinking space for interpreting the content of reading, relating new knowledge to old, and working through implications. It is the weaker readers with less automatic skills who direct their attention to other sources of information within the reading context. Because they have not mastered rapid decoding of text, poor readers rely more on context clues and guesswork (Beveridge and Edmondson, 1989; Webster, 1986; Webster and Wood, 1989).

Supportive evidence for direct visual access to meaning through print has also come from eye movement research, which shows that fluent readers fixate nearly all the words as they read in small windows of text, leaving no time for hypothesis-testing or prediction. The term 'immediacy theory' has been coined to refer to the direct access to meaning through brief word fixations during fluent reading (Just and Carpenter, 1985).

However, from the perspective of this book, the crucial difficulties with top-down theories are that they do not help us identify how children's reading behaviour interacts with the wide range of text forms and challenges presented through the different subject domains of the curriculum. We also need to know much more about what teachers do that makes a difference for children as they cope with print as a medium for learning.

Reading as decoding

Teachers might be forgiven for assuming that many reading researchers, especially psychologists, have a very narrow view of literacy. It is true that much experimental research has tended to focus on the different components which affect an individual's ability to recognize units at the letter or word level in isolation. Cognitive psychologists have a general interest in understanding how humans process information. The study of reading is often undertaken to test aspects of information processing, and not to throw light on the most effective ways of teaching.

For many research psychologists, the reading process works upwards from letter or sound features towards higher levels such as words and sentences. As indicated earlier, these are often referred to as bottom-up models since they characterize reading in terms of an accumulation of sub-skills. This research has provided a sizeable body of evidence on the developmental stages associated with word recognition and production, summarized, for example, in Pumfrey and Reason (1991).

One potential source of information is the features of letter shapes. A reader might use this awareness of the invariant configuration of letter shapes to identify the string of letters which make up individual words. The reader would then have to use this visual representation of the word to recover details about pronunciation, grammatical class and meaning, held in some sort of inner store or lexicon, and built up through teaching and experience. Most teachers are familiar with claims that dyslexic individuals may confuse letter shapes in reading, invert or reverse letters in writing, and that these problems arise from some kind of perceptual deficit. However, there is also a view that dyslexia is part of a spectrum of language-related difficulties involving motor coordination, memory and sound processing (Webster and McConnell, 1987).

Instead of taking the letter as the basic building block, some researchers have argued that the reader identifies whole word patterns. Information may come from spelling regularities, or from the length and distinctive visual character of a word. A number of experiments have attempted to establish whether subjects can more easily identify real words or isolated letters or nonsense strings. The 'word superiority effect' acknowledges that readers do, on the whole, respond to some property possessed by real words but not letters, such that the whole unit is greater than the sum of its parts.

Another line of approach is that the basic building block of reading is sound-based rather than visual, thus, dependent on the set of rules for pronouncing letters, blends and sequences which enable print to be decoded into corresponding speech sounds. Work by Frith (1985) tries to establish whether children's ability to read emerges first through recognition of words as visual wholes (or logographs), or through alphabetic strategies whereby spelling units (orthographs) are used as a basis for pronunciation.

Most theorists agree that children start out, in the logographic stage, by recognizing whole words supported by context. This explains why young children are able to read what they cannot spell. The alphabetic stage is when letter-sound knowledge develops, driven largely by the practice of spelling when writing. Finally, at the orthographic stage children read and spell by a direct route based on automatic grasp of grapheme-phoneme links, which do not require encoding or decoding. It is in this last stage that many psychologists locate the specific reading difficulties of dyslexic children.

Rhyme, alliteration and analogy

Bryant and Bradley (1985) have demonstrated a strong relationship between children's awareness of the phonological patterns in print and development in reading, with an especially strong link for rhyme. Even after controlling for factors such as social background, memory and intelligence, pre-school children's rhyming skills were good predictors of later spelling and reading achievements. They found that training children in rhyme and alliteration could improve reading, whilst weaker readers also had poorer rhyme skills than younger children reading at the same level.

For psychologists, these findings do more than highlight the importance of acquainting children with nursery rhymes and word games in infancy, they also suggest that explicit teaching of phonological skills is critical, especially for children with reading difficulties. However, it has been pointed out that factors thought to be prerequisite to literacy, such as phonological skills, may also develop through reading experience, as a consequence. Determining cause and effect in these issues is problematical (Webster and McConnell, 1987).

Goswami has moved on this work still further (Goswami and Bryant, 1990). She suggests that the link between phonological awareness and reading is through analogies. A child who is good at rhyming may realize that shared sounds between words often also means shared spelling patterns, and that words such as 'rat' and 'hat' not only rhyme, they also share an orthographic unit (or rime): '-at'. Later on, children may work out how to recognize a word which they have not seen before, through analogies with other more familiar words, such as 'head' from 'bread' or 'fright' from 'light'.

Goswami proposes that children's knowledge of both orthography and phonological links develops reciprocally as an interactive process, with the one helping the other. By applying analogies, learning complex spelling rules will help to provide a finer-grained phonological analysis, and vice versa. Goswami says it is time to stop thinking of reading development as a series of stages, since many of the processes involved are interdependent.

Interactive–compensatory model

Finally, we consider here another model of the reading process which, although giving priority to code factors in reading and writing, also attempts to include broader aspects. The interactive–compensatory model drawn up by Stanovich (1980) holds that both bottom-up and top-down processes can occur alongside each other. The reader has several sources of information: letters, sounds, words, syntax which arise upwards from the page. The reader also makes predictions which act downwards on lower levels, each of which operates independently and simultaneously, but which influence each other. So, information gained from the word or sound cues will influence expectations about meaning, whilst the reverse process will also operate.

The interactive-compensatory model differs from the top-down view in its pure form because it emphasizes the critical importance of low-level, data-driven strategies for good readers. Stanovich argues that direct, automatic access to word meanings is necessary to free up the child's thinking and comprehension capacity. When word recognition is slow, readers can compensate by drawing on other sources of information at other levels, such as hypothesis-testing or context-redundancy. But to do this the reader sacrifices thinking space.

In these terms, the crucial difference between good and poor readers is speed of word recognition, an important issue for pupils as they move into the secondary phase of schooling. Poor readers use up attentional capacity because they rely on context, prediction and higher order language skills to work out what words mean. Comprehension and thinking about text suffer as a consequence. It could be that some educators engage in practices which run contrary to the implications of this work. Good readers may be taught to rely more heavily upon context, whilst poor readers are taught low-level decoding skills, such as phonics. The former emulates the strategies of weaker readers, whilst the latter denies poor readers access to supplementary sources of information in text.

Some new reading tasks in school will be best approached by good readers using contextual information, others not. Summarizing the plot of a novel demands different strategies from drawing information out of a biology textbook. This is the issue of identifying and teaching appropriate reading processes to match the nature of the task to the mind of the pupil.

Limitation of code-based models

We said earlier that cognitive psychologists pursue an understanding of how information processing takes place, and this focus for research is unlikely to lead to identifying the most effective way of fostering literacy across the curriculum. Studies of the component skills involved in reading usually take place under controlled experimental conditions, not classrooms, often involving fluent readers completing tasks which are devoid of context. Whilst we may have a richness of data from this field of research on individual differences in reading and the mechanisms involved, questions regarding effective teaching are largely unanswered (Carr and Levy, 1990).

Cognitive research has made an important contribution to the issue of what readers do when they deal with limited samples of text. Reading cannot be understood solely on the basis of informed guess-work: what readers 'expect to see'; nor can it be understood in terms of the successive recognition of separate print units. Much of this work has fostered a view of learning to read and write as the staged acquisition of a hierarchy of target skills to be mastered outside of most subject areas of the curriculum. We strongly reject this interpretation of cognitive research. We wish to emphasize that different demands are made on pupils' retention and recall, speed and automaticity of reading, the collation of information and the drawing together of conclusions, organizational and analytical strategies, in different subject areas.

It follows that, rather than thinking of literacy as a sequence of skills to be mastered outside the curriculum, we should identify those experiences which help to form the distinct literacies of different subject areas. A proficient reader in some contexts may be relatively unproficient in others. Rather than thinking of the cognitive components of reading as skills or abilities, we should see them as processes requiring specific opportunities to become practices, which change when performed in a variety of contexts.

Individualizing failure

What is missing from the focus on target skills is evidence of how young children learn most effectively and under which conditions adults enable children to behave more like readers and writers. Earlier we suggested that, as a teacher, the key to understanding literacy development lies in the relationship between children's critical practice in the classroom, and changes in the child's thinking through using different textual forms for a range of purposes. More effective learning for all children, including those perceived to 'fail', will only come from teachers having greater understanding of those factors in the teaching context which promote development. This book shows how we have attempted to develop such practical understanding with a group of schools.

We are particularly concerned to avoid the problem we have termed the 'individualization of failure'. This uses psychological constructs such as short-term memory, sequencing skills or reasoning capacities, to present a deficit model of why children fail. Even those more positive approaches to raising individual skills such as *Teaching to Objectives* (Solity and Bull, 1987), *Direct Instruction* (Carnine and Silbert, 1979), and *Multi-sensory Teaching* (Hickey, 1977) lead to complaints from teachers that they take no account of the logistics involved in real learning contexts and are based on a mistaken assumption that teaching can be considered as a form of applied child psychology.

Our own view, and the focal point of our enquiry, requires that researchers pay more serious attention to the contexts in which learning encounters take place. If researchers ignore the situation (whether domestic or institutional) of learning, they will continue to ask questions which are unhelpful to teachers.

To summarize, in this section we have considered some of the arguments put forward by different theorists in favour of one model of reading or another. In the main, most reading researchers until this point have detached literacy from its classroom context, focusing on component stages and skills. Others have tried to suggest that in order to become literate all pupils are required to do is to use what they already know about language and the world, and to read. We concluded that it is insufficient to identify what are felt to be skills, stages or rules in literacy development, and then turn these into a recipe for teaching.

As Goswami and Bryant (1990) have recently argued, it is time to stop thinking of literacy development as a sequential series of steps. Instead, we must examine a wide range of overlapping and interdependent processes which make up the specific literacies of specific areas of the curriculum. Most importantly, it is what the teacher does in the context of the classroom, rather than what the pupil has failed to acquire outside the curriculum, which determines effective environments for literacy.

Literacy is an issue for all teachers and for the whole curriculum. The focus of our own research also goes much further than the language difficulties experienced by a few 'special' groups of children. Schools seeking to 'raise standards' of reading and writing will, in our view, make little progress if they start by examining the extent of individual failure to acquire basic skills. To move forward requires a step which hitherto few researchers, psychologists or teachers have taken: examining how literacy is harnessed, within each school subject domain, to the practices of listening, categorizing, thinking and concept-forming, information-seeking, problem-solving, recording, analysing, communicating, reflecting and planning.

The problem is not simply that of teaching the mechanics of reading and writing, but going beyond to nurture a sense of literacy as a tool for wider enquiry and understanding. This is an issue of fundamental importance to both primary and secondary schools. It is out of the sustained challenge to use and think through the language of texts within the functional demands of each subject area, that creative and flexible teaching environments are made, and a strong literate community established for all pupils.

School effects on literacy

It may seem like an impertinence to suggest that we need more information on the way teachers, classrooms and schools make a difference to how and what children learn. They are, of course, not the only sources of differences in children's literacy development. Children arrive in both primary and secondary schools with very disparate stocks of knowledge, strategies and experience. The subtlety with which literacy interpenetrates the family lives of children, together with parental attitudes and support, exert a powerful influence on what pupils of all ages have learned about the purposes and processes of literacy as they enter school (John-Steiner et al., 1994).

In a review of the factors which have an impact on early literacy development, Raban (1991) points out that the children who make the greatest progress in reading are those who have comparatively advanced notions of the functions of reading and writing drawn from their home experience. Raban's own research should not be taken to mean that schools contribute nothing to children's learning; rather, that schools do not significantly alter the overall rank order of children established on entry.

In both primary and secondary phases, surveys have marked out those characteristics of schools associated with high standards of literacy. HMI (DES, 1991), for example, make reference to firm leadership from the head teacher, a language co-ordinator, a school reading policy and a wide variety of resources. In Raban's (1991) review mentioned earlier, high-quality book environments and reference resources are positively associated with high achievement, together with attempts to match children's needs and also challenge pupils with texts of appropriate interest and readability levels. Time spent reading and writing are also important variables. We know that when observations of individuals are made within the same classroom, some pupils spend but a few minutes a day on literacy-related activities, whilst others spend many hours of practice using and composing texts for one purpose or another. Results obtained by Allington (1984), for example, showed that some primary children read as little as sixteen words in a week, whilst other, more competent pupils read several thousand. It is because of this kind of discrepancy that the term 'Matthew effect' has been applied to educational settings which, however unwittingly, support the rich to get richer and the poor to get poorer.

Several studies have provided detailed descriptions of how time is distributed amongst a range of classroom activities, including literacy-related tasks. In the ORACLE study (Galton, Simon and Croll, 1980) of some sixty primary and middle-school classes, teaching is characterized as being 'overwhelmingly factual and managerial' with very little time devoted to problem-solving or collaborative work. Mostly children worked on their own, even when 'grouped'. The majority of their interactions with the teacher consisted of being 'talked at' rather than 'talked with', whilst conversations with other pupils were mostly unrelated to work set.

On average, less than 10 per cent of the teachers' time was spent on reading and this diminished rapidly with age, such that 10-year-olds and their teachers spent about 2 per cent (or twenty minutes per week) of curriculum time on reading. Even less time was spent on oral language work. Writing took up a greater proportion of time, but even here, activities tended to be restricted to extracting information or copying from workcards and books.

The nature of classroom tasks

In a more recent study (although still carried out prior to the National Curriculum), Bennett et al. (1984) considered the nature of the tasks which teachers provide for primary pupils, those crucial features of classrooms which link teachers to learners. The majority of the tasks observed, particularly in language work, demanded rehearsal of familiar routines and existing concepts, a 'staple diet of little new knowledge and large amounts of practice'. Rarely did tasks involve the discovery or construction of new or different ways of perceiving problems, or the application of existing skills to new contexts.

Teachers generally had great difficulty matching tasks to pupils' attainments and achieved such a match on approximately 40 per cent of tasks. Even after specific training most teachers were unable to set tasks on the basis of children's understanding, but relied mainly on direct teaching, with little reference to how children responded.

In writing, there was an emphasis on procedural rather than conceptual processes, with a stress on the physical production and presentation of work. Typically, writing lessons were prefaced by a reiteration of the teacher's rules for spacing, use of word books, neatness. Even when an exciting stimulus had been presented, such as the discovery of a spider in the classroom, lively discussions were often followed by routine writing demands. The teacher had the children copy sentences from the blackboard as a preliminary to writing their own material on spiders. Three-quarters of writing tasks observed were geared to quantity of output or the practising of neatness, punctuation and accuracy. The majority of ideas for writing came from the repertoire of the teacher, whilst classroom interchanges were dominated by spelling requests. When teachers gave feedback to children about their work this was usually done in crisis moments on the basis of performance or output, not on how a task had been tackled in relation to an intended purpose or audience.

The most comprehensive study to date of the use of literacy within primary and secondary schools, was carried out as part of a Schools Council Project involving pupils aged ten to fifteen years (Lunzer and Gardner, 1979). The project studied pupils' capability to use reading for learning, the incidence and context of varied strategies for reading in the classroom. Observations were made in different subject areas on a range of factors, including time spent reading or writing for specific purposes. In the subject area of English, personal writing was found to be the predominant genre of written response; in other subject areas by far the greatest proportion of time was taken up by copying without reflection, or working from textbooks.

Most classroom reading occurred in bursts of less than fifteen seconds in any one minute, suggesting that such reading is discontinuous, fragmentary and uncritical. For primary children, an average 33.4 minutes of reading per day was recorded, but of this time the greatest incidence of continuous reading took place when children were reading privately to suit their own purposes, rather than to complete an assigned learning task. This changed markedly in the secondary school where classroom reading shifted to following instructions or answering questions.

The broad conclusions drawn from Lunzer and Gardner's study are that reading is not widely used in primary and secondary schools as an integral part of teaching or learning, whilst little effort is made to teach more efficient reading as pupils move through the school system. Since many of the secondary teachers in the study regarded reading in lesson-time with suspicion, the authors describe a general 'retreat from print' in secondary school. Teachers appeared to be pessimistic about the virtues of reading for learning, and since opportunities for analysis, discussion and reflection were not taken, there seemed little chance of pupils improving. These authors recommended as 'a fundamental necessity', the provision of a meaningful experience of reading for pupils in science, scoial studies, mathematics and English, together with real opportunities for 'partaking in a discourse which illuminates reading'.

How texts change children's thinking

Beveridge (1991) has drawn attention to the lack of explicit teaching of literacy once children have transferred into secondary education. Furthermore, questions are raised about whether primary teachers are kept sufficiently in touch with the challenges which secondary pupils face, to prepare children adequately for using literacy across the curriculum. Beveridge argues that since the spoken discourse of secondary classrooms is largely inadequate for teaching pupils all they must know, recourse is frequently made to complementary media, such as video, textbooks, diagrams, worksheets and other visual resources. He cites the example of a science text which demands that the pupil extracts precise conceptual relationships.

> In certain parts of Australia crops grew very badly because there was no molybdenum in the soil. When the soil was sprayed with a very diluted solution of molybdenum the plants grew splendidly. Very little molybdenum was needed because too much of a trace element may have a damaging effect on plants.

In this short sample we have an example of how science texts are full of explanations of changing phenomena that emphasize time/space relations. We see language which expresses spatial (where), temporal (when), causal (because) and conditional (may) relationships, together with the introduction of technical vocabulary, indications of relative quantity and quality, and scientific explanation of events. For this kind of text it is inappropriate for pupils to impose their own personal organization upon it; reading and learning depend upon unambiguous recognition of the exact nature of the relationships and technicalities expressed. This is a good example of what Donaldson refers to as the 'language of systematic thought' (Donaldson, 1989).

As we saw earlier in this chapter, most models of the reading process look backwards to the competences which children are expected to bring to learning. We are shifting the focus of interest to the nature of the curriculum and its demands on pupils, rather than viewing literacy as a set of skills acquired outside of the learning context. We emphasize that schools introduce children to a wide range of very specific ways of using print which embody the processes and functions of different subject areas. As a consequence of learning to use these functions properly, children's powers of analysis and problem-solving are changed.

41

Donaldson (1989) gives a number of examples of the kind of impersonal language associated with different subject areas, particularly at secondary level. Words which pupils may have encountered in everyday settings are given very precise meanings. Terms such as 'wave', 'work' or 'power' in physics must be redefined within a scientific context. In maths, notions such as 'raising a number to its power' must be distinguished from terms encountered in humanities, such as 'the power of the law'. Donaldson suggests that the majority of children, especially those for whom reading experience has been confined to stories, will not simply 'pick up' the language of systematic thought. These new forms of language must be explicitly taught. Children's awareness of how language is structured and how it functions in different contexts, must be deliberately planned for and fostered. Donaldson suggests that teaching children the flexibility of language as a tool for thinking should begin in primary school.

The important association between the development of logical thinking and literacy, is a theme taken up by Wood (1988). He dismisses as a gross over-simplification the view that when children learn to read they are acquiring a new and *neutral* code for representing what they already do with and know about speech. Rather, children are introduced to radically new ways of thinking about language itself. Being able to write well demands the capacity to think objectively about language, to take other people's perspectives into consideration, to anticipate any likely sources of misunderstanding and take them into account in the absence of a face-to-face audience. Literacy fosters the ability to plan, to self-regulate, to edit and self-correct, to reflect on the linguistic devices of written language which achieve different emphases and effects.

Wood raises the issue of whether pupils make slow progress in literacy because they have insufficient experience of understanding why different types of writing exist, and ways in which variations in purpose are reflected in stylistic and structural devices. In other words, they do not know how to interact with text; they do not know how to become actively engaged in interpreting what they read (Webster and Wood, 1989).

There is some evidence from American research (Palincsar and Brown, 1984) that intervention techniques can help pupils to become more active interrogators of text: 12- to 13-year-olds with severe reading difficulties were taught to ask relevant questions of text, to resolve ambiguities and speculate about the author's intentions. These researchers claim high success rates in bringing comprehension levels up to age norms, although, prior to the study, the pupils' teachers had persisted in trying to establish 'word-attack' skills, rather than deal with the real problems faced by the pupils in different subject contexts.

Genre theory

A number of attempts have been made to analyse the range of texts which children encounter as they move through the school system, and the demands which these texts make on pupils in order to produce and understand them. The particular discourse forms associated with different subject areas of the curriculum are known as genres. Examples of different genres include narratives, explanations, opinions, arguments and analyses. There is good reason to believe that different genres place different information-handling demands on children (Kress, 1982; Swales, 1990; Beveridge, 1991).

Both the existence of genres as potential written forms of discourse available to the writer, and explanations conveyed by teachers regarding the manner in which genres work, may encourage pupils to organize their thinking in particular ways, to select and emphasize different aspects of their knowledge and understanding in relation to a given audience and intention. However, we are sceptical of claims that a greater *taught* awareness of generic characteristics in writing will on its own improve children's literacy (Christie, 1987; Cope and Kalantzis, 1993).

In our view, the generic characteristics of any given text, whilst being linguistically complex, are less powerful determinants of children's literacy development than social interactions around those texts, during reading or writing. Genre theory runs the risk of overemphasizing the linguistic evidence of different text types at the expense of social context factors, which written genres may reflect, but rarely construct.

The issue of how and when to introduce children to written genres, is still a vexed question for teachers and linguists, and one which our own research has deliberately not pursued to any depth. Where we do make reference to genre, this is mainly to assist our own descriptions of how texts may be organized in different subject areas of the curriculum, not as prescriptions for teaching.

Family literacy and parental partnership

In one important sense, children never approach anything in school completely afresh, without a history. The extent to which parents, family and friends, display and encourage an interest in reading and writing, is the single most important factor associated with children's progress. In relation to literacy, the attitudes, habits and experiences which pupils bring from their home and community, will determine many individuals' motivation and commitment to learning.

For these reasons, some investment has begun to be made in developing family literacy, as a means of influencing children's school progress. For example, the *Adult Literacy Basic Skills Unit*, with Department for

Education (DfE) funding, has recently set up regional family literacy projects aimed at extending the uses of literacy within the day-to-day business
of people's lives. The argument runs that by increasing family literacy and
demonstrating the importance of reading and writing, for example, in
seeking employment, more positive attitudes to literacy and the modelling
of literate behaviours, will transfer to the children.

There is also a body of evidence which demonstrates that direct
parental involvement in reading with their children raises achievements
and improves motivation (Beveridge and Jerrams, 1981; Beveridge et al.,
1987). A number of partnership initiatives have shown that by involving
parents in the classroom and by demonstrating positive strategies which
can be used at home, there can be gains in attitude and general communication between home and school, raised levels of enthusiasm and commitment, together with improvements in confidence, independence and the
quantity of reading undertaken.

The precise form of parental involvement, from family reading group to
paired reading workshop, appears to be less important for success than
organizational issues which sustain momentum. Similarly, the exact nature
of the resources used, from library books to reading schemes, appears to be
less significant for impact on pupil progress than the strategies which adults
adopt for interacting with pupils around text (Topping and Lindsay, 1992).
Quite obviously, any serious attempt by a school to manage the literacy
curriculum effectively must involve parents in the process. This is, of
course, easy to say, but the important question is how this can be sustained.

In the wider perspective of this book, we are concerned with the nature
of schooled opportunities that assist children in becoming literate. Where
there are marked differences between children, for example, on entry to
primary school, these may reflect (and continue to reflect throughout
schooling) distinctive patterns and gaps in literacy experiences at home.
When opportunities are provided for children to extend their use of literacy in classroom contexts, but these fail to be followed-up or enhanced in
the intimacy of the family, the onus on the school increases; making a difference at school becomes much more difficult. Children need both family
and school literacy to recognize and support each other.

The influence of television

One important claim is that children spend a great deal of their time at
home watching television, playing video and computer games, and that
these activities have effectively displaced reading. Television has not only
ousted reading for pleasure, it is argued, but has also reduced time spent
by children making things, such as models from kits, and enjoying shared
activities with peers, family and friends; for example, by scripting plays,
making up adventure stories, or playing boardgames.

It is certainly the case that children spend more time watching television than in pursuit of any other leisure activity. Pre-schoolers in America have been estimated to spend as much as one third of their waking hours watching television (Schiller, 1979). Watching television and playing video games cannot in themselves be considered to be wholly negative. Any potentially damaging or displacement effects are not intrinsic to the media, but grow out of ways in which the media are used. There is a case to be made that television, like other forms of media, should be considered in terms of what children do, in the contexts in which they are familiarly used:

> children's 'cognitive understandings' of television cannot be separated from the social contexts in which they are situated, or from their affective investments in the medium.
>
> Buckingham, 1994, p. 39

Greenfield (1984), in considering the impact of electronic media on children, argues that these newer media forms can be a positive force in children's lives. However, teachers do need to be aware of the influences which electronic media have on children's thinking and attention, and some of the attendant risks of passive long-term television watching.

In just the same way as print literacy introduces children to new ways of using language, which in turn stimulates new ways of thinking and problem-solving, so too television literacy has specific consequences for thinking and behaviour. In watching television programmes, children may be said to 'read' the ways in which images are constructed and narrated in the audio-visual medium, in much the same ways that they learn to interpret features which are represented in the silent and atemporal medium of print. At one level children learn to interpret editing techniques, such as the function of close-up shots, whilst at another level children learn to follow multiple sub-plots and complex formats (such as *NYPD Blue*). In these instances, children are learning about codes of representation and narrative structures which process multiple pieces of information in parallel.

What kinds of thinking are stimulated by the technology of new media, their forms and its code? The characteristic that sets television apart from print media is visual movement which attracts children's attention. However, the continuous movement and rapid pace of most television programmes, unlike print, does not allow for reflection or close analysis. Television is a medium that unfolds in real time and therefore paces the viewer. Evidence shows that heavy television viewing is associated with increased impulsivity and restlessness (Greenfield, 1984). Children who spend a great deal of time watching television are less persistent with other tasks, and may become 'passive assimilators', unused to active engagement in learning.

We have considered the part played by television and electronic media at this point because of the concerns expressed by many teachers that literacy has been displaced by, and cannot compete with the immediacy and visual power of television. So any attempt to manage the literacy curriculum has to harness the positive potential of television (Buckingham, 1992). Inevitably, the media themselves are beyond the control of schools and are here to stay. Many schools depend on television and video as a means of introducing topic material to groups, for example, in a lead lesson. Turning television from a passive to an active medium is central to exploiting its teaching potential, since the stimulus of television, though attention-holding, is not enough to ensure learning.

Greenfield (1984, p. 153) suggests that a pervasive finding of television research is the crucial factor of interacting with children during viewing to develop a more reflective approach, 'adding media to the original medium of face-to-face interaction with the teacher'.

Researching the classroom

In the final section of this chapter we turn to what is perhaps the most important issue for the purposes of the research study we have undertaken: the nature of adult–pupil encounters in teaching and learning. In fact, there is very little empirical evidence which throws light on the quality of encounters enjoyed by teachers and pupils in relation to text, and what appears to make a difference to children's progress and understanding. Some would go so far as to say that we know very little about the quality of children's learning experiences generally (Bennett et al., 1984). As Raban (1991, p. 53) points out, 'What is needed is close observation and cataloguing of teacher behaviours across a range of classrooms in order to detect more or less successful strategies.' However, it is no easy matter to observe busy, complex teaching environments with twenty to thirty individuals and select those aspects which are significant in terms of pupil learning, in order to make systematic records and come up with practical recommendations. How do we know what children are gaining from the tasks and activities set, or even what the teacher intended? How can we probe the nature of their learning to achieve a fine-grained account of those critical features which move children on in their thinking?

Despite the abundance of advice (Desforges, 1988) on how to design more effective learning environments, these suggestions may have very little impact. This is because such advice often depends on some kind of restructured delivery of basic skill teaching to individuals, and ignores the dynamics and organization of classroom life. It has long been recognized that classrooms are social contexts in which much of the teacher's time is devoted to establishing routines, boundaries and adult control, with pupils having to discover what the teacher requires. But classroom-based research has tended to produce over-simplistic analyses and a narrow interpretation of events (Shipman, 1985).

It should also be said that no social context, including classrooms, can be described in full. This limitation is not just one of *data capture*: the difficulty of observing everything that happens. It also derives from the well-recognized point that social data, like all scientific evidence, require a theoretical frame of reference to become meaningful, and that there is a considerable array of such frameworks which apply to classroom life. For example, research into friendship or gender would assemble the data of classroom activity somewhat differently from our own interests in literacy acquisition.

Each research focus requires a theoretical model which generates principles for data organization if it is to be studied usefully and vigorously. It is often the case that no such single agreed model exists for the domains of educational research. However, good research still adopts the practice of leaving the relationship between its theoretical position and its research tools open to inspection.

Adult–child proximation

Addressing the issue of growth in children's understanding and its relationship with the nature of the teaching demands made in different subject domains, requires setting literacy in a conceptual framework which is different from other approaches. Adult–child proximation is a term we have coined to refer to those instances where adults enter into close exchanges with children where information is handed over, explanations are given, and events are interpreted. This is what we mean by mediation: helping children to contruct accounts of events in terms they understand. Adult–child proximation is examined in the nature and quality of interactions, such as conversation, or question and answer routines. Our approach stems partly from recent attempts to study teaching and learning as socially-mediated activity (Wood, 1988; Webster and Wood, 1989; Moll, 1990; Bruner, 1986).

Drawing on the work of Soviet writers, particularly that of Vygotsky, and more recently, Bakhtin, these accounts reject an atomistic or reductionist approach to learning generally, and literacy in particular, as a fragmentation of what transpires during learning, which tends to ignore the complex ways in which new information becomes meaningful (Burgess, 1993; Wertsch and Bustamante Smolka, 1993).

A core idea is that adults frequently help children to accomplish things which they could not do by themselves. Similarly, what adults assist children to achieve collaboratively, prepares children for more independent enquiry in the future. The gap between what children can do on their own and what they can achieve with the help of others more skilled than themselves, is known as the 'zone of proximal development' (Vygotsky, 1978). Through social interaction with the more mature, children are exposed to practices and examples of how others tackle problems and manage their thinking.

Effective teaching, in these terms, is much more than the transmission of information from one individual to another. Rather, successful teaching is constituted in certain styles of cooperation and negotiation. The importance of this view is that learning depends more on the teacher's dialogue with individuals and groups than on the transfer of information in the form of 'true' statements made by the teacher and remembered by the pupils.

Our focus in this book is on the teaching and learning of literacy as both a teacher, school and inter-school process. More precisely, we are concerned to study the teaching of literacy set in a system of classrooms within and between schools. Our research tools must consequently have a generality which is applicable across a range of contexts and yet must be realistic to the teachers concerned. The model we eventually put into use began its development from consideration of how to identify the dialogic approach to literacy as used in everyday teaching through mediation.

Teaching as 'mediation'

We can identify some of the key features of teaching as mediation or proximation in relation to literacy. There is an emphasis on meaning, relevance, the functional uses of literacy and the creation of classroom environments in which many different types of literacies can be explored and developed. Teachers who follow this approach will emphasize the creation of social contexts in which children actively use text to achieve specific purposes, avoiding the reduction of reading and writing to skill sequences or stages.

It is the teacher's task to work towards the pupils' mastery of their own learning. Mature thinking involves a degree of self-regulation, planning, suggesting, reminding and evaluating oneself. Through social interaction with the more mature, pupils are shaped towards more systematic organization and self-control: they achieve a critical reflection on how they went about their learning, what went well, and what could be done better. This critical reflection can operate at many levels of the reading or writing process, including low-level factors such as how letters are formed and spelling units assembled. But it is important that pupils do not lose sight of why something is being read or written, the larger purpose of using literacy as part of the demands, intentions and procedures of different subject areas.

A further issue concerns what it is that is learned or changes. Much of school learning can be characterized as recitation, where the main routines of instruction are those of illustration, explanation and information-giving.

The pupils' task may be construed as that of absorbing and reciting content for assignments and examinations. Effective learning, in proximation terms, is about the pupil coming to know 'how', not 'that'. Knowing 'how' is instantiated in pupils' meaningful grasp of procedures which enable learning to be generalized from one context to another. For example, when children are taught how to manipulate abstract symbols in solving mathematical equations without understanding the concepts which underlie them, or how they can be applied in the real world, empty knowledge – procedures without meaning – is the result.

Rather than simply learning rote facts and information contained *within* the subject, pupils must acquire some of the processes, strategies and objectives which *underpin* the subject and those who practise it. At all levels, effective learning means that children are asked to behave as historians, scientists or readers, from the outset. This is more than simply arranging a set of classroom events in which subject literacy plays a role, for example, re-enacting the Battle of Hastings and writing an account. For effective learning to take place, pupils must be led to internalize some of the thought processes of a historian, such as a consideration of the provenance of available evidence.

The next point concerns how teachers can work effectively as mediators. Teachers have an overview of their subject domains and how small units of enquiry (for example, topics within a scheme of work) relate to the larger direction in which teaching is leading. Hence, teachers are in a good position to identify priorities, to mark out those subject areas which need to be covered thoroughly, and to know which processes have to be mastered.

Effective teachers help pupils make informed choices about their learning, rather than simply directing them to get on with a task. They help pupils select appropriate problems to tackle; draw attention to relevant or overlooked information; negotiate resources, materials and potential strategies. Wherever possible, pupils are asked to think of themselves as sources of information, to be creative in their own questioning and independent in their decision-making. However, this does not preclude rote practice in areas where memorization is required, such as learning to spell unusual words. Similarly, learning to play the trombone or to make a screenprint, requires work with the instrument or equipment. It is an important part of the teacher's role to explore the best ways of achieving the aims set in relation to the pupils' starting points.

Contingencies in teaching

Perhaps the best way to characterize the teacher's role is in terms of contingency. By this we mean the timing of intervention in order to assist children's performance of a task, particularly when difficulties arise. This involves gauging a pupil's (or group's) moment-to-moment understanding of a task, providing more information and help where needed, using questions to move thinking forward, allowing more initiative when pupils succeed.

Wood (1992) argues that most classroom settings are actually very *low* in intellectual challenge. He feels that most of the dialogues teachers hold with pupils do not promote reflection, analysis, enquiry, or sustain interest and motivation. Many questions asked by teachers, for example, are closed, factual questions, with known right answers. Teachers get to ask practically all the questions, whilst pupils strive to provide the right answers. Typically, teachers give pupils around one second of 'wait time' in which to formulate and produce a reply. Simply increasing wait time produces more effective classroom dialogue. Wood suggests that, rather than test questions to check what pupils know, alternative strategies include teachers giving their own thoughts and ideas to pupils, speculating, suggesting, surmising, interpreting, illustrating, listening, planning with, sharing and acknowledging what children have to say.

An important aspect of teachers' lesson management involves devising opportunities in which feedback can be given. Having tackled a task, there is an important review stage when pupils are asked to reflect on their learning, what they have gained, how they could have proceeded any differently, what to move on to next. At this evaluation stage teachers must be careful to respond to the process or strategy that a child has chosen and not simply to mark the product, quantity or output. This is an important phase of helping to make explicit the criteria by which learning is evaluated. Creating an atmosphere which highlights joint hypothesis-raising and problem-solving, also includes a conscious awareness of the language required to comment on the process of learning. This exposes some of the links between learning dialogues and the mental processes acquired by pupils.

Effective teachers recognize that not everything can be left to the pupil's initiative and that some achicvements must be won through sustained, deliberate practice or study. We are not suggesting that the best teaching is informal, or indeed highly structured, since the crucial issue is whether pupils recognize the reasons for embarking on a particular learning route and where it is leading. It is a question of teachers standing with pupils in a shared enterprise, recognizing that while children enjoy solving problems, they may need help to find the right questions and the appropriate means to tackle them.

To do all this makes many demands on teachers themselves, requiring them not only to be experts in the tools, techniques and content of their subject specialisms, but also to have expertise in how children think and learn. This is why we have suggested that literacy, as both tool *and* technique, should be on every teacher's agenda and is interwoven with the whole curriculum.

This brings us to the last, but not least, element in adult–child proxima-tion: the ability of teachers to decentre, to think about the pupils' perspec-tives as well as their subject, to learn from pupils' responses, to adjust their teaching reciprocally as they interact with children in the classroom. Another way of expressing this is to add to the notion of 'apprenticeship' a two-way effect: the events of learning not only influence conceptual changes in pupils, they also produce conceptual changes in the adult. Good quality dialogic literacy teaching occurs when teachers act with particular understandings which are both fluid and responsive.

Summary

We began this chapter by examining the current concerns for standards of attainment in reading and writing, whether these have fallen in recent years and whether teaching methods can be blamed for any apparent changes. Our considered advice is that teachers should be wary of test results, many of which are conflicting, none of which provide a satisfactory basis for moving forward. Importantly, these unproductive arguments about methods and standards reduce the complexity of children's literacy development to unitary, simplistic notions.

In the past, what has fuelled the debate over literacy teaching has been a number of contrasting models of the reading process, derived from quite different research traditions. We have illustrated how models have changed over time, and highlighted some of the constraints attached to analyses of literacy in terms of bottom-up, top-down or compensatory factors. None of this work has adequately addressed how literacy is acquired in real classrooms, and how children's reading behaviour inter-acts with the wide range of text forms and subject challenges, as children pass from primary to secondary school.

We also have scant evidence on what makes a difference to children's learning of literacy, under what conditions, and in response to what kind of teaching. Currently, there is a tendency for many teachers, particularly at secondary level, to view literacy as someone else's specialist respons-ibility, outside the mainstream curriculum and unimportant to most other subject teaching.

Much of the evidence we have reviewed suggests that the teaching of literacy is mostly perceived in terms of discrete steps or skills, which pupils ought to acquire by the later stages of primary school. It also appears that from infant school onwards, less and less attention is given to literacy teaching, such that by secondary school, the likelihood of pupils being given help to cope with the burgeoning literacy demands of different subject areas decreases rapidly. Indeed, there are some alarming figures which show the limited amount of time when pupils engage in literacy-related tasks, particularly for continuous reading. In writing, teachers tend to emphasize secretarial skills, neatness and volume, and writing for personal reasons rather than dealing with the written functions of tasks within subject domains.

On the whole, teachers and curriculum legislators have a tradition of neglecting literacy for learning. In the terms by which teaching was defined earlier in this section, literacy does not appear to be developed in the dialogical forms we have outlined. Given the prescriptive and content-laden philosophy that underlies the National Curriculum, which manages to leave literacy out of its broad context, teachers have been further discouraged from seeing literacy as a challenge for the whole curriculum and an integral part of every teacher's agenda.

In this chapter we have set the scene for a new framework for managing literacy in schools, which will focus on the nature of the curriculum itself and the way in which different subject areas introduce pupils to specific ways of understanding and generating text. These diverse literacies, including television literacy, have the potential for influencing how children think and behave. It is critical, in our view, to try and establish under which social-interactive conditions of teaching and learning children acquire adult approaches to problem-solving. In our view, these processes of systematic thought must be explicitly captured in classroom discourse and experience.

Notes

1   The first two extracts are concerned with visual perception, discrimination of patterns, eye movements, transfer and 'gestalt' theory: the perception of whole units. The extract from Smith includes key constructs of prediction and hypothesis-testing, whilst Wray et al., refer to cooperative exploration and self-images of language users. The changes reflect a shift in the view of how language itself is acquired, away from perceptual, mechanical aspects of decoding, towards outcomes of interactive social experience.

2   Importantly, because we can account for the functioning of complex systems in terms of models or rules, this does not mean that the systems in question are actually being driven by, or rely on, those rules. To take an example, the motion of the planets in the solar system has been represented in terms of specific mathematical rules, but it would not be claimed that Venus or Saturn are *following* such rules. There is a crucial distinction to be made here – one which informs much of our current thinking about literacy – between 'rule-described' and 'rule-following' behaviour.

References

Alexander, R., Rose, J. and Woodhead, C. (1992) *Curriculum Organisation and Classroom Practice in Primary Schools*. London: HMSO

Allington, R. (1984) Content coverage and contextual reading in reading groups. *Journal of Reading Behaviour*, no. 16, pp. 85–96

Bennett, N., Desforges, C., Cockburn, A. and Wilkinson, B. (1984) *The Quality of Pupil Learning Experiences*. London: Lawrence Erlbaum Associates

Beveridge, M. C. (1991) Literacy and learning in secondary school: problems of texts and teaching. In A. Webster (ed.) *Language and Language-related Difficulties. Educational and Child Psychology*, vol. 8, no. 3, pp. 60–71

Beveridge, M. C. and Edmondson, S. (1989) Microcomputer assessment of reading processes under word and phrase presentation. *Journal of Research in Reading*, vol. 12, no. 1, pp. 1–12

Beveridge, M. C. and Jerrams, A. (1981) Preschool children's language: an evaluation of a parental assistance plan. *British Journal of Educational Psychology*, no. 51, pp. 256–66

Beveridge, M. C., Jerrams, A. and Lo, P. (1987) The effects of a school based parental assistance plan on children's social sensitivity. *Journal of Applied Developmental Psychology*, vol. 8, no. 2, pp. 139–81.

Bruner, J. S. (1968) *Toward a Theory of Instruction*. New York: Norton

Bryant, P. and Bradley, L. (1985) *Children's Reading Problems*. Oxford: Blackwell

Buckingham, D. (1992) *Television Literacy: Talk, Text and Context*. London: Falmer Press

—— (1994) Media education. In B. Stierer and J. Maybin (eds) *Language, Literacy and Learning in Educational Practice*. Clevedon: Multilingual Matters in association with The Open University

Burgess, R. (1985) (ed.) *Issues in Educational Research: Qualitative Methods*. London: Falmer Press

Carnine, D. and Silbert, J. (1979) *Direct Instruction Reading*. Orlando, FL: Charles Merrill

Carr, T. and Levy, B. (1990) (eds) *Reading and its Development: Component Skills Approaches*. London: Academic Press

Christie, F. (1987) Young children's writing: from spoken to written genre. *Language in Education*, vol. 1, no. 1, pp. 3–13

Cope, B. and Kalantzis, M. (1993) The power of literacy and the literacy of power. In B. Cope and M. Kalantzis (eds) *The Powers of Literacy: A Genre Approach to Teaching Writing*. London: Falmer Press, pp. 63–89

Department of Education and Science (1975) *A Language for Life* (The Bullock Report). London: HMSO

—— (1992) *The Teaching and Learning of Reading in Primary Schools 1991*. London: HMSO

Desforges, C. (1988) Psychology and the management of classrooms. In N. Jones and J. Sayer (eds) *Management and the Psychology of Schooling*. London: Falmer Press

Donaldson, M. (1989) *Sense and Sensibility: Some Thoughts on the Teaching of Literacy*. Reading: Reading and Language Information Centre

Frith, U. (1985) Beneath the surface of developmental dyslexia. In K. Patterson, M. Coltheart and J. Marshall (eds) *Surface Dyslexia*. London: Lawrence Erlbaum Associates

Galton, M., Simon, B. and Croll, P. (1980) *Inside the Primary Classroom*. London: Routledge and Kegan Paul

Goodman, K. (1967) Reading: a psycholinguistic guessing game. In H. Singer and R. Ruddell (eds) *Theoretical Models and Processes of Reading*. Newark, DE: International Reading Association

—— (1972) Reading: the key is in children's language. *The Reading Teacher*, March, pp. 505–8

Goswami, U. and Bryant, P. (1990) *Phonological Skills and Learning to Read.* Hove: Lawrence Erlbaum Associates

Greenfield, P. (1984) *Mind and Media: the Effects of Television, Computers and Video Games.* London: Fontana

Hammersley, M. (1993) (ed.) *Educational Research: Current Issues.* London: Paul Chapman

Hickey, M. (1977) *Dyslexia: A Language Training Course for Teachers and Learners.* Bath: Better Books

John-Steiner, V., Panofsky, C. P. and Smith, L. W. (1994) *Sociocultural Approaches to Language and Literacy: An Interactionist Perspective.* Cambridge: Cambridge University Press

Just, M. and Carpenter, P. (1985) *The Psychology of Reading and Language Comprehension.* Newton, MA: Allyn and Bacon

Kress, G. R. (1982) *Learning to Write.* London: Routledge and Kegan Paul

Lunzer, E. and Gardner, K. (1979) *The Effective Use of Reading.* London: Heinemann, for the Schools Council

Moll, L. (1990) (ed.) *Vygotsky and Education: Instructional Implications and Applications of Socio-historical Psychology.* Cambridge: Cambridge University Press

Palincsar, A. and Brown, A. (1984) Reciprocal teaching of comprehension-fostering and comprehension-monitoring activities. *Cognition and Instruction.* no. 1, pp. 117–75

Pumfrey, P. (1990) Literacy and the National Curriculum: the challenge of the 1990s. In P. Pumfrey and C. Elliot (eds) *Children's Difficulties in Reading, Spelling and Writing.* Basingstoke: Falmer Press

Pumfrey, P. and Reason, R. (1991) *Specific Learning Difficulties (Dyslexia): Challenges and Responses.* Windsor: NFER/Nelson

Raban, B. (1991) The role of schooling in initial literacy. In A. Webster (ed.) *Language and Language-Related Difficulties. Educational and Child Psychology*, vol. 8, no. 3, pp. 41–59

Reed, M., Webster, A. and Beveridge, M. (1995) The conceptual basis for a literacy curriculum. In P. Owen and P. Pumfrey (eds) *Children Learning to Read: International Concerns. Volume 1: Emergent and Developing Reading: Messages for Teachers.* London: Falmer Press

Schiller, J. (1979) You and that box in the corner. *Australian Journal of Early Childhood* vol. 4, no. 2, pp. 32–6

Schonell, F. J. (1945) *The Psychology and Teaching of Reading.* London: Oliver and Boyd

Shipman, M. (1985) *The Management of Learning in the Classroom.* London: Hodder and Stoughton

Smith, F. (1973) (ed.) *Psycholinguistics and Reading.* New York: Holt, Rinehart and Winston

—— (1978) *Reading.* Cambridge: Cambridge University Press

Solity, J. and Bull, S. (1987) *Special Needs: Bridging the Curriculum Gap.* Milton Keynes: Open University Press

Stanovich, K. (1980) Towards an interactive-compensatory model of individual differences in the development of reading fluency. *Reading Research Quarterly*, vol. 16, no. 1, pp. 32–71

Start, K. and Wells, B. (1972) *The Trend of Reading Standards*. Slough: NFER

Swales, J. (1990) *Genre Analysis: English in Academic and Research Settings*. Cambridge: Cambridge University Press

Topping, K. and Lindsay, G. (1992) Paired reading: a review of the literature. *Research Papers in Education*, vol. 7, no. 3, pp. 199–246

Turner, M. (1990) *Sponsored Reading Failure*. Warlingham: IPSET Education Unit

Tyler, L. and Marslen-Wilson, W. (1982) Speech comprehension processes. In J. Mehler, E. Walker and M. Garrett (eds) *Perspectives on Mental Representation*. Hillsdale, NJ: Lawrence Erlbaum Associates

Vygotsky, L. (1978) *Mind in Society: The Development of Higher Psychological Processes*. Cambridge, MA: Harvard University Press

Waterland, L. (1988) *Read With Me: An Apprenticeship Approach to Reading*. 2nd edn. Stroud: The Thimble Press

Webster, A. (1986) *Deafness, Development and Literacy*. London: Methuen

Webster, A. and McConnell, C. (1987) *Children with Speech and Language Difficulties*. London: Cassell

Webster, A. and Wood, D. J. (1989) *Children with Hearing Difficulties*. London: Cassell

Wertsch, J. V. and Bustamante Smolka, A. L. (1993) Continuing the dialogue: Vygotsky, Bakhtin and Lotman. In H. Daniels (ed.) *Charting the Agenda: Educational Activity after Vygotsky*. London: Routledge

Wilkinson, A. (1971) *The Foundations of Language: Talking and Reading in Young Children*. Oxford: Oxford University Press

Wood, D. J. (1988) *How Children Think and Learn*, Oxford: Blackwell

—— (1992) Language, learning and education. In P. Gray (ed.) *New Concepts, New Solutions: Educational and Child Psychology*, vol. 9, no. 2 pp. 17–25

Wray, D., Bloom, W. and Hall, N. (1989) *Literacy in Action*. London: Falmer Press

3

UNDERSTANDING LITERACY

C. Lankshear

Source: *Literacy, Schooling and Revolution* (1987) Lewes: Falmer, 37–77

Introduction

The study of literacy has become a major academic growth area in the West during recent years. In some ways this trend is not especially surprising. There are many aspects of the practice of reading and writing – social, cultural, historical, etc. – that are intrinsically interesting and, in their own right, offer the researcher wide scope for stimulating investigation. In addition, a powerful instrumental ground has emerged to encourage critical investigation of literacy and its importance for the lives of individuals and societies within (at least) the Western world. This is the fact that during the past two decades the existence of widespread adult and youth illiteracy has been proclaimed within a number of developed nations, including Britain, the US, Canada, Australia, and New Zealand. Dramatic claims have been widely publicized to the effect that in Britain the number of functionally illiterate citizens – excluding recent immigrants and the mentally handicapped – could be anything from around two million to between six and eight million, depending on which reading age is taken to define 'functional literacy'. And since 1975, estimates suggesting the existence of approximately fifty-four to sixty-four million functionally illiterate US adults have been widely reported 'amid cries of alarm'. These estimates follow the 1971 Harris study, commissioned by the National Reading Centre, which concluded that around 15 per cent of US adults – approximately twenty-three million people – 'have serious reading deficiencies'.[1]

While heightened academic interest in literacy may not in itself be surprising, one *may* be surprised at some of the questions which have emerged as key issues for investigation. These include such questions as: what *is* literacy?; what does it *mean* to be literate or illiterate?; what is it about literacy that makes it valuable, and for whom is it (most) valuable? Many people would no doubt regard such questions as pointless; as 'academic' in the pejorative sense of the term. After all, there is a pervasive folk wisdom about literacy. Surely we *all* know what it is and why it is so valuable and important. The crucial significance of reading and writing, for individual and social betterment alike, has been a largely unquestioned assumption in the West from the time that stirrings for mass education as a main ingredient of social progress and reform emerged in the eighteenth and nineteenth centuries.

Conventional wisdom assumes the necessity and value of literacy for social and economic development, for advancing and maintaining democratic institutions, and for individual betterment. What literacy is, and what it means to be literate (or illiterate), are likewise widely regarded as unproblematic. Graff, however, gives us cause for concern about conventional wisdom here. He contrasts our confident everyday assumptions about the nature and meaning of literacy and the value attaching to reading and writing skills with the confusion and ambiguity apparent in many actual discussions of literacy. He claims that almost all attempts to locate the meaning of literacy are shrouded in vagueness, and that there is surprisingly little agreement as to the precise benefits – individually or socially – of literacy. Furthermore, there is little specific evidence for the benefits that are in fact claimed. While the value of literacy

> for achieving fulfilling, productive, expanding, and participating lives of freedom in modern societies is undoubted and unquestioned ... literacy does not seem to be well understood, popularly or academically ... Whether seen as a concept; a skill, tool or technique; or expected consequences from possession of the tool, discussions of literacy suffer from serious confusion.[2]

Increasingly, scholars have seen a need to problematize conventional wisdom about literacy: to address basic questions concerning the nature, role, and significance of literacy within daily life, evaluate different answers that have been given to these questions, and straighten out what they regard as major confusions over literacy. In this chapter I draw on some of the recent work done in this area – particularly that of Harvey Graff and Brian Street[3] – in order to establish ideas about literacy that will underlie my argument in subsequent chapters.

Understanding (and misunderstanding) literacy

I will begin by spelling out three widely-held beliefs about literacy which I regard as mistaken and will refer to here as popular misconceptions. Having elaborated these beliefs I will consider some major arguments advanced against them – arguments I regard as successful. These arguments offer in place of our common misconceptions the basis for a more accurate understanding of literacy. Educationists and lay persons alike are often inclined to think of literacy as something people either have or lack. Those who lack it are assumed to need it, and ought to acquire it. Once they have it they can employ it for all sorts of ends; they can put it to whatever uses they choose. The world is opened up to the literate person in a way that it remains closed to the illiterate person; literacy produces good consequences for and valuable qualities within the literate person – consequences and qualities precluded from illiterate folk.

At least three closely related misconceptions are often to be found lurking within this view: namely, that literacy is *unitary*; that it is a *neutral* process or tool; and that it is an *independent variable*. Let us take these in turn.

(i) The idea that literacy is unitary is simply the idea that literacy is a single 'thing'; that it is essentially the same 'thing' for everyone. Of course those who see literacy this way acknowledge that there exist (significant) differences between people as regards, say, their *level* of literacy and how they use it. That is, some people have more facility with literacy than others: they can read and write more words, or more complex words, or do so more fluently than others. They may be literate in more languages, or use their literacy in more sophisticated ways than other folk. But in the end, what literate people share in common, regardless of such differences in detail, is their possession of this 'thing' called literacy. What illiterate people share in common is the fact that they don't possess it at all, or else have so little of it that it doesn't count.

The basis for perceiving literacy as a unitary 'thing' typically lies in the belief that literacy is a *technology* or, alternatively, the *skill* to employ the technology of print. An analogy may be drawn here with computing. People are either in a position to use computers – they possess the technology and skills to use it – or they are not. Those who are can use the technology for quite different purposes, in more or less complex and sophisticated or more or less basic ways, within a wider or narrower range of purposes, and so on. In the end, though, the world can be divided into those possessing effective use of computer technology and those who lack it. And what it is that they possess or lack is essentially the same thing, whoever and wherever they are. When literacy is conceived in an analogous way, as a technology or the skill to use this technology, it is possible to observe and describe differences between those who use it whilst, nevertheless, regarding literacy as being the same unitary 'thing' in the end, despite these differences.

An influential example of this viewpoint to be found in recent scholarly research is provided by Goody and Watt, who focus on literacy as the technology of alphabetic writing.[4] They seek (for purposes of anthropological research and explanation) a distinction between literate and non-literate societies, and argue that it was only when the technology of alphabetic writing – 'letters' – became available in the Ancient Greek world that we find the emergence of institutions, social practices, and modes of thinking characteristic of all later literate societies. Goody and Watt introduce their idea of literacy by asking

> At what point in the formalization of pictographs or other graphic signs can we talk of 'letters', of *literacy*? And what proportion of the society has to be able to write and read before the culture as a whole can be described as literate?[5]

They suggest that it was only following the Greek adaptation of the Semitic alphabet – through the addition of vowels – during (probably) the fifth and sixth centuries BC, that 'anything like popular literacy, or the use of writing as an autonomous mode of communication by the majority of members of a society' emerged.[6] It is precisely this technology of alphabetic writing in its perfected form (i.e., with vowels added) that constitutes literacy for Goody and Watt. They do not regard the specific literacy *practices* actually engaged in by particular members and groups within given social contexts – i.e., the various ways the technology is used to pursue social goals – as intrinsic to literacy. Rather, it is the technology itself that constitutes literacy: the invention we call alphabetic writing. Behind all actual literacy practices and varying ideas about how reading and writing are to be used, to what ends, etc., there is seen to reside the technology itself – that unitary or singular thing which *is* literacy.

(ii) It is precisely the tendency to regard literacy as a skill or technology *per se* that encourages belief in its neutrality. For on such views literacy is seen as completely independent of specific social contexts.[7] It is seen, instead, as 'pure skill', or as 'a technology/tool purely and simply': as something to be distinguished in itself from the empirical forms it happens to take and the uses to which it is actually put within daily life. Literacy *in itself* is to be distinguished from the content it is used to acquire and convey, and from any advantages or disadvantages accruing from the particular ways it is used or the forms it takes. It is neutral in that it is detached from and impervious to the concerns, values, attitudes, trends, tastes, practices and patterns of power or influence to be found within given social settings.

There are two sides to this alleged neutrality of literacy. First, what literacy *is* in no way reflects matters of social context. Literacy is literacy is literacy. It is not shaped by the facts of particular social settings. As a tool or skill literacy is, of course, used to acquire and convey (certain) values, beliefs, opinions, traditions, etc; or, used to acquire and convey some values and beliefs rather than others. And so its *use* reflects details of social context. But according to those who accept the neutrality of literacy, 'use' is to be distinguished from 'the thing itself'. Literacy, as it were, remains aloof from the actual practices and processes in which it is employed and by which it is transmitted within varying social, political, cultural, etc., milieux.

The other side to this is that literacy does not of itself define, limit, or influence the use actually made of it, or the interests that are served or undermined by its actual use. Just as it is not up to the computer itself whether it will be used in producing an important breakthrough in medicine, or as an arm of Big Brother in the surveillance of citizens, or to guide nuclear missiles, so (allegedly) it is not a function of 'literacy itself' if people use it to read fine literature, or simply to scan magazine or comic stories, or to satisfy their lust by reading pornographic material; if it is employed to purvey false information or doctrinal belief, to transmit a systematically distorted view of reality; to serve the interests of some groups rather than others and keep 'ordinary citizens' at the mercy of 'the experts', rather than opening up important data and accurate information to people at large, thereby enabling citizens to participate in political processes and wider decision-making in an informed manner.

The belief that literacy is itself neutral with respect to the ways individuals actually use it, and to patterns of use that emerge within a given society or cultural setting, is widespread. Neil Postman describes this view, with specific reference to reading, as follows:

> One of the standard beliefs about the reading process is that it is more or less neutral. Reading, the argument goes, is just a skill. What people read is their own business, and the reading teacher merely helps to increase a student's options. If one wants to read about America, one may go to DeToqueville or *The Daily News*; if one wants to read literature one may go to Melville or Jacqueline Susann.[8]

Literacy, then, according to common opinion, has no 'favourites': it favours no particular content, view of the world, habits, practices, group interests, etc. It is simply 'there' for people to use however they choose. People's actual choices will, of course, be shaped by various factors and influences. These include such things as schooling, family background, peer interests, reading and writing models generally available to the individual, advertising, popular taste, social values, religious practice, the range and price of available reading material, and so on. On the view in question, however, such factors are no part of literacy itself. Rather, it is believed that literacy itself can be neatly distinguished – separated off from – all such particularities.

(iii) While literacy is often regarded as being completely independent of specific social practices, processes, values, interests and the like, it is nevertheless widely believed to be responsible for bringing about a number of general – and generally desirable – outcomes. In other words, while it is not in itself a consequence or reflection of outside influences and does not favour/champion one set of social values, interests or practices at the expense of others, it does produce some important outcomes in its own right. This is what is meant by speaking of literacy as an independent variable.[9] Consequences most commonly attributed to literacy as an independent variable (or cause) may be categorized as 'cognitive', 'economic-developmental', and 'social' respectively.

Those who attribute cognitive consequences to literacy argue that it is responsible for the emergence of key forms of cognition integral to rational thought and judgment. Street identifies (and challenges) theorists across different disciplines who claim that there are inherent differences between written and oral forms of communication. They see written language as freeing us from particularities of context to which humans are bound within oral communication. These particularities stand in the way of performing abstractions and other logical operations, making objective judgments, adopting a sceptical attitude toward information, and developing a concern for precision and avoiding ambiguity. With written language humans can transcend the particularities to which they are confined in oral communication, and develop these several dimensions of rational thought. On the basis of arguments about the special qualities of written communication, it is alleged that members of literate societies are enabled to perform logical-rational-cognitive feats precluded from members of non-literate societies.

Literacy has also been seen as responsible for economic-developmental outcomes. Anderson claims that

> there is convergent evidence that literacy of a large minority of males is a precondition for any significant transition of an under-developed economy to one marked by economic growth ... Very broadly, the data appear to support a generalization ... [that] about 40 per cent of adult literacy or of primary enrolment is a threshold for economic development.[10]

Writing in the same volume as Anderson, Kahan argues with regard to Russian agriculture at the turn of the century that the increased level of literacy among higher income groups of peasants and agricultural labourers became 'the precondition for introduction of machinery and more modern farming methods'.[11]

Often these claims that literacy has a causal influence on economic development seem to rest on little more than correlation: wherein the dates coinciding with a period of economic change and 'take off' correlate with literacy levels at or beyond 40 per cent. In some cases, however, more complex rationales have been advanced – as where the idea of a 40 per cent threshold rate of literacy is in turn 'explained' by theories of the type that allege the importance of literacy for the emergence of cognitive and personal qualities conducive, in turn, to economic development. Oxenham, for instance, suggests that the association of literacy with 'a modernization syndrome', 'the concept of modern man', and the development of such attitudes and dispositions as 'flexibility', 'adaptability', 'empathy', 'willingness to accept change' and 'proneness to adopt innovations', were guiding assumptions behind the trend to literacy campaigns in third world countries following World War Two.[12] In this vein, Hägerstrand claims that the demand for education is at times an innovation which must be introduced to a society in order to open it for further innovation. 'Literacy and other new skills', says Hägerstrand, 'eventually transform social communication and resistance' into patterns more susceptible to innovation and the progress that comes with it.[13]

In his book *The Literacy Myth*, Graff lists various social qualities and ends which are often alleged to flow from literacy. These include, for the individual, self-worth, social mobility, moral growth and personal achievement; and for the community as a whole, orderliness and a law-abiding disposition, cultural enrichment, and civilization generally.[14] It is precisely the belief in literacy as an independent variable having these alleged consequences that Graff labels 'the literacy myth'. His book is an attempt to demonstrate – by reference to specific case studies – the extent to which these beliefs are, collectively, in fact a myth: that the social reality is much more complex than the simple, one-way cause and effect relationship suggests, and that literacy does not produce on its own these outcomes at all.

I will turn now to making good the claim that the ideas about literacy outlined in this section are indeed misconceptions.

Toward understanding literacy

The three beliefs about literacy that I have just described are key tenets of what Street calls the 'autonomous' model of literacy. The general assumption behind this model is that literacy has autonomy from the particular social contexts in which it is employed. Its character is not determined by setting. Equally, it remains independent of and impartial toward the patterns and struggles of daily life. There is no conception of literacy being itself an important dimension of social practice: an integral part of the very social order itself – simultaneously *shaped* by wider social processes, and *employed* in defining, maintaining, transmitting, reinforcing, refining, or challenging various practices and values of daily life. Still less is there any idea that dominant forms of literacy may emerge as structured practices in the service of dominant interests.

Street rejects the 'autonomous' view of literacy and argues instead for what he calls an 'ideological' model. According to this view there is no such thing as a 'literacy essence' lying behind the actual social practices of reading and writing. Rather, the nature and meaning of literacy consists in the forms literacy practice actually takes within given social contexts. Those who espouse the 'ideological' view 'concentrate on the specific social practices of reading and writing': that is, on the forms reading and writing practice actually take, and the ways reading and writing skills are used, rather than on some abstracted technology.[15] In other words, what literacy *is* is entirely a matter of how reading and writing are conceived and practised within particular social settings.

Moreover, according to the ideological model, conceptions and practices of reading and writing evolve and exist within power structures and reflect tensions between competing power and interest groups. The views people have of what literacy involves, of what counts as being literate; what they see as 'real' or appropriate uses of reading and writing skills; the ways people actually read and write in the course of their daily lives; these all reflect and promote values, beliefs, assumptions and practices, which shape the way life is lived within a given society and, in turn, influence which interests are promoted or undermined as a consequence of how life is lived there.

Literacy is best understood as 'a shorthand for the social practices and conceptions of reading and writing'.[16] Indeed, for many social contexts we do better to think in terms of literacies rather than literacy. At any rate, literacy should be seen as an integral aspect – a dimension – of social practice as a whole, simultaneously reflecting and promoting certain beliefs, values and processes. And so it is directly linked to the actual consequences for the lives of individuals and groups of social activity and arrangements grounded in these same beliefs, values and processes. Far from being autonomous, or independent, of existing social values, trends and practices, and the consequences of these for people's interests, literacy is really an intrinsic dimension of them.

From the standpoint of the ideological model, the beliefs that literacy is unitary, neutral, and an independent variable, are readily seen to be mistaken. In this section I will employ a number of arguments which are advanced from the ideological perspective on literacy – or are otherwise consistent with this perspective – in order to critique these three beliefs.

(i) Against the view that literacy is unitary, it is apparent that quite distinct and different literacies exist in social practice. What researchers should do, accordingly, is identify and examine the character of these different literacies, and consider the roles they play within the functioning of the society as a whole and in the lives of various groups and individuals within that society. To establish this I will refer to historical and contemporary examples.

Cressy's investigation of illiteracy levels in England between 1530 and 1730 supports the view that a wide range of literacies was to be found during this period. He argues that a broad distinction between *passive* literacy – comprising 'an ability to read without knowledge of writing' – and *active* literacy – 'where writing as well as reading had been mastered' – can safely be assumed to have applied in England at that time. While available documents do not provide any conclusive evidence of the extent and distribution of active and passive literacy respectively during those years, the existence of a sector of the population who possessed a merely passive literacy seems an inevitable consequence of the way the curriculum was ordered in Tudor and Stuart elementary education.[17]

During the sixteenth century a system of 'charity' and 'petty' schools emerged, outside of the grammar and private school system which was available only to those of means. These former schools taught literacy skills in a strictly sequential manner. Mastery of reading was required before a pupil began learning to write. According to Schofield, within charity schools, 'writing was taught only to those who could read "competently well", and figures were taught only after the art of writing had been mastered'.[18] This sequence was still observed in the nineteenth-century monitorial schools, with the (by now measurable and documented) consequence of promoting a passive literacy among those working-class children who attended them. Thus

> the master in charge of the Borough Street School in London, which was the model school of the Lancastrian ... system, reckoned that it took twelve months to teach a child to read and between three and four years to teach it to write well together with some simple arithmetic. The average length of attendance at this school, which was well above the general average, was thirteen months, enough to acquire an ability to read, but not to write well.[19]

It seems both reasonable and historically edifying to acknowledge the existence of different literacies in this context – especially in view of the fact that the practice of teaching reading alone, to the point of positively *excluding* writing, was often a deliberate political ploy on the part of those people educating working-class children. The attitudes and practices of education providers like Hannah More and Andrew Bell – in the late eighteenth and early nineteenth centuries respectively – give force to the notion of a (distinctively) passive literacy, and reveal the acknowledged importance of promulgating such a literacy among the lower orders. Both understood very clearly the political value of promoting a limited ability to read among the labouring classes, while at the same time deliberately withholding writing skills.

Hannah More felt obliged to defend the Sunday schools she established in the Mendips during the 1790s against those who saw dangers of sedition resulting from extending learning to the masses. Her response was to assert 'the political value of religion', which value 'can never be too firmly believed, or too carefully kept in view'. The social order was indeed beautiful, 'When each, according to his place, pays willing honour to his superiors ... when high, low, rich and poor ... sit down satisfied with his own place'. Biblical text and religious tract offered powerful assistance in the service of this end. After all, was it not true that for 'the rich man at his castle [and] the poor man at his gate, God made them high and lowly and ordered their estate'? If the poor possessed rudimentary reading skills (acquired within an appropriate socialization process) they would be opened to such insights, and would constantly have positive affirmation of their proper attitude of passive resignation as close to hand as the nearest bible or tract. More was adamant: 'I allow of no writing for the poor. My object is not to make them fanatics, but to train up the lower classes in habits of industry and piety'.[20] The reference here to 'fanaticism' is revealing. It would appear that More feared the potential inherent in writing for fostering an active stance toward the world, to the extent that she doubted the capacity of Sunday school instruction and discipline to prevent an undesirable growth of religious fanaticism among the poor if they once acquired the art of writing. There was no such perceived danger, however, with a literacy that was confined to reading alone. The view of Andrew Bell, founder of the Anglican system of monitorial schools, was entirely consistent with More's sentiments. He wrote that with regard to the activities of National Society schools

> it is not proposed that the children of the poor be educated in an expensive way, or even taught to write and cypher ... It may suffice to teach the generality ... to read their bible and understand the doctrines of our holy religion.[21]

What was being advocated here was the inculcation of *a particular literacy*. It was not simply a matter of offering the poor a strictly limited access to (the most minimal elements of) a *technology*. It was, more positively, to transmit to working-class children a definite conception of the bounds and uses of a reading practice appropriate to their class. Their literacy comprised a distinctive form, a coherent (and politically viable) 'package': a limited social practice and conception of reading, defined and rationalized by an ideology. As such it is properly to be regarded as a literacy in its own right; standing alongside other distinctive social practices and conceptions of reading and writing diffused among other social groups.

The research of Cressy, Schofield, and others demonstrates that quite different *literacies* were required – and, in fact, acquired – by people bearing different social class roles and status during the periods covered by their investigations. Cressy comments that during the seventeenth century clergymen, lawyers, and schoolmasters possessed a versatile range of reading and writing skills because that was a prerequisite of their vocation. Gentlemen too were expected to be fully and actively literate. Their education normally prepared them for the business of local administration, estate management, political gossip and civilized intercourse which went with their rank. Their literacy was appropriate to their needs.[22]

Between these groups and the working-class literate, as well as among these groups themselves, we are talking about literacies which are as distinctive as, *and commensurate with*, different social rankings and their associated occupations, pursuits, modes and styles of life. To reduce the practices and conceptions of reading and writing of these elite and professional classes to the idea of their having somewhat greater access across a wider range to *the same technology* as was available to the 'literate' portion of the labouring poor, is to grossly distort social reality. In every major sense other than the biological, these people *were* different from the masses. Their respective literacies were an intrinsic dimension of this difference, and integral to patterning relations between the various levels of the social order.

A further and particularly interesting case was that of the yeomanry – 'a thrusting, dynamic group, working hard, amassing land and profits, apeing their betters, and setting their sons up as gentlemen'. They practised a literacy attuned to their economic affairs, social aspirations, and, in the case of forty-shilling freeholders, the formalities of voting and being generally politically active and informed. Again, theirs was a distinctive literacy. It was, moreover, an integral aspect of a *distinctive mode of social being*. The yeoman's literacy was part of the very structure, the very patterning, of that distinctive mode of social existence which was the life and style of the yeomen. Their literacy was a social *form*: an identifiable set of reading and writing practices governed by a conception of what and how to read and write, when, and why. It was a lived practice symmetrical with the wider life lived by the yeomen, and a core part of the very *structure* of that life. To reduce the yeomen's literacy to a (particular) degree and range of access to a unitary technology is, once again, to dissolve away the utterly social character of literacy. Their literacy was inseparable from their very social being. Cressy makes an interesting comment, which feeds directly into the notion of the yeomen having a distinctive social practice and conception of reading and writing, when he notes that yeomen

> were the natural audience for certain types of printed material. Almanacs, guides to good husbandry, even books of etiquette, appear to have a yeoman readership in mind.[23]

The point I am seeking through these historical examples can, I think, be well made by means of an analogy with work. People down the ages and all over the world have engaged in work in order to sustain their existence. If we pose the question, 'what is the nature and meaning of work?', we could confront it in a manner analogous to treating literacy as a neutral technology lying behind the myriad actual social practices and conceptions of literacy. We could say something like, 'work is organized human activity directed toward producing items that are necessary or otherwise desirable for sustaining human existence'. Having grasped the 'essence' of work in this (or some similar) way, we might then suggest that while different people may participate in greater or lesser amounts of work, across a wider or narrower range of item production, employing more or less sophisticated methods of production, under one or other system or logic of producing their respective items (for example, process line assembly versus one person producing an entire item), they are nevertheless all ultimately engaged in the same 'thing': namely, *work*. In other words, work is the same thing in the end – people just happen to do 'it' differently, for different ends and under different conditions.

Clearly this is absurd. There is no single, unitary, unifying essence of work lying behind the myriad actual social practices and conceptions of work. The perceived essence exists as nothing more than a figment of the imagination of the 'essentializing' philosopher or social scientist. The reality of work – what work *is*: its nature; the meaning of 'work' – is what particular individuals and groups engage in as their structured social practice of work. And this social practice is carried out under governing conceptions of what it is they are (having) to do, how, and why. As for work, so for literacy. Both are dimensions, and interrelated dimensions, of human life: of social practice generally. The perceived unitariness of both is illusory.[24] The important thing so far as the social understanding of work and literacy is concerned, is the actual forms they take within and among particular groups and individuals, in particular times and places. The search for unitary essences directs our attention away from these matters and the many issues – social, political, ethical, cultural, etc. – that turn on them. It is a central virtue of the ideological model of literacy that it brings us back to these matters and their related issues.

There are also very important contemporary dimensions to the claim that we should identify and examine different literacies rather than assert or assume a single unitary literacy. We find present day writers distinguishing between 'basic' and 'critical' literacy, 'domesticating' and 'liberating' literacy, 'improper' and 'proper' literacy, 'functional' and 'full' literacy, and even between different 'functional' literacies. In addition, some identify and elaborate different literacies by social class, culture/subculture, ethnic group, etc.[25] Rather than consider such contemporary dimensions of the present issue here, I will offer later in this chapter a detailed analysis of two distinct *functional* literacies. This analysis will be advanced in the light of my arguments against literacy as a unitary phenomenon, as well as arguments which critique the further claims that literacy is neutral and an independent variable.

(ii) I want now to challenge the alleged *neutrality* of literacy. The arguments I have advanced against the view that literacy is unitary also have grave implications for the claim that literacy is a neutral technology or a neutral skill: i.e., that literacy does not itself determine the uses to which it is actually put and is not itself shaped by the uses made of it. This belief is readily shown to be mistaken once the view is adopted that literacy comprises actual social practices and conceptions of reading and writing.

It is helpful here to return to Neil Postman's consideration of reading as a neutral skill. Having acknowledged the common belief that reading is a neutral skill, that what people read is their own business – for example, on the topic of America they are free to read De Toqueville or *The Daily News* – and that the reading teacher, far from shaping in any way the pupils' worldviews, merely helps increase their options, Postman continues as follows:

> In theory, this argument is compelling. In practice it is pure romantic nonsense. *The New York Daily News* is the most widely read newspaper in America. Most of our students will go to the grave not having read, of their own choosing, a paragraph of De Toqueville or Thoreau or John Stuart Mill or, if you exclude the Gettysburg Address, even Abraham Lincoln. As between Jacqueline Susann and Herman Melville – well, the less said, the better. To put it bluntly, among every 100 students who learn to read, my guess is that no more than one will employ the process toward any of the lofty goals which are customarily held [such as opening students' minds to the wonders and riches of the written word, to give them access to great fiction and poetry, to permit them to function as informed citizens, etc.] The rest will use the process to increase their knowledge of trivia, to maintain themselves at a relatively low level of emotional maturity, and to keep themselves simplistically uninformed about the social and political turmoil around them.[26]

Postman is describing here what literacy actually *is* for people in daily life. He is sketching – albeit in a polemical manner – the actual social practices and conceptions of literacy for the population in question. Literacy is largely seen as a means to information about the world via popular daily newspapers, and so people practise the reading of newspapers *en masse* – with only a tiny proportion turning to social or political theory and critique as a basis for interpreting and evaluating what they read about the world in newspapers, or for seeking a deeper and more accurate knowledge of social, political, and cultural reality. Conceptions of literacy include notions of what is to be read, what one can expect to get from particular print media (for example, 'you get the necessary current affairs information from the newspaper', 'you get a good story from Mills and Boon', 'you get interesting – important? – facts from *The Guinness Book of Records*'), and what the purposes or goals of reading are (to be amused, entertained, transported away, kept up to date, kept informed or in touch, etc.). These very conceptions guide our literacy practice. And our practice in turn affirms these conceptions when we *are* amused, or *do* feel informed and kept in touch.

Now what Postman points to is that these conceptions and social practices of literacy are patterned. There are definite patterns, observable *structures* of reading behaviour. The same applies *a fortiori* to writing. To begin with, people are much more inclined to read than to write. Many people who read a great deal actually write only very occasionally. And what of the writing behaviour itself? Here I take licence to paraphrase Postman. My guess is that among every 100 students who learn to write in societies like our own, no more than one will use the process to write a reasoned and scholarly critique of a newspaper article, to research in any depth the logic and consequences of racist beliefs or sexist attitudes, or to critically examine the democratic assumption that our society successfully promotes equality of opportunity – or pursues this goal as fully as possible. Will one writer in 1000 ever seriously address such themes as whether schools *in fact* provide children with a genuine liberal education? Will one in 100,000 use their writing skills to consider whether schools might reasonably be expected to promote a truly critical, liberating education within capitalist society (or other themes of comparable sophistication)? By contrast, we write relatively many letters (and those addressing daily themes are often lamentable from a critical standpoint, as perusing 'Letters to the Editor' columns readily attests), cheques, shopping lists, notes to the children about when we will be back home, and so on.

These comments are not intended as value judgments – although Postman's values do come through clearly and, hopefully, mine will also in due course. Rather, they are intended to repudiate the myth that literacy is a neutral skill or technology. Literacy is not neutral. To use Postman's formula, literacy – that is, the actual social practices and conceptions of reading and writing – is ninety-nine for *The Daily News* and one for De Toqueville. Literacy is aligned ninety-nine to one *against* critical in-depth, evaluative reading. It is aligned ninety-nine to one in *support* of 'increasing one's knowledge of trivia and remaining simplistically uninformed about the social and political turmoil around us'. It is similarly aligned *against* critical, penetrating, evaluative, truth-seeking writing; and *for* the minimal, routine forms and procedures typically followed in daily life.

Against the belief that literacy does not itself determine the uses to which it is put and is not itself shaped by the uses made of it, I argue that literacy *is* the uses to which it is put and the conceptions which shape and reflect its actual use. Once this is admitted we do more than merely achieve relief from the gross reification of literacy involved in the literacy-as-a-neutral-skill-or-technology view. In addition, we are freed to ask a whole range of questions that we are effectively discouraged from asking if we assume that literacy is neutral. For we can now entertain the possibility that the forms reading and writing take in daily life are related to the wider operation of power and patterns of interest within society.

The questions we are freed to ask include, for example: why is it that reading and writing practices are patterned in the way they are?; what forces or practices encourage this patterning?; why are the very options that are often held up as the *real* purposes of reading and writing conspicuous by their near absence?; what are the forces and processes that effectively close off these (pseudo) options from the great majority of readers and writers in our society?; are there particular interests served and/or undermined by the widespread tendency for actual reading and writing practices to be uncritical, superficial, trivializing, un- or mis- informative, etc.?; if so, what are these interests, and how are they related to those forces and processes that pattern literacy practices and their guiding conceptions?; what are the consequences, in historical and biographical terms, of literacy practices (habits?) being what they are?; are there ways of altering these patterns in a more critical direction?; should we attempt to?; when all is said and done, how free *is* the individual to choose for the sorts of options Postman seems to value most highly?

Against this background we can raise the possibility that belief in the neutrality of literacy is, in fact, an important ideological belief. For as long as literacy is presumed to be neutral, teachers and other purveyors of literacy are absolved from having to consider what the end consequences are of their activities. We can rest easy in the belief that it is none of *our* responsibility if learners just happen to end up choosing the more minimal options, and are left to grope their way through life systematically misinformed, as bearers of distorted or naive views of the world, even clinging to 'information' (myths) that undermine their own interests. We are given a moral and political 'holiday': left free to continue teaching under a comforting delusion, oblivious to the actual outcomes of our labours.

Only if we face up to the ways in which, and extent to which, reading and writing *are actually patterned* are we enabled to consider the wider scene in which we, as teachers of reading and writing, are key characters. Only then are we obliged to consider closely the extent to which it is responsible, *or irresponsible*, to continue teaching reading and writing skills without seeking knowledge and understanding of the full and real outcomes of the literacy we facilitate, and the ways in which we might strive to gain some control over and against such outcomes – and thereby bring the outcomes of our educational practice more closely into line with our liberal educational rhetoric. An important first step in this process is to discard the mistaken belief that literacy is neutral. Indeed, it is precisely this kind of belief that shields us from recognizing and questioning our role in a process that claims to educate people for liberal and liberating ends, but succeeds only in socializing generation after generation into uncritical participation in routine practices and beliefs: including routine practices and conceptions of reading and writing.

If it is true that within our own society the social practices of reading and writing are predominantly uncritical, within a world that positively calls out for sensitive critique of so many trends, practices and policies, perhaps educators should be asking whether there exist contemporary equivalents of Hannah More's Sunday schools: that is, forces and processes that effectively maintain a social order in which interests are served differentially, by systematically withholding skills, *including literacy skills first and foremost*, that enable critical investigation and evaluation of this social order. Do mass media networks, advertising, curriculum policies and practices, pedagogies, educational rhetoric, popular taste and opinion (already well and truly shaped by these other forces), play a role in shaping prevailing patterns of literacy? Or, perhaps, might work processes that in no way call for the critical use of literacy skills result in whatever skills people may once have possessed being extinguished, lost through lack of use, or positively discouraged? If so, can we detect interests which are systematically favoured or negated by the literacies (and illiteracies) shaped by these influences, and by the effective 'swamping' of more critical forms of literacy? The belief that we can in fact detect such interests underlies the claim that prevailing practices and conceptions of literacy – and, indeed, *all* forms of literacy – are ideological. It also underlies the claim that belief in the neutrality of literacy is an important ideological view.

(iii) Powerful arguments have been advanced against the alleged cognitive, economic-developmental, and social consequences deriving from literacy as an independent variable. Street provides a comprehensive coverage of the case against cognitive outcomes. Rather than deal with this here I simply refer readers to his work. I want briefly to survey some arguments against the claimed economic-developmental outcomes of literacy, since these will resonate with themes addressed later in reference to literacy and the Nicaraguan Revolution. My main interest here, however, is with a line of argument advanced by Harvey Graff against the alleged social consequences of literacy.

The belief that literacy, as an independent variable, produces important economic-developmental outcomes is readily dispensed with. According to Hunter and Harman, mounting evidence suggests that literacy skills are not sought unless they are generally considered desirable within the culture – that is, unless 'literacy consciousness' is the norm.[27]

If this is true there are grounds for believing that 'literacy skills follow rather than precede development' – including economic development. In other words, perhaps some level of economic development (within wider processes of development) is causally significant in promoting literacy as a relevant goal and enhancing its attainment among the population, *rather than the other way round*. This would certainly help explain some of the massive failures of literacy campaigns within a number of radically 'under-developed' countries. Whatever the precise relationship actually is between literacy and economic dimensions of development, it is obviously more complex than the simple 'literacy causes/produces development' view suggests.

Moreover, insofar as the diffusion of literacy among a population does help enhance development, this will not be literacy as an abstracted, autonomous technology. Only particular forms of literacy – particular practices and ideals of reading and writing – will have significance: namely, forms attuned to the real needs, interests, and perceptions of local people. Just what these forms comprise will be largely determined by factors extrinsic to the mere technique(s) or technology of reading and writing. Street makes precisely this point in a brief but penetrating attack on the ethnocentric mentality of those developmentalists who – albeit with good will – foist literacy programmes (and other development 'initiatives') on third world people without due regard or respect for them and their reality. With reference to the pilot scheme for a literacy project in Tanzania (during 1971), Street notes:

> the literacy that was provided for local farmers was not ... 'rooted in their daily work' [although those promoting the programme believed it would be]: indeed, since the local farmers had no integral use for what they had been taught it soon began to 'atrophy' and the project staff had to construct an artificial 'literacy environment' to try and sustain it.[28]

The message here is that for literacy to assist in promoting or enhancing development it must be grounded in the real development needs of the people concerned, and be seen by them to have this grounding. This, however, will necessarily make it a *particular literacy*, not some contingent application of universal abstracted literacy. If literacy is to continue enhancing development once it has already begun, it must remain open to refinement, alteration, and redefinition in the light of altered circumstances, local experiences, priority shifts, etc. Revised conceptions and practices of reading and writing may prove necessary to maintain development impetus. To repeat, this is in no way the idea of an independent variable acting unilaterally to bring about desirable (or desired) consequences. Literacy and local circumstances are interwoven. We should, of course, expect this since literacy is *used*. And for it to be used it must have a form that is usable and useful within its specific context. It was because the literacy foisted on the Tanzanian farmers had no use for them that it 'atrophied'. To conceive literacy (indeed, *literacies*) this way is to see it as interwoven with wider social practices, goals, interests and processes: as an organic part of a social order and social practice; not as an independent, detached variable producing its own causal outcomes on an external reality. To a large extent literacy is a dependent variable – shaped by the wider social life within which it evolves and is practised.

Let us now turn to arguments advanced by Harvey Graff which bear on the alleged (important) social consequences of literacy. Graff focuses on the everyday belief that literacy is a very important tool for ensuring fulfilling lives and productive citizenship: that literacy brings, simultaneously, advantages to the individual – in terms of personal development, happiness, equal opportunity to pursue advantage, social mobility, job satisfaction, economic reward, personal enrichment and fulfilment – as well as to society – in terms of enlightenment, social cohesion and harmony, respect for the law, enhanced democratic practice, orderliness, variety, enriched institutional life, etc. He takes our largely uncritical belief in the power of literacy to bring about such wide ranging social outcomes and subjects it to close empirical scrutiny, by means of historical case study and analysis. His investigation centres on three cities in Ontario, Canada, during the mid-nineteenth-century. Hamilton, London, and Kingston all had high rates of literacy – in excess of 90 per cent – as defined and measured by census, and documented records for these cities offer good data for analysis.[29]

Each town had a high proportion of migrant citizens: notably, Irish, English, and US born – with many of the latter being black. Graff identifies the (90 per cent) literate and (10 per cent) illiterate populations, observing that

> the ascribed characteristics of Irish birth, Catholicism, colour, and
> female sex, as they intersected with age, constituted the dominant
> forces among the origins of illiteracy.[30]

At this time a well developed rhetoric of achievement was espoused at official levels within the province by such people as Egerton Ryerson, Ontario's Chief Superintendent of Education. Literacy was widely acclaimed as necessary, and even sufficient, to enable those who possessed it to overcome ascribed handicaps and achieve social mobility. Literacy, it was claimed, was not merely instrumental in overcoming inherited economic disadvantage. It would also enable individuals to overcome 'other ascribed characteristics, including those stemming from ethnic origins, family and class backgrounds, and sometimes sex and race'.[31]

To test for the alleged 'personal benefits' outcome of literacy Graff compares the literate and illiterate populations in terms of occupation and income level (the most readily measurable forms of benefit) for the year 1861. He also adds a temporal dimension to the argument by assessing the fortunes ten years on (i.e., in 1871) of those illiterate adults who remained in the one town, and also considers the economic fates of their children. His findings suggest that there is no basis for the view that literacy functions as an independent variable to bring about personal benefits in occupational and economic terms.

He finds that many literate workers shared occupations with illiterate folk – indeed, 75 per cent of unskilled labourers and 93 per cent of semi-skilled workers were literate. On the other hand, almost 20 per cent of illiterate males obtained artisan or skilled work across a wide range of occupations. Moreover, some illiterate adults actually found work within commercial, clerical, and professional pursuits. For many adults, then, being literate provided them with no advantage over others who were illiterate. In fact, significant numbers of illiterate adults actually enjoyed occupational advantage over their literate peers. This advantage was almost entirely the result of ascription: especially the fact of being English and Protestant. More than 50 per cent of illiterate English Protestant males obtained skilled or non-manual work. By contrast, for many Irish Catholics, women generally, and Blacks,

> the achievement of education brought no occupational rewards at all; inherited factors cancelled the potential of advancement through literacy.[32]

The significance of literacy for personal benefit was small, if not negligible, here. Graff claims that the one context in which being illiterate was a disadvantage and being literate an advantage in occupational terms was where an individual *already had* the 'right' ascribed characteristics. Illiteracy seems to have imposed an important barrier against an English Protestant moving upward into skilled labour; but its significance for an Irish Catholic was virtually non-existent. Substantially the same patterns are reflected in income levels. Where being literate *did* intersect with higher income – for example, in gaining skilled work which brought with it higher pay, plus the fact that literate skilled workers earned more than illiterate skilled workers – the major factor operating seems again to have been ascribed characteristics.

Adding the temporal dimension makes no real difference to the overall picture. Ten years later, illiterate adults who had stayed in the same town revealed some modest success in improving their occupational status, wealth, and ownership of property – despite the fact that emerging indus-trialization might have been expected to call for enhanced skills (including literacy skills) in order to maintain one's occupational standing and eco-nomic level, let alone improve it. Illiteracy seems not to have been a disad-vantage in these terms to adults who had learned to 'read' their city through experience. Interestingly, by 1871 not a single illiterate English Protestant in the sample remained poor. All had achieved what Graff calls a middle-class economic standing. By contrast, many literate Irish, Catholics, and Blacks remained poor. A generation on, many literate sons of illiterate fathers enjoyed some measurable mobility over them. Even so, these sons remained within the working-class itself. They moved upward relative to their fathers, but only *within* the working-class. Interclass mobility, says Graff, was 'quite exceptional ... literacy and education did not have *that* kind of impact on the social structure.'[33] In brief, Graff's study suggests that, with regard to personal benefit (defined in quantifiable terms), 'literacy's role was neither as simple nor as direct as contemporary opinion would predict'. There is no basis to be found here for the belief that the role of literacy is 'central and deterministic ... a requirement, in fact, of development ... in respect of individuals'. Far from operating as an independent factor, let alone a major determining factor,

> literacy interacted with ethnicity, age, occupation, wealth, adjust-ment, and family organization, reinforcing and mediating the primary social processes that ordered the population, rather than determining their influences.[34]

What, then, of the alleged consequences of literacy as an independent variable for society more generally? Graff proceeds here by identifying the social benefits that were explicitly sought by those people who promoted education and literacy in mid-nineteenth century Ontario, and considers the nature and role of literacy in relation to achieving these benefits. Once again his argument suggests that literacy did *not* function as an independ-ent causal factor in the achievement of social benefits. Rather, it func-tioned as an integrated and highly conditioned component within a very complex process of schooling. When examining literacy in relation to occupation and income, Graff found it impossible to isolate the effect of literacy from that of ascribed characteristics where literate workers did well or improved their circumstances. Similarly, when examining literacy in relation to achieving social goals Graff finds it impossible to isolate the operation of literacy from that of, say, the process of maintaining control in the school. Moreover, he finds that school literacy – the literacy trans-mitted in school – cannot be understood as a pure skill or technology. Rather it can only be understood as a complex *form*, conditioned and shaped by a 'hidden' curriculum, a definite pedagogy, sector interests, and a valuative position consistent with those sector interests. Far from being an independent variable, the school literacy of working-class youth in Ontario was very much a dependent, conditioned variable.

Three closely related themes run through Graff's argument pertaining to the alleged social consequences of literacy.

(i) Promoting literacy for its own sake, or for whatever ends the individual might choose to employ it, was never on the agenda of those who advocated mass schooling for universal literacy in nineteenth-century Ontario. Indeed, 'literacy alone ... – that is, isolated from its moral basis – was feared as potentially subversive'.[35] *The Christian Guardian* stressed the need to control the use of literacy, in school and home alike. 'No part of education is of greater importance than the selection of proper books'. Especially feared were 'exciting books of fiction', along with the works of such authors as Tom Paine and Voltaire. *The Christian Guardian* insisted that novels be proscribed for young and unmarried women. A religious newspaper was recommended for the needs of all – especially of poor families. The Bible was seen as the best of all possible literature for guiding the new social order. The views of the *Guardian* assume special significance when it is known that Ryerson edited that paper before becoming Education Superintendent.

(ii) A schooling based upon literacy was seen as important for efficiently adjusting working-class children to the social order and for establishing a hegemony attuned to the emerging industrial capitalist society.

> The literacy of properly schooled, *morally restrained* men and women represented the object of the school promoters. As Susan Houston summarizes, 'The campaign against ignorance (and the mandate of the school system) encompassed more than reading; illiteracy was deplored, but more as a visible sign of that other ignorance that was the root of personal and social deviance', and a threat to the emerging capitalist order.[36]

In other words, it was the achievement of 'moral' development and social control, to be effected through school learning, discipline and order, *mediated by literacy* (since literacy is the inevitable medium of education within a print society), that underlay the strong commitment of the school promoters to ensuring universal literacy.

Ryerson's own view was that education should promote principles, habits, and character, in an apprenticeship for life and eternity. Christian duties and discipline were to be central in education. After all,

> high intellectual and physical accomplishments may be associated with deep moral and public debasement. It is the cultivation of

[our] moral powers and feelings which forms the basis of social order and the vital fluid of social happiness.[37]

Literacy was to be the medium of an educational process leading to correct moral development and the growth of discipline and social control. The morality in question would be a shared morality – a morality common to all social classes, drawing them together in social cohesion. It would simultaneously shape a responsible, obedient workforce, and mask the conflicting interests of different classes within the social order by uniting them under a common conception (ideology) of a benign society functioning in the interests of all equally. In Graff's words.

> Community and oneness, the basis for cohesion and hegemony, would be well advanced in common and correct schooling. The classes – rich and poor alike – would share habits and values once more, respect one another, and the lower-class would become respectable and self-respecting. Of course, neither the social classes nor the social order need be disturbed.[38]

(iii) The actual physical characteristics and dynamics of the classroom, together with the pedagogy employed and a hidden curriculum associated with reading, contrived to produce a learning context admirably suited to promoting that 'moral' development and social control sought among working-class children through education. Graff notes, for example, that classrooms were typically crowded – with teacher-pupil ratios of 1:100 by enrolment and 1:70 by typical attendance being commonplace. As a result, maintaining order in the classroom was a major priority. The heavy emphasis accordingly placed on sheer classroom management had obvious implications for the sorts of attitudes and habits each child had to develop in order for learning to proceed. Children were obliged to be quiet and docile, to the point of being virtually inactive, other than when called on to recite the ABCs. Classroom learning effectively became an apprenticeship in passivity and resignation: an exercise in social control. In addition, the pedagogy employed was highly conducive to promoting obedience, quietness and discipline. The dominant method of rote repetition of letters or words actually militated against reading or writing with genuine comprehension. Consequently it was 'safe' in the sense that it was impotent to generate a critical literacy that might in turn encourage questioning of social practices and arrangements, or the values of the hegemony sought by ruling interests. This method did, however, assert the teacher's authority, establish the values and habits of drill, and promote passive attitudes and responses on the part of pupils.

The implications of Graff's inquiry are obvious. To the extent that literacy played a role within educational processes leading to moral development, social control, and cohesion built around a shared view of society as promoting the interests of all, it is clear that literacy did not function as an independent variable. To begin with, it would be impossible to separate off the contribution of literacy *per se* from that of the control mechanisms employed, the pedagogy that operated, or the other components of the schooling process (overt and hidden) as a whole. Moreover, the idea of a socially detached, free-ranging technology of reading and writing giving rise to social (or personal) benefits is entirely out of place here. The literacy sought by those who promoted and controlled education in Ontario was a thoroughly conditioned variable. The social practices of reading and writing they envisaged were grounded in an ideal which was ideological through and through – immersed in the interests of those who stood to gain from maintaining and consolidating existing social relations. Literacy was intended to offer access to moral instruction – which promised social control and cohesion in addition to (though very much informed by) Christian rectitude. Moral instruction and judicious control of reading matter would, in turn, eliminate the risk of potentially 'dangerous' uses of literacy – including those which might lead to critiquing and challenging existing social arrangements. Furthermore, the actual literacy acquired and practised in the classroom (that is, the specific form it took, or the form that it *was*) incorporated the pedagogy itself. In other words, what literacy very largely *was* reflected and embodied the distinctive pedagogy by which it was acquired (as a rote form) and employed by the pupils (in repetition on demand). This is quite alien to the idea of literacy as an abstracted, socially/culturally disembodied technology. It is, rather, the idea of literacy as ideological: as a socially constructed *form*, shaped by and reflecting wider social practices, relations, values, goals, interests, etc. This is precisely the view of literacy I am recommending here.

It follows from what I have argued that to misconstrue literacy as an independent variable is to mystify and distort what actually goes on in education. Furthermore, such confusion is interest serving, as can be illustrated by reference to Graff's study. For in this context it would suggest that social cohesion, orderliness, and 'moral propriety' were the fortunate but spontaneous/uncontrived outcomes of a neutral technology or process – namely, literacy. In fact these outcomes reflect the way in which educational practice was socially constructed and maintained. What is more, these outcomes were especially beneficial to (and desired by) particular sector interests. Cohesion, harmony, obedience, and acceptance by all of the status quo, serve the interests of those who do best out of existing social arrangements. Their interests are doubly served if such social 'values' are seen to result from literacy itself rather than from socially constructed and maintained (educational) practices: since the true origins of advantage and disadvantage, *in social practice*, are masked. What is really socially constructed advantage appears instead to be the natural outcome of a neutral process.

Literacy: a summary statement

I see the major points about literacy to have emerged thus far as these:

(i) Literacy is best understood, in Street's words, as a shorthand for the social practices and conceptions of reading and writing. There is no single, unitary referent for 'literacy'. Literacy is not the name for a finite technology, set of skills, or any other 'thing'. We should recognize, rather, that there are many specific literacies, each comprising an identifiable set of socially constructed practices based upon print and organized around beliefs about how the skills of reading and writing may or, perhaps, should be used.

(ii) The *form* that particular literacies take reflects aspects of the wider social reality within which they are evolved and practised. These aspects include values, goals, beliefs, assumptions, ideals, traditions, interests, institutional procedures, patterned power relations, etc. We have seen, for example, that the school literacy described by Graff reflected social relations of authority and control; patterns of domination and submission. These relations characterized the pedagogy by which reading and writing were taught/acquired, and within which they were employed in the classroom. And so the distinctive practice of school literacy here was *structured* around these relations. The practice of reading and writing actually reflected hierarchical social relations. As such, this particular school literacy accorded well with the views of dominant interest groups as to how life should be lived – for example, harmoniously and obediently within established social goals and hierarchies of power, control and authority – and with the existing hierarchical class, gender, and racial relations of that society.

This does not mean, however, that literacies are merely passive, conditioned reflexes of wider social reality. The relationship between literacy and social beliefs, values, and practices more generally, is dynamic and dialectical. Literacies 'act back on' social reality as well as 'being acted on'. Indeed, as we will see, some practices and conceptions of reading and writing are consciously constructed and practised with a view to transforming existing social reality.

(iii) A given literacy is, then, a *representation* of reading and writing practice. It is a form that reading and writing *can* take and, as a matter of historical fact, *has* taken. As such each form is a response to some values, assumptions, practices, etc., rather than (or more than) others. Literacies are not neutral. They are ideological forms with profound significance for how human life is lived and whose interests are most served by the way life is lived. One literacy may favour engagement with serious literature for contemplation; another with light reading for amusement or diversion. One favours critical investigation and analysis; another is entirely uncritical. These dispositions must be seen as integral to the literacies themselves; not as (merely) contingent features of them. As structured practice, one literacy (or form) *is* critical; the other *is* uncritical. They have different implications for how people approach their world.

(iv) Within a given society definite *patterns* of literacy practice may be apparent. Postman, for example, suggests that the dominant reading practice within the US is superficial, unreflective and uncritical – to the point of promoting *un*awareness. Reflective, evaluative, and genuinely informative reading practice is, in his view, hopelessly marginalized. If this is a reasonable assessment, important questions arise as to how such patterns emerge, and why they emerge: especially in view of our official educational rhetoric which stresses the importance and value of literacy for critical enlightenment, informed participation in democratic processes, etc. In particular, are certain interests served by the patterns of literacy that emerge? And if so, what possibilities exist for those whose interests are undermined by prevailing literacy practices to create new ones which better reflect and promote their interests?

Given the argument in chapter 1, the view that literacies are socially constructed has important implications for the question of literacy and human interests. For if literacy is socially constructed we should expect some people or groups within societies like our own to have greater influence than others in the process of determining what will count as literacy within that social-historical setting. Moreover, this should in turn result in their interests being better served by the literacy which evolves than those of groups with lesser access to power by which to shape social practice.

In the remainder of this chapter I will address the relationship between literacy and human interests, and consider the implications of my account for the politics of literacy. Before turning to this task, though, I want to comment briefly on the emergence of *patterns* of actual literacy within a society, by reference to Graff and the school literacy of nineteenth-century Ontario.

School practice and uncritical literacy

Postman presents us with a contradiction. We 'customarily hold' a whole range of 'lofty goals' for literacy. In fact these goals are negated by the actual reading and writing practice of the overwhelming majority of citizens. How does this come about? How are we to explain the dominant pattern of literacy, in which uncritical and unreflective practice prevails? Graff's work again provides a clue here. If we take his description of classroom practice in the common-schools of Ontario we can see how the practice of a distinctively *uncritical* – even uncomprehending – literacy would become the norm, almost inevitably, for those pupils. Unless there were powerful countervailing influences in their adult lives the only literacy available to them would have been the minimal form acquired in their schooling. Whether or not there *were* countervailing factors is not an issue here. We have already seen, however, that influential opinion at the time stressed the importance of controlling literacy outside school as well as within it. Such control would have worked against the emergence of critical literacy had their been an inclination toward it. What though, of school literacy itself?

In chapter 7 of *The Literacy Myth* Graff inquiries into the quality of literacy promoted by Ontario's common-schools during the 1850s–70s. The evidence he musters suggests that the quality of literacy achieved by most pupils was low. There was generally a minimal comprehension of what was read in class, and minimal ability to actively employ the mechanical skills of reading and writing. Graff notes several factors contributing to this outcome, all of which were *structural* characteristics of the school. These include: the impossible physical conditions teachers and pupils alike had to contend with in the classroom – overcrowding, poor ventilation, freezing conditions in winter, etc.; the fact that most teachers were of low ability and/or poorly trained, and the few good teachers that did exist were so poorly paid and otherwise rewarded that they soon left teaching; a way of organizing the curriculum which inevitably resulted in superficial coverage of the various branches of knowledge – and, thus, of the content that was read and written; and the methods of instruction and classroom management that were employed.

These latter warrant further description. Inadequacies in prevailing methods of teaching reading were recognized by education officials at the time. In the 1850s the dominant method was to teach the alphabet first, and then move to spelling syllables of two or three letters – rather than using whole words as the unit of instruction. Ryerson, for one, found this method inappropriate (favouring an approach based on words). He described the method used as

> tedious to the teacher, stultifying to the student – 'protracted for many months' in its purely mechanical process. Lacking were, in his opinion, meaning, ideas, and applications. Indignantly, Ryerson asked, 'Is it not calculated to deaden rather than quicken the intellectual faculties? Is not such irrational drudgery calculated to disgust the subject of it with the very thought of learning?' In the rote repetition of the letters, sometimes extending to years, the intellectual side – the meaning of what was read – was neglected; obscured were 'the meanings of the words used, the facts narrated, the principles involved, the lessons inculcated'. Children learned neither useful skills nor fluency; they learned

little more than indifference or aversion to reading, and with 'so few pleasant recollections, that they engaged in it with reluctance, and only from necessity'.[39]

Other failings in methodology noted by Graff include an overemphasis on enunciation – in the mistaken belief, perhaps, that it correlates with comprehension – and the failure to take due account of the fact that the style and diction of school and book might be very different from that of home and street – with obvious implications for the transferral of literacy skills outside a classroom setting.[40] Finally, the practices of classroom management were hostile to any desire (let alone propensity) to learn. The schoolroom became

'a prison from which [the child] gladly escapes and to which he unwillingly returns'. The children dared not speak or ask questions; this would violate classroom order. 'His active little mind, playing in his healthy body, looking for and desiring knowledge, is curbed, depressed, broken, under the discipline of the present system'. Fondness for learning and study were presumed to depend on the nature of early encounters with the school. From the beginning, then, desire was being crushed.[41]

The point I am seeking here is this. Given that Graff is describing something like the norm for common-school practice and pupil experience at the time, we would expect the majority of those emerging from the schools to indeed possess a low quality, uncritical literacy. This school literacy would become patterned practice – if reading and writing were kept up to any significant extent at all upon leaving school. The higher the proportion of the population for whom this formed the experience of reading and writing, the more dominant this particular practice of literacy would be. Interestingly, Graff comments that high degrees of literacy skill were not required by most people, for work or welfare alike, in Ontario at this time. The culture simply did not require it. Even among non-manual workers – in clerical work, say – ' "automatic responses" and "rule of thumb techniques" may well have played a more common role than higher, more advanced literacy skills' (let alone a genuinely critical literacy).[42] What is more, the culture *did not desire* a higher literacy for, as we have seen, it was believed that unless literacy was controlled it was potentially subversive. Now it is precisely out of such an interplay as that between structural aspects of schooling hostile to the emergence of high quality critical literacy, and the fact that the culture 'neither required nor desired it', that patterns of literacy practice evolve. When faced with the situation described by Postman, we may ask: what are the contemporary social forces that are the equivalents of those described by Graff for mid-nineteenth century Ontario? I will address this issue in chapter 4.

Literacy and human interests: two models of functional literacy

In this section I will outline two competing models of functional literacy and spell out the very different implications these models have respectively for serving human interests. The first is a model which emerged as an official response (a policy) to the discovery of widespread adult illiteracy in the US during the 1960s and 1970s. The second comprises my own view of how functional literacy *ought* to be understood and approached in practice: an ideal to be pursued in preference to the first model.

'Official' functional literacy

In both Britain and the US, official policy responses to evidence of widespread adult illiteracy saw *functionality* adopted as the appropriate standard of attainment to be pursued by literacy programmes. The US Office of Education defined the literate person as 'one who has acquired the essential knowledge and skills in reading, writing, and computation required for effective functioning in society, and whose attainment in such skills makes it possible for him to develop new attitudes and to participate actively in the life of his times'.[43] In Britain

> *A Right to Read* ... quoted with approval the US National Reading Center's (USNRC) definition: 'A person is functionally literate when he has command of reading skills that permit him to go about his daily activities successfully on the job, or to move about society normally with comprehension of the usual printed expressions and messages he encounters'.[44]

While the latter statement is explicitly minimal in its vision of attainment, the US Office account – which allows for a level of literacy skill making it possible for individuals to *participate actively* in the life of their times – has more expansive potential. Whether this potential is actually realized is, however, another matter altogether. Clearly, the important issue is how official policy is in fact defined and implemented – in theory and practice. There is no doubt that, within Britain particularly, but also within Australia and the US,[45] some of the adult literacy programmes to emerge in the wake of official recognition of adult illiteracy do pursue learning goals which are pedagogically sophisticated and critically demanding. Nevertheless, the best known attempt to date to define in empirical terms what it means to be functionally literate within a modern western society promotes an unacceptably minimal vision of attainment. This is the model of functional literacy advanced by the Adult Performance Level Study (APL), which was undertaken by the Office of Continuing

Education at the University of Texas on behalf of the US Office of Education.

In *Adult Functional Competency: a summary*, APL constructs a model of functional literacy on two dimensions: content and skills. Content refers to the kind of information the individual needs access to and the knowledge they must be able to generate in order to function competently in daily life. APL defined five general knowledge areas which, for them, comprise the *content* of functional literacy. These are consumer economics, occupationally related knowledge, community resources, health, and government and law. On the *skills* side, APL claims that the great majority of requirements placed on adults are accounted for in four primary skills: communication skills (reading, writing, speaking and listening); computation skills; problem-solving skills; and interpersonal relations skills.[46]

Content and skills intersect to provide an empirical account of what is required for functional literacy. For each content area a broad *goal* is specified. To achieve these goals is to be functionally literate. The five goals, by content area, are:

1   consumer economics – to manage a family economy and to demonstrate awareness of sound purchasing principles;
2   occupational knowledge – to develop a level of occupational knowledge which will enable adults to secure employment in accordance with their individual needs and interests;
3   health – to ensure good medical and physical health for the individual and his family;
4   government and law – to promote an understanding of society through government and law and to be aware of government functions, agencies, and regulations which define individual rights and obligations;
5   community resources – to understand that community resources, including transportation, are utilized by individuals in society in order to obtain a satisfactory mode of living.[47]

Each goal statement is then defined more specifically in terms of detailed empirical *objectives*. Within consumer economics twenty objectives are identified. There are ten for occupational knowledge, thirteen for health, six for government and law, and sixteen for community resources (of which nine relate to transportation). Examples of these objectives are revealing.

For example, *consumer economics* objectives include: being able to count and convert coins and currency and to convert weights and measures using mathematical tables and operations; understanding the concepts of sales tax and income tax; developing an understanding of credit systems. *Occupational knowledge* objectives include: being able to identify sources of information – radio, newspapers – which could lead to employment;

knowing how to prepare for job applications and interviews; being aware of vocational testing and guidance methods which may help one recognize job interests and relevant qualifications; knowing which attributes and skills may lead to job promotion and the standards of behaviour for various types of employment. And objectives relating to *government and law* include: developing an understanding of the structure and functioning of the federal government; understanding the relationship between the individual citizen and the government and between the individual and legal system; and exploring the relationship between government and the US tax system.

At the most specific level, functional literacy is defined in terms of situation-specific requirements called *tasks*. APL did not publish examples of tasks in *Adult Functional Competency*, partly because they were revising them at the time and partly because it is 'the *objective* that is the most important element in the requirements for functional literacy'.[48] Explicitly stated tasks would be guidelines at most, rather than fixed and final requirements: examples of how objectives *might* be met, allowing for the considerable variations that may exist within the nation between the detailed circumstances and needs of different people.

To be functionally literate in this sense comprises a minimal, essentially negative, and passive state. The functionally literate person can at best *cope* with their world. They manage to fill in job application forms, having read the advertisement for the job. They may even get the job and, in that event, survive in it assisted by the ability to read bus and train timetables, job instructions, order forms, and the like. To be functional here is to be *not unable to cope* with the most minimal routines and procedures of mainstream existence in contemporary society. (Though, of course, being able to read and write hardly bestows the power to create jobs where none exist, or a livable income where jobs attained are very poorly paid.) It is, then, a negative state – avoiding failure to cope – rather than any optimal achievement, or a *positive* achievement of human capacities. It is, moreover, passive. Functional literacy equips the person to respond to outside demands and standards, to understand and follow. There is no suggestion here of leading, commanding, mastering or controlling.

Indeed, there are good grounds for arguing that this allegedly functional literacy is in fact *dysfunctional* for disadvantaged illiterate adults[49], and functional instead for those people whose interests are best served by maintaining the social relations and practices of the society by which they are already advantaged. For the APL approach to functional literacy is a potent ideological mechanism which, in its content and process aspects alike, affirms the disadvantaged in a view of the world that leads them to accept as inevitable, and to participate actively in, the very practices and relations that disadvantage them.

Three aspects of this ideological role, by which elite interests are served at the expense of those of subordinate groups – subsuming the illiterate themselves – may be identified. First, the very *logic* of the APL approach to functional literacy is ideological. It operates on the model of donating 'competencies' to passive recipients. The latter are thereby invited to perceive themselves as deficit systems, presently struggling because of their own personal deficiencies. A series of messages is powerfully conveyed to the illiterate adult by this logic, with the net effect of adjusting them to the *status quo* in which they are disadvantaged, rather than challenging and enabling them to question it. Consider, for example, the following sequence of assumptions or beliefs transmitted by the logic of donated 'competence':

1   'the problem is within me. If I can't get a job, or the job I want, that is because of my personal inadequacy rather than a fault or weakness in the system' (such as a crisis in capital, a depressed job market, an ever-shrinking number and range of skilled and interesting jobs, etc.);
2   'others do better than I do because they *are* better. There is nothing wrong with the "game" itself. I'm just not a sufficiently skilled "player" ';
3   'to do better I must be assisted by others who will diagnose my problem and provide the assistance I need'.

This, clearly, is a powerful initiation into passivity and political impotence – into accepting unquestioningly personal responsibility for conditions and circumstances which may well have their real origin in, say, the economic, political, and social (including educational) structures of daily life. For the potentially disaffected and politically active to become bearers of such beliefs and assumptions is greatly to the advantage of those whose interests will continue to be privileged so long as existing social arrangements are not challenged and transformed.

This outcome of serving elite interests at the expense of subordinate interests is further enhanced by a second aspect of the ideological role of the APL model of functional literacy. The point here is that the very process leading to successful acquisition of the various skills and content specified by APL is at the same time a thorough immersion in the values and practices of a capitalist-consumer society. It is a process by which disadvantaged adults are 'hooked' even more deeply (and irretrievably) into the very 'game' – the social relations and practices of capitalism and consumerism – in which they are objectively disadvantaged. This is because they are actively involved in 'playing the game' in the very process of learning those rules, skills, beliefs, and values which are held up as the means to successful participation in mainstream society – but which, of course, are in no way *sufficient* means to success. The point here can be demonstrated by building on an idea advanced by Neil Postman.

Postman claims that in a complex society people cannot be *governed*, and so cannot be 'good citizens', if they cannot read rules, signs, regulations, forms, directions, directives, etc.[50] Teaching illiterate adults reading skills in this context, however, goes far beyond the mere mechanics of controlling their *behaviour*. Citizens who are enabled to obey regulations and meet required standards by learning to read are, simultaneously, inducted into a set of values and norms: namely those underlying the regulations, directions, standards, and requirements themselves. Their consciousness, their perception of the world and *what it is to live in the world*, is shaped in this same process. And so, by extension of this argument, to attain the objectives specified by APL is precisely to be inducted into the values and practices of a competitive capitalist-consumer society. (Compare, 'to be aware of the basics of consumer decision-making', 'to know the attributes and skills which may lead to promotion', 'to know basic procedures for the care and upkeep of personal possessions', etc.). Since the minimal skills offered by such a functional literacy cannot possibly transform all – or even many – who acquire them into 'successful' people in capitalist-consumer terms, the act of engaging disadvantaged adults in these values and practices can only further enhance the interests of those who *are* successful within existing social arrangements. Such literacy is, then, *dysfunctional* for those people for whom it is alleged to be functional; and functional for others instead.

Finally, the APL model transmits a particular conception of literacy, which masks from learners the potential reading and writing have for developing critical acumen and stimulating effective political action aimed at promoting the interests of one's group. There is, for example, a minimal emphasis placed on active *writing* skills by APL. The act of merely teaching people to read, as opposed to (also) teaching them to write competently, has important consequences for 'domesticating' a population.[51] Levine argues that, on the whole, it is

> writing competencies that are capable of initiating change. Writing conveys and records innovation, dissent, and criticism; above all it can give access to political mechanisms and the political process generally, where many of the possibilities for personal and social transformation lie.[52]

The functional literacy proposed by APL actively inducts learners into a world view and set of practices which work *against* their interests, while at the same time denying them access to dimensions of literacy with the potential to stimulate informed resistance against processes and circumstances oppressing and otherwise disadvantaging them. In transmitting a set of essentially passive skills and 'knowledges' in the name of literacy, APL assists in defusing potential disaffection and effective transforming action. For one of the 'lessons' learned by clients of such a functional literacy programme is that literacy (thus construed) has no political significance. Or to put it the other way, the insight that literacy *can* have real political significance – opening up a new view of human options, and stimulating active organized pursuit of these options – is systematically withheld from learners here.

Consequently, what APL proposes as functional literacy is, in fact, a classic instance of a literacy which negates personal control and critical, informed, rational engagement with one's world. Instead of enhancing control and understanding, it offers a deeper induction into and further affirmation of that very (distorted) consciousness of daily life which maintains and reinforces social relations and practices of structured advantage and disadvantage. The irony here is that it is precisely these social relations and practices that yield (among other ills) structured adult illiteracy in the first place. Thus a deep paradox emerges: whereas functional literacy is presented as being functional for illiterate disadvantaged persons it appears, rather, to be *dysfunctional* for them, *and functional instead* for those persons and groups whose interests are best served – at the expense of the disadvantaged – by maintaining the economic, political, social, and cultural status quo. Adjusting and accommodating potentially disaffected and politically active people to the status quo is precisely what such (official) functional literacy achieves.

Optimal functional literacy

To describe a form of literacy as *functional* is elliptical. It is an abbreviation. If we are to understand and assess a given description of functionality we must ask: 'functional for whom, and for what, and in what ways or by what means, etc.?' Promoters of such minimal functional literacies as that advanced by APL would fill out the ellipsis/abbreviation by claiming that the literacy they offer enables presently illiterate adults to function more effectively in society, to develop attitudes and skills conducive to achievement and personal success, and to participate actively in the life of their times. If pushed further, as we have seen, they cash these values out in terms of being able to gain employment and to function smoothly within the established workforce, make their (often meagre) income run as far as possible in satisfying objective life needs, to adopt sound purchasing habits tailored to their means, to fill in the myriad forms one faces in daily life, to learn of one's rights *and duties* as a citizen, to be able to cast a vote in an election, and such like.

Now the point is that there is no necessary reason to fill out the ellipsis in this way. There are all sorts of other values that can be used to fill in the 'for whom?', 'for what?', and 'in what ways, or by what means?' variables. Opponents of the APL (or any similar) approach are free to contest the particular values assigned to these variables. They may reject the association of functional literacy with a specific population: namely, illiterate adults within societies where universal literacy is the expectation. Rather, they might argue, a truly functional literacy is what we should be aiming at on behalf of *all* people. Likewise, the assumption that what is to be provided in the way of (functional) literacy should aim at successfully accommodating illiterate adults to established relations and practices of capitalist production and consumerism, is open to challenge. So too is the idea of achieving this accommodation by means of transmitting a set of minimal reading and (perhaps) writing skills employing content and reflecting concerns steeped in an ideology of capitalism and consumerism.

The fact that a given conception and practice of functional literacy is open to challenge, and *is* challenged, in no way guarantees that a single shared alternative will emerge in its place. Competing views as to what comprises an optimal or ideal functional literacy seem inevitable. Rather than enter into lengthy debate here about the relative merits of potential alternatives to the APL model, I intend simply to identify the approach to literacy taken by Paulo Freire as encompassing an ideal of functional literacy.[53] This involves some licence on my own part, since Freire does not himself speak of functional literacy in respect of his theory and practice. Yet, I believe, a notion of functionality is entirely appropriate here: an idea of being functional, however, which has no connotations of being merely (or narrowly) instrumental, minimal, or otherwise 'second best'.

There is neither space nor need here to spell out Freire's conception and practice of literacy at any length. Details of an attempt to implement a functional literacy along broadly Freirean lines will emerge in chapter 5. For my present purposes a brief outline of how the variables involved in talk of functional literacy may be filled out by reference to Freire's work must suffice. As far as the 'functional for whom?' variable is concerned, the point to be noted is that this will be a universal ideal. Given what counts as being literate on Freire's view, the rightful possessors of a genuine functional literacy will be *all human beings*. This is because the achievement of literacy – as understood by Freire – is a necessary aspect of functioning as a human being. Since functioning as a human being is a calling for all humans equally, it follows that a literacy which enables us to function cannot be reserved for a special or limited group targeted to receive distinctive treatment.

For what ends, or to what purposes, may Freirean literacy be regarded as functional? The short answer is that the kind of literacy promoted by Freire's pedagogy is functional in respect of enabling human beings to pursue their common ontological and historical vocation of becoming more fully human, on a basis of equality with one another.[54] According to Freire, to become more fully human is to become ever more critically aware of one's world and in creative control of it. The more one engages in conscious action to understand and transform the world – one's reality –

in a praxis of reflection and action, the more fully human one becomes. As human beings our shared vocation is to each become an active *subject* engaged on an equal basis with others in the process of creating (or 'naming') the world – that is, creating history and culture – rather than existing merely as passive *objects* accepting reality/the world as ready-made by other people. The key point here is Freire's belief that in creating history and culture humans do not merely create and recreate social reality, but simultaneously create their own *being* in this process. In speaking of our vocation as one of becoming more fully human, Freire means that we are to be ever more fully present in determining what we become as human beings. Each of us, equally, is to become more and more a shaper of the form our humanity takes. To live in a world which is ready-made by others is to accept the personal being that is shaped by the processes of living in that world; by the social structures that operate within that world. It is to surrender to others the power to make of ourselves what we become: to surrender our agency, our supreme (human) power of self-creation. To use Freire's language, it is to be dehumanized: to be reduced to an object that is shaped and made, rather than to express our uniquely human potential to be actively involved in creating what we become.[55] Becoming literate, as Freire conceives it, is a necessary part of pursuing our human vocation.

The ways and means by which Freirean literacy is functional for the universal human pursuit of our common vocation are bound up with its character as a distinctive *praxis*. Freire insists that literacy be acquired and employed within an on-going process involving both action and reflection directed at our world. Freire not only identifies a common human vocation to become more fully human. He also recognizes the existence of structured practices and relations of unequal power – of domination and oppression – which deny for many people the pursuit and attainment of their human vocation. These include oppressive practices and relations patterned along lines of gender, race, class, age, ethnicity/culture, etc.[56] If humans are to pursue their vocation on equal terms with one another they must break down these structures of domination and oppression, and increasingly replace them with social arrangements which positively enable all humans to participate in creating history, culture and, ultimately, human *being* itself. This process involves confronting the reality of oppression and dehumanization, identifying those social relations and practices (grounded in structured power differentials) that thwart and deny the human vocation, and proceeding to recover and express our humanity by building enabling alternatives in the place of existing oppressive structures.

A truly functional literacy is both a means and an outcome of this very process. To understand our world as oppressive, and to act to transform it, requires a praxis of reflection *and* action. We come to know our world more critically, more accurately, not merely through reflecting upon it but, rather, by reflecting upon it and acting upon it in the light of our reflection. Conversely, we cannot act meaningfully on our world to transform it into a context in which all humans can equally pursue their vocation unless we act on the basis of critical reflection. Action without reflection is not merely blind; it is also mere *behaviour* and, as such, appropriate to the animal rather than the human world. Human praxis involves a unity of conception and execution, action and reflection, consciousness and expression of that consciousness in action.

Freire proposes that literacy be learned and practised in such a way that humans achieve a progressively critical consciousness of their world and become involved in acting upon it. The *words* that people learn to read and write must stimulate critical investigation of oppression, and enhance the possibility of liberation from this oppression through a process of cooperative human action. Mechanical literacy skills are, then, to be acquired within an expressly ideological context – key words providing the medium for learning are words which call out critical themes for discussion and analysis of the learners' social reality. This discussion and analysis will then suggest possibilities for collective action addressed at overcoming some oppressive aspect of social reality. The *process* by which literacy is transmitted and employed in the praxis of critical reflection and transforming action must itself be non-oppressive: it must be democratic and liberating. According to Freire, the literacy process must be a dialogue: a pedagogical engagement among equals which partakes of the very character of humans, equally and in community with one another, pursuing their vocation of becoming more fully human. In other words, the literacy process must itself be characterized by social relations of equality and liberation, reflecting the values of trust and respect for persons.

Consequently, in Freire's approach humans learn to read and write within an overtly political process: a process aimed at enhancing our understanding of how and where oppression operates, and stimulating informed commitment to overcoming it. The learning context is explicitly ideological. Literacy is acquired in the process of understanding one's world from a particular theoretical perspective. This is a perspective which positively *assumes* the operation of structured oppression. People uncover oppression and become committed to overcoming it in the very process of overcoming the tyranny of illiteracy – which they come to understand as being itself a symptom of oppression. The literacy process itself, and the wider cultural action for freedom born in the context of learning to read and write, reflect the values of equality and activity rather than hierarchy and passivity. Moreover, the literacy which comprises reading and writing words in seen, ultimately, as an intrinsic part of a much larger literacy: the act of 'reading' and 'writing' the world itself. 'Writing' is the act of creating history, culture, and human *being*, in the light of "reading" the text of social reality through the act of critical reflection. The values involved here are, then, the precise antithesis of those inherent in approaches to functional literacy which, in one way or another, effectively adjust and accommodate human beings to a ready-made world in which adult illiteracy is just one symptom of oppression and structured disadvantage.[57]

Kozol provides an example of this ideal in practice by reference to a community-based literacy programme with which he was involved. During the operation of this programme.

> at least 200 persons nightly filled the basement of our church and overflowed into a network of apartments that we rented in the ... neighbourhood in which we worked. [M]ost of us (teachers and learners both) were also taking action on the words we learned and on the world of anguish and injustice which those words revealed. Literacy sessions that evolved around such words as 'tenant', 'landlord', 'lease', 'eviction', 'rat', and 'roach' led to one of the first rent strikes in our city. Words connected to the world, led – not in years but in a matter of days – to the reward of a repainted building, the replacement of illegal exits ... and the reconstruction of a fire escape that served the tenants of a building of five storeys but could not be used because it had rotted into empty air above the second floor.

He adds that none of the adults he worked with in such programmes was prepared to settle in their learning 'for the "functional abilities" of bottom level job slots in available custodial positions'. Many of them became leaders in struggle for structural change, notably involvement in action to desegregate the Boston schools. Employment-wise, some became community advisers, others gained degrees from the Harvard Graduate School of Education (despite lacking a college education), and another became 'a mortgage officer in Boston's largest bank'.[58]

I have contrasted these two models of functional literacy with a view to indicating how they are entirely different literacies, with opposite implications for serving human interests. The APL model is intended to promote the work and welfare interests of people seen as presently disadvantaged in these respects by their illiteracy. But immersed in an ideological perspective which does not recognise the *structured* nature of advantage and disadvantage, 'success' and 'failure', and oblivious – it seems – to their own ideological trappings, the creators of APL come up with a conception and practice of reading and writing that can only reinforce and deepen the disadvantage and powerlessness of those millions in the US who are illiterate.[59] APL ultimately serves the interests of those who benefit most from ensuring that all citizens participate smoothly and unquestioningly in the routines of work and consumerism within a modern capitalist society. In terms of its uncritical character, the social 'benefits' it helps promote, and the interest groups to whom its *real* benefits accrue, APL literacy has much in common with the school literacy described by Graff. Both are literacies which accommodate people to existing circumstances in which the interests of some are systematically elevated at the expense of others. Impotent to address (or even identify) the structures in which such advantage and disadvantage originate, APL literacy effectively serves the interests of elites at the expense, ironically, of precisely those subordinate interests it is intended to benefit.

By contrast, the second model *begins* from the assumption of structured domination and subordination, advantage and disadvantage. As a definite theory and practice of reading and writing it promotes understanding of these structures and, ultimately, their transformation into more truly democratic forms: in which the interests of (class, race, gender, ethnic, etc.) groups disadvantaged by current economic, social, cultural and political arrangements, are promoted to a position of equal status with those of all other human beings, and pursued on that basis. To engage in this literacy *is* to engage in the process of understanding and transforming social relations and practices of oppression and inequality. Accordingly, it works in exactly the opposite historical direction to APL.[60]

Literacy, politics and policy: proper versus improper literacy

The political significance of literacy has to do with the form it takes and the role it plays within the process of humans pursuing interests, goals, and aspirations under conditions in which power is distributed unequally within the social structure. Given the argument in this chapter we are now in a position to clarify this further. It has been shown that literacy is not singular. A wide range of practices and conceptions of reading and writing exists. Both historical and contemporary examples of different literacies have been sketched here, and some aspects of their connection with human interests and aspirations noted. This question of relationship between specific literacies and the interests of various social groups will be considered in greater detail in chapters 3 and 4. Enough has already been said, however, to suggest the manner in which and extent to which particular literacies may systematically favour the interests of some groups over others by legitimating, maintaining, and strengthening social relations and practices in which power is structured unequally. Conversely, a given literacy may – as in the case of the second model of functional literacy – play an important role within activity aimed at identifying, understanding, and challenging social arrangements in which unequal access to power is patterned along class, gender, race, cultural, ethnic, etc., lines. Different literacies, then, may have very different *political* implications.

I want to apply these ideas to Wayne O'Neil's distinction between being properly and improperly literate: that is, between practising a proper or an improper literacy.[61] As amended here, this distinction will offer a useful criterion with which to assess, from a political point of view, educational policies and practices centering on literacy.

O'Neil's original distinction has to do with whether or not a person has control over their life and world and is able to deal rationally with their life and decisions. Proper literacy enhances a person's capacity for genuine control and rational decision-making. Improper literacy reduces and destroys it – offering a mere illusion of control in place of genuine control. One may be able to read and write and yet be improperly literate, says O'Neil.

> Make a distinction: being able to read means that you can follow words across a page, getting generally what's superficially there. Being literate means that you can bring your knowledge and your experience to bear on what passes before you. Let us call the latter proper literacy; the former improper.[62]

An unfortunate feature of our modern schooled society is that 'we have too much improper literacy at the expense of properly literate folk'.[63] And yet it is clearly in people's interests to be properly literate, and against their interests to be improperly literate.

O'Neil believes the way we teach reading in school inevitably leads to many people becoming improperly literate. By the time a child begins school they have already achieved a solid basis for proper literacy. Their ability to 'construct coherence around experience', and to 'deal in words and action with [their] experience' is already well-developed. Unfortunately, the teaching of reading in school destroys this basis for proper literacy: for control and understanding mediated by reading and writing. In place of genuine control it promotes a superficial pseudo-control. What happens is that school reading replaces the child's initial *depth* understanding of the world – their understanding of the layers and complexity of experience – with linear, surface, 'understanding'. Experience of the world is reduced to the surface linear arrangement of letters on a page. 'Knowledge' becomes shallow; instead of the deep and complex process it really is (and is seen to be by children before they are inducted into school reading). Within school, reading is treated 'as if it were another language, another world, not as if it were a highly abstract representation of the world the child already has tacit knowledge of'. Reading is pushed 'into context-less space': the first step in destroying coherence and, with it, the chance for genuine control of and rational dealing with the world.[64]

The subsequent practice of reading and writing within school completes the process of obliterating genuine understanding of and control over experience. Knowledge is still further reduced to superficiality and mis-understanding through the curriculum: by which the child is made to 'review what [they] already know' and to 'learn anew the surfaces of knowledge.' The curriculum reduces geography to a catalogue of names, products and capitals, history to 'a linear succession of dates and events', science to taxonomy, and literature to a chronologically ordered set of the best thoughts humans have uttered. Finally, improperly literate adults take effective control of school administration, and ensure that 'impropriety' is maintained by stamping out any serious attempts made by teachers to actually foster some proper literacy. The remedy for all this, in O'Neil's view, is to let children *learn* to read, by allowing reading to emerge in the context of children and adults talking and telling of the riches youngsters already possess. To promote proper literacy we must 'keep all the words and the world together and [children] involved in it'.[64]

O'Neil's discussion is brief and intentionally schematic. It is suggestive rather than exhaustive. The point to be noted here is that, as far as he goes, O'Neil may have put his finger on a symptom rather than a cause. There are no grounds for believing that if children are somehow helped to 'keep all the words and the world together and themselves involved in it', they will inevitably overcome existing structural impediments to genuine control and rational decision-making in their lives. It can be argued that typical school reading practices have evolved and are maintained (for example, by focusing on problems of quantity rather than quality, on remedial reading rather than promoting critical literacy) *precisely because* they have no significance for identifying and addressing structured inequalities of power and, consequently, for overcoming barriers to the kind of understanding and control that enable people to pursue their inter-ests and aspirations on an equal basis with others. The world in which chil-dren are to be kept involved, and with which all the words are to remain connected, is at present a world in which class, gender, race, age, cultural, and ethnic relations reflect differentials of power: where access to the means by which to articulate and promote individual or group interests is patterned unequally. Achieving genuine control over our lives and the capacity to deal rationally with decisions presupposes coming to under-stand and transform existing *structural* barriers to these ends.

This suggests a necessary modification to O'Neil's distinction between proper and improper literacy, to invest it with *political* force. Proper liter-acy enhances people's control over their lives and their capacity for dealing rationally with decisions by enabling them to identify, understand, and act to transform, social relations and practices in which power is struc-tured unequally. For it is in this inequality that the real barriers to under-standing and control originate: including the power to foist upon others ideological positions which shape their understanding of the world against their interests, and lead them to make decisions to their own disadvantage.

Improper literacy either fails to promote, or else actively impedes, such understanding and action. It follows from this that the functional literacy promoted by APL is an improper literacy: since it further immerses people who are currently disadvantaged in the very ideologies and practices that disadvantage them in the first place. Similarly, the common-school education of working-class children in mid-nineteenth century Ontario made them improperly literate. By contrast, those members of oppressed groups who practise reading and writing along the lines described (and practised) by Freire, are properly literate.

We come, finally, to the implications of the argument in this chapter for educational policy specifically. Here I want to make three brief points. First the distinction between proper and improper literacy, as I have amended it, provides a criterion by which to assess the *politics* of particular educational policies concerned with literacy. That is, one way of describing and evaluating such policy is in terms of whether it enhances or impedes the achievement of genuine control and rational decision-making in people's lives.

Second, the range of policies that may be considered is very wide. Relevant policy is by no means confined to the sphere of formal education. Indeed, some of the most important policy developments concerned directly and explicitly with literacy in recent years have been pitched outside formal education – notably, informal literacy programmes for adults. Moreover, it will be clear from earlier argument that a good deal of policy which is pertinent to literacy is not actually couched or presented as literacy policy *per se*. In many cases, policies addressing school curricula and pedagogy cannot be fully understood and appraised without considering their implications for promoting one or another form of literacy: for example, critical or uncritical?; proper or improper?; etc.

Finally, there is no need to limit discussion to policies framed and enacted by such official organs as ministries, departments, or offices of education, local education authorities, education commissions, etc. In addition, policies, manifestos, recommendations, ideals, and demands advanced by lobbies, pressure groups, political parties, and even revolutionary fronts (as we will see) fall within the legitimate scope of investigation here.

Notes

1 With regard to the British estimates see HARGREAVES, D. (1980), *Adult Literacy and Broadcasting: the BBC's experience*, London, Frances Pinter, 1. The lower estimate is based on a reading age of nine years, and the higher on a thirteen year reading age. For the US reference see HUNTER, C. ST. J. and HARMAN, D. (1979), *Adult Illiteracy in the United States*, New York, McGraw Hill, pp. 26–30.

2 GRAFF, H. (Ed), (1981) *Literacy and Social Development in the West*, Cambridge, Cambridge University Press, p. 1.

3 GRAFF, *ibid.*, and (1979), *The Literacy Myth: literacy and social structure in the nineteenth-century city*, New York, Academic Press. STREET, B.V. (1984), *Literacy in Theory and Practice*, Cambridge, Cambridge University Press. The framework of my discussion in the next section owes much to Street's account of the autonomous model of literacy.

4 GOODY, J. and WATT, I. (1968), 'The Consequences of Literacy', in GOODY, J. (Ed.), *Literacy in Traditional Societies*, London, Cambridge University Press, pp. 27–68.

5 *Ibid.*, my italics.

6 *Ibid.*, p. 40

7 Compare STREET, *op. cit.*, Introduction.

8 POSTMAN, N. (1970) 'The politics of reading', *Harvard Educational Review*, 40, 2, pp. 247.

9 Compare here Street's reference to the tendency on the part of some theorists to isolate literacy as an independent variable and claim to be able to study its consequences, in *op. cit.*, Introduction.

10 In ANDERSON, C.A. and BOWMAN, M. (Eds), (1966), *Education and Economic Development*, London, Frank Cass, pp. 345 and 347.

11 KAHAN, A. (1966), 'Determinents of the Incidence of Literacy in Nineteenth-Century Rural Russia', in *ibid.*, p. 302.

12 Compare STREET, *op. cit.*, p. 185. The reference is to OXENHAM, J. (1980), *Literacy: writing, reading and social organization*, London, Routledge and Kegan Paul.

13 HÄGERSTRAND, T. (1966), 'Quantitative techniques for analysis of the spread of information and technology', in ANDERSON and BOWMAN (Eds), *op. cit.*, p. 244.

14 GRAFF, H. J. (1979), *op. cit.*, Compare XV and 19.

15 STREET, *op. cit.*, p. 2.

16 *Ibid.*, p. 1.

17 See here CRESSY, D. (1981), 'Levels of literacy in England 1530–1730', in GRAFF (1981), *op. cit.*, pp. 105–6.

18 SCHOFIELD, R.S. (1968), 'The Measurement of literacy in pre-industrial England', in GOODY (Ed), *op. cit.*, p. 136.

19 *Ibid.*, p. 137.

20 Hannah More cited in SIMON, B. (1960), *Studies in the History of Education 1780–1870*, London, Lawrence and Wishart, p. 133.

21 Cited *ibid.*

22 CRESSY, *op. cit.*, pp. 109–110. Note that I am speaking here of different literacies and not, merely, of varied skills.

23 On the yeomen, compare *ibid.*, p. 110.

24 This perception may, however, perform a very important ideological function: suggesting that, in the end, all humans are equally workers. We are all workers and, therefore, all really *the same*. This deflects critical attention away from such matters as the fact that some workers get more pay than others, enjoy better working conditions, have more control over their work, etc. Often the better-off 'workers' are more accurately described as capitalists.

25 Of the many references possible here, compare the following as selected examples: BERNSTEIN, B. (1971), *Classes, Codes and Control*, 1, London, Routledge and Kegan Paul; FREIRE, P. (1972), *Pedagogy of the Oppressed*, Harmondsworth, Penguin, (1974), *Education: the practice of freedom*, London, Writers and Readers, (1985), *The Politics of Education*, London, MacMillan; KOZOL J. (1985), *Illiterate America*, New York, Anchor and Doubleday;

LABOV, W. (1973), 'The logic of non-standard English', in KEDDIE, N., (Ed), *Tinker Tailor ... the Myth of Cultural Deprivation*, Harmondsworth, Penguin; O'NEIL, W. (1970), 'Properly literate', *Harvard Educational Review*, 40, 2, pp. 260–3; POSTMAN, N. (1970), *op. cit.*; ROSEN, H. (1972), *Language and Class: a critique of Bernstein*, Bristol, Falling Wall Press; SEARLE, C. (1975), *Classrooms of Resistance*, London, Writers and Readers; (1984), *Words Unchained: language and revolution in Grenada*, London, Zed Press.

26 POSTMAN, *op. cit.*, p. 247.

27 HUNTER and HARMAN, *op. cit.*, p. 15.

28 Compare STREET, *op. cit.*, chapter 7, especially pp. 186–94. The quotation is from p. 190.

29 GRAFF (1979), *op. cit.*, pp. 17–19.

30 *Ibid.*, p. 65.

31 *Ibid.*, p. 71.

32 See *ibid.*, pp. 75–7.

33 See *ibid.*, chapters 3 and 4. The quotation is from p. 189.

34 *Ibid.*, p. 56.

35 Compare *ibid.*, p. 23.

36 Cited *ibid.*

37 Cited *ibid.*, p. 30.

38 *Ibid.*, p. 34.

39 *Ibid.*, p. 279.

40 *Ibid.*, p. 275.

41 *Ibid.*

42 *Ibid.*, p. 303.

43 Cited in LEVINE, K. (1982), 'Functional literacy: fond illusions and false economies', *Harvard Educational Review*, 52, 3, p. 256.

44 Cited *ibid.*

45 In the case of Britain compare, for example, the work of ALBSU, the Friends' Centre, and see also MACE, J. (1979), *Working with Words*, London, Writers and Readers/Chameleon. With regard to the US, compare KOZOL, *op. cit.* Within Australia some very interesting developments in adult literacy have emerged out of the ESL Programmes, 'Women's Work, Women's Lives' and 'Migrant Women and Work', written by Barbara Bee for the Outreach Project at Randwick Technical College, Sydney.

46 Adult Performance Level Study (1975), *Adult Functional Competency*, Austin, University of Texas, 2.

47 *Ibid.*, appendix.

48 *Ibid.*

49 With regard to the relationship between being illiterate and being disadvantaged more generally, compare HUNTER and HARMAN, *op. cit.*, chapter 2.

50 POSTMAN, *op. cit.*, p. 246.

51 Compare FREIRE, (1972, 1973, 1985) all *op. cit.* See also, BERGGREN, C. and L. (1975), *The Literacy Process: a practice in Domestication or Liberation?*, London, Writers and Readers.

52 LEVINE, *op. cit.*, p. 262.

53 Compare FREIRE's various works, *op. cit.* See also his (1973), *Cultural Action for Freedom*, Harmondsworth, Penguin.

54 Compare FREIRE (1972), *op. cit.*, chapter 1. See also my (1986) 'Humanizing functional literacy: beyond utilitarian necessity', *Educational Theory*, 36,4. Much of the argument in this section originally appeared in my article in *Educational Theory*. I am grateful for permission to reproduce that material here.

55 Compare FREIRE, *ibid.*, chapter 1.
56 Compare GIROUX, H.A. (1985), 'Introduction' to FREIRE, *op. cit.*
57 Specifically, Hunter and Harman explore the intersection between being illiterate/educationally deprived, being unemployed and otherwise poor, belonging to a racial or ethnic minority group, having a prison record, and being female. While they do not draw hard and fast conclusions, they produce figures which, for all their incompleteness, are strongly suggestive. Compare HUNTER and HARMAN, *op. cit.*, chapter 2.
58 KOZOL, *op. cit.*, pp. 44–5.
59 O'NEIL, *op. cit.*
60 That is to say, other things being equal. Brian Street reminds me that at least some learners are likely to see through the hidden logic and ideology of a text like APL, and transcend passivity.
61 O'NEIL, *op. cit.*, p. 262.
62 *Ibid.*, p. 263.
63 *Ibid.*
64 *Ibid.*

4

LEARNING THE LITERACIES OF PRIMARY AND SECONDARY SCHOOLING

Frances Christie

Source: Christie, F. and Misson, R. (eds) *Literacy and Schooling* (1998) London: Routledge, 47–73

Introduction

There are at least two myths abroad in literacy education, the one having quite an old history, the other being much more recent in its origins. The first, and older of the two myths (whose origins are in fact some centuries old), is that which holds that the learning of literacy is a particular, even a unique, task for the first years of schooling. Learning to read and write is a matter primarily of mastering the spelling, handwriting and punctuation systems, and hence of being able both to make meaning of the words on the printed page, and to construct meanings oneself by writing. The teacher's role in this view of things, is to focus in particular on teaching these systems, often indeed at the cost of sense and meaning, so insistent can the demand be to teach and reinforce such things as a sense of sound-letter correspondence. The second myth, dating in particular from the 1970s and 1980s, is that which proposes that the learning of literacy is a 'natural' process, and that it is learned in much the same way as is speech. In the model proposed in this case, the teacher's role is to be at best supporter and facilitator as children develop skills with literacy in largely untutored ways.

Both myths are harmful, distorting what are in fact much more complex issues and processes. To take the former myth, we can see that involved here is a conventional view of literacy, as being essentially constructed in writing, spelling and punctuation. Like many other myths, this one has some elements of truth, although it does not do justice to the true situation. English orthography, handwriting and punctuation are very important, especially in the first years of schooling, and where students attempt to proceed up the years of school while still experiencing difficulties in

100

control of these matters, they run into trouble. However, spelling, punctuation and handwriting are also the most visible manifestations of literate behaviour, and it is for that reason very easy to be persuaded that mastery of these things represents the sum total of appropriate literate behaviour. The sum total, as we shall see, is infinitely more complex, involving mastery of the grammatical features of written, as opposed to spoken language, but these features, regrettably, are often not very apparent.

To turn to the second of the myths, this derives from the influence of writers such as Goodman (1982) and also Smith (e.g. 1985), both of whom commenced their writing in the late 1960s and 1970s, and both of whom were influenced by the linguistic theories of Chomsky (though it is notable that Chomsky has never claimed any educational relevance for his theories). Both subscribed to the view that the ability to learn language is innate, and that observation of the ways oral language is learned by normal children encourages the view that they proceed by processes of trial and error to identify the rules by which language is put together and used.[1] The view went on to propose that literacy is best learned in the same ways as speech, and that too much overt intervention on the part of the teacher can be a cause of harm. For Goodman (cited by Reid, 1993: 23) at least, reading was seen as 'the direct counterpart' of listening, and learned in the same 'natural' way. In a paper Goodman gave at the Regional Language Centre Seminar on 'Reading and Writing: Theory into Practice' in Singapore in 1994, he argued a similar view of the learning of writing: it parallels the learning of speech, and should be allowed to develop in 'natural' and untutored ways.[2]

Just as there is an element of truth in the older myth, there is at least some truth in the 'natural' learning theories of Goodman, Smith and others. First-hand observation of children, apart from the wealth of available research evidence about how children learn their mother tongue, makes it clear that engagement in normal everyday activities with caregivers provides the best – and therefore most 'natural' way for children to learn language. Hence – and many good teachers can attest to this – children learn literacy best in ways that provide opportunities to learn and understand it for meaningful and rewarding purposes, so that these too may be understood as 'natural'. But for all that, 'natural' learning theories are in fact very barren, because they fail to grasp both how different written language is from speech, and how critical is the role of the teacher in intervening to teach students literacy.

Where, as in the former myth, it is the view that literate behaviour is all about spelling, punctuation and the writing system, there are at least two unfortunate consequences in educational practice. First, there is an assumption that everything children need to know about being literate should be mastered by about age eight or nine. In this view, literacy is unidimensional. The view holds that some essential skills for reading and writing are established in the early years, and the implication beyond that is that, in some very unproblematic way, these skills get recycled ever after as students grow older, moving up the years of schooling and entering adult life. The second and related unfortunate consequence of the assumption that literacy is all about spelling, writing and punctuation, is that it deskills teachers; it causes them not to acknowledge or to teach for a developing understanding of the nature of literacy, and of the ways it changes, both as students grow older, and as they encounter and deal with different kinds of knowledge and experience. The truth is that literacy is multi-dimensional, not uni-dimensional, that there are many literate practices, and that the learning of literacy takes many years. (See Macken-Horarik and Williams in this volume for related discussions.) Indeed, it can be argued that the learning of literacy is lifelong. Particularly in the contemporary world, and under the pressures of developments in information technology (see Morgan, Lankshear and Knobel, this volume), there is reason to believe that literacy is undergoing frequent rapid change, causing all of us to work at understanding its new potential and possibilities.

As for the second myth, I have already suggested something of its harmful consequences. First, in that the view of language and learning here assumes that written language is learned in the same way as speech, it fails to acknowledge just how different the two modes of using language really are. It therefore has nothing useful to say about the features of written language, and leaves teachers and students alike uninformed. Second, in that the view assumes the benefits of a facilitative rather than an interventionist role on the part of the teacher, this also deskills the teacher, encouraging a sense that there is no expert knowledge to be offered students as they learn literacy.

While the two myths identified have had different historical and theoretical bases, I shall suggest in this chapter that the two are alike in that both hold very limited models of the nature of language generally, and of literacy learning in particular, across the years of schooling. I shall argue that if we adopt a functional model of language and literacy, we can actually trace linguistic evidence for some of the significant milestones in literacy learning that need to occur throughout the years of schooling if students are to emerge with a reasonable degree of proficiency. Additionally, we can suggest something of the knowledge teachers will require in order to teach literacy properly across the years of school.

In order to develop the argument here, I propose to examine below some of the most rudimentary of the texts young children learn to write, and then go on to examine a sampling of those by older students. One might of course, develop a similar or complementary argument by reference to the text types, or genres, students need to read at different stages of their learning. One reason examination of writing is particularly revealing, however, is that it is the productive mode: it reveals something of the actual tasks in composing literate texts that students have to handle in their learning.

First, however, before I commence examination of a selection of written text types or genres across the years of schooling, I want to offer some general observations about spoken and written language, and about the kinds of knowledge that schooling requires students increasingly to handle with respect to literacy. I shall also make some observations about the values of a functional grammar as a tool for exploring the nature of language, spoken and written. I shall suggest that the nature of literacy changes as students grow older, and that there is a relationship between the changing patterns of written language that students need to recognise and use, and the varieties of knowledge they need to learn. A functional grammar, I shall suggest, allows us to trace features of the changes.

Spoken and written language

A variety of twentieth-century research, by linguists (e.g. Halliday, 1975, 1985), psychologists (e.g. Vygotsky, 1962; Luria, 1976; Trevarthen, 1987; Bruner, 1986), anthropologists (e.g. Malinowski, 1923; Goody, 1968) palaeoanthropologists (e.g. Leakey, 1994) and sociologists (e.g. Berger and Luckman, 1966; Bernstein, 1975) has testified to the great significance of language in all human communities. Oral language is the basic resource with which individuals grow and express their identity as well as participate in and comprehend their social groups.

With the advent of literacy humans learned to handle experience in new ways. The greatest change that literacy afforded involved a distancing effect. Both the writer and the reader became distanced from the events and/or information recorded in writing. Thus, events and/or information could be recorded and communicated to persons who were distant over space – say in another region or another country – and over time – say in future unborn generations. To handle information in either sense is to do things differently from the way they are done in speech. Thus, for example, whenever we take events lived and talked about in the immediacy of face-to-face interaction, and reconstruct these for an audience in another time or place, we change the events. We represent them differently, drawing upon graphic means to do so, employing a writing system and a spelling system in the process. In addition, we change the grammatical choices in which we represent the events. That is to say, we build knowledge of the events in new ways.

As Halliday (1985) has suggested, we need to be careful about drawing too neat a parallel between the processes by which humans evolved their languages and subsequently their written modes and the processes by which children learn their mother tongue and thence learn literacy.

Evolution is not the same as growth in learning. Nevertheless, there is a sense in which certain parallels apply. Thus, for most children the first steps in becoming literate appear to emerge from prior efforts in drawing, just as it seems the world's writing systems evolved from earlier experiences in drawing and painting.

Early childhood teachers often encourage children to do drawings and to write about them. One young child in the preparatory or kindergarten year produced a picture of himself and family at the beach, and produced a rudimentary script. The teacher wrote what she understood to be Mark's meanings beneath, referring to his 'beach towel' (see figure 1). The little script is of interest for several reasons. My principal interest here lies in the fact that the child, quite unable to write the words 'beach towel', actually drew a little picture of one, taking its place on the line in what otherwise constitutes a reasonably good attempt to produce written English. He had produced an ideograph. But the general character of the rest of the piece shows he knew he was employing not the semiotic system of drawing, but that of writing. In a study of the early writing development of about fifty-five children over the first three years of their schooling (Christie, 1989), this child was the only one ever to produce such a script with ideograph. It would seem to be uncommon. Herein lies important evidence to suggest that children fairly early learn that drawing and writing are different, and that they achieve different ends. Where drawing represents actual things such as a beach towel, writing represents language. Writing is a symbolic system of a different order from drawing.

Developing proficiency with control of the symbolic system of writing requires that students engage increasingly with the grammatical features of the written mode. However, the processes of learning the grammar of writing take several years. Indeed, the evidence (e.g. Halliday, 1994; Derewianka, 1996; Christie, 1995a, b, c, 1996, 1997) would suggest that control of written language is a development of late childhood and early adolescence, though the pattern varies a great deal with individuals. As the grammar of written language changes, so too do the kinds of knowledge that students are asked to learn.

In the early days and years of schooling, a great deal of what is learned relies upon manipulation of what we will call 'commonsense' knowledge: the knowledge of the familiar and the commonplace, of what is known and observed in family and community. Good early childhood teachers actively exploit knowledge of these matters as, for example, they teach children about such things as good foods to eat (aspects of the school health programme), the passage of the seasons (aspects of the natural science programme), or movement about the streets, including use of safe crossings and traffic lights (aspects of the social science programme), where in all cases, familiar everyday experience provides a commonsense knowledge for teaching and learning. The first writing experiences of

Figure 1 Mark's drawing

young children deal with the familiar and the commonsense, but as students grow older they move increasingly into learning 'un-commonsense' knowledge (Bernstein, 1975): i.e. knowledge that is esoteric in some sense, and not familiarly available.

Un-commonsense knowledge is not a fixed commodity, as it tends to vary in different periods of history: what is commonsense today may well have been un-commonsense in an earlier time. But what is clear is that learning un-commonsense knowledge is effortful, it tends to take time and it normally requires some assistance in its mastery. Such knowledge, while of course often freely talked about, is typically also found in patterns of written language, which by their nature are quite different from the early patterns of commonsense knowledge construction.

Bearing these observations in mind we will examine some instances of written language, initially from the early years of schooling, and then from the later years. Before I commence this discussion, however, I want to say a little of the systemic functional grammar (e.g. Halliday, 1994; Martin, 1992a; Matthiessen, 1995) and associated theories of register and genre used to examine the texts.

Systemic functional grammar, register and genre

There are currently around the world various functional approaches to language studies, and several might well be used to address educational questions. Systemic functional (SF) grammar is distinctive in several senses, and it is because of these that I shall make some selective use of the grammar here. SF grammar has a reasonably well-established history of involvement in education, having been drawn upon in a number of educational projects and reports in the UK (it was drawn upon by Carter and others, for example, in developing the Language in the National Curriculum Project) and in Australia (Christie *et al.*, 1991. See Christie, 1991 and Martin, 1992b for some representative discussions of the ways SF theory has been used to inform language education developments in Australia.) It is partly because the grammar has such an established history of involvement in educational theory and research that I draw on it here: it has a track record.

One of the most distinctive of the features of SF grammar is its claim that all natural languages have three major *metafunctions*: the *ideational* (to do with the experiences, or the 'content' represented in language), the *interpersonal* (to do with the nature of the relationship of the participants involved in using language) and the *textual* (to do with the manner in which sequences of language items 'hang together' to build meanings and hence create texts). When we use language, we select from the total language system those items necessary: to achieve our goals in representing some aspect(s) of experience or information, to construct and/or negotiate our relationships with others, and to build meaningful text.

The particular language choices we make at any time depend in part on the *context of situation* and the *register* associated with it, and partly on the *context of culture* and the associated *genre*. Some examples will suffice to demonstrate the point. In the course of a typical day, the average person will move into many different contexts of situation. Assume a typical day in the life of a teacher who, on leaving home in the morning, stops at the local garage to buy petrol, holding a conversation with the petrol vendor, then travels to school, where she chairs a curriculum planning meeting with other teachers, receives a telephone conversation from a concerned parent about a child, teaches several lessons to different classes, and writes several reports on curriculum matters. Each of the different activities just sketched in represents a different context of situation, requiring different language choices with respect to register. That is to say, interpersonally, the teacher assumes a different relationship with the other participants involved in each context of situation; ideationally, she deals with different experiences or information; while textually, sometimes she engages in face-to-face conversation, sometimes (as in the case of the phone conversation) she holds conversation with an unseen participant, and sometimes (as in the reports) she produces written text for a relatively remote audience. All these subtle shifts with respect to register are known, or are realised, in the different language choices the teacher takes up.

Since the imagined teacher is assumed to be in an English-speaking context of culture, we can expect that the genres involved are all those characteristic of English-speaking cultures. A genre, as the term is used here, is a staged, purposeful, goal-directed activity represented in language. The trade encounter with the petrol vendor (see Ventola, 1987 and Hasan, 1985 for analyses of related genres), for example, will be one representative instance of a genre, while the lessons will constitute 'curriculum genres' (e.g. Christie, 1995a, b, c, 1996, 1997), or perhaps parts of such genres, where they could embrace several lessons. The telephone conversation, the meeting procedure, the written reports will all have distinctive genres: a distinctive series of stages through which the participant(s) must move in order to achieve the goals of the activities involved.

To this point, the only terms I have used from the SF grammar referred to the three metafunctions. Below, as I examine a representative sample of written texts produced by students across the years of schooling, I shall, as appropriate, introduce other terms taken from the SF grammar to describe particular language choices. Two matters should be noted; first, on occasion I shall use terms that will be known to readers familiar with more traditional models of grammar, for many are retained in the functional description; second, a full SF description will not be attempted with respect to any text.

Early writing behaviour

Necessarily, language is learned in face-to-face interaction, and the patterns of speech reflect and reveal much of the immediacy of the ways in which language is used. As noted above, the particular achievement of writing is that it enables people to use language for other than the immediate context of face-to-face interaction: it affords a distancing from the matters written about in terms of time and space. It is these particular distancing features that, more than anything else, account for the grammatical differences between speech and writing.[3] Young children of course understand nothing of this, and it takes some years for a consciousness of the grammatical features of written, as opposed to spoken language to emerge.

A child in Year 1 wrote the following (spelling corrected), which is set out to reveal the two clauses involved:

> I'm going to see a kangaroo and a koala
> but I found my mum and my dad.

Technically, this piece does not qualify as a text, since while it is certainly English, it is difficult to see that the two clauses cohere to create the unity we should expect in a text. Plainly, the young writer uses fragments of personal experience, but without advice about the context(s) from which the child draws the experience, the meaning of the sentence is not clear. Had it been possible to speak to the child, it would no doubt have been possible to retrieve the connections he intended between his apparently disparate clauses. But the opportunity afforded for clarification in speech is not so readily available once one has embarked on use of the written mode. In an important sense, written language removes its experience from the immediacy of the face-to-face interaction, bringing about changes in the grammer which children find hard to grasp.

As students grow a little older and learn to write at more sustained lengths, they produce texts such as the following (with spelling corrected), which I have set out clause by clause to reveal something of its grammatical organisation:

*Text 1 Anakie Gorge**

On Wednesday we went to Anakie Gorge[4]
and «when we went» we went past Fairy Park
and «when we got there» we walked down the path
and we saw a koala
and we saw a lizard
and there was dead foxes hanging on the fence
and we walked on to the picnic place
and then we climbed up the mountain
and I nearly slipped
so I went down
and «when everyone was down» we had lunch
and then we went for a walk to the creek
and found stones
and boys were throwing stones in the water
and «when we were coming back» Jeffrey fell in the creek
and «before we went» we made daisy chains. The End.

The writer of Text 1 narrates personal experience, creating what Rothery (1984) termed a recount. The most distinctive features of such a text are:

- the fact that it recreates personal experience and activities, evident in part in the extensive use of personal pronouns, and also in the many material processes, such as 'we went', 'we got there', 'we walked'. (The functional grammar, identifies different types of processes realised in verbs and their associated participants.)[5]
- its overt and frequent uses of conjunctive relations (marked in bold) to link the clauses through which she reconstructs personal experience;

- the very strong sense of additive connection established in these conjunctive relations;
- the use of the past tense indicating the writer is aware she is reconstructing past events.

The text succeeds as a piece of coherent written language, though it makes few uses of punctuation. For all that, the text is grammatically closer to speech than to mature writing. The reason we can say this is that it strings together a sequence of clauses, overtly linked through uses of conjunctions as already noted, in a manner more characteristic of talk than of writing. The tendency of written language, as opposed to speech, as we shall see later, is to compress independent clauses, often burying the conjunctive relations found between clauses, and re-expressing the information in different grammatical choices.

Another early text type is that found in Text 2.

Text 2 How to make chocolate eggs

Things we need
water
frying pan
moulds
two bowls
brown and white chocolate

How to make them
1 put water in the frying pan
2 put the bowl in the water in the pan
3 put the frying pan on
4 melt the chocolate
5 put chocolate in the mould
6 put the mould in the fridge
7 tip eggs out of mould
8 put eggs on the plate
9 and eat them.

Text 2 has a lot in common with Text 1. Ideationally, it also draws on personal experience, and it is built round a sequence of steps. Like Text 1, it uses material processes ('put', 'melt, 'tip'), constructing actions in fact. But unlike Text 1, Text 2 does not reconstruct events. Interpersonally, the writer of Text 2 takes up a very different relationship *vis à vis* the reader. Text 2 directs the actions of others in the manner of all procedural genres. Where the declarative mood choice was selected in Text 1 for the building of information, Text 2 selects the imperative mood as an important aspect of constructing its meanings.

Simple recounts and procedures in the manner of Texts 1 and 2 would seem to be prototypical, even elemental genres in an English-speaking culture. It is this more than anything else that must explain the enduring nature of such text types in young learners' classrooms. Recreating event and directing others to action would seem to be two quite fundamental ways of making meaning. Early production of such text types is regularly rehearsed in speech, and this explains for example, the role of morning news or show-and-tell sessions in early childhood education, in which young students often practise narrating events to others, or on occasion they practise telling others how to do something.

But the challenge of learning literacy – indeed a significant challenge of school learning – is learning to handle more than personal experience. As we shall see, learning to deal with the researched experience of a gradually expanding curriculum involves learning to handle language in new ways.

Writing in the middle to upper primary school years

Text 3, by a child of eight years old in Year 3 is an interestingly transitional text, since it certainly recreates personal experience, but it also provides evidence of capacity to make deductions from personal experience, in a manner characteristic of Western scientific endeavour. I am indebted to Aidman (in prep.) who collected the text, for permission to use it here.

Text 3 Science works

Record of Events
One Monday 29th April Grade 3V went to Science works.
We went to a science show.
The lady [[that put on the show]] showed us experiments with liquid nitrogen.
One of them was with a flower.
She put the flower in the liquid nitrogen
and then put it on the table.
The flower died.
She did the same thing to a squash ball
but ‹when she warmed it up› it went back to normal.

Results
And that shows
that non-living things can go back to normal
but living things cannot
after being put in liquid nitrogen.

Text 3 is an early, if incomplete, example of what Veel (1992), studying science teaching in the junior secondary school, has identified as a 'procedural recount'. It outlines the procedure or set of steps the lady at the science show carried out in the opening element, but then, critically, it concludes with a subsequent element, shown in italics, in which the implications of the simple procedure are indicated. This latter element of its structure is signalled through several linguistic means:

- the use of the conjunction 'and', building connectedness to the earlier element of the genre, but also heralding the start of the new element, where the student writes 'And that shows . . .';
- the use of the very general referent 'that' in the same clause to refer back in a summary way to the steps in the procedure;
- the use of the verbal or signifying process 'shows' in the same clause signalling that the significance of the events is to be revealed. (See Williams this volume for some discussion of verbal or what he calls 'saying processes'.);
- the shift from the past to the present tense, indicating that the writer adopts a different aspect towards the experience being constructed. The simple present tense choice indicates that the meanings endure, or are in a sense 'timeless'.

The young writer was in fact the only child in her class who wrote such a text type, for none of the others seemed able to write the concluding element in particular. This would suggest that it was for them a difficult thing to do.

The child who wrote Text 3 reproduced the set of steps in which the science lady did her simple experiment in a manner not unlike the young writer who produced Text 2: that is, for each event a separate clause was produced, and the clauses were linked by a conjunctive relation. This is to reproduce experience in a congruent manner: that is to say, for each one step or event, there is one clause to build it. The tendency to reproduce experience this way is the tendency of speech. We string the experiences and events of life together as series of interconnecting clauses, marking their connectedness through frequent use of conjunctive relations. This no doubt makes it easier for our listeners to follow what we are saying than if we produced language closer to true written language. This is not of course to suggest that speech is better than writing, or vice versa. On the contrary, it is to draw attention to the important matter that the two are very different. Written language has evolved over the centuries to do things that speech doesn't do. It necessarily takes many years to master the grammatical organisation of written language. It is not a developmental feature of primary aged children.

Text 4, about the processes by which gold bullion is produced was written by a student in Year 6 of the primary school. It is reproduced here by permission of Sandiford (1988), who collected it in her work with students learning to research and write explanation genres. Once again, I have set it out showing the independent clauses on separate lines, and also marking instances of conjunctive relations in bold. This helps reveal something of the grammatical choices by which the text is put together. The genre has two elements of structure, the opening one in which the phenomenon to be discussed is introduced, and a longer element in which the processes are explained by which that phenomenon comes about. The two elements are labelled, though the student did not write these labels.

Text 4 Gold mining

Phenomenon
Over the years people have thought of many different ways
[[of processing ore]]
to find gold and other precious minerals.
Up to now they used horses and manual strength
but now there is a whole new way [[to process ore]].

Explanation sequence
The process starts
when the ore is blasted from the mine
and brought up to the surface.
The ore is very big
when taken from the mine
so before it can be processed
it has to be crushed.
The first stage [[that the ore goes through]] is 'primary crushing',
when the ore passess through the jaw crusher, the cone crusher
and finally the screen
which only lets particles smaller than 10 mm pass.
The small bits of ore are mixed with water
to form a thick mud [[called slurry]].
In the slurry the heavier particles of gold sink to the bottom,
the lighter parts are then washed away.
The slurry passess through a series of chemical treatment(s).
This treatment is necessary
to separate the gold from waste.
The slurry is pumped into a series of 12 tanks.
Air is blown in
and the slurry and chemicals are mixed together under high temperature
in a process [[known as gold leaching.]]
Then gold with some waste is put into a special tank with pieces of carbon in it.
Gold attaches itself to the carbon.

The carbon with gold is screened out of the tank
and washed with cyanide at high temperatures.
Then an electric current in steel wool attracts the gold particles.
The steel wool is then dissolved into hydrochloric acid
and gold particles are smelted.
Smelting is the last process in gold mining,
which purifies the gold to 99.9% pureness (purity).
Once the gold is pure
it is poured into moulds,
where it cools
and hardens
and becomes gold bullion.

Text 4 shows a student who is dealing with un-commonsense knowledge: knowledge that is, which was quite outside his experience, which required some research to identify it, and which also required some skill in representing that knowledge in a manner that adequately explained the phenomenon. Some linguistic features particularly involved in the construction of such knowledge and such a genre include:

- a number of processes, some of which are material, and involved in building the activities through which the gold is processed (e.g. 'the process starts', 'it can be crushed', 'the slurry is pumped') and several relational processes, involved either in building features of the gold and other elements (e.g. 'the ore is very big') or sometimes in identifying some phenomenon (e.g. 'the first stage [[that the ore goes through]] is "primary crushing" ');
- the use of considerable technical language relevant to the un-commonsense field of knowledge e.g. 'gold bullion', 'a series of chemical treatment(s)', 'gold particles', 'an electric current in steel wool', to mention a few;
- some skill in introducing several technical terms in ways that reveal the terms by reference to their meanings, where these are expressed in less technical or more commonsense ways. In the following examples, the technical term is italicised, and in each case it is in fact a relational process (i.e. a 'being' or sometimes a 'naming' process), either realised in 'is' or in 'called' that helps introduce the technical term:

  i The first stage [[that the ore goes through]] is *'primary crushing'* ...
  ii to form a thick mud [[called *slurry/*]].
  iii Air is blown in and the slurry and chemicals are mixed together under high temperature in a process [[known as *gold leaching*]];

- the series of conjunctive relations, more varied in character than in the simple additive manner that was a feature of Text 1 above, regarding the class visit. Their effect is to build a series of interconnecting steps in the processes described, suggesting a fairly complex series of events, whose sequence and consequential effects are important;

- the very authoritative role taken up by the writer towards the reader, marked in the absence of reference to self (or indeed to any other human agent), and the consistent use of the third person throughout the text.

Before I leave discussion of Text 4, I want to draw attention to some other aspects of the linguistic resources deployed by the young writer, showing evidence of developing maturity in control of written language. The two resources are those of nominal group and circumstance, both of which I shall briefly explain first. The term 'nominal group' refers to any word or group of words that names. A pronoun such as 'he' or 'she' is a nominal group, and so is a noun such as 'gold' or 'ore'. Most commonly, however, a nominal group consists of more than one word, as in 'the small bits of ore' or 'the heavier particles of gold'. In fact, the wonderful resource that is the nominal group is capable of being expanded to 'pack in' a great deal of important information. The young writer of Text 4 very successfully uses this resource, as in the two examples just cited, as well as in for example: 'an electric current in steel wool', or 'a whole new way [[to process ore]]'. If we compare the uses of nominal group with those found in the texts by younger writers, we can see how much simpler are theirs. Consider these instances in Text 1 by a much younger writer, for example: 'we', 'a koala', 'dead foxes', 'the mountain'.

To turn to the notion of circumstance, this is a term which is used when considering processes, which have already been briefly introduced. Often, a process involves an accompanying circumstance, realised either in an adverbial group or in a prepositional phrase. Here are some examples from Text 4:

the ore is blasted *from the mine*
in the slurry the heavier particles of gold sink *to the bottom*
the slurry passes *through a series of chemical treatments*
the slurry is pumped *into a series of 12 tanks*
the carbon with gold is screened *out of the tank*
and washed *with cyanide at high temperatures*.

Again, if we compare the uses of circumstances in Text 4 with examples from Text 1, we can gauge something of the journey the young writer needs to take in learning to deploy language to create meanings, including the un-commonsense meanings of the knowledge of school learning. Thus in Text 1, we find the following instances of circumstances, all of them filling an important role, but all reasonably simple, while in some other clauses there are no circumstances at all:

114

we went *to Anakie Gorge*
we walked *down the path*
we climbed *up the mountain.*

Text 4 makes more frequent use of circumstances than does Text 1, and their collective effect is to build a great deal of important experiential information.

Nominal group and circumstance are two important resources for building experience and information, and always exploited to the full by successful writers. As students enter the secondary school, they often don't use these resources well, instead producing language marked by some of the simplicity of the much younger child. Developing maturity in writing will involve among other matters, learning to exploit such language resources, though there are of course other features of written language for the older writer which we will now consider.

Changing features of writing with the entry to secondary schooling

Above, I noted that the writers of texts such as Texts 1, 2 or 3 tended to create their texts by producing a series of clauses, each of which constructed a particular event, and that these events were then overtly linked through conjunctive relations. The pattern is very similar in Text 4 as well, despite its greater complexity in other ways, as we have seen. The tendency to build experience in this way represents a congruent way to build meaning. That is to say, one clause is used for one event, where the event is realised essentially in a process with accompanying participants and sometimes accompanying circumstances, as in:

From Text 1

On Wednesday	we	went	to Anakie Gorge
Circumstance	Participant	Process	Circumstance

From Text 2

put	water	in the frying pan
Process	Participant	Circumstance

From Text 3

she	put	the flower	in the liquid nitrogen
Participant	Process	Participant	Circumstance

From Text 4

the small bits of ore	are mixed	with water
Participant	Process	Circumstance

The tendency of young writers is to write series of such congruent clauses. But the tendency of much 'true written language' of the kind found in a great deal of adult life is to rearrange the grammar of independent clauses, compressing them in ways that produce incongruent realisations of the meanings involved. The process by which independent, congruent clauses are taken and rearranged is known as that of grammatical metaphor (Halliday, 1994). It compares with lexical metaphor, which is probably more familiar to most readers of this chapter. Examples of lexical metaphors occur when, for example, the poet says of the moon that it is a 'ghostly galleon tossed upon cloudy seas', or more familiarly in speech when we say of someone that 'he is a silly ass'. We sometimes forget in fact, how ubiquitous is the use of lexical metaphor as in commonplace expressions like saying that someone 'is long in the tooth', or advising someone 'to keep his head'. In such cases, we use a term to identify some action or entity that is not literally true. We do this to create a particular effect, perhaps to reinforce the point being made, or to produce a particularly powerful image for the listener or reader. The effect is to create a meaning by incongruent means.

Grammatical metaphor, as already suggested, is so called because the usual grammatical expression of the idea or experience is rearranged to express it, drawing on the grammatical resources in different ways. It is control of grammatical metaphor that is in particular important as students move into secondary education, and into the need increasingly to construct un-commonsense knowledge of many kinds. Successful emergence of grammatical metaphor and hence control of 'true written language' is a feature of late childhood and adolescence.

Let me illustrate the point by reference to a sentence I have taken from a publication giving advice on exercise (Guide to Exercise, Heart Foundation, 1982: 48): 'The possibility of runners [[being affected by heat stress]] is a major problem [[confronting fun runners]].'

This consists of one clause, with two down-ranked or embedded clauses within it, marked with the brackets [[ ]]. It is a very familiar instance of written English. If we convert the sentence to a version closer to the way it might be said in speech, we produce a more congruent version, in which I have marked in bold the conjunctive relations:

If people run
they get hot
and this can stress them
so this makes it hard [[to organise a fun run]].

116

Note what happens in the process of turning this to speech:

- the one clause of writing has become four clauses in speech;
- conjunctive relations between clauses in the speech build a sense of the logical relationships between the messages of the clauses;
- the spoken version says 'if people run /they get hot/ and this can stress them'. Three verbal groups realising three processes are involved here: 'run', 'get' and 'can stress'. These three clauses, their processes and their relatedness are dealt with quite differently in the grammar of writing, where they are captured in a nominal group which involves one embedded clause: 'the possibility of runners [[being affected by heat stress]]'. In fact, the processes of speech and the logical relationships between clauses are transformed by creating two nominal groups 'the possibility of runners' and 'heat stress'. At the same time, the conjunctive relations are buried;
- an effect of all these grammatical changes is that the only process present in the clause is 'is'. This is an instance of a relational process, creating a relationship between two entities. Once you create two things or entities which you name through nominal groups, you can then build a connection between them through a relational process: 'The possibility of runners [[being affected by heat stress]] *is* a major problem [[confronting fun runners]].'

And now note what has happened to the part of the clause which reads 'is a major problem [[confronting fun runners]]'. In speech there is the use of a conjunction 'so' and another clause: 'so this makes it hard [[to organise a fun run]]'.

Overall, the one clause of the written version is very much denser than the four clauses of speech. That is because it is the tendency of writing to 'pack in' or compress information by use of nominal group, while it is the tendency of speech to offer information in a string of interconnected clauses, where there are many more grammatical items in use, including the conjunctions, articles, prepositions, pronouns and so on.

If at this point we look back and review the texts so far examined in this chapter, we can see that they have all tended to produce series of clauses that offered congruent realisations of their information. This tendency is particularly marked for example, in Texts 1, 2 and 3. In the case of Text 4, as we saw, the text is denser than the earlier ones because of the more elaborate use of nominal groups and circumstances, and the conjunctive relations are more varied, as befits the more complex sets of logical relationships constructed between various activities. But even then, there is no use of grammatical metaphor.

It should be noted that the extent to which a text uses grammatical metaphor is in part a condition of the field of knowledge or experience being constructed. Fields vary, though we can say that many of those constructed in the school subjects of the secondary level will use grammatical metaphor to make their meanings. Most of the texts used in this chapter have been chosen from scientific fields, where un-commonsense knowledge is an issue, though this was not of course the point in the instance of Text 1, about a class visit.

Writing in the secondary school

Text 5 was written by a student in Year 8 aged about fourteen. It is an instance of a report genre about arthritis. It is succesful for several reasons, not least that it does make effective use of grammatical metaphor in achieving control of the un-commonsense. A scientific report of the kind set out here has two elements, Classification and Description, and they are labelled. As in the case of the other texts I have examined, I have set it out clause by clause. As in earlier instances, embedded clauses are shown. Where something occurs in rounded brackets ( ), this identifies elliptical elements in the student's text.

Text 5 Arthritis

General classification
Arthritis is a disease [[which affects the joints of the body]], due to a lack of lubrication in the joints.
This causes friction and (it causes) the bones to rub together.
The word arthritis means: inflammations [[afflicting the joints]].

Description: causes
Many of the causes of arthritis are unknown.
Some cases have been known to result from bacterial diseases like syphilis and gonorrhea or viral infections like German measles and hepatitis.
They often can lead to pains in the joints.
Injuries, particularly sport injuries, can cause arthritis to develop in later life.

Description: symptoms
Arthritis affects people of all ages.
It can cause swelling, stiffness, soreness and sharp pains in the joints, limiting mobility and movement in the affected areas.
The area around the joint may be red and (it may) feel warm, creating discomfort.

Description: treatment
Unfortunately, so far no complete cure is known for arthritis.
Doctors may recommend aspirin and other anti-inflammatory drugs to help relieve pain and stiffness.

Antibiotics [[to drain pus from affected joints]] may also be beneficial for cases [[resulting from bacterial infections.]]

Injections of gold salts have proved helpful in some cases.

A long list of other drugs are questionable.

Exercises or physiotherapy may also give the sufferers relief and (they may) help to keep the joints mobile.

Description: state of knowledge

Even though signs of arthritis have been found in dinosaur fossils, very little is known about the disease.

But during recent times, as the awareness of the disease has grown, more research and studies are being carried out.

(From McNamara *et al.*, 1987: 18)

This text abounds in instances of grammatical metaphor, only some of which I have identified in table 1. It is not the case that each pair in the table 'says the same thing'. However, in each pair at least we can say that there is a considerable similarity in the experiential information represented. Furthermore, a comparison of the two throws light on the issue of how the grammar changes partly out of the need to shift from speech to writing and partly out of the pressure to represent un-commonsense knowledge.

We can see that in several cases, the causal relationships between events or items of information which are made explicit in speech are buried or at least realised very differently. Consider the case of the

Table 1 Grammatical metaphor

Incongruent realisation	Congruent realisation
Arthritis is a disease [[which affects the body]] due to a lack of lubrication in the joints.	Arthritis is a disease which people get in many parts of their bodies. It develops because the body joints are not lubricated properly.
This causes friction and (it causes) the bones to rub together.	The bones begin to rub together because the joints are not lubricated and they develop friction.
The word arthritis means: inflammations [[afflicting the joints]].	The word arthritis refers to what happens when the joints of the body become inflamed.
Many of the causes of arthritis are unknown.	Researchers do not know why people get arthritis.
Doctors may recommend aspirin and other anti-inflammatory drugs to help relieve pain and stiffness.	Doctors may recommend aspirin and other drugs which help control inflammation.

opening sentence: 'Arthritis is a disease [[which affects the joints of the body]], due to a lack of lubrication in the joints.' In order to re-express the ideas here in a more congruent realisation, we have used three clauses. In addition, note that the causal connection captured in 'due to' in the written version is now made more overt with the use of the conjunction 'because' when we create the separate clause 'because the joints are not lubricated'. Finally, looking again at the written version, we can see that it has created a large nominal group 'a lack of lubrication in the joints'. The process involved in 'the joints are not lubricated' is now turned into a thing we can name as a phenomenon. This process of creating phenomena in this way is very much a part of the effect of grammatical metaphor, and it tells us something of its value. The phenomena we create become part at least of the substance of the un-commonsense learning of schooling.

We can see the same process at work for example in the instance of 'Doctors may recommend aspirin and other anti-inflammatory drugs to help relieve pain and stiffness.' The nominal group 'other inflammatory drugs' would be represented in speech as 'drugs which control inflammation'. It is important and useful to create the nominal group because it creates a thing or phenomenon important in the total pattern of building knowledge about arthritis and its treatment.

There is another sense in which the tendency of the incongruent realisations of written language is worthy of comment: it is that its effect is often to remove human agency. Consider for example 'Many of the causes of arthritis are unknown.' In the spoken or more congruent version, 'Researchers do not know why people get arthritis', two lots of humans are identified – 'researchers' and 'people'. Why might it be useful or desirable sometimes to remove humans in this way? The answer in this case is that the removal of human agency enables the writer to foreground or make prominent 'the causes of arthritis', rather than the issue of who gets it, or who researches it.

The tendency of much written language to bury human agency and hence responsibility, it should be noted, is often identified as an issue we should worry about. Where human agency is removed, it is often the case that human responsibility for events and happenings in the world is simply removed. Consider for example the following sentence which I have made up, but which draws attention to a genuine contemporary problem: 'The destruction of the rain forests in many parts of the world has caused a decline in a range of animal and plant species which hitherto lived in the forests.' The nominal group 'the destruction of the rain forests in many parts of the world' in itself obscures the fact that it is humans who destroy the forests. If the writer of the imagined text from which this sentence is drawn were not to acknowledge this, then this would be a failure to drive home the issue of whose responsibility is really involved.

Construction of nominal groups of the kind I have identified is an important aspect of the ways in which un-commonsense knowledge is constructed. The grammatical tendencies involved can be shown to be capable of being used in the construction of knowledge we may want to disagree with or to challenge. An important part of preparing students to be competent to challenge is teaching them aspects of how the grammar works to build knowledge so that they can make judgments for themselves about the values of the knowledge involved. This should be part of building the critical literacy discussed by Macken-Horarik elsewhere in this volume.

By way of bringing to a close this discussion of texts in the secondary school, I want briefly to turn to some writing in English and geography. I shall use extracts only, drawn from much longer passages of writing. I shall argue that the extracts used illustrate features of the written language students need to write and read as they grow older and move up the secondary school.

One student in Year 12 had been studying the novella by Janet Lewis called *The Wife of Martin Guerre*, and she was asked to write an argumentative text in which she discussed the characters. Her opening paragraph read:

> The strength of the novel *The Wife of Martin Guerre* is the portrayal of human qualities and values. We see in Bertrande a strong sense of right and wrong; dutifulness, we see in Bertrande and Pierre. Martin shows that he values individual freedom while Arnaud is someone who values love.

Here the student constructs qualities through use of quite elaborate nominal groups. On the one hand the qualities are in the book, as in 'the strength of the novel *The Wife of Martin Guerre*' and 'the portrayal of human qualities and values'. On the other hand, the qualities are in the characters as in 'a strong sense of right and wrong' or in 'individual freedom'.

In order to write in this manner, the writer needed to distance herself from the events of the novel to construct an argument and an interpretation, not about the details of who did what to whom, but rather about the values and moral positions that give the novel its point. To build such an argument, she had considerable recourse to the grammar of written language in order to construct statements about the moral positions of some of the characters. Herein lie some of the critical features which English students must master in order to construct abstract thought and reasoning in their writing.

Another student, this time in Year 9, and aged about sixteen years, was working on a major unit of work on World Heritage sites around the world. One of the sites he studied was Kakadu National Park, a huge tract of land in northern Australia, famous for its flora and fauna and for its sacred Aboriginal sites. In the course of a fairly substantial piece of written work in which maps and other sources were also used, one student wrote:

> The main reason for Kakadu National Park's achievement of World Heritage status is its beautiful attractions of cultural and natural significance.

Two large nominal groups here, linked by the relational process, 'is' create the one clause. As speech it would be something like the following:

> Kakadu National Park has achieved World Heritage status
> because it has many items
> that are significant culturally and naturally
> and they attract many people.

My own research in secondary schools (Christie, 1995b, 1995c, 1997), sampling students' learning in several different school subjects shows that students vary enormously in the extent to which they take up and use all the grammatical resources with which to produce written language of the kind we have been reviewing. Many students write what their teachers often recognise is language closer to speech, and they regularly receive poor grades because of this. The processes of preparing students for control of written language should commence in the primary school, and where students receive plenty of guided assistance from their teachers in studying and using the models of literate language, they will be in a strong position to enter secondary schooling. However, whatever students know at the end of primary school, it will need to be consolidated and extended at the secondary level, and here their teachers will play an important role. Development of control of many aspects of written language is a feature of late childhood and adolescence. Where teachers are aware of the particular linguistic requirements of their subjects to build their un-commonsense knowledge, they will be able to anticipate their students' needs, and to direct their learning by drawing attention to the features of literate language to be used.

Conclusion

I began this chapter with the observation that there are myths about literacy and literacy education. One myth holds that the learning of literacy is primarily a task of the early years of schooling and that thence-forth, students simply recycle the skills mastered in the first four years or so of schooling. The other myth holds that the learning of literacy is a 'natural' process, best fostered in non-interventionist ways, where the teacher's role is mainly to facilitate learning, not to direct learning of literacy. Both myths I suggested are harmful. The former is harmful because it does not acknowledge the considerable learning over years about literacy that needs to take place for students to be judged truly literate, and able to function in the contemporary world. The latter is harmful because it diminishes, sometimes even denies, the important role of the teacher in guiding and directing students' literacy. Both myths, and the models of literacy and literacy learning they represent, I suggested, suffer from an inadequate and limited understanding of language and literacy.

In this chapter I have sought to provide a sense of a better model of language and literacy by developing aspects of a functional account. While I have looked most closely at instances of written texts in this chapter, I have tried to demonstrate some of the ways in which written language differs from speech. I have suggested that the two differ grammatically and that the grammatical differences are born of the different purposes the two modes serve. Whereas speech is learned in face-to-face interaction and continues to be used that way throughout life, writing evolved to deal with experience at some remove, and it is for that purpose that it continues to be used. Thus, the grammatical features of writing reflect the fact that it creates information for the audience that is removed in terms of space and time. It is the distancing effect this generates which causes the grammatical changes as language moves from speech to writing.

Children's first attempts at writing necessarily draw upon the grammatical features of language most readily available to them, and they thus produce early texts which show aspects of the grammatical organisation of speech. In particular their tendency is to produce sequences of independent clauses, linked by a series of conjunctive relations, where each clause offers congruent representation of the experience at issue. Moreover, early writers, while certainly using nominal groups and circumstances in their writing, have yet to learn how to exploit both fully. As students grow older, a developmental task they face is that of learning how to represent experience and knowledge by the incongruent means made available through grammatical metaphor. This allows them, among other matters, to exploit the resources of the nominal group and in other ways to build written texts marked by the density that is more characteristic of writing than of speech.

I have noted that emergence of control of written language, while it certainly commences in the primary school, is a developmental feature of late childhood and adolescence. However, it is clear that not all adolescents learn to handle written language well, often struggling to deal with the uncommonsense knowledge that is a feature of the secondary school and of its increasingly differentiated curriculum. Much conventional wisdom about literacy learning never really acknowledges the very considerable developmental process that is involved in learning literacy, nor does it acknowledge the important role of teachers in both understanding the features of writing, and in teaching students to be aware of these features, in order to become effective users of literacy themselves.

Notes

* The symbols « » indicate a clause that is said to be enclosed within another. Thus the clause 'when we went' is enclosed within 'and we went past Fairy Park'.
1   A useful discussion and critique of the 'natural' learning theories of Goodman and Smith will be found in Reid, 1993.
2   I heard Goodman give the paper – one of several invited keynote papers – but regrettably it did not subsequently appear in the Conference Proceedings published by the SEAMEO Regional Language Centre, and edited by M. L. Tickoo.
3   These matters are discussed in detail in Halliday, 1985.
4   Incidentally, the child is writing here of a park in the Australian bush, a few kilometres from her school.
5   The notion of a process is useful because it helps us establish the type of experience being established in language through the verbal group and its associated participants. This helps us say more about the nature of the meaning constructed than does the label 'verb'. For example, 'walked', 'smiled', 'thought', 'was' are all instances of verbs, and we can label them as such. But use of the functional grammar enables us to indicate the type of process realised in each case. Respectively, they are as follows: material (having to do with action), behavioural, mental and finally relational.

References

Berger, Peter and Luckmann, Thomas, 1966 *The Social Construction of Reality*. Middlesex, England: Penguin Books.

Bernstein, Basil, 1975 *Class, Codes and Control, Vol. 3. Towards a Theory of Educational Transmissions*. London: Routledge & Kegan Paul.

Bruner, Jerome, 1986 *Actual Minds, Possible Worlds*. Cambridge, Mass.: Harvard University Press.

Christie, F., 1989 'Curriculum genres in early childhood education: a case study in writing development.' Unpublished Ph.D. thesis, University of Sydney.

—— 1991 'Literacy in Australia' in *Annual Review of Applied Linguistics*, 12, 142–155.

—— 1995a 'Pedagogic discourse in the primary school' in *Linguistics & Education*, No 3, Vol. 7, 221–242.

—— 1995b, 'The teaching of literature in the secondary English class'. *Report 1 of a Research Study into the Pedagogic Discourse of Secondary School English*. A study funded by the Australian Research Council. University of Melbourne.

—— 1995c The teaching of story writing in the junior secondary school. *Report 2 of a Research Study into the Pedagogic Discourse of Secondary School English*. A study funded by the Australian Research Council. University of Melbourne.

—— 1996 *Geography. Report of a Research Study into the Pedagogic Discourse of Secondary School Social Sciences*. A study funded by the Australian Research Council. University of Melbourne.

—— 1997 'Curriculum genres as forms of initiation into a culture' in F. Christie and J. R. Martin (eds) *Genres and Institutions: Social Processes in the Workplace and School*. London: Cassell Academic, 134–160.

Christie, F., Devlin, B., Freebody, P., Luke, A., Martin, J., Threadgold, T. and Walton, C., 1991 *Teaching English Literacy. A Project of National Significance on the Preservice Preparation of Teachers to Teach English Literacy*. Department of Education and Training & The Centre for Studies of Language in Education, Northern Territory University, Darwin, Australia.

Derewianka, B., 1996 'Language development in the transition from childhood to adolescence: the role of grammatical metaphor.' Unpub. PhD thesis, Macquarie University, Australia.

Goodman, K. S., 1982 in K. K. Gollasch (ed.) *Language and Literacy: the Selected Writings of Kenneth S. Goodman*. London: Routledge & Kegan Paul.

Goody, J. (ed.), 1968 *Literacy in Traditional Societies*. Cambridge, Cambridge University Press.

Halliday, M. A. K., 1975 *Learning How to Mean: Explorations in the Development of Language*. London: Edward Arnold.

—— 1985 *Spoken and Written Language*. Geelong Victoria: Deakin University Press (republished by Oxford University Press, 1989).

—— 1994 *An Introduction to Functional Grammar*. London: Arnold.

Hasan, R., 1985 in M. A. K. Halliday and R. Hasan *Language, Context and Text: a Social Semiotic Perspective*. Geelong Victoria: Deakin University Press (republished by Oxford University Press, 1989).

Heart Foundation, 1982 *Guide to Exercise*. National Heart Foundation of Australia, ACT.

Leakey, R., 1994 *The Origin of Mankind*. London: Weidenfeld & Nicolson.

Luria, A. R., 1976 *Cognitive Development, Its Cultural and Social Foundations*. (ed. M. Cole) Harvard: Harvard University Press.

McNamara, J., McCoughlin, R. and Baker, G., 1987 *Putting Pen to Paper: A Manual for Teachers. Practical Ideas for Writing in Science and History*. Richmond, Australia: Detail Printing.

Malinowski, B., 1923 'The problem of meaning in primitive languages' in G. K. Ogden and I. A. Richards (eds) *The Meaning of Meaning: A Study of the Influence of Language upon Though and the Science of Symbolism*. London: Routledge & Kegan Paul.

Martin, J. R., 1992a *English text. System and Structure*. Amsterdam: John Benjamins.

—— 1992b 'Genre and literacy – modelling context in educational linguistics' in *Annual Review of Applied Linguistics*, 141–174.

Matthiessen, C., 1995 *Lexicogrammatical Cartography: English Systems*. Tokyo: International Science Publishers.

Reid, J., 1993 'Reading and spoken language: the nature of the links' in R. Beard (Ed.) *Teaching Literacy, Balancing Perspectives*. London: Hodder & Stoughton, 22–34.

Rothery, J., 1984 'The development of genres – primary to junior/secondary school' in Deakin University *Children Writing Study Guide*. Geelong, Victoria: Deakin University Press, 67–114.

Sandiford, C. 1998 'Teaching Explanations to Primary School Children. The how and the why'. Unpub. M. Ed thesis.

Smith, F. (2nd edn), 1985 *Reading*. Cambridge: Cambridge University Press.

Trevarthen, Colwyn, 1987 'Sharing makes sense: intersubjectivity and the making of an infant's meaning' in R. Steele and T. Threadgold (eds) *Language Topics. Essays in Honour of Michael Halliday*. Amsterdam: John Benjamins, Volume 1, 177–199.

Veel, R., 1992 'Engaging with scientific language: a functional approach to the language of school science' in *Australian Science Teachers Journal*, 38, 4.

Ventola, E., 1987 *The Structure of Social Interaction*. London: Pinter.

Vygotsky, L. S. 1962 *Thought and Language*. Massachusetts: MIT Press.

5

A SURVEY OF INSTRUCTIONAL PRACTICES OF PRIMARY TEACHERS NOMINATED AS EFFECTIVE IN PROMOTING LITERACY

Michael Pressley, Joan Rankin and Linda Yokoi

Source: *Elementary School Journal* (1996) 96(4): 363–384

What is the nature of effective primary literacy instruction? Many theories and models have been proposed in response to this question (Chall, 1967; Flesch, 1955; K. S. Goodman & Y. M. Goodman, 1979), each emphasizing particular processes and instruction stimulating those processes. Invariably, advocates of a model hypothesize that children will be more literate if they experience the model that they espouse rather than other forms of literacy instruction. Such hypotheses have led to tests of various types of primary-level literacy instruction (Barr, 1984).

The most famous set of such evaluations was the "first-grade studies" in the 1960s, sponsored by the U.S. Office of Education (Adams, 1990, chap. 3; Barr, 1984; Bond & Dykstra, 1967). A strength of these studies was that each of various approaches to reading instruction was tested in several different experiments and, typically, by different research teams. By most accountings, however, there was no clear overall winner in the first-grade studies (Barr, 1984; Bond & Dykstra, 1967), nor in extensions of the comparisons to grade 2 level (Dykstra, 1968). Although word reading sometimes was improved in programs targeted at increasing decoding skills and knowledge of letter-sound consistencies in words, vocabulary and comprehension were affected little by alternatives to the traditional basal approach. (See Guthrie and Tyler, 1978, for a more optimistic appraisal of the linguistic and the phonics plus basal approaches, which they concluded produced at least slightly greater reading achievement than the alternatives.) Given the ambiguity in the results of the first-grade studies, the great debate about the nature of the optimal beginning reading instruction raged on (Chall, 1967).

The models in the debate have shifted since the late 1960s, however. A popular contemporary approach, whole language, emphasizes language processes and the creation of learning environments in which students experience authentic reading and writing (Weaver, 1990). Both linguistic and cognitive development are presumed to be stimulated by experiencing good literature and attempting to compose new meanings (e.g., see Y. M. Goodman, 1990). There is opposition to explicit, systematic teaching of reading skills, especially elements of decoding (e.g., see King & K. S. Goodman, 1990). According to whole-language theorists, any skills instruction that occurs should be in the context of natural reading and only as needed by individual readers. Consistent with psycholinguistic models of development, whole-language advocates believe that the development of literacy is a natural by-product of immersion in high-quality-literacy environments.

In contrast, other reading educators argue that learning to break the code is a critical part of primary-level reading and that breaking of the code is most likely when students are provided systematic instruction in decoding (e.g., see Chall, 1967). There is a growing data base showing that such instruction increases reading competence (Adams, 1990), especially for students who experience difficulties in learning to read when instruction is less explicit (Mather, 1992; Pressley & Rankin, 1994).

Increasingly, explicit decoding instruction is conceived in cognitive-science terms, largely because much recent evidence supporting it has been generated by cognitive psychologists and cognitively oriented reading researchers. For example, some cognitive scientists believe that the development of strong and complex connections between words and their components (Adams, 1990; Foorman, 1994) follows from explicit instruction in phonemic awareness, letter recognition, attention to the sounds of words, blending of sounds, and practice in reading and writing words, to the point that they are automatically recognized and produced. Beyond word-level decoding, many cognitive scientists conceive of text comprehension as the application of particular information processes to text (e.g., relating new text to prior knowledge, asking questions in reaction to text, visualizing text content, and summarizing). Skilled comprehension requires self-regulated use of such information processes. A start on the development of such self-regulation is teaching of comprehension strategies that stimulate processes used by good comprehenders, for example, instruction of prior-knowledge activation as a prereading strategy, self-questioning during reading, construction of mental images capturing the ideas covered in text, and finding main ideas (Brown, Bransford, Ferrara, & Campione, 1983; Pressley et al., 1992).

There has been much research about the effectiveness of whole language, traditional decoding, and cognitive science-inspired primary-level instruction. The evidence is growing that whole language experiences stimulate children's literate activities and positive attitudes toward literacy, as well as increased understanding about the nature of reading and writing (e.g., see Graham & Harris, 1994; Morrow, 1990, 1991, 1992; Neuman & Roskos, 1990, 1992). Even so, a disturbing finding is that, compared with conventional instruction, whole language programs do not seem to have much of an effect on early reading achievement as measured by standardized tests of decoding, vocabulary, comprehension, and writing (Graham & Harris, 1994; Stahl, McKenna, & Pagnucco, 1994; Stahl & Miller, 1989). In contrast, programs explicitly teaching phonemic awareness, phonics, and letter-sound analysis have promoted standardized-test performance and have proved superior to programs, such as whole language, that emphasize meaning-making (Adams, 1990; Pflaum, Walberg, Karegianes, & Rasher, 1980). In addition, reading programs that explicitly teach students to use repertories of comprehension strategies have proved their worth in promoting understanding of text (Bereiter & Bird, 1985; Palincsar & Brown, 1984), including when this is measured by standardized assessments (e.g., see Brown, Pressley, Van Meter, & Schuder, 1995).

The hypothetico-deductive studies comparing various types of primary reading instruction with traditional instruction, however, have not provided a satisfactory answer to the question posed in the first line of this article, "What is the nature of effective primary reading instruction?" Most critically, close examination of many recent studies supporting explicit teaching of decoding and instruction of comprehension strategies reveals that there are often many elements of whole language in such teaching, including the reading of outstanding children's literature and daily writing (Pflaum et al., 1980; Pressley et al., 1991, 1992). What has emerged in recent years, in part from the realization that explicit decoding and comprehension instruction typically occur in the context of other components, is a new hypothesis: Effective primary literacy instruction is multifaceted rather than based on one approach or another (e.g., see Adams, 1990; Cazden, 1992; Delpit, 1986; Duffy, 1991; Fisher & Hiebert, 1990; McCaslin, 1989; Pressley, 1994; Stahl et al., 1994). On the basis of available data, however, few details can be added to the generalization that effective instruction often integrates whole language, letter- and word-level teaching, and explicit instruction of comprehension processes. The investigation reported here was designed to provide a window on the details.

We used a research method very different from the hypothetico-deductive approach that has predominated in prior research in this area. Our assumption, consistent with expert theory (Chi, Glaser, & Farr, 1988; Ericsson & Smith, 1991; Hoffmann, 1992), was that effective primary reading teachers would have a privileged understanding of literacy instruction. That is, they would be aware of the elements of their teaching, in part because their teaching is the result of many decisions about what works in their classrooms and what does not. Moreover, we expected that such teachers would be able to relate their knowledge of teaching in response to focused questions, just as other professionals can relate their expertise when questioned (Diaper, 1989; Meyer & Booker, 1991; Scott, Clayton, & Gibson, 1991). Thus, in this study we pursued a detailed description of effective primary reading instruction by surveying reputationally effective primary reading teachers about their instruction.

In doing so, we begin to fill a somewhat surprising gap in the literature. We could find no systematic study of effective primary reading teachers' knowledge about the components that need to be included in primary literacy instruction. There are testimonials about the practice and power of particular approaches to reading instruction, most notably, about whole language (e.g., see Ohanian, 1994; Shannon, 1994; Weaver, 1990; Whitmore & Y.M. Goodman, 1992; see the bibliography in Smith, 1994, for many examples). And entire practitioner journals, such as *Reading Teacher* and *Journal of Reading*, regularly publish the perspectives of certain teachers about specific reading instructional methods. Still, those providing testimonies about or descriptions of particular methods were not selected because of their effectiveness as teachers but, rather, because of the methods that they used in their classrooms. In contrast, in this study a number of teachers were selected on the basis of their perceived effectiveness.

Method

Participants

Our goal in selecting participants was to identify a sample of effective primary-level literacy teachers. We included participants from across the country, to avoid local and regional biases. Fifty reading supervisors were selected randomly from the International Reading Association's list of elementary language arts supervisors. In a letter, they were asked to identify the most effective kindergarten, grade 1, and grade 2 literacy educators in their jurisdiction, with "effective" defined as "successful in educating large proportions of their students to be readers and writers." Forty-five of the supervisors replied to this request, with each nominating one kindergarten, one grade 1, and one grade 2 teacher. As part of the nomination process, the reading supervisors were asked to specify indicators and sources of information informing their opinions of nominated teachers. The possibilities included the following: (*a*) achievement records of students within a teacher's classes (58% of nominees), (*b*) conversations in which the nominated teacher has described sound teaching philosophy and practices that the teacher has used in the classroom (96% of nominees), (*c*) direct observations of the teacher's teaching (88% of nominees), (*d*) interactions with the teacher during in-service sessions that suggested that the teacher can integrate and apply sound principles of reading instruction (89% of nominees), and (*e*) positive comments, from other teachers, administrators, or parents, regarding the skills and effectiveness of the teacher (94% of nominees). Nominating supervisors were encouraged to provide additional explanation supporting their positive view of the teacher and were asked to rate their confidence in their evaluation of the teacher, by indicating whether they were (*a*) absolutely certain, (*b*) highly confident, (*c*) confident, (*d*) somewhat confident, or (*e*) not confident in their opinion. For all teachers in the study, the nominators supported their nomination with at least three of the indicators and rated their confidence in the nomination as being "absolutely certain" or "highly confident."

Of the 135 teachers nominated, 113 replied to the first-round, short questionnaire sent to them in this study; 86 of these 113 replied to the second and final questionnaire, with 83 of the 86 providing usable responses. The first questionnaire was completed in fall 1992; the second was completed in spring 1993.

Teacher characteristics. The 83 participants who provided usable responses to the final questionnaire (23 kindergarten teachers, 34 grade 1 teachers, and 26 grade 2 teachers) came from 23 states and represented all major geographic regions of the United States. Forty-two participants held a bachelor's degree only; 41 also held a master's degree. The teachers were generally experienced, with 3–35 years of teaching and a mean of 16.7 years.

School characteristics. The schools in which participants worked included the diversity of the 1990s American population of school children. For example, the percentage of students in a teacher's school who qualified for free lunch ranged from 0% to 95% (mean = 38%). The percentage of students receiving special education services in these classrooms ranged from 0% to 36% (mean = 10%). Across all of the schools served by participating teachers, 17% of students in the schools in which the teachers taught were African American (classroom range = 0%–100%; eight teachers from majority African American schools), 9% were Mexican American (school range = 0%–81%; four teachers from majority Mexican American schools), 6% were Asian American (school range = 0%–100%), and 7% were native American (school range = 0%–100%; four teachers served majority-Native American schools).

Questionnaire

First short questionnaire. The overarching goal of the study was to solicit information from the teachers about their literacy instruction. First, all nomiated teachers were asked to respond to a short questionnaire requesting three lists of 10 practices that they believed to be "essential in their literacy instruction." Each teacher generated one list for good readers, one for average readers, and one for weaker readers. A letter accompanying this short questionnaire emphasized that the recipients were among a select sample of teachers who had been identified as effective primary reading teachers by their supervisors, and it stated that we were seeking insights into what actually occurs in their classrooms. The response rate to this request was more than 83%: 113 of the 135 nominated teachers responded.

Final questionnaire. The 300 practices that the teachers cited in response to the short questionnaire were categorized. Some practices were logically related to one another, however—such as some teachers reporting that phonics should never be taught in isolation and others arguing for daily phonics instruction based on workbook exercises. We used all 300 practices to develop a final questionnaire assessing reading and writing instruction, items that teachers could respond to objectively (e.g., measuring the frequency of the teacher's use of an instructional practice, on a seven-point Likert scale from never to several times daily). Every practice cited in response to the initial questionnaire was represented on the final questionnaire. As a means of broadening the categories of response with respect to educational practices that might be targeted at weaker students, we also sent a short survey to a sample of special educators. The special education teachers mentioned a few instructional practices that the regular education teachers did not cite, such as varying instruction with learning style and teaching attending skills. These practices were also assessed on the final questionnaire.

The final questionnaire requested 436 responses of various kinds. It was 27 pages long and was sent to the 113 teachers who responded to the initial questionnaire. The teachers were informed that the survey would require about 45 minutes to complete and were asked to return it within 3 weeks of receiving it. After 3 weeks, we sent a postcard reminder.

The general directions accompanying the questionnaire were the following:

> Many thanks for your reply to the initial round of our survey. The responses we received were exceptionally illuminating. There were so many elements of effective instruction mentioned by teachers, however, that we need to ask more focussed questions in order to produce quantifiable data for the survey. The enclosed items are intended to be answered quickly. All of these items are tapping what you know very well, your own instructional practices and thus, we suspect most items will be answered without hesitation on your part. This knowledge that you possess about your primary reading instruction is extremely valuable.

A total of 86 questionnaires were returned (76% response rate). Three returned questionnaires were not usable, however, because they were provided by teachers with teaching assignments other than kindergarten, grade 1, *or* grade 2 (e.g., teaching a combined grades 1–3).

A variety of question types were used, in order to have questions sensitively tapping each practice suggested in the responses to the first questionnaire. In designing questions, we tried to describe practices by using terms that appeared in the responses to the first questionnaire.

Two hundred thirty-one times teachers were asked to check a particular strategy, emphasis, practice, technique, or material if it was present in their classroom. For example, if teachers indicated that they taught concepts of print, they responded to a follow-up item of this type:

> Which of the following concepts of print do you teach? —none, —directionality of print, —concept of a letter, —concept of a word, —punctuation, —parts of a book, —sounds are associated with print. [Such items involving numbers of teachers reporting a practice were analyzed nonparametrically.]

Sixty-six items asked teachers to indicate the frequency of an instructional technique or area of emphasis on eight-point rating scales (e.g., from 0 = never to 7 = several times a day, with midpoint 4 = weekly):

> Do you use "big books"? [scale: never to several times a day]
> After a story, do you ask students "comprehension questions"? [scale: not at all to all stories] [Such items involving numerical values generated by teachers, one value per teacher, were analyzed parametrically.]

Another 65 items asked teachers to estimate the percentage of time or the number of minutes allocated to an activity, as in the following example:

> What percentage of the material read by your students is outstanding children's literature? ... written at a "controlled" reading level? ... written to provide practice in phonetic elements and/or patterns ... high interest, low vocabulary materials?

Thirty-three items requested teachers to categorize their use of instructional practices as "always, sometimes, or never" or "regularly, occasionally, or never," as in the following examples:

> Which of the following extension activities do you use regularly, occasionally, or never?: arts/crafts with print attached, cooking activities, dramatics or puppet plays, drawing or illustrating stories, movement activities, field trips, games.

Are home/parents involved in your reading instruction for good readers? ... average readers? ... weaker readers?

Forty-three items, such as the following questions, required yes/no responses:

Do you teach reading across the curriculum?
Do you teach critical thinking skills?

Sixteen items required a written explanation or clarification of a response, with most of these items requesting "other" responses. (These "other" responses were not informative, for the most part, and they are not included in the results section.) A few of these open-ended questions probed issues that we considered especially important to illuminate, on the basis of review of the first-round lists generated by the teachers. These probes included the following:

If you consider yourself only somewhat consistent with whole language, please clarify.
If ... [you teach reading across the curriculum], please describe your practice.
[Such items were analyzed both quantitatively and qualitatively.]

For 22 of the items, teachers were required to respond separately for good, average, and weaker students, as illustrated by this example:

How much of your instructional time in reading involves individual oral reading by students? [Teachers were asked to respond, in terms of minutes, for good, average, and weaker readers.]

Results

We recognized from the outset that the diverse question types on our instrument would preclude many traditional approaches to analyzing questionnaire data, especially ones aggregating over items that assessed related issues. The response distributions to many of the items made aggregation over items untenable anyway (e.g., a number of elements of instruction were endorsed either by most teachers or few teachers, so that responses to the items were not normally distributed). Thus, here in the Results section, we focus on analysis of individual items.

More positively, the responses were striking and orderly for many items—that is, responses did not have the randomness associated with unreliability. In addition, there were many indications that the teachers took great care in responding to the items (e.g., explanations offered about

134

responses in the margins of the questionnaire, all questions answered by most teachers, and extreme neatness in responses). Thus, we concluded that some important sources of error (e.g., carelessness) were probably minimized.

This Results section is organized around issues addressed in the questionnaire, with many issues addressed by several questions and different types of questions. A number of findings are described prosaically in what follows, on the basis of Likert means (e.g., an instructional practice rated 6.72 on a "never" [0] to "several times a day" [7] scale is reported as occurring "several times a day," the whole-number value closest to 6.72).

On the basis of responses to the first, short questionnaire, we expected that the reports would vary by grade level, and they did somewhat. That is, items were analyzed either parametrically or nonparametrically, depending on the type of item, with respect to grade level ($p < .05$ for grade-level effects and all other effects taken up in Results). The most important grade-level differences are summarized in Tables 1 and 2. In general, with increasing grade level, and as students master prereading skills and learn to decode, instruction of higher-order competencies was reported more often. Analogously, reports of picture books and patterned books gave way to reports of more sophisticated materials with advancing grade. Also, teachers claimed greater attention to mechanics, such as punctuation and spelling, with grades 1 and 2 students than with kindergarten students. There was also increased reporting of planning and editing of writing, from kindergarten to grade 2. Although, with increasing grade, there were more reports of traditional approaches to instruction—such as round-robin reading, use of basals, spelling tests, and homework—the teachers did not report these approaches as predominating in their classrooms but, rather, as blended with many other components. Important differences in grade-level reports are highlighted in what follows.

In responses to the first questionnaire, there were reports of some differences in the explicitness and extensiveness of instruction, as a function of student reading achievement. Thus, 32 of the final survey items requested teachers to estimate the explicitness and/or extensiveness of their instruction, separately for good, average, and weaker readers. For the most part, statistical analyses of these items suggested similar instruction for students, regardless of ability, although there were also some differences as a function of student ability, summarized in Table 3. In general, more explicit/extensive instruction was reported for weaker readers, with respect to letter- and word-level skills such as decoding and sight word learning. Nonetheless, we emphasize that the reported instruction differences as a function of reader ability were few.

General characteristics of learning environments

Teachers described classrooms filled with print. All teachers in the sample indicated that they attempted to create a literate environment in their classrooms, including an in-class library. All but one claimed to display student work in the room. All but three teachers reported chart stories and chart poems. Most (71%) reported posting of word lists and use of signs/labels in the classroom (67%; for grade-level differences, however, see Table 1). The teachers reported learning centers (i.e., listening, reading, or writing centers), although their use declined with advancing grade level.

These classrooms were rich with stories. On average, the teachers reported reading to their students daily, with rereading less common and decreasing with increasing grade level. The teachers reported telling stories to students, weekly on average. Sixty-six percent reported audio-taped stories, and 33% prerecorded videotaped stories.

When asked whether they were whole language teachers, 54% responded yes and 43% claimed that they were somewhat whole language teachers. One possibility that we explored was that reported instruction might have been different among those teachers claiming to be wholly committed to whole language than among teachers less committed. For each grade level, we examined the correlations between teacher commitment to whole language and all other variables. There was one striking, consistent correlation, across grades, between commitment to whole language and reported practice: Fully committed whole language teachers were less likely to use basals than were less committed teachers, $r = .49$ at kindergarten, $r = .59$ at grade 1, and $r = .66$ at grade 2.

General teaching processes

Participants in this study reported applying many effective conventional instructional methods in the service of literacy education.

Modeling. The teachers reported overt modeling of reading for students on a daily basis; that is, they reported reading aloud for students, making clear to them what is meant by reading. They also reported overt modeling of comprehension strategies several times a week, and modeling of the writing process weekly. The love of reading was reported as modeled daily, the love of writing as modeled weekly.

Practice and repetition. Practice of isolated skills (e.g., on a computer, skill sheets, workbooks, and songs) was estimated as averaging 13% of the literacy instructional day. The majority, (59%) of the sample reported using drills, with drilling for letter recognition—which decreased with increasing grade level—and for phonics/letter-sound association, and spelling—which increased with increasing grade level.

Table 1 Classroom characteristics and instructional practices reported less often with increasing grade level

	Kindergarten	Grade 1	Grade 2
Learning environment:			
Signs and labels (% of teachers)	78	76	46
Learning centers (% of teachers)	100	85	73
General teaching processes:			
Letter-recognition drills (% of teachers)	65	26	8
Small-group work and instruction (% of instruction)	. . .	33	17
Songs (e.g., Alphabet Song) (% of teachers)	100	79	73
Teaching of reading:			
Teaching letter recognition (% of teachers)	100	91	50
Copying/tracing letters (% of instruction)	. . .	13	2
Teaching alphabetic principle:			
Good readers (% of teachers)	90	75	43
Average readers (% of teachers)	95	81	67
Teaching focusing on sounds of words (% of teachers)	100	85	65
Teaching concepts of print:	Daily	Daily	Weekly
Concept of a letter (% of teachers)	100	85	42
Directions of print (% of teachers)	96	82	42
Phonics drills (% of teachers)	43	21	12
Teaching of phonics using games and puzzles (% of teachers)	91	56	50
Letter of day/week (% of teachers)	57	18	8
Decoding strategies instruction to weaker readers	. . .	Daily	Several times a week
Explicit attempts to develop sight word vocabulary:			
Good readers (% of teachers)	. . .	79	54
Average readers (% of teachers)	83	82	54
Teacher rereading stories	Several times a week	Weekly	Several times a year to monthly
Shared big-book reading	Several times a week	Several times a week	Several times a year
Rereading of big books:			
Good readers (% of teachers)	100	85	50
Average readers (% of teachers)	100	91	75
Chart stories and poems	. . .	Several times a week	Monthly

continued

Table 1 continued

	Kindergarten	Grade 1	Grade 2
Picture books (% of materials)	46	30	...
Patterned books (% of materials)	32,	27,	11,
	Several times a week	Weekly to several times a week	Monthly
Reading aloud of patterned books (% of teachers)	85	82	54
Controlled reading-level materials	...	40	22
Materials providing practice in reading specific phonetic elements (% of materials)	...	28	8
"Easy" reading (% of reading)	54	33	31
"Frustration"-level reading:			
Good readers	20	11	11
Average readers	21	12	12
Teaching of writing:			
Student dictation of stories to adults (including whole-class dictation to teacher)	Monthly	Several times a year	Each semester
Shared writing	...	Several times a week	Monthly
Accountability:			
Parent conferences	...	Several times a year	Each semester

NOTE.

$p < .05$ for each effect summarized in this table. When only two grade levels are indicated in the table, the trend involving third-grade level was in the other direction and not statistically significant.

Grouping. The teachers reported a combination of whole-group, small-group, and individual instruction, as well as individual seatwork, as part of the literacy instructional day. More whole-group instruction (about half of total instruction) was reported than small-group instruction, which varied with grade level—it was about a third of instruction at kindergarten and grade 1 and about a sixth of instruction at grade 2. More small-group instruction was claimed than individual instruction, reported as about one-sixth of total literacy instruction. The teachers believed that only about 10% of their students' time was spent in seatwork. They reported cooperative grouping for 46% of their instruction on average.

Notably, some traditional approaches to primary literacy grouping were

Table 2 Classroom characteristics and instructional practices reported more often with increasing grade level

	Kindergarten	*Grade 1*	*Grade 2*
General teaching processes:			
Round-robin reading	Each semester	Each semester	Several times a year
Individually guided reading for weaker readers (% of reading)	33	53	52
Teaching of reading:			
Teaching decoding strategies to weaker readers	Several times a week	Daily	...
Teaching use of syntax cues for decoding (% of teachers)	35	88	81
Teaching common phonics rules (% of teachers)	13	71	85
Teaching morphemic-structural analysis for decoding (% of teachers)	17	76	92
Teaching syllabification rules for decoding (% of teachers)	0	29	46
Spelling drills (% of teachers)	9	41	69
Spelling tests (% of teachers)	0	65	88
Sight word drills (% of teachers)	35	50	...
Teaching comprehension strategies:			
Activating prior knowledge (% of teachers)	70	91	92
Question generation (% of teachers)	57	82	100
Finding main ideas (% of teachers)	61	85	100
Summarization (% of teachers)	70	76	100
Using story grammar cues (% of teachers)	22	58	58
Teaching of the critical thinking skills:			
Webbing (% of teachers)	61	88	96
Identifying causes and effects (% of teachers)	61	94	100
Preteaching of vocabulary (% of teachers)	30	68	69
Choral reading (% of teachers)	57	82	92
Homework (% of teachers)	32	79	85
Student reading aloud to other people	Weekly	Several times a week	Several times a week
Student reading aloud:			
Poetry (% of teachers)	60	85	88
Trade books (% of teachers)	40	91	...
Basal stories (% of teachers)	10	67	73
Silent reading	11 minutes daily	17 minutes daily	21 minutes daily

continued

Table 2 continued

	Kindergarten	Grade 1	Grade 2
Chapter books (% of materials)	3	7	12
Basal use (frequency, % of materials)	Each semester, 2	Monthly, 22	Monthly, 21
Controlled-reading level materials (% of materials)	24	40	...
Materials providing practice with specific phonetic elements (% of materials)	10	28	...
"Instructional"-level reading:			
Average readers (% of reading)	45	60	...
Weaker readers (% of reading)	40	50	55
Teaching of writing:			
Student story writing (% of teachers)	61	94	96
Writing in response to reading	Several times a year	Weekly	Weekly
Planning before writing (% of teachers)	48	82	92
Revising during writing (% of teachers)	13	71	88
Publishing story collections (% of teachers)	27	59	69
Teaching punctuation:	52	88	96
Out of context (% of all teaching of punctuation)	5	9	27
Accountability:			
Writing portfolios (% of teachers)	48	79	85

NOTE.

$p < .05$ for each effect summarized in this table. When only two grade levels are indicated in the table, the trend involving third-grade level was in the other direction and not statistically significant.

not endorsed. Of the 55 teachers indicating use of ability grouping, only 19 reported use of the traditional three-group approach (i.e., high, medium, and low reading groups). Round-robin reading was reported as occurring rarely (i.e., once a month), although slightly more in grades 1 and 2 than in kindergarten.

Sensitivity to students and individual student needs. The teachers claimed sensitivity to student needs. For instance, 96% of the teachers indicated that they permitted progress in literacy at students' own paces, with 89% reportedly attempting to assess the learning styles of their students and with 92% reportedly attempting to adjust instruction to students' learning style. The teachers claimed that 46% of their total instructional time involved minilessons, targeted at "things students

Table 3 Instructional practices reported as more explicit/extensive for weaker compared to stronger readers

	Good	Average	Weaker
Grade 1:			
Activities requiring students to focus on the sounds of words	Weekly	Weekly	Several times a week
Teaching of letter-sound associations (% of teachers)	71	85	97
Individually guided writing (% of teachers)	25	31	37
Decoding-strategies instruction	Several times a week	Several times a week	Daily
Grades 1 and 2:			
Teaching of the alphabetic principle (% of teachers):			
Grade 1	71	76	100
Grade 2	35	54	77
Teaching of visual discrimination (% of teachers):			
Grade 1	65	74	85
Grade 2	65	88	92
Teaching of alphabetic recognition (% of teachers):			
Grade 1	35	50	91
Grade 2	12	15	46
Grade 2:			
Teaching of auditory discrimination (% of teachers)	65	88	92
Development of sight vocabulary (% of teachers)	54	54	85
Rereading of big books (% of teachers)	46	69	77
Individual oral reading	16 minutes daily	16 minutes daily	25 minutes daily

NOTE.
$p < .05$ per effect.

needed to know at this moment." The teachers estimated that they spent 17% of their instructional time in reteaching the entire class and 21% of their instructional time in reteaching small groups or individual students. Grades 1 and 2 teachers reported that, for weaker students, the majority of instruction involved individually guided reading.

Integration with other curricula and activities. The teachers reported that literacy instruction was integrated with the rest of the curriculum: 93% indicated that reading instruction occurred across the curriculum; the corresponding figure for writing was 88%; for listening, 88%; and for speaking, 75%. Ninety-four percent reported the use of themes extending to other parts of the curriculum to organize reading and writing instruction. In response to an open-ended question, teachers mentioned reading as part of science instruction (35%), social studies (31%), and math (23%), with another 11% simply claiming that reading instruction occurred in all content areas.

All teachers reported using extension activities. These included arts and crafts associated with print experiences, illustration of stories read, games, cooking, and movement activities.

Teaching of reading

What is taught. When asked to divide a total of 100% of their literacy instruction into the percentage dedicated to meaning-making versus decoding, meaning-making predominated, by 71%–27%. This translated into the teaching of the content and processes summarized in this subsection.

Thus, more than 89% of the teachers reported teaching skills and knowledge pre-requisite to reading, such as auditory discrimination skills, visual discrimination skills, concepts of print (e.g., punctuation, print-sound association, parts of a book, concept of a word; see Table 1 for grade-level differences, however), and letter-sound associations. Some very basic skills were taught by most kindergarten teachers but were much less prominent with increasing grade. These included letter-recognition activities and copying/tracing of letters. Especially important, the proportion of teachers claiming to teach the alphabetic principle—that all 26 letter symbols are worth learning because each stands for sounds in spoken words (Adams, 1990)—declined with increasing grade. Consistent with the decline with increasing grade in teaching of the alphabetic principle, with advancing grade level there were fewer reports of activities requiring focus on the sounds of words.

An important finding was that, for every basic skill, the majority of teachers who reported teaching it claimed to do so in the context of actual reading and writing. Even so, for every basic skill except concepts of print, at least 88% of the teachers who reported teaching the skill also reported some isolated skills instruction, most often involving games and puzzles to teach the skill or to provide practice with it.

The teachers reported that teaching of decoding strategies and word-level skills and knowledge occurred at least several times a week. Several decoding strategies were reported as taught by most teachers: using context cues to decode words (98% of teachers), using picture cues to decode words (96%), and sounding out words by using letter-sound knowledge (92%). Other strategies were taught little in kindergarten but much more by grade 2: (*a*) using syntax cues to decode words; (*b*) using common phonics rules; (*c*) using morphemic structural analysis clues, including prefixes, suffixes, and base words; and (*d*) syllabification rules.

The commitment to teaching decoding also came through in the response to questions about the explicit teaching of phonics, which 95% of the teachers said they did. Teachers reported that they used a variety of procedures for doing so, most prominently (*a*) in the context of real reading (90% of teachers), (*b*) during discussion of sounds as part of writing (84%), and (*c*) through invented spelling (84%). Teaching of phonics outside the context of natural reading was reported as well, however, with 43% of the teachers claiming use of workbooks and skill sheets and with 32% reporting use of a phonics program. At least half of teachers at each grade reported use of games and puzzles to teach phonics, although the proportions of teachers claiming to do so decreased with advancing grade. Only at kindergarten level was use of the letter-of-the-day or -week approach reported by a majority of teachers. The teachers decided which phonics elements to teach either according to class/small-group needs (77% of teachers), individual student needs (74%), the sequence prescribed in a basal series or phonics program (40%), or the sequence in a scope-and-sequence chart (14%). In short, there was much more commitment to teaching of phonics in ways that were consistent with ongoing reading and writing and with students' needs during reading and writing than to teaching phonics in isolation, although there were reports of phonics instruction in isolation and/or as prescribed by a standard approach.

The reported explicit teaching of spelling increased with grade level, for example, as reflected in increased reporting of spelling drills and tests with advancing grade. Grades 1 and 2 teachers indicated diverse sources for words tested, including published spelling curricula (38% of teachers), words selected from basal or other stories (33%), items selected from students' writing (30%), lists (Dolch or Chall) of frequently used words (27%), a district-developed spelling program (17%), and student self-selected words (14%). When teachers were asked to respond to the open-ended item "How do you react to children's invented spellings?" all teachers indicated at least acceptance of invented spellings much of the time. Even so, at times, correct spellings were expected. Thus, 11 of the grade 2 teachers indicated, in response to an open-ended question about spelling, that correct spelling (e.g., of high-frequency words) was expected in final drafts of writing for publication.

The teachers (96%) reported explicitly attempting to develop new vocabulary. Most (95%) reported that they did so in the context of other reading and writing, a claim consistent with other claims, including 93% of the teachers reporting that new vocabulary came from stories read in class and 65% of the teachers reporting instruction of vocabulary that students wanted to use in their writing.

Most teachers reported attempting explicitly to develop sight word vocabulary, although less so for good and average readers with advancing grade level. Most teachers (87%) who attempted to develop sight word competence reported doing so in the context of other reading and writing activities. Nonetheless, there were also reports of isolated development of vocabulary, for example, by sight word drilling, which was reported more by grade 1 teachers than by kindergarten teachers.

Critical to meaning-making is comprehension, including understanding of text elements, with 96% of the teachers reporting that they taught text elements and with at least three-quarters of the teachers reporting instruction in each text element (i.e., theme/main idea, details vs. main idea, plot, sequencing, cause-and-effect relations in stories, story mapping/webbing, character analysis, and the idea of the illustrator as an interpreter of a story).

All teachers reported that they taught comprehension strategies, with this commitment holding for readers of all ability levels. A dramatic finding was that all teachers at all grades reported teaching prediction. Seventy-three percent reported teaching visualization as a strategy. Other comprehension strategies (i.e., activating prior knowledge, asking questions, delineating the main idea, summarization, and looking for story grammar elements) were reported more frequently with advancing grade.

All teachers claimed to teach critical thinking strategies. More than 93% reported teaching brainstorming, categorizing, and recalling details. At least the majority reported teaching students how to make distinctions, how to make evaluations, webbing, and identifying causes and effects, with the latter two strategies increasingly endorsed with increasing grade.

Because possession of background knowledge is critical to understanding text, it is notable that teachers reported that they attempted to develop students' background knowledge, on average, for more than half the stories that they covered (i.e., through prereading discussion, related reading, hands-on experiences, or videos/movies). They indicated developing students' understanding of important concepts (e.g., through preteaching of vocabulary) before or as they encountered them in a story, again for more than half the stories on average. The proportion of teachers endorsing such preteaching increased with advancing grade.

Types of reading and reading-related activities. Teachers reported involving students in many types of reading experiences. The percentage of teachers reporting choral reading increased with grade, as did the percentage of teachers assigning reading homework. Most (i.e., 90% or more) of the teachers reported the following activities: shared reading, including reading along with big books (see Table 1, however, for evidence of grade-level differences); student read-alouds to peers, teachers, other adults, or older and younger children—an activity increasing in frequency with advancing grade level—of poetry, trade books, and basals; student re-

readings of stories, books, and big books; silent reading (increasing in frequency with advancing grade level); and student discussions of stories and literature. Many teachers (69%) reported student book sharing as part of literacy instruction—for example, in the form of book reports or informal comments to other students about books that they have read.

What is read. The teachers on average reported that 73% of the reading in their classrooms was of outstanding children's literature. In contrast, only 6% was described as expository material, reflecting a heavy bias toward narratives and other clearly literary genres. The teachers reported that a mean of 12% of their reading was of poems.

Picture books and predictable books declined in prominence with advancing grade. Chapter books increased in occurrence, from kindergarten to grade 2, as did the percentage of reading from basal materials. Reported basal use was highly variable, however, ranging from no use of basals to daily use of them. (See the earlier result relating basal use to whole-language commitment.) Consistent with the reported use of basals, which often attempt to use controlled vocabulary and provide practice in specific phonetic elements, the teachers reported that a nontrivial proportion of reading was of materials with a controlled reading level: 24% of reading materials in kindergarten, 40% in grade 1, and 22% in grade 2. The teachers also reported some reading of material designed to provide practice with specific phonetic elements: 10% of the materials read in kindergarten, 28% in grade 1, and 8% in grade 2.

In this study, one traditional way of classifying what students read was telling—the percentage of easy, instruction-, and frustration-level reading. In general, the percentage of easy reading decreased with increasing grade level. Although there was relatively little frustration-level reading reported, also reported were decreases in frustration-level reading with increasing grade. Reports of instruction-level reading increased with grade.

The teachers indicated that they used author studies (i.e., several pieces by the same author, with background information about the author, author's style, etc.), but for less than half of what is read. Ninety-four percent of the teachers indicated that they tried to teach their students about the illustrators of stories and texts.

Teaching of writing

Types of writing. Most teachers (86%) reported that their students wrote stories and developed written responses to readings, with both of these responses increasing in frequency with increasing grade level. Eighty-seven percent of the teachers reported journal writing by their students, several times a week on average. Students were reported as writing poems only a few times a year.

Composition activities were not precluded in kindergarten simply because students lacked translation skills: kindergarten teachers reported that student dictation of stories to other people occurred once a month on average. They also reported that whole-class dictation of stories to the teacher as scribe occurred about once a month on average. Such dictations were reported as less frequent in grades 1 and 2.

Just as shared reading was reported, so was shared writing (see Table 1). A majority of the teachers reported that they encourage home reading, and 59% reported that they encourage home writing.

Teaching the writing process. Teachers claimed to encourage planning before writing, increasingly from kindergarten to grade 2. Teaching of revising—for example, through student-teacher and peer editing conferences—was also reported more often with advancing grade level. All but one kindergarten teacher and five grade 1 teachers reported some publication of students' work.

The majority of respondents at each grade level reported teaching mechanics, for example, punctuation, with such teaching reported more frequently with advancing grade. Most teaching of punctuation was reported as occurring in context, with the percentage of out-of-context instruction of punctuation increasing with advancing grade, however. A minority (30%) of teachers reported using the computer as part of writing instruction.

Making literacy and literacy instruction motivating

The teachers reported extensive efforts to make literacy and literacy instruction motivating. In general, the teachers strongly endorsed (i.e., there was a mean rating of at least 5 on a seven-point scale) the following practices: (*a*) classroom as a risk-free environment; (*b*) positive feeback; (*c*) conveying the importance of reading/writing in life; (*d*) setting an exciting mood for reading, adding color and humor, and so on; (*e*) encouraging an, "I can read, I can write" attitude; (*f*) accepting where the child is right now and working to improve literacy from that point; (*g*) conveying the goal of every lesson and why the lesson is important to students; (*h*) encouraging students to find and read stories/books that they like, as part of the literacy program (i.e., self-selection of materials that are read); (*i*) encouraging students' ownership of their reading, by having them make for themselves many decisions about what to read; (*j*) encouraging personal interpretations of text; (*k*) selecting class reading materials on the basis of students' interest; and (*l*) encouraging student ownership of writing (e.g., students' selection of writing topics).

Accountability

Most teachers (i.e., more than 88%) reported regular checks of student comprehension of stories heard and read, by asking students questions after most readings and by requesting students to retell stories. Reading portfolios were reported by 34% of the teachers. Writing portfolios were reported by many more teachers, however, and were reported increasingly with advancing grade level. On average the teachers claimed to communicate with home about student literacy progress once a month. All but three of the teachers reported regular conferences with parents (i.e., at least two a year; see Table 1).

Discussion

The teachers in this study reported an integration of literacy instructional components, many of which enjoy empirical support as improving particular aspects of literacy: it is notable that the teachers reported doing much to create classroom environments supportive of literacy, because placing young children in environments that invite and support literacy stimulates them to do things that are literate (e.g., see Morrow, 1990, 1991; Neuman & Roskos, 1990, 1992). The teachers' claimed commitments to outstanding literature are sensible, given the increasing evidence that, when such literature drives instruction, there are positive effects on students' autonomous use of literature and on their attitudes toward reading (e.g., see Morrow, 1992; Morrow, O'Connor, & Smith, 1990). The literature emphasis reported by the teachers in this study is also striking in light of increasing evidence (e.g., see Feitelson, Kita, & Goldstein, 1986; Morrow, 1992) that consistent experiences with high-quality literature foster growth in understanding the structure of stories, which improves both comprehension and writing, as well as the sophistication of children's language. Just as broad reading expands the knowledge of adults (Stanovich & Cunningham, 1993), extensive experiences with stories expand children's knowledge of the world, as reflected, for example, by breadth of vocabulary (e.g., see Elley, 1989; Robbins & Ehri, 1994).

The claimed attention to the alphabetic principle, development of letter-sound associations, and activities focusing on the sounds of words makes sense in view of the clear associations between such instruction and success in reading (Adams, 1990) and other competencies, such as spelling (e.g., see Ball & Blachman, 1991; Lie, 1991; Nelson, 1990; Tangel & Blachman, 1992; Uhry & Shepherd, 1993). The respondents' reported modeling and explaining of literacy skills and strategies are also sound, for consistent use of these techniques has long-term positive effects on literacy achievement (Duffy et al., 1986, 1987; Duffy, Roehler, & Herrmann, 1988).

147

That writing was reported as involving instruction to plan, draft, and revise also is sensible: a growing body of data substantiates that children's composing abilities and understanding of writing increase substantially as a function of such instruction (Graham & Harris, 1994).

Primary-level language arts classrooms vary greatly in the extent to which they motivate children's literacy (e.g., see Turner, 1993). Thus, it is striking that sample teachers reported great commitment to motivation of literacy. Each of the 12 items on the final questionnaire pertaining to motivation of literacy received a mean rating near the top of the scale on which it was rated, with very low variability. That is, this sample of teachers claimed to do much to stimulate their students' engagement in reading and writing, from providing immediate positive feedback to fostering long-term beliefs that students can become good readers and writers.

What is also interesting is what was downplayed. Some common classroom instructional elements that have been criticized as potentially undermining reading achievement (e.g., see Allington, 1983; Hiebert, 1983) were reported as infrequent by the sample. For example, little ability-based reading grouping was reported, a practice that probably does not promote student achievement (Slavin, 1987) and that can, in some cases, affect it adversely during the primary years (e.g., see Juel, 1990). Also, the survey teachers did not report round-robin reading as the predominant type of reading but, rather, claimed a variety of types of reading, consistent with the perspective that different types of classroom reading stimulate improvements in different abilities (e.g., see Freppon, 1991; Hoffman, 1987; Reutzel, Hollingsworth, & Eldredge, 1994).

In short, a number of contemporary reading-instructional theorists have argued for balanced reading instruction, meaning the meshing of holistic literacy experiences and skills instruction (e.g., see Adams, 1990; Cazden, 1992; Delpit, 1986; Duffy, 1991; Fisher & Hiebert, 1990; McCaslin, 1989; Pressley, 1994; Stahl et al., 1994). Consistent with that outlook, the teachers in this study depicted their classrooms as integrating the attractive features of whole language with explicit skills. (See Groff, 1991, for complementary data.)

Education of students experiencing difficulties

Although the teachers reported delivering a common curriculum to their students, they also claimed to tailor instruction to individual differences. The teachers' commitment to meeting the needs of individual students came through most clearly with respect to their stance on the literacy education of students experiencing difficulties in learning to read and write. In recent years the literacy instruction offered to weaker readers has been criticized, with observers such as Allington (1991) arguing that weaker readers are often given heavy doses of lower-order, skills-oriented instruction aimed at improving decoding only, with a concomitant reduction in instruction aimed at promoting higher-order meaning-making (e.g., see Bean, Cooley, Eichelberger, Lazar, & Zigmond, 1991). Such compensatory instruction is often disconnected from the curriculum that stronger students experience.

That is not what this sample of teachers claimed to do for their weaker students, however. Although the teachers reported attending more to lower-order skills with weaker readers compared with good readers, there were few differences in instruction reported for good, average, and weaker readers. The teachers depicted their instruction as providing the more explicit lower-order (i.e., letter- and word-level) instruction that weaker students need without sacrificing weaker students' exposure to and experiences with good literature or their introduction to higher-order skills and strategies. Compensatory instruction for weaker students was described as integrated with the curriculum received by all students. (See Wendler, Samuels, & Moore, 1989, for complementary data that exceptional literacy teachers are especially attuned to providing assistance to students on an as-needed basis.)

Implications for teacher education

On the basis of the data reported here, a case can be made that a teacher's education should include exposure to a number of approaches and practices intermingling different types of instruction. As Duffy (1991, pp. 13–14) put it: "I think we do better by teaching teachers multiple alternatives, by teaching them how to network these so they can be accessed appropriately when needed, and by helping them understand that teaching demands fluid, multiple-dimensional responses to an infinite number of classroom situations, not narrow, uni-directional responses.... I want [teachers] ... to select among theories and procedures according to their judgement about what the situation calls for." Duffy (1991) came to this conclusion after his immersion in an elementary-teaching community for a year, as he studied teaching and teacher change. His perspective was informed by classroom observations and interviews with teachers. We come to the same conclusion, on the basis of information from the participants in the detailed survey summarized here.

Caveats, potential limitations, and future research

The data obtained in this survey were very orderly. Such orderliness is striking, in light of potential criticisms of a survey of instruction conducted at a distance from actual teaching. First, it could be argued that the criteria for selecting teachers would translate differently in different settings. If our selection criteria had been ineffective, what would be expected would be a sample of teachers widely varying in ability and effectiveness. Such a variable sample might be expected to produce highly variable outcomes, which is not what we obtained. A similar criticism that could be made is that some terms of reference in the survey—terms such as "whole language" and "good," "average," and "weaker" readers—might have had different meanings for different participants. Such a criticism is not consistent, however, with outcomes obtained here. For example, teachers identifying themselves as fully committed to whole language reported that they do not use basals as much as do those teachers who were somewhat committed to whole language, an outcome that would be expected. Our use of the terms "good," "average," and "weaker" readers was not so ambiguous as to preclude teachers from reporting more explicit and extensive teaching of lower-order skills to weaker compared with other readers, consistent with many observations in the reading-instructional literature (e.g., see Harris & Sipay, 1990). In short, although there was certainly some fuzziness in the meanings of some terms in this survey, that is because ideas such as whole language and reading ability classifications are fuzzy concepts. Fuzzy concepts typically can be understood, however, even if precise meanings are elusive (e.g., see Mancuso & Eimer, 1982), and we believe that the orderliness in outcomes obtained in this study suggests that teachers understood the terms in the survey. We carefully designed the questions to describe practices as the teachers themselves, in response to the first, open-ended questionnaire, described the practices.

Another potential concern is that, by relying on nominations from supervisors who are members of the International Reading Association (IRA), the bias would be too much in favor of some literacy perspectives that the supervisors perceived to be favored by the IRA—whole language philosophy in particular. Three realities must be confronted in reflecting on this criticism. First, without a doubt, whole language is one of the main conceptions of reading that is driving primary literacy instruction in North America in the 1990s (see Symons, Woloshyn, & Pressley, 1994), and thus it is hard to imagine a sampling procedure that would not produce many supervisors or teachers who were not extensively exposed to whole language and frequently committed to some version of it. Second, the members of the IRA are diverse in their outlook. The IRA includes the most prominent proponents of a number of instructional practices and perspectives that conflict with the tenets of whole language. Moreover, publications of the IRA reflect diversity of perspective about literacy instruction, more than unanimity with respect to any one stance, including whole language. Our interaction with professionals working in schools who are members of the IRA, most of whom are language arts supervisors, indicates that the grass-roots members are analogously diverse in their outlooks. Third, the criticism that this study may have been biased toward extremism of any type would have to explain away one of the principal findings—that there was balance in perspective, reflected throughout the reports. The teachers in this survey reported integration of diverse practices as part of literacy instruction. Moreover, the teachers claimed many instructional practices not consistent with whole language philosophy, such as isolated skills instruction and, for many, some use of basal readers (e.g., see Weaver, 1990).

One strength of the survey approach used here was that the questions on the final instrument were based on teachers' responses to the initial survey. That is, all practices probed on the final survey were mentioned in responses to the preliminary survey. A weakness of this approach is that there were other practices that teachers did not cite initially, ones that are common in education but that are not considered effective by outstanding teachers. For example, in the preliminary round, no teachers cited pull-out remediation instruction as important in their instruction of weaker readers. It seems likely that such instruction occurs in at least some of the classrooms served by the teachers participating in this survey study. We expect that our future final surveys will largely be teacher driven but that we will also be more proactive in attempting to generate potential teaching elements not identified initially by teachers, in order to tap a fuller range of issues about instruction than we tapped in this survey.

Surveying can provide information about many elements of instruction—but not much insight into teachers' unique implementations of the elements: might effective teachers be especially talented at story telling, modeling reading and writing processes, communicating with parents, or any of the other elements of instruction? Surveying also does not generate much information about how elements of instruction are blended—either how teachers plan their lessons and, hence, anticipate mixing elements or how they make instructional decisions while they teach and, thus, combine the elements of instruction from minute to minute. Finally, some who remain unconvinced that verbal reports can reflect actual behavior well are reluctant to make *any* inferences about teaching that are based on teachers' questionnaire responses.

For all of those reasons, we are now observing and interviewing a smaller sample of effective primary literacy teachers. What is reported here is the first of what we hope will be converging data about effective primary literacy instruction, data generated by using multiple methods. What the methods across this program of research will have in common, however, will be a focus on effective literacy teachers. With regard to beginning reading instruction, we believe that the great debates to come will be better informed than the great debates of the past—if the debaters know a great deal about the teaching of effective literacy teachers.

Note

This research was funded in part by the National Reading Research Center, an Office of Educational Research and Improvement, U.S.

Department of Education, research and development center, headquartered at the University of Maryland and the University of Georgia. Authors Pressley and Rankin are principal investigators of the center. Additional funding was provided by the University at Albany, State University of New York (in the form of a graduate stipend and tuition for Linda Yokoi), and the University of Nebraska. The opinions in this article are ours and do not represent the views of the funding agencies. Nazy Kaffashan assisted with the data analysis, and Jennifer Mistretta and Ruth Wharton-McDonald commented on the manuscript as it was being prepared, in part as they prepared to conduct follow-up research documenting effective grade 1 literacy instruction more fully. Correspondence regarding this article and the research program in general can be directed to Michael Pressley, Department of Educational Psychology and Statistics, University at Albany, SUNY, Albany, NY 12222.

References

Adams, M. J. (1990). *Beginning to read*. Cambridge MA: Harvard University Press.

Allington, R. L. (1983). The reading instruction provided readers of differing reading abilities. *Elementary School Journal*, **83**, 548–559.

Allington, R. L. (1991). The legacy of "Slow it down and make it more concrete." In J. Zutell & S. McCormick (Eds.), *Learner factors/teacher factors: Issues in literacy research and instruction: Fortieth yearbook of the National Reading Conference* (pp. 19–29). Chicago: National Reading Conference.

Ball, E. W., & Blachman, B. A. (1991). Does phoneme awareness training in kindergarten make a difference in early word recognition and developmental spelling? *Reading Research Quarterly*, **26**, 49–66.

Barr, R. (1984). Beginning reading instruction: From debate to reformation. In P. D. Pearson (Ed.), *Handbook of reading research* (pp. 545–581). New York: Longman.

Bean, R. M., Cooley, W. W., Eichelberger, T., Lazar, M. K., & Zigmond, N. (1991). Inclass or pullout: Effects of setting on the remedial reading program. *Journal of Reading Behavior*, **23**, 445–464.

Bereiter, C., & Bird, M. (1985). Use of thinking aloud in identification and teaching of reading comprehension strategies. *Cognition and Instruction*, **2**, 131–156.

Bond, G. L., & Dykstra, R. (1967). The cooperative research program in the first-grade reading instruction. *Reading Research Quarterly*, **2**, 5–142.

Brown, A. L., Bransford, J. D., Ferrara, R. A., & Campione, J. C. (1983). Learning, remembering, and understanding. In J. H. Flavell & E. M. Markman (Eds.), *Handbook of child psychology*, Vol. **3**. *Cognitive development* (pp. 77–166). New York: Wiley.

Brown, R., Pressley, M., Van Meter, P., & Schuder, T. (1995). *A quasi-experimental validation of transactional strategies instruction with previously low-achieving grade-2 readers*. Manuscript submitted for publication, University at Buffalo, State University of New York, Department of Educational and Counseling Psychology.

Cazden, C. (1992). *Whole language plus: Essays on literacy in the United States and New Zealand*. New York: Teachers College Press.

Chall, J. S. (1967). *Learning to read: The great debate*. New York: McGraw-Hill.

Chi, M. T. H., Glaser, R., & Farr, M. J. (Eds.). (1988). *The nature of expertise*. Hillsdale, NJ: Erlbaum.

Delpit, L. D. (1986). Skills and other dilemmas of a progressive black educator. *Harvard Educational Review, 56*, 379–385.

Diaper, D. (Ed.). (1989). *Knowledge elicitation: Principles, techniques, and applications*. New York: Wiley.

Duffy, G. G. (1991). What counts in teacher education? Dilemmas in educating empowered teachers. In J. Zutell & S. McCormick (Eds.), *Learner factors/teacher factors: Issues in literacy research and instruction: Fortieth yearbook of the National Reading Conference* (pp. 1–18). Chicago: National Reading Conference.

Duffy, G., Roehler, L., & Herrmann, G. (1988). Modeling mental processes helps poor readers become strategic readers. *Reading Teacher, 41*, 762–767.

Duffy, G. G., Roehler, L. R., Meloth, M., Vavrus, L., Book, C., Putnam, J., & Wesselman, R. (1986). The relationship between explicit verbal explanation during reading skill instruction and student awareness and achievement: A study of reading teacher effects. *Reading Research Quarterly, 21*, 237–252.

Duffy, G. G., Roehler, L. R., Sivan, E., Rackliffe, G., Book, C., Meloth, M., Vavrus, L., Wesselman, R., Putnam, J., & Bassiri, D. (1987). Effects of explaining the reasoning associated with using reading strategies. *Reading Research Quarterly, 22*, 347–368.

Dykstra, R. (1968). Summary of the second grade phase of the Cooperative Research Program in primary reading instruction. *Reading Research Quarterly, 4*, 49–70.

Elley, W. B. (1989). Vocabulary acquisition from listening to stories. *Reading Research Quarterly, 24*, 174–187.

Ericsson, K. A., & Smith, J. (Eds.). (1991). *Toward a general theory of expertise*. Cambridge: Cambridge University Press.

Feitelson, D., Kita, B., & Goldstein, Z. (1986). Effects of listening to series stories on first graders' comprehension and use of language. *Research in the Teaching of English, 20*, 339–356.

Fisher, C. W., & Hiebert, E. H. (1990). Characteristics of tasks in two approaches to literacy instruction. *Elementary School Journal, 91*, 3–18.

Flesch, R. (1955). *Why Johnny can't read*. New York: Harper & Row.

Foorman, B. R. (1994). The relevance of a connectionist model of reading for "The great debate." *Educational Psychology Review, 6*, 25–47.

Freppon, P. A. (1991). Children's concepts of the nature and purpose of reading in different instructional settings. *Journal of Reading Behavior, 23*, 139–163.

Goodman, K. S., & Goodman, Y. M. (1979). Learning to read is natural. In L. B. Resnick & P. A. Weaver (Eds.), *Theory and practice of early reading* (Vol. 1, pp. 137–154). Hillsdale, NJ: Erlbaum.

Goodman, Y. M. (Ed.). (1990). *How children construct literacy: Piagetian perspectives*. Newark, DE: International Reading Association.

Graham, S., & Harris, K. R. (1994). The effects of whole language on children's writing: A review of literature. *Educational Psychologist, 29*, 187–192.

Groff, P. (1991). Teachers' opinions of the whole language approach to reading instruction. *Annals of Dyslexia*, **41**, 83–95.

Guthrie, J. T., & Tyler, S. J. (1978). Cognition and instruction of poor readers. *Journal of Reading Behavior*, **10**, 57–78.

Harris, A. J., & Sipay, E. R. (1990). *How to increase reading ability: A guide to developmental and remedial methods*. New York: Longman.

Hiebert, E. H. (1983). An examination of ability grouping for reading instruction. *Reading Research Quarterly*, **18**, 231–255.

Hoffman, J. V. (1987). Rethinking the role of oral reading in basal instruction. *Elementary School Journal*, **87**, 367–373.

Hoffmann, R. R. (1992). *The psychology of expertise: Cognitive research and empirical AI*. New York: Springer-Verlag.

Juel, C. (1990). Effects of reading group assignment on reading development in first and second grade. *Journal of Reading Behavior*, **22**, 233–254.

King, D. F., & Goodman, K. S. (1990). Whole language: Cherishing learners and their language. *Language, Speech, and Hearing Services in Schools*, **21**, 221–227.

Lie, A. (1991). Effects of a training program for stimulating skills in word analysis in first-grade children. *Reading Research Quarterly*, **26**, 234–250.

Mancuso, J. C., & Eimer, B. N. (1982). Fitting things into categories. In J. C. Mancuso & J. R. Adams-Webber (Eds.), *The construing person* (pp. 130–151). New York: Praeger.

Mather, N. (1992). Whole language reading instruction for students with learning disabilities: Caught in the cross fire. *Learning Disabilities Research & Practice*, **7**, 87–95.

McCaslin, M. M. (1989). Whole language: Theory, instruction, and future implementation. *Elementary School Journal*, **90**, 223–229.

Meyer, M., & Booker, J. (1991). *Eliciting and analyzing expert judgement: A practical tour*. London: Academic Press.

Morrow, L. M. (1990). Preparing the classroom environment to promote literacy during play. *Early Childhood Research Quarterly*, **5**, 537–554.

Morrow, L. M. (1991). Relationships among physical designs of play centers, teachers' emphasis on literacy in play, and children's literacy behaviors during play. In J. Zutell & S. McCormick (Eds.), *Learner factors/teacher factors: Issues in literacy research and instruction: Fortieth yearbook of the National Reading Conference* (pp. 127–140). Chicago: National Reading Conference.

Morrow, L. M. (1992). The impact of a literature-based program on literacy achievement, use of literature, and attitudes of children from minority backgrounds. *Reading Research Quarterly*, **27**, 251–275.

Morrow, L. M., O'Connor, E. M., & Smith, J. K. (1990). Effects of a story reading program on the literacy development of at-risk kindergarten children. *Journal of Reading Behavior*, **22**, 255–275.

Nelson, L. (1990). The influence of phonics instruction on spelling progress. In J. Zutell & S. McCormick (Eds.), *Literacy theory and research: Analyses from multiple paradigms* (pp. 241–247). Chicago: National Reading Conference.

Neuman, S. B., & Roskos, K. (1990). The influence of literacy-enriched play settings on preschoolers' engagement with written language. In J. Zutell & S. McCormick (Eds.), *Literacy theory and research: Analyses from multiple paradigms* (pp. 179–188). Chicago: National Reading Conference.

Neuman, S. B., & Roskos, K. (1992). Literacy objects as cultural tools: Effects on children's literacy behaviors in play. *Reading Research Quarterly*, **27**, 203–225.

Ohanian, S. (1994). "Call me teacher" and "Who the hell are you?" In C. B. Smith (Moderator), *Whole language: The debate* (pp. 1–15, 58–61). Bloomington, IN: EDINFO Press.

Palincsar, A. S., & Brown, A. L. (1984). Reciprocal teaching of comprehension-fostering and comprehension-monitoring activities. *Cognition and Instruction*, **1**, 117–175.

Pflaum, S. W., Walberg, H. J., Karegianes, M. L., & Rasher, S. P. (1980). Reading instruction: A quantitative analysis. *Educational Researcher*, 9(7), 12–18.

Pressley, M. (1994). Commentary on the ERIC whole language debate. In C. B. Smith (Moderator), *Whole language: The debate* (pp. 155–178). Bloomington, IN: ERIC/REC.

Pressley, M., El-Dinary, P. B., Gaskins, I., Schuder, T., Bergman, J., Almasi, L., & Brown, R. (1992). Beyond direct explanation: Transactional instruction of reading comprehension strategies. *Elementary School Journal*, **92**, 511–554.

Pressley, M., Gaskins, I. W., Cunicelli, E. A., Burdick, N. J., Schaub-Matt, M., Lee, D. S., & Powell, N. (1991). Strategy instruction at Benchmark School: A faculty interview study. *Learning Disability Quarterly*, **14**, 19–48.

Pressley, M., & Rankin, J. (1994). More about whole language methods of reading instruction for students at risk for early reading failure. *Learning Disabilities Research & Practice*, **9**, 156–167.

Reutzel, D. R., Hollingsworth, P. M., & Eldredge, J. L. (1994). Oral reading instruction: The effect on student reading development. *Reading Research Quarterly*, **29**, 40–59.

Robbins, C., & Ehri, L. C. (1994). Reading story-books to kindergartners helps them learn new vocabulary words. *Journal of Educational Psychology*, **86**, 54–64.

Scott, A. C., Clayton, J. E., & Gibson, E. L. (1991). *A practical guide to knowledge acquisition*. Reading, MA: Addison-Wesley.

Shannon, P. (1994). "The answer is yes . . ." and "People who live in glass houses . . ." In C. B. Smith (Moderator), *Whole language: The debate* (pp. 48–51, 81–99): Bloomington, IN: EDINFO Press.

Slavin, R. E. (1987). Grouping for instruction in the elementary school. *Educational Psychologist*, **22**, 109–128.

Smith, C. B. (Moderator). (1994). *Whole language: The debate*. Bloomington, IN: EDINFO Press.

Stahl, S. A., McKenna, M. C., & Pagnucco, J. R. (1994). The effects of whole language instruction: An update and reappraisal. *Educational Psychologist*, **29**, 175–186.

Stahl, S. A., & Miller, P. D. (1989). Whole language and language experience approaches for beginning reading: A quantitative research synthesis. *Review of Educational Research*, **59**, 87–116.

Stanovich, K. E., & Cunningham, A. E. (1993). Where does knowledge come from? Specific associations between print exposure and information acquisition. *Journal of Educational Psychology*, **85**, 211–229.

Symons, S., Woloshyn, V. E., & Pressley, M. (Guest eds.). (1994). Scientific evaluation of whole language [Special issue]. *Educational Psychologist*, **29**(4).

Tangel, D. M., & Blachman, B. A. (1992). Effect of phoneme awareness instruction on kindergarten children's invented spelling. *Journal of Reading Behavior*, **24**, 233–261.

Turner, J. C. (1993). Situated motivation in literacy instruction. *Reading Research Quarterly*, **28**, 288–290.

Uhry, J. K., & Shepherd, M. J. (1993). Segmentation/spelling instruction as part of a first-grade reading program: Effects on several measures of reading. *Reading Research Quarterly*, **28**, 218–233.

Weaver, C. (1990). *Understanding whole language: From principles to practice.* Portsmouth, NH: Heinemann.

Wendler, D., Samuels, S. J., & Moore, V. K. (1989). Comprehension instruction of awardwinning teachers, teachers with master's degrees, and other teachers. *Reading Research Quarterly*, **24**, 382–401.

Whitmore, K. F., & Goodman, Y. M. (1992). Inside the whole language classroom. *School Administrator*, **49**(5), 20–26.

6

THE CHARACTERISTICS OF EFFECTIVE TEACHERS OF LITERACY

Jane Medwell, David Wray, Louise Poulson and Richard Fox

Source: *Education 3 to 13* (1999) 27(1): 46–52

Introduction

This article gives a preliminary report of the results of research, commissioned by the Teacher Training Agency, into the characteristics of teachers who can be shown to be effective in teaching literacy to primary pupils. The findings are based on a close study of a sample of teachers whose pupils make effective learning gains in literacy and of a sample of teachers who were less effective in literacy teaching.

The aims of this research were to:

1 identify the key factors in what effective teachers know, understand and do which enable them to put effective teaching of literacy into practice in the primary phase;
2 identify the strategies which would enable those factors to be more widely applied;
3 examine aspects of continuing professional development which contribute to the development of effective teachers of literacy.

Effective teaching and effective teachers

The literature on effective teaching has a number of predominant themes. These include school effect issues and issues related to the likely characteristics of effective teachers. Given the lack of value added data on which to base valid assertions, variations in children's literacy achievements must be treated cautiously. One recent review suggests that a child's background (prior learning, intelligence, home background, parents etc.) contributes 85% to what is learned in school: the other 15% is contributed by schooling (Harrison, 1996). This is a pessimistic estimate and is confounded by the evidence that individual children vary hugely in terms of the experiences of literacy they get in school. It is also the case that particular school effects are unlikely to affect all children equally (Allington, 1984).

The project reported here focused on the contribution made by the teacher and the school to what children learn. Research on school effectiveness suggests that variations in children's literacy performance may be related to three types of effect: whole school, teacher, and methods/materials. Of these three, the consensus is that the effect of the teacher is the most significant (Barr, 1984; Adams 1990). Of the range of models put forward to explain the various components of school/teacher/pupil interactions, one we found particularly useful was the concept of 'curricular expertise', as advanced by Alexander, Rose & Woodhead (1992). By this they meant "the subject knowledge, the understanding of how children learn and the skills needed to teach subjects successfully." Effective teaching, they argued, depends on the successful combination of this knowledge, understanding and skill.

Most of the research into effective teaching is generic rather than specific to literacy teaching. In the 1970s a number of large scale studies in the USA attempted of look at the effects of the teacher by searching for links between teacher classroom behaviour and pupil achievement. (See Brophy & Good (1986) for a review). More recent studies have taken a more complex view of the classroom and used multi-faceted methods of research. Studies such as that of Bennett et al (1984) looked at the classes of teachers deemed to be effective and Mortimore et al (1988) studied teaching in junior schools. At the same time official inspections by HMI have sought to identify and describe effective teaching.

Whilst the research offers little literacy-specific information it does give a range of findings concerning:

- teacher classroom behaviour, such as classroom management, task setting, task content and pedagogic skills – "the skills needed to teach subjects successfully", in the words of Alexander, Rose & Woodhead (1992).
- teacher subject knowledge and beliefs, in which we can include content knowledge in a subject, an understanding of how children learn in that subject and the belief systems which interact with and enable such knowledge to be put into operation in the classroom.

Effective teaching and effective teachers of literacy

There have been numerous attempts to establish the nature of effective teaching in literacy. Most of these have begun by analysing the processes involved in being literate and from this putting forward a model to guide instruction in literacy (for example, Chall, 1967; Flesch, 1955; Goodman & Goodman, 1979). The argument has been that effective teaching in literacy is that which produces effective literate behaviour in learners. This sounds like an eminently sensible position but its main problem has been the difficulty researchers and teachers have found in agreeing on what exactly should count as effective literate behaviour, especially in reading. The major disagreement has centred around the relative importance given in views of literacy to technical skills such as word recognition, decoding and spelling or to higher order skills such as making meaning. Such lack of agreement has led to proponents of radically different approaches to teaching literacy claiming superiority for their suggested programmes, but using very different criteria against which to judge the success of these programmes.

An example of this can be found in recent debates about literacy teaching. An approach known in the USA and other parts of the world as 'whole language' emphasises language processes and the creation of learning environments in which children experience authentic reading and writing (Weaver, 1990). Both linguistic and cognitive development are presumed to be stimulated by the experience of reading good literature and of writing original compositions. Whole language theorists and teachers stress that skills instruction should occur within the context of natural reading and writing rather than as decontextualised exercises. The development of literacy tends to be seen as a natural by-product of immersion in high quality literacy environments.

In contrast, other researchers and teachers argue that learning the code is a critical part of early reading and that children are most likely to become skilled in this when they are provided with systematic teaching in decoding (e.g., Chall, 1967). There is growing evidence that such teaching increases reading ability (Adams, 1990), especially for children who experience difficulties in learning to read (Mather, 1992; Pressley & Rankin, 1994).

There have been several studies comparing the effectiveness of teaching programmes using a whole language approach and programmes emphasising traditional decoding. The evidence suggests that teaching based on whole language principles (i.e. the use of whole texts, good literature and fully contextualised instruction) does stimulate children to engage in a greater range of literate activities, develop more positive attitudes toward reading and writing, and increase their understanding about the nature and purposes of reading and writing (e.g. Morrow, 1990, 1991, 1992; Neuman & Roskos, 1990, 1992). Evidence also indicates, however, that whole language teaching programmes have less of an effect upon early reading achievement as measured by standardised tests of decoding, vocabulary, comprehension, and writing (Graham & Harris, 1994; Stahl,

McKenna, & Pagnucco, 1994; Stahl & Miller, 1989). Teaching which explicitly focuses on phonemic awareness and letter-sound correspondences does result in improved performance on such standardised tests (Adams, 1990). The picture emerging from research is, therefore, not a simple one.

There is an issue which has potential bearing on understanding of the nature of effective literacy teaching and which may, in fact, be the focal point around which apparently conflicting research findings may be synthesised. This concerns the near impossibility of finding, and thus testing, 'pure' teaching approaches in literacy. Close examination of many recent studies which appear to support the explicit teaching of decoding and comprehension strategies suggests that embedded in these programmes there are often many elements of what could be described as whole language teaching, including, for example, the reading of high quality children's literature and daily original writing by children (Pressley et al., 1991, 1992). Similarly, when the programmes described by whole language advocates are examined closely, it is quite apparent that they do contain a good deal of systematic teaching of letter-sound correspondences, for example (cf. Holdaway, 1979). These teaching approaches, in fact, are tending to become more and more alike and commentators such as Adams (1991) have suggested that there is no need for a division between teaching approaches styled as 'whole language' or 'explicit code teaching' in orientation. What has emerged in recent years is a realisation that explicit decoding and comprehension instruction are most effectively carried out in the context of other components.

Such rapprochement between previously contrasting positions suggests that effective literacy teaching is multifaceted (e.g., Adams, 1990; Cazden, 1992; Duffy, 1991; Stahl et al., 1994). That is to say that effective teaching often integrates letter- and word-level teaching with explicit instruction of comprehension processes and sets these within a context meaningful to the children in which they read and write high quality whole texts. Such an approach implies an informed selection by the teacher from a range of teaching techniques and approaches on the basis of a detailed understanding of the multifaceted nature of literacy and of the needs of a particular group of children. It does not, as Rose (1996) points out, mean the naive use of a range of teaching methods in the hope that, like shotgun pellets, at least some of them will hit the target.

The likely characteristics and manifestations of effective teaching of literacy, therefore, can be described, to some extent. The focus of our research was to consider what it was that effective teachers knew and believed about this teaching, and how this contributed to their effectiveness.

Designing the study

In the research, we aimed to compare the practices, beliefs and knowledge of a group of teachers identified as effective at teaching literacy with those of a group of teachers not so identified. To do this we identified two main sample groups:

1 the main sample of 228 primary teachers identified as effective in the teaching of literacy;
2 the validation sample of 71 primary teachers not so identified.

The effective teachers were chosen from a list of teachers recommended as effective by advisory staff in a number of LEAs. The key criterion for this choice was whether we could obtain evidence of above-average learning gains in reading for the children in the classes of these teachers.

Teachers in both groups completed a questionnaire designed to enquire into their beliefs about literacy and literacy teaching approaches, their feelings about children's needs in literacy development, their reported use of a range of teaching techniques and their professional development experience in literacy.

We then identified sub-samples of the two main groups, including:

1 a sub-sample of 26 teachers from the group of teachers identified as effective in the teaching of literacy;
2 a validation sub-sample of 10 of the primary teachers from the validation group.

The teachers in both these sub-samples were twice observed teaching and then interviewed about each of these teaching episodes. The first observation/interview focused on teaching strategies, classroom organisation and the genesis of these in terms of the teachers' experiences of professional development. The focus in the second observation/interview was on lesson content and teachers' subject knowledge. During the second interview, teachers completed a 'quiz' designed to test their knowledge about aspects of literacy.

We also collected two sets of reading test results from the children being taught by these teachers. One of these sets indicated the children's reading abilities before they arrived in this teacher's class and the other these abilities after a year in this class. These two sets of results were used to provide an objective measure of the effectiveness of these teachers in teaching literacy.

Main findings of the research

In the space available here all we can do is summarise the major findings of the research. Much greater detail about these findings can be found in the book arising from the project (Wray et al, 2002).

Teachers' subject knowledge in literacy

Both the effective teachers and the validation teachers knew the requirements of the National Curriculum well and could describe what they were doing in terms of these. The effective teachers, however, placed a great emphasis on children's knowledge of the purposes and functions of reading and writing and of the structures used to enable these processes. They taught language structures and were concerned to contextualise this teaching and to present such structures functionally and meaningfully to children.

Even the effective teachers, however, had limited success at recognising some types of words (e.g. adverb, preposition) in a sentence and some sub-word units (e.g. phoneme) out of context. Units such as phonemes, onsets and rimes and morphemes were problematic for them and even using more everyday terminology for these units still did not guarantee success for the teachers in recognising them out of the lesson context. Despite this apparent lack of explicit, abstract knowledge of linguistic concepts, the effective teachers used such knowledge implicitly in their teaching, particularly that connected with phonics. It seems that the teachers knew the material they were teaching in a particular way. They appeared to know and understand it in the form in which they taught it to the children, rather than abstracted from the teaching context. This is an important finding, which we feel has implications for the content of teachers' continuing professional development.

Teachers were also asked to examine and judge samples of children's reading and writing. All the teachers were able to analyse the children's mistakes in these samples, but the way the two groups carried out this task was different. The effective teachers were more diagnostic in the ways they approached the task and were more able to generate explanations as to why children read or wrote as they did. In examining pieces of writing, the two groups eventually mentioned similar features, but the effective teachers were quicker to focus on possible underlying causes of a child's writing behaviour. Although both groups reached broadly similar conclusions about children's reading and writing, the effective teachers were able to offer many more reasons for their conclusions and to make these detailed judgements more quickly. This suggests a firmer command of subject knowledge relating to literacy processes.

Teachers' beliefs about literacy

The effective teachers of literacy tended to place a high value upon communication and composition in their views about the teaching of reading and writing. They were more coherent in their belief systems about the teaching of literacy and tended to favour teaching activities that explicitly emphasiscd the understanding of what was read and written.

The effective teachers translated their beliefs about purpose and meaning into practice by paying systematic attention to both the goals they had identified for reading and writing (the understanding and production of meaningful text) and to technical processes such as phonic knowledge, spelling, grammatical knowledge and punctuation. They tended to approach these technical skills in distinctive ways by using an embedded approach; that is, they gave explicit attention to word and sentence level aspects of reading and writing within whole text activities which were both meaningful and explained clearly to pupils. Teachers in the validation sample with less coherent approaches were less likely to show how technical features of reading and writing fitted within a broader range of skills. They did not necessarily ensure that pupils understood the connections between the aims and the processes of reading and writing.

Coherence and consistency emerged as being an important and distinctive characteristic of the effective teachers in several senses:

- their beliefs were internally consistent;
- their practice lived up to their aspirations;
- their beliefs included a belief in making connections between the goals of literacy teaching and learning activities and the activities themselves.

Teaching practices: connections and contexts

The effective teachers were generally much more likely to embed their teaching of reading into a wider context and to understand and show how specific aspects of reading and writing contributed to communication. They tended to make such connections implicit and explicit. For example, when teaching skills such as vocabulary, word recognition and the use of text features, they made heavy use of whole texts or big books as the context in which to teach literacy. They were also very clear about their purposes for using such texts. They also used modelling extensively. They regularly demonstrated reading and writing to their classes in a variety of ways, often accompanying these demonstrations by verbal explanations of what they were doing.

Because of this concern to contextualise their teaching of language features by working together on texts, these teachers made explicit connections for their pupils between the text, sentence and word levels of language study.

The lessons of the effective teachers were all conducted at a brisk pace. They regularly re-focused children's attention on the task at hand and used clear time frames to keep children on task. They also tended to conclude their lessons by reviewing, with the whole class, what the children had done during the lesson.

Links with recent developments in literacy teaching

This research was begun before the National Literacy Strategy was put in place. There are, however, some specific points of connection between the model of literacy teaching implicit in the National Literacy Strategy and our research findings. We found that the effective teachers of literacy tended to teach literacy in lessons which were clearly focused on this subject (literacy hours). Within these lessons they used a mixture of whole class interactive teaching and small group guided work, with occasional individual teaching usually undertaken by a classroom assistant or volunteer helper. A good deal of their teaching involved the use of shared texts such as big books, duplicated passages and multiple copies of books, through which the attention of a whole class or group was drawn to text, sentence and word level features.

Implications of the research

There are several implications emerging from the research in terms of future policy and practice in continuing professional development.

Access to in-service courses

There has been a tendency for literacy curriculum specialists (school English co-ordinators) to be targeted for in-service opportunities in literacy. There is evidence in our findings that this policy has had a positive effect on these teachers but that teachers who had not been designated as school English co-ordinators were somewhat restricted in the in-service opportunities available to them. We feel strongly that *all* teachers need professional development in this crucial area.

The nature of professional development experience

Our findings suggest that a particularly valuable form of professional development is teachers' involvement in longer term projects where they have to work out practical philosophies and policies regarding literacy and its teaching, for example, through doing and using research. This contrasts with the predominantly 'short-burst' nature of much current professional development experience.

The content of in-service courses

The most effective in-service content seemed from our findings not to be that which focused on knowledge at the teachers' own level, but rather that which dealt with subject knowledge in terms of how this was taught to children. This implies a more practical approach and the teachers in this study confirmed that one of the most successful forms of in-service was that which gave them guided opportunities to try out new ideas in the classroom.

While we found little evidence that the effective teachers of literacy had an extensive command of a range of linguistic terminology, it seems likely that having a greater command might help them further improve their teaching of literacy. Such terminology could be introduced (or reintroduced) to teachers not as a set of definitions for them to learn but as the embodiments of linguistic functions with a strong emphasis upon the ways these functions might be taught.

The evidence from this project also suggests that the experience of being an English co-ordinator makes a significant contribution to teachers' development as literacy teachers. Schools need to consider how appropriate elements of this experience can be replicated for other teachers.

Conclusion

The research project described in this article is unique in this country in focusing not on features of the teaching of literacy but on the characteristics of the teachers who perform this teaching well. We feel that we have made a significant contribution to understandings in this area and, we hope, have initiated a debate about teacher preparation, knowledge and development which has the potential to lead to major improvements in the quality of literacy teaching. We welcome any comments or feedback on any of our findings.

References

Adams, M. J. (1991) Why not phonics and whole language? In Ellis, W. (ed.) *All Language and the Creation of Literacy*. Baltimore, MA: The Orton Dyslexia Society.

Adams, M. J. (1990) *Beginning to Read: Thinking and Learning About Print*. Cambridge MA: MIT Press.

Alexander, R., Rose, J. and Woodhead, C. (1992) *Curriculum Organisation and Classroom Practice in Primary Schools*. London: HMSO.

Allington, R. (1984) Content coverage and contextual reading in reading groups. *Journal of Reading Behaviour*. 16.

Barr, R. (1984) Beginning reading instruction: from debate to reformation. In David Pearson (ed.) *Handbook of Reading Research*. New York: Longman.

Bennett, S. N., Desforges, C., Cockburn, A. and Wilkinson, B. (1984) *The Quality of Pupil Learning Experiences*. London: Lawrence Erlbaum.

Brophy, J and Good, T. (1986) Teacher behaviour and student achievement. In Wittrock, M. C. (ed.) *Handbook of Research in Teaching*. London: Collier Macmillan.

Cazden, C, (1992) *Whole Language Plus: Essays on Literacy In The United States and New Zealand*. New York: Teachers' College Press.

Chall, J. (1967) *Learning to Read: the Great Debate*. London: McGraw-Hill.

Duffy, G. (1991) What counts in teacher education? Dilemmas in educating empowered teachers. In J. Zutell and McCormack, S. (eds) *Learner Factors / Teacher Factors: Issues in Literacy Research and Instruction: Fortieth Yearbook of the National Reading Conference*. Chicago: NRC.

Flesch, R. (1955) *Why Johnny Can't Read*. New York: Harper Row.

Goodman, K. and Goodman, Y. (1979) Learning to read is natural. In Resnik, L. B. and Weaver, P. A. (eds) *Theory and Practice of Early Reading*. Hillsdale, NJ: Erlbaum.

Graham, S. and Harris, K. R. (1994) The effects of whole language on children's writing: a review of the literature. *Educational Psychologist*. 29, 187–192.

Harrison, C. (1996) *Teaching Reading: What Teachers Need to Know*. Cambridge: United Kingdom Reading Association.

Holdaway, D. (1979) *The Foundations of Literacy*. Auckland: Ashton Scholastic.

Mather, N. (1992) Whole language reading instruction for students with learning abilities; caught in the crossfire. *Learning Disabilities Research and Practice*. 7, 87–95.

Morrow, L. M. (1990) Preparing the classroom environment to promote literacy during play. *Early Childhood Research Quarterly*. 5, 537–554.

Morrow, L. M. (1991) Relationships among physical design of play centres, teachers' emphasis on literacy play, and children's behaviours during play. In Zutell, J. and McCormack, S. (eds) *Learner Factors/Teacher Factors: Issues In Literacy Research and Instruction: Fortieth Yearbook of The National Reading Conference*. Chicago: NRC.

Morrow, L. M. (1992) The impact of literature based programmes on literacy achievement, use of literature and attitudes of children from ethnic minority backgrounds. *Reading Research Quarterly*. 27, 251–275.

Mortimore, P., Sammons, P., Stoll, L., Lewis, D. and Ecob, R. (1988) *School Matters*. Wells, Somerset: Open Books.

Neuman, S. B. and Roskos, K. (1990) The influence of literacy enriched play settings on pre-schoolers engagement with written language. In J. Zutell and McCormack, S. (eds) *Literacy Theory and Research: Analyses From Multiple Paradigms*. Chicago: NRC.

Neuman, S. B. and Roskos, K. (1992) Literacy objects as cultural tools: effects on children's literacy behaviours at play. *Reading Research Quarterly*. 27, 203–225.

Pressley, M. and Rankin, J. (1994) More about whole language methods of reading instruction for students at risk for early reading failure. *Learning Disabilities Research and Practice*. 9, 156–167.

Pressley, M., Gaskins, I., Cunicelli, E. A., Burdick, N. J., Schaub-Matt, M., Lee, D. S. and Powell, N. (1991) Strategy instruction at Benchmark School: a faculty interview study. *Learning Disability Quarterly*. 14, 19–48.

Pressley, M., El-Dinary, P. B., Gaskins, I., Schuder, T., Bergman, J., Almasai, L. and Brown, R. (1992) Beyond direct explanation: transactional instruction of reading comprehension strategies. *Elementary School Journal*. 92, 511–554.

Rose, J. (1996) What our schools must teach. In *The Times*, 8th May, 1996.

Stahl, S. A. and Miller, P. D. (1989) Whole language and language experience approaches for beginning reading: a quantitative research synthesis. *Review of Educational Research*. 59, 87–116.

Stahl, S. A., McKenna, M. C. and Pagnucco, J. R. (1994) The effects of whole language instruction: an update and reappraisal. *Educational Psychologist*. 29, 175–186.

Weaver, C. (1990) *Understanding Whole Language: From Principles to Practice*. Portsmouth NH: Heinemann.

Wray, D., Medwell, J., Poulson, L. & Fox, R. (2002) *Teaching Literacy Effectively*. London: RoutledgeFalmer.

167

7

WHAT NO BEDTIME STORY MEANS*

Narrative skills at home and school

Shirley Brice Heath

Source: *Language in Society* (1982) 11: 49–76

In the preface to *S/Z*; Roland Barthes' work on ways in which readers read, Richard Howard writes: "We require an education in literature ... in order to discover that *what we have assumed* – with the complicity of our teachers – *was nature is in fact culture, that what was given is no more than a way of taking*" (emphasis not in the original; Howard 1974:ix).[1] This statement reminds us that the *culture* children learn as they grow up is, in fact, "ways of taking" meaning from the environment around them. The means of making sense from books and relating their contents to knowledge about the real world is but one "way of taking" that is often interpreted as "natural" rather than learned. The quote also reminds us that teachers (and researchers alike) have not recognized that ways of taking from books are as much a part of learned behavior as are ways of eating, sitting, playing games, and building houses.

As school-oriented parents and their children interact in the pre-school years, adults give their children, through modeling and specific instruction, ways of taking from books which seem natural in school and in numerous institutional settings such as banks, post offices, businesses, or government offices. These *mainstream* ways exist in societies around the world that rely on formal educational systems to prepare children for participation in settings involving literacy. In some communities these ways of schools and institutions are very similar to the ways learned at home; in other communities the ways of school are merely an overlay on the home-taught ways and may be in conflict with them.[2]

Yet little is actually known about what goes on in story-reading and other literacy-related interactions between adults and preschoolers in communities around the world. Specifically, though there are numerous diary accounts and experimental studies of the preschool reading experiences of mainstream middle-class children, we know little about the specific literacy features of the environment upon which the school expects to draw. Just how does what is frequently termed "the literate tradition" envelope the child in knowledge about interrelationships between oral and written langauge, between knowing something and knowing ways of labelling and displaying it? We have even less information about the variety of ways children from *non-mainstream* homes learn about reading, writing, and using oral language to display knowledge in their preschool environment. The general view has been that whatever it is that main-stream school-oriented homes have, these other homes do not have it; thus these children are not from the literate tradition and are not likely to succeed in school.

A key concept for the empirical study of ways of taking meaning from written sources across communities is that of *literacy events*: occasions in which written language is integral to the nature of participants' interac-tions and their interpretive processes and strategies. Familiar literacy events for mainstream preschoolers are bedtime stories, reading cereal boxes, stop signs, and television ads, and interpreting instructions for com-mercial games and toys. In such literacy events, participants follow socially established rules for verbalizing what they know from and about the written material. Each community has rules for socially interacting and sharing knowledge in literacy events.

This paper briefly summarizes the ways of taking from printed stories families teach their preschoolers in a cluster of mainstream school-oriented neighborhoods of a city in the Southeastern region of the United States. We then describe two quite different ways of taking used in the homes of two English-speaking communities in the same region that do not follow the school-expected patterns of bookreading and reinforcement of these patterns in oral storytelling. Two assumptions underlie this paper and are treated in detail in the ethnography of these communities (Heath forthcoming b): (1) Each community's ways of taking from the printed word and using this knowledge are interdependent with the ways children learn to talk in their social interactions with caregivers. (2) There is little or no validity to the time-honored dichotomy of "the literate tradition" and "the oral tradition." This paper suggests a frame of reference for both the community patterns and the paths of development children in different communities follow in their literacy orientations.

Mainstream school-oriented bookreading

Children growing up in mainstream communities are expected to develop habits and values which attest to their membership in a "literate society." Children learn certain customs, beliefs, and skills in early enculturation experiences with written materials: the bedtime story is a major literacy event which helps set patterns of behavior that recur repeatedly through the life of mainstream children and adults.

In both popular and scholarly literature, the "bedtime story" is widely accepted as a given – a natural way for parents to interact with their child at bedtime. Commercial publishing houses, television advertising, and children's magazines make much of this familiar ritual, and many of their sales pitches are based on the assumption that in spite of the intrusion of television into many patterns of interaction between parents and children, this ritual remains. Few parents are fully conscious of what bedtime storyreading means as preparation for the kinds of learning and displays of knowledge expected in school. Ninio and Bruner (1978), in their longitudinal study of one mainstream middle-class mother-infant dyad in joint picture-book reading, strongly suggest a universal role of bookreading in the achievement of labelling by children.

In a series of "reading cycles," mother and child alternate turns in a dialogue: the mother directs the child's attention to the book and/or asks what-questions and/or labels items on the page. The items to which the what-questions are directed and labels given are two-dimensional representations of three-dimensional objects, so that the child has to resolve the conflict between perceiving these as two-dimensional objects and as representations of a three-dimensional visual setting. The child does so "by assigning a privileged, autonomous status to pictures as visual objects" (1978: 5). The arbitrariness of the picture, its decontextualization, and its existence as something which cannot be grasped and manipulated like its "real" counterparts is learned through the routines of structured interactional dialogue in which mother and child take turns playing a labelling game. In a "scaffolding" dialogue (cf. Cazden 1979), the mother points and asks "What is x?" and the child vocalizes and/or gives a nonverbal signal of attention. The mother then provides verbal feedback and a label. Before the age of two, the child is socialized into the "initiation-reply-evaluation sequences" repeatedly described as the central structural feature of classroom lessons (e.g., Sinclair and Coulthard 1975; Griffin and Humphry 1978; Mehan 1979). Teachers ask their students questions which have answers prespecified in the mind of the teacher. Students respond, and teachers provide feedback, usually in the form of an evaluation. Training in ways of responding to this pattern begins very early in the labelling activities of mainstream parents and children.

Maintown ways

This patterning of "incipient literacy" (Scollon and Scollon 1979) is similar in many ways to that of the families of fifteen primary-level school teachers in Maintown, a cluster of middle-class neighborhoods in a city of the Piedmont Carolinas. These families (all of whom identify themselves as "typical," "middle-class," or "mainstream,") had preschool children, and the mother in each family was either teaching in local public schools at the time of the study (early 1970s), or had taught in the academic year preceding participation in the study. Through a research dyad approach, using teacher-mothers as researchers with the ethnographer, the teacher-mothers audio-recorded their children's interactions in their primary network – mothers, fathers, grandparents, maids, siblings, and frequent visitors to the home. Children were expected to learn the following rules in literacy events in these nuclear households:

1   As early as six months of age, children *give attention to books and information derived from books.* Their rooms contain bookcases and are decorated with murals, bedspreads, mobiles, and stuffed animals which represent characters found in books. Even when these characters have their origin in television programs, adults also provide books which either repeat or extend the characters' activities on television.

2   Children, from the age of six months, *acknowledge questions about books.* Adults expand nonverbal responses and vocalizations from infants into fully formed grammatical sentences. When children begin to verbalize about the contents of books, adults extend their questions from simple requests for labels (What's that? Who's that?) to ask about the attributes of these items (What does the doggie say? What color is the ball?)

3   From the time they start to talk, children *respond to conversational allusions to the content of books; they act as question-answers who have a knowledge of books.* For example, a fuzzy black dog on the street is likened by an adult to Blackie in a child's book: "Look, there's a Blackie. Do you think *he's* looking for a boy?" Adults strive to maintain with children a running commentary on any event or object which can be book-related, thus modelling for them the extension of familiar items and events from books to new situational contexts.

4   Beyond two years of age, children *use their knowledge of what books do to legitimate their departures from "truth."* Adults encourage and reward "book talk," even when it is not directly relevant to an ongoing conversation. Children are allowed to suspend reality, to tell stories which are not true, to ascribe fiction-like features to everyday objects.

5   Preschool children *accept book and book-related activities as entertainment.* When preschoolers are "captive audiences" (e.g., waiting in a doctor's office, putting a toy together, or preparing for bed), adults reach for books. If there are no books present, they talk about other objects as though they were pictures in books. For example, adults point to items, and ask children to name, describe, and compare them to familiar objects in their environment. Adults often ask children to state their likes or dislikes, their view of events, and so forth, at the

end of the captive audience period. These affective questions often take place while the next activity is already underway (e.g., moving toward the doctor's office, putting the new toy away, or being tucked into bed), and adults do not insist on answers.

6   Preschoolers *announce their own factual and fictive narratives* unless they are given in response to direct adult elicitation. Adults judge as most acceptable those narratives which open by orienting the listener to setting and main character. Narratives which are fictional are usually marked by formulaic openings, a particular prosody, or the borrowing of episodes in story books.

7   When children are about three years old, adults discourage the highly interactive participative role in bookreading children have hitherto played and children *listen and wait as an audience*. No longer does either adult or child repeatedly break into the story with questions and comments. Instead, children must listen, store what they hear, and on cue from the adult, answer a question. Thus, children begin to formulate "practice" questions as they wait for the break and the expected formulaic-type questions from the adult. It is at this stage that children often choose to "read" to adults rather than to be read to.

A pervasive pattern of all these features is the authority which books and book-related activities have in the lives of both the preschoolers and members of their primary network. Any initiation of a literacy event by a preschooler makes an interruption, an untruth, a diverting of attention from the matter at hand (whether it be an uneaten plate of food, a messy room, or an avoidance of going to bed) acceptable. Adults jump at openings their children give them for pursuing talk about books and reading.

In this study, writing was found to be somewhat less acceptable as an "anytime activity," since adults have rigid rules about times, places, and materials for writing. The only restrictions on bookreading concern taking good care of books: they should not be wet, torn, drawn on, or lost. In their talk to children about books, and in their explanations of why they buy children's books, adults link school success to "learning to love books," "learning what books can do for you," and "learning to entertain yourself and to work independently." Many of the adults also openly expressed a fascination with children's books "nowadays." They generally judged them as more diverse, wide-ranging, challenging, and exciting than books they had as children.

The mainstream pattern. A close look at the way bedtime story routines in Maintown taught children how to take meaning from books raises a heavy sense of the familiar in all of us who have acquired mainstream habits and values. Throughout a lifetime, any school-successful individual moves through the same processes described above thousands of times.

Reading for comprehension involves an internal replaying of the same types of questions adults ask children of bedtime stories. We seek *what-explanations*, asking what the topic is, establishing it as predictable and recognizing it in new situational contexts by classifying and categorizing it in our mind with other phenomena. The what-explanation is replayed in learning to pick out topic sentences, write outlines, and answer standard-ized tests which ask for the correct titles to stories, and so on. In learning to read in school, children move through a sequence of skills designed to teach what-explanations. There is a tight linear order of instruction which recapitulates the bedtime story pattern of breaking down the story into small bits of information and teaching children to handle sets of related skills in isolated sequential hierarchies.

In each individual reading episode in the primary years of schooling, children must move through what-explanations before they can provide *reason-explanations* or *affective commentaries*. Questions about why a particular event occurred or why a specific action was right or wrong come at the end of primary-level reading lessons, just as they come at the end of bedtime stories. Throughout the primary grade levels, what-explanations predominate, reason-explanations come with increasing frequency in the upper grades, and affective comments most often come in the extra-credit portions of the reading workbook or at the end of the list of suggested activities in text books across grade levels. This sequence characterizes the total school career. High school freshmen who are judged poor in compo-sitional and reading skills spend most of their time on what-explanations and practice in advanced versions of bedtime story questions and answers. They are given little or no chance to use reason-giving explanations or assessments of the actions of stories. Reason-explanations result in config-urational rather than hierarchical skills, are not predictable, and thus do not present content with a high degree of redundancy. Reason-giving explanations tend to rely on detailed knowledge of a specific domain. This detail is often unpredictable to teachers, and is not as highly valued as is knowledge which covers a particular area of knowledge with less detail but offers opportunity for extending the knowledge to larger and related con-cerns. For example, a primary-level student whose father owns a turkey farm may respond with reason-explanations to a story about a turkey. His knowledge is intensive and covers details perhaps not known to the teacher and not judged as relevant to the story. The knowledge is unpre-dictable and questions about it do not continue to repeat the common core of content knowledge of the story. Thus such configured knowledge is encouraged only for the "extras" of reading – an extra-credit oral report or a creative picture and story about turkeys. This kind of knowledge is allowed to be used once the hierarchical what-explanations have been mastered and displayed in a particular situation and, in the course of one's academic career, only when one has shown full mastery of the hierarchical skills and subsets of related skills which underlie what-explanations. Thus, reliable and successful participation in the ways of taking from books that teachers view as natural must, in the usual school way of doing things, precede other ways of taking from books.

These various ways of taking are sometimes referred to as "cognitive styles" or "learning styles." It is generally accepted in the research literature that they are influenced by early socialization experiences and correlated with such features of the society in which the child is reared as social organization, reliance on authority, male-female roles, and so on. These styles are often seen as two contrasting types, most frequently termed "field independent-field dependent" (Witkin et al. 1966) or "analytic-relational" (Kagan, Sigel, and Moss 1963; Cohen 1968, 1969, 1971). The analytic field-independent style is generally presented as that which correlates positively with high achievement and general academic and social success in school. Several studies discuss ways in which this style is played out in school – in preferred ways of responding to pictures and written text and selecting from among a choice of answers to test items.

Yet, we know little about how behaviors associated with either of the dichotomized cognitive styles (field-dependent/relational and field-independent/analytic) were learned in early patterns of socialization. To be sure, there are vast individual differences which may cause an individual to behave so as to be categorized as having one or the other of these learning styles. But much of the literature on learning styles suggests a preference for one or the other is learned in the social group in which the child is reared and in connection with other ways of behaving found in that culture. But how is a child socialized into an analytic/field-independent style? What kinds of interactions does he enter into with his parents and the stimuli of his environment which contribute to the development of such a style of learning? How do these interactions mold selective attention practices such as "sensitivity to parts of objects," "awareness of obscure, abstract, nonobvious features;" and identification of "abstractions based on the features of items" (Cohen 1969: 844–45)? Since the predominant stimuli used in school of judge the presence and extent of these selective attention practices are written materials, it is clear that the literacy orientation of preschool children is central to these questions.

The foregoing descriptions of how Maintown parents socialize their children into a literacy orientation fit closely those provided by Scollon and Scollon for their own child Rachel. Through similar practices, Rachel was "literate before she learned to read" (1979: 6). She knew, before the age of two, how to focus on a book and not on herself. Even when she told a story about herself, she moved herself out of the text and saw herself as author, as someone different from the central character of her story. She learned to pay close attention to the parts of objects, to name them, and to provide a running commentary on features of her environment. She learned to manipulate the contexts of items, her own activities, and language to achieve book-like, decontextualized, repeatable effects (such as puns). Many references in her talk were from written sources; others were modelled on stories and questions about these stories. The substance of her knowledge, as well as her ways of framing knowledge orally, derived from her familiarity with books and bookreading. No doubt, this development began by labelling in the dialogue cycles of reading (Ninio and Bruner 1978), and it will continue for Rachel in her preschool years along many of the same patterns described by Cochran-Smith (1981) for a mainstream nursery school. There teacher and students negotiated story-reading through the scaffolding of teachers' questions and running commentaries which replayed the structure and sequence of story-reading learned in their mainstream homes.

Close analyses of how mainstream school-oriented children come to learn to take from books at home suggest that such children learn not only how to take meaning from books, but also how to talk about it. In doing the latter, they repeatedly practice routines which parallel those of classroom interaction. By the time they enter school, they have had continuous experience as information-givers; they have learned how to perform in those interactions which surround literate sources throughout school. They have had years of practice in interaction situations that are the heart of reading – both learning to read and reading to learn in school. They have developed habits of performing which enable them to run through the hierarchy of preferred knowledge about a literate source and the appropriate sequence of skills to be displayed in showing knowledge of a subject. They have developed ways of decontextualizing and surrounding with explanatory prose the knowledge gained from selective attention to objects.

They have learned to listen, waiting for the appropriate cue which signals it is their turn to show off this knowledge. They have learned the rules for getting certain services from parents (or teachers) in the reading interaction (Merritt 1979). In nursery school, they continue to practice these interaction patterns in a group rather than in a dyadic situation. There they learn additional signals and behaviors necessary for getting a turn in a group, and responding to a central reader and to a set of centrally defined reading tasks. In short, most of their waking hours during the preschool years have enculturated them into: (1) all those habits associated with what-explanations, (2) selective attention to items of the written text, *and* (3) appropriate interactional styles for orally displaying all the know-how of their literate orientation to the environment. This learning has been finely turned and its habits are highly interdependent. Patterns of behaviors learned in one setting or at one stage reappear again and again as these children learn to use oral and written language in literacy events and to bring their knowledge to bear in school-acceptable ways.

But what corresponds to the mainstream pattern of learning in communities that do not have this finely tuned, consistent, repetitive, and continuous pattern of training? Are there ways of behaving which achieve other social and cognitive aims in other sociocultural groups?

The data below are summarized from an ethnography of two communities – Roadville and Trackton – located only a few miles from Maintown's neighborhoods in the Piedmont Carolinas. Roadville is a white working-class community of families steeped for four generations in the life of the textile mill. Trackton is a working-class black community whose older generations have been brought up on the land, either farming their own land or working for other landowners. However, in the past decade, they have found work in the textile mills. Children of both communities are unsuccessful in school; yet both communities place a high value on success in school, believing earnestly in the personal and vocational rewards school can bring and urging their children "to get ahead" by doing well in school. Both Roadville and Trackton are literate communities in the sense that the residents of each are able to read printed and written materials in their daily lives, and on occasion they produce written messages as part of the total pattern of communication in the community. In both communities, children go to school with certain expectancies of print and, in Trackton especially, children have a keen sense that reading is something one does to learn something one needs to know (Heath 1980). In both groups, residents turn from spoken to written uses of language and vice versa as the occasion demands, and the two modes of expression seem to supplement and reinforce each other. Nonetheless there are radical differences between the two communities in the ways in which children and adults interact in the preschool years; each of the two communities also differs from Maintown. Roadville and Trackton view children's learning of language from two radically different perspectives: in Trackton, children "learn to talk," in Roadville, adults "teach them how to talk."

Roadville

In Roadville, babies are brought home from the hospital to rooms decorated with colorful, mechanical, musical, and literacy-based stimuli. The walls are decorated with pictures based on nursery rhymes, and from an early age, children are held and prompted to "see" the wall decorations. Adults recite nursery rhymes as they twirl the mobile made of nursery-rhyme characters. The items of the child's environment promote exploration of colors, shapes, and textures: a stuffed ball with sections of fabrics of different colors and textures is in the crib; stuffed animals vary in texture, size, and shape. Neighbors, friends from church, and relatives come to visit and talk to the baby, and about him to those who will listen.

The baby is fictionalized in the talk to him: "But this baby wants to go to sleep, doesn't he? Yes, see those little eyes gettin' heavy." As the child grows older, adults pounce on word-like sounds and turn them into "words," repeating the "words," and expanding them into well-formed sentences. Before they can talk, children are introduced to visitors and prompted to provide all the expected politeness formulas, such as "Bye-bye," "Thank you," and so forth. As soon as they can talk, children are reminded about these formulas, and book or television characters known to be "polite" are involved as reinforcement.

In each Roadville home, preschoolers first have cloth books, featuring a single object on each page. They later acquire books which provide sounds, smells, and different textures or opportunities for practicing small motor skills (closing zippers, buttoning buttons, etc.). A typical collection for a two-year-old consisted of a dozen or so books – eight featured either the alphabet or numbers, others were books of nursery rhymes, simplified Bible stories, or "real-life" stories about boys and girls (usually taking care of their pets or exploring a particular feature of their environment). Books based on Sesame Street characters were favorite gifts for three- and four-year-olds.

Reading and reading-related activities occur most frequently before naps or at bedtime in the evening. Occasionally an adult or older child will read to a fussy child while the mother prepares dinner or changes a bed. On weekends, fathers sometimes read with their children for brief periods of time, but they generally prefer to play games or play with the children's toys in their interactions. The following episode illustrates the language and social interactional aspects of these bedtime events; the episode takes place between Wendy (2;3 at the time of this episode) and Aunt Sue who is putting her to bed.

[Aunt Sue (AS) picks up book, while Wendy (W) crawls about the floor, ostensibly looking for something]
W: uh uh
AS: Wendy, we're gonna read, uh, read this story, come on, hop up here on this bed.
[Wendy climbs up on the bed, sits on top of the pillow, and picks up her teddy bear]
[Aunt Sue opens book, points to puppy]
AS: Do you remember what this book is about? See the puppy? What does the puppy do?
[Wendy plays with the bear, glancing occasionally at pages of the book, as Aunt Sue turns. Wendy seems to be waiting for something in the book]
AS: See the puppy?
[Aunt Sue points to the puppy in the book and looks at Wendy to see if she is watching]

W: uh huh, yea, yes ma'am

AS: Puppy sees the ant, he's a li'l
[Wendy drops the bear and turns to book.]
fellow. Can you see that ant? Puppy has a little ball.

W: ant bite puppy
[Wendy points to ant, pushing hard on the book]

AS: No, the ant won't bite the puppy, the [turns page] puppy wants to play with the ant, see?
[Wendy tries to turn the page back; AS won't let her, and Wendy starts to squirm and fuss]

AS: Look here, here's someone else, the puppy
[Wendy climbs down off the bed and gets another book]

W: read this one

AS: Okay, you get back up here now. [Wendy gets back on bed]

AS: This book is your ABC book. See the A, look, here, on your spread, there's an A. You find the A. [The second book is a cloth book, old and tattered, and long a favorite of Wendy's. It features an apple on the cover, and its front page has an ABC block and ball. Through the book, there is a single item on each page, with a large representation of the first letter of the word commonly used to name the item. As AS turns the page, Wendy begins to crawl about on her quilt, which shows ABC blocks interspersed with balls and apples. Wendy points to each of the A's on the blanket and begins talking to herself. AS reads the book, looks up, and sees Wendy pointing to the A's in her quilt.]

AS: That's an A, can you find the A on your blanket?

W: there it is, this one, there's the hole too. [pokes her finger through a place where the threads have broken in the quilting]

AS: [AS points to ball in book] Stop that, find the ball, see, here's another ball.

This episode characterizes the early orientation of Roadville children to the written word. Bookreading time focuses on letters of the alphabet, numbers, names of basic items pictured in books, and simplified retellings of stories in the words of the adult. If the content or story plot seems too complicated for the child, the adult tells the story in short, simple sentences, frequently laced with requests that the child give what-explanations.

Wendy's favorite books are those with which she can participate: that is, those to which she can answer, provide labels, point to items, give animal sounds, and "read" the material back to anyone who will listen to her. She memorizes the passages and often knows when to turn the pages to show that she is "reading." She holds the book in her lap, starts at the beginning, and often reads the title, "Puppy."

Adults and children use either the title of the book or phrases such as "the book about a puppy" to refer to reading material. When Wendy acquires a new book, adults introduce the book with phrases such as "This is a book about a duck, a little yellow duck. See the duck. Duck goes quack quack." On introducing a book, adults sometimes ask the child to recall when they have seen a "real" specimen such as that one treated in the book: "Remember the duck on the College lake?" The child often shows no sign of linking the yellow fluffy duck in the book with the large brown and grey mallards on the lake, and the adult makes no efforts to explain that two such disparate looking objects go by the same name.

As Wendy grows older, she wants to "talk" during the long stories, Bible stories, and carry out the participation she so enjoyed with the alphabet books. However, by the time she reaches three and a half, Wendy is restrained from such wide-ranging participation. When she interrupts, she is told:

> Wendy, stop that, you be quiet when someone is reading to you.
> You listen; now sit still and be quiet.

Often Wendy immediately gets down and runs away into the next room saying "no, no." When this happens, her father goes to get her, pats her bottom, and puts her down hard on the sofa beside him. "Now you're gonna learn to listen." During the third and fourth years, this pattern occurs more and more frequently; only when Wendy can capture an aunt who does not visit often does she bring out the old books and participate with them. Otherwise, parents, Aunt Sue, and other adults insist that she be read a story and that she "listen" quietly.

When Wendy and her parents watch television, eat cereal, visit the grocery store, or go to church, adults point out and talk about many types of written material. On the way to the grocery, Wendy (3;8) sits in the backseat, and when her mother stops at a corner, Wendy says "Stop." Her mother says "Yes, that's a stop sign." Wendy has, however, misread a yield sign as *stop*. Her mother offers no explanation of what the actual message on the sign is, yet when she comes to the sign, she stops to yield to an oncoming car. Her mother, when asked why she had not given Wendy the word "yield," said it was too hard, Wendy would not understand, and "it's not a word we use like *stop*."

Wendy recognized animal cracker boxes as early as 10 months, and later, as her mother began buying other varieties, Wendy would see the box in the grocery store and yell "Cook cook." Her mother would say, "Yes, those are cookies. Does Wendy want a cookie?" One day Wendy saw a new type of cracker box, and screeched "Cook cook." Her father opened the box and gave Wendy a cracker and waited for her reaction. She started the "cookie," then took it to her mother, saying "You eat."

The mother joined in the game and said "Don't you want your *cookie*?" Wendy said "No cookie. You eat." "But Wendy, it's a cookie box, see?", and her mother pointed to the C of *crackers* on the box. Wendy paid no attention and ran off into another room.

In Roadville's literacy events, the rules for cooperative discourse around print are repeatedly practiced, coached, and rewarded in the preschool years. Adults in Roadville believe that instilling in children the proper use of words and understanding of the meaning of the written word are important for both their educational and religious success. Adults repeat aspects of the learning of literacy events they have known as children. In the words of one Roadville parent: "It was then that I began to learn ... when my daddy kept insisting I *read* it, *say* it right. It was then that I *did* right, in his view."

The path of development for such performance can be described in three overlapping stages. In the first, children are introduced to discrete bits and pieces of books – separate items, letters of the alphabet, shapes, colors, and commonly represented items in books for children (apple, baby, ball, etc.). The latter are usually decontextualized, not pictured in their ordinary contexts, and they are represented in two-dimensional flat line drawings. During this stage, children must participate as predictable information-givers and respond to questions that ask for specific and discrete bits of information about the written matter. In these literacy events, specific features of the two-dimensional items in books which are different from their "real" counterparts are not pointed out. A ball in a book is flat; a duck in a book is yellow and fluffy; trucks, cars, dogs, and trees talk in books. No mention is made of the fact that such features do not fit these objects in reality. Children are not encouraged to move their understanding of books into other situational contexts or to apply it in their general knowledge of the world about them.

In the second stage, adults demand an acceptance of the power of print to entertain, inform, and instruct. When Wendy could no longer participate by contributing her knowledge at any point in the literacy event, she learned to recognize bookreading as a performance. The adult exhibited the book to Wendy: she was to be entertained, to learn from the information conveyed in the material, and to remember the book's content for the sequential followup questioning, as opposed to ongoing cooperative participatory questions.

In the third stage, Wendy was introduced to preschool workbooks which provided story information and was asked questions or provided exercises and games based on the content of the stories or pictures. Follow-the-number coloring books and preschool "push-out and paste" workbooks on shapes, colors, and letters of the alphabet reinforced repeatedly that the written word could be taken apart into small pieces and one item linked to another by following rules. She had practice in the linear, sequential nature of books: begin at the beginning, stay in the lines for coloring, draw straight lines to link one item to another, write your answers on lines, keep your letters straight, match the cutout letter to diagrams of letter shapes.

The differences between Roadville and Maintown are substantial. Roadville adults do not extend either the content or the habits of literacy events beyond bookreading. They do not, upon seeing an item or event in the real world, remind children of a similar event in a book and launch a running commentary on similarities and differences. When a game is played or a chore done, adults do not use literate sources. Mothers cook without written recipes most of the time; if they use a recipe from a written source, they do so usually only after confirmation and alteration by friends who have tried the recipe. Directions to games are read, but not carefully followed, and they are not talked about in a series of questions and answers which try to establish their meaning. Instead, in the putting together of toys or the playing of games, the abilities or preferences of one party prevail. For example, if an adult knows how to put a toy together, he does so; he does not talk about the process, refer to the written material and "translate" for the child, or try to sequence steps so the child can do it.[3] Adults do not talk about the steps and procedures of *how* to do things; if a father wants his preschooler to learn to hold a miniature bat or throw a ball, he says "Do it this way." He does not break up "this way" into such steps as "Put your fingers around here," "Keep your thumb in this position," "Never hold it above this line." Over and over again, adults do a task and children observe and try it, being reinforced only by commands such as "Do it like this," "Watch that thumb."

Adults at tasks do not provide a running verbal commentary on what they are doing. They do not draw the attention of the child to specific features of the sequences of skills or the attributes of items. They do not ask questions of the child, except questions which are directive or scolding in nature, ("Did you bring the ball?" "Didn't you hear what I said?"). Many of their commands contain idioms which are not explained: "Put it up," or "Put that away now" (meaning to put it in the place where it usually belongs), or "Loosen up," said to a four-year-old boy trying to learn to bat a ball. Explanations which move beyond the listing of names of items and their features are rarely offered by adults. Children do not ask questions of the type "But I don't understand. What is that?" They appear willing to keep trying, and if there is ambiguity in a set of commands, they ask a question such as "You want me to do this?" (demonstrating their current efforts), or they try to find a way of diverting attention from the task at hand.

Both boys and girls during their preschool years are included in many adult activities, ranging from going to church to fishing and camping. They spend a lot of time observing and asking for turns to try specific tasks, such as putting a worm on the hook or cutting cookies. Sometimes adults say "No, you're not old enough." But if they agree to the child's attempt at the task, they watch and give directives and evaluations: "That's right, don't twist the cutter." "Turn like this." "Don't try to scrape it up now, let me do that." Talk about the task does not segment its skills and identify them, nor does it link the particular task or item at hand to other tasks. Reason-explanations such as "If you twist the cutter, the cookies will be rough on the edge," are rarely given, or asked for.

Neither Roadville adults nor children shift the context of items in their talk. They do not tell stories which fictionalize themselves or familiar events. They reject Sunday School materials which attempt to translate Biblical events into a modern-day setting. In Roadville, a story must be invited or announced by someone other than the storyteller, and only certain community members are designated good storytellers. A story is recognized by the group as a story about one and all. It is a true story, an actual event which occurred to either the storyteller or to someone else present. The marked behavior of the storyteller and audience alike is seen as exemplifying the weaknesses of all and the need for persistence in over-coming such weaknesses. The sources of stories are personal experience. They are tales of transgressions which make the point of reiterating the expected norms of behavior of man, woman, fisherman, worker, and Christian. They are true to the facts of the event.

Roadville parents provide their children with books; they read to them and ask questions about the books' contents. They choose books which emphasize nursery rhymes, alphabet learning, animals, and simplified Bible stories, and they require their children to repeat from these books and to answer formulaic questions about their contents. Roadville adults also ask questions about oral stories which have a point relevant to some marked behavior of a child. They use proverbs and summary statements to remind their children of stories and to call on them for simple comparisons of the stories' contents to their own situations. Roadville parents coach children in their telling of a story, forcing them to tell about an incident as it has been pre-composed or pre-scripted in the head of the adult. Thus, in Roadville, children come to know a story as either an accounting from a book, or a factual account of a real event in which some type of marked behavior occurred and there is a lesson to be learned. Any fictionalized account of a real event is viewed as a *lie*; reality is better than fiction. Roadville's church and community life admit no story other than that which meets the definition internal to the group. Thus children cannot decontextualize their knowledge or fictionalize events known to them and shift them about into other frames.

When these children go to school they perform well in the initial stages of each of the three early grades. They often know portions of the alpha-bet, some colors and numbers, can recognize their names, and tell someone their address and their parents' names. They will sit still and listen to a story, and they know how to answer questions asking for what-explanations. They do well in reading workbook exercises which ask for identification of specific portions of words, items from the story, or the linking of two items, letters, or parts of words on the same page. When the teacher reaches the end of story-reading or the reading circle and asks questions such as "What did you like about the story?", relatively few Roadville children answer. If asked questions such as "What would you have done if you had been Billy [a story's main character]?", Roadville children most frequently say "I don't know" or shrug their shoulders.

Near the end of each year, and increasingly as they move through the early primary grades, Roadville children can handle successfully the initial stages of lessons. But when they move ahead to extra-credit items or to activities considered more advanced and requiring more independence, they are stumped. They turn frequently to teachers asking "Do you want me to do this? What do I do here?" If asked to write a creative story or tell it into a tape recorder, they retell stories from books; they do not create their own. They rarely provide emotional or personal commentary on their accounting of real events or book stories. They are rarely able to take knowledge learned in one context and shift it to another; they do not compare two items or events and point out similarities and differences. They find it difficult either to hold one feature of an event constant and shift all others or to hold all features constant but one. For example, they are puzzled by questions such as "What would have happened if Billy had not told the policemen what happened?" They do not know how to move events or items out of a given frame. To a question such as "What habits of the Hopi Indians might they be able to take with them when they move to a city?", they provide lists of features of life of the Hopi on the reservation. They do not take these items, consider their appropriateness in an urban setting, and evaluate the hypothetical outcome. In general, they find this type of question impossible to answer, and they do not know how to ask teachers to help them take apart the questions to figure out the answers. Thus their initial successes in reading, being good students, following orders, and adhering to school norms of participating in lessons begin to fall away rapidly about the time they enter the fourth grade. As the importance and frequency of questions and reading habits with which they are familiar decline in the higher grades, they have no way of keeping up or of seeking help in learning what it is they do not even know they don't know.

Trackton

Babies in Trackton come home from the hospital to an environment which is almost entirely human. There are no cribs, car beds, or car seats, and only an occasional high chair or infant seat. Infants are held during their waking hours, occasionally while they sleep, and they usually sleep in the bed with parents until they are about two years of age. They are held, their faces fondled, their cheeks pinched, and they eat and sleep in the midst of human talk and noise from the television, stereo, and radio. Encapsuled in an almost totally human world, they are in the midst of constant human communication, verbal and nonverbal. They literally feel the body signals of shifts in emotion of those who hold them almost continuously; they are talked about and kept in the midst of talk about topics that range over any subject. As children make cooing or babbling sounds, adults refer to this as "noise," and no attempt is made to interpret these sounds as words or communicative attempts on the part of the baby. Adults believe they should not have to depend on their babies to tell them what they need or when they are uncomfortable; adults know, children only "come to know."

When a child can crawl and move about on his own, he plays with the household objects deemed safe for him – pot lids, spoons, plastic food containers. Only at Christmastime are there special toys for very young children; these are usually trucks, balls, doll babies, or plastic cars, but rarely blocks, puzzles, or books. As children become completely mobile, they demand ride toys or electronic and mechanical toys they see on television. They never request nor do they receive manipulative toys, such as puzzles, blocks, take-apart toys or literacy-based items, such as books or letter games.

Adults read newspapers, mail, calendars, circulars (political and civic-events related), school materials sent home to parents, brochures advertising new cars, television sets, or other products, and the Bible and other church-related materials. There are no reading materials especially for children (with the exception of children's Sunday School materials), and adults do not sit and read to children. Since children are usually left to sleep whenever and wherever they fall asleep, there is no bedtime or naptime as such. At night, they are put to bed when adults go to bed or whenever the person holding them gets tired. Thus, going to bed is not framed in any special routine. Sometimes in a play activity during the day, an older sibling will read to a younger child, but the latter soon loses interest and squirms away to play. Older children often try to "play school" with younger children, reading to them from books and trying to ask questions about what they have read. Adults look on these efforts with amusement and do not try to convince the small child to sit still and listen.

Signs from very young children of attention to the nonverbal behaviors of others are rewarded by extra fondling, laughter, and cuddling from adults. For example, when an infant shows signs of recognizing a family member's voice on the phone by bouncing up and down in the arms of the adult who is talking on the phone, adults comment on this to others present and kiss and nudge the child. Yet when children utter sounds or combinations of sounds which could be interpreted as words, adults pay no attention. Often by the time they are twelve months old, children approximate words or phrases of adults' speech; adults respond by laughing or giving special attention to the child and crediting him with "sounding like" the person being imitated. When children learn to walk and imitate the walk of members of the community, they are rewarded by comments on their activities: "He walks just like Toby when he's tuckered out."

Children between the ages of twelve and twenty-four months often imitate the tune or "general Gestalt" (Peters 1977) of complete utterances they hear around them. They pick up and repeat chunks (usually the ends) of phrasal and clausal utterances of speakers around them. They seem to remember fragments of speech and repeat these without active production. In this first stage of language learning, the repetition stage, they imitate the intonation contours and general shaping of the utterances they repeat. Lem 1;2 in the following example illustrates this pattern.

Mother: [talking to neighbor on porch while Lem plays with a truck on the porch nearby] But they won't call back, won't happen =
Lem: =call back
Neighbor: Sam's going over there Saturday, he'll pick up a form =
Lem: = pick up on, pick up on [Lem here appears to have heard *form* as *on*]

The adults pay no attention to Lem's "talk," and their talk, in fact, often overlaps his repetitions.

In the second stage, repetition with variation, Trackton children manipulate pieces of conversation they pick up. They incorporate chunks of language from others into their own ongoing dialogue, applying productive rules, inserting new nouns and verbs for those used in the adults' chunks. They also play with rhyming patterns and varying intonation contours.

Mother: She went to the doctor again.
Lem (2;2): [in a sing-song fashion] went to de doctor, doctor, tractor, dis my tractor, doctor on a tractor, went to de doctor.

Lem creates a monologue, incorporating the conversation about him into his own talk as he plays. Adults pay no attention to his chatter unless it gets so noisy as to interfere with their talk.

In the third stage, participation, children begin to enter the ongoing conversations about them. They do so by attracting the adult's attention with a tug on the arm or pant leg, and they help make themselves understood by providing nonverbal reinforcements to help recreate a scene they want the listener to remember. For example, if adults are talking, and a child interrupts with seemingly unintelligible utterances, the child will

185

make gestures, extra sounds, or act out some outstanding features of the scene he is trying to get the adult to remember. Children try to create a context, a scene, for the understanding of their utterance.

This third stage illustrates a pattern in the children's response to their environment and their ways of letting others know their knowledge of the environment. Once they are in the third stage, their communicative efforts are accepted by community members, and adults respond directly to the child, instead of talking to others about the child's activities as they have done in the past. Children continue to practice for conversational participation by playing, when alone, both parts of dialogues, imitating gestures as well as intonation patterns of adults. By 2;6 all children in the community can imitate the walk and talk of others in the community, or frequent visitors such as the man who comes around to read the gas meters. They can feign anger, sadness, fussing, remorse, silliness, or any of a wide range of expressive behaviors. They often use the same chunks of language for varying effects, depending on nonverbal support to give the language different meanings or cast it in a different key (Hymes 1974). Girls between three and four years of age take part in extraordinarily complex stepping and clapping patterns and simple repetitions of hand clap games played by older girls. From the time they are old enough to stand alone, they are encouraged in their participation by siblings and older children in the community. These games require anticipation and recognition of cues for upcoming behaviors, and the young girls learn to watch for these cues and to come in with the appropriate words and movements at the right time.

Preschool children are not asked for what-explanations of their environment. Instead, they are asked a preponderance of analogical questions which call for non-specific comparisons of one item, event, or person with another: "What's that like?" Other types of questions ask for specific information known to the child but not the adults: "Where'd you get that from?" "What do you want?" "How come you did that?" (Heath 1982). Adults explain their use of these types of questions by expressing their sense of children: they are "comers," coming into their learning by experiencing what knowing about things means. As one parent of a two-year-old boy put it: "Ain't no use me tellin' 'im: learn this, learn that, what's this, what's that? He just gotta learn, gotta know; he see one thing one place one time, he know how it go, see sump'n like it again, maybe it be the same, maybe it won't." Children are expected to learn how to know when the form belies the meaning, and to know contexts of items and to use their understanding of these contexts to draw parallels between items and events. Parents do not believe they have a tutoring role in this learning; they provide the experiences on which the child draws and reward signs of their successfully coming to know.

Trackton children's early stories illustrate how they respond to adult views of them as "comers." The children learn to tell stories by drawing heavily on their abilities to render a context, to set a stage, and to call on the audience's power to join in the imaginative creation of story. Between the ages of two and four years, the children, in a monologue-like fashion, tell stories about things in their lives, events they see and hear, and situations in which they have been involved. They produce these spontaneously during play with other children or in the presence of adults. Sometimes they make an effort to attract the attention of listeners before they begin the story, but often they do not. Lem, playing off the edge of the porch, when he was about two and a half years of age, heard a bell in the distance. He stopped, looked at Nellie and Benjy, his older siblings, who were nearby and said:

Way
Far
Now
It a church bell
Ringin'
Dey singin'
Ringin'
You hear it?
I hear it
Far
Now.

Lem had been taken to church the previous Sunday and had been much impressed by the church bell. He had sat on his mother's lap and joined in the singing, rocking to and fro on her lap, and clapping his hands. His story, which is like a poem in its imagery and line-like prosody, is in response to the current stimulus of a distant bell. As he tells the story, he sways back and forth.

This story, somewhat longer than those usually reported from other social groups for children as young as Lem,[4] has some features which have come to characterize fully-developed narratives or stories. It recapitulates in its verbal outline the sequence of events being recalled by the story-teller. At church, the bell rang while the people sang. In the line "It a church bell," Lem provides his story's topic, and a brief summary of what is to come. This line serves a function similar to the formulae often used by older children to open a story: "This is a story about (a church bell)." Lem gives only the slightest hint of story setting or orientation to the listener; where and when the story took place are capsuled in "Way, Far." Preschoolers in Trackton almost never hear "Once upon a time there was a——" stories, and they rarely provide definitive orientations for their stories. They seem to assume listeners "know" the situation in which the narrative takes place. Similarly, preschoolers in Trackton do not close off their stories with formulaic endings. Lem poetically balances his opening and closing in an inclusio, beginning "Way, Far, Now." and ending "Far, Now.". The effect is one of closure, but there is no clearcut announcement of closure. Throughout the presentation of action and result of action in their stories, Trackton preschoolers invite the audience to respond or evaluate the story's actions. Lem asks "You hear it?" which may refer either to the current simulus or to yesterday's bell, since Lem does not productively use past tense endings for any verbs at this stage in his language development.

Preschool storytellers have several ways of inviting audience evaluation and interest. They may themselves express an emotional response to the story's actions; they may have another character or narrator in the story do so often using alliterative language play; or they may detail actions and results through direct discourse or sound effects and gestures. All these methods of calling attention to the story and its telling distinguish the speech event as a story, an occasion for audience and storyteller to interact pleasantly, and not simply to hear an ordinary recounting of events or actions.

Trackton children must be aggressive in inserting their stories into an ongoing stream of discourse. Storytelling is highly competitive. Everyone in a conversation may want to tell a story, so only the most aggressive wins out. The content ranges widely, and there is "truth" only in the universals of human experience. Fact is often hard to find, though it is usually the seed of the story. Trackton stories often have no point – no obvious beginning or ending; they go on as long as the audience enjoys and tolerates the storyteller's entertainment.

Trackton adults do not separate out the elements of the environment around their children to tune their attentions selectively. They do not simplify their language, focus on single-word utterances by young children, label items or features of objects in either books or the environment at large. Instead, children are continuously contextualized, presented with almost continuous communication. From this ongoing, multiple-channeled stream of stimuli, they must themselves select, practice, and determine rules of production and structuring. For language, they do so by first repeating, catching chunks of sounds, intonation contours, and practicing these without specific reinforcement or evaluation. But practice material and models are continuously available. Next the children seem to begin to sort out the productive rules for speech and practice what they hear about them with variation. Finally, they work their way into conversations, hooking their meanings for listeners into a familiar context by recreating scenes through gestures, special sound effects, etc. These characteristics continue in their story-poems and their participation in jump-rope rhymes. Because adults do not select out, name, and describe features of the environment for the young, children must perceive situations, determine

how units of the situations are related to each other, recognize these relations in other situations, and reason through what it will take to show their
correlation of one situation with another. The children can answer questions such as "What's that like?" ["It's like Doug's car"] but they can
rarely name the specific feature or features which make two items or
events alike. For example, in the case of saying a car seen on the street is
"like Doug's car," a child may be basing the analogy on the fact that this
car has a flat tire and Doug's also had one last week. But the child does
not name (and is not asked to name) what is alike between the two cars.

Children seem to develop connections between situations or items not
by specification of labels and features in the situations, but by configuration links. Recognition of similar general shapes or patterns of links seen
in one situation and connected to another, seem to be the means by which
children set scenes in their nonverbal representations of individuals, and
later in their verbal chunking, then segmentation and production of rules
for putting together isolated units. They do not decontextualize; instead
they heavily contextualize nonverbal and verbal language. They fictionalize their "true stories," but they do so by asking the audience to identify
with the story through making parallels from their own experiences. When
adults read, they often do so in a group. One person, reading aloud, for
example, from a brochure on a new car decodes the text, displays illustrations and photographs, and listeners relate the text's meaning to their
experiences asking questions and expressing opinions. Finally, the group
as a whole synthesizes the written text and the negotiated oral discourse to
construct a meaning for the brochure (Heath forthcoming a).

When Trackton children go to school, they face unfamiliar types of
questions which ask for what-explanations. They are asked as individuals
to identify items by name, and to label features such as shape, color, size,
number. The stimuli to which they are to give these responses are two-
dimensional flat representations which are often highly stylized and bear
little resemblance to the "real" items. Trackton children generally score in
the lowest percentile range on the Metropolitan Reading Readiness tests.
They do not sit at their desks and complete reading workbook pages;
neither do they tolerate questions about reading materials which are structured along the usual lesson format. Their contributions are in the form of
"I had a duck at my house one time." "Why'd he do that?" or they imitate
the sound effects teachers may produce in stories they read to the children. By the end of the first three primary grades, their general language
arts scores have been consistently low, except for those few who have
begun to adapt to and adopt some of the behaviors they have had to learn
in school. But the majority not only fail to learn the content of lessons,
they also do not adopt the social interactional rules for school literacy
events. Print in isolation bears little authority in their world. The kinds of
questions asked of reading books are unfamiliar. The children's abilities to

metaphorically link two events or situations and to recreate scenes are not tapped in the school; in fact, *these abilities often cause difficulties*, because they enable children to see parallels teachers did not intend, and indeed, may not recognize until the children point them out (Heath 1978).

By the end of the lessons or by the time in their total school career when reason-explanations and affective statements call for the creative comparison of two or more situations, it is too late for many Trackton children. They have not picked up along the way the composition and comprehension skills they need to translate their analogical skills into a channel teachers can accept. They seem not to know how to take meaning from reading; they do not observe the rules of linearity in writing, and their expression of themselves on paper is very limited. Orally taped stories are often much better, but these rarely count as much as written compositions. Thus, Trackton children continue to collect very low or failing grades, and many decide by the end of the sixth grade to stop trying and turn their attention to the heavy peer socialization which usually begins in these years.

From community to classroom

A recent review of trends in research on learning pointed out that "learning to read through using and learning from language has been less systematically studied than the decoding process" (Glaser 1979: 7). Put another way, how children learn to use language to read to learn has been less systematically studied than decoding skills. Learning how to take meaning from writing before one learns to read involves repeated practice in using and learning from language through appropriate participation in literacy events such as exhibitor/questioner and spectator/respondent dyads (Scollon and Scollon 1979) or group negotiation of the meaning of a written text. Children have to learn to select, hold, and retrieve content from books and other written or printed texts in accordance with their community's rules or "ways of taking," and the children's learning follows community paths of language socialization. In each society, certain kinds of childhood participation in literacy events may precede others, as the developmental sequence builds toward the whole complex of home and community behaviors characteristic of the society. The ways of taking employed in the school may in turn build directly on the preschool development, may require substantial adaptation on the part of the children, or may even run directly counter to aspects of the community's pattern.

At home. In *Maintown* homes, the construction of knowledge in the earliest preschool years depends in large part on labelling procedures and what-explanations. Maintown families, like other mainstream families, continue this kind of classification and knowledge construction throughout the child's environment and into the school years, calling it into play in response to new items in the environment and in running commentaries on old items as they compare to new ones. This pattern of linking old and new knowledge is reinforced in narrative tales which fictionalize the teller's events or recapitulate a story from a book. Thus for these children the bedtime story is simply an early link in a long chain of interrelated patterns of taking meaning from the environment. Moreover, along this chain, the focus is on the individual as respondent and cooperative negotiator of meaning from books. In particular, children learn that written language may represent not only descriptions of real events, but decontextualized logical propositions, and the occurrence of this kind of information in print or in writing legitimates a response in which one brings to the interpretation of written text selected knowledge from the real world. Moreover, readers must recognize how certain types of questions assert the priority of meanings in the written word over reality. The "real" comes into play only after prescribed decontextualized meanings; affective responses and reason-explanations follow conventional presuppositions which stand behind what-explanations.

Roadville also provides labels, features, and what-explanations, and prescribes listening and performing behaviors for preschoolers. However, Roadville adults do not carry on or sustain in continually overlapping and interdependent fashion the linking of ways of taking meaning from books to ways of relating that knowledge to other aspects of the environment. They do not encourage decontextualization; in fact, they proscribe it in their own stories about themselves and their requirements of stories from children. They do not themselves make analytic statements or assert universal truths, except those related to their religious faith. They lace their stories with synthetic (nonanalytic) statements which express, describe, and synthesize actual real-life materials. Things do not have to follow logically so long as they fit the past experience of individuals in the community. Thus children learn to look for a specific moral in stories and to expect that story to fit their facts of reality explicitly. When they themselves recount an event, they do the same, constructing the story of a real event according to coaching by adults who want to construct the story as they saw it.

Trackton is like neither Maintown nor Roadville. There are no bedtime stories; in fact, there are few occasions for reading to or with children specifically. Instead, during the time these activities would take place in mainstream and Roadville homes, Trackton children are enveloped in different kinds of social interactions. They are held, fed, talked about, and rewarded for nonverbal, and later verbal, renderings of events they witness. Trackton adults value and respond favorably when children show they have come to know how to use language to show correspondence in function, style, configuration, and positioning between two different things or situations. Analogical questions are asked of Trackton children, although the implicit questions of structure and function these embody are never made explicit. Children do not have labels or names of attributes of items and events pointed out for them, and they are asked for reason-explanations not what-explanations. Individuals express their personal responses and recreate corresponding situations with often only a minimal adherence to the germ of truth of a story. Children come to recognize similarities of patterning, though they do not name lines, points, or items which are similar between two items or situations. They are familiar with group literacy events in which several community members orally negotiate the meaning of a written text.

At school. In the early reading stages, and in later requirements for reading to learn at more advanced stages, children from the three communities respond differently, because they have learned different methods and degrees of taking from books. In comparison to Maintown children, the habits Roadville children learned in bookreading and toy-related episodes have not continued for them through other activities and types of reinforcement in their environment. They have had less exposure to both the content of books and ways of learning from books than have mainstream children. Thus their need in schools is not necessarily for an intensification of presentation of labels, a slowing down of the sequence of introducing what-explanations in connection with bookreading. Instead they need *extension of these habits to other domains* and to opportunities for practicing habits such as producing running commentaries, creating exhibitor/questioner and spectator/respondent roles. Perhaps most important, Roadville children need to have articulated for them *distinctions in discourse strategies and structures*. Narratives of real events have certain strategies and structures; imaginary tales, flights of fantasy, and affective expressions have others. Their community's view of narrative discourse style is very narrow and demands a passive role in both creation of and response to the account of events. Moreover, these children have *to be reintroduced to a participant frame of reference to a book*. Though initially they were participants in bookreading, they have been trained into passive roles since the age of three years, and they must learn once again to be active information-givers, taking from books and linking that knowledge to other aspects of their environment.

Trackton students present an additional set of alternatives for procedures in the early primary grades. Since they usually have few of the expected "natural" skills of taking meaning from books, they must not only learn these, but also *retain their analogical reasoning practices* for use in some of the later stages of learning to read. They must *learn to adapt the creativity in language, metaphor, fictionalization, recreation of scenes and exploration of functions and settings of items they bring to school*. These children already use narrative skills highly rewarded in the upper primary grades. They distinguish a fictionalized story from a real-life narrative. They know that telling a story can be in many ways related to play; it suspends reality, and frames an old event in a new context; it calls on audience participation to recognize the setting and participants. They must now *learn as individuals to recount factual events in a straightforward way* and *recognize appropriate occasions for reason-explanations and affective expressions.* Trackton children seem to have skipped learning to label, list features, and give what-explanations. Thus they need to *have the mainstream or school habits presented in familiar activities with explanations related to their own habits of taking meaning* from the environment. Such "simple," "natural" things as distinctions between two-dimensional and three-dimensional objects may need to be explained to help Trackton children learn the stylization and decontextualization which characterizes books.

To lay out in more specific detail how Roadville and Trackton's ways of knowing can be used along with those of mainstreamers goes beyond the scope of this paper. However, it must be admitted that a range of alternatives to ways of learning and displaying knowledge characterizes all highly school-successful adults in the advanced stages of their careers. Knowing more about how these alternatives are learned at early ages in different sociocultural conditions can help the school to provide opportunities for *all* students to avail themselves of these alternatives early in their school careers. For example, mainstream children can benefit from early exposure to Trackton's creative, highly analogical styles of telling stories and giving explanations, and they can add the Roadville true story with strict chronicity and explicit moral to their repertoire of narrative types.

In conclusion, if we want to understand the place of literacy in human societies and ways children acquire the literacy orientations of their communities, we must recognize two postulates of literacy and language development.

1   Strict dichotomization between oral and literate traditions is a construct of researchers, not an accurate portrayal of reality across cultures.
2   A unilinear model of development in the acquisition of language structures and uses cannot adequately account for culturally diverse ways of acquiring knowledge or developing cognitive styles.

Roadville and Trackton tell us that the mainstream type of literacy orientation is not the only type even among Western societies. They also tell us that the mainstream ways of acquiring communicative competence do not offer a universally applicable model of development. They offer proof of Hymes' assertion a decade ago that "it is impossible to generalize validly about 'oral' vs. 'literate' cultures as uniform types" (Hymes 1973: 54).

Yet in spite of such warnings and analyses of the uses and functions of writing in the specific proposals for comparative development and organization of cultural systems (cf. Basso 1974: 432), the majority of research on literacy has focused on differences in class, amount of education, and level of civilization among groups having different literacy characteristics.

"We need, in short, a great deal of ethnography" (Hymes 1973: 57) to provide descriptions of the ways different social groups "take" knowledge from the environment. For written sources, these ways of taking may be analyzed in terms of *types of literacy events*, such as group negotiation of meaning from written texts, individual "looking things up" in reference books, writing family records in Bibles, and the dozens of other types of occasions when books or other written materials are integral to interpretation in an interaction. These must in turn be analyzed in terms of the specific *features of literacy events*, such as labelling, what-explanation, affective comments, reason-explanations, and many other possibilities. Literacy events must also be interpreted in relation to the *larger sociocultural patterns* which they may exemplify or reflect. For example, ethnography must describe literacy events in their sociocultural contexts, so we may come to understand how such patterns as time and space usage, caregiving roles, and age and sex segregation are interdependent with the types and features of literacy events a community develops. It is only on the basis of such thorough–going ethnography that further progress is possible toward understanding cross-cultural patterns of oral and written language uses and paths of development of communicative competence.

Notes

* One of a series of invited papers commemorating a decade of *Language in Society*.

1 First presented at the Terman Conference on Teaching at Stanford University, 1980, this paper has benefitted from cooperation with M. Cochran-Smith of the University of Pennsylvania. She shares an appreciation of the relevance of Roland Barthes' work for studies of the socialization of young children into literacy; her research (1981) on the story-reading practices of a mainstream school-oriented nursery school provides a much needed detailed account of early school orientation to literacy.

2 Terms such as *mainstream* or *middle-class* cultures or social groups are frequently used in both popular and scholarly writings without careful definition. Moreover, numerous studies of behavioral phenomena (for example, mother-child interactions in language learning) either do not specify that the subjects being described are drawn from mainstream groups or do not recognize the importance of this limitation. As a result, findings from this group are often regarded as universal. For a discussion of this problem, see Chanan and Gilchrist 1974, Payne and Bennett 1977. In general, the literature characterizes this group as school-oriented, aspiring toward upward mobility through formal institutions, and providing enculturation which positively values routines of promptness, linearity (in habits ranging from furniture arrangement to entrance

into a movie theatre), and evaluative and judgmental responses to behaviors which deviate from their norms.

In the United States, mainstream families tend to locate in neighborhoods and suburbs around cities. Their social interactions center not in their immediate neighborhoods, but around voluntary associations across the city. Thus a cluster of mainstream families (and not a community – which usually implies a specific geographic territory as the locus of a majority of social interactions) is the unit of comparison used here with the Trackton and Roadville communities.

3   Behind this discussion are findings from cross-cultural psychologists who have studied the links between verbalization of task and demonstration of skills in a hierarchical sequence, e.g., Childs and Greenfield 1980; see Goody 1979 on the use of questions in learning tasks unrelated to a familiarity with books.

4   Cf. Umiker-Sebeok's (1979) descriptions of stories of mainstream middle-class children, ages 3–5 and Sutton-Smith 1981.

References

Basso, K. (1974). The ethonography of writing. In R. Bauman & J. Sherzer (eds.), *Explorations in the ethnography of speaking.* Cambridge University Press.

Cazden, C. B. (1979). Peekaboo as an instructional model: Discourse development at home and at school. *Papers and Reports in Child Language Development* **17**: 1–29.

Chanan, G., & Gilchrist, L. (1974). *What school is for.* New York: Praeger.

Childs, C. P., & Greenfield, P. M. (1980). Informal modes of learning and teaching. In N. Warren (ed.), *Advances in cross-cultural psychology*, vol. 2 London: Academic Press.

Cochran-Smith, M. (1981). The making of a reader. Ph.D. dissertation. University of Pennsylvania.

Cohen, R. (1968). The relation between socio-conceptual styles and orientation to school requirements. *Sociology of Education* **41**: 201–20.

——. (1969). Conceptual styles, culture conflict, and nonverbal tests of intelligence. *American Anthropologist* **71** (5): 828–56.

——. (1971). The influence of conceptual rule-sets on measures of learning ability. In C. L. Brace, G. Gamble, & J. Bond (eds.), *Race and intelligence.* (Anthropological Studies, No. 8, American Anthropological Association). 41–57.

Glaser, R. (1979). Trends and research questions in psychological research on learning and schooling. *Educational Researcher* **8** (10): 6–13.

Goody, E. (1979). Towards a theory of questions. In E. N. Goody (ed.), *Questions and politeness: Strategies in social interaction.* Cambridge University Press.

Griffin, P., & Humphrey, F. (1978). Task and talk. In *The study of children's functional language and education in the early years.* Final report to the Carnegie Corporation of New York. Arlington, Va.: Center for Applied Linguistics.

Heath, S. (1978). *Teacher talk: Language in the classroom.* (Language in Education 9.) Arlington, Va.: Center for Applied Linguistics.

——. (1980). The functions and uses of literacy. *Journal of Communication* **30** (1): 123–33.

——. (1982). Questioning at home and at school: A comparative study. In G. Spindler (ed.), *Doing ethnography: Educational anthropology in action.* New York: Holt, Rinehart & Winston.

——. (forthcoming a). Protean shapes: Ever-shifting oral and literate traditions. To appear in D. Tannen (ed.), *Spoken and written language: Exploring orality and literacy*. Norwood, N.J.: Ablex.

——. (forthcoming b). *Ways with words: Ethnography of communication in communities and classrooms*.

Howard, R. (1974). A note on S/Z. In R. Barthes, *Introduction to S/Z*. Trans. Richard Miller. New York: Hill and Wang.

Hymes, D. H. (1973). On the origins and foundations of inequality among speakers. In E. Haugen & M. Bloomfield (eds.), *Language as a human problem*. New York: W. W. Norton & Co.

——. (1974). Models of the interaction of language and social life. In J. J. Gumperz & D. Hymes (eds.), *Directions in sociolinguistics*. New York: Holt, Rinehart and Winston.

Kagan, J., Sigel, I., & Moss, H. (1963). Psychological significance of styles of conceptualization. In J. Wright & J. Kagan (eds.), *Basic cognitive processes in children*. (Monographs of the society for research in child development.) **28** (2): 73–112.

Mehan, H. (1979). *Learning lessons*. Cambridge, Mass.: Harvard University Press.

Merritt, M. (1979). Service-like events during individual work time and their contribution to the nature of the rules for communication. NIE Report EP 78–0436.

Ninio, A., & Bruner, J. (1978). The achievement and antecedents of labelling. *Journal of Child Language* **5**: 1–15.

Payne, C., & Bennett, C. (1977). "Middle class aura" in public schools. *The Teacher Educator* **13** (1): 16–26.

Peters, A. (1977). Language learning strategies. *Language* **53**: 500–73.

Scollon, R., & Scollon, S. (1979). The literate two-year old: The fictionalization of self. *Working Papers in Sociolinguistics*. Austin, TX: Southwest Regional Laboratory.

Sinclair, J. M., & Coulthard, R. M. (1975). *Toward an analysis of discourse*. New York: Oxford University Press.

Sutton-Smith, B. (1981). *The folkstories of children*. Philadelphia: University of Pennsylvania Press.

Umiker-Sebcok, J. D. (1979). Preschool children's intraconversational narratives. *Journal of Child Language* **6** (1): 91–110.

Witkin, H., Faterson, F., Goodenough, R., & Birnbaum, J. (1966). Cognitive patterning in mildly retarded boys. *Child Development* **37** (2): 301–16.

8

INVOLVING PARENTS IN THE TEACHING OF READING

A study of current school practice

P. W. Hannon and P. Cuckle

Source: *Educational Research* (1984) 26(1): 7–13

Introduction

Teachers of reading often acknowledge the important role that parents can play in fostering their children's reading development, especially in the pre-reading and early stages. Recently, however, there has been interest in involving parents (particularly working-class parents) more directly by the simple expedient of sending school reading books home with children and encouraging parents to hear their children read. A pioneer experiment along these lines has been carried out with six- to eight-year-olds in two schools in Haringey, London (Tizard, Schofield and Hewison, 1982). A second is in progress in the north of England (Jackson and Hannon, 1981). Both have received a certain amount of publicity (e.g. Wilby, 1981), and a number of other schools elsewhere are known to have embarked on similar projects (e.g. Ashton and Jackson, 1982).

These initiatives are bound to raise several questions in the minds of those concerned with the teaching of reading. One of the most obvious concerns effectiveness. Does this form of parental involvement help or hinder early reading development? Here, encouraging results have been reported. Children in the Haringey experiment seem to have progressed further in terms of reading test scores than children in certain control groups (Hewison, 1981; Tizard, Schofield and Hewison, 1982).

There is another, more sceptical, question to be considered too. What is all the fuss about? Have not many schools already been sending school books home with infants and junior children as standard practice? If the practice is in fact widespread the recent research can be considered as reassuring rather than challenging. The purpose of this paper is to try to examine existing practice in schools more closely to see whether what has been tried in recent experiments is in any way something new.

197

One point which needs to be recognized at the outset is that parents already involve themselves to a considerable extent in children's early reading development. In a series of surveys in working class areas of London, Hewison and Tizard (1980) found that about half of children aged seven to eight were 'regularly heard to read' by their parents. Only about 10 per cent were never helped. A similar picture is emerging from surveys in the north of England (Hannon and Jackson, 1983) and from earlier work in the 1960s in Nottingham (Newson and Newson, (1977). Not much is known about class differences in this kind of parent involvement but the Newsons' study indicated that they were not as great as might be expected. Therefore the question of whether schools do or do not involve parents may be rather beside the point. It may be more important to ask what attitude schools take to the reality of parents' existing involvement. Do they, for example, accept it, deny it or welcome it?

There are two aspects of schools' practice which are particularly important here. The first concerns what support or advice they offer parents. The Newsons' findings led them to make the following complaint about schools.

> That over 80 per cent of our sample claimed in fact to have given help with reading would suggest that, in their varying ways, most parents see themselves as having some part to play in this basic aspect of their children's education, and yet this willingness is too often mis-channelled for lack of advice, encouragement and appreciation from those best qualified to give it.
>
> (Newson and Newson, 1977, p. 150)

A second aspect of school practice, which might have an impact is the provision of books and other materials geared to children's reading needs. This could be very important in the case of working-class children for the Newsons found what they described as a 'massive class difference in book ownership'. Not only were middle-class children more likely to have sizeable collections of books; they also had more comics bought for them, and were twice as likely to belong to a public library.

It is precisely these two aspects of school practice which appear to have been developed in recent projects. In the Haringey Project, for example, parents were encouraged and guided in hearing their children read at home through meetings at school and two or three home visits per term by researchers. Mostly books were sent home on a minimum of three or four nights per week in one school and two or three nights per week at the second (Tizard, Schofield and Hewison, 1982).

To what extent do schools already do this kind of thing? One obvious source of information to turn to in answering this question is the recent NFER study *Parental Involvement in Primary Schools* (Cyster, Clift and

Battle, 1980). In this research a national sample of almost 1,700 primary schools of all kinds was surveyed by a postal questionnaire of more than 100 items. There was an 83 per cent response rate. A parallel survey was undertaken of LEA policies in the areas of the schools. In a later stage of the research 10 of the schools surveyed were selected for case studies in which all teachers and one in 10 parents were interviewed. In short this is the most comprehensive study to date of how schools involve parents of children in the primary years.

Unfortunately no information appears to have been sought in the NFER study about school practice in relation to parents helping their children with reading *at home*. The study concentrated on parents' involvement in *school*-based activities. For example it was found that, in relation to reading, parents helped in school libraries, covering books, etc., in 29 per cent of schools, and heard children read under the supervision of a teacher in 26 per cent of schools. Home visits by teaching staff were reported by 20 per cent of schools but little is said about their purpose. The whole issue of parental involvement in home-based educational activities, even homework, seems to have been rather overlooked. Therefore it is worth considering how we might fill this gap in our knowledge of current school practice.

A study

There are certain methodological difficulties in determining the exact nature of school practice in this area. One can ask heads what goes on but they may not always be able to give a full and accurate picture, even when willing to do so, particularly concerning what happens at the classroom level or in individual parent teacher interactions. For example a head might report having a policy to send reading material home and to encourage parents to hear children read but, of itself, this does not mean it happens on a significant scale (although such an attitude might be a precondition for it to happen at all). To find out what really happens one has to probe further and discover the policies of individual class teachers which do not always accord with those of their heads. Even then one could find individual teachers in favour of sending books home but overestimating the frequency with which it happens. Further probing might then involve looking at whether records are kept by teachers, and indeed whether any monitoring of home reading is carried out at all. Finally one might even question children and parents about what happens.

If such methods are necessary to gain a true picture of current practice it suggests that one should look at a small number of cases in depth rather than try to cover too large a sample at a superficial level. The research reported below attempted to do this by studying a small number of schools and by restricting itself to investigating practice in relation to children in one age level within schools – children aged six to seven in the top infants year. This age group was chosen because it had been in the target age range in recent projects and most of the children would be in the early stages of reading where parental help could be most helpful.

The schools studied

Sixteen infant and first schools within four electoral wards of a northern local education authority were studied in the summer term 1981, when most of the top infants children were aged seven. Initially some of the schools were chosen through university contacts with educational psychologists who, together with heads, were known to be interested in reviewing this aspect of school practice. All other schools with children in the target age range within the same wards were then asked to collaborate in the study too, and all agreed to do so.

Information was obtained from heads about a number of school characteristics which could be compared to those reported for the NFER national sample. The two samples were fairly similar in terms of school size, type of school building, ethnic origins of children, pupil turnover, church affiliation, staff:pupil ratio and pattern of class grouping. The samples differed to some extent in that more schools in this study were situated in council estates and, according to heads' judgments, fewer mothers went out to work. Just over half the heads in this study (nine out of 16) judged that their schools' parents were largely manual workers rather than largely professional/management or mixed. In the NFER sample rather less than half of heads (46 per cent) characterized their parents this way.

Method

Each school was visited by one of the writers (PC). Interviews were carried out with the heads, with all available teachers of the top infants age group and with three randomly selected children in each teacher's class (Cuckle, 1981).

The interviews with heads took from half an hour to an hour each, the schedule covering a number of issues including basic characteristics of the school and locality, reading standards and teaching provision in the school, and heads' general views about parental involvement in the teaching of reading. In relation to advice and support for parents, heads were asked whether parents were encouraged to help their children with reading and whether they received any instruction or guidance in doing so from teachers either formally or informally. In relation to providing reading materials for home use, heads were asked whether children were allowed to take school reading books home and, if so, whether it was actually encouraged.

The interviews with class teachers were shorter but covered some of the same points about their views of the parent's role. Class teachers were specifically asked whether they allowed children to take reading or library books home. If so, they were asked how many children were so permitted and whether they monitored how often it happened. The teachers were also asked how they thought parents did help at home, whether they were offered any guidance, and whether parents helped with their children's reading in any other ways.

Finally, the interviewer asked to meet children in the appropriate age group taught by each class teacher. The interviewer was herself a trained infants teacher of several years' experience familiar with the hazards of seeking views and information from young children. She sat down with a group of children chosen at random, and selected one child to interview by counting round the group in a clockwise direction until she reached a randomly determined number between 1 and 10. Three children in each class were chosen in this manner, wherever possible from different groups in the classroom. In this way it was hoped to minimize any unconscious bias which might have operated if either teacher or interviewer had selected children by more informal means.

The interviewer's conversation with the children varied according to whether their teachers allowed books home but was planned to cover a number of points including whether each child did take his or her reading book home (sometimes or always), whether they liked doing so, and who they read to. Those allowed to do so were specifically asked whether they had taken a book home and read to anyone the previous night.

Findings

All interviews with heads were satisfactorily completed (N = 16). Of the 23 teachers of top infants in the schools, one could not be interviewed due to absence and in one school the head asked the interviewer not to approach two teachers (N = 20). Some general information was obtained from heads about the practices of the three teachers not interviewed but this is not included in the report below. Three children were interviewed for each teacher interviewed (N = 60). Full cooperation was given by all interviewed, including the children.

The head teachers

The heads' interviews revealed a generally positive attitude to parents. About half stressed the importance of their close relationship with parents although others were slightly more guarded, pointing out the difficulties of over-anxious 'pushy' parents, or the incapacity of some parents to help their children. Two heads welcomed parental interest but indicated that they preferred parents to let schools get on with the job of teaching. In only one interview was there a definite suggestion of antipathy between parents and the school. When asked how parents can help their children's progress at school most heads referred to general points such as having a positive relationship with the school, providing general encouragement and being familiar with school procedures but four heads specifically mentioned parental involvement in reading or maths.

When asked directly how parents could help with reading, many of the heads (11 out of 16) immediately mentioned listening to children read, the rest considered talking about books or reading to children preferable. In six cases the schools had occasional talks or workshops for parents about children's reading books.

Possibly the most important point to emerge from the interviews with heads concerned the variety of views held about providing school reading books for use at home. Three heads did not allow reading books to be taken home at all (although two were prepared to allow other kinds of books to be taken). One said that the school could not afford sufficient reading books, another suggested that children's relations with their parents might somehow be adversely affected, and the third argued that it might lead to children reading 'parrot fashion'.

A further three heads allowed reading books to go home but definitely preferred them not to, on the grounds that in one way or another parents' efforts would hinder rather than help the teaching of reading in school. Four heads allowed books home but expressed some reservation either about the dangers of too much pressure on children or about children being bored by reading the same book at home and in school. Consequently there were just six heads who allowed books home without expressing any reservations, and indeed most of these seemed to be warmly in favour of the practice. Each of the 13 heads who allowed books home said that the final decision rested with the class teacher.

The class teachers

The 20 class teachers interviewed clearly recognized the importance of parents in children's early reading development. All of them mentioned specific ways in which parents could help. The most common suggestion (made by 11 out of 20) was that parents should read *to* their children, but almost as many (10) said that they gave word lists or flash cards for children to learn at home with their parents. Amongst other suggestions given for parental involvement were for parents to help children use the school library (three teachers) and for workcards or reading games to be sent home (three teachers).

On the question of sending reading book home, the teachers' opinions were more divided Three of the 20 were in no position to send books home since their heads did not permit it. Of the remaining 17, five did not allow it. The reasons given were that there were insufficient books, that there would be confusion over different teaching methods, that the material was inappropriate, that children would memorize the books, and that the practice diminished the value of teachers' training.

Twelve of the 20 did allow books home, but a majority of this group (nine) still expressed reservations or misgivings. (In the classes where books were allowed home at all it applied to all of the children in the teacher's class.) The difficulties referred to included confusion over different teaching methods (three teachers), books not returned, damaged books, boredom due to reading the same book twice, parental pressure causing children's anxiety and children unfairly comparing parents with teachers. Only three teachers out of the 20 interviewed allowed books home without expressing reservations.

The 12 teachers who allowed books home were asked if any guidance was given to parents. Five teachers gave no particular guidance, simply allowing books to be used as parents thought best. Four teachers offered guidance through informal discussions with parents in school but this was limited to children having specific problems with reading. Three teachers seemed to offer guidance to all parents: one asked parents 'just to listen', another gave each child a specific book to read at home, and the third suggested specific activities for parents like helping the child to learn new words for a page or to practise a particular page. Overall, however, the impression gained from the interviews was that the majority of parents receive little or no guidance.

The teachers who allowed books home were also asked whether they monitored how often children actually took them home. Three of the 12 appeared to have virtually no way of knowing whether and how often particular children were taking books and reading at home. Six felt that in one way or another they would be aware of what was happening. One said she gave children an informal comprehension test on material they had been asked to read at home. Only two teachers kept a written record of home reading – in one case in a special book, in the other by means of cards on which parents were asked to note what had been read. Overall, therefore, there was very little evidence of systematic monitoring of children's reading at home.

The children

According to the accounts children gave in conversation with the interviewer, about a third (18 out of 60) did read at home to their parents, and nearly half (27) read either to their parents or to siblings. Nearly all the rest said they read to themselves, but there were four children who appeared not to read at all at home and who may well have had no suitable books at home.

Each of the 36 children in classes where it was allowed was asked how often he or she did take reading books home. Twelve said they never did so, 24 said they did sometimes. None said they always did. As a further check, all the children were asked whether they had a school reading book at home 'last night'. Five children said they had taken one home the previous night. These children were gently asked to show the interviewer the book and pages they had read or a card which had been marked. Two children were able to do this; one said he had taken his book home but forgotten to read it, and the replies from the other two did little to convince the interviewer that they had actually taken a book and read it to anyone at home.

An attempt was made to discover whether children liked taking books home where it was allowed. Most (21 out of 36) said they liked doing it, and the two-thirds of these who were able to give reasons were fairly evenly divided between those who felt it made them better readers and those who simply liked reading generally or reading aloud particularly. The 15 who did not like taking books home included several who said they did it anyway. The main objections given were dislike of the reading book, forgetting to return it, and already being a 'good reader'.

Discussion

The findings summarized above relate to three levels within the life of schools – heads, teachers and children. Taken separately, the validity of the interview method to study each of them is, of course, vulnerable to the usual criticisms, even though it may be superior to, say, a postal questionnaire technique. However, it is possible to combine findings from all three levels to gain a more comprehensive view than would be possible by focusing on any one level. Here and there some cross-checking between findings from different levels may improve validity too. Three issues can usefully be discussed in this way.

1 Support and advice for parents

Children's own accounts in this study confirm what is already known from other research, that a substantial number of young children read aloud to someone at home. However, the attitude of this sample of schools is generally to *encourage alternative forms of parental involvement* such as reading stories to children or helping them learn particular words. This was particularly the case with the class teachers. Certainly support and advice for parents hearing their children read is scarce. Only three class teachers out of 20 offered any form of such guidance to *all* parents (although a further four did so with certain problem readers). Other support might have come from school-organized workshops and talks but four out of the eight teachers who worked in schools having such activities did not allow books home. Taking the most optimistic view of what was offered, and adding together all forms of support and advice reported, parents were only helped in about a third of classes.

2 School reading books for home use

This study provides information about a carefully defined sample of 20 top infants classes. In principle all 20 sets of children might have been taking their school reading books home to read to their parents. However the findings already given show how the potential figure was reduced by the operation of various factors.

First there was the refusal of some heads to permit their teachers to send books home. That reduced the potential number of classes where it could happen from 20 to 17. Next there were class teachers who had decided individually not to allow it. That left 12 classes but in most of those the teachers had reservations about the desirability of children taking school reading books home. It is doubtful whether many were sufficiently convinced of its desirability to actually encourage it. If one takes some system of recording of home reading as a sign that it might happen (or be intended to happen) on a significant scale one is left with just two classes out of the original 20. The evidence therefore suggests that school reading books are not likely to be widely used for home reading.

The situation is summarized in Table 1 which shows how the number of teachers who might have sent books home was reduced by the cumulative effect of these factors. It would of course, be a mistake to suppose that the exact proportions in the table could be generalized to all areas throughout

Table 1 Factors affecting use of school reading books at home

Factor	How often found amongst class teachers	
	Proportion of interviews	*Number of teachers*
Whether teacher acknowledges the importance of parental involvement	100%	20
Whether head permits teacher to send books home	85%	17
Whether teacher allows children to take books home	60%	12
Whether teacher allows books home without expressing reservations	15%	3
Whether teacher keeps some record of the use of books at home	10%	2

the country. What can be said with some confidence, however, is that these factors will everywhere limit the extent to which schools provide reading materials for home use.

3 Take-up of what is available

If there was a widespread use of school reading books at home, it would surely have emerged in the interviews with children. From a sample of 60 children the interviewer could only find two children whom she could be reasonably sure had taken a book home and read it on a given date. There was nothing unusual about the date of interview and it may not be unreasonable therefore to assume that this proportion reflects the true frequency of this form of parental involvement. Even in classes where children were allowed to take books home there seem to be no grounds for supposing the frequency to be much higher than one in 20 per night. Whatever the true frequency, it is almost certainly lower than might have been expected without this study. In the absence of greater teacher commitment to this form of parental involvement, and more systematic monitoring of take-up, it would be unrealistic to expect a higher figure.

Conclusions

This study does not of itself constitute a criticism of current school practice, merely a description of it. Some changes may be desirable on the grounds that more parental involvement helps children's reading development or for other reasons. However that would require the examination of other evidence and some fundamental questions about the nature of schooling which require separate consideration. What this report does is to cast considerable doubt on claims to the effect that schools are *already* assisting children's reading at home through the provision of reading materials and support for parents. In relation to this form of parental involvement it does not seem to be the case that 'We've all been doing it all the time'.

Acknowledgements

Our thanks for their time and interest to staff and children of the schools studied.

References

ASHTON, C. and JACKSON, J. (1982). ' "Lies, damned lies and statistics": or a funny thing happened in a reading project', *AEP Journal*, **5**, 10, 43–6.
CUCKLE, P. (1981). A survey of parental involvement in the reading development of seven year old children. Unpublished MSc Special Study, Division of Education, University of Sheffield.

CYSTER, R., CLIFT, P. S. and BATTLE, S. (1980). *Parental Involvement in Primary Schools.* Windsor: NFER.

HANNON, P. W. and JACKSON, A. (1983). Intervention to involve parents in their children's early reading development. Unpublished working paper, Division of Education, University of Sheffield.

HEWISON, J. (1981). 'Home is where the help is', *Times Educational Supplement*, 16 January.

HEWISON, J. and TIZARD, J. (1980). 'Parental involvement and reading attainment, *British Journal of Educational Psychology*, **50**, 209–15.

JACKSON, A. and HANNON, P. W. (1981). *The Belfield Reading Project.* Rochdale: Belfield Community Council.

NEWSON, J. and NEWSON, E. (1977). *Perspectives on School at Seven Years Old.* London: George Allen & Unwin.

TIZARD, J., SCHOFIELD, W. N. and HEWISON, J. (1982). 'Collaboration between teachers and parents in assisting children's reading', *British Journal of Educational Psychology*, **52**, 1–15.

WILBY, P. (1981). 'The Bellfield experiment', *Sunday Times*, 29 March.

9

PARENTAL INVOLVEMENT
AND READING ATTAINMENT

Jenny Hewison and J. Tizard

Source: *British Journal of Educational Psychology* (1980) 50: 209–215.

Introduction

The research reported here is concerned with the influence of parental help on the reading attainments of 7- and 8-year-old children. The work forms part of a more wide-ranging investigation by Hewison (1979) into relationships between the child's home background and his success in school. It is well established that scores obtained by children on tests of academic attainments are strongly associated with demographic character-istics, as measured by social class, material circumstances and size of family—also that attitudinal factors such as parents' newspaper reading habits and the number of books in the home are related to children's edu-cational success (Douglas, 1964; Davie *et al.*, 1972). The aim of Hewison's (1979) study was to investigate whether differences in school achievement *within* a working-class population could be related to differences in the home backgrounds of the children; demographic, cultural and attitudinal variables were to be taken into account, but the main concern was to be with characterising parental *behaviour* and day-to-day child-rearing activ-ities.

Children aged 7–8 years were chosen for study, because that is the age of transfer from infants to junior school and because social class differ-ences in achievement are already well established by that age. Reading attainment was chosen as the measure of school achievement in the studies because at 7–8 years of age it is not only the best index of how well a child is currently doing in school but also the best single predictor of sub-sequent school achievement.

The pilot inquiry and the two subsequent studies were all carried out in a very homogeneous working-class area, which contained a negligible pro-portion of families of immigrant origin. All of the families included in the studies were white, and there was little variation in their material and social conditions. In all three studies, information was obtained from reading tests given to the children, and parental interviews.

The pilot study

Method

The pilot study was carried out in two infant schools. An attempt was made to interview the mothers of all children in final-year classes at the two schools. Introductory letters were sent to the homes, then an interviewer (J.H.) called at each house and asked the mother if she would agree to be interviewed. Eighty-one homes were contacted in this way. Three mothers did not wish to participate in the study, and seven repeatedly broke interview appointments. Incomplete information was obtained from six homes, where the interviewee was not the full-time guardian of the child. Thus the size of the final interview sample was 65.

In the pilot study structured open interviews were used to obtain the home background information. Topics covered included attitudes to children's play and discipline, the sharing of activities and conversation, reading to the child and hearing him read, a series of questions about how the child spent his leisure time and another on attitudes to school. The time taken to carry out the pilot interview ranged from 30 minutes to two and a half hours.

The reading attainment of the children was assessed using the Southgate Reading Test I. Reading test scores were not obtained on two children who were repeatedly absent from school, so the final sample size for the pilot study was 63. The study took place towards the end of the school summer term, i.e., in June and July when the age range of the children in the sample was 6 : 11 to 7 : 09.

Results

In general, Bernstein's (Bernstein and Brandis, 1970; Brandis, 1974) and others' findings of modest correlations between aspects of the child's behaviour and circumstances at home and his level of attainment were confirmed. There was, however, one question to which replies correlated strongly with the children's reading attainments. This was whether or not the mother regularly heard the child read. Most of the other significant findings between reading ability and parental practices could be accounted for statistically by the fact that parents who displayed attitudes and behaviour which appeared to favour the development of reading ability in their children were also more likely to have the habit of hearing the child read ('coaching'). Analysis by partial correlation showed that, for example, the association between 'attitudinal' factors and reading attainments came about because the 'attitudes' were correlated with 'coaching'—children whose parents had good 'attitudes' but who did not receive 'coaching' were not advanced in their reading.

The main study method

The results of the pilot inquiry were both striking and unexpected. In the second study of the series, the ideas generated in the pilot were put to the test on new data.

The names of 30 children were randomly drawn from the first year roll in each of four junior schools. As in the pilot study, introductory letters were sent to the parents of the selected children before an interviewer (J.H.) visited them at home. Once contacted, no mother refused to be interviewed, and none persistently broke appointments: interviewing was terminated when a minimum of 25 successful interviews had been carried out in each school area, 107 interviews being carried out in all.

A closed interview schedule, based on the framework of response coding developed in the pilot study, was used to obtain the home background information. Topics covered in the interviews again included attitudes to school and parental help with reading at home. Aspects of the mother's language behaviour were assessed using two scales devised and employed by members of Bernstein's research team (Brandis, 1970; Henderson, 1971; Brandis, 1974). The first of these scales was designed to assess a mother's willingness to chat to her child in a number of different physical circumstances, and the second her willingness to answer a variety of different 'awkward' questions. The time taken to carry out each interview ranged from 30 minutes to one hour. Scores on a standardised reading test, (the NFER Test 'A') and on the WISC were obtained for the sample children. The IQ tests were administered by trainee educational psychologists from the London Institute of Education. The testers were not informed about the purpose of the main investigation and since their work was carried out under the supervision of their course tutor, the results are probably as valid, and the testing as reliable as is normally the case.

One child was absent from the reading testing, and six from the IQ testing. The final sample size for whom full reading, IQ and home environment information was available, was therefore 100. The study took place in the autumn term, when the age range of the sample children was 7 : 02 to 8 : 02.

Results

Significant correlations were again obtained between a number of different aspects of the home environment and reading performance. As in the pilot study, the factor which was found to be most strongly associated with reading success was whether or not the mother regularly heard the child read—not whether she read to the child but whether she heard the child read. Taking this factor into account substantially reduced the correlations of the other home environment variables (including whether or not the mother read to the child) with reading performance.

Analysis of variance calculations revealed no significant differences in reading performance among the four schools in the study, nor between boys and girls. No significant school or sex differences were found in the proportions of mothers who heard their children read, and no interactions were found between these variables and the 'coaching' factor in the determination of reading performance, i.e., the 'coaching' effect was observable in all four schools, and for both boys and girls.

Reading attainments and 'coaching'

Of the 100 children in the sample, 47 had mothers who heard them read at home ('coached') and 53 had not. Table 1 presents the reading attainments of the two groups, tested on the NFER Reading Test A.

As in the pilot study, the differences in reading scores between the coached and not-coached samples was very great, amounting to almost one standard deviation. The point biserial correlation between Coaching and Reading Score was $r = 0.61$, i.e., 36 per cent of the variance in reading scores would be accounted for statistically by the factor of coaching.

Reading attainments, coaching and mother's language behaviour

The interrelationship of these three variables is of particular theoretical importance. Mothers' scores on both the language behaviour scales were found to be significantly correlated with their children's reading ability. (Pearson's $r = 0.23$, $P < 0.05$ for the 'Chat' scale; and $r = 0.33$, $P < 0.001$ for the 'Awkward questions' scale.) However, as in the pilot study, it was found that mothers who had educationally favourable language behaviour were also more likely to hear their children read. When this was taken into account, only a very weak and statistically non-significant relationship

Table 1 Age standardised readings test scores of children who were coached or not coached

Sample	N	Mean	SD
Coached	47	101.7	10.35
Not coached	53	87.6	7.79
Total	100	94.2	11.46

Note
F ratio = 59.7, df = 1,98, P < 0.0001

211

remained between maternal language behaviour and reading performance. (Partial r = 0.05 for the 'Chat' scale, and partial r = 0.16 for the 'Awkward questions' scale, neither coefficient being significant at the 0.05 level). Controlling for language behaviour, on the other hand, had very little effect on the association between coaching and reading performance. After adjusting for both language variables, partial r = 0.56, P < 0.001.

Reading attainments, coaching and IQ

As expected, a highly significant relationship existed between reading score and IQ (Pearson's r = 0.54, P < 0.001). In addition, Coaching and IQ were strongly associated, as shown in Table 2. The point biserial correlation between coaching and IQ was 0.37, P < 0.001.

Using multiple regression methods it was established that the IQ differences shown in Table 2 were insufficient to account for the superior reading attainments of the coached children. To demonstrate the interrelationships of the three variables in another way, groups of children banded for IQ were studied. Table 3 was produced when the banded chil-

Table 2 Full scale WISC IQ scores of children who were coached or not coached

Sample	N	Mean	SD
Coached	47	108.2	14.59
Not coached	53	97.2	13.04
Total	100	102.4	14.80

Note
F ratio = 16.0, df = 1,98, P < 0.0001

Table 3 The relationships between coaching and reading performance in groups of children banded for IQ

IQ band (Mean IQ = 102.4)		'Poor readers' test score ≤94	'Good readers' test score ≥95	Total
87 or less	Not coached	10	0	10
	Coached	1	1	2
88–102	Not coached	21	5	26
	Coached	6	10	16
103–117	Not coached	9	3	12
	Coached	2	14	16
118 or above	Not coached	4	1	5
	Coached	2	11	13
Total		55	45	100

dren were classified by their level of reading attainment (above or below the sample mean of 94.2), and at coached or not coached.

Table 3 shows, first, that the effect of being coached is observable at all levels of IQ; and second, that the higher the IQ band, the higher the proportion of children receiving this form of help with their reading.

A replication study

Method

A weakness of the studies so far was that no assessment was attempted as to the amount of coaching children were receiving at the time or had received in the past. To get an idea of this, a further sample of children and their parents was studied. Unfortunately it was not possible this time to assess the children's IQs. The study was a quick one designed simply to find out whether the amount of coaching was related to reading attainment score.

The procedure followed in the main study for obtaining a sample was again adopted. The names of 30 children were randomly drawn from the first-year rolls of the same four junior schools (the study took place 12 months after the previous one) and the contacting and interviewing of parents carried out as before. One hundred and six mothers were contacted, and 105 agreed to be interviewed. One child missed the reading testing, so the final sample size for the study was 104.

Detailed questioning of parents, using a closed interview schedule, made it possible to classify the amount of help their children had received into one of the following five categories: *regular*, or *occasional*, help in the juniors; *regular*, or *occasional*, help in the infants only; *no help* at any time.

Results

Table 4 gives the mean reading scores of children in the five 'coached' categories.

An analysis of variance carried out on the data revealed that the relationship between amount of help given and reading performance was highly significant statistically (F = 18.5, df = 4.99, P <0.0001).

The results are very consistent indeed. They fully confirm the earlier findings, and suggest in addition that reading attainment scores vary in stepwise fashion with the amount of coaching in reading which the children have received.

Discussion

There is an increasing awareness of the need for co-operation between the home and the school. Also, the significant part that a child's home

Table 4 Mean reading scores of children in five 'coached' categories

Help received	Mean reading score	SD	N
Regular help in juniors	104.9	10.9	39
Occasional help in juniors	98.3	8.8	23
Regular help in infants only	91.2	9.3	19
Occasional help in infants only	86.7	9.0	11
No help at any time	81.1	10.3	12
Total sample	96.3	12.8	104

environment plays in determining his educational progress has been well documented in, for example, the two longitudinal studies carried out by J. W. B. Douglas (Douglas, 1964) and the National Children's Bureau (Davie *et al.*, 1972). Both the Plowden Report (1967) and the Bullock Report (DES, 1975) discussed co-operation between parents and teachers and made constructive suggestions as to how this could be improved.

In general, these recommendations have been concerned with ways of changing the attitudes of teachers and parents. What matters most, according to the Plowden Report is "whether there is a genuine mutual respect, whether parents understand what the schools are doing for their individual children and teachers realise how dependent they are on parental support".

There has been much less discussion of parental involvement in children's actual school work. The Plowden and Bullock Reports both made some reference to parents helping their children with work at home, but neither report made explicit its views as to the desirability or otherwise of this practice. The 'Survey among parents of primary school children', carried out for the Plowden Committee, did, however, yield factual information on the extent to which schools encouraged children to take work home, and on parents' attitudes to homework.

According to their parents' report, 26 per cent of children in the top infants, and 39 per cent in the bottom juniors were given work to do at home. In classes where such work was given, only around 16 per cent of parents disapproved of this, or thought the children were given too much (only 2 per cent thought this); about 60 per cent thought they were given the right amount, and about 20 per cent thought they were given too little (Plowden Report Vol. II, Appendix 3, Table 25). Social class differences in parental response to this question were found to be remarkably small, though significantly more children of parents in social classes I and II were

214

in fact given homework to do (Table 26). Parental help with homework was also found to be widespread, with 73 per cent of children in the top infants receiving help. Less than a third of parents were, however, reported to have asked the school for homework, or how to help their child at home.

The Bullock Report was primarily concerned with the teaching of reading and other language skills in a school setting. Discussion of parental involvement was restricted to general remarks about the role of parents in extending children's language development, and fostering positive attitudes to books and reading. Talking to children and reading to them were considered the most appropriate activities for parents to engage in, and specific warnings were issued against the use by parents of more formal techniques, such as helping their children work through the books in a reading scheme. The Bullock Report did not at any stage address itself to the issues raised by the Plowden inquiry, which had shown that large numbers of children were already being given active help with school work by their parents.

The present study, like the Plowden survey, was concerned with learning more about existing parental practices. It showed, firstly, that many parents (about half, in these samples of white working-class parents) did spend time coaching children in the mechanics of reading, though practically none of these had consulted the school about this, and none at all claimed to have had any encouragement from the school. Secondly, this coaching was undoubtedly related strongly to reading performance. The 'Coaching factor' accounted for 36 per cent of the variance in reading scores—a proportion of variance accounted for which was, incidentally, more than twice the amount of the variance in educational performance within schools accounted for by all variables defined as 'parental attitudes' in the National Survey commissioned by Plowden (Vol. I, Table 1, p. 53.) The effect could be explained, statistically, neither by between-schools differences, nor by IQ effects—the relationship between coaching and reading attainment remaining highly significant even after both these factors had been taken into account. There were no significant sex effects in the data.

IQ and coaching both had independent contributions to make to the prediction of reading performance. This fact established, it remained the case that children who were coached had IQs which were 11 points higher, on average, than those who were not.

The relationship between these two variables may be accounted for in a number of ways which the data cannot distinguish. It may be that more intelligent pupils are more keen to have themselves heard reading by their parents, or that more intelligent parents have more intelligent children whom they are likely to want to see get on well at school. Another possibility is that coaching which leads to better reading also boosts IQ.

The study leaves unanswered the major question as to why some parents coach and others do not. Those who coached were a self-selected group. It is possible that what was chiefly responsible for their children's success in learning to read was not the practice in reading the parents gave them but rather the interest parents took in their schooling, of which coaching was merely an indicator. The fact that scores on other, 'attitudinal' questions relating to parental interest in the child's education correlated only very modestly with reading attainment score goes against this last hypothesis, but questioning by parental interview may be only a poor indicator of parental 'style' in upbringing.

Survey findings obtained from members of self-defined groups throw no light on the question of how far parental styles of upbringing are subject to change. This can only be decided in practice. Fortunately we had the opportunity, in collaboration with W.N. Schofield, and the local education authority primary advisers to carry out an experiment in the London borough of Haringey. In this study, an effort was made to get *all* parents of children in selected school classes to hear their children read at home. Results of this experiment are in process of analysis and will be presented in subsequent papers.

Acknowledgment

This paper is based on a doctoral thesis submitted by J. Hewison in partial fulfilment of the requirements for the degree of Ph.D. at the University of London. The empirical work was supported by an MRC postgraduate scholarship, and carried out under the direction of the late Professor J. Tizard. The authors would like to express their gratitude to the Director of Education, London Borough of Barking, for permission to carry out these studies, and to all the head teachers, teachers and parents, for their assistance and co-operation.

References

BERNSTEIN, B., and BRANDIS, W. (1970). Social class differences in communication and control. In BRANDIS, W., and HENDERSON, D. (Eds.), *Social Class, Language and Communication*. London: Routledge and Kegan Paul.

BRANDIS, W. (1970). Appendix II: A measure of the mother's orientation towards communication and control. In BRANDIS, W., and HENDERSON, D. (Eds.), *Social Class, Language and Communication* London: Routledge and Kegan Paul.

BRANDIS, W. (1974). Personal communication.

DAVIE, R., BUTLER, N., and GOLDSTEIN, H. (1972). *From Birth to Seven: A Report of the National Child Development Study*. London: Longman.

DEPARTMENT OF EDUCATION AND SCIENCE (1975). *A Language for Life*, (The Bullock Report). London: HMSO.

DOUGLAS, J. W. B. (1964). *The Home and the School*. London: MacGibbon and Kee.

HENDERSON, D. (1973). Contextual specificity, discretion and cognitive socialization: with special reference to language. IN BERNSTEIN, B. (Ed.), (1973), *Class, Codes and Control: Volume 2*. London: Routledge and Kegan Paul.

HEWISON, J. (1979). Home environment and reading attainment: a study of children in a working class community. Unpublished Ph.D. thesis, University of London.

PLOWDEN REPORT (1967). *Children and their Primary Schools*. Report of the Central Advisory Council for Education. London: HMSO.

10

RHETORIC AND RESEARCH IN FAMILY LITERACY

Peter Hannon

Source: *British Educational Research Journal* (1999) 26(1): 121–138

The term 'family literacy' now figures prominently in the discourses of early childhood education, literacy and adult education, in several English-speaking countries. In this article I wish to draw attention to some strands of the rhetoric of family literacy. By 'rhetoric' is meant discourse largely 'calculated to persuade or influence others' (the 'others' here being policy-makers, educators, and citizens with some interest in education). Examining the rhetoric of family literacy means examining explicit and implicit claims for certain programmes. I also wish to explore how those claims relate to educational research and hope to show that, although rhetoric has sometimes been informed by research, it has also obscured, misinterpreted, ignored and exaggerated research findings. Although many studies will be described or quoted, the purpose of this article is not to provide a review of the field but to show through examples that there is a rhetoric and to seek research evidence for claims made within that rhetoric.

The focus is on what will be termed 'restricted' programmes in family literacy. To explain what is meant by this it is necessary to review the use of the term 'family literacy'. Ten years ago it was not much used or known in education. It had some currency within a relatively small circle of literacy researchers who were interested in young children's literacy development before school and out of school. Taylor (1983) in the USA had coined the term to refer to the interplay of literacy activities of children, parents and others which she found in six families studied over periods ranging from months to years. She concluded that 'literacy is a part of the very fabric of family life' (p. 87). There were other studies around the same time (e.g. Heath, 1983; Teale, 1986) which took a similar sociocultural approach to understanding literacy development in communities and families, although they did not use the term 'family literacy'.

Later in the 1980s in the USA, 'family literacy' acquired a different meaning, referring not to a *research focus* but instead to *educational pro-*

grammes. This meaning subsequently reached Britain and other English-speaking countries. Two main concepts of family literacy programmes can be distinguished from that period.

The first, broad concept of family literacy programmes included any approach which explicitly addressed the family dimension in literacy learning, e.g. parental involvement in schools, pre-school interventions, parenting education, family use of libraries, community development, and extensions of adult literacy education to include children (McIvor, 1990; Nickse, 1990b). In terms suggested by Nickse (1990b), some of these programmes focused directly on children and only indirectly, if at all, on parents as literacy learners. Others focused on parents and only indirectly on children. What they all had in common, however, was a recognition that individual literacy learners were members of families, and that families affected, and were affected by, the individuals' learning. When the focus was on children this usually meant parental involvement in children's learning.

This broad concept has been reflected in publications from the International Reading Association, detailing schemes across the USA in the early 1990s (Morrow, 1995; Morrow *et al.*, 1995). Wolfendale & Topping (1996) adopted a similar perspective in their compilation and review of developments in Britain, Australia and New Zealand. In this sense family literacy programmes have been around for two or more decades but the new descriptor 'family literacy' is more inclusive and useful than, say, 'parental involvement', which tends to convey the idea that parents are the only members of a family worth involving in children's literacy development. 'Family literacy' can also convey the idea that there is pre-existing literacy activity in families, that older family members may be engaging children in those activities (and vice versa), and that in practice most programmes often do not deal with isolated individuals but with members of a family.

The second concept of family literacy programmes referred to programmes which combined direct adult basic education for parents with direct early childhood education for children, i.e. where there was a dual, simultaneous focus on two generations. Often these programmes also sought to change how parents interacted with their children and supported their literacy development. A prime example was the 'Kenan model', promoted with great vigour by the National Center for Family Literacy (NCFL), established for that purpose in Louisville, Kentucky (Perkins & Mendel, 1989). Thus, Sharon Darling, president and founder of the NCFL, defined family literacy in these terms:

> At NCFL we prefer to define family literacy as a holistic, family-focused approach, targeting at-risk parents and children with intensive, frequent, and long-term educational and other services.

Total family literacy programs include four components which are integrated to form a unique, comprehensive approach to serving families: (1) basic skill instruction for parents or caregivers, (2) preschool or literacy education for young children, (3) regular parent and child interaction, and (4) parent education/support activities.

(Darling, 1993a, p. 3)

This concept of a 'family literacy' programme (developed by others as well as the NCFL) was basically new. Several years later there is still no commonly accepted term by which it can be distinguished from the 'broad' concept of family literacy programme described earlier. Not being able to draw this distinction makes for difficulties in discussing family literacy programmes because it may not be clear which kind of programme is being referred to, and what is said about one kind may not apply to the other. It is at this point that issues of rhetoric arise, for the choice of term can itself be an act of persuasion. Darling, in the quotation cited earlier, used the word 'total', which implies that other kinds of programme are 'partial'—something less than the real thing. It is not easy to find a term which is neutral and accurate ('combined', for example, will not do because most family literacy programmes combine different components). For the purposes of this article I choose to use the term 'restricted'. This might be regarded as having somewhat negative connotations but that may be no bad thing if it offers an alternative rhetoric to that to be described later. 'Restricted' is an accurate term because the programmes concerned are restricted to families who participate in *all* components and because the programmes constitute a restricted subset of family literacy programmes in general. It is not suggested here that the family literacy addressed in such programmes is restricted (it may or may not be) but that the programmes are restricted in the sense of setting very specific entry requirements for families. The rhetoric to be discussed in this article relates mainly to restricted programmes.

Most of the rhetoric associated with restricted programmes is found in the USA but echoes of it can be detected in other countries, including Britain where, in 1993, the government-funded Adult Literacy and Basic Skills Unit (ALBSU, since renamed the Basic Skills Agency, BSA) launched a family literacy initiative which promoted restricted programmes. Demonstration programmes funded in this initiative had to provide '1. accredited basic skills instruction for parents; 2. early literacy development for young children; 3. joint parent/child sessions on supporting pre-reading, early reading and reading skills' (ALBSU, 1993a, p. 4). The similarity of the ALBSU concept to that of the NCFL, quoted earlier, was later acknowledged.

In developing this model we looked at the development of family literacy in the United States and tried to learn from the best of what was going on in the US as well as avoid less effective practices.

(BSA, 1996, p. 3)

From the start, family literacy programmes, particularly restricted ones, had an uneasy relationship with family literacy research. Programmes and research studies both acknowledged the importance of the family as a site for literacy activities and literacy learning but, as Auerbach (1989) pointed out, the assumptions underpinning programmes were often at odds with research findings. For example, according to family literacy research, very few, if any, families could be said totally to lack literacy or concern for children's development and education yet some programmes appeared to be premised on such beliefs. Auerbach noted 'a gap between research and implementation: existing models for family literacy programs seemed not to be informed by ethnographic research' (Auerbach, 1989, p. 167).

Throughout the 1990s, the term 'family literacy' became steadily more familiar to policy-makers and practitioners on both sides of the Atlantic in discourse about literacy education, standards of literacy, and teaching methods. In part this was due to government funding of restricted programmes (in the USA, the Federal 'Even Start' programme; in England and Wales, the ALBSU/BSA Family Literacy Initiative). In part it reflected the development of broader forms of practice at local level (Hannon, 1995; Morrow, 1995; Wolfendale & Topping, 1996). There may also have been deeper cultural currents in this period—relating to anxieties about national literacy levels and the position of families in society—which made programmes labelled 'family literacy' particularly attractive to policy-makers and funders. Whatever the reasons, the result is that 'family literacy' has figured prominently in educational discourse, for example, in special issues of journals (*Language Arts*, 1993; *Journal of Reading*, 1995; *RaPAL Bulletin*, 1994; *Reading*, 1995; *Reading and Writing Quarterly*, 1995; *Australian Journal of Language and Literacy*, 1994; *The Reading Teacher* 1995; *Viewpoints*, 1993), in special conferences, in numerous references in broadcast and print media, and in government documents such as the National Literacy Act (P.L. 102–73) 1991 in the USA or the Education White Paper for England, *Excellence in Schools* (Department for Education and Employment [DfEE], 1997).

There have been many criticisms concerning the alleged 'deficit view' of families implicit in some family literacy rhetoric (a collection of such criticisms, and alternative conceptions of families' literacies, has been assembled by Taylor [1997]). In this regard Auerbach (1997) and Grant (1997) have examined specific claims and myths in family literacy in the USA and

Australia. There is no need to go over the same ground in this article. Instead, other features of family literacy rhetoric which are no less important but which have not received equal attention will be examined. The examination relates to two countries, the USA and Britain, and focuses on five areas: (1) usage of the term 'family literacy'; (2) targeting of programmes for selected families; (3) accessibility and take-up of programmes; (4) educational effects; and (5) socio-economic effects. In respect of rhetoric in each area, one can ask, 'How does this relate to research?' The article concludes with a discussion of what research is needed to develop practice and policy in this field.

(1) Usage of the term 'family literacy'

Earlier, a distinction was made between 'family literacy' as a term which referred to a research focus and as a term which referred to certain forms of educational programmes. The former meaning came first historically but has now been almost entirely obliterated by the latter. For example, notice in the earlier quotation, from Darling, that she says, 'we prefer to define family literacy as a holistic, family focused approach, targeting at-risk parents and children'. 'Family literacy' is now commonly used to refer only to programmes—as shorthand for 'family literacy programme'. Sometimes it is only restricted programmes that are referred to as if there were no other kind. Such are the resonances of the words 'family' and 'literacy' at the present time that it is a great rhetorical advantage for politicians and advocates of certain kinds of programmes to be able to refer them simply as 'family literacy'. The rightness and merit of such programmes for funding seems irresistible.

This has two consequences. First, the vocabulary of educational research is weakened by the loss of a term which defined a valuable line of research thus rendered less visible. It should be noted, however, that such research has continued. In the USA, following the work by Taylor, Heath and Teale mentioned earlier, there have, for example, been studies of families' literacies by Taylor & Dorsey-Gaines (1988), Baker *et al.* (1994), Purcell-Gates (1995) and Voss (1996). In Britain, Weinberger (1996), Gregory (1996), and Barton & Hamilton (1998) have illuminated aspects of family literacy in different communities. This line of research has become obscured by discourse in which family literacy research means research into family literacy programmes.

A second consequence is that, as this line of family literacy research is obscured, it becomes more difficult for practitioners and policy-makers to draw on it to develop family literacy programmes. If 'family literacy' always refers to programmes it is harder to conceive of it as something which could occur independently of programmes. The situation lamented by Auerbach (1989) is in danger of getting worse. Auerbach (1995) has

222

gone on to suggest that there is a continuum of programmes from those which ignore pre-existing family literacy to those which see the social context as a rich resource that can inform rather than impede learning. The former, she argues, are inevitably prescriptive and interventionist; the latter can be participatory and empowering. It does seem likely that programme developers who remain ignorant of existing patterns of family literacy will work at one end of the continuum without being fully aware of possibilities at the other end. The rhetorical restriction of the term 'family literacy' just to programmes devalues research which could inform those programmes.

(2) Targeting of programmes for selected families

Crucial to the rhetoric of restricted programmes is the claim that there is a significant number of families in which parents have literacy difficulties and in which children also have (or will later have) low literacy achievement. That is the justification for restricting programmes to families willing to address both parental and child literacy simultaneously. Although it is undoubtedly the case that there are families in which parents have literacy difficulties and that there are families in which children have low literacy achievement, it is necessary to ask how many of each kind there are, and to what extent they are the *same* families. There is likely to be some overlap between the two kinds of family but it is often implied that they coincide completely and constitute a large number which ought to be selected as the target of family literacy programmes.

The rhetoric asserts (a) that parents with literacy difficulties will have low achieving children, and (b) that low achieving children have parents with literacy difficulties. Obviously, (a) and (b) are logically distinct propositions but they are often taken together as if each entailed the other. It is claimed that children can be identified as at risk of literacy underachievement on the basis of parental literacy difficulties. The parents' literacy, or lack of it, is put forward as a *cause* of the children's difficulties. The literature on family literacy abounds with references to a 'cycle of underachievement' which can be broken by targeting parents' and children's literacy at the same time in the same programme.

Examples of this rhetoric from the USA are provided by Darling (1993b) and Nickse (1990a).

> Family literacy programs recognise that these two groups—undereducated adults and educationally 'at risk children' interlock; they are bound so tightly together that excellence in public school education is an empty dream for youths who go home each afternoon to families where literacy is neither practised or valued.
>
> (Darling, 1993b, p. 2)

The goal of family literacy programs is to enhance the lives of both parent and child: to improve skills, attitudes, values, and behaviors linked to reading. These programs try to break the cycle of low literacy, a cycle which limits lives.

(Nickse, 1990a, p. 4)

This powerful intervention holds great promise for breaking the intergenerational cycle of undereducation and fulfilling America's broadest educational aims.

(Darling, 1993b, p. 5)

In Britain ALBSU echoed these claims.

Programmes which offer a combination of teaching for parents and children can prevent failure, break the cycle of under attainment and raise confidence and achievement across the generations.

(ALBSU, 1993b, p. 1)

Gillian Shephard, a former Secretary of State for Education in England, has stated:

Family literacy schemes break the vicious circle where parents pass on poor literacy and numeracy to their children.

(Department for Education, 1995)

There is a surface plausibility about the assumptions underlying these statements but how well do they relate to research evidence? Do children who achieve poorly in school in fact have parents with literacy difficulties? Can parental literacy difficulties be used to identify children likely to fail and for whom a family literacy programme would be appropriate?

To answer these questions one needs to survey a representative sample of families and examine the association between parents' and children's literacy. Such a study has been carried out in Britain. It has been cited in support of the earlier claims but when examined closely it can be seen that it actually contradicts them.

The research in question was carried out in 1991 for ALBSU by a team from the City University, London. Using a subsample of 1761 families with 2617 children drawn from the fifth sweep of the British National Child Development Study, children's reading was tested on the Peabody Individual Achievement Test Reading Recognition Assessment and parents were asked as part of a longer interview whether they had problems with reading, writing or spelling (ALBSU, 1993c). Data were also collected on other family characteristics and children's attainment in mathematics.

Children's reading achievement was categorised in four levels, 1–4, according to quartiles of age-standardised scores. Table 1 shows some of the findings as presented by ALBSU (1993c). It can be seen from Table 1 that there was a clear association between children's reading test scores and parents' reported reading difficulty. It is particularly interesting that 48% of the children whose parents had reading difficulties were in the 'low' reading group (compared to 24% from other families). One can agree with the Director of ALBSU, Alan Wells, who claimed that the study provided 'the first objective evidence of the link between a parent's competence in basic skills and the competence of their children' and that it indicated 'a very strong correlation between low basic skills of parents and low attainment of children' (Wells, 1993, p. 3). Correlation, however, is one thing, identification quite another.

Further analyses in the ALBSU study showed that in low income families and in families where parents had no educational qualifications as well as reading difficulties the proportion of low reading children rose to 72%. The proportion of children who were low in either mathematics or reading in such families was 76%. The study concluded:

> The combination of parental literacy and numeracy problems, with a low level of parental education or low family income, *can be used to identify the children who were most likely to perform badly* in the maths and reading tests.
>
>   (ALBSU, 1993c, p. 19, emphasis added)

This statement is highly misleading. The fact that certain parental characteristics are associated with children's low reading achievement does not mean that they can be used to identify those children. To understand why, return to Table 1. Data were presented there by ALBSU

Table 1 Relation between children's reading achievement and parents' reported reading difficulties as presented by ALBSU (1993)

Child's reading test score	Parent reading difficulty?	
	Yes %	No %
1. Low	48	24
2.	22	25
3.	17	25
4. High	13	26
n (100%)	107	2500

Source: ALBSU (1993c), Table 1, p. 10.

(1993c) in a manner likely to persuade—perhaps even calculated to persuade—that parental literacy difficulties account for much of children's poor literacy achievement, but if the data are recast in the form of Table 2 it can be seen that this is not so. In Table 2 children in the higher three quartiles on reading test scores have been grouped together as 'other' to clarify comparisons with the 'low' group and instead of percentages there are the inferred numbers of children in each cell (calculated by reference to the cell percentages and column totals given in Table 1). The figures in Table 2 were directly inferred from Table 1 although they were never presented in this form by ALBSU.

It can be seen from Table 2 that 51 out of the 107 children whose parents had reading difficulties were in the low reading group (this is the 48% referred to earlier) but the table also enables a judgement to be made of the value of parental reading difficulty as a method for identifying children with low reading. It shows that it is very insensitive for it only identifies 8% (51 out of 651) of the low reading group. Any programme targeted on this basis would miss 92% of the lowest achieving children. Almost as bad is the fact that 52% (56 out of 107) of the children identified would be in the higher reading achievement groups and would be targeted for a programme they might not need with a consequent waste of educational resources and the families' time.

It might be argued that the method of identification could be improved by adding identifiers of low family income and parents' lack of qualifications and combining them to identify children whose achievement was low in either mathematics or reading (as described by ALBSU, 1993c, in the quotation given earlier). Table 3 shows the relevant figures, derived from another table in the ALBSU report (as before, the cell figures were calculated by reference to the percentages and column totals given in the report). Data were not presented in this form by ALBSU but it can be seen that the 76% of children mentioned earlier (as having parents with reading difficulties, low income and no qualifications who were in the low reading group) comprised 22 out of 29 children.

Table 3 reveals that the sensitivity of this method is now absurdly low in

Table 2 Data from Table 1 expressed in terms of inferred numbers of children

Child's reading test score	Parent reading difficulty?		
	Yes	No	Totals
Low	51	600	651
Other	56	1900	1956
Totals	107	2500	2607

Source: Derived from ALBSU (1993c), Table 1, p. 10.

Table 3 Inferred numbers of children with low scores in reading or mathematics according to parental characteristics

Child's test score in reading or mathematics	Parent reading difficulty, low income and no qualifications?		
	Yes	No	Totals
Low in either	22	921	943
Other	7	1669	1676
Totals	29	2590	2619

Source: Derived from ALBSU (1993c). Table 8, p. 18.

that it identifies only 2% of all the children in the low reading group. It should also be noted that the target group, comprising 29 out of 2619 children, is only 1% of the population. The best that can be said for this as a method of identification is that it does not falsely identify as low achievers quite so many of the children in the higher groups as did the previous method (24% of those identified being false positives compared to 52% previously).

The rhetoric that family factors identify poor readers is therefore not borne out by this research. There is an overlap between families where parents have literacy difficulties and families where children have low literacy achievement but it is an extremely small overlap. Targeting just those families will not meet the needs of many others.

Might other studies, using different measures and different populations, find better methods of identification? Possibly, but the examination of this particular study highlights pitfalls likely to be encountered by research in any country which seeks to identify children with low literacy achievement on the basis of family characteristics. One is the tendency to believe that a significant correlation implies an acceptable method of identification. It has been shown that this does not necessarily follow. Another is that the prevalence of reported literacy difficulties in families is relatively low in countries such as the USA or Britain. If one devised a broader concept of parental literacy difficulty with higher prevalence one could expect to identify a greater proportion of children who were poor readers but the proportion of better readers falsely identified could also rise.

The search for methods of identification is often driven by policy-makers' wish for the 'magic bullet' which, targeted selectively at a few families, eliminates social problems. There is no evidence that targeting restricted programmes on the basis of parental literacy difficulty can be sufficiently accurate. One policy alternative to restricted programmes is universal, literacy-oriented early childhood education (including pre-school education). This could include ongoing assessment of children's literacy learning, accompanied by appropriate intervention as and when needed. Such early literacy education could seek to include parental involvement and provide opportunities for adults to develop their literacy too if they wanted to. There would in effect be a broad range of family literacy programmes within which restricted programmes would be just one variety. This would be a larger scale, more expensive option than a policy of providing restricted programmes, which claims to achieve the same with less resources.

(3) Accessibility and take-up of programmes

Even if there was an accurate method of selecting families for programmes the rhetoric glosses over some potentially fatal difficulties in practice. It cannot be taken for granted that parents will take up the programmes offered. There are several factors which might prevent this happening. First, parents may not accept that they have the educational needs which professionals ascribe to them (whether for basic literacy or other adult education). Second, even if they agree they have needs, they may not wish to do anything about them. Third, they may not wish to get involved in promoting their children's literacy. Fourth, even if none of these factors apply and parents are willing to join family literacy programmes, practical problems of programme organisation may reduce take-up. Is there research which can help assess the seriousness of these factors?

Regarding the readiness of parents to accept professionals' definitions of their educational needs, it is hard to identify directly relevant research but professional educators experienced in working with adults outside institutional settings will surely recognise that many poorly educated adults simply do not feel the needs which well-educated professionals expect them to feel. They may judge that their literacy competence is not a significant problem compared to others they face. In the US context, for example, Gadsden (1994) has suggested how this can be so.

> In low-income communities where many family literacy programs are targeted for African-American and other families of color, the programs address only a small, and, for some participants, relatively unimportant part of the problems facing them, problems that they see as centered in the ability to obtain employment. The appearance, if not reality, of a declining economy and labor force have been evidenced in low-income communities through increases in lay-offs, the reminders of 'last hired-first fired' for many people of color, a growing crisis of labor force participation among African-American males, and crime and hopelessness that occur in tandem or shortly after economic hardship and crisis.
>
> (pp. 18–19)

Suppose, in such circumstances, that parents nevertheless accept that they have literacy needs, how many are prepared to do anything about them? Research suggests that it might be only a small minority. A British study by Bynner & Fogelman (1993), using the National Child Development Study sample when adults were aged 33, found that less than one-fifth of those who reported literacy problems had ever attended an adult literacy class.

One can be more optimistic about parents' willingness to be involved in their children's literacy. Many parental involvement programmes have secured near 100% take-up and continuing high levels of participation even in neighbourhoods considered disadvantaged (Hannon, 1995). Much depends upon how parents are invited to take part, what they are asked to do, and the programme's responsiveness to different families' circumstances. The research evidence suggests that this factor does not present insuperable difficulties.

Regarding the fourth factor, whether programmes can be organised so as to be accessible in practical terms to all parents wanting to participate, there must be doubts. It is known, for example, that centre-based parent involvement programmes typically achieve lower take-up and participation rates than home-based ones. Parents' circumstances vary so much (in terms of domestic commitments, ages of children, housing, travel, and work hours if employed) that programmes which rely on only one format (e.g. a weekly daytime class) are bound to be inaccessible for some families. If the parent and child components take place simultaneously, in parallel groups, the flexibility of programmes is further reduced.

Doubts relating to these factors could be allayed if there was evidence that take-up of restricted programmes was in fact satisfactorily high. That would mean that in practice none of the factors had a seriously adverse effect. Since take-up is crucial to programme success (where it is low the programme fails even in reaching, never mind benefiting, its target group), one might expect it to have been researched across a range of programmes. This has not happened. Sometimes the issue is treated in terms of whether or not places are filled on a programme or whether families in programmes are from the target population (e.g. St Pierre et al., 1995; Brooks et al., 1996) but this provides no information about what proportion of the target group takes up the programme. Research into take-up can be difficult in that it requires a target group to be defined and its size measured or estimated, as well as some agreement about what counts as an invitation to participate, but in principle it is a perfectly researchable issue.

Meanwhile, it is interesting that the most common barriers identified by Even Start programmes in the USA, according to St Pierre et al. were 'difficulties in the recruitment, retention, attendance and motivation of families' (p. 86). In Britain, a later phase of the ALBSU initiative funded over 400 small-scale restricted programmes but an evaluation by Poulson et al. (1997) implied, even if it did not explicitly so state, that recruitment difficulties may have led some programmes to be less than frank initially with parents about their aim to help them with basic skills or to recruit parents without such needs. The rhetoric will carry more conviction when it can cite evidence that a high proportion of families judged to need restricted programmes in family literacy do take them up.

(4) Educational effects

The rhetoric of restricted programmes is quite emphatic about their effectiveness. For example, in the USA, Darling (1992) claimed that 'A recent study of Kenan Model programs has shown lasting educational benefits for both parents and children' (p. 23). Padak & Rasinski (1997) have stated, 'Family literacy programs do work, and their benefits are widespread and significant' (p. 2). In Britain, ALBSU claimed that family literacy 'shows greater gains, for adults and children, than in separate programmes, and better retention rates' (ALBSU, 1993b, p. 3).

Before turning to available research to see whether it can support such claims, it is worth pausing to ask what would count as 'success' for restricted programmes, and how rigorously it should be demonstrated. 'Success' requires, first, that children and parents derive clearly identifiable benefits from participating in programmes. However, that is not enough, for the rhetoric makes a further claim that because restricted programmes focus simultaneously on both parents and children they are more effective than programmes that focus on either parents or children separately. Thus, Darling (1992) claimed:

> Family literacy programs place equal emphasis on two generations and two goals, maximising the effects of early education for children and literacy instruction for adults. The synergy of reciprocal learning and teaching among family members creates a home environment that both supports and enhances learning.
>
> (p. 23)

Brooks & Hayes (1998) have described what is expected thus:

> high-quality, comprehensive family literacy programs should be *designed* to encourage maximum positive interaction among the parts to produce a result that is much more than the sum of the results of the separate parts. That interaction is intended to result in an added value of comprehensive family literacy programs over single-service programs, even if a family is provided all the services of family literacy program but as separate services.
>
> (Brooks & Hayes, 1998, p. 3)

In Britain, Wells (1995) explained, 'Family literacy programmes offer what the Americans describe as "double duty dollars" because they target both parents and their children' (pp. 1–2).

The suggestion here is that something extra can be expected from restricted programmes, that parents will gain more than they would from conventional adult education programmes and also that children will gain more than they would from early childhood education parental involvement programmes. If this were not so, the basic case for restricted programmes would collapse. Research, therefore, has to compare not just 'restricted programmes versus no programme' but, more importantly, 'restricted programmes versus other programmes'. Hence, it is not enough to say of restricted programmes simply that 'they work'. Rhetoric using the word 'work' implies that criteria for success are as unproblematic as those for telling whether a washing machine works. It may 'work' in the sense of meeting a narrow functional criterion but may fail in relation to other criteria or in comparison to other methods. A key question is whether restricted programmes work better than the obvious policy alternatives, which in this case is not 'no programme at all' but separate adult education and early childhood literacy parent involvement programmes or flexible family literacy programmes. A further issue is whether, as Wells (1995) has implied, restricted programmes are more cost-effective than other provision.

The most convincing way to demonstrate that any educational programme is more effective than another is through a true experimental design in which there is random allocation—in this case of families—to each programme (and to a control no-programme condition) followed by a comparison of educational outcomes across groups. It is not easy to conduct such a study in field conditions but given the resource implications of national family literacy policies one would expect it to be done. If a true experimental design cannot be followed, then a good quasi-experimental design is the next best thing. It is important to evaluate outcomes for all those invited to participate in programmes, not just those who take up an invitation and continue to participate. Evaluation should be open to the possibility (hinted at by family literacy advocates) that restricted programmes might be more effective because they have higher retention.

The quality and extent of research into restricted programme effects falls well short of what is required. Take, for example, the claim by Darling (1992) quoted earlier that there are 'lasting educational benefits for both parents and children'. No reference is given to the 'recent study' mentioned but it is presumably one reported by Seaman et al. (1991) and Seaman (1992) of 14 programmes which had concluded that the Kenan model was 'a successful intervention strategy for breaking the cycle of illiteracy which plagues millions of families in the United States' (Seaman, 1992, p. 80). Yet this 'finding' was reached without representative sampling of participants in programmes, without considering families who dropped out, without any comparison of programme participants to a control group (or even to a quasi-experimental comparison group) and without independent measures of educational outcomes. Making totally unsupported claims for the success of an educational programme without citing evidence is bad enough but to imply that there is research evidence when that evidence is seriously inadequate is perhaps worse.

Several commentators have noted the lack of research. Nickse (1993) observed that 'there is but modest evidence to date that family and inter-generational literacy programs work' (p. 34). Gadsden (1994) has commented, 'Studies that explore the parameters of literacy programs are limited, and the potential impact of the activities in them on the families that they are intended to serve is relatively unknown' (p. 2). Topping & Wolfendale (1995) commented, 'It seems that although the evaluation research on parental involvement in reading is generally positive, the picture for family literacy is still incomplete. Evaluative evidence to date is very varied in quality and quantity' (p. 31). However, since these rather bleak comments were made, findings from two well-designed evaluations of restricted programmes—one in the USA (St Pierre *et al.*, 1995) and one in England (Brooks *et al.*, 1996)—have become available.

St Pierre *et al.* (1995) reported the final evaluation of the Even Start family literacy programme. This included an experimental study in which 200 families were allocated at random to programme or control conditions. Programme effects in the experimental group were rather disappointing. There were no significant gains for parents' literacy in terms of an adult reading achievement test. Children in the programme, despite doing well in the early stages, were eventually no better than the control group on measures of emergent literacy, vocabulary and school readiness. The researchers suggest that this may be 'because control children enrolled in preschool or kindergarten, and because some Even Start children no longer participated in an Even Start early childhood program' (p. 246). Another way to interpret the findings is to see the experiment as actually a comparison between restricted programmes (prone to drop-out) and more conventional early childhood education programmes (which might well have included some parental involvement), which shows that both produce gains for children but neither is any more effective than the other. The experimental study was only one part of a larger evaluation which used data from 270 projects nation-wide in 1992–93 involving over 16,000 families. This was inevitably less rigorous than the experimental study but it did find evidence of benefits for parents and children, although none to support the claim that restricted programmes are superior to others.

Brooks *et al.* (1996) reported an evaluation of four demonstration programmes, involving over 300 families, established as part of the ALBSU initiative. The study found benefits, including gains on literacy measures, for both parents and children and a follow-up study was able to demonstrate that these were maintained 20–34 months later (Brooks *et al.*, 1997). Children's gains were shown by comparing their progress in reading test scores to that of a national sample of children tested in an earlier survey but, unlike the Even Start study, there was no direct comparison of the restricted programme with any other kinds of programme. Neither was programme take-up directly investigated. This study is in many ways a model evaluation—evidence-based, well designed, efficient in use of resources, technically highly competent and clearly reported—but its weakness is that it leaves unanswered the central question about the effectiveness of restricted programmes, namely whether or not they are any better for children or parents than stand-alone programmes or flexible family literacy programmes. It did not answer this question because it did not address it. It did not address it because ALBSU, which commissioned the research, did not ask for it to be addressed.

In summary, there is now evidence from evaluations in Britain and the USA to support claims that restricted programmes have positive educational effects for parents and children but there is none to show that they have greater effects, or are more cost-effective, than separate child-focused or adult-focused programmes. To that extent rhetoric about restricted programmes lacks research support.

(5) Socio-economic effects

Finally, one strand of family literacy rhetoric which cannot go unremarked is the extravagance of claims made for the socio-economic benefits of restricted programmes. Examples are confined to the USA and—perhaps exclusively—to the National Center for Family Literacy.

> At its most basic level, the power of family literacy is the power of change. It is enabling at-risk families with little hope to reverse the cycle of undereducation and poverty in their own lives. The empowerment they attain through the education and knowledge they acquire in a family literacy program allows them to take control of their lives, and consequently, to change the destiny of their families for generations to come.
>
> (National Center for Family Literacy, 1994, p. 1)

> Family literacy can help break the intergenerational cycle of poverty and dependency. Family literacy improves the educational opportunities for children and parents by providing both learning experiences and group support. In the process, family

literacy provides parents with skills that will improve their incomes. It provides disadvantaged children with educational opportunities that can enable them to lift themselves out of poverty and dependency.

(Brizius & Foster, 1993, p. 11)

A child's first classroom, the home, can be changed from a hopeless environment to one in which an attitude of appreciation and respect for education are modeled for the children. These changes pave the way for school successes, and thereafter life successes. The message to policy makers and legislators, then, is that family literacy can reduce the number of people on government assistance and increase the number of productive citizens.

(National Center for Family Literacy, 1994, p. 1)

In Britain, the claims have been more modest. Writing of the ALBSU initiative, Hempstedt (1995) has stated, 'We have tried to avoid some of the more inflated claims, found in some American programmes, which suggest that family literacy has the capacity to effect wider social and economic change' (p. 10).

There are several reasons to treat the US claims with caution. The long-term effects of well-designed pre-school programmes reported by Lazar *et al.* (1982) show that, although they can bring welcome socio-economic benefits for children later in life, these are not nearly as dramatic as those promised in the earlier cited quotations. Research in Britain using the National Child Development Study sample suggests that thus far education has had limited success in changing the socio-economic circumstances of families (Feinstein, 1998). Bernstein's (1970) dictum, 'Education cannot compensate for society' would be one way to summarise the position. Graff (1991) has shown that claims that literacy produces economic benefits (rather than vice versa) cannot easily be substantiated. It is likely that Freire (1972) was nearer the mark when he pointed out:

Merely teaching men [*sic*] to read and write does not work miracles; if there are not enough jobs for men able to work, teaching more men to read and write will not create them.

(Freire, 1972, p. 25)

Against this background it would be surprising if restricted programmes in family literacy were more effective than others in overcoming the effects of poverty, bearing in mind that there are unanswered questions about the take-up of such programmes and that they have not been shown to be any more effective in educational terms than other programmes. One must wonder, then, about the rhetoric which is being employed. It may be motivated by the need to secure funding from employers, business and government for specific programmes. However, as Auerbach (1995) points out, the consequences of such rhetoric could be unfortunate:

> Suggesting that enhanced family literacy interactions will break the cycle of poverty or compensate for problems facing the educational system only reinforces the ideology that blames poor people for their own problems and leaves social inequities intact.
>
> (p. 23)

Apart from the rhetoric, what?

One has to conclude that rhetoric about restricted programmes in family literacy is poorly linked to available research evidence. The rhetoric obscures research findings about family literacy as something which occurs in most families, quite independently of any programmes, and which is worth understanding better. It misleadingly suggests stronger links between parental and child literacy than actually exist. It fails to appreciate the paucity of research on take-up and participation levels and ignores that which suggests there could be serious problems. Its claims for educational effects are not supported by available evidence and its claims for socio-economic effects are implausible.

It might be objected that this verdict fails to give due recognition to the positive findings of St Pierre *et al.* (1995) and Brooks *et al.* (1996)—two well-designed studies which found benefits for children and parents in restricted programmes. However, these studies do not indicate the proportion of families willing to participate in such programmes and therefore what proportion of children and parents stand to gain—other evidence discussed suggests that it could be a rather small minority. Neither, of course, do these studies indicate that there is only one kind of family literacy programme.

This critique is not meant to deny the many positive achievements of family literacy programmes in general. The rhetoric which causes so many difficulties mainly concerns restricted programmes. Most of the problems with restricted programmes would disappear if the *insistence* on combining adult basic education with other components was dropped. This would of course make them like other forms of flexible family literacy programmes. One can imagine a range of literacy programmes for adults, including parents, in which parent involvement in children's literacy could be an *option* but not a prerequisite for entry to the programme. Ideally, it ought to be possible for all adults, including parents, to access basic education in different ways according to their interests and circumstances (Bird & Pahl, 1994). Similarly, one can imagine a range of programmes mainly concerned with children's literacy education and parental involvement in which adult basic education for parents would be an *option* for those who want it. There is very reason to incorporate adult basic education in family literacy programmes *as a response to the adults' interests*, just as it is desirable to have it as an adjunct to many forms of community education or workplace training. Parental involvement (a form of adult education in itself) is not the same as basic literacy or numerary education and should not have to be combined with it unless it clearly meets parents' interests to do so. Within the range of family literacy programmes there could be some in which, where it suited families, all components were combined in the manner of restricted programmes but this would only be one choice among many.

Relieved of the necessity to include all components in a programme there would be less need for the questionable ideology of a cycle of low literacy. Problems of recruitment and take-up could be eased and programme advocates might be under less pressure to make extravagant claims about effectiveness. There would still be problems and dilemmas common to all such programmes (e.g. relating to conceptions of literacy, avoidance of deficit characterisations of families, programme delivery, and effectiveness) but most of these have to be faced in any form of education.

There are alternatives to restricted programmes. Several models have been documented by McIvor (1990), Morrow (1995), Morrow, Tracey and Maxwell (1995), Wolfendale & Topping (1996), and Hannon (1998b). They need to be systematised and evaluated more stringently by programme developers and researchers. The family literacy policy options are certainly wider than 'restricted programmes or nothing'. The policy difficulty posed by reliance on restricted programmes is that parents' readiness to undertake a certain form of adult basic education, at a certain time and place, becomes the price of children's admission to a programme. If the parent's interest in adult basic education coincides with their interest in getting involved in their children's education then there is evidence that restricted programmes can be valuable but there is as yet no research evidence to justify such programmes being the paradigm into which all families must be squeezed.

Practice and policy needs to be informed by research into the broad category of family literacy programmes. Where possible, practitioners in the field should be supported in doing research themselves so that they can act on what they find and be better prepared to make use of other researchers' findings (Hannon, 1998a). Alternatives to restricted programmes need to be identified, documented and evaluated in terms of feasibility and outcomes and, if possible, compared to restricted programmes. The theoretical base for programme design, and particularly the vexed question of linking home and school literacies without denying the existence of either, could be helped by more research, in more communities, into existing patterns of family literacy. The issues of recruitment, take-up, participation and drop-out need to be investigated directly rather than regarded as inconvenient complications in evaluation studies. More needs to be known about programme effects, what can be expected from specific approaches used singly and in combination. The meaning of programmes to participants needs to be explicated in order to understand the effectiveness or ineffectiveness of programmes.

It is frustrating for educational researchers to see developments in their field driven by rhetoric rather than research but family literacy is not the first case of this happening and it will not be the last. Researchers are not—and, it is to be hoped, never will be—solely responsible for developments in policy and practice. However, they are responsible for the quality of their work and for showing its relation to policy and practice. It is in that spirit that this critique is offered.

Acknowledgements

I am grateful to many practitioners and researchers for discussing with me the issues addressed in this article and also to Valerie Hannon, Angela Jackson, Elaine Millard, Cathy Nutbrown and Jo Weinberger, who commented on an earlier version of the paper. Responsibility for the views expressed about research studies and for the arguments presented in the article remain with me.

References

ADULT LITERACY AND BASIC SKILLS UNIT (ALBSU) (1993a) *Framework for Family Literacy Demonstration Programmes* (London, Adult Literacy and Basic Skills Unit).

ADULT LITERACY AND BASIC SKILLS UNIT (ALBSU) (1993b) *Family Literacy News, No. 1* (London, Adult Literacy and Basic Skills Unit).

ADULT LITERACY AND BASIC SKILLS UNIT (ALBSU) (1993c) *Parents and Their Children: the intergenerational effect of poor basic skills* (London; Adult Literacy and Basic Skills Unit).

AUERBACH, E.R. (1989) Toward a social-contextual approach to family literacy, *Harvard Educational Review*, 59 pp. 165–181.

AUERBACH, E.R. (1995) Which way for family literacy: intervention or empowerment?, in: L.M. MORROW (Ed.) *Family Literacy: connections in schools and communities*, pp. 11–27 (Newark, DE, International Reading Association).

AUERBACH, E.R. (1997) Reading between the lines, in: D. TAYLOR (Ed.) *Many Families, Many Literacies: an international declaration of principles*, pp. 71–82 (Portsmouth, NH, Heinemann).

BAKER, L., SONNENSCHEIN, S., SERPELL, R., FERNANDEZ-FEIN, S. & SCHER, D. (1994) *Contexts of Emergent Literacy: everyday home experiences of urban pre-kindergarten children*, Reading Research Report No. 24 (Athens, GA/College Park, MD, National Reading Research Center).

BARTON, D. & HAMILTON, M. (1998) *Local Literacies: reading and writing in one community* (London, Routledge).

BASIC SKILLS AGENCY (1996) *Update*, No. 13 (London, Basic Skills Agency).

BERNSTEIN, B. (1970) Education cannot compensate for society, *New Society*, 26 February, pp. 344–347.

BIRD, V. & PAHL, K. (1994) Parent literacy in a community setting, *RaPAL Bulletin*, No. 24, pp. 6–15.

BRIZIUS, J.A. & FOSTER, S.A. (1993) *Generation to Generation: realizing the promise of family literacy* (Ypsilanti, MI, High/Scope Press).

BROOKS, G., GORMAN, T., HARMAN, D. & WILKIN, A. (1996) *Family Literacy Works* (London, Basic Skills Agency).

BROOKS, G., GORMAN, T., HARMAN, J., HUTCHISON, D., KINDER, K., MOOR, H. & WILKIN, A. (1997) *Family Literacy Lasts* (London, Basic Skills Agency).

BROOKS, G. & HAYES, A. (1998) Issues in Evaluating Family Literacy Programs in Britain and the United States, paper presented to the *Reading Research Conference, International Reading Association Annual Convention*, Orlando FL, 2 May.

BYNNER, J. & FOGELMAN, K. (1993) Making the grade: education and training experiences, in: E. EERRI (Ed.) *Life at 33: the fifth follow-up of the National Child Development Study* (London, National Children's Bureau).

DARLING, S. (1992) Toward a unified vision of US education, *Reading Today*, June/July p. 23.

DARLING, S. (1993a) Focus on family literacy: the national perspective, *NCFL Newsletter*, 5, p. 3.

DARLING, S. (1993b) Family literacy: an intergenerational approach to education, *Viewpoints*, 15, pp. 2–5.

DEPARTMENT FOR EDUCATION (1995) Break the vicious circle—Shephard, *News* 36/95 (Press Release) (London, Department for Education).

DEPARTMENT FOR EDUCATION AND EMPLOYMENT (1997) *Excellence in Schools* (White Paper, Cm 3681) (London, The Stationery Office).

FEINSTEIN, L. (1998) Which children succeed and why, *New Economy*, June, pp. 99–104.

FREIRE, P. (1972) *Cultural Action for Freedom* (Harmondsworth, Penguin).

GADSDEN, V. (1994) *Understanding Family Literacy: conceptual issues facing the field*, NCAL Technical Report TR94–02 (Philadelphia, PA, National Center on Adult Literacy, University of Pennsylvania).

GREGORY, E. (1996) *Making Sense of a New World: learning to read in a second language* (London, Paul Chapman).

GRAFF, H. (1991) *The Literacy Myth: cultural integration and social structure in the nineteenth century*, 2nd edn (New Brunswick, NJ, Transaction Publishers).

GRANT, A. (1997) Debating intergenerational family literacy: myths, critiques, and counterperspectives, in: D. TAYLOR (Ed.) *Many Families, Many Literacies: an International declaration of principles*, pp. 216–225 (Portsmouth, NH, Heinemann).

HANNON, P. (1995) *Literacy, home and School: research and practice in teaching literacy with parents* (London, Falmer Press).

HANNON, P. (1998a) An ecological perspective on educational research, in: J. RUDDUCK & D. MCINTYRE (Eds) *Challenges for Educational Research* (London, Paul Chapman Publishing/Sage).

HANNON, P. (1998b) How can we foster children's early literacy development through parent involvement? in: S.B. NEUMAN & K.A. ROSKOS (Eds) *Children Achieving: best practices in early literacy* (Newark, DE, International Reading Association).

HEATH, S.B. (1983) *Ways with Words: language life and work in communities and classrooms* (Cambridge, Cambridge University Press).

HEMPSTEDT, A. (1995) 'A good start for learning': family literacy work by the Basic Skills Agency, *Reading*, 29, pp. 10–14.

LAZAR, I., DARLINGTON, R., MURRAY, H., ROYCE, J. & SNIPPER, A. (1982) Lasting effects of early education, *Monographs of the Society for Research in Child Development*, 47, (2–3, Serial No. 195).

McIVOR, M.C. (1990) *Family Literacy in Action: a survey of successful programs* (Syracuse, NY, New Readers Press).

MORROW, L.M. (Ed.) (1995) *Family Literacy: connections in schools and communities.* (Newark, DE, International Reading Association).

MORROW, L.M., TRACEY, D.H. & MAXWELL, C.M. (Eds) (1995) *A Survey of Family Literacy in the United States* (Newark, DE, International Reading Association).

NATIONAL CENTER FOR FAMILY LITERACY (1994) Communicating the power of family literacy, *NCFL Newsletter*, 6, p. 1.

NICKSE, R. (1990a) Foreword, in: M.C. McIVOR, (Ed.) *Family Literacy in Action: a survey of successful programs*, pp. 4–5) (Syracuse, NY, New Readers Press).

NICKSE, R.S. (1990b) *Family and Intergenerational Literacy Programs: an update of 'Noises of Literacy'* (Columbus, OH, ERIC Clearinghouse on Adult, Career and Vocational Education, Ohio State University).

NICKSE, R.S. (1993) A typology of family and intergenerational literacy programs: implications for evaluation, *Viewpoints*, 15, pp. 34–40.

PADAK, N. & RASINSKI, T. (1997) *Family Literacy Programs: who benefits?* (Kent, OH, Ohio Literacy Resource Center (EDRS No. ED 407 568).

PERKINS, D. & MENDEL, D. (1989) *A Place to Start: the Kenan Trust family literacy project* (Louisville, KY, National Center for Family Literacy).

POULSON, L., MACLEOD, F., BENNETT, N. & WRAY, D. (1997) *Family Literacy: practice in local programmes* (London, The Basic Skills Agency).

PURCELL-GATES, V. (1995) *Other People's Words: the cycle of low literacy* (Cambridge, MA, Harvard University Press).

SEAMAN, D. (1992) Follow-up study of the impact of the Kenan Trust model of family literacy. *Adult Basic Education*, 2, pp. 71–83.

SEAMAN, D., POPP, B. & DARLING, S. (1991) *Follow-up Study of the Impact of the Kenan Trust Model for Family Literacy* (Louisville, KY, National Center for Family Literacy).

ST PIERRE, R., SWARTZ, J., GAMSE, B., MURRAY, S., DECK, D. & NICKEL, P. (1995) *National Evaluation of the Even Start Family Literacy Program* (Washington, DC, US Department of Education, Office of Policy and Planning).

TAYLOR, D. (1983) *Family Literacy: young children learning to read and write* (Exeter, NH, Heinemann).

TAYLOR, D. (Ed.) (1997) *Many Families. Many Literacies: an international declaration of principles* (Portsmouth, NH, Heinemann).

TAYLOR, D. & DORSEY-GAINES, C. (1988) *Growing up literate: learning from inner-city families* (Portsmouth, NH, Heinemann).

TEALE, W.H. (1986) Home background and young children's literacy development, in: W.H. TEALE & E. SULZBY (Eds) *Emergent Literacy: writing and reading*, pp. 173–206 (Norwood, NJ, Ablex).

TOPPING, K. & WOLFENDALE, S. (1995) The effectiveness of family literacy programmes, *Reading*, 29, pp. 26–33.

VOSS, M. (1996) *Hidden Literacies: children learning at home and at school* (Portsmouth, NH, Heinemann).

WELLS, A. (1993) Foreword to ALBSU, *Parents and Their Children: the intergenerational effect of poor basic skills* (London, Adult Literacy and Basic Skills Unit).

WELLS, A. (1995) Foreword to Basic Skills Agency, *Family Literacy Works: key findings from the NFER evaluation of the Basic Skills Agency's demonstration programmes* (London, Basic Skills Agency).

WEINBERGER, J. (1996) *Literacy goes to School: the parents' role in young children's literacy learning* (London, Paul Chapman).

WOLFENDALE, S. & TOPPING, K. (Eds) (1996) *Family Involvement in Literacy: effective partnerships in education* (London, Cassell).

11

A LONGITUDINAL STUDY OF CHILDREN'S EARLY LITERACY EXPERIENCES AT HOME AND LATER LITERACY DEVELOPMENT AT HOME AND SCHOOL

Jo Weinberger

Source: *Journal of Research in Reading* (1996) 19(1): 14–24

Introduction

Studies of early home literacy, home-school links and school reading achievements are critical for an understanding of children's early literacy development. Indeed, children spend most of their time outside school, and much of their literacy learning occurs within a family context at home. This means that information about family literacy can inform an understanding of children's development, especially if this is collected over a number of years so that continuing patterns of literacy learning can be traced. In the study reported here children with differing literacy experiences and abilities were studied from age 3, to discover what aspects of family-based literacy seemed to make a difference for literacy attainment at age 7. It investigated the likely importance for literacy development not just of school-entry factors (at age 5), as revealed by previous research, but of pre-nursery factors (at age 3) too.

Previous research

A number of lines of research are relevant to the significance of home factors for literacy development: surveys of children's development, studies of children who read early, ethnographic studies of literacy practices, studies investigating home factors and longitudinal studies.

Surveys of children's development at home that have included relevant findings about literacy, have shown a relationship between literacy achievement and social class (Douglas, 1964; Morton-Williams, 1964; Davie, Butler and Goldstein, 1972; Newson and Newson, 1968, 1977). The Newsons' work showed how involved many parents were with their children's literacy learning at home.

Studies of children who learn to read early (Durkin, 1966; Clark, 1976; Anbar, 1986) highlighted many likely contributory factors such as children being read to from a young age, reading materials in the home and parents encouraging their children's literacy. What these studies do not show is whether these experiences were also common for children who did not read early.

Ethnographic studies have provided additional insight into home literacy practices. Heath (1983) found different ways of engaging with literacy events in separate communities in the Carolinas, United States, a white and a black working class community, and teachers' families living in town. In both working class groups discontinuities between home and school often made literacy learning problematic at school. Taylor (1983) studied six middle class families living on the periphery of New York City, with a preschool child learning to read and write. She interpreted learning at home as a highly contextualised, complex cultural activity. Taylor and Dorsey-Gaines (1988), exploring home literacy in the context of lower class black children living in urban poverty in the States, found parents in their sample interested in studying. The children often engaged in reading and writing activities, which were encouraged and valued by the parents. Teale (1986) in a study of 24 pre-school children from Anglo, Black and Mexican American low-income families in San Diego found literacy occurring in all the homes, although there was considerable variation between families. Although these studies provide qualitative data on literacy learning in families in different contexts, they do not provide quantitative evidence to show its consequences for school attainment.

The effects on reading development of children reading aloud to parents has been investigated in both descriptive and intervention studies (Hewison and Tizard, 1980; Tizard, Schofield and Hewison, 1982; Hannon, 1987). Some studies have pointed to the relationship between teacher-parent contacts, and children's reading (Iverson, Brownlee and Walberg, 1981; Epstein, 1991).

Two major longitudinal studies in Britain have investigated aspects of children's home background which relate to literacy achievement. Wells (1987) reported findings from the Bristol Language Development Programme, which found that children's knowledge of literacy was the best predictor of overall achievement at age 7. Those children who knew most about literacy tended to have parents who read more and owned more books, and read more often with their children. Children with limited preschool literacy experiences had less understanding about the purposes of literacy or how to derive meaning from print than their peers. This study contributed significantly to understanding the impact of home literacy, but as its design was principally concerned with oral language, only a limited number of factors directly concerned with reading and writing were considered.

In a longitudinal study of children's school achievements and progress starting at school entry, Tizard et al. (1988) found that children who performed well on tests of literacy just before compulsory schooling were most likely to be performing well at age 7. Children of parents who provided more exposure to books and who had the most positive attitude towards helping the children at home, scored more highly on tests of reading and writing than other children. Letter identification at school entry was the strongest predictor of reading at age 7 and handwriting skills at school entry were also related to later reading. The study showed wide differences between children in their knowledge about print at school entry. This study commenced just before school entry, and did not trace the influence of very early literacy experiences on later development.

The present study aims to provide greater detail about home literacy experiences from an earlier age, and to explore their relation with literacy achievement in school.

Method

The literacy development of 42 children, at home and at school, was followed from age 3 to 7. Children attended a nursery where the writer was then a teacher. Children were involved from before the start of nursery (age 3) to the end of Infant school (age 7).

Sample

All families in the sample were white and spoke English as a first language, apart from one family where English was a second language. There were 24 boys and 18 girls: 27 were working class, and 15 middle class, by OPCS (1991) classifications.

Methods of data collection

When children were aged 3 (pre-nursery), data were collected through interviews conducted with parents at home. All the parents contacted agreed to be interviewed, and most were keen to do so, never having been asked about their children's literacy development by anyone in a professional capacity before. The interview provided information on children's family background, and issues relating to literacy resources and activities at home, including the children's access to reading and writing materials, book ownership, their experience of being read to, the parents' approach to reading and writing with their child, information and advice given to parents, details of children acting like a reader and writer and having favourite books. At age 5 (school entry), assessments were made of the children's vocabulary, writing, letter knowledge, access to stories at home and use of books in nursery. To assess vocabulary, two standardised vocabulary tests were used (English Picture Vocabulary Test, EPVT, Brimer and Dunn, 1963 and WPPSI Vocabulary Subtest, Wechsler, 1967). To assess writing, children were asked to write their first name unaided, and copy a phrase. Letter knowledge was assessed by presenting the children with letters out of alphabetical sequence, to see which they could recognise. Parents were asked if children listened to stories at home at this stage, and if so, how often. Finally, to see if children chose to look at books in nursery, teacher observations were recorded as to whether children voluntarily looked at or read books. At age 7 (end of Infant School), children were interviewed, and a second parent interview was conducted, providing updated information about families, and literacy in the home including whether the child brought books home from school, read out loud at home, listened to stories, used home computers, their involvement in literacy activities with parents, and parents' own involvement and reading and writing at home. More details are reported in Weinberger (in press).

Outcome measures for children at age 7 were the child's level of reading book, and whether the child was judged to be experiencing literacy difficulties or not; a wider range of measures are reported in more detail elsewhere (Weinberger, 1993).

Reading books were divided into 13 levels based on a system devised by Moon (1980), *Individualised Reading*. This system divided all readily available, commercially produced reading schemes, and many other children's books, into graded levels, according to the difficulty of the text. The level of reading book, which did not rely on how a child performed on the day, provided in indication of what the children were actually reading in school.

Children whose scores fell within the bottom third on two or more outcome measures of literacy were deemed to be having literacy difficulties. The outcome measures in question were children's scores on Young's Group Reading Test, (Young, 1989); a writing score including story writing, expository writing and level of independence in writing; children's level of reading book, and levels reached on Standard Assessment Tasks for English (SEAC, 1991, 1992). Children identified in this way were also those who according to teachers' judgements were experiencing problems with literacy.

Results

Pre-nursery home experiences and later reading book level

Figure 1 shows how children's reading book levels at age 7 were distributed. Predictor variables were examined in relation to reading book level. Whether children had favourite books at age 3 emerged as a significant factor. Having favourite books or not provides a composite measure of early book experience, including children's access to materials, interactions with parents, and children's own inclinations through making choices (Weinberger, 1993). The 15% of children who were reported as *not* having favourite books at age 3 had a mean reading book level of 4.9, compared to 7.8 for the others, $(F(1,40) = 9.6, p < .01)$. This is not just statistically significant. The educational significance can be seen by considering the type of book the children were reading as defined by Moon and Raban (1975). The definition for Levels 4–6, describing books read by weaker readers, is

> "Less and less dependence on illustration and consequently text is fairly limited, *vocabulary range is narrow* within a particular book. New words should be obvious from the illustration. Ideally a *text form more akin to transcribed oral language form is used rather than the standard written form.*"
>
> (p. 78) (emphasis added)

In contrast, here is the definition of Levels 7–9, describing books read by more competent readers,

> " 'Developmental reading'. Stories becoming longer, print smaller, style *conforming to standard written form, wider vocabulary*

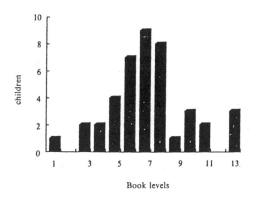

Figure 1 Level of child's reading book at age 7. Number of children = 42.

content. Most books are still short enough to be read at a sitting. Ideally these books are phrased in print format according to 'units of meaning'."

(p. 79) (emphasis added)

Children reading these books were more likely to be reading complete stories, and acquiring a richer vocabulary than children reading at lower levels.

There were other factors that seemed to be educationally significant too, in the sense that they were associated with differences of the order of at least two reading book levels. Employment and social class showed significant associations with later reading book level. Thirteen mothers were employed outside the home when the children were aged 3, mostly on a part-time, casual basis. Their children's mean reading book level was 8.7 compared with a mean level of 6.6 for the children whose mothers had not been employed, $(F(1,40) = 6.5, p < .01)$. In terms of class, children from middle class homes had a mean reading book level of 8.5, while children from working class homes had a mean level of 6.5, $(F(1,40) = 6.3, p < .05)$.

Sensitivity to rhyme has been shown in other studies to be connected with later literacy performance (Maclean, Bradley, and Bryant, 1987, Goswami and Bryant, 1990). In the present study, the children's reported knowledge of nursery rhymes was used as a measure of rhyme sensitivity. Parents of 15 children reported that they knew more than a dozen nursery rhymes at age 3. Their children later had a mean reading book level of 8.5. The remaining children knew fewer rhymes and had a mean reading level of 6.5, $(F(1,40) = 3.9, p < .05)$. For very young children, much of their knowledge of nursery rhymes was likely to come from experiences at home.

Whether the child was a library member at age 3 showed a relationship with the level of reading book. It was the child's parents who would have chosen whether to enrol their child in the library. Only 11 children were library members at this stage. Their later reading book level was 8.7, compared with a level of 6.7 for the other children, $(F(1,40) = 3.9, p < .05)$. Other studies have also reported the significance of access to books via the library (for example, Clark, 1976).

Parents were asked what sorts of material they read with their children. Six children were not read to from books containing stories. They later had a lower mean level of reading book than the other children (a level of 5.3 compared with 7.6, $F(1, 40) = 3.9 p < .05$).

These findings suggest that parents' interactions with books with their children had a positive influence on later literacy development. Those children with the least experience of books at home at age 3 (without favourite books, not having access to library books, and without being read to from storybooks), were the children faring less well with their reading at school at age 7.

School entry measures (age 5) and later reading book level (age 7)

Several assessments of children's literacy achievements at school entry related significantly to their reading book level at age 7. The highest correlation was for the WPPSI Vocabulary Subtest, $r = 0.55$, $p < .001$, and for the EPVT, $r = 0.53$, $p < .001$. Also highly significant was the child's ability to write their first name, $r = 0.53$, $p < .001$. The children's ability to write their name at this stage would have been influenced by their own inclinations and abilities, but also by the help and guidance of supportive adults. During parent interviews, 33 said they were helping their child to write their name. Also highly significant was the relationship between whether the child knew some letters or not and the level of reading book at age 7, $r = .51$, $p < .001$. This relationship has also been reported by other studies (Muehl and DiNello, 1976, Zifcak, 1981, Wells, 1987, Tizard et al., 1988, Blatchford, 1991). The children's ability to copy a phrase was significantly related to later reading book level. Those that could do so later had a mean reading level of 8.0 compared with a mean level of 6.3, ($F(1,39) = 5.0$, $p < .05$). This assessment gave an indication of the child's familiarity with reproducing standard letter shapes. Blatchford (1991) reported similar results. This finding indicates the interrelatedness of reading and writing.

Parents were asked how frequently children listened to stories at home. Fifteen children did so at least once a day, and they had a higher mean reading book level (8.1) than those for whom this was more infrequent, (6.5, $F (1,39) = 4.4$, $p < .05$). Children's familiarity and enjoyment of books at home probably made the children more likely to choose to look at books on their own when they came to nursery. Twenty-nine of the 42 children did so of their own initiative, and this was significantly associated with the level of reading book at age 7 (mean reading levels of 8.0 and 5.5, $F(1,40) = 9.4$, $p < .01$).

Home experiences at age 7 and reading book level

A number of home experiences at age 7 related to the children's reading book level. Fourteen of the children had access to a computer at home at this stage. Many parents gave examples of how this helped the children's literacy. This opportunity, provided by parents, made a significant impact on children's reading book level, with the children having a mean reading book level of 8.1 compared with a mean level of 5.5 for the other children, ($F(1,40) = 11.4$, $p < .01$). It is not however clear from this study whether it was the interaction with the computer as such that was important, or whether this provided a proxy variable referring to some underlying feature of the home, for instance the level of resourcing or interest in education.

Parent's perceptions of their role with regard to literacy and school were significant in relation to children's level of reading book. Only 12 of the 42 parents felt they knew how reading was taught in school. Their children had a mean reading book level of 8.9 compared with the mean level of the other children of 6.6, $(F(1,40) = 4.4$, p $<.01)$. Other research (Tizard et al., 1988) has reported similar findings. Similarly, only 10 parents said they knew about writing in school. Their children had a mean reading book level of 8.7, while the other children had a mean level of 6.8, $(F(1,40) = 4.4$, p $<.05)$. It is not surprising that the connection was stronger with reading, but the fact that there was a relationship points to the inter-connectedness of reading and writing, and to school communication with parents having a relationship with children's progress.

Thus those parents who had more knowledge of school literacy practices tended to have children with a higher level of reading book at this stage. This is in keeping with findings elsewhere that parent teacher contact can have a positive affect on children's reading (Iverson et al., 1981, Epstein, 1991).

At age 7, most of the children, at least occasionally, took books from school and read at home. Teachers were asked about which children did so, and they only mentioned four children that never did so. These latter children had a lower mean level of reading book, 4.7, compared with a mean of 7.5 for the rest, $(F(1,40) = 4.2$, p $<.05)$. Those children who could have most benefited from assistance with school initiated reading at home were those whom the teachers thought were not being given this help.

Children were asked if they were aware of seeing someone reading at home. Two-thirds (28) of the children said they were. Their mean reading book level, at 7.9, was higher than that for the other children, at 5.9, $(F(1,40) = 6.5$, p $<.01)$. In this way, parents, acting as models for literacy, probably had an impact on the children's reading at school.

Taken as a whole, these findings show a significant relationship between parent and family context and children's level of reading at school. Children reading well were those whose literacy was resourced at home, allowing them experience of favourite books; whose parents read stories to them, and who, maybe as a consequence, chose to look at books in nursery. The children saw their parents read at home, and the parents themselves had some idea about literacy teaching in school.

Children with literacy difficulties

In educational terms, it is helpful to know whether there are factors likely to predict literacy problems at age 7. In this study, fourteen children were identified (using a process described in the method section of this paper) as having particular literacy problems. Analyses, using non-parametric measures of association, revealed that the same factors relating to reading book level also related specifically to a statistically significant degree (p <.001) to children with literacy difficulty, namely their vocabulary score (EPVT), how well they could write their name, copy a phrase, and whether they knew some letters or not. Other factors which related to reading book level to a statistically significant degree (p <.01) were whether the child had favourite books at age 3, and the number of nursery rhymes the child knew, the children's vocabulary score (WPPSI Vocabulary Subtest), and whether they chose to look at books at nursery. Parents of children having difficulties were less likely to know how reading was taught in school and therefore less in a position to know how to offer help with literacy problems at school.

However, additional factors also emerged. Children with literacy difficulties were less likely to read out loud to someone frequently at home, ($\chi^2(1) = 8.9$, p <.01), and were less likely, according to their teacher, to take school reading books home, ($\chi^2(1) = 5.8$, p <.01). Thus the more problems children had, the less likely they were to read voluntarily, so making it hard to get the practice they needed to improve. Their parents were also amongst those who, when asked questions relating to day-to-day literacy learning activities at home, were not able to provide examples, ($\chi^2(1) = 5.8$, p <.01). It may well be that this reflected a lack of parental awareness about children's literacy learning.

Resourcing of literacy was relevant here. Children with literacy problems owned on average fewer books than other children at this stage, ($\chi^2(2) = 7.1$, p <.05), and were less likely to have access to a computer at home at age 7, ($\chi^2(1) = 3.9$, p <.05). These factors were also reflected in the teachers' judgement that these children were receiving less support for literacy from home than the other children ($\chi^2(1) = 3.6$, p <.05).

The picture which emerges of children with literacy difficulties is that they come from homes where there were fewer literacy resources (books, computers), the children read less, and had less support generally for literacy at home. Their parents knew less than others about literacy in school, and were less likely to be able to give examples of everyday literacy occurring at home.

Discussion

The study highlights a number of home factors which would merit further investigation. It suggests the significance of texts in relation to literacy learning, from children having favourite books at age 3, to the book they were actually reading at school at age 7, for children's literacy development. Whether or not a child had favourite books before entry to nursery was identified as showing a correlation with children's later literacy development. This is a new finding, which could merit further research to explore and explain the distinctive contribution of this factor. The use of child's level of reading book at age 7 as an outcome measure has the advantage of revealing the types of texts children of different abilities actually used. Since assigning levels of difficulty to reading books is a system used in many schools, this could be adopted in future studies.

What this study does is point to the need for literacy learning that takes place in families to be made more visible to teachers, so that it can be built on, and enhanced, at school. In practical terms, it would, for instance, be beneficial for children's literacy for teachers to talk with parents about literacy occurring as a part of everyday family activities at home, and the parent's role in providing resources and opportunities, acting as a model for literacy, and interacting with their child on literacy. Teachers could provide more information to all parents about the literacy teaching in school. In encouraging reading books to go home, it would be helpful if teachers ensured all children were reminded that they could take their book.

For early years teachers, it would seem to be particularly beneficial to find out more about the home experiences of children who did not choose books for themselves in a nursery setting. It would also be useful to discover how many rhymes the children knew already, and to encourage saying rhymes at home, particularly for those children whose experience here was limited. Teachers could also find out about children's storybook experience at home, and opportunities for writing, and add encouragement. Teachers of young children could ask parents about children's favourite books. For those without favourites, teachers could suggest the family borrow books, show parents the range of books available for young children, and explain the importance of children having the opportunity and encouragement to choose a favourite book for later literacy development.

Conclusions

Many of the children's previous experiences were significantly related to their literacy achievements by the age of 7.

Some of the preschool factors that were significantly related to later attainment were whether children had favourite books at age 3 (a predictor that has not been reported in previous studies), whether parents read to them from storybooks or not, and how many nursery rhymes they knew.

Measures at school entry that were predictors of children's literacy development at age 7 confirmed findings from previous studies: vocabulary scores on standardised texts, letters known, and name and phrase writing. In addition, whether children chose to look at books at nursery, how often they were read to at home, and whether they could attend to stories at nursery were also significant.

Once the children were in school other factors of significance were whether their parents knew how reading and writing were taught in school, and if the child had access to a computer at home.

For children with particular literacy difficulties, what was significant was whether they took a reading book home from school, the frequency with which children read to their parents, and whether parents could provide examples of everyday literacy activities at home.

These quantitative correlations imply the likelihood of a positive contribution of home factors in children's literacy development. They confirm findings by others, and highlight new factors of significance, including the influence of children having favourite books *prior* to school entry. The study paves the way for further qualitative research to show in more detail how home factors have a significant part to play in early literacy development.

References

ANBAR, A. (1986) Reading acquisition of pre-school children without systematic instruction, *Early Childhood Research Quarterly*, 1, 1, 69–83.

BLATCHFORD, P. (1991) Children's writing at seven years: associations with handwriting on school entry and pre-school factors. *British Journal of Educational Psychology*, 61, 73–84.

BRIMER, A. and DUNN, L. (1963) *English Picture Vocabulary Test (EPVT)*. Windsor, Berks: NFER.

CLARK, M.M. (1976) *Young Fluent Readers*. London: Heinemann Educational Books.

DAVIE, R., BUTLER, N. and GOLDSTEIN, H. (1972) *From Birth to Seven*. London: Longman.

DOUGLAS, J.W.B. (1964) *The home and the school: a study of ability and attainment in the primary school*. London: MacGibbon and Kee.

DURKIN, D. (1966) *Children who Read Early*. New York: Teachers College Press.

EPSTEIN, J.L. (1991) Effects of parent involvement on change in student achievement in reading and math. In Silvern, S. (ed.), *Literacy through Family, Community, and School Interaction*. Greenwich, Conn.: Jai.

GOSWAMI, U. and BRYANT, P. (1990) *Phonological Skills and Learning to Read*. Hove, East Sussex: Lawrence Erlbaum Associates.

HANNON, P. (1987) A study of the effects of parental involvement in the teaching of reading on children's reading test performance. *British Journal of Educational Psychology*, 57, 1, 56–72.

HEATH, S.B. (1983) *Ways with words: language, life and work in communities and classrooms*. Cambridge: Cambridge University Press.

HEWISON, J. and TIZARD, J. (1980) Parental involvement and reading attainment. *British Journal of Educational Psychology*, 50, 209–215.

IVERSON, B.K., BROWNLEE, G.D. and WALBERG, H.J. (1981) Parent-teacher contacts and student learning. *Journal of Educational Research*, 24, 6, 394–396.

MACLEAN, M., BRYANT, P. and BRADLEY, L. (1987) Rhymes, Nursery Rhymes and Reading in Early Childhood. *Merrill-Palmer Quarterly*, 33, 3, 255–281.

MOON, C. (1980) *Individualised Reading.* Reading: Centre for the Teaching of Reading, University of Reading.

MOON, C. and RABAN, B. (1975) *Question of Reading.* London: Ward Lock Educational.

MORTON-WILLIAMS, R. (1967) The 1964 National Survey among parents of primary school children. In D.E.S. (1967), *Children and their Primary Schools, Vol. 2, Research and Surveys.* London: HMSO.

MUEHL, S. and DINELLO, M.C. (1976) Early first-grade skills related to subsequent reading performance: A seven-year follow-up study. *Journal of Reading Behaviour,* 8, 67–81.

NEWSON, J. and NEWSON, E. (1968) *Four Years Old in an Urban Community.* London: Allen and Unwin.

NEWSON, J. and NEWSON, E. with BARNES, P. (1977) *Perspectives on School at Seven Years Old.* London: Allen and Unwin.

Office of Population, Censuses and Surveys (OPCS) (1991) *Standard Occupational Classification.* London: HMSO.

School Examinations and Assessment Council (SEAC) (1991, 1992) *Standard Assessment Tasks.* London: HMSO.

TAYLOR, D. (1983) *Family literacy: young children learning to read and write.* London: Heinemann Educational Books.

TAYLOR, D. and DORSEY-GAINES, C. (1988) *Growing up Literate: learning from inner-city families.* Portsmouth, N.H.: Heinemann.

TEALE, W.H. (1986) Home background and young children's literacy development. In Teale, W.H. and Sulzby, E. (eds.), *Emergent Literacy.* Norwood, N.J.: Ablex.

TIZARD, B., BLATCHFORD, P., BURKE, J., FARQUHAR, C. and PLEWIS, I. (1988) *Young Children at School in the Inner City.* Hove and London: Lawrence Erlbaum Associates.

TIZARD, J., SCHOFIELD, W.N. and HEWISON, J. (1982) Collaboration between teachers and parents in assisting children's reading. *British Journal of Educational Psychology,* 52, 1–15.

WECHSLER, D. (1967) *WPPSI Manual (Wechsler Preschool and Primary Scale of Intelligence).* New York: The Psychological Corporation.

WEINBERGER, J. (1993) *A Longitudinal Study of Literacy Experiences, the Role of Parents, and Children's Literacy Development.* Division of Education, University of Sheffield: Unpublished Ph.D. thesis.

WEINBERGER, J. (in press) *Literacy Goes to School.* London: Paul Chapman.

WELLS, G. (1987) *The Meaning Makers: children learning language and using language to learn.* London: Hodder and Stoughton.

YOUNG, D. (1989, 3rd edition) *Manual for the Group Reading Test.* Sevenoaks: Hodder and Stoughton.

ZIFCAK, M. (1981) Phonological awareness and reading acquisition. *Contemporary Educational Psychology,* 6, 117–126.

12

LITERACY OBJECTS AS CULTURAL TOOLS

Effects on children's literacy behaviors in play

Susan B. Neuman and Kathy Roskos

Source: *Reading Research Quarterly* (1992) 27: 203–225

While a great deal of attention has been drawn to the pedagogical, psychological, and social factors involved in learning to read, the organizational dimensions that might influence children's opportunities to actively engage in literacy learning have remained relatively unexplored. Rarely has the impact of the ways in which the literacy environment is structured been considered, though evidence suggests that such considerations may be critically important (Atwell, 1987; Graves, 1983; Morrow & Weinstein, 1986). Weinstein's (1979) integrative review of the impact of classroom environments, for example, reveals a limited body of knowledge regarding how the physical features of classrooms and settings may be constructed to enhance learning.

Acknowledging the importance of the environment-behavior relationship, recent research on early childhood has taken a more "ecological" perspective, attempting to describe how particular environments, communities as well as classrooms, might impact children's behavior as it naturally occurs (Fernie, 1985; Gump, 1989). This approach is based on the work of ecological psychologists who posit that individuals and environments are interdependent: Human behavior not only influences the surrounding environment but is influenced by it (Barker, 1978; Barker & Wright, 1951). Human ecologists, as well (Brofenbrenner, 1977; Day, 1983), conceive of environments as interrelated at many different contextual levels, from microsystems (e.g., schools) to macrosystems (e.g., culture). Each level of context and its participants transact, affecting and being affected by each other.

In particular, ecologists have examined early childhood classroom indoor play environments to explore those features of architecture and settings that may enhance the value of play in children's development. Their research suggests that variables of materials and setting exert a strong pull on the nature and quality of children's learning through play (Fein, 1975; Quilitch & Risley, 1973; Vandenberg, 1981). For example, in a study by Fein (1975), when abstract blocks were replaced with realistic replicas of objects, the quality of young children's pretend play was enhanced.

That the physical environment may "coerce" behavior (Gump, 1989) has important implications for literacy learning in early childhood as well. With physical design changes in play environments, we may be able to extend the range of literacy opportunities for young children and thereby encourage developmentally appropriate literacy activities. For example, in a preliminary study examining the impact of literacy-enriched play areas on children's literacy behaviors, we found that preschool children spontaneously used almost twice as much print in their play than prior to the environmental intervention (Neuman & Roskos, 1990b). Given the potential of environmental factors for learning, then, changes in the structural features of the play environment that are literacy based may have important consequences for children's emerging conceptions of literacy.

Of course, play as a process in and of itself provides a particularly rich medium for children's exploration of literacy: its cultural roles, routines, scripts, and tools (Roskos, 1987). As a medium for exploration, play has been described as providing a "courage all its own" (Bruner, 1983). Liberated from situational constraints, children in play are free to construct microworlds in which actions and objects need not conform to reality or convention. For example, in the play context a toy block may become a telephone or a car or whatever meaning is instrumental to the play sequence.

In their transforming of one thing into another, children are thought to begin to separate meaning from objects, providing the foundation for understanding other representational systems, like written language (Piaget, 1962; Vygotsky, 1962). To anchor the transformation, the process appears to require initially a relatively familiar context with common objects, that is, good exemplars of a general category (Fein, 1975). Once children's mental representations are well established, objects and contexts may be replaced by more abstract forms.

Experimental studies in free play settings generally confirm the use of objects as substitutes or "meaning-markers" (Vygotsky, 1962). Young children tend to show richer and more elaborated sequences of play with highly prototypical objects (Fein & Robertson, 1975; McLoyd, 1983). Correspondingly, there is some evidence that the relationship of pretend behavior to object prototypicality may change between the ages of 4 and 8 when children's language becomes explicit enough to convey the meaning of objects without their physical presence (Pulaski, 1973).

Although much of the research on play transformations has concentrated on the quality of pretend play (Chaille, 1978; El'Konin, 1966), a number of recent studies have focused on how the uses of objects and symbolic transformation in play contexts may influence children's emerging conceptions of literacy (see reviews by Christie & Johnsen, 1983; Pellegrini, 1985). One type of analysis, for example, looks at the transformational process per se, and examines the predictive relations between symbolic play and early literacy. This research is based on the theoretically demonstrated parallels between the use of symbols in play and the use of signs in emergent reading processes (Pellegrini, 1980, 1985). In recent longitudinal studies, however, Pellegrini and his associates (Galda, Pellegrini, & Cox, in press; Pellegrini, Galda, Dresden, & Cox, 1990) found that although symbolic transformations predict emergent writing status, they do not predict emergent reading status or oral language related to reading. This finding led the authors to suggest that reading and writing may have different ontological roots.

A second type of analysis has been more ecological in orientation, examining the influence of literacy objects within the play environment on children's playful literacy behaviors. This research is based on the premise that by using literacy-related objects in play environments, young children will engage in "run-ups" to literacy (Bruner, 1984) in their early attempts to understand it as a "pattern of discourse" (Goelman, 1984). Research of this type was initiated on the basis of observational studies documenting children's natural engagement in literacy-like tasks in play (Jacob, 1984; Neuman, 1991; Roskos, 1987).

Most surveys, however, indicate that there is a paucity of literacy objects and materials in child care settings which have been purposely designed to facilitate natural interactions with written language (Morrow, 1990a; Robinson, 1990; Schickedanz, 1986). Consequently, to examine the influence of objects on children's emerging concepts of literacy, several studies have attempted to enrich particular play centers with literacy materials (Neuman & Roskos, 1990a; Morrow, 1990a; Vukelich, 1989). Vukelich (1989), for example, transformed two play centers into a flower shop with sales forms and receipts and a bank with literacy materials including withdrawal slips, instructions on how to use a cash machine, and loan application forms. Similarly, Morrow (1990b) created a veterinary corner, with forms and books to accompany the play. Although these enriched environments produced more literacy-related play, it is not clear whether the settings and related objects in these studies represent prototypical contexts and objects of meaning to young children. Thus, the utility of these objects in building up stores of represented meanings to be used at some later time in more abstract forms of literacy use may be limited.

In contrast, the research reported here was designed to analyze the influence of physical design changes in the play environment through the insertion of common literacy-related objects in prototypical contexts on preschoolers' literacy behaviors in spontaneous free play. The settings and literacy objects were designed to serve as pivots for children to develop an array of new strategies, associations, and behavioral prototypes that might later be used in other contexts. Further, we questioned whether the inclusion of typical literacy objects in play settings might produce more sustained and elaborated sequences of literacy in play, as reported in our previous research (Neuman & Roskos, 1990a, 1990b). Specifically then, the study was designed to answer the following questions:

1 Do play settings enriched with literacy objects influence the frequency of literacy demonstrations in the spontaneous play of preschoolers?
2 Does the inclusion of literacy objects in play environments influence the duration and complexity of literacy-related free play?
3 How are literacy objects used in children's spontaneous play?

Studies of ecological influences in children's play have noted the important distinction between play and exploration with objects (Berlyne, 1960; Hutt, 1979). Reflecting a locus-of-control factor, in exploration the child asks, "What can this object do?", whereas in play the question becomes "What can I do with this object?" Over time, exploration, which is dominated by children's actions, is thought to decrease while the amount of time spent playing with an object, using more explicit language, is said to increase (Hutt & Bhavnani, 1976). Consequently, this research was conducted over a 7-month period to allow sufficient time for the novelty of objects to wear off.

Method

Subjects and setting

Ninety-one preschoolers, 3–5 years old, from two day-care centers in an urban metropolitan area participated in the study. Each center served families from diverse ethnic backgrounds; the sample included 62% Caucasian, 31% Black, 5% Southeast Asian, and 2% Hispanic children.

Ms. K., the Program Director, administered both day-care centers, which were located in close proximity to each other. Programs were similar in philosophical orientation: Children were encouraged to select many of their own activities from a variety of learning areas, to be physically and mentally active, and to learn through active exploration and interaction with adults, other children, and materials. Both programs were state licensed and met the accreditation standards of the National Academy of Early Childhood Programs. Each program included a teacher-to-child ratio of 1:10, a planned curriculum incorporating science, social studies, language, art, and motor coordination activities integrated throughout the day, and approximately 180 minutes per day for indoor and outdoor free play.

The sites were similar in their physical organization of play areas. Book corners, housekeeping areas, blocks, small manipulatives, and art centers were placed around the perimeter of each classroom with an open space in the middle of the room. Although typical play objects were plentiful in both sites, few literacy-related objects, aside from books in the book corner and paper at the arts and crafts table, were readily accessible to children. Both centers, however, did include some print displays such as the alphabet, chart stories, and lists of children's names. Figures 1 and 2 illustrate these classroom settings.

Centers were randomly selected into nonintervention (Site A) and intervention (Site B) classrooms. Forty-five children (25 boys, 20 girls), with a mean age of 4.17, were in Site A, and 46 children (24 boys, 22 girls), mean age 3.68, were in Site B.

To obtain some measure of prior knowledge in literacy and comparability across the two sites, the Test of Early Reading Ability (TERA) (1981) was individually administered to each child in the sample. Designed to assess reading behaviors that emerge during the preschool years, the 5-to-10-minute test measures children's ability to attribute meaning to printed symbols and the functions of print, their knowledge of the alphabet, and their understanding of the conventions of print. A t test indicated no statistically significant differences between intervention and nonintervention groups ($t = 1.23$, $df = 83$, ns). Descriptive statistics for participant children in the two sites are presented in Table 1.

Procedures

Table 2 details the time-sampling schedule and specific tasks of the study. Prior to the intervention phase of the study, two measures of literacy behavior in play were obtained to examine the frequency of literacy demonstrations in preschoolers' spontaneous play and the uses of literacy-related objects in four play settings: housekeeping, book corner, small manipulatives, and arts/crafts table.

Four graduate students in early childhood education and reading were trained over three 1-hour sessions to observe and record the number of literacy demonstrations each child engaged in during free play. Literacy demonstrations (Neuman & Roskos, 1990b; Roskos, 1990) were defined as instances of handling (focusing on the physical exploration of a literacy object), reading (attributing meaning to printed marks or symbols), and writing (attempting to use printed marks as a form of communication). Using videotapes from earlier research (Neuman & Roskos, 1990b), observers practiced identifying and tallying observable demonstrations in each category. Intercoder reliability indicated .97 agreement between observers following the training period.

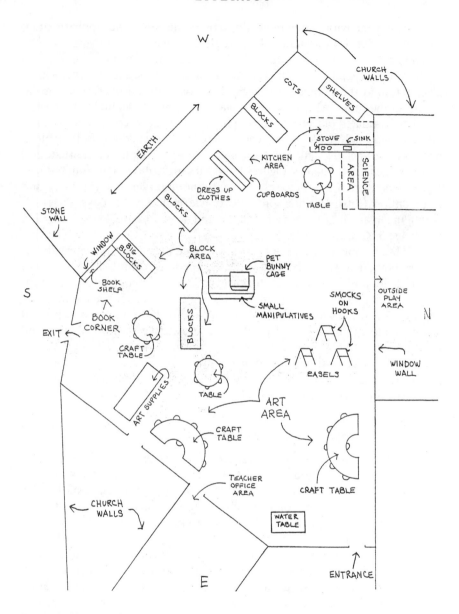

Figure 1 Classroom A: nonintervention classroom

Over a 2-week period, each child's play was observed and the number of literacy demonstrations was tallied during four 15-minute segments of spontaneous play, for a total of 60 minutes of play observed per child.

To examine the uses of literacy-related objects, children's spontaneous play activity was videotaped for 30 minutes, four different times, in four

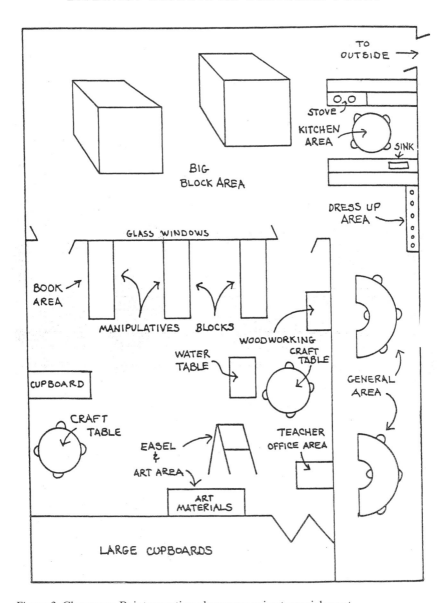

Figure 2 Classroom B: intervention classroom prior to enrichment

different areas (housekeeping, book corner, small manipulatives, and arts/crafts table) for a total of 2 hours per play area. Rather than focusing on an individual child, the goal of the videotaping was to obtain samples of children's play themes and their uses of objects in play.

Videotaping was conducted by two graduate students in communications

Table 1 Description of the sample

Center	Site	
	Nonintervention (Site A)	*Intervention (Site B)*
Ethnicity	Number of children	
Caucasian	27	29
Black	14	14
Hispanic	1	1
Asian	3	2
Gender		
Male	25	24
Female	20	22
Age	Means (and *SD*s)	
Male	4.34 (0.59)	3.72 (0.70)
Female	3.98 (0.77)	3.63 (0.51)
	Percentile scores (and *SD*s)	
Test of Early Reading Ability (TERA)	41.25 (29.90)	35.22 (24.87)

who had previous experience in videotaping play behavior in early childhood settings. Both had been trained to identify play themes, using videotapes and transcripts from earlier research (Roskos, 1987). Prior to the data collection period, both familiarized themselves with the sites, noting play tendencies and potential technical problems, such as light levels, traffic patterns during play time, and acoustics. On the basis of this information, a strategy was developed for videotaping play themes as they naturally occurred in both intervention and nonintervention sites.

Using a camcorder and a microphone system,[1] the two worked in tandem, skirting a preselected play area for a 30-minute time period. If the children began a play topic, but then abandoned it in less than 30 minutes, the two remained in the area to fulfill the time period. If the children initiated a play theme, then left the area to pursue it, the pair would follow the children in an effort to capture the play action and language. Thus, it was possible for the video recorders to successfully video children's play actions and language as they naturally occurred, without confining children's play to predetermined areas or requiring them to wear individual microphones.

Intervention design

Investigations of play activity reveal that children create play contexts, situations, and plans based on what they already know, using objects to support this endeavor (Bruner, 1983; Fein, 1975; Garvey, 1977). Studies

Table 2 Time line of study

Tasks	Months								
	1	2	3	4	5	6	7	8	9
Gathering baseline data									
Administration of TERA	• (Month 1)								
Observations of individual children's play behavior	• (Month 1)								
Videotape observations of 4 play areas	• (Month 1)								
Intervention	•————(1.5 weeks)————————————————————•(7.5 Months)								
Mid-enrichment phase									
Videotape samples of play activities in centers			•——————•(Month 3 + 4)					
Late-enrichment phase									
Videotape samples of play activities					•————(Month 5.5–6.5)————•(7.5 Months)			
Observations of individual children's play behavior							•(7.5 Months)		
Analysis of data									
ANCOVA pre/post observations								•(Month 8)	
Identification and analysis of play frames (216)								•——•(Month 8–8.5)	
Identification of literacy-related play frames (74)								•(Month 8.5)	
Sampling and transcription of 5 literacy-related play frames from baseline, mid-enrichment, and late-enrichment								(Month 8.5–9) •——•	
Coding of frames into behavioral units									•(Month 9)

indicate that spatial organization, the functional complexity of play materials, and classroom organization influence the quality of play in an environment (Emmerich, 1977; Hutt, 1979; McLoyd, 1983; Proshansky & Wolfe, 1975). Specifically, the more familiar the children are with play contexts and their corresponding objects, the more they tend to play in increasingly complex ways, using elaborated language in the process.

Considering the importance of familiarity, informal discussions were held with day-care teachers and with parents to determine what literacy contexts and objects were already known to the children. In addition, baseline videotapes were scanned to note children's play preferences, interests, and instances of literacy behaviors. Such information provided clues as to potential play settings, literacy objects, and spatial arrangements that might be particularly appealing and familiar from the child's point of view.

On the basis of existing research and specific site-based information, three principles of design were established in planning the literacy enrichment in the intervention site.

> Principle #1: For literacy enrichment purposes, the play space should be arranged so as to encourage sustained play interactions, yet allow for adequate adult presence and supervision.

Research on the characteristics of play environmental design has demonstrated that small, intimate play areas encourage more interactive and sustained play activity (Neill, 1982; Zifferblatt, 1972). Day-care teachers in our study, however, expressed concern that if play spaces were too private, teachers could not adequately monitor children's play activities. To accommodate these concerns yet allow for more intimacy in various play areas, the play space was more sharply defined, using semifixed features such as cupboards, screens, tables, directional signs, and hanging mobiles.

In addition, items in the children's play environment were inventoried and labelled in ways that resembled real-world print displays. For example, storage bins for small manipulatives were identified by print and picture much like hardware store items. Art materials were identified by means of a large chart that contained printed names of items and their corresponding pictures. Teachers were also encouraged to display the children's drawings and writing attempts throughout the play environment. Directional signs (words + pictures + arrows) were strategically placed about the environment to serve as reference points for locations. In these ways, the environment was spatially organized using print and picture.

> Principle #2: The literacy enrichment should include play settings that reflect authentic literacy contexts in the children's real-world environment and are natural adaptations of existing play areas.

Since young children seem to play best about what they know, literacy-enriched play settings were created that reflected real-life literacy situations for these children. For instance, parents and teachers reported that the children had considerable background about libraries and offices, having frequently visited these settings as a part of their day-care and real-world experiences. Many of them, however, had much less experience with post offices or banks, since they spent most of their day in the day-care setting.

Further, concerned that abrupt changes in play areas might prove overwhelming to the children, day-care teachers suggested that rather than create a totally new environment, we modify or enhance existing centers to include more literacy. On the basis of these considerations, three play settings were developed: the kitchen/house setting, the cozy corner library, and the office. These centers resembled contexts where children might have witnessed or experienced literacy activities, according to their parents and day-care teachers. Thus the centers were designed to capitalize on print contexts already known to the children.

> Principle #3: The literacy enrichment should include a network of common literacy objects in appropriate contexts that are safe for children to use.

Since object familiarity appears to be instrumental in the early phases of symbolization and meaning-making (Vygotsky, 1962), an essential criterion in choosing literacy objects was that they be prototypical of children's experiences in similar contexts in their daily lives. For example, items in the kitchen/house center included cookbooks, coupons, recipe cards, actual grocery packages, children's books, and materials for list-making, such as pencils and notepads. In short, we attempted to insert familiar literacy objects into equally familiar print-based contexts for these children, with the idea that these ecological factors might assist children's meaning-making with literacy in their play.

Three additional criteria drawn from our earlier work also guided the insertion of literacy objects into each play center: appropriateness (item naturally and safely used by young children), authenticity (a real item in the child's general environment), and utility (item useful to children in their imitative literacy attempts) (Neuman & Roskos, 1990a). Table 3 gives a comparison of the nonliteracy and literacy-related objects and settings in Site A and Site B before and after intervention.

No changes in the play environment were made at the nonintervention site; teachers were encouraged to organize play areas "as usual." Floor plans illustrating the design differences in the play environment of Site B after enrichment are shown in Figure 3. Changes in the structural configuration of the classroom remained stable throughout the study.

During free play periods, teachers and aides in both sites were encouraged

Table 3 Nonliteracy and literacy objects in targeted play areas by site before and after enrichment

Play area	Before enrichment				After enrichment			
	Site A		Site B		Site A		Site B	
	Nonliteracy objects	Literacy objects	Nonliteracy objects	Literacy objects	Nonliteracy objects	Literacy objects	Nonliteracy objects	Literacy objects
Housekeeping	kitchen setup pots/pans plastic fruit tableware	none	kitchen setup pots/pans plastic fruit tableware	none	same	same	same + tree telephone	books (10 est.) telephone book cookbooks (5) recipe cards small plaques stationary coupons store ads play money grocery packages message board calendars notepads pens, pencils markers decals
Book corner	bean bag chair small chairs	books (12 est.) ABC chart	bean bag chair child's rocker book rack	books (8 est.) wall poster	same	same	couch area rug tree telephone table	return cards library stamps books (70 est.) bookmarks magazines pens, pencils markers paper signs calendars

Manipulatives	Legos
	lock-blocks
	beads
	plastic
	  animals
	straws
	small
	  blocks
		none	same	same +
				buttons
					telephone book
					wall posters
					file folders
					stickers
					labelled bins
					magazines
					maps
					paper
					pencils

Arts/crafts	easel paints brushes paper aprons	none	same	same	inventory art posters pencils labelled supplies

Office	—	—	—	table
				chairs
				telephone
				computer
				  keyboard
				file racks
				in/out trays
				clipboards
				plastic clips
				small bins
					calendars
					appointment
					  book
					message pads
					  (10 est.)
					signs
					books
					pamphlets
					magazines
					file folders
					business cards
					forms
					ledger sheets
					paper
					pencils, pens
					markers
					small notebooks
					stencils

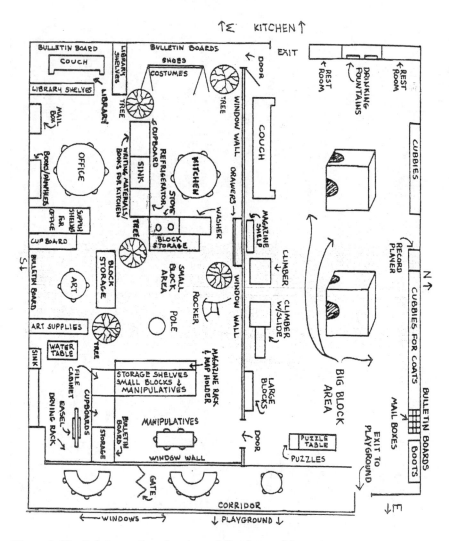

Figure 3 Site B: intervention classroom following enrichment

not to restrict any play areas, but to allow children to move about freely in all the play settings. The role of the adult in these sites was to set the stage and observe children's play; rarely did adults directly intervene in the play activity.

Over the next 6 months, videotaped samples of children's spontaneous free play in the newly established kitchen/house, library, and office settings at Site B and the housekeeping, book corner, small manipulatives and arts/crafts table settings at Site A were collected weekly, using procedures similar to those in the preintervention phase. This was done throughout the study for a total of 18 hours of videotaped play per site (see Table 4).

Table 4 Comparisons of sites by play area and amount of videotaping before and after enrichment

Play areas	Before enrichment				After enrichment			
	Site A	Videotaping time	Site B	Videotaping time	Site A	Videotaping time	Site B	Videotaping time
Housekeeping	✓	1 hour	✓	1 hour	✓	5 hours	Kitchen	5 hours
Book corner	✓	1 hour	✓	1 hour	✓	5 hours	Library	5 hours
Small manipulatives	✓	1 hour	✓	1 hour	✓	4 hours	✓	1 hour
Arts/crafts	✓	1 hour	✓	1 hour	✓	4 hours	✓	1 hour
Office	0	—	0	—	✓	—	—	6 hours
Blocks								
Large	✓	—	✓	—	✓	—	✓	—
Small	✓	—	✓	—	✓	—	✓	—
Sand/water table	✓	—	✓	—	✓	—	✓	—
Large muscle	✓	—	✓	—	✓	—	✓	—
Outdoor play	✓	—	✓	—	✓	—	✓	—

During the final 2-week period of the study, each child's spontaneous play activity was systematically observed, once again using the same preintervention procedure. Eighty-five children comprised the final number of subjects in the study, representing a loss of 7% of the sample due to child absences and family relocations.

Data analysis

Frequencies of children's handling, reading, and writing behaviors were tallied prior to and following the intervention to determine the influence of these physical design changes on the number of literacy demonstrations in children's spontaneous free play. A one-way analysis of covariance was conducted, with the corresponding baseline score serving as covariate, for each category of response.

Videotaped play activity was qualitatively analyzed to examine the duration and complexity of children's play sequences with print, and the function of literacy objects in these settings. Through repeated viewings and discussion, 44 hours of videotaped play (8 hours baseline; 36 hours throughout study) were scanned, and play frames—defined by Sutton-Smith (1971) as play that is bound by a location and a particular focus or interaction—were established. This analysis yielded a total of 216 play frames.

These play frames were examined for evidence of literacy behaviors—

Table 5 Literacy-related play frames in each of the play settings by site

Site	Number of play frames			
	Baseline phase	Mid-enrichment phase	Late-enrichment phase	Total
Nonintervention (Site A)				
Housekeeping	1	0	2	3
Book corner	2	2	2	6
Small manipulatives	2	2	1	6
Arts/crafts	0	1	0	1
Total	5	5	5	15
Intervention (Site B)				
Housekeeping [kitchen/house]	1	3	6	10
Book corner [library]	5	14	11	30
Small manipulatives [office]	0	6	13	19
Arts/crafts	0			
Total	6	23	30	59
				74

handling, reading, or writing activities. Of the 216 frames, 74 or 34% were literacy-related. Each was numbered by date, and the play frames were grouped by site into three time periods: baseline, mid-enrichment, and late-enrichment. Table 5 illustrates the number of literacy-related play frames in each of the play settings by site.

Five play frames from each time period in the intervention and nonintervention groups were selected for subsequent analysis to examine the influence of literacy enrichment on the duration and complexity of the literacy-related play (see Appendix C for additional information on these play frames).[2] Duration was calculated by determining the amount of time children spent on literacy-related play in each play frame. Complexity was analyzed by counting the number of contingent sequences of literacy demonstrations: consecutive instances of handling, reading, or writing within play frames. Contingent sequences of play behavior are regarded by play researchers (Sylva, Roy, & Painter, 1980) as providing the best empirical evidence of complexity. As reported in our previous research, these sequences of literacy demonstrations indicated more complex literacy-related play (Neuman & Roskos, 1990b). Table 6 illustrates the coding procedures.

Differences between groups on duration and complexity were analyzed using one-way repeated measures analysis of variance (ANOVA) across the three time periods.

Finally, the 30 play frames were transcribed verbatim, including children's talk, gesture, physical action, and object use, to examine how literacy objects functioned in the play frame. Since researchers have shown that specific changes in context result in specific changes in language used (Halliday, 1975), the frames were coded according to the type of speech acts and actions the preschoolers used and their purpose in relation to literacy objects.

Each play frame was divided into behavioral units, defined as individual segments of speech or specific action (Barker, 1978). Units were classified as serving one of the following roles in a play exchange: requestives, responsives, performatives, and nonverbal actions. This typology was derived from Dore's (1978) extensive observations of young children's speech acts in preschool classrooms; it is used to describe the ways in which children learn to use the pragmatic aspects of language. Actions were included because interactions between children are thought to be first through gesture and action, and then through symbol. Language is seen as very much predicated on gesture (Lock, 1978).

Using this system, we classified each behavioral unit as a requestive, responsive, performative, or a nonverbal action. We then examined how the literacy objects were used through children's language and actions. Through repeated readings of transcripts, we were able to divide the uses of literacy objects into eight categories: labeling, pretending to read,

Table 6 Segment of a coded transcript analyzing complexity and duration of literacy demonstrations in a play frame, office play area

Literacy demonstration	Speaker	
Writing	Claire [to Carol]:	Betcha can't make this Carol (shows her a big letter M on paper).
Writing	Carol [to Claire]:	I know how [writes a letter M].
Writing	Claire [to Gwen]:	I can make something better than you [makes a C].
Reading	Gwen [to Claire]:	See I made a C.
Writing	Claire [to Gwen]:	Yeah, but I bet you can't make this [refers to some marks on her paper].
Writing	Gwen [to Claire]:	Wow. Do you know how to write? [attempts to scribble like Claire]
Writing	Claire [to Gwen]:	Yup! [tries to write a letter]
Writing	Shameika [to Claire]:	You can't make this [writing on paper].
Handling	Claire [to Shameika]:	Bet you can't make this [holds up her paper].
Writing	Shameika [to the others]:	I'm making letters [writes the letter *e* on her paper].
Handling	Claire [to Shameika]:	We don't care. [to others] Right? We don't care about your picture. Who cares? Nobody cares about your picture. Look at mine! [holds up her paper for everyone]
Writing	Shameika:	[Making more lines on paper]
Writing	Claire:	I can make that [attempts to write what Shameika is writing].
Writing	Gwen:	I can make that too-o-o [writes on paper].
Writing	Shameika [to the others]:	When you write, you just hafta make lines [demonstrates by writing].
Writing	Claire [to the others]:	We know how to make lines ... lines is very easy. We don't need no help to make lines [writes on her paper].
End of sequence	Supraja [coming into office area]:	Guess what! I saw *Batman* at the movies.

Note
Total number of literacy demonstrations = 16. Total duration: 450 seconds.

pronouncing words or letters, exploring objects, writing, transforming, no reference to object, and off-task behavior. For example, the behavioral unit, "Watch, Claire, how I can write," was coded as a performative speech act (P), in which the child made reference to writing (w). By cross-referencing speech acts and action behavioral units with reference to how the objects were used, then, it was possible to analyze in what ways literacy-related play was extended through the uses of objects. Further, this procedure allowed us to examine the extent to which the objects might influence a variety of linguistic repertoires (see Tables 7 and 8 for coding system).

Each segment was coded holistically for gist, which, according to Corsaro (1979), yields an accurate measure of a behavioral unit for preschool children.

Table 7 Coding system for children's speech acts and nonverbal actions

Category	Code
Requestive: Solicits information or action	S
Question: Seeks either judgment or information. "Wanna write a valentine?"	
Action request: Seeks the performance of an action by hearer. "Give me that book!"	
Suggestion: Recommends the performance of an action by hearer or speaker. "Let's play librarian"	
Responsive: Supplies solicited information	R
Answer: Provides solicited judgment of proposition. "A little boy from China drinked your milk."	
Explanation: States justifications and predictions. "Cause I readed that Chinese book."	
Performative: Accomplishes acts and establishes facts by being said	P
Claim: Establishes rights of speaker. "That's my letter."	
Declarative: Announces facts or rights of speaker. "I know how to write my name."	
Qualification: Provides unsolicited information to requestives. "That is not an *a*."	
Nonverbal: Expresses meaning through actions or gestures	N

Table 8 Coding system for reference to object

Category	Code
Labelling: A literacy object is identified.	1
Pretending to read: A child attempts to read.	b
Pronouncing words or letters: Specific words or letters are pronounced.	w
Exploring objects: A literacy object is manipulated or handled.	e
Writing: Writing is used to communicate with others.	wr
Transforming: Child assigns new meaning to a literacy object.	t
No reference to object: Child makes a statement that makes no reference to literacy object.	n
Off-task: An object is used inappropriately.	o

Transcripts were coded by one of the authors, then reviewed by the other to ensure consistency of coded categories. Disagreements were resolved through discussion. A sample of a coded transcript is shown in Table 9.

In total, 325 behavioral units were reported for the intervention group, 111 for the nonintervention group. In order to examine potential differences in the uses of literacy objects, these frequencies were converted to percentages. Due to the relatively limited number of literacy-related behavioral units from the nonintervention group, data were collapsed across all three time periods. Following a procedure developed by Alvermann and Hayes (1989), we constructed graphs displaying the uses of literacy objects as revealed through language and action during play.

Results

Frequency of literacy demonstrations

Our first analysis was designed to measure differences between groups in the number of literacy demonstrations in children's spontaneous free play.

Table 9 Sample of a coded transcript analyzing the use of literacy objects through speech acts and actions

Code	Speaker	Behavioral units
Swr	Elisha	Claire, I know how to write my Mom's name, wouldya like to watch me?
Rwr	Claire	Yeah.
Nwr	Elisha	[She holds the pencil and starts to
Rw		write.] Want me to make an *A*?
Rwr,	Claire	Yeah. [She watches as Elisha begins
Nwr		to make a mark.] I'm gonna make an
Pw		*A*.
Sw	Elisha	What's that?
Rw Pw	Claire	That's the *A*. It's not very good
Ne		[She scratches furiously on her paper
Swr		as Elisha looks on.] I did it wrong again, right? [She begins to scribble on her paper very hard.]
Ne	Elisha	[She begins to scribble on her paper.]
Pe, Pe	Claire	Let me see. Oh yuck! We're making
Pe		yucky ones.
Pe, Ne	Elisha	Oh yuck! [She continues to scribble.]
Pw		Now lemme make a better *A*.

Note
See Tables 7 and 8 for explanations of codes.

Table 10 Means (and standard deviations) for number of literacy demonstrations by site before and after intervention

Type of demonstration	Site			
	Nonintervention		Intervention	
	(Site A)		(Site B)	
	Pre (Month 1)	Post (Month 7)	Pre (Month 1)	Post (Month 7)
Handling	1.36 (2.90)	1.53 (2.16)	1.70 (3.80)	7.30 (6.54)
Reading	1.17 (2.67)	0.67 (0.82)	0.56 (1.22)	2.09 (2.32)
Writing	0.05 (0.22)	0.31 (0.75)	0.30 (0.86)	2.60 (2.89)

Note
Duration of each videotape from which literacy demonstrations were determined = 30 minutes.

Table 10 presents the mean scores for the preenrichment frequencies and the adjusted means for the postenrichment scores on the number of handling, reading, and writing literacy demonstrations.

Significant differences were reported in each category of response. Children in Site B engaged in significantly more handling ($F(1,82) = 29.99$, $p < .001$), reading ($F(1,82) = 13.43$, $p < .001$), and writing ($F(1,82) = 26.89$, $p < .001$) demonstrations in play than children in Site A. These data indicated that the infusion of literacy objects along with physical design changes in play settings significantly influenced the nature of children's literacy behaviors.

Duration and complexity of literacy-related play themes

Table 11 presents mean scores for intervention and nonintervention groups for the duration and complexity of literacy-related play themes across baseline, mid-enrichment and late-enrichment periods.

One-way repeated measures ANOVAS of literacy-related play frames in the representative sample indicated statistically significant differences between the two groups across the three time periods, with the intervention group engaging in lengthier ($F(1,8) = 109.13$, $p < .001$) and more complex literacy-related play ($F(1,8) = 26.78$, $p < .001$), than those children in the nonintervention group.

Figures 4 and 5 display these differences between groups in the average duration and complexity of literacy-related play themes across the three time periods.

As expected, only slight differences in duration and complexity of literacy-related play themes were reported for the two groups prior to literacy enrichment. However, following the infusion of literacy-related objects,

Table 11 Means (and standard deviations) for duration and complexity of play themes

Period and group	Average duration[a]			Complexity[b]		
	M	SD	R	M	SD	R
Baseline phase						
Intervention	101.00	117.44	9–300	1.80	1.30	1–4
Nonintervention	90.60	73.89	18–200	2.00	0.00	0
Mid-enrichment phase						
Intervention	604.00	310.03	200–1037	13.00	3.46	10–18
Nonintervention	57.00	25.87	38–102	1.80	0.84	1–3
Late-enrichment phase						
Intervention	683.20	291.60	358–1032	20.00	9.92	10–33
Nonintervention	52.00	29.50	30–100	1.60	0.89	1–3

Notes
a In seconds.
b Number of demonstrations in each play frame

there were striking differences in both variables. Children in the intervention group engaged in over 10 times the amount of literacy-related play. Related to this finding, there was a marked change in the complexity of play frames, with the intervention group engaging in more contingent

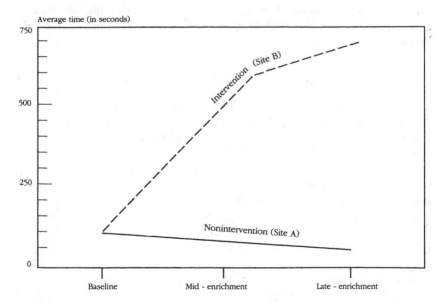

Figure 4 Duration of literacy-related play frames: baseline, mid-, and late-enrichment phases

274

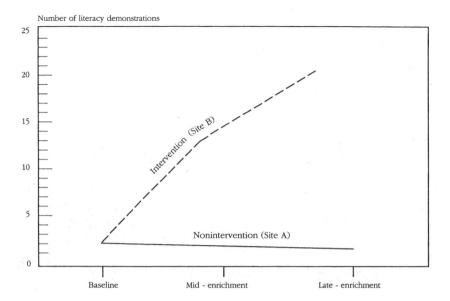

Figure 5 Complexity of literacy-related play frames: baseline, mid-, and late enrichment periods

sequences of literacy behavior. Further, these effects were maintained and even extended in the late-enrichment period, demonstrating the impact of settings and literacy objects on play even after the effects of novelty wore off.

In summary, children in the intervention group spent more time engaging in handling, reading, and writing activities in play than the nonintervention group. These demonstrations became more sustained and more interconnected as literacy was increasingly integrated in children's ongoing play themes over the 7 month period of the study.

Children uses of literacy objects in play

Figures 6 and 7 describe how literacy objects were used in play as communicated by the preschoolers' speech acts and actions. Speech acts in each category were aggregated to examine differences between nonintervention and intervention groups. (See Appendices B and C for percentages of behavioral units in each category and reference to the literacy object for intervention and nonintervention groups.)

Children in Site B tended to rely more on language in communicating with others in literacy-related play than the nonintervention group; only 14% of the play in the intervention group was dominated by nonverbal action, compared to 41% in Site A. In the nonintervention group, for

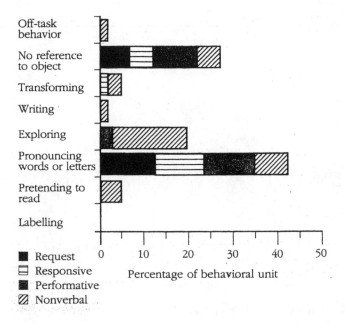

Figure 6 Percentage of behavioral units for each speech act or action and type of reference to the literacy object: nonintervention group

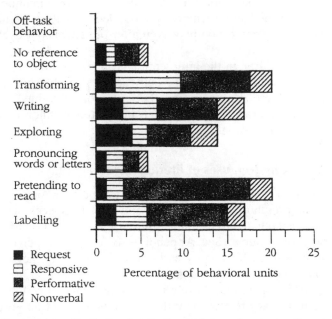

Figure 7 Percentage of behavioral units for each speech act or action and type of reference to the literacy object: intervention group

example, meaning was often conveyed through actions, as in one play theme where we observed a little girl attempting to engage her friend in play by pointing to a paper as if it were a map. In contrast, children in the intervention group more often negotiated meaning through language, as in the following episode:

Katie: [referring to her book]: Here's the name. Oh, no! (She flips through the book.)

Supraja: [looking at the pages] This is a cooking book. This is a cooking book, Katie. That's OK.

Katie: [sweeping her hand across the print] There's words. It's a word book.

Supraja: A check book!

Katie: [closing the book and smiling] Yeah, like a checkbook.

Closely associated with these trends, the nonintervention group's reliance on nonverbal actions was accompanied by more exploratory behavior, as in "what can this object do," in comparison with the intervention group, where literacy was situated in the context of pretend play. For example, children's use of writing instruments (markers, pencils, crayons) in the nonintervention group consisted largely of experimenting with the various colors or making marks on paper. On the other hand, children in the intervention group frequently used writing instruments in more functional ways, such as to "write valentines," to record "library" rules, and to write down "directions." In this respect, the literacy behaviors demonstrated by the nonintervention group tended to be guided by the object, externally driven, with action subordinated to the object, whereas those demonstrated by the intervention group were more internally driven, with action subordinated to the children's intentions.

Children in the intervention group also used literacy objects to engage in a wide variety of literacy behaviors. They focused their interactions on the labeling of objects, reading, writing, and using literacy in their pretend play activities more frequently than the nonintervention group. For example, children in Site A most often engaged in identifying words and letters seen on the available print such as a calendar or a list of children's names in the classroom. In Site B, however, play settings provided a broad diversity of literacy activities, as in the office, where children spent time preparing and sending mail, writing each other's names, reading messages, and assuming the roles of office workers.

Further, striking differences were reported between groups in the role of the literacy object in play. Even when a literacy object was physically present, a good deal of talk and action among preschoolers in the nonintervention group made no reference at all to it, indicating that the object was not the focus of learning and interaction. For example, in one episode,

277

two boys were playing "sleep" in the library corner, holding books, yet making no mention of the content of the books. Children in the intervention group, however, frequently incorporated the literacy objects into their play themes, using them to further their play purposes. For example, the children's use of a "Trapper-Keeper" notebook became a central prop in a number of family play themes about "doing homework":

Sharonda: Good afternoon!
Julia: [carrying the Trapper-Keeper]. Oh hello, mother. [Pointing to it] I gotta study for class, Mom.
Sharonda: Hurry up! We gotta go to Gramma's house.
Julia: Guess what? I gotta show you something. [She opens the Trapper-Keeper.] I gotta bad test!
         [She shows her a folded piece of paper.]
         Look! I've been studying a lot.
Sharonda: Don't study tomorrow a really lots. I don't need it.

Finally, contrary to some teachers' beliefs that play with real objects encourages more "real-life" play (Paley, 1990), children in the intervention group actually engaged in more object transformations with the literacy props than those in the nonintervention group. For example, the children changed cookbooks into "magic, genie books" and pieces of paper into detailed directions for "ballet lessons." These children used literacy objects in creative ways as they pretended to be magicians, mail carriers, or librarians, indicating that object prototypicality and familiarity might have actually encouraged more meaningful and imaginative literacy-based play.

In sum, our data indicated that children in the intervention group relied more often on the language of literacy over gestures and actions alone to elicit, respond to, and perform activities in play. In addition, they incorporated literacy objects into their play in more diverse and functional ways. These differences indicate that the physical presence of objects in their related settings may have assisted children in the use of more explicit language in literacy-based play.

Discussion

Ecologists have argued that early childhood classroom settings exert a "coercive power" over their inhabitants, constraining certain behaviors and permitting others (Gump, 1989; Weinstein, 1979). Factors such as room size, intimacy of setting, and material resources have been shown to elicit differences in the quality of children's pretend play, social interaction, and constructive activity (Fernie, 1985). Specifically, empirical evidence suggests that young children first use objects and settings they already know to construct meaning from experiences in play; these are replaced by more representational forms as they grow older (Elder & Pederson, 1978; Fein, 1975). How children use objects and settings within their environment is thought to reflect their growing capacity to create analogies (or symbols) that become increasingly independent of external stimulation, and increasingly representational of the events to which they refer (Werner & Kaplan, 1963). Consequently, in structuring play environments to enhance literacy interactions, we embedded common literacy objects in known settings to encourage young children to engage spontaneously in literacy-like behaviors, using their prior knowledge as well as that of their peers to extend their associations and understandings of literacy.

The results of this study indicate that the deliberate enrichment of the play environment with familiar literacy objects in equally familiar contexts of literacy use enhanced young children's literacy activity in play. Over the period of the intervention, the frequency, duration, and complexity of children's playful literacy activities increased, suggesting that, unlike toys, the objects encouraged children's self-generated literacy activity in richer and more elaborated play sequences.

Further, through their language and actions, children's uses of literacy objects became increasingly varied, incorporating a greater repertoire of questions, responses, and behaviors involving literacy. These findings support our previous research, indicating that children's collaborative engagement in literacy through play may provide substantive input in their learning about written language as reflected in their discourse. In our study, we found children's instructional discourse focused on designating the names of literacy objects, on negotiating their meaning, and on coaching another child in some literacy task (Neuman & Roskos, 1991). Taken together, these results suggest that more challenging and complex language use may be produced in play environments that are literacy based with objects and settings that are not only familiar but instrumental in nature. In short, the physical play environment permitted the creation of situational contexts in which literacy may be used.

In addition, the results indicate that within this enriched play environment children incorporated literacy objects and roles into their play, creating new play themes to express their ideas about literacy. In the process of play, the constellation of objects-contexts-roles provided a network, luring children into the language and actions of literacy while simultaneously enhancing the quality of their literacy-based play. In this respect, the play environment scaffolded the children's "comprehension of the act" of literacy prior to their formal induction via instruction. Wood, Bruner, and Ross (1976) have argued that this form of recruitment is the first stage of scaffolding, to be replaced by later assistance in more and more conventional forms.

Findings from this study indicate the need for certain ecological considerations related to the literacy enrichment of play environments. That the children in the intervention site evidenced more and qualitatively different literacy activities in play appears to be linked more to the conscientious application of environmental design principles than to the simple littering of play areas with literacy objects. What seems key here is the insertion of known literacy objects embedded within familiar play areas. This kind of nested familiarity within well-designed play environments tended to create networks of literacy behaviors easily incorporated into children's naturally developing play themes. In this manner, literacy settings and objects appeared to serve as pivots (Vygotsky, 1967), supporting the play and assisting the use of language over action as a means of conveying meaning about literacy.

In particular, these findings suggest that a more calculated approach to the design of literacy enrichment in early childhood play environments is needed—one that uses information from a variety of sources. Specifically, parents need to be surveyed as to the kinds of literacy activities and situations that naturally occur outside the early childhood program; teachers, as well, need to rework play centers to include familiar literacy objects and routines. This implies that literacy-enriched play settings and objects will vary across programs, reflective of the broader cultures of their participants. In this respect, "travel agency" and "restaurant" play centers may be appropriate to one early childhood environment but not to others, where the generic "offices" and "grocery stores" may more likely represent real-world literacy contexts to children.

There are several important limitations to consider in this research. While clearly significant, physical dimensions of an educational setting represent only one factor in the definition of a learning environment; the role of the teacher, parent involvement, the curriculum, and program philosophy have a critical influence in providing literacy opportunities for children. This suggests that further research focusing on the role of the adult in enhancing preschoolers' literacy-related play is sorely needed to explore how properly timed interventions may assist and enrich play as a medium for literacy learning. Since internal control and intrinsic motivation are fundamental to the definition of play (Garvey, 1977), such adult interactions must be subtly introduced so as not to disrupt or control the play flow, but to accentuate certain features of the literacy task that are relevant to children.

Further, creating opportunities for literacy engagement is certainly not sufficient to bring about literacy acquisition. This study makes no claim that increased frequency in literacy-enriched play directly impacts the broad array of abilities associated with literacy achievement. In fact, we suspect that the linkage between these settings and literacy learning would be more closely associated with a greater understanding of the functions of contextualized print directly related to the play settings themselves. In a current study, we are examining the effects of literacy-related play in an office area on children's knowledge of functional print associated with working in an office.

Finally, although creating environments for literacy may provide opportunities to engage in these practices, the very nature of play suggests that it is child initiated, spontaneous, and voluntary. Children in this study were free to enter into the literacy play settings or not, raising the issue of self-selection. For example, it could be that the children who may benefit the most from these types of settings will be the least inclined to enter them. This suggests that these play settings represent only one potential route to effective engagement; early childhood learning environments must include multiple routes to literacy interactions.

With these considerations in mind, however, this research suggests that children's functional engagement with literacy objects in play settings may serve an important role in their early attempts to gain power and control over written language. Through play, children may explore the cultural tools of literacy, making them a functional and valued part of their own experience.

Appendices

Appendix A Percentage of behavioral units for each speech act or action and type of reference to the literacy object: Nonintervention group

Object references	Speech act and actions					
	Requestive	*Responsive*	*Performative*	*Nonverbal*	*Total*	*N*[a]
Labelling					0%	0
Pretending to read				5%	5%	6
Pronouncing words or letters	12%	12%	11%	7%	42%	47
Exploring			2%	18%	20%	22
Writing				1%	1%	1
Transforming		1%		3%	4%	4
No reference to object	6%	5%	10%	6%	27%	30
Off-task behavior				1%	1%	1
Total	18%	18%	23%	41%	100%	111

Note
a Number of behavioral units.

Appendix B Percentage of behavioral units for each speech act or action and type of reference to the literacy object intervention group

Object references	Speech act and actions					
	Requestive	Responsive	Performative	Nonverbal	Total	N[a]
Labelling	2%	4%	9%	2%	17%	55
Pretending to read	1%	2%	15%	2%	21%	68
Pronouncing words or letters	1%	2%	2%	1%	7%	23
Exploring	4%	2%	5%	3%	12%	39
Writing	3%	4%	7%	3%	17%	55
Transforming	2%	8%	8%	2%	20%	65
No reference to object	1%	1%	3%	1%	6%	20
Off-task behavior					0%	0
Total	14%	23%	49%	14%	100%	317

Note
a Number of behavioral units

Appendix C Summary of representative play frames for intervention and nonintervention groups

Phase of study and group	Play frames			
	Duration	Number of children		Topic of play
		Boys	Girls	
Preenrichment phase Intervention				
	8 sec.	2		Spelling a word on the typewriter
	9 sec.		3	Reading in the book corner
	39 sec.		3	Flipping pages of a book in the book corner
	112 sec.		1	Reading in the book corner
	300 sec.		1	Reading in the book corner
Nonintervention				
	26 sec.		2	Pretending to have a picnic and reading a book
	18 sec.		1	Sitting in a chair reading
	109 sec.		1	Reading names of children in the class
	200 sec.		1	Singing the alphabet song in housekeeping corner
	100 sec.		1	Turning pages of a book in the book corner

Mid-enrichment phase
Intervention

700 sec.		2	Reading books in the library
1,037 sec.	3	4	Playing mail carrier and writing in the office
200 sec.	1	1	Reading books in the library
450 sec.		1	Reading a book in the library
633 sec.		4	Doing "homework" in the kitchen

Nonintervention

50 sec.		3	Reading in the book corner
38 sec.		2	Pretending to fall asleep holding a book in the book corner
53 sec.		2	Showing a friend a paper in the big block area
102 sec.		2	Pretending that a paper is a "map" in the big block area
42 sec.	1		Scribbling with a marker in the arts and crafts area

Late-enrichment phase
Intervention

925 sec.	2		Playing with a "magic genie" recipe book in kitchen
1,032 sec.	2	4	Making and sending valentines in the office
648 sec.	1	3	Organizing a "show" in the office
358 sec.		1	Reading a recipe book in the kitchen
453 sec.	2	3	Writing letters and mailing them in the office

Nonintervention

60 sec.		5	Turning pages of a book in book corner
100 sec.		1	Reading names of the children in the class off the back of carpet squares
40 sec.		3	Setting up a library for storybook reading
30 sec.	1		Reading letters off an alphabet chart
30 sec.	2		Reading letters off an alphabet chart

Notes

This research was supported by an Elva Knight Research Grant awarded through the International Reading Association.

1 A Panasonic Camcorder was used for videotaping. Two table-top cordless microphones and a portable mixer were used for audiotaping play talk. One microphone was centrally placed in the play area and the other hand-held by an observer who moved with the children. The observer also controlled the mixer, which was positioned near the different videotaped play areas.

2 Due to differences in the number of literacy-related play frames across sites, all frames from Site A were used for qualitative analysis, while a random sample of frames was selected from Site B.

References

ALVERMANN, D., & HAYES, J. (1989). Classroom discussion of content area reading assignments: An intervention study. *Reading Research Quarterly, 24*, 305–335.

ATWELL, N. (1987). *In the middle*. Portsmouth, NH: Heinemann.

BARKER, R. (1978). Stream of individual behavior: In R. Barker & Associates (Eds.), *Habitats, environments, and human behavior* (pp. 3–16). San Francisco: Jossey-Bass.

BARKER, R., & WRIGHT, H. (1951). *One boy's day*. New York: Harper & Row.

BERLYNE, D. (1960). *Conflict, arousal and curiosity*. New York: McGraw-Hill.

BROFENBRENNER, U. (1977). Toward an experimental ecology of human development. *American Psychologist, 32*, 513–531.

BRUNER, J. (1983). Play, thought and language. *Peabody Journal of Education, 60*, 60–69.

BRUNER, J. (1984). Language, mind and reading. In H. Goleman, A. Oberg, & F. Smith (Eds.), *Awakening to literacy* (pp. 193–200). Portsmouth, NH: Heinemann.

CHAILLE, C. (1978). The child's conceptions of play, pretending, and toys: Sequences and structural parallels. *Human Development, 21*, 201–210.

CHRISTIE, J., & JOHNSEN, E.P. (1983). The role of play in social-intellectual development. *Review of Educational Research, 53*, 93–115.

CORSARO, W. (1979). We're friends, right? Children's use of access rituals in a nursery school. *Language in Society, 8*, 315–336.

DAY, D. (1983). *Early childhood education: A human ecological approach*. Glenview, IL: Scott, Foresman.

DORE, J. (1978). The structure of nursery school conversation. In K. Nelson (Ed.), *Children's language* (Vol. 1, pp. 397–444). New York: Gardner Press.

ELDER, J., & PEDERSON, D. (1978). Preschool children's use of objects in symbolic play. *Child Development, 49*, 500–504.

EL'KONIN, D. (1966). Symbolics and its functions in the play of children. *Soviet Education, 8*, 35–41.

EMMERICH, W. (1977). Evaluating alternative models of development: An illustrative study of preschool personal-social behaviors. *Child Development, 48*, 1401–1410.

FEIN, G. (1975). A transformational analysis of pretending. *Developmental Psychology, 11*, 291–296.

FEIN, G., & ROBERTSON, A.R. (1975). Cognitive and social dimensions of pretending in two-year olds. Detroit: Merrill-Palmer Institute. (ERIC Document Reproduction Service N. ED 119 806)

FERNIE, D. (1985). The promotion of play in the indoor play environment. In J. L. Frost & S. Sunderlin (Eds.), *When children play* (pp. 285–290). Wheaton, MD: Association for Childhood Education International.

GALDA, L., PELLEGRINI, A.D., & COX, S. (in press). A short-term longitudinal study of preschoolers' emergent literacy. *Research in the Teaching of English.*

GARVEY, C. (1977). *Play.* Cambridge, MA: Harvard University Press.

GOELMAN, H. (1984). The discussion: What was said. In H. Goelman, A. Oberg, & F. Smith (Eds.), *Awakening to literacy* (pp. 201–213). Portsmouth, NH: Heinemann.

GRAVES, D. (1983). *Writing: Teachers and children at work.* Portsmouth, NH: Heinemann.

GUMP, P. (1989). Ecological psychology and issues of play. In M. Bloch & A.D. Pellegrini (Eds.), *The ecological context of children's play* (pp. 35–56). Norwood, NJ: Ablex.

HALLIDAY, M.A.K. (1975). *Learning how to mean: Explorations in the development of language.* London: Edward Arnold.

HUTT, C. (1979). Exploration and play. In B. Sutton-Smith (Ed.), *Play and learning* (pp. 175–194). New York: Gardner Press.

HUTT, C., & BHAVNANI, R. (1976). Predictions from play. In J.S. Bruner, A. Jolly, & K. Sylva (Eds.), *Play* (pp. 216–219). New York: Penguin.

JACOB, E. (1984). Learning literacy through play: Puerto Rican kindergarten children. In H. Goelman, A. Oberg, & F. Smith (Eds.), *Awakening to literacy* (pp. 73–83). Portsmouth, NH: Heinemann.

LOCK, A. (Ed.) (1978). *Action, gesture and symbol: The emergence of language,* London: Academic Press.

MCLOYD, V. (1983). The effects of the structure of play objects on the pretend play of low-income preschool children. *Child Development, 54,* 626–635.

MORROW, L.M. (1990a). *Relationships between adult modeling, classroom design characteristics and children's literacy behavior.* Paper presented at the National Reading Conference, Miami Beach, FL.

MORROW, L.M. (1990b). Preparing the classroom environment to promote literacy during play. *Early Childhood Research Quarterly, 5,* 537–554.

MORROW, L.M., & WEINSTEIN, C.S. (1986). Encouraging voluntary reading: The impact of a literature program on children's use of library corners. *Reading Research Quarterly, 21,* 330–346.

NEILL, S. (1982). Experimental alternations in playroom layout and their effect on staff and child behavior. *Educational Psychology, 2,* 103–109.

NEUMAN, S.B. (1991). *Literacy in the television age.* Norwood, NJ: Ablex.

NEUMAN, S.B., & ROSKOS, K. (1990a). Play, print and purpose: Enriching play environments for literacy development. *The Reading Teacher, 44,* 214–221.

NEUMAN, S.B., & ROSKOS, K. (1990b). The influence of literacy enriched play settings on preschoolers' engagement with written language. In S. McCormick & J. Zutell (Eds.), *Literacy theory and research: Analyses from multiple paradigms* (pp. 179–187). Chicago: National Reading Conference.

NEUMAN, S.B., & ROSKOS, K. (1991). Peers as literacy informants: A description of young children's literacy conversations in play. *Early Childhood Research Quarterly, 6,* 233–248.

PALEY, V. (1990). *The boy who would be a helicopter.* Cambridge, MA: Harvard University Press.

PELLEGRINI, A. (1980). The relationship between kindergartners' play and achievement in prereading, language, and writing. *Psychology in the Schools, 17,* 530–535.

PELLEGRINI, A. (1985). The relations between symbolic play and literate behavior: A review and critique of the empirical literature. *Review of Educational Research, 55,* 207–221.

PELLEGRINI, A.D., GALDA, L., DRESDEN, J., & COX, S. (1990). *A longitudinal study of the predictive relations among symbolic play.* Paper presented at the American Educational Research Association Conference, Boston, MA.

PIAGET, J. (1962). *Play, dreams, and imitation.* New York: Norton.

PROSHANSKY, E., & WOLFE, M. (1975). The physical setting and open education. In T.G. David & B.D. Wright (Eds.), *Learning environments* (pp. 31–48). Chicago: University of Chicago Press.

PULASKI, M.A. (1973). Toys and imaginative play. In J.L. Singer (Ed.), *The child's world of make-believe* (pp. 74–103). New York: Academic Press.

QUILITCH, H., & RISLEY, T. (1973). The effects of play materials on social play. *Journal of Applied Behavioral Analysis, 6,* 573–578.

ROBINSON, S. (1990). *A survey of literacy programs among pre-schools.* Paper presented at the American Educational Research Association Annual Conference, Boston, MA.

ROSKOS, K. (1987). *The nature of children's literate behavior in pretend play episodes.* Unpublished doctoral dissertation, Kent State University, Kent, OH.

ROSKOS, K. (1990). A taxonomic view of pretend play. *Early Childhood Research Quarterly, 5,* 495–512.

SCHICKEDANZ, J. (1986). *More than the ABC's: The early states of reading and writing.* Washington, DC: National Association for the Education of Young Children.

SUTTON-SMITH, B. (1971). Boundaries. In R.E. Herron & B. Sutton-Smith (Eds.), *Child's play* (pp. 103–106). New York: Wiley.

SYLVA, K., ROY, C., & PAINTER, M. (1980). *Childwatching at play group and nursery school.* London: Grant McIntire.

VANDENBERG, B. (1981). Environmental and cognitive factors in social play. *Experimental Child Psychology, 31,* 169–175.

VUKELICH, C. (1989). *Materials and modeling: Promoting literacy during play.* Paper presented at the National Reading Conference, Austin, TX.

VYGOTSKY, L.S. (1962). *Thought and language.* Cambridge, MA: M.I.T. Press.

VYGOTSKY, L. (1967). Play and its role in the mental development of the child. *Soviet Psychology, 12,* 62–76.

WEINSTEIN, C.S. (1979). The physical environment of the school: A review of the research. *Review of Educational Research, 49,* 577–610.

WERNER, H., & KAPLAN, B. (1963). *Symbol formation.* New York: Wiley.

WOOD, D., BRUNER, J., & ROSS, G. (1976). The role of tutoring in problem solving. *Journal of Child Psychology and Psychiatry, 17,* 89–100.

ZIFFERBLATT, S. (1972). Architecture and human behavior: Toward increasing understanding of a functional relationship. *Educational Technology, 12,* 52–57.

13

THE EMERGENT LITERACY CONSTRUCT AND KINDERGARTEN AND READINESS BOOKS OF BASAL READING SERIES

Elfrieda H. Hiebert and Jacqueline M. Papierz

Source: *Early Childhood Research Quarterly* (1990) 5(3): 317–334

Reading instruction is beginning earlier and earlier for American children. This study examined the nature of reading instruction, as evidenced in the early childhood components of the basal reading materials that guide a majority of American teachers. Basal activities were examined from the emergent literacy perspective which suggests developmentally appropriate experiences that build on what and how young children learn in natural settings. Activities in student and teacher books of kindergarten and readiness components of four basal reading series were analyzed to answer two questions. The first related to the match between basal activities and the emergent literacy construct. Analyses showed that conventional readiness activities like visual, shape, and color discrimination dominated kindergarten books and that auditory discrimination activities dominated readiness books. Emergent literacy activities that experts identified as appropriate for instructional materials were not prominent in either student or teacher books. The second question pertained to differences between meaning- and decoding-oriented series in implementation of literature and decoding activities. Although series did not differ from one another in the amount of attention devoted to either literature or decoding, descriptive analyses of comprehension and decoding instruction showed that meaning-oriented series incuded more high-quality literature for teacher read-alouds, whereas decoding-oriented series allowed more connections between letter-sound correspondences and word identification. The implications of assumptions underlying these materials on children's reading acquisition and adaptations in materials that implement the emergent literacy construct are discussed. Expectations for young children's participation in academic activities are moving lower and lower (Elkind, 1987; Gallagher & Sigel, 1987). Not only are programs for 4-year-olds being modeled on those of the kindergarten but the kindergarten curriculum has come to look more and more like that of first grade (Durkin, 1987). Questions about developmental appropriateness most often pertain to reading since reading typically comprises the primary academic activity in early school programs. The present study considered the developmental appropriateness of activities in early childhood components of basal reading programs which serve as the main source of elementary curriculum.

Developmental appropriateness was examined through the lens of the emergent literacy view. This label has come to be used for a perspective on young children's literacy acquisition that stems from recent work in psycholinguistics and cognitive psychology. The perspective derives from research that shows the "spontaneous expertise" (Hatano & Inagaki, 1983) regarding literacy that has developed in young children. As a result of interacting with and observing those in their environments using print, preschool children come to understand the language of books (Sulzby, 1985) and the functions of print in the environment (Lomax & McGee, 1987). They even invent spelling systems as they scribble and write (Read, 1986). These concepts are not the product of direct instruction but result from natural activities in homes and preschools, such as storybook reading (Teale, 1986).

The manner in which the emergent literacy perspective that emanates from work on children's development prior to formal instruction can influence school literacy experiences has been given considerable thought. For example, Holdaway (1979) has shown how the features of home storybook reading can be translated to settings with a teacher and a group of children through the use of enlarged or "big" books. Sulzby (1985), in documenting a developmental progression in book reading, has suggested experiences for children who have not had many book experiences at home. The understandings about written language that children develop as they draw, scribble, and write with invented spelling argue for extensive involvement in similar activities in school (Dyson, 1986; Read, 1986).

The emergent literacy perspective stands in sharp contrast to the reading readiness perspective that has dominated beginning reading instruction for decades. The reading readiness concept has evolved to be part of the skills-oriented perspective in which children follow a fairly strict hierarchy in the acquisition of literacy, moving from letters to letter-sound correspondences to sight words. In this perspective, a view of readiness has been very critical since reading requires correct identification of letters and letter-sound correspondences. In this context, it is reasonable to question young children's participation in literacy activities since they are often asked to work on isolated units of language in paper-and-pencil exercises.

In contrast, the emergent literacy perspective argues for young children's participation in activities of a very different sort. Although this view recognizes that children of different developmental levels need to be involved in different aspects of literacy activities, the mechanism for acquiring literacy is participation in authentic literacy activities like following along in a big book as the teacher reads aloud or telling a story through a drawing. While for some children this reading experience may be the context for initial concepts about stories and books, others may be acquiring an understanding of the relationship between oral and written language. Still other children may be focusing on particular words. The kinds of literacy experiences that evolve from the emergent literacy perspective are quite different than many of the experiences that have come to mean beginning reading. The experiences of emergent literacy such as storybook reading, drawing or scribbling stories, and independently looking through favorite storybooks are quite different than testing children on letters and sight words and practicing these skills on worksheets.

This study established a set of classroom applications from the emergent literacy research and examined the degree to which these ideas have been applied in early childhood components of basal reading programs. A major source of direction for elementary teachers' literacy instruction comes from commercial reading materials (Shannon, 1983), and kindergarten teachers are not an exception to this pattern. Seventy-five percent of kindergarten teachers in a recent survey reported that they used the materials from a commercial reading series (Educational Research Service, 1986). This use indicates that the developmental appropriateness of literacy activities for young children will be influenced in large part by basal reading materials.

A particular interest of the study was to determine the developmental appropriateness of activities in series having different historical roots. The role of specific information about letters and sounds in learning to read continues to generate considerable debate (e.g., Carbo, 1988; Chall, 1989). Historically, differences in the nature of the beginning reading task have been framed in the "decoding-meaning" dichotomy made by Chall (1983). Although all programs are now aiming to integrate high-quality literature into their beginning reading materials (e.g., English-Language Arts Curriculum Framework & Criteria Committee, 1987) and all series have many decoding activities (Chall, 1983), their differences that stem from historical roots may create distinct beginning reading experiences which vary in their developmental appropriateness for young children.

In this study, kindergarten and readiness materials of four basal reading series, two from a meaning-oriented tradition and two from a decoding-oriented tradition, were analyzed to answer two questions:

1   Do basal reading materials implement the emergent literacy perspective?

2   Do meaning- and decoding-oriented series differ in implementation of comprehension and decoding activities?

Method

Materials

Most recent copyrights of basal series at the study's initiation, those presented for the Texas textbook adoption, were examined. To permit comparison, two series from each orientation were chosen. Two series were randomly selected from the four meaning-oriented series adopted in Texas (Macmillan: Arnold & Smith, 1987; Scott Foresman: Allington et al., 1987). The series chosen by Texas for its decoding slot (Scribner: Cassidy, Roettger, & Wixson, 1987) and the other major contender for that position (Economy: Matteoni, Sucher, Klein, & Welch, 1986) represented decoding-oriented series.

The first two student books of each series and accompanying teachers' manuals comprised the sample of materials. The first two books of Scott Foresman and Economy were labeled as kindergarten and readiness. The intended level for kindergarten is straightforward. Although publishers continue to place the readiness book as a review at the beginning of first grade, many schools use this book at the end of kindergarten (Educational Research Service, 1986). The first books of Scribner and Macmillan were labeled as kindergarten-readiness and readiness. The reason for Scribner's designation is uncertain because no explanations were given nor was either a kindergarten book or kit described in any promotional materials.[1] Well over 2 years after the kindergarten-readiness book had been on the market, Macmillan issued a kit aimed at kindergarten, which consisted of various materials, including an accompanying student book and teacher's manual (Arnold, Smith, Flood, & Lapp, 1988). Because Macmillan's kindergarten-readiness book was described for "extension and reinforcement," the use of this book as the first component seemed justified since a program's philosophy toward beginning reading would be expected to be most evident in materials for extension and reinforcement. Furthermore, an analysis of the activities in the student book from the kindergarten kit and the kindergarten-readiness student book of Macmillan showed no substantial differences in distribution or type of exercises. For the purposes of this study, first books of all series will be referred to as kindergarten.

Macmillan's kindergarten kit illustrates the many ancillary components of basal reading programs. Because it was necessary to limit the study, however, ancillary components such as picture and concept cards and tests were not analyzed.

Procedure

The match between activities in basal reading materials and the emergent literacy construct

The comparison of activities in the basal programs and the emergent literacy construct was accomplished through three steps. First, activities in student books of the basal programs were established by reviewing the scope and sequence of materials. These categories were used to establish interrater agreement between two researchers on 20% of the pages in each student book. The two researchers achieved a level of 97% agreement, leading to the conclusion that these categories characterized the activities in the student books. One investigator then evaluated the remainder of the materials according to these categories. A similar procedure was used to achieve interrater agreement for the remaining analyses in the study.

The second step in the comparison was to establish the activities that exemplify the emergent literacy construct. Emergent literacy activities that might be translatable into commercial reading materials were established in the following manner. Issues of five major journals in reading and writing (*Reading Research Quarterly, Research in the Teaching of English, Journal of Reading Behavior, Reading Teacher*, and *Language Arts*), covering 1976 to 1987, were examined, as were several recent books on emergent literacy (Sampson, 1986; Teale & Sulzby, 1986; Yaden & Templeton, 1986). This process generated a list of instructional applications of the emergent literacy research which was given to five experts who have conducted research on emergent literacy. All five experts agreed to participate in the rating of categories despite reservations by several experts about commercial reading programs. Experts were given the categories and definitions that appear in Table 1 and were asked to rate each from 7 (high) to 1 (low). Categories that achieved an average rating of 6 or more made up the final set.

Finally, the two sets of categories taken from the review of the student books and the analysis of emergent literacy research were compared. Suggestions in teachers' manuals also were analyzed according to the emergent literacy categories. Because teachers' manuals averaged 109 pages, a sampling procedure was necessary. An element of interest (e.g., teacher read-aloud) was analyzed in lessons from the first and last units. The rationale underlying this decision was that changes across the program should be most evident in the first and last units. The plan was to add lessons from intervening units if differences existed between the first and last units. Activities across first and last units were consistently similar, making it unnecessary to add lessons from intermediate units. The same procedure was used throughout the study to sample activities in the teachers' manuals.

Table 1 Instructional activities from recent research on emergent literacy

Activity	Research base
1 *The language of reading:* Students are given labels for process of reading and units of written language (e.g., oral reading, silent reading, letter, word, sentence, story).	Downing, 1986; Johns, 1986
2 *Comprehension activities as part of teacher read-aloud:* Within teacher read-aloud activities that have been encouraged for decades, increased attention has been paid to comprehension activities such as retelling, predicting outcomes, elements of the story such as characters, and vocabulary. Numerous activities are variants of teacher read-aloud activities such as big books and repeated reading of stories.	Morrow, 1984; Roser & Martinez, 1985
3 *Student reading of books:* Students read tradebooks or specially developed books with predictable patterns. There are several early forms of student reading of books—even before children can recognize any words such as pretend reading of very familiar books and even just looking at books.	Bridge, 1986; McCormick & Mason, 1986; Rhodes, 1981; Snow & Ninio, 1986; Sulzby, 1985
4 *Familiar words in the environment:* Reading activities involve words from traffic signs, food products, and so forth, as well as labelling of familiar objects in classroom environment.	Goodman & Goodman, 1979; Hiebert, 1978
5 *Invented spelling:* Students write words, using their own spelling. Invented spelling can occur as part of composing or simply as experimentation with written language. Spelling activities can be with preformed letters (e.g., magnetic letters) or pens and pencils.	Chomsky, 1979; Read, 1986
6 *Composing:* Students compose stories, messages, lists, and other genres. Students' composing may involve a scribe (e.g., teacher, aide) who takes their dictation.	Clay, 1975; Dyson, 1986

Differences between meaning- and decoding-oriented series

First, student book activities were analyzed statistically for differences across meaning- and decoding-oriented series. Next, comprehension and decoding activities in student books and teachers' manuals were analyzed descriptively.

For comprehension, the focus of the descriptive analysis was on characteristics of stories and comprehension activities. From the emergent literacy perspective, early literacy experiences should immerse young children in high-quality literature that captivates them (Strickland, 1987) and encourages their participation through predictable story patterns (Bridge, 1986). Consequently, literature in the series was analyzed in two ways. First, two experts in children's literature rated passages for literary quality from 5 (high) to 1 (low). Second, the predictable nature of passages was analyzed. Bridge (1986), building on the ideas of Smith (1978) and others, has identified five patterns that make books predictable for children as they listen or read. The present concern was with presence or absence of patterns rather than with representation of different patterns. Stories were rated as having (1) or not having (0) a pattern.

Advice to teachers on comprehension instruction was analyzed with a set of categories from recent research on comprehension (Anderson, Hiebert, Scott, & Wilkinson, 1985). The intention was to add categories if, in analyzing suggestions in teachers' manuals, this set of categories was not complete. The set of categories consisted of activation/development of background knowledge, making predictions, purpose setting, discussion of unfamiliar vocabulary, teacher questioning, and retelling. One category, rereading of passages for different purposes, was added in reviewing teachers' manuals. Information in target lessons was rated from 5 (always) to 1 (never).

The descriptive analysis considered two aspects of decoding: the characteristics of words for children to identify, and guidance for teachers in children's use of letter-sound information in identifying words. The underlying philosophy of a program is manifested in the characteristics of words children are asked to identify. If knowledge of letters and sounds is important, words will be ones with high regularity, fitting letter-sound patterns that children are learning. Words also be chosen on the basis of their meaningfulness. While high-frequency words may not be very meaningful to children, one standard for word choice has been the frequency with which words appear in text (e.g., *the*, *and*, *can*, and *for*). In this study, of interest were words that fit other criteria for meaningfulness, such as words that occur in compelling stories or words that have high interest to children, such as the words *dinosaur* and *robot* (Ashton-Warner, 1963).

A second dimension of decoding instruction is the guidance given to teachers. While many high-frequency words also have high regularity (e.g., *and*, *can*), the philosophy in teachers' manuals may encourage teaching these words by sight. Suggestions regarding word identification were examined to determine whether letter-sound correspondences that children had already been taught as part of decoding exercises were applied when they identified words.

Results

The match between activities in basal reading materials and the emergent literacy construct

Results are presented in three steps: (a) description of activities in materials for students, (b) establishment of the emergent literacy criteria, and

(c) comparison of activities in student books and teachers' manuals with the emergent literacy criteria.

Basal categories

Five categories, which are presented in Table 2, accounted for all activities in students' kindergarten and readiness books. Four of the categories closely mirror the conception of reading readiness that was first described in 1925 (National Society for the Study of Education, 1925): auditory discrimination, visual discrimination and letter naming, listening comprehension, and general readiness (which consisted primarily of shape, color, and number discrimination). The fifth category, that of word identification, constitutes reading in the traditional sense.

Emergent literacy categories

Experts gave a rating of 6 or higher (7 was the highest) to five of the six key categories from the review of the emergent literacy literature (comprehension activities as part of teacher read-alouds, student reading of books, environmental print, invented spelling, and composing). The average rating for the sixth category, the language of reading, was substantially lower than 6 and consequently was not included in the analysis.

Comparison of basal and emergent literacy categories: student books

The only category common to the textbook and emergent literacy category sets was comprehension activities. Even here, the activities in student books differed substantially from the definition of comprehension

Table 2 Distribution of categories in kindergarten (K) and readiness (R) books

	Scott Foresman		Macmillan		Economy		Scribner	
	K	R	K	R	K	R	K	R
Auditory discrimination	35.5[a]	55.5	32.5	40.5	46.6	46.1	4.0	32.5
Comprehension	20.8	15.8	7.5	6.0	4.5	5.3	15.0	12.0
Visual discrimination	26.0	4.3	3.0	9.5	16.6	9.9	17.1	8.0
Readiness	48.2	35.8	53.0	23.0	58.1	33.4	55.7	39.5
Word identification	1.5	22.5	0.0	9.0	0.0	15.0	0.0	0.0

Note

a Figures represent raw numbers of pages. A page could consist of several exercises, which were represented as fractions of pages. The failure of pages for a book to total to a whole number is due to rounding off the numbers within categories.

in the emergent literacy view. From that perspective, comprehension consists of discussions or retellings of stories and responding to stories through art, movement, or writing. The analysis of student books showed that a sizable amount of attention was given to a group of "listening comprehension" activities. Unlike comprehension activities from the emergent literacy construct, listening comprehension activities involved sequencing events or identifying details in pictures rather than illustrating a favorite part of a story. In Scott Foresman and Macmillan, the pictures came from stories which the teacher had read aloud. Economy and Scribner's listening comprehension activities were not story based but relied primarily on pictures of commonplace occurrences such as the order of events during a day.

Occasional activities that involved elements of other emergent literacy categories were found, but typically these were not integral to the program. The difference in interpretation was most evident in the emergent literacy category "students' reading of books." In all cases, kindergarten and readiness books of the basal programs were workbooks with exercises rather than books with stories. The finding that the first materials of basal reading series consist of workbooks and not of books with illustrated stories should not be overlooked. To give appropriate acknowledgment, it should be noted that two of the series, Scott Foresman and Economy, provided several "little books" within their workbooks. Scott Foresman's little books consisted of a page which children were to detach and fold to form a book. Economy's little books varied from Scott Foresman's in intention and design in that several pages that formed a "story" began to appear halfway through the readiness workbook as exercises for application of word identification skills. These were much different from the wordless and predictable books that are characteristic of children's literature.

Environmental print was included in at least one workbook page in each student book, but the objective was to teach children awareness of signs rather than to foster literacy. For example, an activity in Macmillan's kindergarten book required children to discriminate between signs, some with words (stop, walk) and some without (symbols for railroad and school crossing).

Workbook pages did not encourage children to attempt the spelling of a word (i.e., invented spelling) or to compose. Children participated in handwriting and tracing activities that were aimed to teach formation of letters and visual discrimination, rather than in the drawing, scribbling, and invented spelling activities that have been described as children's means of entering into writing (Dyson, 1986; Read, 1986).

Comparison of basal and emergent literacy categories:
teachers' manuals

The guidance given to teachers varied considerably from that which has been proposed in the literature on emergent literacy. Comprehension, the category that the two schemes shared, will be treated in more detail in the comparison of meaning- and decoding-oriented series. However, a critical feature of stories that were used for teacher read-aloud and concomitant comprehension activities was clear immediately and should be noted. None of the series had actual books from which teachers read to children. Read-aloud stories were presented in dense print in the teachers' manuals, clearly intended for the eyes of the teacher only. Read-aloud experiences provided no opportunities for children to see the written message. The illustrations that are such a salient part of children's literature were either missing or limited to a single page in the teachers' manuals. All of the teachers' manuals listed supplementary books related to topics. However, these books and stories were not integral to the program. Furthermore, teachers' use of such books, when they need to find them in school and public libraries, is questionable. The finding that the stories for instruction in the basal programs did not include real books for teachers to share with children, coupled with the presence of workbooks rather than storybooks in materials for students, captures the nature of early childhood components of basal reading programs. Programs emulated the workbook, skill-and-drill model of elementary schools, not the model of the home where storybooks play a major role in children's literacy acquisition.

The use of familiar words from the environment, such as *stop* from a sign, to guide students in learning letter names and letter-sound correspondences was completely lacking. Although many environmental words cannot be included in printed materials because of copyrights, suggestions to point out familiar words in the classroom and school could be made. For example, after the word *boy* has been introduced in Scott Foresman's manual, teachers could be encouraged to draw children's attention to this word in the school. Suggestions of this type were not made. Recommendations about labeling objects in the classroom environment were also considered. For example, teachers could be encouraged to label desk, door, and drawer when studying *d* and /d/. Again, no evidence for implementation of this type was found. Furthermore, teachers' manuals suggested no activities that would involve children in invented spelling or composing through scribbling or writing.

Differences between meaning- and decoding-oriented series

Differences across the two types of series were considered, first, in a statistical analysis of distributions of categories and second through descriptions of comprehension and decoding activities.

In considering differences in distributions of categories within student books (data were presented in Table 2), the first step was to establish a common metric because student books varied in length. Page counts were converted to percentages which were then multiplied by the minimal number of pages in any book (88 pages). Distributions of categories within books could then be statistically treated as if all books were of similar length.

A hierarchical log-linear analysis allows the examination of relationships among a set of ordinal categorical variables such as those in the present data set (Haberman, 1978; Norusis, 1985). The analysis begins with data organized in a multidimensional cross tabulation table, like that on Table 2. Observed cell frequencies are compared against those predicted from a model. Because the page counts had been adjusted to yield the same number of total pages, the two main effects of series and level, which test for total differences, were not of interest. The relationship of interest was the three-way interaction of series, level, and category, which tests for a differential distribution of emphases within each book that cannot be predicted on the basis of either series or level. The Chi-square of 29.52 (df = 12) was significant at the .003 level, indicating that the three-way effect cannot be ignored. An examination of the data in Table 2 made it apparent that the distributions of categories varied substantially across different series within the same orientation (i.e., meaning or decoding) as well as across different levels within the same series.

Because of these idiosyncratic patterns, two additional analyses were conducted. These analyses contrasted the meaning-oriented and decoding-oriented series on features that have been hypothesized as the strength of each type of series—listening comprehension activities for the meaning-oriented series and auditory discrimination activities for the decoding-oriented series. For each feature of listening comprehension and auditory discrimination, a log-linear analysis was conducted. For auditory discrimination, the test of the equal-probability model indicated differences between texts, $\chi^2(7) = 44.26$, $p = .001$. However, the differences were not along the meaning-decoding dimension as indicated by the results of an additional analysis that contrasted the decoding-oriented and meaning-oriented texts. This analysis showed no differences between texts of different orientations. An examination of the data in Table 2 indicates that the largest discrepancy between predicted and actual pages lay in Scribner's lack of attention to auditory discrimination at kindergarten.

The log-linear analysis for the listening comprehension category showed a marginal difference across texts, $\chi^2(7) = 14.98$, $p = .036$, but an analysis contrasting meaning-oriented and decoding oriented texts again showed no differences along the meaning or decoding dimensions. Differences across texts were idiosyncratic rather than linked to series' historical roots.

Comprehension

Comprehension features were considered by examining features of teacher read-aloud passages and comprehension instruction. Data on characteristics of passages in Table 3 show that one of the decoding-oriented series, Economy, had substantially more stories than the other three series. However, the analysis of literary quality showed these stories, as well as those of the other decoding-oriented series, to be quite different than those of the two meaning-oriented series. Experts on children's literature gave low ratings to passages in the decoding-oriented series, whereas ratings for passages in meaning-oriented series were consistently high. The passages in Scribner and Economy had been specifically written to convey particular concepts. For example, the purpose of the many short passages in Economy was for children to hear words with a particular target letter-sound correspondence such as "Amos the Ape" which introduced long /a/. In contrast, the stories for meaning-oriented series were fairy tales and modern classics. However, the literature experts declined to give the highest rating to the latter passages because they regarded illustrations as a critical component of literature at this level and the single-page illustrations in the teachers' manuals did not meet this criterion.

Data on predictability of passages which appear in Table 3 indicate that the meaning-oriented series varied on this feature, but at least some of their passages were predictable. Many stories had a phrase or sentence that was repeated at various points in the story (e.g., *Millions of Cats* in Macmillan) or a repetitive-cumulative pattern in which a phrase or sentence is repeated in each succeeding episode and a word or phrase is added (e.g., *Ask Mr. Bear* in Scott Foresman). In contrast, passages in decoding-oriented series uniformly did not have predictable patterns.

Comprehension activities in teachers' manuals are summarized in Table 4 A clear pattern between meaning- and decoding-oriented series was not

Table 3 Ratings of teacher read-aloud passages

	Scott Foresman		Macmillan		Economy		Scribner	
	K	R	K	R	K	R	K	R
Raw number	7	4	4	3	29	24	3	3
Literary quality[a]	4	4	4	4	1	1	1	1
Predictable pattern[b]	1	0.25	0.75	0.67	0	0	0	0

a Literary quality ranged from 5 (high) to 1 (low). Score is the average of two experts across all stories for Scott Foresman, Macmillan, and Scribner. For Economy, the score is based on a sampling of the stories.

b Score represents an average across stories which were each given a score of 1 (presence of a predictable pattern) or 0 (absence of a predictable pattern).

Table 4 Ratings of comprehension suggestions in teachers' manuals

	Scott Foresman		Macmillan		Economy		Scribner	
	K	R	K	R	K	R	K	R
Activation/development of background knowledge[a]	4	3	4	2	5	5	1	1
Elicitation of predictions	5	5	1	1	5	5	1	1
Listening for purpose	4	5	3	2	5	5	5	5
Rereading of passage	5	5	3	4	1	1	1	1
Discussion of unfamiliar vocabulary	4	5	4	4	5	5	1	1
Retelling by children	5	5	2	2	5	5	5	5
Teacher questioning	5	5	3	4	5	5	5	5

a Suggestions for comprehension activities ranged from 5 (high) to 1 (low).

evident in suggested comprehension activities. One meaning-oriented series, Scott Foresman, consistently developed the comprehension activities that have been substantiated by recent research. Economy, a decoding-oriented series, contained all elements except for rereading of passages. The other decoding-oriented series, Scribner, lacked many comprehension elements such as activation of background knowledge, prediction-making, and discussion of unfamiliar vocabulary. Macmillan's treatment of comprehension was not as sparse as Scribner's, nor was it as rich as that of Scott Foresman and Economy.

Decoding

The nature of decoding in early word identification was examined by considering, first, the source of words children are asked to read (high regularity, high frequency, high interest) and, second, guidance for teachers in connecting letter-sound information to word identification.

While independent word identification was not an expectation in kindergarten books of any series, it was an expectation in the readiness books of all series. As data in Table 5 indicate, series varied considerably in number and kinds of words that children were expected to identify. A strict difference in kinds of words occurred along the meaning-decoding line. Words in decoding-oriented series had been chosen for high regularity, whereas words in meaning-oriented series had been chosen for high frequency. The term *meaning-oriented* may be a misnomer in that high-frequency words such as *the*, *has*, *to*, and *is* are not highly meaningful to young children.

Table 5 The match between decoding and word identification in readiness books

High-frequency words or high-regularity words for which instruction of major patterns had not been provided	High-regularity words for which instruction of major patterns had been provided
Scott Foresman boy, a, likes, sees, cat, has, runs, the, girls, is, makes	
Macmillan Nan, Ben, can, Don, read, the, see, Kim, go, to, park	
Economy I a	team, need, bat, see, meet, Sue, cat, boat, man, made, am, in, pond, paint, not, tire, it, on, and, hat, leaf, hop, sun, hot
Scribner	and, ran, Dan, Ann, Nan

Although some of the high-frequency words in the meaning-oriented series had regular letter-sound patterns, the word identification strategies which teachers were to guide children in using did not make use of this feature of words. The initial word identification strategy was "sight word recognition" or memorization, with information presented only about discrete parts of words (almost entirely initial consonants). Unlike the two meaning-oriented series, the decoding-oriented series attempted to teach children about letter-sound information in a manner that allowed application to an entire word. Although both series attempted to have children apply knowledge of letter-sound information in identifying words, the two decoding-oriented series provided different techniques. In Economy, after a pattern such as vowel digraphs with long /e/ had been presented, students were to apply their knowledge to a group of words that included *team*, *need*, *see*, and *meet*. Scribner took a more direct blending strategy. First, /a/, /u/, /d/, and /n/ were presented and practiced thoroughly. Then these letters were combined in words such as *Dan*, *Nan*, and *and*.

Discussion

The first question of this study can be answered quite simply. The emergent literacy construct is not reflected in the kindergarten and readiness components of widely-used commercial reading programs. The early childhood components of basal reading programs reflect a view of reading readiness that has come to be heavily influenced by a skill-oriented perspective of reading over the decades. The emergent literacy construct that has emanated from cognitive psychology and psycholinguistics over the past several decades does not underlie student materials or guidance given to teachers. Characteristics of current programs bear evidence to at least three assumptions about young children and how they learn.

The most basic assumption is that reading acquisition is a hierarchical process that moves from letters, then to words, and finally to sentences and paragraphs. Students were only exposed to words once they had learned letters. When a corpus of words has been acquired at the readiness level, students move on to stories in the preprimers. The assumption for such a strict hierarchy in reading acquisition lacks verification in either practice or research. According to the Commission of Reading, "Learning to read appears to involve close knitting together of reading skills that complement and support one another, rather than learning one skill, adding a second, then a third, and so on" (Anderson et al., 1985, p. 97).

Closely related to the assumption of hierarchical acquisition of skills is the assumption that these skills are acquired in a rote, repetitive manner rather than by understanding patterns and making generalizations based on these understandings. Instruction of each letter and letter-sound correspondence followed the same routine. The tenth and nineteenth letters were introduced in precisely the same way as the introduction of the first and second letters. This approach departs from the view of literacy acquisition that comes from work in cognitive psychology and psycholinguistics. The work of Brown (1973) and others suggests that young children possess the ability to generalize their knowledge about language. When exemplars of a concept or skill are introduced in ways that encourage children to generalize, all examples of a class do not have to be taught directly. Cunningham's (1988) study of phonemic awareness in kindergarten children confirms this suggestion. Acquisition of phonemic awareness proceeded more quickly when teachers made connections between letter-sound correspondences rather than when teaching each letter in an isolated manner.

A third assumption concerns young children's prior knowledge about literacy. Instruction in all series proceeded as though children knew nothing about literacy or had never had any exposure to it in their environments. Research on emergent literacy has created quite a different view of young children's literacy knowledge prior to school. This research suggests that most children possess at least some concepts and skills related to reading and writing. For example, young children produce a special register when asked to read books that differ from their conversational speech (Sulzby, 1985). Young children write messages (Clay, 1978) even though these typically are inventive representations of the spelling system (Read, 1986). They also give meaning to words on signs and labels (Hiebert, 1978), although they most likely cannot identify these words out of the environmental context. Even with regard to the curriculum of the

kindergarten and readiness books, many young children are quite proficient as evidenced by their ability to name a substantial number of letters
(Mason, 1980). None of the teachers' manuals acknowledged that young
children possess concepts about literacy nor was there any encouragement
of a stance on the part of teachers to look at young children as possessing
expertise about literacy.

Although series with origins in meaning and decoding traditions are
more similar than disparate in their general approach to beginning
reading, series retain distinctive features that are in line with their historical roots. The two meaning-oriented series took the route of asking children to identify high-frequency words, even though considerable time had
been spent on auditory discrimination. Interestingly, despite the label of
meaning-oriented, word learning in these series was not connected to comprehension activities that occurred within the context of teacher read-
aloud stories. In the context of high-frequency words, children were
advised to use letter-sound correspondences but only for segments of
words. In terms of the criterion of meaningfulness, the meaning-oriented
series fell far short. Not only were young children expected to memorize
high-frequency words, many of which have little intrinsic meaning to
young children, but they were also expected to apply knowledge to isolated units of words, rather than to entire words.

The two decoding series gave children better opportunities to make the
connection between letter-sound information and word identification.
Serious questions can be raised, however, about the feasibility of any of
these approaches for children who come to school without hundreds of
hours spent listening to parents or preschool teachers read books aloud,
looking at words as adults point them out on signs and labels, and drawing
and scribbling messages. The process of learning words and letter-sound
patterns occurred out of the context of interesting books and writing activities in all series. Children who have had extensive literacy experiences in
their home and environments may be able to make sense of such instruction. For children who depend on the school to learn to read, the complete
separation of learning about words and listening comprehension from
books undoubtedly makes the introduction to literacy formidable, if not
incomprehensible.

Extensive changes are required, if the first levels of basal reading programs are to provide the context for successful reading acquisition, especially for children at risk. The records of schools are not outstanding in
teaching at-risk youngsters to read. Although many complex factors enter
into illiteracy and dropout rates, children's early experiences in school
condition later outcomes (Psacharopoulos, 1981). Increasing numbers of
at-risk children demand programs that better build on the manner in
which young children learn.

First and foremost, programs can provide children with opportunities to see written language in books as their teachers read to them and as they look at books independently and with peers. There can be little doubt that participation in workbooks as an initial introduction to literacy does not build on or foster the ways in which young children learn. Books by Mayer, Martin, Seuss, and many others show that delightful books can be written with few words in a manner that captures young children's interest. Opportunities for children to retell stories, look at books with predictable patterns, write messages with invented spelling, and respond to literature through drawing would go a long way in improving initial reading experiences.

Changes are also needed in the guidance given to teachers. General guidelines for teachers, rather than the specific play-by-play presentation that now constitutes lessons in teachers' manuals, are needed for teachers to act as reflective decision makers. When a teacher is guided in giving 41 directives, as was the case in a typical page from one of the teacher's manuals in this study, the teachers' and children's passivity is inevitable.

The present examination indicates that kindergarten and readiness books are based on some doubtful assumptions about the ways young children learn and what it means to become literate. A long road still lies ahead in making changes in materials that create the context for many children's initiation into reading. Guidelines for changes exist in the emergent literacy research. Hopefully, the next decade will be a time when inventive books provide the commonplace context for young children's introduction to reading instruction.

Note

1 This description of a kindergarten-readiness may also reflect the separate adoption of materials for kindergarten in Texas. Books labeled only kindergarten would not be appropriate for Grades 1 to 8 adoption in Texas.

References

Allington, R.L., Blachowicz, C., Cramer, R.L., Cunningham, P.M., Perez, G.Y., Robinson, C.F., Sebesta, S.L., Smith, R.G., & Tierney, R.J. (1987). *Here we are (K). Come along (R)*. Glenview, IL: Scott Foresman.

Anderson, R.C., Hiebert, E.H., Scott, J.A., & Wilkinson, I.A.G. (1985). *Becoming a nation of readers*. Champaign, IL: Center for the Study of Reading.

Arnold, V.A., & Smith, C.B. (1987). *Getting started (K–R). I think I can (R)*. New York: Macmillan.

Arnold, V.A., Smith, C.B., Flood, J., & Lapp, D. (1988). *Once upon a time (K)*. New York: Macmillan.

Ashton-Warner, S. (1963). *Teacher*. New York: Bantam.

Bridge, C.A. (1986). Predictable books for beginning readers and writers. In M.R. Sampson (Ed.), *The pursuit of literacy: Early reading and writing* (pp. 81–96). Dubuque, IA: Kendall/Hunt.

Brown, R. (1973). *A first language: The early stages*. Cambridge, MA: Harvard University Press.

Carbo, M. (1988). Debunking the great phonics myth. *Phi Delta Kappan, 70*, 226–240.

Cassidy, J., Roettger, D., & Wixson, K. (1987). *Hello sunshine (K–R). Let's begin (R)*. New York: Scribner.

Chall, J.S. (1983). *Learning to read: The great debate* (2nd ed.). New York: McGraw-Hill.

Chall, J.S. (1989). Learning to read: The great debate 20 years later: A response to "Debunking the great phonics myth." *Phi Delta Kappan, 70*, 521–538.

Chomsky, C. (1979). Approaching reading through invented spelling. In L.B. Resnick & P.A. Weaver (Eds.), *Theory and practice in early reading* (Vol. 2, pp. 43–65). Hillsdale, NJ: Erlbaum.

Clay, M. (1975). *What did I write?* Portsmouth, NH: Heinemann.

Cunningham, A.E. (1988, April). *A developmental study of instruction in phonemic awareness*. Paper presented at the annual meeting of the American Educational Research Association, New Orleans.

Downing, J. (1986). Cognitive clarity: A unifying and cross-cultural theory for language awareness phenomena in reading. In D.B. Yaden, Jr. & S. Templeton (Eds.), *Metalinguistic awareness and beginning literacy: Conceptualizing what it means to read and write* (pp. 13–30). Portsmouth, NH: Heinemann.

Durkin, D. (1987). A classroom-observation study of reading instruction in kindergarten. *Early Childhood Research Quarterly, 2*, 275–300.

Dyson, A.H. (1986). Children's early interpretations of writing: Expanding research perspectives. In D.B. Yaden, Jr. & S. Templeton (Eds.), *Metalinguistic awareness and beginning literacy: Conceptualizing what it means to read and write* (pp. 201–218). Portsmouth, NH: Heinemann.

Educational Research Service. (1986). *Kindergarten programs and practices in public schools*. Arlington, VA: Author.

Elkind, D. (1987). *Miseducation: Preschoolers at risk*. New York: Alfred A. Knopf.

English-Language Arts Curriculum Framework & Criteria Committee. (1987). *English-Language arts framework for California public schools: Kindergarten through grade twelve*. Sacramento: California State Department of Education.

Gallagher, J.M., & Sigel, I.E. (Eds.). (1987). Introduction to special issue: Hot-housing of young children. Early Childhood Research Quarterly, 2, 201–202.

Goodman, K.S., & Goodman, Y.M. (1979). Learning to read is natural. In L.B. Resnick & P.A. Weaver (Eds.), *Theory and practice of early reading* (pp. 137–154). Hillsdale, NJ: Erlbaum.

Haberman, S.S. (1978). *Analysis of qualitative data* (Vol. 1). New York: Academic.

Hatano, G., & Inagaki, K. (1983). Two courses of expertise. *Annual report: Research and clinical center for child development*. Sapporo, Japan: Hokkaido University Faculty of Education.

Hiebert, E.H. (1978). Preschool children's understanding of written language. *Child Development, 49*, 1231–1238.

Holdaway, D. (1979). *The foundations of literacy*. Exeter, NH: Heinemann.

Johns, J.L. (1986). Students' perceptions of reading: Thirty years of inquiry. In D.B. Yaden, Jr. & S. Templeton (Eds.), *Metalinguistic awareness and beginning literacy: Conceptualizing what it means to read and write* (pp. 31–40). Portsmouth, NH: Heinemann.

Lomax, R.G., & McGee, L.M. (1987). Young children's concepts about print and reading: Toward a model of word reading acquisition. *Reading Research Quarterly, 22,* 237–256.

Mason, J.M. (1980). When do children begin to read: An exploration of four-year-old children's letter and word reading competencies. *Reading Research Quarterly, 15,* 203–227.

Matteoni, L., Sucher, F., Klein, M., & Welch, K. (1986). *Sunrise Song (K). First light (R).* Oklahoma City, OK: The Economy Company.

McCormick, C.E., & Mason, J.M. (1986). Intervention procedures for increasing preschool children's interest in and knowledge about reading. In W.H. Teale & E. Sulzby (Eds.), *Emergent literacy Writing and reading* (pp. 90–115). Norwood, NJ: Ablex.

Morrow, L.M. (1984). Reading stories to young children: Effects of story structure and traditional questioning strategies on comprehension. *Journal of Reading Behavior, 16,* 273–288.

National Society for the Study of Education. (1925). *Report of the National Committee on Reading.* (24th Yearbook of the National Society for the Study of Education). Bloomington, IN: Public School Publishing.

Norusis, M.S. (1985). *Advanced statistics guide SPSS.* New York: McGraw-Hill.

Psacharopoulos, G. (1981). Returns to education: An updated international comparison. *Comparative Education, 17,* 321–341.

Read, C. (1986). *Children's creative spelling.* Boston: Routledge & Kegal Paul.

Rhodes, L.K. (1981). I can read! Predictable books as resources for reading and writing instruction. *The Reading Teacher, 34,* 511–518.

Roser, N., & Martinez, M. (1985). Roles adults play in preschoolers' response to literature. *Language Arts, 62,* 485–490.

Sampson, M.R. (Ed.). (1986). *The pursuit of literacy: Early reading and writing.* Dubuque, IA: Kendall/Hunt.

Shannon, P. (1983). The use of commercial reading materials in American elementary schools. *Reading Research Quarterly, 19,* 68–85.

Smith, F. (1978). *Understanding reading* (2nd ed.). New York: Holt, Rinehart, & Winston.

Snow, C.E., & Ninio, A. (1986). The contracts of literacy: What children learn from learning to read books. In W.H. Teale & E. Sulzby (Eds.), *Emergent literacy: Writing and reading* (pp. 173–206). Norwood, NJ: Ablex.

Strickland, D.S. (1987). Literature: Key element in the language and reading program. In B. Cullinan (Ed.), *Children's literature in the reading program* (pp. 68–76). Newark, DE: International Reading Association.

Sulzby, E. (1985). Children's emergent reading of favorite storybooks: A developmental study. *Reading Research Quarterly, 20,* 458–481.

Teale, W.H. (1986). Home background and young children's literacy development. In W.H. Teale & E. Sulzby (Eds.), *Emergent literacy: Writing and reading* (pp. 173–206). Norwood, NJ: Ablex.

Teale, W.H., & Sulzby, E. (Eds.). (1986). *Emergent literacy: Writing and reading.* Norwood, NJ: Ablex.

Yaden, D.B., Jr., & Templeton, S. (Eds.). (1986). *Metalinguistic awareness and beginning literacy: Conceptualizing what it means to read and write.* Portsmouth, NH: Heinemann.

14

PREPARING THE CLASSROOM ENVIRONMENT TO PROMOTE LITERACY DURING PLAY

Lesley Mandel Morrow

Source: *Early Childhood Research Quarterly* (1990) 5: 537–554

A classroom's physical environment is usually given less consideration than instructional planning. Concentrating on pedagogical and interpersonal factors, teachers tend to give little attention to the space, materials, and physical setting of teaching and learning. Even at the early childhood level, where relatively more time is spent arranging classroom space and materials, teachers tend to think of the learning environments' background scenery.

By contrast, a more dynamic view proposes that by purposefully arranging the environment, teachers can use physical setting as an active and pervasive influence on their own activities and attitudes as well as on those of their students.

The present study sought to describe the effects that physical design changes in preschool classroom play centers can have on children's literacy behaviors during play time. Materials for reading and writing were added to dramatic play areas and design changes implemented to determine if children's voluntary literacy behaviors (attempted and conventional reading and writing) could be increased during free-play periods.

The literature review that follows focuses on: (a) the importance of physical environment in promoting learning; (b) the contribution of play to emergent literacy; (c) the purposeful manipulation and use of play centers in early childhood classrooms; (d) the selection of specific literacy behaviors measured in the study; and (e) the role of the adult in all these activities.

Historically, early childhood education has emphasized the importance of carefully designed physical environment in fostering learning. Pestalozzi's object lessons stressed manipulative experiences, and Froebel's gifts and occupations were systemically planned, as was Montessori's prepared environment (Morrison, 1988). Piaget (1962) also held that the learning of young children requires interaction with materials.

More recently research has documented the critical role that physical environment, combined with clearly defined teaching purposes, plays in classroom learning experiences (Loughlin & Suina, 1983; Rivlin & Weinstein, 1984). Indeed, careful classroom design has been termed essential to the success of instruction (Loughlin & Martin, 1987; Weinstein, 1977). Spatial arrangements alone affect children's behavior in the classroom. Field (1980) observed that rooms partitioned into smaller spaces facilitated such behaviors as peer and verbal interaction, fantasy, associative, and cooperative play more than did rooms with large open spaces. Nash (1981) and Moore (1986) found that children in carefully arranged rooms showed more creative productivity and greater use of language-related activities than did children in randomly arranged rooms. Children also demonstrated more engaged and exploratory behavior and more social interaction and cooperation than children in moderately or poorly defined settings.

Joining the block and housekeeping areas of a classroom increased mixed-sex groupings among 3- and 4-year-olds, as well as relevant, constructive use of the block area by girls (Kinsman & Berk, 1979). Montes and Risley (1975) found that storing toys on open shelves rather than in boxes led to easier selection, more time spent playing, and more immediate involvement.

The introduction of thematic play materials into the dramatic play area of a laboratory playroom and of a preschool classroom, led children to more elaborate and longer play sequences (Dodge & Frost, 1986; Woodward, 1984). Pelligrini (1983) found that dramatic props in the block center elicited more imaginative language than playing with blocks alone. That appropriate physical arrangement of furniture, selection of materials, and the aesthetic quality of a room, contribute to teaching and learning is evident also in studies by Bumsted (1981), Phyfe-Perkins (1979), and Sutfin (1980).

The role of play in emergent literacy

Vygotsky (1966) maintains that play allows a child to go beyond the bounds of stimulus and learn to use symbolic, abstract levels of thought. Piaget (1962) stressed the importance of play in developing representational skills—that is allowing something to stand for something else out of the immediate context. Play gives children the chance to incorporate new information into their behaviors and to elaborate and extend known information or familiar skills into new contexts.

Early childhood classroom are typically arranged into activity centers—almost always including dramatic play areas. Can such areas be designed to stimulate and reinforce emergent literacy behaviors? Can activities suggested by the teacher facilitate the children's use of written language to represent spoken language, assigning pretend play a specific role in developing the child's representational skills?

Literacy behaviors have already been observed in very young children long before school enrollment or formal instruction (Durkin, 1974; Ferreiro & Teberosky, 1982; Teale & Sulzby, 1986). Emergent literacy is evident in children's awareness of reading and writing and in their exploration with such materials for reading and writing as paper, pencils and books (Lomax & McGee, 1987; Schickedanz, 1986), in scribbling, drawing, dictation, story composition, and functional writing (Clay, 1985; Ehri, 1989; Harste, Woodward, & Burke, 1984), and in listening to stories, handling books, pretend reading, telling stories, playing with letters, and exposure to environmental and functional print (Clay, 1985; Hiebert, 1981; Lomax & McGee, 1987; Mason & Kerr, 1988; Morrow, 1985; Sulzby, 1985).

Appropriate physical environment is essential in supporting and actively influencing the amount and type of literacy behaviors in which children engage (Morrow, 1987, 1989; Morrow & Weinstein, 1982, 1986). Children's voluntary use of literature materials, for instance, can be increased during free-play time by designing a visible, accessible, attractive library corner and encouraging teacher guidance in its use.

The dramatic play area seems especially promising for the practice, elaboration, and extension of emergent literacy. Roskos (1988) observed such literate behaviors as paper handling, storytelling, and early reading and writing among very young children at play. Pellegrini (1980) found a relationship between levels of play and achievement in emergent reading, writing, and language. Dramatic play has improved story production and comprehension, including recall of details and the ability to sequence and interpret (Mandler & Johnson, 1977; Saltz, Dixon & Johnson, 1977; Saltz & Johnson, 1974). Similar positive effects resulted when children played out familiar fairy tales during thematic-fantasy play sessions (Pellegrini, 1982; Silvern, Taylor, Williamson, Surbeck, & Kelly, 1986).

Connections between play and emergent writing abilities have been delineated by Christie and Noyce (1986) possibly because in solitary dramatic play children use solo techniques, developing story lines, organizing narrative, and developing clarity of expression and precise vocabulary.

The role of the adult in promoting literacy in play

Physical environment apparently affects both teacher behaviors and youngsters' behaviors (Kritchevsky & Prescott, 1977). Teachers who worked in higher quality space were more likely to be sensitive and friendly toward children, to encourage children in self-chosen activities, and to teach consideration for the rights and feelings of others. Teachers in poorer quality space were less involved, more restrictive, and more likely to teach arbitrary rules of social living. Teachers also play a vital role in guiding students in using different physical settings (Moore, 1986). Preschool teachers can promote writing development by modelling functional writing during play sessions and by introducing functions of print (Schrader, 1989). Vygotsky (1966) maintains that the adult provides a social context for the child's learning that enables the child to perform at a higher level than is possible on the child's own.

Holdaway (1979) views literacy development similarly. The supportive adult provides an emulative model that the child first observes, then carries out in a collaborative effort with encouragement and necessary assistance from the adult. The child then goes on to practice the new behavior and eventually reaches independence. Natural learning is shaped and supported by adult intervention based on the child's needs and current level of ability.

Purpose of the present study

The present study set out to determine if and how children's voluntary literacy behaviors could be increased during free-play periods through the design and equipping of dramatic play areas. It addressed four specific questions:

1   Are the type and amount of literacy play activities increased by incorporating books, paper, and pencils into dramatic play areas?
2   Does the purposeful design of thematic play areas increase the type and amount of literacy play activities in rooms that include books, paper, and pencils?
3   Does teacher guidance during play affect the amount of literacy behaviors that occur?
4   Do the sexes differ in the type and amount of literacy behavior participation?

Methods

Subjects

The study employed 13 preschool classrooms with an average class size of 12. All were located in suburban, middle class areas. Of 170 children in the study, 84 were girls, 86 boys. Taught by student teachers enrolled in a teacher education program, classes were selected for the study if: (a) both student-teacher and cooperating teacher were willing to participate; (b) free-play periods of 20–30 min were scheduled daily; (c) teachers had made no specific environmental provisions or suggestions for literacy activities during play before the start of the present research project.

Physical design of dramatic play areas

Physical attributes of the dramatic play areas before and after the intervention were compared to check on design change manipulation. Results indicated that before the investigation, none of the 13 rooms had literacy materials purposefully placed in the dramatic play area, and none of the rooms had created a thematic play situation with literacy materials included. The dramatic play areas in the preschools had been set up like kitchens containing a table and chairs, a stove, cabinets, dishes, pots and pans, dress-up clothing, dolls, a mirror, and sometimes a telephone.

Procedures

Settings

Classrooms were randomly distributed among one control and three experimental conditions. The three control classrooms served 19 girls and 19 boys. Treatment for the three classrooms in Experimental Group 1, E1, (E1 = 18 girls, 21 boys) consisted of teacher-guided introduction books, paper, and pencils into the dramatic play area. Treatment for the four classrooms in Experimental Group 2, E2, (E2 = 28 girls, 29 boys) consisted of teacher-guided thematic play with books, paper, and pencils incorporated into the play area. Treatment for the three classrooms in Experimental Group 3, E3, (E3 = 19 girls, 20 boys) was similar to that for E2, but without teacher guidance.

Intervention

Before the beginning of data collection, the 13 participating student-teachers attended a workshop introducing them to the materials for the intervention periods of the study. The workshops were separate for each condition. Procedures for the study were described at each workshop and the student-teachers were provided with scripts for introducing play periods to the children. During the study, they guided play periods and collected anecdotal data. Research assistants, one per classroom, were also present at the workshops. They prepared and placed classroom materials according to particular treatment and collected data on the children's literacy behaviors.

Preintervention or baseline data were collected twice a week for 3 weeks. In all rooms, the research assistants and student-teachers observed and recorded the number of children participating in literacy activities in the dramatic play areas, and the type of activities in which they were engaged. Four observations were conducted each day approximately 5–7 min apart. Literacy behavior during play was defined as reading-like and writing-like acts such as using printed materials with attention to their symbolic aspects and the production of printed materials. More specifically, literacy behaviors for observation included: (a) Paper Handling—sorting, shuffling, and scanning (Clay, 1985; Harste et al., 1984); (b) Writing—drawing, scribbling, tracing, copying, dictating, writing on a computer or typewriter, thematic play related to writing, story writing, and invented writing (Clay, 1985; Harste et al., 1984); and (c) Reading—browsing, pretend reading, book handling, storytelling, reading aloud to oneself or others, and reading silently (Clay, 1985; Heibert, 1981; Lomax & McGee, 1987; Mason & Kerr, 1988; Morrow, 1985; Schickedanz, 1986, Sulzby, 1985). This list of observed behaviors reflects the work of Roskos (1988). Throughout the study, behavior checklists were provided to the research assistants, one checklist per session.

After 3 weeks, research assistants in the experimental classrooms implemented physical changes in the dramatic play areas. The same materials were placed in all three groups of experimental classrooms, E1, E2, and E3: (a) stacks of different sized paper and types; (b) materials for making books, such as construction paper and a stapler; (c) ready-made blank booklets; (d) magazines and books; and (e) pencils, felt tip pens, crayons, and colored pencils. Each kind of material had its own storage container and storage location.

In both E2 classrooms (thematic play with teacher guidance) and E3 classrooms (thematic play without teacher guidance), dramatic play areas were designed to represent veterinarians' offices. Each included a waiting room with chairs, a table, magazines, books, and pamphlets. On the wall were posters about pets, a list of doctor's hours, a "No Smoking" sign, and a sign that said, "Check in with the nurse when you arrive." The "nurse" was given forms and a clipboard to use with "patients". Also in the office were a telephone, address and telephone books, appointment cards, a calendar, patient folders, prescription pads, white coats, masks, gloves, bandages, and doctor's kits.

In E1 and E2 classrooms, teachers discussed the materials with the children and suggested how children could play with them. In E1 classrooms, dramatic play areas were designed to represent kitchens. At the beginning of each play period, teachers suggested that the children try such activities as reading to dolls, writing notes to friends, writing recipes, making shopping lists, and taking telephone messages. In E2 classrooms, teachers also discussed potential uses of materials at the beginning of each play period: for example, reading to pets in the waiting room, filling out prescription forms and appointment cards at the nurse's desk. Because the children were preschoolers, they were also told that they could pretend to read and write. In E3 classrooms (unguided thematic play), teachers introduced the new materials only the first time they were added to the area for free-time

311

use. Teachers in the control classrooms implemented no changes in the dramatic play areas, nor did they suggest any literacy behaviors during play.

With the addition of materials in the experimental groups, a 1-week pause in data collection allowed the novelty of the changes to wear off. Then data collection was resumed for another 3 weeks, the intervention period for purposes of the study. Again, observations were conducted twice a week during free-play periods. After a second lapse, 1 month in duration, observations were again conducted twice a week for 3 weeks to measure the effects of intervention over a longer period of time.

Research assistants visited the classrooms twice a week to ensure that the physical plans for each of the conditions were in place, to replenish supplies, and to monitor student-teacher ability to study parameters and guidelines. Twice during the observation period, research assistants and student teachers were checked for observer-reliability in recording literacy behaviors during play. They agreed on 90% of their observations of the number of children participating in literacy activities on a 95% of their observations of the kinds of activities observed.

Results

Research design

The classroom was used as the unit of analysis, since the behavior of children during free-play time is likely to be interdependent. This interdependence would violate the assumption of independence of experimental units underlying conventional analyses that use the child as the unit of analysis. In addition, because children could not be randomly assigned to conditions, intact classrooms were used. For each of the measures used in the analysis, the classroom mean for that measure was considered to be the observation. Because the major focus of this research was to contrast literacy behavior during play in three different time periods (preintervention, during intervention, and delayed), a repeated measures analysis of variance was used. The F statistic corresponding to Wilk's Lambda will be reported for all analyses. The factors in the design were group (experimental, with three different treatments and a control), sex (male and female), and time (pre, during, and delayed). In the analysis, the primary dependent variable was the total number of different children who participated in particular literacy behaviors during each free-play period in the four different groups. There were 18 data points available for each classroom, 6 preintervention, 6 during intervention, and 6 after a 1-month delayed period of time. In order to attain a reliable index of classroom behavior for each period, these six data points were averaged for each period.

312

Number of children and types of literacy activities

Literacy activities were divided into four major categories: paper handling, writing, reading, and the total score for all three categories. Although several categories of paper handling, writing, and reading were designated as items to record if observed, the amount of participation in each subcategory was so small that statistical analyses could be done only for each main category.

Table 1 presents the means and standard deviations for paper handling in the four groups in each of the three time periods. The analysis indicated that there was a significant group by time interaction, $F(6,34) = 2.54$, $p<.03$. A univariate analysis of variance was done on each of the three time periods to see where the differences occurred. Significant differences were not found between the groups in the preintervention period. There were significant differences between groups in time period two, $F(3,18) = 4.86$, $p<.01$, and in time period three, $F(3,18) = 4.54$, $p<.01$, on the amount of paper handling. Post hoc comparisons for group means using the Duncan test indicated that in time period two (intervention) and time period three (delayed), the three experimental groups were significantly different from the control and that they did more paper handling activity than the control group. None of the experimental groups were different from each other. Figure 1 displays the results. It is clear that roughly equal gains occur for the experimental groups during the intervention and maintain for at least 1 month following the intervention.

There were no significant main effects or interactions for sex on the paper handling or for any other of the variables tested.

Table 2 presents the means and standard deviations for writing in the

Table 1 M (and *SD*) for paper handling

Groups	Pre	Intervention during	Delayed
(E1) Thematic play with teacher guidance[1]	0.03[a] (0.04)	2.77[a] (0.29)	2.75[a] (0.28)
(E2) Paper, pencil, books with teacher guidance[2]	0.05[a] (0.05)	3.00[a] (0.30)	2.73[a] (0.30)
(E3) Thematic play without teacher guidance[3]	0.03[a] (0.02)	2.50[a] (0.20)	2.45[a] (0.21)
Control[4]	0.01[a] (0.17)	0.07[b] (0.00)	0.06[b] (0.00)

Notes
M in any column are significantly different, $p<.05$, if they do not share the same superscript.
1 $N = 39$
2 $N = 57$
3 $N = 39$
4 $N = 38$

Literacy During Play

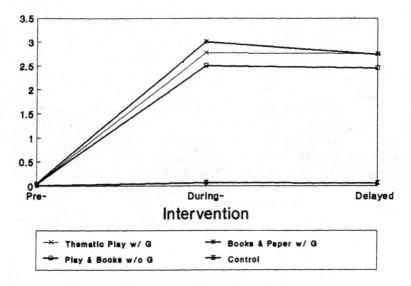

Figure 1 Paper handling (means)

Table 2 *M* (and *SD*) for writing

Groups	Pre	Intervention during	Delayed
(E1) Thematic play with teacher guidance[1]	0.01[a] (0.01)	2.85[a] (0.25)	2.65[a] (0.28)
(E2) Paper, pencil, books with teacher guidance[2]	0.02[a] (0.02)	3.76[b] (0.22)	3.68[b] (0.25)
(E3) Thematic play without teacher guidance[3]	0.02[a] (0.25)	2.85[c] (0.13)	0.76[c] (0.12)
Control[4]	0.01[a] (0.01)	0.05[d] (0.01)	0.08[d] (0.01)

Notes
M in any column are significantly different, $p<.05$, if they do not share the same superscript.
1 $N = 39$
2 $N = 57$
3 $N = 39$
4 $N = 38$

four groups in each of the three time periods. The analysis indicated that there was a significant group by time interaction, $F(34) = 8.15$, $p<.001$. A univariate analysis of variance was done on each of the three time periods to see where the differences occurred. No significant differences were found between the groups in the preintervention period. There were significant differences between groups in time period two, $F(3,18) = 26.67$, $p<.001$, and in time period three, $F(3,18) = 21.14$, $p<.001$, in the amount of writing. Post hoc comparisons for group means using the Duncan test indicated that in time period two (intervention) and time period three (delayed), all groups were significantly different from each other. The books, paper, and pencils groups (E1) demonstrated the most writing, next was the thematic play with teacher guidance (E2), next was the thematic play without teacher guidance (E3), and the control group showed the least amount of writing behavior. Figure 2 displays the results. It is clear that roughly equal gains occur for the experimental groups during the intervention and maintain for at least 1 month following the intervention.

Table 3 presents the means and standard deviations for reading in the four groups in each of the three time periods. The analysis indicated that there was a significant group by time interaction, $F(6,34) = 3.05$, $p<.01$. Univariate analysis of variance was done on each of the three time periods to see where the differences occurred. No significant differences were found between the groups in the preintervention period. There were differences between groups in time period two, $F(3,18) = 7.94$, $p<.01$, and in time period three, $F(3,18) = 6.63$, $p<.01$, on the amount of reading. Post hoc comparisons for group means using the Duncan test indicated that in both time periods two and time period three, thematic play with teacher guidance (E2) did significantly more reading than the other three groups. The books, paper, and pencils group (E1) and thematic play without guidance (E3) were similar to each other and were significantly different from

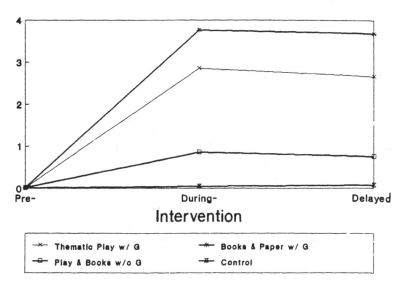

Figure 2 Writing (means)

315

Table 3 M (and *SD*) for reading

Groups	Pre	Intervention During	Delayed
(E1) Thematic play with teacher guidance[1]	0.02[a] (0.02)	3.90[a] (0.28)	3.78[a] (0.32)
(E2) Paper, pencil, books with teacher guidance[2]	0.11[a] (0.12)	1.18[b] (0.09)	1.22[b] (0.07)
(E3) Thematic play without teacher guidance[3]	0.02[a] (0.02)	1.20[b] (0.15)	1.21[b] (0.15)
Control[4]	0.02[a] (0.29)	0.05[c] (0.02)	0.04[c] (0.00)

Notes
M in any column are significantly different, $p<.05$, if they do not share the same superscript.
1 $N = 39$
2 $N = 57$
3 $N = 39$
4 $N = 38$

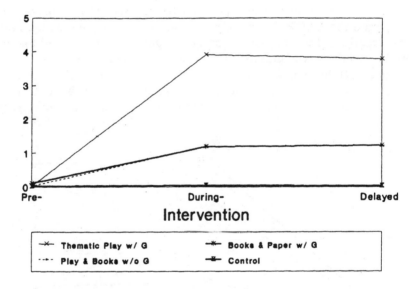

Figure 3 Reading (means)

the control group, with more reading in those groups than in the control group. Figure 3 displays the results. It is clear that roughly equal gains occur for the experimental groups during the intervention and maintain for at least 1 month following the intervention.

Table 4 presents the means and standard deviations for total literacy behaviors in the four groups in each of the time periods. The analysis

Table 4 M (and *SD*) for total literacy

Groups	Pre	Intervention During	Delayed
(E1) Thematic play with teacher guidance[1]	0.02[a] (0.03)	3.20[a] (0.19)	3.06[a] (0.21)
(E2) Paper, pencil, books with teacher guidance[2]	0.06[a] (0.17)	2.64[a] (0.14)	2.54[a] (0.23)
(E3) Thematic play without teacher guidance[3]	0.02[a] (0.01)	1.51[b] (0.13)	1.47[b] (0.12)
Control[4]	0.01[a] (0.38)	0.05[c] (0.00)	0.06[c] (0.02)

Notes

M in any column are significantly different, $p<.05$, if they do not share the same superscript.

1 $N = 39$
2 $N = 57$
3 $N = 39$
4 $N = 38$

indicated that there was a significant group by time interaction, $F(6,34) = 7.23$, $p<.001$. A univariate analysis of variance was done on each of the three time periods to see what periods had differences. Significant differences were not found between the groups in the preintevention period. There were significant differences between groups in time period two, $F(3,18) = 47.89$, $p <.001$, and in time period three, $F(3,18) = 36.64$, $p <.001$, in the amount of total literacy behavior. Post hoc comparisons for group means using the Duncan test indicated that in time periods two and three, E1 and E2 were similar to each other and they were significantly different from the other groups in using the most literacy behaviors. The E3 group was significantly different from E1 and E2, both demonstrated more literacy behaviors than E3, but E3 used significantly more literacy behaviors than the control group. The control group was significantly different from the experimental groups and used the least literacy behaviors. Figure 4 displays the results. It is clear that roughly equal gains occur for the experimental groups during the intervention and maintain for at least one month following the intervention.

Separate analyses were not done for the individual items in each of the main categories observed (paper handling, writing, and reading), because there was insufficient child participation in any one of them for a statistical analysis to be carried out. Observations of the data revealed that in paper handling, children mostly did sorting of paper; in writing, mostly drawing, scribbling, copying, and writing related to thematic play; and in reading, browsing, pretend reading, looking at books, and pretending to read to others.

Literacy During Play

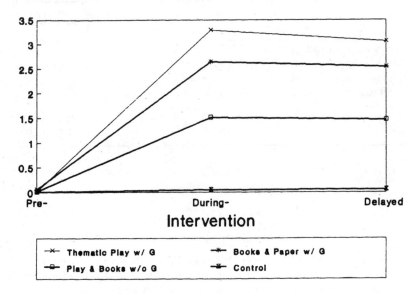

Figure 4 Total literacy (means)

Discussion

The physical design changes implemented in the present study were effect-ive in increasing the level of voluntary literacy behaviors during play. The data support the recommendations of researchers concerning the powerful impact of design changes on behavior. Altman and Wohlwill (1979) claim that young children are quite sensitive to modification of the environment. This study clearly indicates that teachers cannot overlook the physical setting of the classroom in their preoccupation with curricular and inter-personal concerns. By providing well-designed classrooms, teachers are able to facilitate literacy behaviors and possibly enhance cognitive devel-opment. Certainly the present study indicates that the effort involved in providing literacy materials in dramatic play areas and thematic settings yields gratifying results.

Literacy settings and literacy during play

The study implemented two physical design strategies to determine the effect of both on the amount and type of literacy behavior that occurred. In the first group (E1), paper, pencils, books, and magazines were added to the dramatic play area. In the second group (E2), a thematic setting was designed, a veterinarian's office, with paper, pencils, books, and magazines. Overall, thematic setting produced more literacy behaviors in total than occurred in E1, the group supplied only with literacy materials. When viewed more specifically, however, it was found that children in E1 participated in more writing activities than did the children in E2, and the children in E2 participated in more reading activities than the children in E1.

Another important finding was that even after a delayed period of time, literacy behaviors continued and did not taper off. It should also be noted, however, that although treatment did significantly increase the use of literacy behaviors during play, that use was still limited to only a few children per classroom.

Anecdotal observations

Anecdotal observations by the teachers and research assistants of conversations and activities that occurred among children during the free-play periods in the different groups add insights into the observed behavior. According to those anecdotes, children in the thematic play group interacted with each other a great deal in their literacy activity during play. Their play involved associative and cooperative role playing focused on the theme of a veterinarian's office. The play was elaborate and its sequences long. Similar results were found by Dodge and Frost (1986) and Woodward (1984).

When observing in the thematic play setting, it was typical to see children in the veterinarian's waiting rooms reading to their stuffed animal pets while waiting to see the doctors. Some children read to themselves and some to each other. Children also used the crayons and paper to draw pictures. Pet owners checked with the nurses, who recorded that they were waiting, filled out forms, and made appointments that were written down in the appointment book. The doctors and pet owners talked about their pets' problems. The doctors examined the pets and prescribed medicine on prescription pads. Doctors also made notes in the pets' folders. Specific incidents that occurred during play illustrate such findings:

> Jessica was waiting to see the doctor. She told her stuffed dog not to worry, that the doctor wouldn't hurt him. She pretended to read *Are You My Mother* to her pet and showed him the pictures as she read.
>
> Jennie ran into the doctor's office shouting, "My dog got runned over by a car." The doctor bandaged the dog's leg. Then the two children decided that the incident must be reported to the police. Before calling the police, they got out the telephone book and turned to a map to find the spot where the dog had been hit. Then they called the police on the toy phone to report the incident.

Preston examined a pet teddy bear. He took the bear's temperature and blood pressure and recorded the numbers. Then he gave the bear a shot and said, "I'm sorry, I hope I didn't hurt you." He wrote out a prescription in scribble writing, then read it to the bear and its owner. As he pointed to the paper, he said, "Now, this says that you make sure you take 100 of these pills every hour until you're better." Preston wrapped the bear in a blanket and added, "Now, you stay nice and warm, and call me if you have any more problems."

Israel, who was playing the doctor, told Jessica, his nurse, to send a letter to Mrs. Smith telling her it was time to bring her dog for a checkup. Jessica did what Israel told her.

Joshua had just examined a dog. He was going to write in the patient's folder and said, "You know what? I'm going to write his name in dog language. How do you spell *Ruff*?"

The E1 classrooms (teacher-guided materials) generated a great deal of excitement. Children were delighted to use the materials; however, literacy behaviors were, for the most part, not tied to any particular themes. When children wrote they tended to explore and experiment with the literacy materials. They did not look at books very often. The writing materials seemed more attractive and the children used them readily, but reading materials not identified to a specific thematic purpose or function did not engage much interest. Nor were children's literacy behaviors in this group as collaborative or cooperative as those of children in the thematic groups. Rather, many children played alone with the literacy materials. They also tended to move quickly from one activity to the next, their literacy behaviors more random, less elaborate, and less purposeful. In the thematic play groups, by contrast, children read more often and the reading was almost always related to the theme: for example, child reading to pet in the waiting room, looking up information about medicine, and so forth.

Anecdotes from the E1 group illustrate the nature of their literacy behaviors:

Matthew picked up some paper and began copying letters from a chart on the wall. Jonathan asked him what he was doing, then got himself some paper and a pencil and started doing the same thing. They compared each other's writing, then started to write their own names.

Claire found a quiet place on the floor, took some pencils and crayons, and began to draw.

Marsha picked up a book and said, "I'm reading." Josh sat at the table with some paper and said, "I'm doing my homework." Taylor chimed in and said, "Look, I wrote my name!"

320

Children did play school occasionally. They liked to take down each other's telephone numbers and addresses. Otherwise, the literacy activity was a series of unrelated acts of copying charts, pretend writing, trying to write letters, and modelling each other's work. In reality, the literacy was not really tied to play, but it took place in a free-play period when children had the opportunity to select activites of a wide range.

Teacher guidance

All three experimental conditions implemented physical design changes in their dramatic play areas by adding materials and organizing space in specific ways. It was evident that the children in the experimental groups participated in more literacy behaviors during play than did children in the control group. Two of the experimental treatments included teacher guidance. In those classrooms in which teachers introduced literacy materials and made frequent suggestions for their use, children participated in more literacy activities in greater variety than did children in classrooms where teacher guidance was not provided. The results of this investigation support the role of the adult during play as discussed in the literature review, especially in Vygotsky's (1966) theory that children learn higher psychological processes through social environment and specifically with adult guidance within a child's "zone of proximal cognitive development." The results also reinforce Holdaway's (1979) model that a child reaches independence by modelling behaviors in collaboration with an adult, profiting from encouragement and assistance.

Classrooms in which teachers provided guidance produced more literacy behaviors than those in which no such guidance was offered. Morrow (1982; 1987) and Morrow and Weinstein (1982, 1986) found that although appropriate environmental design can increase children's voluntary use of literature, it must be supported by adult guidance to be totally effective.

Implications

The results of this study lend empirical support to the importance of the physical environment as a catalyst for changing behavior and, in this case, increased use of literacy activities by preschool children. Each of the experimental conditions resulted in more literacy behaviors than were evident in the control group. Thematic settings encouraged role playing; literacy activity in those settings focused almost entirely on theme and was based on meaning and function. Classrooms in which literacy materials were unrelated to specific theme produced activities that were more experiemntal, exploratory, random, and less focused. Teacher guidance also obviously played an important role in increasing quantity and variety of literacy behaviors among children. Finally, effects of experimental treatments seemed to last over a period of time.

Additional studies should investigate the effects of such treatments on literacy development, with treatments extended over longer periods of time. It is also assumed that thematic settings would need to be changed from time to time in order to maintain children's interest. Literacy materials should be varied in type and quantity periodically, with new kinds of materials introduced. Although the present study was not carried out long enough to measure changes in literacy development, dated samples of children's writing from the experimental groups showed more scribble writing early in the project, with more attempts later at letter-like forms and random letters. Generally the theories of Vygotsky (1966) and Piaget (1962) seemed to be validated in the results of the study. Play apparently did enable children to assimilate new information and consolidate past experience through symbolic means.

It seems appropriate and beneficial, based on the results of this investigation, that teachers prepare their environments to include literacy materials in play centers in the classroom. Such materials in such settings increase children's voluntary involvement in varied literacy experiences. Future research may reveal that play-related literacy activity has the potential to increase literacy development as well.

Acknowledgements

This research was supported by the Rutgers University Research Council. I would like to extend my gratitude to the individuals who helped to carry out the study. They are: Maria Antonucci, Michele Biasucci, Danielle DeLorenzo, Pamela Dobrzynski, Julie Friel, Patricia Kennely, Margaret Keilly, Jill Locotos, Maureen Malvarony, Ann Pacciano, Maria Perillo, Jill Rosen, Laura Scott, Doreen Tandries. Finally, I want to acknowledge the statistical assistance of Jeffrey Smith.

References

Altman, I., & Wohlwill, J. (1979). *Children and the environment.* New York: Plenum.

Bumsted, L.A. (1981). *Influencing the frequency of children's cooperative and social behavior through change in the design and management of the classroom.* Unpublished master's thesis, Cornell University, Ithaca, NY.

Christie, J., & Noyce, R. (1986). Play and writing: Possible connections. In B. Mergen (Ed.), *Cultural dimensions of play, games and sport.* Champaign, IL: Human Kinetics.

Clay, M. (1985). *Early detection of reading difficulties* (3rd ed.), Portsmouth, NH; Heinemann.

Dodge, M., & Frost, J. (1986). Children's dramatic play: Influence of thematic and nonthematic settings. *Childhood Education*, 166–170.

Durkin, D. (1974). A six year study of children who learned to read in school at the age of four. *Reading Research Quarterly, 10*, 9–61.

Ehri, L. (1989). Movement into word reading and spelling. In J.M. Mason (Ed.), *Reading and writing connections*. Needham Heights, MA: Allyn & Bacon.

Ferreiro, E., & Teberosky, A. (1982). *Literacy before schooling*. Portsmouth, NH: Heinemann.

Field, T. (1980). Preschool play: Effects of teacher/child ratios and organization of classroom space. *Child Study Journal, 10*, 191–205.

Harste, J.C., Woodward, V.A., & Burke, C.L. (1984). *Language stories and literacy lessons*. Portsmouth, NH: Heinemann.

Hiebert, E. (1981). Developmental patterns and interrelationships of preschool children's print awareness. *Reading Research Quarterly, 16*, 236–260.

Holdaway, D. (1979). *Foundations of literacy*. New York: Ashton Scholastic.

Kinsman, C., & Berk, L. (1979). Joining the block and housekeeping areas: Changes in play and social behavior. *Young Children, 35*, 66–75.

Kritchevsky, S., & Prescott, E. (1977). *Planning environments for young children: Physical space*. Washington, DC: National Association for the Education of Young Children.

Lomax, R.G., & McGee, L.M. (1987). Young children's concepts about print and reading: Toward a model of word reading acquisition. *Reading Research Quarterly, 22*, 237–256.

Loughlin, C.E., & Martin, M.D. (1987). *Supporting literacy: A developing effective learning environment*. New York: Teachers College Press.

Loughlin, C.E., & Suina, J.H. (1983). Reflecting the child's community in the classroom environment. *Childhood Education, 60*, 18–21.

Mandler, J., & Johnson, N. (1977). Remembrance of things parsed: Story structure and recall. *Cognitive Psychology, 9*, 111–151.

Mason, J., & Kerr, B. (1988). *Transmission of literacy to young children*. Paper presented at the annual CORR preconvention of the International Reading Association, Toronto, Canada.

Montes, F., & Risley, T. (1975). Evaluating traditional day care practices: An empirical approach. *Child Care Quarterly, 4*, 208–215.

Moore, G. (1986). Effects of the spatial detinition of behavior settings on children's behavior: A quasi experimental field study. *Journal of Environmental Psychology, 6*, 205–231.

Morrison, G. (1988). *Early childhood education today* (4th ed.). Columbus, OH: Merrill.

Morrow, L. (1982). Relationships between literature programs, library corners and children's use of literature. *Journal of Educational Research, 75*, 339–344.

Morrow, L. (1985). Retelling stories: a strategy for improving young children's comprehension, concept of story structure, and oral language complexity. *Elementary School Journal, 85*, 647–661.

Morrow, L. (1987). Promoting inner city children's recreational reading. *Reading Teacher, 24*, 266–276.

Morrow, L. (1989). *Literacy development in the early years: Helping children read and write*. Englewood Cliffs, NJ: Prentice Hall.

Morrow, L., & Weinstein, C. (1982). Increasing children's use of literature through programs and physical design changes. *The Elementary School Journal, 83*, 132–137.

Morrow, L., & Weinstein, C. (1986). Encouraging voluntary reading: The impact of a literature program on children's use of library centers. *Reading Research Quarterly, 21*, 330–346.

Nash, B. (1981). The effects of classroom spatial organization on 4- and 5-year-old children's learning. *British Journal of Educational Psychology, 51*, 144–155.

Pellegrini, A. (1980). The relationship between kindergarteners' play and achievement in prereading, language, and writing. *Psychology in the Schools, 17*, 530–535.

Pellegrini, A. (1982). The construction of cohesive text by preschoolers in two play contexts. *Discourse Processes, 5*, 101–108.

Pellegrini, A. (1983). Sociolinguistic contexts of the preschool. *Journal of Applied Developmental Psychology, 4*, 389–397.

Phyfe-Perkins, E. (1979). Children's behavior in preschool settings: A review of research concerning the influence of the physical environment. In L. Katz (Ed.), *Current topics in early childhood education* (Vol. 3, pp. 91–125). Norwood, NJ: Ablex.

Piaget, J. (1962). *Play, dreams and imitation in childhood*. New York: Norton.

Rivlin, L., & Weinstein, C. (1984). Educational issues, school settings, and environmental psychology. *Journal of Environmental Psychology, 4*, 347–364.

Roskos, K. (1988). *A summary of an exploratory study of the nature of literate behavior in the pretend play episodes of 4- and 5-year-old children*. Unpublished manuscript.

Saltz, E., Dixon, D., & Johnson, J. (1977). Training disadvantaged preschoolers on various fantasy activities: Effects on cognitive functioning and impulse control. *Child Development, 48*, 367–380.

Saltz, E., & Johnson, J. (1974). Training for thematic-fantasy play in culturally disadvantaged children: Preliminary results. *Journal of Educational Psychology, 66*, 623–630.

Schickedanz, J. (1986). *More than the ABCs: The early stages of reading and writing*. Washington, DC: National Association for the Education of Young children.

Schrader, C. (1989). Written language use within the context of young children's symbolic play. *Early Childhood Research Quarterly, 4*, 225–244.

Silvern, S., Taylor, J., Williamson, P., Surbeck, E., & Kelly, M. (1986). Young children's story recall as a product of play, story familiarity and adult intervention. *Merrill-Palmer Quarterly, 32*, 73–86.

Sulzby, E. (1985). Children's emergent reading of favorite storybooks: A developmental study. *Reading Research Quarterly, 20*, 458–481.

Sutfin, H. (1980). *The effect on children's behavior of a change in the physical design of kindergarten classroom*. Unpublished doctoral dissertation, Boston University.

Teale, W., & Sulzby, E. (1986). Emergent literacy as a perspective for examining how young children become writers and readers. In W.H. Teale & E. Sulzby (Eds.), *Emergent literacy: Writing and reading*. Norwood, NJ: Ablex.

Vygotsky, L. (1966). Play and its role in the mental development of the child. *Soviet Psychology, 12*, 62–76.

Weinstein, C.S. (1977). The physical environment of the school: A review of the research. *Review of Educational Research, 49*, 577–610.

Woodward, C. (1984). Guidelines for facilitating socio-dramatic play. *Childhood Education, 60*, 172–177.

15

LITERACY KNOWLEDGE IN PRACTICE

Contexts of participation for young writers and readers

Susan B. Neuman and Kathleen Roskos

Source: *Reading Research Quarterly* (1997) 32(1): 10–32

Children's earliest discoveries about written language are learned through active engagement with their social and cultural worlds (Bissex, 1980; Teale & Sulzby, 1986). They interact with others in writing and reading situations, explore print on their own, and experiment with different forms, inventing their own literacies. As they engage in these meaningful activities, children develop knowledge about the forms and functions of written language in situational contexts (Goodman, 1986; Lass, 1982). Consequently, environments that are embedded with rich written language experiences provide opportunities for children to become naturally involved in literacy-related events. Such settings include not only physical surroundings, but human relationships that determine when, how often, and in what situations children may engage in using the cultural tools of literacy—materials, uses, and meanings (Neuman & Roskos, 1992; Tharp & Gallimore, 1988).

The developing child, however, is not merely a tabula rasa on which the environment makes its impact, but part of a dynamic system (Bronfenbrenner, 1977). Children use the resources and constraints of the social and physical environment, as well as their relevant knowledge and skills, to analyze and construct their understandings of print and their world. As emphasized by Vygotsky (1978), in these contexts they practice using the cognitive tools (i.e., books, paper, writing tools) in problem-solving situations through interaction with peers and more experienced members of society. Thinking develops out of this external social activity through internalization of the processes and practices provided by the sociocultural context. Therefore, children's learning about literacy is integrally tied with practical action, resulting from their need to control, manipulate, and function in their environment.

As children enter more formal learning contexts in school, literacy activities tend to become removed from the context of socially relevant action, to contexts in which "words are the major invitations to form concepts rather than the action" (Bruner, Olver, & Greenfield, 1966, p. 62). Unlike everyday situations, verbal rules or generalizations in school learning may precede or, in some cases, substitute for their referents in practical contexts. Much of children's formal education may typically involve them in learning techniques for processing information (e.g., identifying letters, sounds, and words; computation skills), apart from their functional relation, with the assumption that what is learned at the time may be useful later on. According to Scribner and Cole (1973a) in their classic article comparing formal and informal instruction, such learning practices by their very nature are discontinuous with those of everyday life and may contradict the kinds of learning situations and cultural practices that exist in the society outside of school. In contrast to "out of context school learning" (p. 556), involvement with written language includes a range of activities that vary in different cultural contexts and for a variety of functional purposes.

Consequently, the concept of moving everyday life into schools to reflect more authentic situations has become regarded as essential in the process of enculturating literacy learning (Brown, Collins, & Duguid, 1989). Authentic activities reflect practices that individuals typically exercise in day-to-day situations. They are the ordinary practices of the culture—what people do in daily, weekly, and monthly cycles of activity. Such practices, for example, include shopping for the best bargain, figuring out the fat content of a favorite food, and examining health care options on an insurance policy.

These activities, shown in a large number of ethnographic studies of everyday cognition (Childs & Greenfield, 1980; Lave, Murtaugh, & de la Rocha, 1984; Scribner, 1984; Scribner & Cole, 1973b), appear to be different than school-related tasks. Lave et al. (1984), for example, examining the routines of grocery shopping, found that the dialectic of arithmetic in grocery shopping was shaped by the context of the activity. The problem-solving arithmetic tasks that were generated in this context involved shoppers' values and beliefs, as well as opportunistic solutions—behaviors that bore little resemblance to paper-and-pencil arithmetic tasks. Rather than the use of explicit, formal rules, it was the activity that shaped and refined how the tool (in this case, arithmetic) was used for subsequent action.

Social practice proponents argue that knowledge in practice constitutes a more powerful source of socialization than traditional, didactic teaching (Collins, Brown, & Newman, 1989; Lave, 1988; Scribner, 1986). In practice, the occasions and conditions for using literacy or arithmetic arise directly out of the context and are framed by the way in which other members of that community see the world (Brown et al., 1989). The apprentice, for example, becomes expert by observing, being coached by a mentor, and practicing the skills to be learned. Similar to Wood, Bruner, and Ross's (1976) conception of comprehending the act, observation first provides a global picture, which then acts as a guide to subsequent learning. The conceptual model then is used to monitor progress as the apprentice becomes increasingly proficient through successive approximations. In the course of learning through activity and social interaction, the apprentice becomes enculturated in a community of practice (Brown et al., 1989).

Thus, in contrast to formal schooling, an apprenticeship model embeds the learning of skills, strategies, and knowledge in their social and functional context. In this context, learners have access to experts as well as novice learners, who may serve as benchmarks for their own progress. In fact, several aspects of this apprenticeship model have been used successfully for teaching processes that experts use to handle complex tasks. Collins et al. (1989), for example, described a learning model of *cognitive apprenticeship*, which focuses on learning through guided experience and highlights the cognitive and metacognitive processes, rather than the physical skills and processes of a traditional apprenticeship, which comprise expertise in areas like reading, writing, and math. The cognitive apprenticeship model involves alternating responses between expert and novice in a shared problem-solving situation; in this manner, students are made sensitive to the details of expert performance as they are encouraged to make incremental adjustments in their own performance. Palincsar and Brown's (1984) reciprocal teaching model and Scardamalia and Bereiter's (1985) procedural facilitation in writing are examples of approaches in this tradition.

Yet, the cognitive apprenticeship model still relies on decontextualizing knowledge, assuming transferability of these knowledge, skills, and strategies to new settings (Collins et al., 1989). Another approach to situated learning in school is to create authentic contexts for which literacy can be used to meet the demands of a situation. This approach focuses on thinking in practice, rather than on thinking as separate from doing. Consistent with the sociocultural theory of Vygotsky (1978) and Leont'ev (1981), context and the child's activity are seen as inseparable, their meanings derived as jointly producing psychological events. Through activity, it assumes that occasions for thinking are subjectively experienced, that cognitive and metacognitive processes are employed to meet the problem solver's functional needs, and that these processes are adapted and extended with each new experience (Rogoff, 1982). In this view activities create an arena that may stimulate active knowledge construction.

Thus, if children's earliest conceptions of literacy are closely tied to practices in which they are embedded, one way to examine their development is to study literacy knowledge in practice. In this case, the practices or activities themselves become objects of analysis (Leont'ev, 1981; Scribner,

1984). Observing a child's attempts at reading a letter or writing a grocery list, for example, may reveal important understandings about how literacy is used and adapted to get things done and what strategic processes may be involved in these situations.

Using activity as the basic unit of analysis, however, carries several important implications for what we study. First, the focus on activity as a basic unit emphasizes children's adaptations of literacy objects and tools in active terms, highlighting processes more than outcomes or products. Second, and relatedly, the activity as the unit of analysis emphasizes literacy as social adaptation applied in the course of practical action, thereby varying across different contexts and problem-solving situations. And third, the focus on activity emphasizes what children actively do (e.g., exploring, problem solving) rather than who they are in terms of their status characteristics (e.g., socioeconomic status).

Specifically, a focus on children's literacy-related activity may address the following questions: (a) What features distinguish literacy in practice? (b) What knowledges do these activities require? and (c) What cognitive and metacognitive operations may be involved in these activities? Responses to these questions may reveal a rich repertoire of knowledge and understandings that children, through interactions with their world, bring to literacy and may serve as an important foundation for building more complex concepts. Further, an examination of literacy in practice could reveal important aspects of context that support literacy learning in these early years. Incorporating these aspects into classroom instruction could potentially provide better continuity between home and school practices, integrating literacy learning with practical everyday activity.

Although the importance of context in early literacy learning is certainly not a new concern, much of the research to date has focused on context as a scaffold for children's developing awareness of print (Goodman & Altwerger, 1981; Masonheimer, Drum, & Ehri, 1984; McGee, Lomax, & Head, 1988; Neuman & Roskos, 1993). In contrast, this study was designed to investigate young children's literacy activity as it was intricately interwoven within settings designed to reflect literacy-related situations in children's real-world environment. Since play is where much of young children's exploration and learning takes place (Bruner, 1972), three literacy-related play settings reflecting design principles of real-life environments became the arena in which to observe children's literacy in practice. Our goal was to capture the multifaceted knowledge and behaviors that may constitute early literacy practices for these developing 3- and 4-year-old children, viewing literacy in its development not as a series of acquisitions of skills but as a series of transformations and adaptations across events and settings.

Method

Subjects and setting

Thirty preschoolers (fifteen 3-year-olds; fifteen 4-year-olds), from a collaborative state-funded (Massachusetts early childhood initiative) multicultural preschool project and federally funded Even Start program in a diverse low- to middle-income community participated in the study. Six of the 30 families received public assistance. Serving families from 14 ethnic communities, the program was designed for children from non-English-speaking or bilingual homes and/or low-income families. The majority of the children were born in the U.S. and spoke English as their primary language, with some facility in the family's native language. Thirty percent of the children were bilingual.

Prior to children's entrance in the program, teachers were required by a national Even Start evaluation team to individually administer the Peabody Picture Vocabulary Test (PPVT) to children. PPVT scores for the 3-year-olds averaged 20% (SD = 24.47) and for the 4-year-olds, 24% (SD = 28.66). Descriptive statistics of the sample are presented in Table 1.

The program was administered by Marcia Krasnow and supported by a program coordinator, three certified early childhood teachers, and a

Table 1 Description of the sample (N = 30)

Category	3-year-olds	4-year-olds
Age in months	M = 42.56 (SD = 2.38)	M = 56.56 (SD = 2.45)
Gender		
Males	5 boys	7 boys
Females	10 girls	8 girls
Peabody Picture		
Vocabulary Test (PPVT)	M = 20.21 (SD = 24.47)	M = 24.34 (SD = 28.66)
Ethnicity		
European American	2	1
Greek	1	1
Haitian	1	0
Italian	3	4
Brazilian	1	1
Portuguese	2	1
Ugandan	1	0
Honduras	1	1
Vietnamese	1	0
German	2	0
Lebanese	0	2
Syrian	0	1
Nigerian	0	1
Colombian	0	2

telecommunications specialist. As part of its service to the community, an innovative feature of the program was to disseminate information on early childhood practices and parenting education for those families with children over the target age or children unable to attend a preschool program. The preschool was technically equipped as a studio to videotape children's activities in centers throughout the room. Three remote control cameras and seven omnidirectional microphones with six additional wireless microphones distributed throughout the area provided picture and sound capabilities of broadcast quality. In a separate studio, the telecommunications specialist directed the cameras to follow the children's actions and to continuously monitor the audio quality. An edited version with teacher narration of the children's activities for the day was then broadcast to the surrounding community on a local-access cable channel.

Three-year-old children attended Tuesday and Thursday mornings and 4-year-olds on Monday, Wednesday, and Friday, from 9.00 to 11.00 a.m. Daily activities included inquiry-based projects, art, music, motor coordination activities, and approximately 30 to 40 minutes per day for indoor or outdoor free play. Teachers incorporated multiculturalism, using parents as a primary resource, through many of the children's activities in storybook reading, music, art, and snack time. In this English immersion program, however, the language spoken by teachers and children was English.

Prior to our involvement, the physical organization of the 50' × 50' preschool room included a book corner, a little writing table, and art, kitchen, and block areas. As part of the collaborative effort with Even Start (i.e., a focus on family literacy), the director sought to enhance these play areas in ways that might demonstrate children's early literacy activity to the families served in the program as well as to the local community. Eliciting ideas from parents as well as the children themselves, the teachers and the researchers designed three literacy-related play areas: a post office, a family restaurant, and a doctor's office.

Intervention design

Reviewing ecological studies from play research and cognitive performance (Bjorklund, Muir-Broaddus, & Schneider, 1990; Morrow, 1990; Neuman & Roskos, 1992; Rogoff, 1982; Weinstein, 1979), we examined environmental design factors that might best provide opportunities for literacy in practice activity. Several factors appeared especially important for creating these activity settings for young children: (a) organization, (b) familiarity of objects and operations, (c) meaningfulness of activity, and (d) social resources.

Organization of settings. Children reveal what they know and can do to the extent that an environment is supportive of their efforts (Bjorklund et al., 1990). It is widely accepted, for example, that children perform better in situations that are familiar to them (DeLoache & Brown, 1987; Perkins, 1993). Similarly, contexts that incorporate everyday literacy practices of family and community suggest settings with identifiable frameworks (i.e., names, scripts) that encourage children to use what they know to generate new information.

Familiarity of objects and operations in settings. Children show more advanced thinking when highly typical materials are available for use with a task (Bruner, 1983; Neuman & Roskos, 1992). The value of object familiarity and prior experience is well documented in play research (Garvey, 1977; McLane & McNamee, 1990). Pretense is facilitated by prototypical objects and settings that evoke everyday experiences, especially in its early stages. Thus, the relative familiarity children have with objects and operations to be performed with them facilitates their ability to use what they know, to demonstrate their competence, and to create new behavioral combinations.

Meaningfulness of activity in settings. A setting's potential is realized only to the extent its activity has meaning for its participants. Studies of young children's problem solving and planning skills demonstrate the power of purpose for revealing cognitive competence (DeLoache & Brown, 1987; Rogoff, Mosier, Mistry, & Goncu, 1993; Rubin, Fein, & Vandenberg, 1983). For young children, purposeful, goal-directed activity is often embedded in game-like or play situations, which afford greater opportunity to pursue goals that are personally motivating and meaningful. Play provides a means to practice what has been observed in the home and community with reduced risk of censure and to experiment with ideas and objects with less fear of consequences (Bruner, 1972; Vygotsky, 1967). Pretend play allows children to borrow and create roles, adopt and change roles, exploit and alter procedures, use language to make sense, and negotiate and persuade; in sum, they play with symbols and conventions of their culture.

Social resources in settings. The richest and most elaborate resource available to children in their natural environment is observing other people in that setting. Studies of collaboration between peers suggest that joint work stimulates initiative, attention to details of performance, and commitment to activity (Brown et al., 1993; Forman & McPhail, 1993; Neuman & Roskos, 1991). In addition, there is some evidence that more expert play partners can facilitate the social pretense in low-play peers and not at their own expense (Fryer & Fein, 1995). Their more capable demonstrations of "just pretend" appear to teach their less skilled peers how to think symbolically with a greater store of information available in their environment.

A synthesis of research, therefore, suggests that authentic arenas for literacy action should reflect what children see in their everyday contexts and include relevant, familiar literacy objects and tools within the realm of their experiences. Settings that invite explorations of literacy objects, routines, scripts, and roles enable children to demonstrate their developing understandings and interaction with others. Regardless of whether settings are real or imagined, as Lave (1988) has argued, these settings should provide for *authentic dilemmas* that offer children opportunities to use literacy, create problem-solving situations, and improvise solutions.

Using these criteria the teachers and researchers created three literacy-enriched settings specifically adapted to our young children's abilities, interests, and prior experiences: the post office, a restaurant, and the doctor's office. All three represented arenas of activity that incorporated literacy practices commonly found in the children's immediate environment as reported by their parents and teachers. The children, for example, were particularly familiar with the local post office because their parents, as recent immigrants, frequently exchanged mail and packages with relatives in their native countries.

The settings were supplied with relevant literacy objects, props, and environmental print that were familiar and functional to the children and were organized to encourage sustained play activity, accommodating 3 to 4 children at a time. As indicated in Figure 1, each setting was clearly marked in the environment using architectural features to define its space and printed signs to indicate its purpose. Objects and props were attractively arranged to draw children into pretend play activity and were of sufficient complexity to elicit multiple interactions. For example, the post office included various sized bins and trays for organizing paper, sorting mail, or storing and stacking supplies. Transfer of props from one setting to another encouraged flexibility in the use of the materials. Table 2 summarizes the environmental features of the settings tailored to our sample.

Procedure

The study was conducted over a 7-month period, beginning in November and ending in May. Data were collected through observations, videotape analyses, and weekly informal conversations with teachers and the telecommunications specialist. Since our goal was to discover how 3- and 4-year-old children used literacy in practice, all observations were conducted in the control room to avoid distractions from any outside observers.

Children were introduced to the literacy-related play settings in several steps following an apprenticeship model. Prior to creating the post office play area, teachers talked and read stories to children about visiting a post office. Several days later, they visited the local post office, spoke to postal workers, and brought back a number of artifacts (e.g., posters, express mail envelopes, and cartons). Following their visit, teachers gave a grand

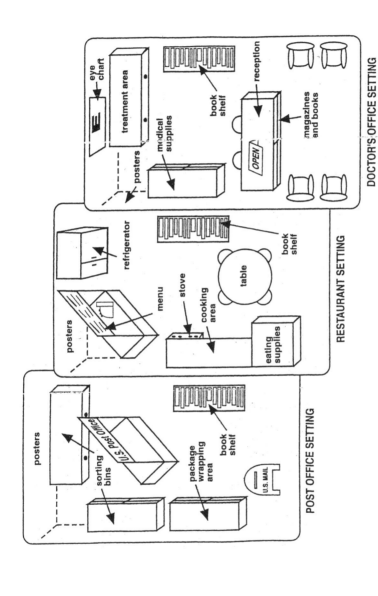

Figure 1 Three literacy-related play settings

Table 2 Description of authentic play settings

| Setting | Organization | Familiarity | Meaningfulness | Potential meaning | Social |
		Objects	*Typical operations in real-life settings*	*making activities*	*resources*
Post office	local post office	paper stationery envelopes pencils markers stamps greeting cards express mail mailbag mailbox sorting trays hat/pouch stampers stamp pads related signs (e.g., MAIL) packages wrapping paper weight scale bins/trays labels markers related books	writing letters mailing letters receiving letters sending packages receiving packages	pretending to write letters pretending to receive letters pretending to be a postal worker/ mail officer	peers, occasional teacher visits
Restaurant	fast-food restaurant	menus order pad pencil markers	ordering food	pretending to cook food pretending to serve food pretending to be a customer	peers, parents, teachers

Center	Materials	Activities	Dramatic play	Participants
	wall menu related signs (e.g., EXIT) order form food placemats utensils bill credit cards play money bank checks cash register related books (e.g., cookbooks)	serving food paying for food	pretending to own a restaurant	peers, parents, teachers
Doctor's office health clinic	appointment book pencils markers calendars note paper insurance forms bank checks play money file folders related signs (e.g., OFFICE) related books (e.g., visits to the doctor's office) paper clipboard eye chart emergency procedures memo paper pill boxes	making appointment paying bills pretending to be a receptionist recording symptoms writing prescriptions	pretending to be sick pretending to be a doctor pretending to be a nurse playing hospital	

tour of the new play setting that the teachers and the researchers had developed together, describing the materials and the names of the objects (e.g., mailbag), and modeling several pretend scenarios. In the days that followed, teachers participated in play activity as coplayers (Roskos & Neuman, 1993) when they perceived that children would benefit from an adult presence; however, as play progressed, they increasingly shifted their role to that of observers. In this respect, we attempted to follow the crucial features of traditional apprenticeship from a teacher's point of view through modeling, coaching, and fading (Collins et al., 1989). Using similar procedures, after a 2-week period teachers introduced the redesigned second setting, the family restaurant (they visited a fast-food restaurant), followed 3 weeks later by the doctor's play office setting (a doctor and her nurse visited the classroom). Once play in these areas was established, teachers adopted an observer role (rather than coplayer), allowing us to focus on child-initiated activity.

The telecommunications specialist followed children's literacy play activity 1 day per week for each program (3- and 4-year-olds) over the next 20 weeks. Children were free to play in any area for approximately 25–30 minutes, with space considerations the only restriction (no more than 5 in a setting). No attempt was made to control the number of times a child played in these areas or to ensure every child's participation. Instead, we were interested in capturing as well as possible their interactions in these settings. Rather than focus on a preselected area, cameras followed the children's free play activity. If there was little activity in one setting and much activity in another, for example, the cameras would pursue the activity and record the setting in which it took place. If there was no activity in any of the three settings, the cameras would fade and turn on only if children came into one of the areas. Thus, the emphasis was on the activity and the setting, and not on the individual child.

A video log was maintained throughout the study indicating the number of children and the settings most frequently visited. Other activities such as block-building or art in the other play areas were not recorded at these times.

Weekly observations were conducted in the control room to ensure that the play settings provided children with opportunity to use literacy in authentic situations, to examine whether children were stimulated to play in these areas, and to regularly infuse new materials and multicultural artifacts in the settings. Following observations, informal conversations were held with administrators and teachers to elicit their feedback and to discuss the quality of children's language activity and play. Over 20 hours of videotaped play were recorded: 7.7 hours in the post office, 6.2 in the family restaurant, and 6.9 in the doctor's office.

Data analysis. The focus of our analysis was to examine children's literacy knowledge and strategies in practice and the key features of these interactions. Data analysis was carried out in several phases. First, all tapes were reviewed to establish literacy-related play episodes. An episode was defined as an interrelated set of goal-directed actions and dialogue in literacy play activity (Kantor, Miller, & Fernie, 1992). We eliminated independent play actions, such as playing with the cash register keys or playing with a stamp pad, because they appeared more exploratory in nature. We also eliminated literacy episodes that were prompted or directed by the teacher. Included in the analysis, however, were those episodes that might involve the teacher or a parent as participant in a minor role. Seventy-six episodes, in total, were recorded. Each episode was transcribed verbatim and annotated with field notes from observations, recording the setting, the number of children, and the play activity (see Table 3).

We examined these transcriptions for the features of literacy in practice (e.g., how children go about solving literacy-related problems in authentic situations), the knowledges and purposes for writing and reading, and the types of strategies that children seemed to use in the process of their goal-directed actions. Using the constant-comparative method to analyze and reduce the primary data into codifiable categories (Glaser & Strauss, 1967), we first sought to identify salient characteristics of contextualized literacy practice. Through repeated readings, viewings, and discussions, we compared episodes across settings to determine features that best reflected context as a jointly produced event. Typological dimensions of context were generated, then refined by comparing these features with previous episodes. For example, accessibility to literacy tools, recorded as an important feature of context in our initial analysis, was examined across all episodes so that generalized statements about tool availability and use could be developed.

Second, we examined through typological analysis the types of domain-specific literacy knowledge employed in activities. Typological analysis

Table 3 Summary of literacy episodes (N = 76)

Category	3-year-olds	4-year-olds
Total number of episodes	28	48
Number of episodes per setting		
Post office	16	16
Restaurant	7	18
Doctor's office	5	12
Total number of children		
visiting play areas	14	13
Average number of children		
in each episode	3	4
Total number of hours		
videotaped	10:37	10:43

involves dividing observed phenomena into categories that appear to describe events or relationships in settings (Goetz & LeCompte, 1984). Our readings indicated two types of working knowledge: declarative and procedural.

For example, in one interaction, Kara tells Lisa, "They're stamps. You use them to mail a letter." This type of interchange was labeled *declarative knowledge*, indicating *I know that* (Bruner, 1972; Farnham-Diggory, 1994). In this instance, Kara's statement indicated that she knew the name and function of a literacy object.

Children's activities also indicated information about how to go about various literacy-related actions. Following Kara's interchange, for example, she put a letter in the mailbox. Here, her actions indicated *procedural knowledge*, reflecting information about a literacy routine (Bruner, 1972; Farnham-Diggory, 1994; Paris, Lipson, & Wixson, 1983). In this example, Kara's actions demonstrated that the *knew how to* mail a letter. Situations that included both knowing that and knowing how were multiple coded.

Third, our readings also indicated evidence of *strategic knowledge*, not bound to a particular domain, that enabled children to accomplish their communicative goals (Paris et al., 1983). We found evidence, for example, of self-monitoring behaviors such as requests for help, self-correcting, or correcting others as children assumed specific literacy roles (like a postal worker) and practiced routines. Since learners tend to be strategic only when they need to be (Garner, 1990), coding in this analysis consisted of marking those literacy-related speech or gestural units (e.g., mailing a letter) reflecting some type of monitoring device and placing them in appropriate categories. In one interaction, Lisa's attempt to be a postal worker was corrected by Sebastian, who said "Uuh, I'm not that guy [the postal worker)—see, you're that guy." Other types of self-monitoring behaviors, as well, were recorded throughout the data.

Last, we categorized declarative and procedural knowledge according to the purposes for literacy in each activity. Here, categories were induced from the data reflecting *why* writing and reading were used on a continuum of literacy purposes. Each episode was coded by marking chunks of discourse reflecting a literacy purpose. Strategies were then cross-referenced with literacy purposes to examine why and how literacy was used in each setting.

Coding consisted of marking each literacy-related speech or gestural unit (e.g., mailing a letter) holistically for gist and placing it in an appropriate category. Corsaro (1979) found that this approach yielded an accurate measure of behavior for preschool children. Non-literacy-related talk, such as "I'm a monster and I'm going to eat you up," within the context of these episodes was not coded for this analysis.

Selected transcripts were coded by both of us to establish and refine coding categories. The validity of categories and examples was then established by asking an external coder, a graduate research assistant trained in early childhood observation, to code a number of transcripts according to these definitions. In addition, we asked her to examine transcripts for potential behaviors that might not be included in our coding system. This validation procedure served as a check on whether we had adequately captured the literacy behaviors in context and whether the examples we selected represented the same behaviors to someone not involved with data collection. Following discussions and modifications, transcripts were coded by one of us, then reviewed by the other, to ensure consistency of coded categories. Disagreements were resolved by reviewing videotape episodes and observational notations (see Appendix for a coded transcript).

We conducted three levels of analyses. Our first analysis was designed to broadly describe the key features of literacy in practice across the three settings. The second analysis examines types of knowledge displayed in practice, focusing on domain-specific and strategic behaviors. And the final analysis describes the relation between domain-specific and strategic activity in literacy in practice.

Results

Features of literacy in practice

Viewing literacy as an activity spanning the roles of person and context, the first analysis examined critical features of literacy in practice, providing a framework for why and how writing and reading were used in authentic activity. Five features of literacy in practice throughout the 76 episodes were identified and described.

Presence of other people. Activities in these settings involved children in collaboration with others to solve problems. In some episodes, children engaged in parallel activities, with each child carrying on concurrent activity, while in others there was more social interaction; however, virtually all episodes involved group problem solving of one kind or another. In the presence of others children tested their solutions, shared their expertise, and assisted one another's performance. For example, playing post office, Matthew asked his friend, "Hey, man, could you get me an enn ..., an ennnn ..." "An envelope?" Joey replied. "Yup, and make it a big one." All 76 episodes involved children engaging with others in literacy activity (see Table 3).

Feedback from others. Related to the presence of others, children received feedback in the context of these activities, allowing them to quickly adjust their actions to meet the demands of the situation. A typical example follows in the post office setting.

Kara and Lisa are side by side in the post office, near the cash register.

Kara: Lisa, if you want something, you have to give us money.
Lisa: OK [and begins to write on the money].
Kara: Lisa, you don't write on money.
Lisa: I need something [and starts putting stickers on the money].
Kara: Lisa, you don't put stickers on money.
Lisa: I know.

Feedback in these situations was frequent, immediate, and often subtle (e.g., the nod of a head). It came in many forms—correcting, modeling, demonstrating, and, in some cases, even instructing. Regardless of its form, however, feedback appeared to provide tracking information, which would then be used by the child or children to regulate the next phase of activity.

Access to tools and related supplies. Children's communication and collaborative activities involved the use of literacy objects and tools (e.g., paper, pencils, menus). From a Gibsonian perspective (Gibson, 1979), these objects appeared to afford opportunities to explore routines and to suggest certain activities. For example, children used pens, stationery, and a mailbox to write and send letters, menus to read and order selections from the restaurant, and eye charts to examine a patient's eyesight in the doctor's office. In fact, when accessibility to objects became unavailable, activities would be curtailed. For example, Colleen asked, "Can I have a stamp, please?" "There's no more," Cindy replied, and Colleen answered, "Now I can't write a letter for my mother, my father, and my brother."

Multiple options for activity. Although settings certainly imposed frames of reference that activated particular scripts (e.g., ordering from a menu, buying stamps), there were multiple options for activities within them. In fact, literacy often served the function of deciding between many options (e.g., menu selection, form of payment, shopping needs). Settings provided a familiar framework for activity that invited children to form goals—intentions—and to execute them in a series of action sequences. In this respect, children were able to create, invent, and innovate flexible solutions in problem-solving situations, like in the following scenario.

Christine, Lisa, and a parent are in the doctor's office.

Christine: (to the parent patient) I need your card. You can use your Blue Cross/Blue Shield card. (to Lisa) I need to print your card too, [grabs a card from Lisa]. Medical, I need it. I'll give you back your card next week.
Parent: You won't give me back my card? Why not?
Christine: 'Cause you have too much blood of the shot we just gave you. When you come back, the blood will go away. . .

Parent: So when the blood goes away, I can get my medical card back?
Christine: Yes, that's right [writes on her chart].

Problem-solving situations. Applied to a varied and open set of options, literacy activity in these contexts was in the service of action. Reading and/or writing occurred within situations and was engaged in for reasons other than literacy itself. Whether children were writing prescriptions, sending letters, or communicating with loved ones, literacy served as an integral aspect of practical activity. Thus, rather than a set of skills that was the same everywhere at all times, reading and writing demonstrations were adapted to the nature of the activity. For example, children's writing, slow and laborious when addressing a letter in the post office setting, was cryptic in the restaurant where fast service was a necessity. Varying tasks posed different problems and novel solutions, requiring dynamic adaptations and transformations of literacy in context.

Literacy in practice as defined by these five features, therefore, was not a primary focus nor an individual matter. Rather, mediating other meaningful activity, the cultural tools and artifacts of literacy were explored and exploited by children as they set about to purposefully participate in their social world.

Literacy knowledge in practice

Within these contexts of participation, our second analysis examined the types of knowledge displayed in practice. Our analysis revealed a rich storehouse of literacy knowledge: Children's activities in authentic play contexts were embedded with domain-specific declarative and procedural knowledge as well as non-domain-specific strategic knowledge of literacy.

Declarative and procedural knowledge. As shown in the typology in Table 4, children's *declarative knowledge* illustrated understandings about individuals and their roles in familiar literacy-related contexts (mail carriers, waiters, doctors, nurses) as well as implicitly held understandings of the ways these individuals functioned in their roles. In the following episode, for example, Christine demonstrates not only explicit, but also implicit, knowledge of the authority role of the doctor.

Christine: [with a clipboard and pen] to Kara (the patient) We need ... we have to have you take these pills. (declarative) [whispers to Colleen who is acting like a nurse and following Christine with pencil and pad] 14–45–14 (declarative; procedural)
Christine: OK. And 45–45–45 (declarative) [to the girls at the reception desk who are keeping the patient's chart]. (procedural)
Christine: (to the patient) And you gotta take these pills ... Don't drink juice or ginger ale or coke with 'em. (declarative)
Kara: Just water?

Table 4 Children's declarative knowledge about literacy in play

Category	Description	Examples
Roles of individuals common to the setting		
Post office	cashier, postal officer, customer, package handler, letter writer	"I'm the mailman. You're supposed to write a letter and give it to me."
Restaurant	customer, waiter/waitress, chef, restaurant owner	"Want to be the waiter?" says Joey. "No, I want to be the chef," says Justin. "Well, who's going to be the customer?"
Doctor's office	Doctor, nurse, receptionist, patient	"Hey, where's the doctor's place?" asks Analisa. Joey says, "I'm a doctor. She very sick?"
Implicit knowledge about setting		
Post office	Busy mail officers, importance of mail and money transactions, importance of writing correctly	"This is your package. That will be five dollars, five dollars," says Cindy. "OK, here's the box," says Johnny. "No, no, you got to write carefully on it."
Restaurant	Testy waiters, impatient customers, inappropriate customer behavior	Joann yells to Lisa, "Stop stuffing that pizza in your purse, or you'll never come back to this restaurant."
Doctor's office	Authoritarian doctor, docile patient, assisting nurse responding to doctor's orders.	Christine, with stethoscope around neck and pad and paper, "Nurse, check this baby because her weight is low."
Names and functions of literacy objects		
Post office	stamps, envelopes, pencil, letter, dollars, money, mailbox, color names	Johnny says to Lisa, "We have no dollars." Lisa answers, "You mean no moneys?"
Restaurant	Food names, menu, bill, check	Cindy [pointing to the picture on the menu] says to the waitress, "I'd like a BLT."
Doctor's office	Pills, scale, blood pressure, insurance card, eye chart, credit cards	"Lisa, we need all your credit cards. Give me your Blue Cross one, too."

Christine: Yeah, or tea. Something that will agree. Remember, take this pill with milk, this one with tea, and this one with water. (declarative) (then to Colleen who is writing this down) 72–22–79. (declarative; procedural)

The doctor's role is defined by the activity (dispensing medicine and providing clear directions) and the tone of the interaction; here, Christine uses the repetition of random numbers spoken to her assistants (who carefully write them down), implicitly conveying her understanding of the doctor's authority role over others. As noted in Table 4, such explicit and implicit understandings of literacy-related roles (postal officers, waiters, receptionists) were common in each setting.

Further, as noted in the example above, the names of common literacy objects and their functions were also integrally tied to practical action in these settings. Literacy objects like envelopes, menus, checks, credit cards, and eye charts were identified and described in the course of a play activity. For example, replying patiently to Johnny's inquiry about a literacy object, mail officer Mary Kate reminded him that "They're stamps. You put them on this [envelope]. Stickers doesn't look like this." Interactions like these indicated domain-specific knowledge about the labels and the structures of common literacy-related activities in these everyday settings.

Setting-specific procedural knowledge indicated children's understanding of the actions and behaviors associated with literacy tasks. Routines, or subroutines of more extended tasks, illustrated *how to* perform literacy-like activities. As shown in Table 5, they reflected a conceptual understanding of how to use literacy to carry out everyday activities for organizing, sharing, and transactive purposes—getting, giving, and writing down important information and conveying information to others. In the family restaurant, for example, the large menu in the setting served as the informational resource for ordering, as Joey pretends to be a waiter:

Joey: (to the customer) What do you want? [looking at the menu and pointing] This or that or that or that. Eggs? (procedural)

Michael: I want eggs. I want my eggs. Fried eggs. [Joey writes this down.] Two more eggs. (declarative) [Joey continues to write.] (procedural)

[Joey hands the customer a check.] (procedural)

Michael: Here, here. Hey, wake up here [and gives him the money]. (declarative, procedural)

Often resembling imitations of adult behavior, these routines tended to have a character all their own. Children practiced, tried to perfect, and slightly varied situationally specific routines in striking detail. For example, literacy-related subroutines recorded in the doctor's office play

343

Table 5 Children's procedural knowledge of how to use literacy in play activities

Setting	Common routines	Examples
Post office	How to get stamps How to put together a letter How/where to mail a letter How to address a letter How to deliver mail	Matthew says to Colleen, "How do you put this [letter] in [the envelope]?" "You have to wrap it up. See, it's too big." [She folds it in three parts, puts it in envelope, and licks the envelope.]
Restaurant	How to take an order How to order from the menu How to pay for food 　Look at bill, review items, 　give money, get change, 　leave tip exchange pleasantries How to take inventory	To customer, Michael asks, "What do you want? [looking at the menu.] Egg? (to the other customer.) And what do you want? You want what he gets?" "Yes," Johnny says. Michael yells, "Oh Chef, I want eggs. Fried eggs.
Doctor's office	How to take down information How to give prescriptions How to sign in How to get pulse, weight How to give an eye test How to pay for services How to describe emergency 　procedures How to give assignments to 　others How to get referrals from other 　doctors	To parent, Kara says, "Now look at the eye chart and read the letters" [coaching parent]. The parent says, "A-E-E." Kara says, "Now try it again." "Did I make a mistake?" the parent asks. "Just read the chart again. You did very good."

Table 6 Number and percentage of behavioral units for knowledge category by setting

Type	Setting					
	Post office		Restaurant		Doctor's office	
	No.	%	No.	%	No.	%
Declarative knowledge (knowing that)	62	25%	59	33%	54	31%
Procedural knowledge (knowing how)	75	30%	101	56%	69	40%
Total number of domain-specific knowledge units	137		160		123	

setting included signing in, taking information and documenting a patient's vital signs, describing emergency procedures using a chart, giving prescriptions, getting referrals from other doctors, giving assignments to nurses, and paying for services with money, insurance, or credit cards. These data reveal a wide range of setting-specific knowledge involving how to execute various literacy actions in these contextualized settings.

Table 6 describes the number and percentage of behavioral units for each knowledge category in these activities. Reflecting Bruner's (1972) thesis that actions, or know how, precede verbal knowledge, or know that, these data indicate that observations of procedural knowledge were recorded more frequently than declarative knowledge. Consequently, it was children's actions and routines, even more than their verbal capacity, that gave evidence of the considerable literacy-related knowledge they brought to bear in the course of their playful activities.

Strategic knowledge of literacy. Practical problems often required children to monitor the success of their understandings by seeking information and by checking them against their own existing hypotheses. Unlike domain-specific declarative and procedural knowledge, however, these metacognitive behaviors, defined here as *strategic knowledge*, included self-monitoring devices that were employed across settings. Six types of strategies were identified: (a) seeking information, (b) correcting, (c) self-correcting, (d) assigning roles and resources, (e) checking, and (f) gathering resources (see Table 7 for definitions).

Self-monitoring was evident in Sebastian and Brian's play in the post office, for example:

Sebastian: (to everyone) Hey, come here, the post office is open. (declarative)

Brian: No, it's closed. I think it's closed [points to the sign that says *closed*]. (declarative)

Sebastian: It's not closed, right? (checking)
Brian: Yes, because this is closed [the sign—points to it]. (declarative)
Sebastian: Yes, it says I am closed. (self-correcting)
Brian: (looking at the sign) Yeah. (declarative)
Sebastian: You read it? (checking)
Brian: Closed, c-l-o-s-e-d. (declarative)
Sebastian: I'll put an open sign up and then you read it. (assigning resources) When it gets dark we'll put on closed. (declarative) [Pauses, looks at the open sign] P-O-M open. It says open. (declarative)

As noted in this example and others, children sought from one another information, resources, and feedback to resolve ambiguities, formulate new solutions, and direct future communicative efforts.

Examining frequencies of behavioral units in strategic activity, Table 8 reveals that higher frequencies of strategic behaviors were recorded in the post office setting (where declarative and procedural knowledge were lower) than in the other two settings. This suggests that strategic behaviors may have been used as tools for knowledge generation. As shown in Table 8, the social interactive devices of seeking information and assigning roles and resources were used most frequently in two of the three settings, fol-

Table 7 Definitions and examples of strategies in episodes

Definition	Example
Seeking Information Requesting help, a question	Mary Kate, playing post officer, asks, "What is this, Johnny?" [holding stamps]
Correcting Giving feedback to others	Cindy, responding to Colleen who is putting money in an envelope, says "You can't send money in the mail."
Self-correcting Correcting self in a in the process of completing a task	Lisa, after putting a letter in the cash register, says, "Oops, that doesn't go there."
Assigning roles and resources Suggesting a role and describing objects that specify activity in the role	Christine, in the restaurant, asks her friend, "Want to go to the restaurant with us? I'll give you some clothes," [gets dress, shoes, and purse].
Checking Examining or checking specific behaviors against some standard	Writing letters together in the post office, Natasha, showing Christine her work, asks, "Is this the way you make an *O*?"
Gathering resources Gathering relevant literacy materials before beginning a task	Kara runs up to the teacher in the post office, saying, "We don't have any more stamps. We need more stamps to mail our letters."

Table 8 Distribution of strategies in episodes: percentage (and number) of units in each setting

Behavioral units	Setting		
	Post office	Restaurant	Doctor's office
Seeking information	24%	25%	45%
	(36)	(13)	(20)
Correcting	20%	13%	14%
	(30)	(7)	(6)
Self-correcting	5%	2%	5%
	(7)	(1)	(2)
Assigning roles and resources	20%	30%	0%
	(20)	(15)	(0)
Checking	11%	4%	22%
	(16)	(2)	(10)
Gathering resources	20%	26%	14%
	(30)	(13)	(6)
Total percent	100	100	100
Total number of strategies	148	50	44

lowed by correcting, gathering resources, and checking information with peers. Self-correcting was least common among the strategic behaviors documented. Activities in these everyday settings, therefore, seemed to naturally provide opportunities for children to use strategies to examine, reexamine, and solve problems together.

Thus, in the context of activity in these three settings it was evident that children brought setting-specific declarative and considerable procedural knowledge to bear to these literacy-related tasks. Further, they intentionally applied a variety of strategies to generate new information and to solve practical problems. Throughout their activity, 3- and 4-year-old children displayed and pursued new knowledge about how things worked, using literacy as a tool to serve their communicative needs.

Domain-specific and strategic knowledge in practice

Our final analysis examined the interaction of literacy-related domain-specific and strategic knowledge in practice. Specifically, we asked how and when strategies were used for knowledge generation. To conduct this analysis, we first categorized declarative and procedural knowledge routines in six domains reflecting their communicative purpose. These domains included: (a) sharing information, (b) making transactions, (c) authenticating information, (d) remembering, (e) making choices, and (f) organizing activity (see Table 9 for definitions and examples).

Table 9 Definitions and examples of purposes for writing and reading

Purpose for writing and reading	Example
Sharing information	
Literacy was used as a communications tool, to explain one's actions, to interact with others, to teach a literacy routine	"Lisa, I'll show you how to write an *a*—watch me."
Making transactions	
Literacy was used to conduct business transactions	Sara exclaims, "I need money money, so I can buy, buy, buy."
Authenticating information	
Literacy was used as a legitimating device, to document events /observations, or to verify decisions	"Don't come in cause we're closed. You see what the sign says."
Remembering	
Literacy was used as a memory device, to take down an order, to remember directions	"Excuse me, I have to write down something so I won't forget."
Making choices	
Literacy was used to make decisions or to demonstrate preferences	Looking at menu, Cindy says, "Mmm, I'll have some ice cream."
Organizing activity	
Literacy was used to arrange or allocate materials and assign various roles	"You get the envelope, and I'll get the paper, and we'll make a letter."

For example, literacy routines, like paying for stamps, insurance, or credit cards, were categorized as making transactions; taking orders, writing down vital signs, and making lists were categorized as remembering. We then cross-referenced literacy purposes with strategies employed for each setting. Figures 2–4 describe each setting.

As illustrated in these Figures, patterns and purposes varied dramatically across settings. In the post office setting as shown in Figure 2, for example, strategies were invoked most frequently to organize activity and to conduct transactions. Both purposes seemed to involve some level of difficulty and detail for translating what children knew about literacy into action, provoking them to frequently engage in requesting information and correcting one another as well as arranging and gathering literacy resources. At the cash register in the setting, for example, Sebastian checks and is corrected by Mary Kate in a typical transaction routine.

Sebastian and Mary Kate at the cash register.

Sebastian: (to Mary Kate) Put on the price 269293 for those stamps. (declarative) Oops, I'm the guy who does that, right? [the cashier] (self-correcting). I can do that, right? [looks at Mary Kate] Because I'm the guy, I'm supposed to do it. (checking)

Mary Kate: [nods] (correcting)

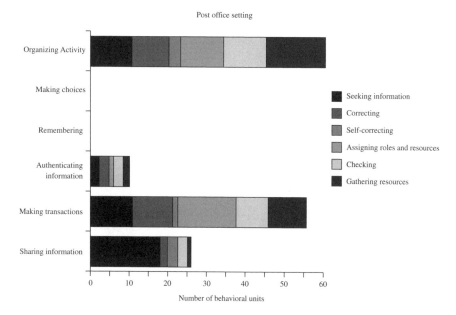

Figure 2 Purposes for using strategies in post office setting

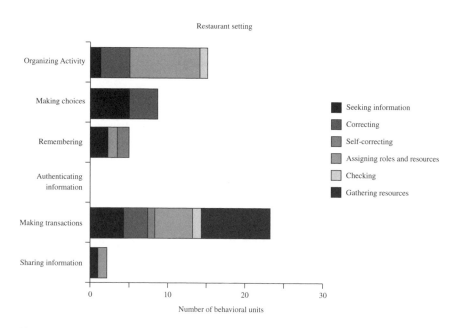

Figure 3 Purposes for using strategies in restaurant setting

349

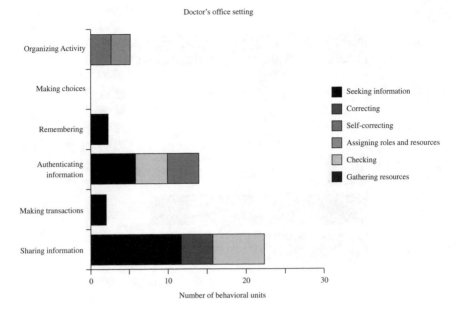

Figure 4 Purposes for using strategies in doctor's office setting

Sebastian: This is three dollars, right? (checking). What's a letter? (seeking information)
Mary Kate: That's how much for a letter [shows him]. (correcting)
Sebastian: A letter is three dollars? (checking)
Mary Kate: A letter is one dollar. (correcting)

Greater frequencies of strategic activity for transacting and organizing purposes were also recorded in the restaurant setting in Figure 3. Like the post office, children in this setting repeatedly practiced these situationally specific routines, calling upon a slightly diffcrent series of monitoring devices than in the post office setting to correct and check information with their peers. For example:

Cindy: [pretending to be a waitress]. You have to pay for your food. (declarative) [looks] Oooo, you have no money. (checking)
Jason: I don't care. So who cares? (correcting)
Cindy: [goes over to her friends] What do we do? The customer is not paying money. (seeking information) [They bring him a hamburger anyway.]
Jason: Thank you [pretends to eat]. (procedural)
Cindy: Give me one dollar, five dollars. (gathering resources)
Jason: Here's some [gives her a credit card]. (assigning resources)

350

Routines such as these seemed to elicit inventive heuristics (Brown et al., 1989)—strategies to assist children in refining a procedural skill (in this case paying for food). Less complex or more automated routines, on the other-hand, appeared to make strategic behaviors unnecessary. In these episodes, children seemed to monitor their activity less rigorously than when acting out specific literacy-related routines. For example, ordering food in the restaurant for children typically involved a routine, like "Whatta ya want?" "I'll have pizza," rarely involving strategy use.

On the other hand, there was less evidence of strategic behaviors in situations that were less familiar to young children. As shown in Figure 4, for example, although literacy was used primarily for authenticating and sharing purposes, these activities seemed to involve a knowledge base that many of these young novices did not have; thus, they seldom called upon strategic behaviors. For example:

Analisa: Where's the doctor's place? [She's holding a pencil and a pad.] (seeking information)
Joey: I'm the doctor. (declarative) [talks on the phone]
Analisa: [plays with the baby]
Joey: [Holds the clipboard and quietly talks to himself]

Unlike cases in which a basic procedure was known, children did not appear to assess or seek verification from others against an existing model.

Strategic behaviors, therefore, appeared to be used to refine procedural routines that were neither too automatic nor too complex. Certain settings, like the post office, seemed to elicit greater strategy use than others, like the doctor's office. Further, certain types of literacy purposes were more likely to elicit a variety of strategies than others. For example, strategies to use literacy for transactions and for organizing activity were recorded more frequently in the post office and the restaurant than were other types. Different settings, therefore, provided children with different opportunities for using literacy to explore the physical and social resources of their environment.

This analysis of activities indicated the variable and dynamic nature of literacy for these 3- and 4-year-old children. In these settings the occasions and conditions for use arose out of the context of activity, resulting in a unique pattern of strategic behavior and purposes applied to each setting. In contexts of participation, young children adapted their uses of literacy to meet the demands of different situations, thus extending and enriching their knowledge of the multifaceted nature of literacy.

Discussion

Reading and writing are embedded in the everyday lives of young children, closely tied to specific relationships and specific contexts (Teale &

Sulzby, 1986). Through participating in activities that require cognitive and communicative functions, children are drawn into the uses of these functions by their caregivers in ways that may nurture and develop them. Consequently, children's earliest conceptions of literacy and strategies for reading and writing are likely to be formed through socially mediated activity.

Much of what is transmitted about literacy will be tacit and context specific, however. What is learned by children through these apprenticing situations, as is true of many other special skills, will likely be practiced in playful activity (Bruner, 1972). And it is within this context of purposeful, pressure-free play in familiar environments that children may best display and extend their knowledge about literacy and how it may function in their worlds (Fantuzzo et al., 1995).

Our study focused on how literacy was practiced in the context of activity. From the sociocultural theories of Vygotsky (1978) and Leont'ev (1981), cognition is an activity spanning the roles of person and context. Consistent with this approach, we examined the literacy practices as they were embedded in activity, focusing on dynamic processes rather than underlying abilities of individuals. In emphasizing the centrality of activity, we sought to highlight the context-dependent, situated, and enculturated nature of literacy learning for emergent learners, and how the context might support their uses of these cognitive tools in authentic domain activity.

This study examined key features of contexts that supported literacy in practice activities. These features included the presence of other people, feedback from others, access to literacy tools, multiple options for activity, and purposeful situations other than literacy learning itself. Of course, these contexts only approximated authentic, everyday settings because it would be impractical for preschool or elementary schools to create true apprenticeship sites. Still, even in these simulated settings, activity was performed in the context of some shared task that was distributed across people and applied for specific purposes. In sharp contrast to skillbased instructional settings in which children are expected to learn and perform individually independent of props, or purpose (Resnick, 1989), literacy activities engaged children in processes of meaning construction tied to their actual use.

We would argue that these contexts produced physical and social support systems for activating children's knowledge and strategies. Familiar settings, authentic objects, and other people provided children with accessible representations, needed knowledge, and materials (e.g., clipboard, pencil, and paper) to support their interactions with print. Lave and Wenger (1991) have argued that mental activity cannot be considered an individual activity, but one that stretches over persons, activities, and settings. The immediate physical and social resources outside the person are said to form a cognitive partnership, or what Perkins (1993) has described as *person-plus-surround*. Thus, from an activity perspective, these contexts were not merely backdrops or external sources of stimulation; rather, they were critical vehicles of thought that shaped and helped to direct children's ongoing activities.

Our study indicated that in these contexts children engaged in a wide range of literacy practices. Using knowledge of their social and cultural worlds in situations that evoked familiar activity, children were able to call up appropriate context-sensitive rules and routines derived from their daily experiences. Three- and 4-year-olds adapted the tools of literacy for specific purposes and engaged in strategic behaviors in a variety of problem-solving situations, giving evidence of the rich repertoire of literacy knowledge and inventive heuristics they bring to these informal settings. These results strongly suggest that long before formal instruction, children use legitimate reading and writing behaviors as an integral part of their everyday lives.

Such knowledge of literacy purposes and strategic behaviors, embedded in practice, may have traditionally gone unnoticed in school contexts, however. Literacy demonstrations in their contextualized form reflected *knowing how*, or procedural knowledge, more than *knowing that*, or declarative knowledge. Even though procedural modes of transmitting knowledge have been considered to precipitate language growth (Bruner, 1972), literacy-related action sequences and routines as critical cognitive activity in literacy development have not been fully recognized in previous studies or measures of early literacy behavior. Yet, these literacy actions and routines in this study appeared to reveal an important form of domain-specific knowledge. These results, therefore, argue for a broader framework for interpreting young children's knowledge base about literacy and the learning processes that constitute its early development. As a legitimate form of early literacy, participation in writing and reading practices represents an important phase of literacy learning, engaging children in practicing not only what written language is for, but how it works.

Across these settings children used a variety of strategies to monitor their understandings. Until recently, it had been assumed that children younger than age 5 were incapable of such intentional behaviors (Brown & DeLoache, 1978; Gelman, 1978): Nevertheless, recent studies (DeLoache & Brown, 1987; Revelle, Wellman, & Karabenick, 1985; Rowe, 1994) have revealed that even preschoolers show signs of being intentional at the level of demonstrating an awareness of a goal and show an understanding that something should be done in order to reach that goal. Our study substantiates this research, suggesting that in familiar, supportive environments with prompts or cues, children are capable of activating strategies in situations that *they* judge to be important and in which *they* are interested in the outcome and the goal.

Whether or not or to what extent strategic activities will be used, however, is likely to vary from setting to setting. In this study, children used strategies most often for transacting and organizing purposes as they attempted to refine and expand domain-specific knowledge. Fewer strategies were used in situations where literacy rules were either very well known or not known well enough. Confirming Gamer's (1990) theory of settings, strategy use was strongly dependent on the context in which the activity occurred. Children adjusted their strategic activity according to the context of participation.

This research raises several important issues for engaging young literacy leamers in more formal instruction. Much of what children learn about literacy before entering school is holistic, unintentional, and incidental (Iran-Nejad, McKeachie, & Berliner, 1990). Creating contexts in such a way that these dynamic learning approaches continue to work for children may represent a particularly important activity in early childhood classrooms.

In this study, for example, we orchestrated classroom settings to more closely approximate authentic learning opportunities in real-world contexts. In these contexts, we found children engaging in a variety of literacy purposes and strategies in rather complex and diverse literacy routines, reflecting approximations of literacy activity in everyday life. Exposed to the domain's conceptual tools in practical activity, these children appeared to adapt through the mechanism of acculturation some of the cultural practices and discourse patterns of literate learners. Such participation in practice applied to multiple settings, according to Hatano (1993), enhances the construction of mental models, enabling generalization of a multitude of literacy practices across various contexts. Participation in authentic activity, therefore, not only provides opportunity for using knowledge and strategies; it also represents critical cognitive work in literacy development.

Nevertheless, participation in practice as the major activity through which learning occurs may have its limitations. Enculturating leamers by modeling authentic real-life practices does not suggest how print conventions and literacy skills are formed by young learners. For example, children's literacy actions and routines did not appear to significantly change or become more embellished over the 7-month period of the study. This could suggest, of course, only limited occasions for demonstrations of knowledge or lack of stimulating options within settings. Or it could reflect a limitation of our research. Because our study focused on children's activity and not teacher-child interactions, long-term apprenticeship involving the teacher in an extended period of modeling, coaching, and fading (Collins et al., 1989) was not conducted; it might be that greater teacher participation could have encouraged more active knowledge construction. But it also could suggest that such activities do not support children's knowledge about literacy, apart from its functional uses. Situating literacy

354

learning in authentic contexts, for example, cannot address how literacy is used to think and reason in a variety of other domains (Brown et al., 1993). Engaging children in authentic literacy practices, therefore, may represent an important form of learning but only one form. Children need instruction that stimulates conceptual and factual knowledge about literacy.

Providing opportunities for both situated learning and formal school learning, therefore, could create dynamic and active classroom contexts for participation in literacy development. Classrooms like these provide both academic instruction and real-world opportunities for children to engage in literacy practices around self-initiated problem-solving situations, creating continuity between the rich contexts of home and school literacy practices. In this respect what children bring, in terms of their multiple literacy capabilities, would be used and practiced to manage complex activities, requiring them to adjust and strategically adapt their purposes for literacy in different situations. In these settings children may engage in such social practices as using literacy to remember, generalize, form concepts, operate with abstractions, and reason logically—activities identified with literate individuals. Such an approach might help children apply their multiple ways of knowing to novel problems, enculturating them into the community of literacy practitioners.

Appendix Sample of coded episode

Three-year-old Stephania, Analisa, and Lisa are in the post office. Lisa is
  protecting the cash register.

Stephania:	I need the money; this is mine. (gathering resources)
Analisa:	Why, I had to take the money, [from the cash register] (seeking information)

Stephania leaves, then returns in a minute.

Stephania:	Give me a pen; please. Where is the pen? Where is the pen? (gathering resources)
Analisa:	Is this the pen? [giving her an index card] (seeking information)
Stephania:	This is not a pen, it's a paper. [throws it, goes to get a pen] (correcting). This is a pen (declarative) This is my pen. [starts writing] I'm going to put the dollar in there. [in an envelope] (procedural)
Analisa:	You have to pay for money. (declarative)
Stephania:	No, no. (correcting)
Analisa:	Give me the money. You have to share. [grabs it] (gathering resources)
Stephania:	No, I need these and you need these. [attempting to share] (assigning resources)
Analisa:	I need two dollars. (gathering resources)
Stephania:	And this is mine. This is mine. This is all my money, OK. [then gives it to Analisa] (gathering resources)

References

BISSEX, G. (1980). *GNYS at work: A child learns to write and read*. Cambridge, MA: Harvard University Press.

BJORKLUND, D.F., MUIR-BROADDUS, J., & SCHNEIDER, W. (1990). The role of knowledge in the development of strategies. In D.F. Bjorklund (Ed.), *Children's strategies* (pp. 93–128). Hillsdale, NJ: Erlbaum.

BRONFENBRENNER, U. (1977). Toward an experimental ecology of human development. *American Psychologist, 32*, 513–531.

BROWN, A., ASH, D., RUTHERFORD, M., NAKAGAWA, K., GORDON, A., & CAMPIONE, J. (1993). Distributed expertise in the classroom. In G. Salomon (Ed.) *Distributed cognitions* (pp. 188–228). New York: Cambridge University Press.

BROWN, A.L. & DELOACHE, J.S. (1978). Skills, plans and self-regulation. In R. Siegler (Ed.), *Children's thinking: What develops?* (pp. 3–36). Hillsdale, NJ: Erlbaum.

BROWN, J.S., COLLINS, A. & DUGUID, P. (1989). Situated cognition and the culture of learning. *Educational Researcher, 18*, 32–42.

BRUNER, J. (1972). Nature and uses of immaturity. *American Psychologist, 27*, 687–708.

BRUNER, J. (1983). Play, thought and language. *Peabody Journal of Education, 60*, 60–69.

BRUNER, J., OLVER, R.R., & GREENFIELD, P.M. (1966). *Studies in cognitive growth*. New York: Wiley.

CHILDS, C.P., & GREENFIELD, P.M. (1980). Informal modes of learning and teaching: The case of Zinacanteco weaving. In N. Warren (Ed.), *Studies in cross-cultural psychology, Vol. 2* (pp. 235–257). London: Academic Press.

COLLINS, A., BROWN, J.S., & NEWMAN, S.E. (1989). Cognitive apprenticeships: Teaching the crafts of reading, writing, and mathematics. In L.R. Resnick (Ed.), *Knowing, learning and instruction* (pp. 453–491). Hillsdale, NJ: Erlbaum.

CORSARO, W. (1979). We're friends, right? Children's use of access rituals in a nursery school. *Language in Society, 8*, 315–336.

DELOACHE, J.S. & BROWN, A.L. (1987). The early emergence of planning skills in children. In J.S. Bruner & H. Weinreich-Haste (Eds.), *Making sense: The child's construction of the world* (pp. 108–130). New York: Methuen.

FANTUZZO, J., SUTTON-SMITH, B., COOLAHAN, K.C., MANZ, P.H., CANNING, S., & DEBNAM, D. (1995). Assessment of preschool play interaction behaviors in young low-income children: Penn interactive peer play scale. *Early Childhood Research Quarterly, 10*, 105–120.

FARNHAM-DIGGORY, S. (1994). Paradigms of knowledge and instruction. *Review of Educational Research, 64*, 463–477.

FORMAN, E., & MCPHAIL, J. (1993). Vygotskian perspective on children's collaborative problem-solving activities. In E. Forman, N. Minick, & C.A. Stone (Eds.), *Contexts for learning: Sociocultural dynamics in children's development* (pp. 213–229). New York: Oxford University Press.

FRYER, M.G., & FEIN, G. (1995, April). *Social pretend play in young children: Partner effects*. Paper presented at the annual meeting of the American Educational Research Association, San Francisco, CA.

GARNER, R. (1990). When children and adults do not use learning strategies: Toward a theory of settings. *Review of Educational Research, 60*, 517–529.

GARVEY, C. (1977). *Play*. Cambridge, MA: Harvard University Press.

GELMAN, R. (1978). Cognitive development. *Annual Review of Psychology, 29*, 297–332.

GIBSON, J.J. (1979). *The ecological approach to visual perception*. Boston: Houghton-Mifflin.

GLASER, B.G., & STRAUSS, A.L. (1967). *The discovery of grounded theory: Strategies for qualitative research*. New York: Aldine.

GOETZ, J., & LECOMPTE, M. (1984). *Ethnography and qualitative design in educational research*. Orlando, FL: Academic.

GOODMAN, Y. (1986). Children coming to know literacy. In W. Teale & E. Sulzby (Eds.), *Emergent literacy* (pp. 1–14). Norwood, NJ: Ablex.

GOODMAN, Y., & ALTWERGER, B. (1981). *Print awareness in preschool children: A working paper*. Tucson, AZ; University of Arizona.

HATANO, G. (1993). Time to merge Vygotskian and constructivist conceptions of knowledge acquisition. In E. Forman, N. Minick, & C.A. Stone (Eds.), *Contexts for learning: Sociocultural dynamics in children's development* (pp. 153–166). New York: Oxford University Press.

IRAN-NEJAD, A., MCKEACHIE, W.J., & BERLINER, D. (1990). The multisource nature of learning: An introduction. *Review of Educational Research, 60*, 509–516.

KANTOR, R., MILLER, S. & FERNIE, D. (1992). Diverse paths to literacy in a preschool classroom: A sociocultural perspective: *Reading Research Quarterly, 27*, 184–201.

LASS, B. (1982). Portrait of my son as an early reader. *The Reading Teacher, 36*, 20–28.

LAVE, J. (1988). *Cognition in practice*. New York: Cambridge University Press.

LAVE, J., MURTAUGH, M., & DE LA ROCHA, O. (1984). The dialectic of arithmetic in grocery shopping. In B. Rogoff & J. Lave (Eds.), *Everyday cognition* (pp. 67–94). Cambridge, MA: Harvard University Press.

LAVE, J., & WENGER, E. (1991). *Situated learning*, New York: Cambridge University Press.

LEONT'EV, A.N. (1981). The problem of activity in psychology. In J.W. Wertsch (Ed.), *The concept of activity in Soviet psychology* (pp. 37–71). Armonk, NY: M.E. Sharpe.

MASONHEIMER, P., DRUM, P., & EHRI, I. (1984). Does environmental print identification lead children into word reading? *Journal of Reading Behavior, 16*, 257–271.

MCGEE, L., LOMAX, R., & HEAD, M. (1988). Young children's written language knowledge: What environmental and functional print reading reveals. *Journal of Reading Behavior, 20*, 99–118.

MCLANE, J.B. & MCNAMEE, G.D. (1990). *Early literacy*. Cambridge, MA: Harvard University Press.

MORROW, L.M. (1990). Preparing the classroom environment to promote literacy during play. *Early Childhood Research Quarterly, 5*, 537–554.

NEUMAN, S.B., & ROSKOS, K. (1991). Peers as literacy informants: A description of children's literacy conversations in play. *Early Childhood Research Quarterly, 6*, 233–248.

NEUMAN, S.B., & ROSKOS, K. (1992). Literacy objects as cultural tools: Effects on children's literacy behaviors in play. *Reading Research Quarterly, 27*, 202–225.

NEUMAN, S.B., & ROSKOS, K. (1993). Access to print for children of poverty: Differential effects of adult mediation and literacy-enriched play settings on environmental and functional print tasks. *American Educational Research Journal, 30*, 95–122.

PALINCSAR, A.S., & BROWN, A. (1984). Reciprocal teaching of comprehension-fostering and monitoring activities. *Cognition & Instruction, 1*, 117–175.

PARIS, S., LIPSON, M., & WIXSON, K. (1983). Becoming a strategic reader. *Contemporary Educational Psychology, 8*, 293–316.

PERKINS, D.N. (1993). Person-plus: A distributed view of thinking and learning. In G. Salomon (Ed.), *Distributed cognitions* (pp. 88–110). New York: Cambridge University Press.

RESNICK, L. (1989). Introduction. In L. Resnick (Ed.), *Knowing, learning, and instruction: Essays in honor of Robert Glaser* (pp. 1–24). Hillsdale, NJ: Erlbaum.

REVELLE, G.L., WELLMAN, H.M., & KARABENICK, J.D. (1985). Comprehension monitoring in preschool children. *Child Development, 56*, 654–663.

ROGOFF, B. (1982). Integrating context and cognitive development. In M.E. Lamb & A.L. Brown (Eds), *Advances in developmental psychology* (pp. 125–161). Hillsdale, NJ: Erlbaum.

ROGOFF, B., MOSLER, C., MISTRY, J., & GONCU, A. (1993). Toddlers' guided participation with their caregivers in cultural activity. In E. Forman, N. Minick, & A. Stone (Eds.), *Contexts for learning: Sociocultural dynamics in children's development* (pp. 230–253). New York: Oxford University Press.

ROSKOS, K., & NEUMAN, S.B. (1993). Descriptive observations of adults' facilitation of literacy in young children's play. *Early Childhood Research Quarterly, 8*, 77–98.

ROWE, D.W. (1994). *Preschoolers as authors*. Cresskill, NJ: Hampton Press.

RUBIN, K., FEIN, F., & VANDENBERG, B. (1983). Children's play. In B. Hetherington (Ed.), *Handbook of child psychology: Social development* (pp. 693–772). New York: Wiley.

SCARDAMALIA, M. & BEREITER, C. (1985). Fostering the development of self-regulation in children's knowledge processing. In S.F. Chipman, J.W. Segal, & R. Glaser (Eds.), *Thinking and learning skills: Research and open questions* (pp. 563–577). Hillsdale, NJ: Erlbaum.

SCRIBNER, S. (1984). Studying working intelligence. In B. Rogoff & J. Lave (Eds.), *Everyday cognition* (pp. 9–40). Cambridge, MA: Harvard University Press.

SCRIBNER, S. (1986). Thinking in action: Some characteristics of practical thought. In R. Sternberg & D. Wagner (Eds.), *Practical intelligence* (pp. 13–30). New York: Cambridge University Press.

SCRIBNER, S., & COLE, M. (1973a). Cognitive consequences of formal and informal education. *Science, 182*, 553–559.

SCRIBNER, S., & COLE, M. (1973b). *The psychology of literacy*. Cambridge, MA: Harvard University Press.

TEALE, W., & SULZBY, E. (1986). *Emergent literacy: Writing and reading* Norwood, NJ: Ablex.

THARP, R., & GALLIMORE, R. (1988). *Rousing minds to life*. Cambridge, MA: Cambridge University Press.

VYGOTSKY, L.S. (1967). Play and its role in the mental development of the child. *Soviet Psychology, 12*, 62–76.

VYGOTSKY, L.S. (1978). *Mind in society: The development of higher psychological processes*: Cambridge, MA: Harvard University Press.

WEINSTEIN, C.S. (1979). The physical environment of the school: A review of the research. *Review of Educational Research, 49*, 577–610.

WOOD, D., BRUNER, J., & ROSS, G. (1976). The role of tutoring in problem solving. *Journal of Child Psychology and Psychiatry, 17*, 89–100.

16

EMERGENT LITERACY

Synthesis of the research

Barbara K. Gunn, Deborah C. Simmons
and Edward J. Kameenui

Source: University of Oregon/NCITE (1995) http://idea.uoregon.edu/~ncite/documents/ techrep/tech 19.html

Introduction

Although most preschool-age children cannot read and write in the conventional sense, their attempts at reading and writing show steady development during this stage (Hiebert, 1988). Typically, reading research in this developmental period has focused on discrete skills that are prerequisite to reading, such as letter-sound correspondences and letter naming. By highlighting the processes and products of initial reading instruction, however, this research has largely excluded the role that writing (van Kleeck, 1990) and early childhood literacy learning play in facilitating reading and writing acquisition. In contrast, the emergent literacy perspective, which emanated from cognitive psychology and psycholinguistics, takes a broader view of literacy and examines children's literacy development before the onset of formal instruction (Hiebert & Papierz, 1990; Mason & Allen, 1986; McGee & Lomax, 1990; Sulzby & Teale, 1991).

From an emergent literacy perspective, reading and writing develop concurrently and interrelatedly in young children, fostered by experiences that permit and promote meaningful interaction with oral and written language (Sulzby & Teale, 1991), such as following along in a big book as an adult reads aloud or telling a story through a drawing (Hiebert & Papierz, 1989). Through the concept of emergent literacy, researchers have expanded the purview of research from reading to literacy, based on theories and findings that reading, writing, and oral language develop concurrently and interrelatedly in literate environments (Sulzby & Teale, 1991). Thus, this contemporary perspective stresses that developmental literacy learning occurs during the first years of a child's life (Mason & Allen, 1986) and is crucial to literacy acquisition (McGee & Lomax, 1990).

The purpose of this chapter is to identify and discuss areas of emerging evidence on the relationship between early childhood literacy experiences and subsequent reading acquisition. We do not wish to minimize the role of oral language in early literacy development, for it serves as a companion to the development of reading and writing. However, our focus is on aspects of literacy acquisition that are related to awareness and knowledge of print. First, dimensions of literacy knowledge and literacy experiences are discussed, based on data from recent primary studies and reviews of emergent literacy research. Then areas of emerging evidence are examined for instructional implications for children entering school with diverse literacy experiences.

Methodology

Types of sources

We reviewed 24 sources including 13 primary studies (Brown & Briggs, 1991; Crain-Thoreson & Dale, 1992; Dickinson & Tabors, 1991; Ehri & Sweet, 1991; Hiebert & Papierez, 1990; Hildebrand & Bader, 1992; Katims, 1991; Morrow, 1990; Morrow, O'Connor, & Smith, 1990; Roberts; 1992; Scarborough, Dobrich, & Hager, 1991; Snow, 1991; Stewart, 1992). Secondary sources included ten overviews of research (Copeland & Edwards, 1990; Mason & Allen, 1986; Pellegrini & Galda, 1993; Sulzby & Teale, 1991; Teale & Sulzby, 1987; van Kleeck, 1990; Hiebert, 1988; McGee & Lomax, 1990; Smith, 1989; Weir, 1989), and one quantitative synthesis (Stahl & Miller, 1989).

Participant characteristics

Participants in the research reviewed included children identified as normally achieving, at-risk, linguistically diverse, and, in one study (Katims, 1991), children identified with cognitive, physical, emotional, behavioral, learning, and developmental disabilities. Due to the emergent literacy focus, the age of the subjects ranged from preschoolers to seven-year olds, with the majority being preschool and kindergarten children.

Measures

Morrow et al. (1990) observed that the measures selected for a study influence the findings and conclusions of that study. Measure selection is a significant consideration in any research design, but is particularly important in emergent literacy where researchers address issues raises by other researchers and relate data across studies to consolidate existing research (Sulzby & Teale, 1991).

Measures in the research reviewed reflected the observational/descriptive nature of emergent literacy investigations and included direct observation of literacy behaviors, parent/child questionnaires about home literacy activities, and researcher-developed measures to assess listening comprehension and letter and word knowledge. Other, less frequently used measures included Clay's (1979) *Concepts about Print Test*, the *School-Home Early Language and Literacy Battery Kindergarten* (SHELL-K), and standardized measures such as the *Peabody Picture Vocabulary Test* – Revised (PPVT-R) and the *California Achievement Test* (subtests of visual and auditory discrimination, sound recognition, vocabulary, and oral comprehension).

Overview of emergent literacy research

Definitions of emergent literacy. Our review of research revealed numerous but complementary definitions of emergent literacy. Researchers agreed that emergent literacy (a) begins during the period before children receive formal reading instruction, (Stahl & Miller, 1989; Teale & Sulzby, 1987; van Kleeck, 1990), (b) encompasses learning about reading, writing and print prior to schooling (Sulzby & Teale, 1991), (c) is acquired through informal as well as adult-directed home and school activities, and (d) facilitates acquisition of specific knowledge of reading. Emergent literacy differs from conventional literacy as it examines the range of settings and experiences that support literacy, the role of the child's contributions (i.e., individual construction), and the relation between individual literacy outcomes and the diverse experiences that precede those outcomes.

Definitions of emergent literacy terms

The term "emergent" denotes the developmental process of literacy acquisition and recognizes numerous forms of early literacy behavior. While frequently discussed in the research we reviewed, these early literacy behaviors (or areas of knowledge) are characterized by terms that are defined in different ways by different authors. The following definitions of emergent literacy terms represent the most commonly used meanings of those terms, and will facilitate understanding of the review of emergent literacy.

- **Conventional literacy:** reading, writing, and spelling of text in a conventional manner.
- **Conventions of print:** knowledge of the semantic and visual structure of text.
- **Purpose of print:** knowledge that words convey a message separate from pictures or oral language.

361

- **Functions of print:** awareness of the uses of print from specific (e.g., making shopping lists, reading street signs, looking up information) to general (e.g., acquiring knowledge, conveying instructions, maintaining relationships).
- **Phonological awareness:** conscious ability to detect and manipulate sound (e.g., move, combine, and delete), access to sound structure of language, awareness of sounds in spoken words in contrast to written words.

Dimensions of emergent literacy

Children begin school with diverse experiences and understandings of print: what it is, how it works, and why it is used. These experiences and understandings give rise to general literacy-related knowledge, as well as specific print skills and oral language competencies (Dickinson & Tabors, 1991; Mason & Allen, 1986). Our review revealed that through exposure to written language (e.g., storybook reading and daily living routines) many children develop an awareness of print, letter naming, and phonemic awareness. Additionally, through exposure to oral language, preschool children develop listening comprehension, vocabulary, and language facility. These initial understandings about print are particularly important considering that children who are behind in their literacy experiences upon entering school become "at risk" in subsequent years (Copeland & Edwards, 1990; Mason & Allen, 1986; Smith, 1989). For example, Scarborough et al. (1991) examined the relation of preschool development to later school accomplishment using parental reports about literacy activities in children's homes during their preschool years and assessments of reading achievement. They found that by the time poor readers entered school they had accumulated substantially less experience with books and reading than those who became better readers. Similarly, Ferreiro and Teberosky (cited in Mason & Allen, 1986) found that children who entered school without understanding the link between their oral language experiences and formal instruction did not advance at the same rate in learning to read and write as children who did make the connection.

Characteristics of emergent literacy research

To understand the implications of emergent literacy for initial reading acquisition, it is helpful to examine the characteristics of the research in this area. To date, emergent literacy research is comprised of more descriptive and correlational studies than experimental investigations (Mason & Allen, 1986; Teale & Sulzby, 1987). This emphasis on descriptive research is not atypical of an area of emerging interest as such a phase is important for identifying the features and dimensions of the phenomenon of interest. One area, phonological awareness, has been the subject of extensive experimental research, and has garnered more attention and examination at the experimental level. This is reflected in both the level of sophistication and the detail of findings, and as such, we exempt phonological awareness from subsequent discussions of emergent literacy research.

Studies of emergent literacy have multiple foci (Sulzby & Teale, 1991; van Kleeck, 1990). To learn about the role of family environment and literacy development, researchers have relied upon descriptive research in the form of naturalistic observations. Ethnographic studies, for example, have described literacy artifacts in preschool children's environment and provided details about the literacy events to which they are exposed and in which they participate. Such studies are useful as they provide information about the literacy experiences of children from various cultures and backgrounds. Examples of ethnographic observation were found in Hiebert's (1988) overview of emergent literacy research, including studies examining the role of word games (e.g., Tobin, cited in Hiebert, 1988), storybook reading (e.g., Snow & Ninio, cited in Hiebert, 1988), and chalkboards (Durkin, cited in Hiebert, 1988) in familiarizing children with the functions of literacy.

A second type of naturalistic observation has looked more specifically at the nature of adult-child interactions surrounding literacy events (Mason & Allen, 1986; Scarborough et al., 1991; Snow, 1991; Teale & Sulzby, 1987) to discern how adults foster literacy development. One example is a longitudinal study of the relation between preschool literacy development and later school achievement. Here Scarborough et al. (1991) interviewed middle-class parents about adult reading, parent-child reading, and children's solitary book activities in the home. Similarly, Hildebrand and Bader (1992) investigated the family literacy-related activities of 59 parents of children ages three to $5\frac{1}{2}$ to determine the contributions parents make to the home literacy environment.

A third type of research has moved beyond descriptive methodologies to determine which aspects of preschool literacy experience best predict reading achievement. For example, Dickinson and Tabors (1991) administered the *School-Home Early Language and Literacy Battery Kindergarten* (SHELL-K) to a sample of five-year-olds to identify the components of their language and literacy development and the experiences that contributed to those components.

Descriptive, correlational methodologies and experimental designs are beginning to be used in complement to examine factors associated and causally linked with early literacy acquisition (Mason & Allen, 1986; Sulzby & Teale, 1991). As researchers continue to investigate factors that influence pre-conventional reading and writing, measures of effectiveness and methods of assessment should become more refined and validated

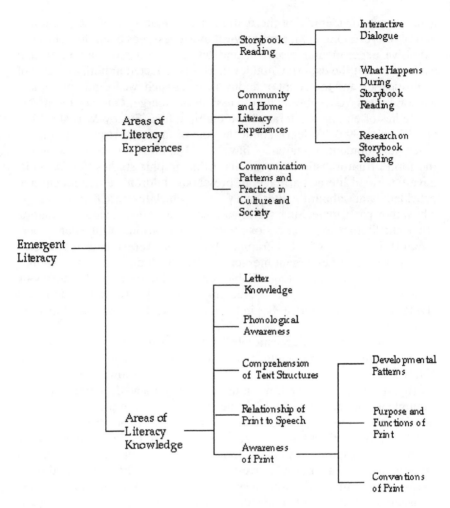

Figure 1 Overview of chapter on emergent literacy.

across studies, which should result in a more consistent examination of data. Moreover, as findings from descriptive studies are used to plan interventions and as the effects of those interventions upon literacy development are examined, the emergent literacy knowledge base will grow. To date, experimental interventions examining causal relations are limited; therefore, areas of emerging evidence should be interpreted with caution.

In this chapter, we focus first on converging themes in emergent literacy research and examine what is known about five areas of emergent literacy: awareness of print, relationship of print to speech, text structure, phonological awareness, and letter naming and writing. Next, we present conclusions about general areas of literacy experiences that facilitate that knowledge, including cultural communication practices and community/home literacy experiences. Finally, we examine the specific contributions of interactive dialogue, storybook reading, and symbolic play to literacy knowledge.

Areas of literacy knowledge

Numerous frameworks have been set forth for categorizing areas of literacy knowledge (Mason & Allen, 1986; Morrow et al. 1990; Stahl & Miller, 1989; van Kleeck, 1990). Although these frameworks differ in structure, certain areas of literacy knowledge are common across the emergent literacy literature. The following structure, adapted from van Kleeck (1990) reflects those areas: (a) awareness of print, (b) knowledge of the relationship between speech and print, (c) text structure, (d) phonological awareness, and (e) letter naming and writing. Each of these areas develops concurrently and interrelatedly, and continues to develop across the preschool and kindergarten period. Moreover, acquisition of these skills is an important part of early childhood literacy development, and substantially affects the ease with which children learn to read, write, and spell (Hiebert, 1988; van Kleeck, 1990; Weir, 1989).

Awareness of print

Experiences with print (through reading and writing) give preschool children an understanding of the conventions, purpose, and function of print—understandings that have been shown to play an integral part in learning to read. Because certain terms are used differently across the emergent literacy research, the way we use a term may differ slightly from the way a particular author uses it; nonetheless the gist of the concept is retained. Generally, "awareness of print" refers to a child's knowledge of the forms and functions of print. For this review, we define "forms" as knowledge of the conventions of print, and "functions" as the purposes and uses of print. In this section, each of these types of print awareness is discussed in relation to the contribution it makes to a child's literacy knowledge.

Conventions of print. Children learn about print from a variety of sources, and in the process come to realize that although print differs from speech, it carries messages just like speech (Morrow et al. 1990). Eventually, children learn that print – not pictures – carries the story. As preschool children listen to stories they learn not only how stories are structured semantically in terms of ideas but also visually in terms of their appearance on the printed page. That is, text begins at the top of the page, moves from left to right, and carries over to the next page when it is turned (Ehri & Sweet, 1991).

Attention to conventions of print is also seen in the development of written language. Children begin writing even before they can form letters, and this early writing reveals children's early attention to the conventions of written language (van Kleeck, 1990). Hiebert (1988) characterized this as a developmental progression in which early attempts at messages may take the form of scribbles that take on characteristics of the writing system, such as linearity. Eventually, the scribbling is superseded by letter-like forms which, in turn, are replaced by letters, generally familiar ones such as those in the child's name.

Functional and varied experiences in reading and writing print help children develop specific print skills, which appear to play an integral part in the process of learning to read (Dickinson & Tabors, 1991; Mason & Allen, 1986). Because of differences in parental support for literacy, however, children do not come to school with the same range of print related experiences (Mason & Allen, 1986). The failure of some children to pick up on physical cues to the nature of reading (e.g., sounds are arranged temporally, whereas writing is arranged permanently in space) means that teachers may need to assess children's level of understanding about print concepts and, when necessary, plan instruction to develop such understanding (Jagger & Smith-Burke, cited in Mason & Allen 1986). This may be accomplished by extending opportunities for children to interact with oral and written language in meaningful contexts such as story reading sessions in which book-handling skills are discussed (Weir, 1989).

Purpose and functions of print. Children understand the purpose of print when they realize that words convey a message; they understand the function of print when they realize that messages can serve multiple purposes (van Kleeck, 1990). While knowledge about the conventions of print enables children to understand the physical structure of written language, the conceptual knowledge that printed words convey a message – that is, the printed words contain meaning independent of the immediate social context – also helps young children bridge the gap between oral and written language. Additionally, as a result of interacting with and observing adults in their environment using print, preschool children also understand the vocabulary of reading in instructional contexts such as read, write, draw, page, and story (Morgan cited in Weir, 1989; van Kleeck, 1990). When formal instruction begins, the child who has this vocabulary about print-related phenomena is more likely to understand the basic vocabulary in the classroom.

Print serves a broad variety of functions. The scope of print functions ranges from very specific (e.g., making shopping lists, reading product labels, writing checks, reading street signs, looking up information) to very general (e.g., acquiring knowledge, conveying instructions, and maintaining relationships). Because all preschool children are not exposed to the same range of print-related experiences, their knowledge of these functions varies considerably. This variation in knowledge of the functions of print is related to daily routines in the child's home; it will be developed more fully in a subsequent section on the role of family environment.

Developmental patterns. Our review of research revealed that conclusions about factors that promote the development of awareness of print (i.e., knowledge of the purposes and processes of reading and the ability to recognize print embedded in environmental contexts) are limited. Lomax and McGee (cited in Hiebert, 1988; Weir, 1989) analyzed developmental patterns of children ages three to six on a hierarchy of reading-related skills and the ability to recognize print embedded in environmental contexts. According to their model of developmental patterns, awareness of print preceded graphic awareness, followed by phonemic awareness, grapheme-phoneme correspondence knowledge, and word reading.

Specifically, pre-kindergarten children demonstrated facility with only the early developing capabilities (e.g., awareness of print and graphic awareness), while gains by older children with succeeding capabilities (e.g. word reading) were reported to depend on proficiency with earlier skills. It appears that levels of preschool literacy competency do exist, and furthermore, these competencies may play a role in facilitating subsequent reading related skills (Weir, 1989).

Relationship of print to speech

The ability to map oral language onto print is important for early reading and writing experiences. Through interaction with others who model language functions, children learn to attend to language and to apply this knowledge to literacy situations. In English, the relationship between oral language (speech) and written language (print) uses the equivalence between phonemes and graphemes. However, since talking and reading are different processes and produce different outcomes (Akinnaso, cited in Mason & Allen, 1986), we cannot assume that children learn this equivalence solely by mapping their knowledge of oral language onto written language (Mason & Allen, 1986). Typically, it has been viewed as a developmental process, rather than an accumulation of discrete skills. Letter knowledge and phonological awareness are constituent skills in children's ability to realize this relationship (Ehri & Sweet, 1991; van Kleeck, 1990), but even before progressing to that level of knowledge, they may participate in less conventional forms of reading and writing that reflect their initial ideas about the relationship between speech and print (Hiebert, 1988; van Kleeck, 1990). For example, children may initially adopt a strategy in which they use one grapheme to represent one sound in an entire syllable or word, such as "Sio" to represent Santiago (Ferreiro, cited in van Kleeck, 1990). This may be followed by invented spelling which although not yet conventional, does adhere to the correspondence in the English orthography (van Kleeck, 1990).

Although the communicative function of oral language might make the acquisition of written language a natural process (Goodman & Goodman, cited in Mason & Allen, 1986), research suggests that written language acquisition can be problematic – due in part to basic differences between the linguistic properties of oral and written language.

Citing Perera's framework, Mason and Allen (1986) summarized the physical, situational, functional, form, and structural differences between oral and written language, and considered the impact of those differences on language instruction in the classroom.

For example, certain *physical differences* exist between written and spoken language. Print is processed by eye while speech is processed by ear (Kavanagh & Matingly, cited in Mason & Allen, 1986). This means, for example, that it may take six minutes to write a paragraph from a speech, but only one minute to read it.

Because of differences in early literacy experiences, children may come to school with varying concepts about the distinctions between the physical cues of reading and the aural cues of spoken language. For example, Ferreiro and Teberosky (cited in Mason & Allen, 1986) found that children varied in their ability to distinguish between oral conversation and a fairy tale or a news item when a researcher "read" to them from a storybook or a newspaper. Such failure to pick up on physical cues that differentiate written from spoken language can be problematic for beginning readers. To help children succeed in relating oral language to print, teachers may need to assess children's knowledge about the differences between speech and print, then clarify and expand their understanding (Jagger & Smith-Burke, cited in Mason & Allen, 1986).

Situational differences between oral and written language are apparent. Oral language most often occurs in a face-to-face context where the listener has the opportunity to ask for clarification or information. In written language or text, however, readers and writers are usually separated. Consequently, the writer must assume that the reader has the knowledge to process and comprehend the text. The reader in turn, must move backward or forward in the print to clarify information (Mason & Allen, 1986).

The multiple *functions* of language children use depends upon the context and the desired function of a given communication. Whereas oral language is generally used to express, explore, and communicate, written language is used as a means for expanding one's own thinking, by prompting comparisons and analysis (Mason & Allen, 1986). If children have not had extensive interaction with adults who model these language functions before coming to school, then the teacher must incorporate opportunities into the curriculum.

368

When English is seen in print *form*, each letter is a distinct visual form, and each word is distinct due to the spaces between the words (Mason & Allen, 1986). Other physical characteristics include indentation, punctuation, and capitalization. By contrast, in speech the boundaries between words and even phonemes may be obscured as Ehri (cited in Mason & Allen, 1986) illustrated in comparing the written "Give me a piece of candy" with the spoken "Gimme a pieca candy" (p.6).

Finally, spoken and written language differ in *structure*. For example, speakers tend to be more redundant than writers, and speech is also more informal than writing, as evidenced by the greater frequency of incomplete sentences, slang expressions, and meaningless vocalizations that function as place holders for thought in spoken language (Perera, cited in Mason & Allen, 1986). For children who come to school with differing exposures to the written and spoken discourse structures, awareness of the structural differences between spoken and written language may not be evident and, therefore, may negatively affect the transfer from listening to reading comprehension.

Given the differences between oral and written language, what are the instructional implications for children who have difficulty making the link between their oral language experiences and formal instruction in reading and writing? Several studies have suggested that when text is designed to resemble speech, beginning readers can process it more readily. Allen (cited in Mason & Allen, 1986) found that primary-grade children performed better on inferential comprehension tasks when the texts were closely linked to the children's oral language. Seventy children of varied reading ability read dictated, peer-written, and textbook stories. Allen observed that even the least able readers inferred well when reading their own texts, and they inferred somewhat better on peer stories than textbook stories. Similarly, Amstersam (cited in Mason & Allen, 1986) reported that children who repeated and later recalled natural language versus primerese versions of fables gave more complete recalls and fewer unnecessary repetitions of the text than children who used the language of the text.

These general manipulations of beginning reading instruction designed to lessen the differences between speech and print may be helpful for at-risk children. However, further research is needed to determine the specific sources of difficulty which at-risk populations experience in transferring speech to print, and how those children might best be helped (Mason & Allen, 1986).

Comprehension of text structures

As the ability to map oral language onto print is important for early reading and writing experiences, awareness of story grammar or text structures is important in facilitating children's comprehension of spoken and written language (Just & Carpenter; Perfetti, cited in van Kleeck, 1990). Children come to school with differing exposures to grammatical and discourse structures (Mason & Allen, 1986). Those who have had exposure to oral or written texts through storybook reading dialogue in the home may be sensitive to the schematic structure of stories from a very young age (Applebee, cited in van Kleeck, 1990). In fact, children recognize such features as formal opening and closing phrases (e.g., "Once upon a time") as early as two years of age. They also abstract a structure for the organization of stories and use this structure in their own comprehension and writing.

In their analysis of the writing of 16 kindergarten children, Brown and Briggs (1991) found that age, prior knowledge, level of social interaction, and environmental experiences influenced the participants' awareness of story elements. Moreover, repeated reading activities as well as reading a wide variety of discourse structures can influence the content and organization of children's stories by facilitating comprehension and developing story knowledge (Brown & Briggs, 1990; Mason & Allen, 1986; van Kleeck, 1990).

Although comprehension of text structures facilitates children's comprehension, few empirical investigations have been conducted in this area, thus limiting converging evidence.

Phonological awareness

Phonological awareness is reviewed extensively in another chapter; however, in this chapter we review its role and integral relation to emergent literacy.

In an alphabetic writing system such as English, beginning readers must use the alphabetic code to understand the link between the sounds of speech and the signs of letters (Mason & Allen, 1986; Sulzby & Teale, 1991). Phonological awareness, or the ability to perceive spoken words as a sequence of sounds, is a specific auditory skill which is of crucial importance to reading ability in an alphabetic system. Because research has established a correlational, if not causal relation between phonological awareness and reading (Ehri & Sweet, 1991; Mason & Allen, 1986; Sulzby & Teale, 1991; van Kleeck, 1990), phonological awareness is often raised in discussions of early childhood literacy education (Sulzby & Teale, 1991). Indeed, of all the areas of literacy knowledge developed during the preschool years, none has been studied as extensively or related as directly to early reading as phonological awareness (van Kleeck, 1990).

However, Sulzby and Teale (1991) noted that while phonological awareness has long been tied to research and practice in the teaching of phonics and other decoding skills, it has been neglected in emergent literacy due to the tendency to view phonological awareness research as traditional and bottom-up in theory. Despite this perspective, some researchers have argued that the ability to deal with the codes of alphabetic language does not automatically arise out of environmental print awareness. Instead, they suggested that young children must be helped to notice that words encode sounds as well as meaning (Dickinson & Snow; Mason; Masonheimer, Drum, & Ehri, cited in Sulzby & Teale, 1991).

Precursory phonological awareness skills such as rhyming and alliteration can emerge in informal contexts before school, and are seen in young children who can neither read nor spell (Snow, 1991; van Kleeck, 1990). A general order for the emergence of other phonological awareness abilities typically begins when children divide sentences into semantically meaningful word groups. According to Fox and Routh (cited in van Kleeck, 1990), the ability to segment sentences into words emerges next, followed by the more phonologically based skill of segmenting words into syllables. The ability to segment words into phonemes comes last (in their study, one quarter of words were segmented into phonemes by age three years). This general order of emergence has been supported in other investigations; however, the children in those studies tended to be older (Ehri; Holden & MacGinitie; Huttenlocher; Liberman; Liberman, Shankweiler, Fisher, & Carter, cited in van Kleeck, 1990).

In contrast to the informal context in which they acquire other emergent literacy skills, most children require specific instruction to acquire the phonological awareness skill of segmentation, or the ability to segment words into their component phonemes, and often master it later than other foundations for print literacy (van Kleeck, 1990). It has also been suggested that general phonological awareness skills be taught in conjunction with letter-sound knowledge to facilitate reading acquisition. Based on their review of research on instruction in phonological awareness, Ehri and Wilce (cited in Sulzby & Teal, 1991) reported that young children can be taught phonological awareness prior to formal reading instruction if they have a certain amount of letter knowledge. Training studies reviewed by Mason and Allen (1986) also revealed the advantages of knowledge of letter-sound principles for reading and spelling. They reported that when children understand that words contain discrete phonemes and that letters symbolize these phonemes, they are able to use more efficient word recognition strategies than when they rely on non-phonetic strategies.

Mason and Allen (1986) summarized their review of phonological awareness research by noting that instructional studies have led to improved outcomes in reading, but questions remain about how to employ information about word-and-letter recognition strategies to improve instruction. The authors concluded that while it is important for children to learn about letter-sound relationships, it should not be at the expense of reading comprehension opportunities or independent reading activities. Similarly, Sulzby and Teale (1991) proposed that without fundamental understandings of the functions and uses of literacy (e.g., storybook reading, language play, written language use in everyday practices), children may not profit from phonological awareness instruction. They suggested that future investigations of phonological awareness combine rigorous classroom-based research on phonological awareness training and its relation to overall early childhood curriculum.

Letter knowledge

Both phonological awareness and letter recognition contribute to initial reading acquisition by helping children develop efficient word-recognition strategies such as detecting pronunciations and storing associations in memory. Letter knowledge, like phonological awareness, may be acquired either though formal instruction or incidentally. Through incidental learning, for example, many children gain at least some concepts and skills related to the formal aspects of print prior to school (Hiebert & Papierz, 1990). They learn about the functions of written language in storybooks and poems while they learn about the forms (e.g., letter naming and visual discrimination) of written language (Hiebert, 1988).

Letter knowledge, which provides the basis for forming connections between the letters in spellings and the sounds in pronunciations, has been identified as a strong predictor of reading success (Ehri & Sweet, 1991) and has traditionally been a very important component of reading readiness programs (van Kleeck, 1990). Knowing the alphabet and its related sounds is associated with beginning literacy. In fact, letter knowledge measured at the beginning of kindergarten was one of two best predictors of reading achievement at the end of kindergarten and first grade – the other predictor was phonemic segmentation skill (Share, Jorm, Maclean, and Matthews, cited in Ehri & Sweet 1991). Furthermore, an analysis of the relationship between literacy development and participation in literacy activities at home revealed that children's exposure to letter names and sounds during the preschool years was positively associated with linguistically precocious performance on selected literacy measures (Crain-Thoreson & Dale, 1992).

Within the scope of this review, several reasons were offered for the effect of letter knowledge in reading acquisition. Based on observations of 5-year-old children in New Zealand, Clay (cited in Mason & Allen, 1986) concluded that:

> before children learn to decode words in and out of context, they become able to use some letter-sound information to recognize, remember, and spell words. This is possible even if they are not taught the letter sounds, because the names of the alphabet letters provide clues to the phonemic representations in words.
>
> (p. 18)

Ehri and Wilce (cited in Ehri & Sweet, 1991) hypothesized that letter knowledge enables beginning readers to adapt to the task of pointing to words as they read them and figure out how printed words correspond to spoken words. It may also enable them to remember how to read the individual words they encounter in the text. "This knowledge of letters provides the basis for forming connections between the letters seen in spellings and the sounds detected in pronunciations, and for storing these associations in memory in order to remember how to read those words when they are seen again" (p.446).

Although letter knowledge may be a strong component in preschool programs, children may also learn these skills at home. In a study of 59 parents of preschool children, Hildebrand and Bader (1992) found that children who performed high on three emergent literacy measures, including writing letters of the alphabet, were more likely to have parents who provided them with alphabet books, blocks, and shapes. The authors suggested that as children exhibit behaviors indicative of emergent literacy, parents and teachers can seize the teachable moments, and provide developmentally appropriate materials and interactions to further literacy development.

Whether letter knowledge is learned at home or at school, through word games or letters on the refrigerator, it appears to foster the development of subsequent reading strategies. However, further research is needed to provide more precise information about the kinds of instruction that are appropriate for children at varying stages of development and ability levels.

In this section, we focused on emerging evidence in emergent literacy research and examined what is known about five areas of emergent literacy knowledge: awareness of print, relationship of print to speech, text structures, phonological awareness, and letter naming and writing. We also identified the following three areas of emerging evidence that have instructional implications for preschool and early elementary children.

- Experiences with print (through reading and writing) help preschool children develop an understanding of the conventions, purpose, and functions of print. These understandings have been shown to play an integral part in the process of learning to read.
- Children learn how to attend to language and apply this knowledge to literacy situations by interacting with others who model language functions.
- Phonological awareness and letter recognition contribute to initial reading acquisition by helping children develop efficient word recognition strategies (e.g., detecting pronunciations and storing associations in memory).

Areas of literacy experiences

Development of literacy knowledge cannot be fully understood without understanding the contexts in which literacy is experienced (Mason & Allen, 1986; Teale & Sulzby, 1990). Some studies of emergent literacy have focused on the print-literacy environment of young children, while others have been interested in children's early literacy skills. Findings from both types of studies inform researchers about the role of contexts (i.e., culture, community, and family) in early literacy development and the kind of literacy knowledge children typically acquire during preschool years (van Kleeck, 1990). In the following section, we examine the social contexts that facilitate this knowledge, beginning with the larger context of culture, and then narrowing the focus to community/home environments, and finally family interactions.

Communication patterns and practices in culture and society

"The purposes for literacy vary both within and across countries, and those purposes affect literacy practices and achievement" (Mason & Allen, 1986, p. 5). For example, in Israel, Jewish children learn to read Hebrew in order to read the Bible, even though they do not speak Hebrew (Downing, cited in Mason & Allen, 1986). Similarly, in Japanese reading instruction, story selection is used to emphasize moral development (Sakamoto & Makita, cited in Mason & Allen, 1986), as in India where cultural values and socialization are stressed in reading primers. Therefore, "we cannot consider the literacy of a child or an adult without also considering the context and perspective or purpose in their culture" (Mason & Allen, 1986, p. 5).

Literacy acquisition is also influenced by societal expectations, and the value a culture places upon literacy for its members (Mason & Allen, 1986). For example, in Nepal, lower-caste children, particularly girls, are not encouraged to learn to read and write (Junge & Shrestha, cited in Mason & Allen, 1986). Similarly, minority cultures in the United States as in other countries have often received inadequate reading and writing instruction. Feitelson (cited in Mason & Allen, 1986) cautioned that in societies such as Israel that have accepted large numbers of families from underdeveloped countries, the literacy traditions of the main culture may be missing among immigrants. Yet, research on well-educated parents in mainstream cultures whose children make the transition to literacy does not inform educators about how to work with children from less-literate immigrant families (Mason & Allen, 1986).

Literacy values can also influence how children view the significance and function of written language and may provide a basis for their interest and success in reading and writing (Clay, cited in Copeland &

Edwards, 1990). In observations of Maori and Samoan children in New Zealand Clay noted that while the two groups were about equal in oral language development at age 7, the Samoan children had made significantly better progress in reading than the Maori children – progress that was equal to that of the Pakehas (the Maori word for New Zealand whites). Clay suggested that a critical difference was ... "the parental attitudes of Samoans favoring education and their influence as models for reading [at church] and writing letters home [to Samoa]" (cited in Mason & Allen, p. 6).

These studies reveal the impact of social expectations and context on literacy learning. What families and communities believe and value about literacy is reflected in the level of preparation children bring to formal instruction, and affects the role of schools in providing literacy experiences and instruction.

Community and home literacy experiences

Literacy activities in the more immediate environments of home and community largely influence a child's literacy development (Morrow, 1990). Thus, a number of studies have documented the positive relation between children's literacy experiences at home and the ease with which children transition to school (Copeland & Edwards, 1990; Mason & Allen 1986; van Kleeck, 1990). However, family literacy environments differ along several dimensions. For example, although some development of print awareness seems to be common across cultures, significant differences exist in the quantity of exposure children have with written language, particularly storybook reading (Stahl & Miller, 1989).

Furthermore, parents' perceptions of the roles they can play in their child's literacy experiences also vary. In Heath's ethnographic study of Roadville (cited in Copeland & Edwards, 1990), a white working class community, and Trackton, a black working-class community, parents wanted their children to achieve in school, yet parents in both communities did not know they could help foster that success by writing extended pieces of prose or enriching their children's oral language experiences.

Research cautions against using group membership as a yardstick for measuring children's literacy preparation. In a meta-analysis of nearly 200 studies, White (cited in van Kleeck, 1990) concluded that it was not socioeconomic status that contributed most directly to reading achievement, but rather other family characteristics related to context such as academic guidance, attitude toward education, parental aspirations for the child, conversations and reading materials in the home, and cultural activities. In the next section then, we examine more specific research on literacy experiences in the context of the family: parent-child interactions, and the role of imaginative play and storybook reading.

Storybook reading

Throughout the literature, storybook reading or reading aloud to children emerges as a key component in facilitating early literacy acquisition (Hiebert, 1988; Mason & Allen, 1986; Morrow et al., 1990; Teale & Sulzby, 1987). For example, Morrow et al. (1990) noted that numerous correlational studies have documented the relationship between reading to children and subsequent success on reading readiness tasks (citing Burrough, 1972; Chomsky, 1972; Durkin, 1974–75; Fodor, 1966; Irwin, 1960; Moon & Wells, 1979). Further, substantial evidence documents that children who are read to acquire concepts about the functions of written language in books (Hiebert, 1988; Mason & Allen, 1986). Children also learn that print differs from speech (Morrow et al., 1990; Smith, 1989) and that print, not pictures, contains the story that is being read. Mason and Allen (1986) observed that "... while additional research is needed to identify factors on the causal chain, a reasonable conjecture is that story reading at home makes important, if not necessary, contributions to later reading achievement" (p. 29).

Storybook reading takes on additional significance when one considers findings indicating that most successful early readers are children who have had contact at home with written materials (Hiebert, 1988; Hildebrand & Bader, 1992; Smith, 1989; Teale & Sulzby, 1987). It is evident that by the time poor readers enter school, they have had substantially less experience with books and reading than those who become better readers. Scarborough et al. (1991) asked parents of preschoolers about the frequencies of adult reading, parent-child reading, and children's solitary book activities in the home, and compared those responses to the children's reading achievement in second grade. Their findings indicated that the children who became poorer readers had less experience with books and reading than children who became better readers. Moreover, children entering school with meager literacy experiences, or less exposure to books and reading, had much to learn about print and were easily confused if they could not map words onto their oral language or could not recognize or distinguish letters (Dyson, cited in Mason & Allen, 1986).

An investigation of the effects of a storybook reading program on the literacy development of urban at-risk children focused on how school instructional programs might address meager literacy experiences (Morrow et al., 1990). Children in four experimental classes followed a daily program of literature experiences that included reading for pleasure, story retelling, repeated reading of favorite stories, interactive story reading, and recreational reading. While students in four control groups followed the district prescribed reading readiness program emphasizing letter recognition and letter-sound correspondence. The experimental groups scored significantly higher than the control groups on story retells, attempted reading of favorite stories, and comprehension tests. However, no significant differences existed between the groups on standardized measures of reading readiness.

Based on these findings, Morrow et al. (1990) suggested that a blend of approaches, coupling some elements of more traditional reading readiness programs with a strong storybook reading component, may be a sound choice for development of literacy instruction package. These findings have implications for preliterate children, in general, and at-risk learners, in particular. Without sufficient storybook reading experience in early childhood – whether at home or at school – students may be missing a key part of the initial foundation of reading. In the following section, we look at the nature of the research on these print experiences, the activities that comprise storybook reading, and the role of interactive dialogue.

Research on storybook reading. Sulzby and Teale (1991) noted that historically, storybook reading has received more research attention than any other aspect of young children's literacy experiences. While it continues to be a significant area of study, they suggested that storybook reading research has evolved in at least four significant ways. First, the methodology has become descriptive in an effort to analyze what goes on during the activity. That is, researchers have moved toward methods that analyze the language and social interaction of storybook reading to gain clues about causal as well as correlational relationships. Second, much of the early storybook reading research focused on the one-to-one or one-to-few readings that typifies parent-child readings at home. By including group storybook reading sessions simulating classroom settings, several studies have examined the similarities and differences between home and school literacy situations. A third change has been the focus on children's independent reading attempts in addition to the focus on adult-child interactions in order to infer what concepts the child is using in reading situations.

Finally, descriptive methodologies and experimental designs are being used in a complementary manner. Information from descriptive studies is being used to design intervention studies and to examine the effects of those interventions upon children's literacy development. These shifts in storybook reading research expand upon previously reported data and serve to inform us about how storybook reading contributes to children's writing, intellectual, emotional, and oral language development (Sulzby & Teale, 1991).

What happens during storybook reading. Storybook reading practices are characterized by routines that help explain how storybook reading contributes to literacy learning (Sulzby & Teale, 1991). These routines appear to have developmental properties, with the adult acting as a scaffold – initially controlling those elements of the task that are beyond the child's ability, then gradually guiding and confirming the child's independent reenactments and attempts at decoding (Mason & Allen, 1986; Sulzby & Teale, 1991).

377

Based on their review of literacy acquisition in early childhood, Sulzby and Teale (1991) described these developmental properties in the context of parent-child reading sessions: (a) labeling and commenting on items in discrete pictures, (b) weaving an oral recount of the pictures in order, (c) creating a story with the prosody and wording of written language, and (d) attending to and decoding the actual printed story. More specifically, they highlighted several studies that clarified the applicability of the scaffolding concept for describing changes in storybook reading.

In an examination of the structure and content of picture book interactions of 30 mothers and their 12-, or 18-month-old infants, DeLoache and DeMendoza (cited in Sulzby & Teale, 1991) observed that the content of mother-child interactions varied as a function of age; the older children's input became increasingly verbal, and the information supplied by the mother became increasingly complex. Sulzby and Teale (1991) found similar changes in the patterns of parent-child readings in eight Hispanic and Anglo families. The parent would frequently focus the very young child on specific objects or characters in the pictures of the books as opposed to the entire story. Then, as the children became toddlers, the parents would expand by telling the main points or reading selected parts of a story (Teale & Sulzby, 1987).

Similarly, in their analysis of emergent literacy research, Mason and Allen (1986) reviewed descriptive studies reporting on parent-child reading routines. Harkness and Miller (cited in Mason & Allen, 1986) also observed mother-child interactions during storybook reading. Although questions or comments to initiate book reading interactions continued throughout book reading sessions, mothers gradually increased the length of time between each interchange by reading longer text sections. Likewise, Ninio and Bruner (cited in Mason & Allen, 1986) analyzed mothers' dialogues that accompanied picture-book reading to young children. They found that mothers directed their children's attention to particular features in a book, asked questions, provided labels, and gave feedback by repeating or extending children's remarks.

In sum, the scaffolded routines of storybook reading create predictable formats that help children learn how to participate in and gradually take more responsibility for storybook reading activities. These routines, as well as the language and social interactions that surround the text, appear to explain what makes storybook reading such a powerful influence in literacy development (Sulzby & Teale, 1991).

Interactive dialogue. While access to print in storybook reading may facilitate literacy acquisition, it has been suggested that how the parent reads to the child is also important (Morrow et al., 1990; Teale & Sulzby, 1987). General consensus has been reached on the key role that adult mediation appears to play in literacy growth (Mason & Allen, 1986; Morrow, 1990; Morrow et al., 1990; Stahl & Miller, 1989; Sulzby & Teale,

1991; Teale & Sulzby, 1987). Thus, the language and social interaction between a parent (or older sibling) and child during shared book experiences may aid in (a) developing language skills (Snow, 1991), (b) familiarizing the child with conventions of print (Dickinson & Tabors, 1991; Stahl & Miller, 1989), and (c) serving as a model of reading (Morrow et al., 1990).

In a review of recent studies on the importance of verbal interactions during storybook reading Mason and Allen (1986) found that the quality and quantity of interactions, not just the presence of reading materials and a story time routine shaped early reading development. They described the effects of verbal interactions in a study comparing early readers with nonearly readers (Thomas, cited in Mason & Allen, 1986). Early readers talked more frequently about literacy with family members, their interactions contained more instances of extending a topic, and they exhibited more accountability (requiring the completion of a language interjection). Because storybook reading is a social activity, children encounter an interpretation of the author's words, which is subsequently shaped by the interpretation and social interaction of the child and the adult reader (Morrow et al., 1990).

The ways in which adults mediate storybooks for children are as varied as the range of settings in which this activity takes place. Parents of early readers (Thomas, cited in van Kleeck, 1990) and parents of children who are successful in school (Heath; Wells, cited in van Kleeck) do more than read books and elicit labels, objects, and details of events. They guide children to relate information in books to other events, and engage them in discussing, interpreting, and making inferences (Teale & Sulzby, 1991; van Kleeck, 1990).

These representations of storybook reading as a scaffolded activity are consonant with Hiebert's (1988) premise that during story reading, adults act as scaffolds for children by connecting story elements with what the child already knows, by asking questions, and by encouraging the children to ask questions. Vygotsky's (1966) theory (cited in Morrow, 1990) that children learn higher psychological processes through their social environment and specifically with adult guidance within a child's "zone of proximal development" also reinforces the idea that children acquire literacy behaviors by interacting/collaborating with an adult aided by their encouragement and assistance (Morrow, 1990).

In this section, we examined the social contexts that facilitate literacy knowledge, beginning with the larger context of culture, then narrowing the focus to community/home environments, and family interactions. We also identified the following two broad areas of emerging evidence:

#1 Socioeconomic status does not contribute most directly to reading achievement. Rather, other family characteristics related to context are more explanatory such as academic guidance, attitude toward education, parental aspirations for the child, conversations in the home, reading materials in the home, and cultural activities. (Note: this conclusion was derived by White from his 1982 meta-analysis, (cited in van Kleeck, 1990), and has been reinforced by recent literature on socioeconomic status and academic achievement.)

#2 Storybook reading, as well as the nature of the adult-child interactions surrounding storybook reading, affects children's knowledge about, strategies for, and attitudes towards reading.

Summary

Our review of the emergent literacy literature suggested that early childhood literacy experiences affect successful reading acquisition along several dimensions. These literacy experiences are, in turn, influenced by social contexts and conditions as diverse as the individual literacy outcomes they help to shape. The challenge for the preschool or elementary classroom teacher is clear: They are charged with designing and delivering reading instruction that not only builds on what the individual child knows, but also accommodates the myriad individual literacy backgrounds present in the classroom.

To summarize, five areas of emerging evidence have implications for addressing those differences and making a closer match between a child's literacy background and classroom instruction:

- Experiences with print (through reading and writing) help preschool children develop an understanding of the conventions, purpose, and functions of print.
- Children learn how to attend to language and apply this knowledge to literacy situations by interacting with others who model language functions.
- Phonological awareness and letter recognition contribute to initial reading acquisition by helping children develop efficient word-recognition strategies (e.g., detecting pronunciations and storing associations in memory).
- Socioeconomic status does not contribute most directly to reading achievement. Rather, other family characteristics related to context are more explanatory such as academic guidance, attitude toward education, parental aspirations for the child, conversations in the home, reading materials in the home, and cultural activities.
- Storybook reading, as well as the nature of the adult-child interactions surrounding storybook reading, affects children's knowledge about, strategies for, and attitudes towards reading.

Acknowledgements

We would like to acknowledge Scott Baker, David Chard, Shirley Dickson, Sylvia Smith and Katie Tate for their contributions to this manuscript. Preparation of this manuscript was supported in part by The National Center to Improve the Tools of Educators (H180M10006) funded by the U. S. Department of Education, Office of Special Education Programs.

Appendix 1 Primary studies

Author	Emergent literacy dimension	Participants	Purpose
Brown & Briggs (1991)	Story writing / text structure.	Kindergarten students N = 16	Examine kindergarten literacy development through writing
Crain-Thoreson & Dale (1992)	Story reading / letter names and sounds.	Linguistically precocious children N = 25 (Studied from 20 months–4.5 years)	Examine relation between language and literacy skills
Dickinson & Tabors (1991)	Impact of settings and experiences on early literacy development.	5-year old children N = 3	To use multiple measures to assess early language and literacy development
Ehri & Sweet (1991)	Print knowledge and fingerpoint-reading.	Children proficient in English N = 36 M = 5.1 years	To investigate kinds of print-related knowledge needed for fingerpoint-reading.
Hiebert & Papierz (1990)	Emergent literacy focus in reading basal activities.	N/A	To examine reading instruction in the early childhood component of basal reading activities.
Hildebrand & Bader (1992)	Home literacy environments.	Parents of preschool children N = 59	To examine relation between parents involvement in literacy activities and their child's emerging literacy behaviors.
Katims (1991)	Development of emergent literacy behaviors in young children with disabilities.	Children identified with disabilities N = 21 M = 5.3 years	To determine if exposure to structured, print-rich environments would develop pre-literate behaviors in children with disabilities.

Appendix 1 continued

Author	Emergent literacy dimension	Participants	Purpose
Morrow (1990)	Role of physical environment in classroom learning experiences.	Preschool children N = 170	To determine the effects of physical design changes in preschool classroom play centers on children's literacy behaviors during play time.
Morrow, O'Connor, & Smith (1990)	Storybook reading.	At-risk Chapter I kindergarten students N = 62	Effects of a storybook reading program on the literacy development of urban at-risk children.
Roberts (1992)	Development of the concept of *word* as a unit of spoken and written language.	K-2nd grade students N = 32	(1) To describe development of concept of *word* related to beginning reading. (2) To investigate relation between cognitive development and acquisition of concept of word.
Scarborough, Dobrich, & Hager (1991)	Preschool literacy activities on the home.	Poor and normal readers N = 56 (Studied from preschool-grade 2)	To examine the relation between preschool literacy experience and later reading achievement.
Snow (1991)	Role of oral language development and reading acquisition.	Low-income families with preschoolers N = 80	To describe environmental supports for literacy development in the home and at school for children from low-income families.
Stewart (1992)	Children's awareness of learning to read.	Kindergarten students N = 56	To investigate children's awareness of how they are learning to read.

Appendix 2 Secondary studies

Author	Emergent Literacy Dimension	Participants	Purpose
Copeland & Edwards (1990)	Writing.	Studies reflected varied populations of preschool to primary-age children.	To examine the social aspects of young children's writing development.
Hiebert (1988)	Preschool literacy experiences.	Studies reflected varied populations of preschool to primary-age children.	To provide an overview of emergent literacy research and its importance for beginning reading programs.
Mason & Allen (1986)	Social/linguistic contexts of literacy, oral and written language, and early reading and writing skills.	Studies reflected varied populations of preschool to primary-age children.	To review emergent literacy research and studies on reading acquisition.
McGee & Lomax (1990)	Beginning reading instruction.	Studies reflected varied populations of preschool to primary-age children.	Response to Stahl & Miller's (1989) meta-analysis of reading instruction approaches.
Pellegrini & Galda (1993)	Symbolic play and literacy.	Studies reflected varied populations of preschool to primary-age children.	To review research on the ways in which symbolic play is related to emergent literacy.
Smith (1989)	Preschool literacy experiences.	Focus on preschool children.	To discuss the concept of emergent literacy.
Stahl & Miller (1989)	Beginning reading instruction.	Studies reflected varied populations of preschool to primary-age children.	Meta-analysis of reading instruction approaches.
Sulzby & Teale (1991)	Storybook reading, writing, metalinguistic awareness, phonemic awareness.	Studies reflected varied populations of preschool to primary-age children.	To review recent research on emergent literacy.

Appendix 2 continued

Author	Emergent Literacy Dimension	Participants	Purpose
Teale & Sulzby (1987)	Storybook reading.	Studies reflected varied populations of preschool to primary-age children.	To discuss recent research on the role of access and mediation in storybook reading.
van Kleeck (1990)	Preschool literacy experiences.	Studies reflected varied populations of preschool to primary-age children.	To discuss recent research on emergent literacy.
Weir (1989)	Prekindergarten literacy programs.	Preschool children.	To discuss implications of recent research on emergent literacy for prekindergarten programs.

References

Brown, D. L., & Briggs, L. D. (1991). Becoming literate: The acquisition of story discourse. *Reading Horizons, 32* (2), 139–153.

Clay, M. (1979). *Stones – The Concepts About Print Test.* Portsmouth, NH: Heinemann Educational Books.

Copeland, K. A., & Edwards, P. A. (1990). Towards understanding the roles parents play in supporting young children's development in writing. *Early Child Development and Care, 56,* 11–17.

Crain-Thoreson, C., & Dale, P. S. (1992). Do early talkers become early readers? Linguistic precocity, preschool language, and emergent literacy. *Developmental Psychology, 28* (3), 421–429.

Dickinson, D. K., & Tabors, P. O. (1991). Early literacy: Linkages between home, school, and literacy achievement at age five. *Journal of Research in Childhood Education, 6* (1), 30–46.

Ehri, L. C., & Sweet, J. (1991). Fingerpoint-reading of memorized text: What enables beginners to process the print? *Reading Research Quarterly, 26* (4), 442–462.

Hiebert, E. H. (1988). The role of literacy experiences in early childhood programs. *The Elementary School Journal, 89* (2), 161–171.

Hiebert, E. H., & Papierz, J. M. (1990). The emergent literacy construct and kindergarten and readiness books of basal reading series. *Early Childhood Research Quarterly, 5* (3), 317–334.

Hildebrand, V. L., & Bader, L. A. (1992). An exploratory study of parents' involvement in their child's emerging literacy skills. *Reading Improvement, 29* (3), 163–170.

Katims, D. S. (1991). Emergent literacy in early childhood special education: Curriculum and instruction. *Topics in Early Childhood Special Education, 11*, 69–84.

Mason, J., & Allen, J. B. (1986). A review of emergent literacy with implications for research and practice in reading. *Review of Research in Education, 13*, 3–47.

McGee, L. M. & Lomax, R. G. (1990). On combining apples and oranges: A response to Stahl and Miller. *Review of Educational Research, 60* (1), 133–140.

Morrow, L. M. (1990). Preparing the classroom environment to promote literacy during play. *Early Childhood Research Quarterly, 5*, 537–554.

Morrow, L. M., O'Connor, E. M., & Smith, J. K. (1990). Effects of a story reading program on the literacy development of at-risk kindergarten children. *Journal of Reading Behavior*, 22(3), 255–275.

Pelligrini, A. D., & Galda, L. (1993). Ten years after: A reexamination of symbolic play and literacy research. *Reading Research Quarterly, 28*, 163–175.

Perera, K. (1984). *Children's writing and reading: Analyzing classroom language.* Oxford, England: Blackwell.

Roberts, B. (1992). The evolution of the young child's concept of word as a unit of spoken and written language. *Reading Research Quarterly, 27* (2), 125–138.

Scarborough, H. S., Dobrich, W., & Hager, M. (1991). Preschool literacy experience and later reading achievement. *Journal of Learning Disabilities, 24* (8), 508–511.

Smith, C. B. (1989). Emergent literacy – an environmental concept. *The Reading Teacher, 42* (7), 528.

Snow, C. E. (1991). The theoretical basis for relationships between language and literacy in development. *Journal of Research in Childhood Education, 6* (1), 5–10.

Stahl, S. A., & Miller, P. D. (1989). Whole language and language experience approaches for beginning reading: A quantitative research synthesis. Review of *Educational Research, 59* (1), 87–116.

Stewart, J. (1992). Kindergarten students' awareness of reading at home and in school. *Journal of Educational Research, 86* (2), 95–104.

Sulzby, E., & Teale, W. (1991). Emergent literacy. In R. Barr, M. L. Kamil, P. B. Mosenthal, & P. D. Pearson (Eds.), *Handbook of reading research* (Vol. 2, pp. 727–757). New York: Longman.

Teale, W. H., & Sulzby, E. (1987). Literacy acquisition in early childhood: The roles of access and mediation in storybook reading. In D. A. Wagner (Ed.), *The future of literacy in a changing world* (pp. 111–130). New York: Pergamon Press.

van Kleeck, A. (1990). Emergent literacy: Learning about print before learning to read. *Topics in Language Disorders, 10* (2), 25–45.

Weir, B. (1989). A research base for pre kindergarten literacy programs. *The Reading Teacher, 42* (7), 456–460.

17

PROGRESS AND PERFORMANCE IN NATIONAL LITERACY STRATEGY CLASSROOMS

Ros Fisher, Maureen Lewis and Bernie Davis

Source: *Journal of Research in Reading* (2000) 23(3): 256–266

Introduction

September 1998, saw the introduction of a daily Literacy Hour into most primary schools (5–11 years) in England as part of the UK government's *National Literacy Strategy* (NLS). The government set the target that 'By 2002 80% of 11 year olds should reach the standard expected in English for their age (i.e. Level 4) in the Key Stage (KS) 2 National Curriculum tests' (DfEE, 1997, para 1). To reach these 'ambitious targets' the government implemented a programme of reform of literacy teaching. The methods that are being promoted are the use of explicit teaching, for 100% of the teacher's time, within a clearly defined framework of teaching objectives at whole text, sentence and word levels. This is managed within a carefully structured hour long session: the Literacy Hour. It includes specific teaching strategies such as shared and guided reading and writing and structured phonic work (DfEE, 1998).

This paper reports on a small-scale study of 20 classrooms in small schools located in a rural area of England during the first year of the implementation of the NLS. Early evidence from government-sponsored research, national testing and inspection findings showed that children taught according to the structure laid down by the literacy strategy made more than the expected progress (Sainsbury, Schagen and Whetton, 1998; Ofsted, 1999). This paper supports this evidence and considers in more depth the nature of this progress and the contexts in which it occurred.

The forerunner to the NLS, *The National Literacy Project*, based in approximately 250 schools, was evaluated by the National Foundation for Educational Research (NFER) by means of reading tests for all age groups, a survey of children's attitudes to reading in KS2 (ages 7–11) and questionnaires completed by head teachers. Sainsbury, Schagen and Whetton (1998) claimed that test results revealed a significant and substantial improvement in children's scores over the first 18 months of the project. Although pupils had come into the project with scores below the national average, their final test scores showed an improvement of approximately six standardised score points. This meant that the children in these schools, although still below national average, had come significantly closer to the national average.

The present study offers further evidence to show that although children made progress in the first year of the NLS, that progress was variable. Evidence from our case studies gives more detail about the nature of this progress. Also proposed is a concern that the NLS is being implemented in different ways in different classes and that not all teachers have really changed the way in which they organise their teaching. Reynolds (1998) commented on the growing evidence of 'context specificity' in the factors associated with learning gains (see also Borich, 1996; Hallinger and Murphy, 1986). Reynolds argued that there was a danger that the 'one size fits all' approach of the NLS might result in doing no more than maximising pre-existing differences. This would be consistent with studies showing that individual teachers make more difference than the actual programme (Goodacre, 1971; Chall, 1967). In an overview of research into the effectiveness of literacy programmes, Adams (1990), with particular reference to phonics instruction, said that statistical analyses showed that research into methods indicated many 'method effects' but also many 'side effects' (such as community, school, classroom, teacher and pupil characteristics). Adams concluded that both the programme used and 'classroom delivery' affected learning. Results from the classes in this study give some support to the view that individual teachers make a difference but also show children making progress in classrooms where attainment had previously been low.

Method

The research consisted of detailed case studies from 20 classrooms, in which multiple sources of evidence were gathered. Ten schools were selected from those that had shown neither exceptionally good nor exceptionally bad performance in the national tests for 11-year-olds in the previous year. Within each school two classes were identified, one with children under 7 years (KS1) and one with children between 7 and 11 years (KS2).

For each school, the most recent inspection report and an interview with the class teacher were used to gain an impression of teachers' attitudes and practice in literacy teaching before the NLS was introduced. Standardised tests in literacy were administered at the beginning and end of the year to provide limited evidence of pupils' attainment in reading within each target class. Each teacher was observed in Literacy Hour sessions in each classroom (one per month from October onwards). The observation data, gathered during the visits, included details of the lesson focus; room layout; resources used; observations of the teacher at predetermined intervals; observations of target children; and the observer's subjective field notes, which gave an account of the lesson and any discussion held afterwards with the teacher. Also collected were teachers' planning documents and target children's work samples. Teachers were interviewed again at the end of the year.

The tests used were standardised tests intended for the appropriate age group and the same ones that had been used by the NFER in the evaluation of the first cohort of the *National Literacy Project* (Sainsbury et al, 1998). In Reception (4/5 year olds) the *Language and Reading Readiness Test of Emergent Literacy* (LARR; Downing, Schaefer and Ayres, 1982) was used on both occasions. In KS1 the *Primary Reading Test* (PRT; France, 1979) was used: in October as a word recognition test and in June as a comprehension test. At KS2 the *Progress in English* (PIE; Kispal, Hagues and Ruddock, 1994) tests were used: Test 8 in October and 9 in June for Years 3 and 4; Test 10 in October and 11 in June for Years 5 and 6. These tests, while generally accepted as useful measures, focus mainly on reading, although PIE also has a spelling component. The period between tests was relatively short, due partly to the late starting of the project because of a delay in the confirmation of funding, and partly to a decision made by the research team that the final round of testing should begin in June in order to ensure that all schools were able to complete tests within the academic year. This meant that the period over which progress was measured was only 8 months.

Results

Progress in reading

Overall statistics could not be analysed because of the different tests that were used. However, the main purpose of this study was not to judge progress. The sample had been deliberately kept small to allow detailed observational data to be collected. The reason for the testing was to contribute to the identification of teachers who had been more successful than other teachers in the literacy progress made by their pupils over the first year of the NLS.

The distribution of the scores within each of the classes can be examined in Figure 1, which shows a box plot of the progress made in standard scores for 19 of the 20 classes (one class was judged to have invalid scores due to errors in the testing procedure). In each plot the box represents the

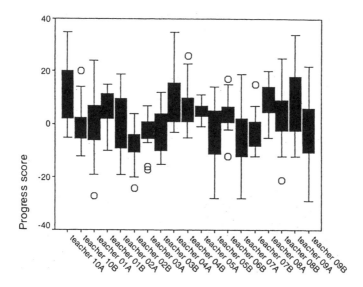

Figure 1 Box plot for progress scores by class.

interquartile range (i.e. the lower boundary of the box is the 25th centile and the upper boundary is the 75th centile) and the horizontal line in the box represents the median. Fifty percent of cases have values inside the box. Outliers are marked with a circle and the largest and smallest values that are not outliers are marked with cross bars. From these plots it can be seen that there was a large variation between classes with only a few children in some classes showing any gain and other classes in which most children made gains.

The study reported here was set up specifically to examine how teachers of mixed age classes in small rural schools managed the NLS in its first year. This was seen as particularly interesting as the NLS is set up in such a way that teaching objectives are prescribed for each term for each age group regardless of age or grouping within the class. Cross tabulation and chi square were used to examine distribution of the progress scores. These showed no significant differences between children in classes of different sizes (some small schools have very low class sizes), number of year groups in the class, nor the age position of the year group in a mixed age class. That is, there was no difference between progress made by the youngest year group in a two, three or four year group class, nor among progress of the oldest year group in a mixed age class. This was contrary to expectations at the start of the project. An analysis of the features of practice of those teachers whose classes made most progress is currently in preparation.

Progress in writing

One of the key features of the NLS is the clear focus given to the development of writing alongside reading. The framework of teaching objectives (DfEE, 1998) is divided into three elements: *word level* (which covers spelling and vocabulary use), *sentence level* (which encompasses grammar and punctuation), and *text level* (which includes development of the structures and linguistic features of various fiction and non-fiction text types).

Writing samples (n = 408) were collected from target children, one sample in each month of the period of observation. These children (n = 51) (one from each year group in each class) had been selected from their October test scores as those with the standardised reading score nearest to 100. The work samples of these children reveal interesting information about the kind of writing experience in each of the classes. They also provide another measure of progress.

The writing samples were analysed according to the following criteria and, for the purposes of measurement, an overall judgement was made as to whether children had made good progress or not.

- *Handwriting* (to include legibility, correctness of letter formation and whether joined or print script).
- *Spelling* (to include accuracy, phonic knowledge, number of words spelled correctly, use of spelling rules and correct spelling of homophones).
- *Punctuation* (to include knowledge of punctuation marks and correct usage).
- *Vocabulary* (to include range, quality and figurative use).
- *Sentence structure* (use of simple, compound and complex sentences, and range of connectives used).
- *Personal voice* (as evidenced by individual style and engagement with the topic).
- *Use of Standard English*.

In the NLS classroom one would expect to see children being introduced to a range of text types through shared and guided reading and writing and just a short 20-minute period during which children can work independently. In practice, many schools have adopted a period during each week when children are able to write independently for a longer duration. This information has not been included with this analysis as different schools changed their practice at different times during the year and no comparison is possible.

Each classroom was visited eight times at monthly intervals during the year, and one hour of literacy teaching was observed. Notes were taken, using an observation schedule that recorded what the teacher was doing at seven predetermined points during the hour, to coincide with the Literacy Hour structure. Of the 158 hours observed, 126 had each element of the whole class parts of the hour in place. Of the 20 classes, seven classes chose to do a complete Literacy Hour for every visit and a further five did so on seven of the eight visits. This reflects what teachers reported to be their usual practice in the end of year interviews.

One of the key features of the NLS is the importance given to teachers actually teaching for 100% of the time during the Literacy Hour. This would normally involve 15 minutes with the whole class on text level objectives, 15 minutes with the whole class on sentence or word level objectives, 20 minutes where teachers teach a small group or groups differentiated by ability in guided reading or writing while the rest of the class work independently, and a 10-minute plenary with the whole class where objectives are reviewed.

Although in interviews at the end of the year teachers said they had mainly used the Literacy Hour, our observations show variations from the normal pattern. These can be seen in Table 1.

One of the key features of the Literacy Hour is the 20-minute period where most of the class work independently and the teacher teaches reading or writing strategies to one small group for 20 minutes (KS2) or to two small groups for 10 minutes each (KS1). This is the opportunity for teachers to work on particular areas for development with children of similar levels of attainment. The major difference between the Literacy Hours observed in the different classes was in this time. In eight of the classes the teacher working with small group(s) was observed to be in place on less than three occasions and in only seven of the classes was this observed on a regular basis. At KS2, only three teachers were observed to use the guided slot on a regular basis and two of these more usually undertook guided reading.

The classes where guided writing was observed to be used regularly were those in which children had made good progress with their writing. This can be seen in Table 2. Chi-squared analysis showed that this difference was significant [$\chi^2 = 8.89$, df = 1, p = 0.003]. Although only one Literacy Hour was observed each month, it may be argued that if teachers were not using this element of the Hour when their Literacy Hours were under observation, it is unlikely that they would use it at other times. This judgement was also borne out by examination of teachers' weekly planning sheets.

Case study 1: Heidi

Heidi was five-and-a-half years old at the start of the year; she was anxious about writing and needed encouragement to have a go. She needed help identifying initial sounds, was unsure of how to group letters into words

Table 1 Observed use of the Literacy Hour in the study

Pupils	Total no. of observations	No. of whole text sessions observed	No. of word/ sentence sessions observed	No. of guided sessions observed	No. of independent sessions observed	No. of plenary sessions observed
4–7 years KS 1	80	78	71	79/160* 45 read 34 write	79	73
7–11 years KS2	78	78	70	40/78 25 read 15 write	78	72

Note
* In 80 observed sessions with the younger children (KS1), 160 guided sessions could have been observed, as teachers of the younger children are expected to work with two guided groups in the 20 minute slot. 13 such 'double sessions' were observed in the 80 observations, and 53 'single sessions'.

Table 2 Numbers of children making good or poor progress in writing in classes where the teacher does or does not do guided writing.

	Good progress	*Poor progress*	
Teacher does guided writing	15	5	20
Teacher does not do guided writing	10	21	31
	25	26	51

and her understanding of sentence structure was weak. In the first week of September she wrote unaided this piece about herself:

> mays Heidi 1 ay5yer o-

During the year Heidi wrote mainly narrative from texts read in class but also wrote from personal experience, and a letter to Father Christmas. Although her reading score changed little, showing an increase of only 1 point, her writing developed well. She learned to spell many common words correctly and make good phonetic attempts at others, e.g. *sked* for scared and *masv* for massive. Her letter formation, which was quite correct at the start of the year, remained good and her print script became neat with correct use of ascenders and descenders. Her use of vocabulary was varied and interesting. By July she was using full stops correctly to mark the end of sentences. She could write for an extended length of time and used complex sentences with an increasing range of connectives. In July she could write a page of writing, as can be seen from the following extract from her account of a visit to Exmoor.

> ... and in the cave it was pech black. and in the cave there was a conv (cavern) and I got sked when it was pech blcak. and when the conv came up. there was a rock. and I got sked and I neley trod on a tadpol but I did't like it. and at the End there was a watr fol and Jade's mum had to hlap us. and then we climbed up a hill ...

Case study 2: Wayne

Wayne was 10 years old at the start of the year in a class with three year groups. In October he wrote the following letter in preparation for an imaginary trip.

> Dear madam/sir,
> I've book Site B for June the 20th–30th 1999. We will be going with Ingen. We will see Dinosaurs, lizards and snakes. You will

need: ten T-shirts, a hat, ten pairs of underwear, ten trousers, twenty pairs of socks, wash things, fives towels, two tents, sleeping bag, p.j.'s, camra with no flash, gun (hand), vidio camra and game boy. It will cost twenty pounds ...

During the year Wayne wrote a good range of text types, including narratives, persuasive writing, and instructions. His writing increased in length. He had joined most of his letters at the start of the year, but over the year the number of letters joined increased and his writing retained its neatness. His use of complex sentences developed, using a wide range of connectives. He spelled most words correctly and those that were not showed good phonic knowledge. He continued to use full stops and capitals correctly and learned to use commas to mark grammatical boundaries and even used semi-colons correctly. His vocabulary contained an interesting use of adjectives and adverbs, which made what he wrote more interesting. The following is part of the second draft of a myth he wrote in February to explain the first snow.

In the land of giants, there lived a sherperd giant named Getrude, Gertrude was a one eyed giant, with two of the hairiest legs you ever seen. Gertrude was intelligent, his face could scare people away with his ugly face with a very unending ragged, beard. Gertrude sat on a rock watching his goat.

The progress demonstrated by Heidi and Wayne is typical of children in their class and in a few others in our sample. Interestingly, the average reading score of children in Heidi's class went down by 1 point and in Wayne's class by 2.5 points. In contrast, there were other classes in which little progress in writing was seen although, in some of these, considerable increase was shown in reading test scores. Clearly the small size of the sample can give rise to such anomalies, nevertheless the richness of the descriptive data gives indications that are worthy of further consideration.

Discussion

The UK government has set the target of 80% of 11-year-olds reaching level 4 in national tests by 2002. Whereas results from end-of-year national tests in 1998 showed 65% of children had reached this level – an increase of only 2% from the previous year – evidence from test scores in 1999, following the introduction of the NLS, showed 69% gaining level 4. This appeared to put the government's targets for 2002 within reach and suggests considerable initial success for the NLS. However, this overall figure concealed the large disparity between attainment in reading and attainment in writing. Whereas 81% of 11-year-olds reached level 4 on the reading tests – an increase of 10% on 1998, only 56% reached level 4 in writing – an increase of only 3% (Stannard, 1999).

The questions of concern to policy makers and educationalists alike are the extent to which any improvement comes as a result of the NLS and why writing has not shown the same improvement found for reading. The advantage of studies of the kind reported here is that there are qualitative data to give possible indications of features of practice within classes where children have shown improvement in writing that may have contributed to this effect.

Use of guided work

Use of guided work is one of the key features of the Literacy Hour, yet the major difference observed in the different classes was in this time. Those teachers who did not use the guided section for group teaching either worked with individual children or moved around the class overseeing the tasks set. They responded to perceived individual needs and answered children's questions. In addition to missing the opportunity to teach small groups, this resulted in the children in these classes being less able to work independently, which made further attempts at guided work more difficult for the teacher.

Range of writing

Another aspect of teacher behaviour that may have contributed to the difference in progress in writing in the different classes was the way in which some teachers were reluctant to give up practices that they had used in the past. Don, aged 5 at the start of the project, was in a class whose pupils made good overall progress in reading. However, his writing experience did not match up to the expectations of the Literacy Hour. Firstly, his teacher did not let him write independently: he was always given the spelling of words he did not know. In September, with the help of a classroom assistant he wrote:

At the weekend I wet to buy A new carpet it was gold and blue.

In contrast to the variety of writing experience in other classes, Don's teacher decided to retain the previous practice of children writing their news each Monday morning; Don also wrote some stories. His reading score increased significantly by 12 points but his writing showed far less progress. At the start of the year his letter formation was inaccurate and this did not improve, although it was even and written on lines. He learned to use full stops. He increased the length of his writing but continued to use mainly simple or compound sentences joined by 'and' and 'then'. As the demands made on his written expression were very similar, his writing tended to follow the same pattern of his first piece. His vocabulary was unadventurous although, by the end of the year, he had begun to use adjectives to add interest to his writing. At the end of June, he wrote a story about a Secret Garden, with the support of the teacher in providing spellings:

> Once upon a time there was a secret house I went in the house and I found the rusty key I opened the creaky door. There was a beautiful Garden. It had a fountain and a pond and I saw blue-bells.

Use of focused teaching objectives

Another difference that the NLS was intended to introduce into teachers' work was the pre-specification of focused objectives in literacy teaching. This has been particularly problematic for teachers who had tended to adopt a version of the process model for the teaching of writing, in which little instruction was given, and a largely individualised approach was adopted to the teaching of reading. Thus, while teachers had become skilled at facilitating and motivating reading and writing, planned and focused teaching was more unusual for some teachers and intervention was largely responsive to perceived individual need.

The teachers in this study had clearly worked over the summer to develop long- and and medium-term plans for the teaching of literacy over the year. However, although all classes had medium-term plans in place with teaching objectives linked to the new literacy framework, their use of these objectives varied. Fifteen of the twenty teachers used daily plans with objectives written in for work at text level and either word or sentence level. However, in the judgement of the research team only six of these teachers used objectives in the way advised by the NLS (focused and explicit). Typical variations from this were where the teacher had chosen too many objectives and the focus was impossible to determine. Other teachers, although they had planned to cover NLS objectives, introduced others that bore no relation to the planned programme of work. Alternatively, although clear NLS objectives were addressed these were at a very general level, e.g. where the NLS objective stated 'to understand the need for punctuation', which one teacher interpreted as *to draw attention to* punctuation marks.

In classes in which children had made progress in writing, there was evidence that teachers had modified the process model to include planned instruction in shared and guided sessions and had encouraged development of the process of writing through the modelling of planning, drafting, and revising procedures and providing time for children to work independently at this. With younger children there were examples of the sort of facilitative strategies described by Bereiter and Scardamalia (1987), such as whole class brainstorming or children taking a known text as a model. There were cases in which there was a clear relationship between lessons taught and children's performance, e.g. Wayne's writing (above) was part of a block of work on myths that followed work on adjectives and the development of characters. Here, clear links can be seen between aspects of language that have been taught through the NLS framework and the writing that children produced.

The intention of the NLS is to provide teachers with a framework for teaching that tells them what to teach as well as giving them a structure for the lesson. The evidence from this study shows that children can make progress in reading in the Literacy Hour. Also, in classrooms where teachers have made full use of the framework, writing also showed improvement.

It is encouraging that early evidence both from the *National Literacy Project* (Sainsbury, Schagen and Whetton, 1998) and National Curriculum tests has shown children making progress in reading. However, as was seen above, where progress is measured according to criteria related to progress in writing, different children can be seen to have made progress. This raises important questions about the danger of complacency in schools where reading test results are high.

Also raised by this study is the question of the extent to which some schools may not have adopted the full scope of the NLS. The research reported earlier, that emphasised the importance of the individual teacher in the success of teaching programmes, must not be forgotten. It is clear that, whereas the literacy strategy has been welcomed by many teachers (Fisher and Lewis, 1998), the way in which the strategy is implemented in different classrooms around the country will have significant impact on the success of the programme.

Indications of practice that may contribute to the difference in progress arise from the classroom observations in this study. In particular, children made good progress in writing where teachers used the format of the Literacy Hour to target their teaching on particular groups (guided writing) and where children were given a wide range of text types to use as models for writing. In addition, different teachers made different use of the framework of objectives. There were clear examples where focused use of objectives gave rise to improved features of writing.

Acknowledgements

This paper draws upon data collected as part of the Economic and Social Research Council funded research project, *The Implementation of the Literacy Hour in Small Rural Schools* (ESRC ref. R000 22 2608) directed by

Dr Ros Fisher and Maureen Lewis, Rolle School of Education, University of Plymouth, UK.

References

ADAMS, M.J. (1990) *Beginning to Read: Thinking and learning about print.* Cambridge MA: MIT Press.

BEREITER, C. and SCARDAMALIA, M. (1987) *The Psychology of Written Composition.* Hillsdale, NJ: Lawrence Erlbaum.

BORICH, G. (1996) *Effective Teaching Methods.* 3rd edition. New York: Macmillan.

CHALL, J.S. (1967) *Learning to Read: The great debate.* New York: McGraw-Hill.

DFEE (1997) *The Implementation of the National Literacy Strategy.* London: Department for Education and Employment.

DFEE (1998) *National Literacy Strategy Framework.* London: Department for Education and Employment.

DOWNING, J., SCHAEFER, B. and AYRES, J.D. (1982) *LARR Test of Emergent Literacy* (Revised edition). Windsor, Berks.: NFER-Nelson.

FISHER, R. and LEWIS, M. (1998) Anticipation or trepidation? Teachers' views on the Literacy Hour. *Reading*, 33, 24–28.

FRANCE, N. (1979) *Primary Reading Test.* Windsor, Berks.: NFER-Nelson.

GOODACRE, E. (1971) *Children and Learning to Read.* London: Routledge and Kegan Paul.

HALLINGER, P. and MURPHY, J. (1986) The Social Context of Effective Schools. *American Journal of Education*, 94, 328–355.

KISPAL, A., HAGUES, N. and RUDDOCK, G. (1994) *Progress in English Tests.* Windsor, Berks.: NFER-Nelson.

OFSTED (1999) *National Literacy Strategy – an Evaluation of the First Year.* London: Department for Education and Employment.

REYNOLDS, D. (1998) Schooling for literacy: a review of research on teacher effectiveness and school effectiveness and its implications for contemporary educational policies. *Educational Review*, 50, 147–162.

SAINSDURY, M., SCHAGAN, I., and WHETTON, C. (1998) *Evaluation of the National Literacy Project: Cohort 1, 1996–1998.* Slough: National Foundation for Educational Research.

SCHEERENS, J. (1992) *Effective Schooling: Research Theory and Practice.* London: Cassell.

STANNARD, J. (1999) *Unpublished lecture given to literacy consultants.* Sunderland, November 1999.

18

LITERACY TRANSFER

A review of the literature

Larry Mikulecky, Peggy Albers and Michele Peers

Source: National Center on Adult Literacy, University of Pennsylvania, Technical Report TR94–05 (1994) http://www.literacyonline.org/products/ncal/pdf/TR9405.pdf

Introduction

Effective learning involves much more than acquiring knowledge. Learners must be able to organize, manipulate, and use or transfer initial learning to new situations. A tacit assumption of much literacy learning is that literacy learned in one situation will transfer to most other situations.

Research and theorizing on what constitutes transfer have occurred in many fields. Two definitions of transfer that are particularly useful for the field of literacy study come from Perkins and Salomon (1989) and Bigge and Shermis (1992). Perkins and Salomon (1989) define transfer as the ability to apply knowledge, skill, and specific strategies from one domain to other novel situations. Bigge and Shermis (1992, p. 218) suggest that "transfer of learning occurs when a person's learning in one situation influences that person's learning and performance in other situations." These two definitions of transfer will serve as guidelines for discussion in this monograph.

Definitions of literacy are many and sometimes situational. They range from attempts to describe the complex interactions between reading and writing to more encompassing descriptions of written language usage embedded in cognitive, metacognitive, and social communication theories. In the workplace, comprehension and use of graphic, tabular, and quantitative displays also enter into the discussion. For the purposes of this report, we maintain that literacy is both a process of developing and learning a range of specific uses of print and other information displays and a collection of life-long habits and processes that enable one, through practice and reflection, to further develop, improve, and expand the literacy abilities one already has. Langer's (1987) concept of learners assuming "ownership for their literacy activities" is central to this later notion. In

399

examining the relationship of literacy and transfer, this report discusses a wide range of literacy studies which address the mastery of specific literacy abilities as well as the increased ownership and control of broader literate strategies, practices, and behaviors.

A key issue for workplace literacy training is the degree to which literacy learned in workplace programs transfers to new situations on the job and in other segments of the learner's life. Typical workplace literacy programs provide less than 50 hours of instruction a year; only a rare few provide as many as 100 hours of instruction per year. There is little opportunity for instructors to provide extensive experience in a broad array of literacy tasks. If newly learned improvements in reading and writing automatically transfer to most new situations a learner encounters, then instructors and program planners need not be overly concerned about the nature of curricula and what sorts of materials are used with learners. If, on the other hand, transfer is often absent or severely limited, then what is covered during instruction must be carefully considered so that it may be of later use to learners.

For the last decade, discussion of the topic of literacy transfer to the workplace has occurred from two potentially contradictory viewpoints. At a very basic level, it seems reasonable to assume that mastery of certain aspects of reading and writing (i.e., the alphabet, key vocabulary, word order) is likely to transfer from one literacy task to most others. These basic aspects of literacy seem a foundation for accomplishing nearly any literacy task one can imagine. In addition to these basic aspects of literacy, some have suggested that a good deal more literacy transfers from one situation to others within the workplace. In the early '80s, Greenan (1982) postulated a list of transferable, generic, workplace literacy skills based upon surveys of vocational education instructors who named comparable skills across several different occupation categories. This trend of looking for similarities among tasks and occupations has continued into the late '80s and early 90s. Brizius and Foster (1987) postulate the existence of "portable skills" that might be carried from job to job, and the U.S. Department of Labor's (1991) SCANS commission suggests that most jobs require mastery of five basic skill areas (most of which involve literacy). The assumption is that mastery of the general skill areas will transfer to most new jobs.

At the same time that these discussions about generic or portable skills were taking place, a growing body of research began to suggest that literacy transfer may be quite limited and that one must master literacies rather than literacy. Literacy skills that seem similar to an outside observer who has already mastered them, may not appear so similar to a new learner. Proponents of this view cite evidence indicating that seeing connections and being able to apply freshly learned strategies to new situations may not occur often and easily for most learners. As one moves into the wide array of literacy challenges facing adults, the problem of transfer becomes even more complex. Duffy (1985) points out the different information-processing demands of reading various types of text (i.e., newspaper, job manual, computer screen, poem, weather graphic). Sticht (1982) found that enlisted men who improved in general literacy classes were not able to perform particularly well on job-reading tasks, although enlisted men who learned with job-related materials did show improvement on job-reading tasks. The National Assessment of Educational Progress survey of Young Adult Literacy (Kirsch & Jungeblut, 1986) found only about 25% shared variance or overlap among performances on the test's three scales (Prose Reading, Document Reading, and Quantitative Reading).

It seems likely that there is some degree of literacy learning transfer as one moves from literacy task to literacy task. It also seems likely that the degree of transfer is less than many have thought. Policy planners and developers of workplace literacy programs need a clearer understanding of literacy transfer in order make program choices about literacy transfer in specific situations. When, if ever, are general literacy programs best? When, if ever, are programs using custom-designed materials and tasks from a particular workplace best?

This report will address the question of literacy transfer by first examining what research has revealed about transfer in general, then specifically examining studies that focus upon literacy transfer, and finally discussing instructional approaches that evidence suggests will facilitate literacy transfer among adults in workplace and other settings. Three key questions will guide the discussion:

- What is the nature of transfer?
- To what extent does literacy transfer exist?
- How can literacy transfer best be facilitated?

What is the nature of transfer?

The nature of transfer has interested psychologists and educators for more than a century. Useful studies and analyses have appeared in three major areas: (a) intelligence definition and scope, (b) expert-novice differences, and (c) transfer theory development.

Intelligence-definition and scope

In the process of defining intelligence, psychologists noticed a tendency for some people to be better able to learn and to relate information from one area to another. They labeled this ability as the "g" or general intelligence factor. They posited that this factor was related to ability to learn and to move from one cognitive situation to another. Success in new situations related not so much to transfer of knowledge, but to transfer of the ability to learn quickly. This factor was often believed to be inherited and therefore fixed and immutable.

The validity of both the "g" concept and the immutability of intelligence has been challenged. One of the earliest challenges came from Franz Gall in the nineteenth century. Gall posited that different forms of perception (music, memory, etc.) exist and that people have differing strengths in each form of perception (Gardner, 1983, p. 12). Throughout the twentieth century, Piaget, Vygotsky, and a host of other psychologists offered evidence of intellectual growth occurring as a result of interaction between society and the individual. If there is a general intelligence, it may well be influenced by sociocultural factors and not be truly inherent.

Although general intelligence is no longer acknowledged as the universal explanation for cognitive ability, it still has some defenders. Jensen (1985), in analyzing 20 of compensatory programs data (Headstart and others), notes that these programs do succeed in socializing children and help them remain in school and often improve their grades. The evidence suggests that such programs do not, however, improve children's relative performance on IQ tests or any other test of cognitive ability (i.e., standardized reading and mathematics tests). Jensen attributes this to information-processing deficits that are part of a fairly stable "g" factor. Hunter and Hunter (1984), in a meta-analytic synthesis of adult job-performance data, note that measures of general cognitive ability are better predictors of future job performance than every other indicator except performance on similar job tasks. This, too, may support arguments for some form of general intelligence that undergirds individual differences in ability to learn new tasks.

Most recent psychological research has moved away from single measure indicators of intelligence. As an alternative to using end product test results as measures of intelligence, a good deal of recent psychological research has examined how the mind processes information. These studies have led to several concepts that have a direct bearing on the nature of transfer. Gardner (1983, p. 60) suggests that intelligence "must entail a set of skills of problem solving ... and must also entail the potential for finding or creating problems—thereby laying the groundwork for the acquisition of new knowledge." Gardner identifies several naturalistic areas of human reasoning that might legitimately be termed intelligences (i.e., language, musical thinking, logical-mathematical analysis, spatial representation, bodily-kinesthetic understanding, and personal). Sternberg (1988) finds intelligence to be represented best by a triarchic combination of processes. Sternberg combines analytical, synthetic, and adaptive factors in defining intelligence.

As one element of his definition, Sternberg discusses the degree to which the individual can focus attention and use strategies to monitor, analyze, and use reason in any given situation. Experience may have a great deal to do with intelligence and the ability to transfer learning from situation to situation. Motivation and will also have a great deal to do with working intelligence and transfer. When we examine the literature on transfer, it becomes clear that psychologists are looking at multiple areas of intelligence to see what transfers (skill, knowledge, or adaptability) from one situation to others.

To summarize, although there is some indication that general intelligence is related to transfer, much recent work suggests that the concept of a single general intelligence is misleading. There may be multiple aspects of intelligence, and intelligence is highly likely to be influenced by experience. This implies the need to much more clearly define what is being learned and link instruction with what the learner will be expected to do with new learning.

Expert–novice difference

The nature of expertise has been studied in various fields from chess, physics, and mathematics to athletics and music. In the 1970s, it was thought that experts were primarily different from novices in that they used more sophisticated strategies for thinking and problem solving (Sweller, 1990). Subsequent reasoning suggested that if one could teach those strategies to a novice, he or she could transfer them and become more expertlike. Careful research has shown the differences between novice and expert to be more complex.

Experts know a good deal. They have highly organized and extensive knowledge bases in the domains for which they are expert (Chi, Feltovich, & Glaser, 1981). Researchers have also found that the experts' more thorough understanding of their expert area allows them to "chunk" large pieces of information into meaningful patterns (Chase & Simon, 1973; Chi et al., 1981; Schoenfeld & Hermann, 1982). With this vast amount of interconnected knowledge, experts use more sophisticated thinking and problem-solving strategies. They formulate multiple and flexible alternate theories about what they see (Dawson & Zeitz, 1989), and reflect on problems by using past knowledge and by monitoring current application in order to move them to the best acceptable solution (Chi et al., 1981).

Moving from novice to expert involves two basic premises: acquiring more knowledge and knowing what to do with that knowledge. Experts' inherent curiosity propels them to continually nurture their knowledge bases with practice and extensive experimentation. This regular and extensive practice enables them to retrieve information spontaneously and make valuable connections to past knowledge quickly. Novices, on the other hand, rely primarily on surface features and explicit details to understand problems (Schoenfeld & Hermann, 1982). The goal of the novice is often to move toward an immediate solution, whereas the goal of an expert is to thoroughly understand the problem before contemplating solutions (Chi et al., 1981).

The study of expert-novice differences, seen in the light of what we know about intelligence, indicates that transfer does not come easily. One must diligently work to develop a large knowledge base, practice to make links between ideas within that knowledge base, and master metacognitive strategies to monitor learning. Berryman and Bailey (1992) cite a growing body of research often labeled *situated cognition*, which indicates that learning transfers best when it is done in real situations in which both knowledge and strategies are learned at the same time. When electronic technicians receive extensive classroom training in electronics and the theory of trouble-shooting, they are not able to transfer the knowledge to improved trouble-shooting on the job (Morris & Rouse, 1985). Expert carpet layers who can do flawless arithmetic on the job, fail arithmetic tests that decontextualize learning (Scribner & Fahrmeir, 1982). They are able to transfer their skills to the situations in which they learned them, but not much further. Learning strategies and knowledge at the same time in realistic situations appears to be key to successful transfer.

Transfer theory development

Theories of learning transfer, both informal and formal, have abounded for centuries. This discussion will provide a brief historical overview of the extensive development of theoretical frameworks that have appeared in the research literature.

Doctrine of formal discipline

The doctrine of formal discipline, dating back to Plato, suggests that by teaching some specific form of knowledge and the discipline involved with learning it (i.e., Latin, computer programming, or mathematics), most learners automatically strengthen certain other abilities such as memory or logic. Recently, the academic discussion of this notion has revolved around the claim that learning the computer language of Logo would bring about improvement in problem-solving skills (Au & Leung, 1991; Grandgenett & Thompson, 1991). Earlier discussions have suggested that learning Latin would bring about improved mastery of English (Lederer, Orlando, & Cevoli 1983). Although an individual will occasionally report making links between learning in one area and learning in other areas, large group studies have detected no evidence for general transfer for the majority of learners. Syntheses of over 100 transfer studies find no substantiation for this theory of transferring logic or problem solving or any other benefit after learning a target subject (De Corte & Verschaffel, 1986; Salomon & Perkins, 1987a, 1987b). Although this notion of formal discipline or extra benefit has been largely discredited by research, it continues to reappear in many general discussions of transfer as if it were a proven theory.

Theories of identical elements and general principles, and interference

An alternative theory of transfer, which postulated that transfer would occur in the presence of shared elements, became important in the early history of experimental psychology. One of Thorndike and Woodworth's (1901) widely recognized studies investigated the transfer of perceiving words with certain letters rapidly and accurately to the accurate and rapid perception of new words containing different letters. It was reasoned, and partially documented, that the degree to which both tasks shared identical features determined positive transfer on the part of the learner. A related but competing theory (Judd, 1908) posited that understanding a general principle (rather than a distinct element) would transfer to several situations. Learning the principle of light refraction in water in one case or situation was shown to transfer to new cases and situations. Studies of transfer throughout the first half of this century occurred both in the laboratory and in classrooms. Variations of identical elements studies occurred in laboratories using a multitude of techniques and instruments from stop watches to tachistascopes to measures of galvanic skin response. During the same time period, several broad (and untestable) theoretical formulations were proposed to account for transfer (or more often lack of transfer) in classrooms. In 1949, Osgood reviewed a half-century of transfer research and expressed his frustration at the vagaries of inconsistent measurement, the lack of specification for what should be measured, and at the sometimes atheortical nature of research. He complained:

> There are no clear-cut generalizations which satisfactorily bind the data together. The difficulty may be traced, in part, to the bewildering variety of procedures, materials, and experimental designs employed by different investigators ... But some of the confusion can also be laid to the fact that in a large proportion of experiments the theoretically relevant relations are patently unspecifiable.
>
> (p. 132)

Cormier and Hagman (1987), in commenting upon this period, note that the conceptual understanding of transfer did not advance as fast as empirical findings accumulated. Some researchers were finding examples of negative transfer and of interference. The terms *proactive* and *retroactive inhibition* entered transfer discussions as attempts to explain how forgetting, learning, and transfer difficulties can result from interference between new and older learnings. Other researchers presented the results of experiments of *stimulus predifferentiation*, which documented the need to become generally acquainted with the learning environment before the learner could even notice the subtlety of some new transfer situations. The examination of interference in relation to learning and transfer characterized much of the research throughout the 1950s and early 1960s.

During the 1960s and 1970s, transfer research declined within the framework of interference theory as attention shifted to more cognitive-based accounts of learning. Given the expansion beyond a single methodological approach, the discussion of transfer became more diffused and subsumed within the context of other issues. In many studies, examination of transfer was only a secondary or a tertiary goal. In such studies, attention to specifying degree of transfer and how to measure transfer was often lax and results related to transfer were relegated to a few paragraphs in discussion sections of articles.

Near and far transfer, vertical and horizontal transfer

From the early 1900s to the 1970s, the study of transfer became increasingly more complex. Researchers (primarily in psychology) continued to perform transfer research using modifications of Thorndike's identical elements theory. In an attempt to differentiate the degree to which identical elements were shared, terms like *near transfer* and *far transfer* evolved. Gagne (1965) expanded the near/far concept with the terms *vertical transfer* and *horizontal transfer*. Vertical transfer referred to increased complexity within very similar tasks and horizontal transfer to increased complexity within increasingly dissimilar tasks. Near and far were relevant on both continua. These terms also provided a conceptual framework for differentiating between *learning* and *transfer*. Learning referred to mastering a task in the exact context in which it was taught, whereas transfer referred to the ability to successfully apply learned abilities to new tasks which shared several, but not all (near transfer) or few (far transfer) central elements with the learning task.

Carefully controlled laboratory studies attempted to specify and operationalize these terms by specifying transfer in terms of slight variations in simple tasks (associating sound tones with other stimuli, rapid perception of relationships, etc.). Difficulties arose, however, when other researchers attempted to extend the theoretical structures to more complex problem-solving and educational tasks (Mayer, 1975; Royer, 1979). The problems of clearly specifying which elements in tasks are identical, whether the specified elements are central, and whether the same elements are central for different learners clouded study results. Other difficulties revolved around how to specify near and far in a way that allowed one to draw conclusions across studies. Further, if distance needs to be considered in both vertical and horizontal terms, the concepts of near and far become even more difficult to specify. Much research in this area has been equivocal, inconsistent, and does not allow for generalization across studies. Cormier and Hagman (1987), in reviewing transfer research to the mid-1980s, state:

> In our view, there are four generic issues important to a comprehensive description of transfer, both as a learning phenomenon and as an event with substantial importance to real-life situations. These issues are: (a) how transfer should be measured, (b) how training for transfer differs from training for rapid acquistion, (c) how direction and magnitude of transfer are determined, and (d) whether different principles of transfer apply to motor, cognitive, and metacognitive elements.
>
> (p. 1)

High and low road transfer

In the late 1980s, a new theoretical framework began to emerge as a way to describe transfer productively and account for the sometimes conflicting results of previous studies. Salomon (working with Globerson and Perkins), in a series of analytic syntheses of transfer research in the 1970s and 1980s, has attempted to organize, categorize, and theorize from the evidence available for transfer. After reviewing two decades of transfer studies, Perkins and Salomon (1989, p. 19) observe that:

> To the extent that transfer does take place, it is highly specific and must be cued, primed, and guided; it seldom occurs spontaneously. The case for generalizable, context-independent skills and strategies that can be trained in one context and transferred to other domains has proven to be more a matter of wishful thinking than hard empirical evidence.

Salomon and colleagues have constructed a theory of transfer which can explain why in some studies transfer seems to be verified and in others it is not. They suggest that transfer is actually a multifaceted phenomenon rather than a singular one. Some skills, like driving a stick shift car, become automatic through intense practice without mindful attention. Such skills can easily transfer from driving a car to driving a truck. Comparable intensive practice of literacy skills would be tracking print lines on a page or recognizing very familiar vocabulary. This sort of automatic ability is termed *low road transfer*. Intense, long-term practice is key to such transfer and little or no conscious thought is involved. Not all transfer is of this automatic sort, however.

Some transfer requires the mindful application of abstract concepts to new situations. For example, time-management strategies learned in junior high school might be drawn upon to solve new problems in college. Delay strategies taught to a child unable to control his temper can be mindfully recalled to help an adult dieter delay and overcome impulsive food purchases. Comparable literacy strategies would be consciously applying a previously learned note-taking technique to a new situation or a trained reader of philosophical writings consciously looking for counter-examples when reading the political claims of candidates. These strategies are termed *high road transfer* (Perkins & Salomon, 1989; Salomon & Globerson, 1987). Although for some experts, these strategies can become nearly automatic, they are usually mindfully chosen and applied. In the field of literacy study, many of the strategies described as metacognitive (i.e., setting goals, asking questions, making predictions, summarizing ideas) would qualify as examples of high road transfer in Salomon's framework.

To what extent does literacy transfer exist?

Very few studies have directly addressed the question of literacy transfer. Almost none of them directly address a theoretical framework related to transfer or specify degree of transfer clearly. In some cases, this makes it problematical to compare the results of various studies. What some researchers label as transfer to new situations might be argued to be simple learning by other researchers because assessment tasks do not differ enough or in a measurable way from instructional tasks. Most of the information available comes from studies primarily designed to address research goals other than transfer. A number of studies have addressed core psychological abilities associated with beginning literacy. This core of abilities can be construed to be central to all literacy, and therefore, possibly transferable. Other, more anthropological studies have examined what aspects of literacy which are present in one context are present or missing in other contexts. Some psychometric analyses of literacy test performance attempt to define statistically the extent or limits of transfer. Finally, studies of literacy performance on school tasks and workplace literacy tasks have attempted to define the degree of transfer from school literacy to workplace literacy.

Cross-national and anthropological studies of literacy

In his historical examination of literacy definitions, Venezky (1990, pp. 10–11) notes that:

Cross-national studies of reading process suggest that a common core of psychological abilities may exist for reading and, in particular, for reading alphabetic and syllabic writing systems. These processes involve primarily the coordination of eye movements into fixations and subsequent saccadic jumps, the acquisition and utilization of symbol-sound correspondences, the building of rapid identification of word units through the integration of information from a variety of sources, and the use of local and global processes to obtain meaning.

Nearly all of the above processes are developed through intensive practice, become automatic as opposed to mindful, and are usually mastered by U.S. children with four to five years of schooling. In Salomon's theoretical framework for explaining learning transfer, these processes would constitute low road transfer of basic literacy processes.

Evidence for transfer beyond this most basic literacy level becomes more problematic. Scribner and Cole (1978) studied literacy among the Vai in Africa. The Vai culture has a variety of different types of literacy—one used for schooling, one for commerce, and one for social purposes. In the Vai culture, it is possible to examine literacy in conjunction with schooling as well as separate from schooling since many people learn only a single literacy. Scribner and Cole concluded that many of the cognitive abilities often associated with literacy (i.e., using abstractions, drawing conclusions based on logic, etc.) were more accurately associated with schooling. These cognitive abilities were not associated with all forms of literacy—only the form of literacy learned in schools. People who were proficient only in the literacy of commerce or the literacy of letter writing did not automatically develop abstract cognitive abilities. To develop these cognitive skills, one needed to learn a particular type of literacy. In fact, Scribner and Cole (1978) concluded that "the effects of literacy and perhaps of schooling as well are restricted ... generalizable to only closely related practices" (p. 457).

Psychometric analyses of literacy abilities

For nearly seven decades, literacy researchers have noted that there is some connection—but very little—between learner scores on tests measuring different sorts of literacy abilities. Ritter and Lofland (1924) and Salisbury (1934) found very low correlations between general reading ability, as measured by standardized tests, and ability to read and reason. In 1944, Artley tested 242 eleventh-grade students with six different general reading, social studies reading, and nonverbal intelligence tests. Artley found correlations among subtests to vary widely, with most correlations being in the $r = .3$ to $r = .5$ range (i.e., 9% to 25% shared variance or overlap). He concluded that "every classroom teacher has the direct responsibility for developing those reading skills and abilities essential for adequate comprehension within his particular area of instruction." This research finding, and others like it, fueled the move to legislatively mandate content area reading courses for high school content area teachers. The general finding of only moderate correlations among an individual's scores on tests for reading different types of materials is echoed by comparable correlations ($r = .4$ to $r = .5$) among Prose, Document, and Quantitative Reading scores on the National Assessment for Educational Progress Test of young adult readers (Kirsch & Jungeblut, 1986). Reder's (1994) analysis of correlations among Prose, Document, and Quantitative Reading scores on the National Adult Literacy survey data gathered in 1992 reveals higher intercorrelations among test scales. Explanations for differences between 1986 and 1992 data are not yet available.

Carroll (1981), in his invited remarks to the International Reading Association, observed that drawing conclusions about transfer, even from relatively high correlations, is somewhat suspect. Good students are absent from school less frequently than poor students, and they are likely to encounter a wider variety of reading materials in the home. As a result, good students may improve in several different skill areas at the same time while poor students, who practice little, do not improve much at all. This situation would produce moderately high correlations among test scores, thereby inflating the degree of transfer one might suppose exists between one type of reading and others. Good students practice nearly everything and improve in nearly everything. This does not indicate that there is a transfer between performance in one area and performance in others. In other words, instruction that leads to improvement in one area is not necessarily likely to lead to improvements in correlate areas. The actual amount of real transfer is likely to be much lower than what 16%–25% shared variance would suggest.

General literacy, workplace literacy, and job performance

Determining the extent to which general literacy can transfer to performance in the workplace is a difficult task. The U.S. Department of Defense (1984), in comparing job performance to performance on the ASVAB test (essentially a multiple-choice standardized test that correlates extremely highly with other standardized reading tests), notes the following correlation ranges: (a) .36 to .52 for jobs in communications, (b) .39 to .77 for jobs in data processing, and (c) .53 to .73 for clerical and supply specialties. This suggests that scores on a test that is essentially a vocational literacy test can predict anywhere from 13% to 60% of the variance for job performance, depending upon the job.

Hunter and Hunter (1984) meta-analyzed the results of hundreds of studies designed to predict job performance. They found that reading tests and other cognitive measures (as limited as they are) were more effective predictors of job performance than were either perceptual or motor abilities and were more effective predictors than biographical inventories, interviews, expert recommendations, or amount of previous education. People who scored highly on the tests tended to perform better on the job. This is strong circumstantial evidence that general literacy transfers somewhat to job performance. Carroll's criticism that the correlations may be inflated because top performers learn many things at the same time is also valid in this situation.

Mikulecky and Winchester (1983) and Mikulecky and Ehlinger (1986) interviewed, observed, and tested nurses and electronic technicians at three levels of experience (i.e., in-training, experienced, and supervisory). The researchers were attempting, in part, to determine the relationship of literacy abilities to actual job performance. In each study, there was no significant relationship between job performance and general literacy, as measured by CLOZE test constructed from a newspaper passage. There was, however, a relationship between job performance and employees' actual daily use of metacognitive literacy practices (i.e., summarizing, making predictions based on reading, focussing by using notes or underlining, and consciously looking for applications).

Studies that approach this problem of workplace literacy transfer by studying the performances of learners before and after receiving training cause us to question the extent of transfer from general training to workplace application. Sticht (1982) reports on a study of 700 enlisted men who received either job-related literacy training or general literacy training. All learners improved while receiving 120 hours of instruction. On tests of job-related reading, however, those receiving job-related literacy training outperformed the regular literacy learners by 300%. Although there was some slight transfer to job-related reading performance from the general training, the transfer was negligible compared to the performance of learners who received specific job-literacy training. Mikulecky and Lloyd (1992) used pre- and post-interviews, supervisor ratings, and tests to assess the impact of various types of literacy training on changes in learners' literacy beliefs, practices, performances, and plans at home and on the job. Learners at two different worksites participated in one of several different types of literacy class (i.e., general literacy training, ESL literacy & communication, and workplace specific literacy & communication training). Classes were effective in that learners made gains. Gains were limited to what instruction focused upon. When instruction addressed workplace materials and tasks, there were improvements in these areas. When instruction focused upon increasing literacy practice at home, there were improvements in the amount of reading done at home. When instructors taught

411

strategies for reading training or workplace materials, learner literacy strategies became more sophisticated and performance improved. When class discussion addressed future choices and possibilities, learners' plans for future education became more distinct and elaborate. No class addressed all the literacy goals and there was virtually no evidence of learners transferring practices and abilities beyond what had been directly addressed by instruction. Mikulecky (1992) reports that extending the workplace literacy evaluation framework to four additional worksites reinforced the conclusions derived at the initial two worksites.

To summarize, there appears to be only a limited relationship between general literacy ability and the ability to use literacy on the job. This relationship is probably only at the most basic level of literacy processes (i.e., eye movement, letter/sound relationships, word recognition). Correlations between general literacy performance and workplace performance range from slight to moderate, but even this circumstantial evidence for transfer may be overinflated because top performers tend to learn several types of literacy at the same time. Studies that compare workplace learner performance before and after short-term instruction (i.e., 30–200 hours) demonstrate almost no literacy transfer beyond what has been directly taught.

Impact of intelligence on transfer

During the past decade, there has been a good deal of controversy about the nature of intelligence. The few studies that analyze the relationship of learning transfer to intelligence have been done with children and adolescents and have employed traditional IQ tests to assess intelligence. Findings from these studies will be considered here, but results must be viewed with a great deal of caution until further research is performed with adults to determine the relationship between measured intelligence and literacy transfer.

Compione, Brown, Ferrara, Jones, and Steinberg (1985) and Ferrara, Brown, and Campione (1986) have performed a series of experiments to more clearly delineate the relationship between transfer and intelligence. These studies focus on performances of seven-year-olds, ten-year-olds, and mentally retarded fourteen-year-olds whose IQ test performance indicates an average mental age of ten.

In the 1985 study, ten-year-olds with average intelligence were compared to mentally retarded fourteen-year-olds with a tested mental age equivalent to the normal ten-year-old. Each group was taught strategies for solving picture problems which involved adding, subtracting, or visually rotating parts of diagrams. The mentally retarded group, through intense, structured instruction (up to three days), was able to reach a level of performance equal to that of the normal ten-year-olds. Learning was possible. One day after training, both groups were given new problems to test how well they had maintained what they had learned and how well they could transfer strategies. The transfer problems were completely new problems that introduced changes to move learners progressively further away from the practice problems. Although the mentally retarded adolescents were able to maintained some of what they had learned after a day's rest, it was significantly less than the performance of normal ten-year-olds. The performance gap was even wider for transfer problems, with almost no transfer among the mentally retarded group. Campione et al. (1985, p. 313) note, "the lower the ability level of the student, the smaller the change required to generate some disruption of performance."

Ferrara et al. (1986) performed additional experiments with average and high IQ seven-year-olds and ten-year-olds. The children were asked to pretend that they were spies trying to decode messages in strings of letters. They were taught strategies for identifying patterns among letters. When six problems could be solved without assistance, training was considered complete. Two days after training, children were asked to "think out loud" as they tried to identify patterns. The children were told that hints would be given, if needed, to solve the problems, which ranged from exact problems from training (i.e., maintenance problems) to problems which became increasingly different from training (i.e., transfer problems). Results indicate that older children outperformed younger children in both maintenance and transfer tasks and that high IQ children outperformed average IQ children. The higher the IQ, the fewer the prompts required. The gap between high IQ and average IQ in number of prompts required to solve problems increased as transfer problems increasingly differed from practice problems.

To summarize, this series of studies suggests that for children and adolescents the amount of transfer is related to measured intelligence. In addition, the more dissimilar the transfer task is from initial training, the larger role measured intelligence appears to play in independent transfer performance. The authors of all studies in this area express caution that their work not be overgeneralized, since some learners who score low on IQ measures are able to transfer what they have learned.

Transfer and learning disability

Discussions of transfer and learning disability are important to the discussion of adult literacy. There is some evidence that a significant number of adults who have passed through years of schooling and still read at very low levels also have significant learning disabilities. Adult literacy programs that teach for transfer need to be based, in part, on what we know about transfer and learning disability. Keefe and Meyer (1988, p. 615) tested over 100 adults in an adult literacy program. Among adults with the lowest literacy levels (i.e., third-grade level and below), the authors report that approximately 78% had tested learning and language disabilities. There are few studies of adult learning disability that determine the impact of these disabilities upon learning and transfer. The few studies that have examined the relationship of transfer to learning disability have focused upon children and adolescents.

Gelzheiser (1984) examined how well learning-disabled adolescents (compared with a nondisabled control group and a learning-disabled control group) could learn and transfer strategies for organizing and retrieving information from memory. Results indicate that the learning-disabled adolescents were able to learn and transfer the strategies that they were taught. Recall of facts by learning-disabled students who received strategy instruction was significantly better than their learning-disabled peers who did not receive this instruction. All learning-disabled groups still scored significantly lower than the nondisabled control group.

Collins, Carnine, and Gersten (1987) found that adolescent learning-disabled and remedial students trained in simple reasoning problems could transfer this training to paragraphs with embedded reasoning problems. The training was highly structured using five 20–30 minute sessions with a computer program. Those in the experimental group who gave incorrect answers were provided elaborated corrective feedback while those in the control group were simply informed when answers were wrong. Results show that students trained with elaborated corrective feedback significantly transferred their training. They were able to identify the reasoning problems in embedded paragraphs at a higher level than were students in the basic correction group. Given sufficient training time, learning-disabled adolescents were able to learn and transfer logical reading strategies.

Kerchner and Kistinger (1984) studied whether fourth-, fifth-, and sixth-grade learning-disabled students could transfer their training in process writing on the computer to process writing using pencil and paper. For seven months during a portion of each day, students received literacy instruction. In the control group, students used extensive language experience with no word processing. Reading instruction involved a variety of texts and students concentrated on developing spelling skills through teacher dictation of sentences. The experimental group used the *Bank Street Writer* word processing program. They composed at the keyboard, participated in editing conferences, edited at the keyboard, and illustrated compositions. The experimental group outperformed the control group on thematic maturity, word usage, style, and overall writing test score. There were no significant differences on vocabulary, spelling, and handwriting or reading ability. The authors conclude that when learning disabled-students are provided with extensive training, they are able to transfer writing skills from computer composition to handwritten composition.

These studies of learning-disabled children and adolescents provide evidence for the ability of disabled learners to transfer literacy training to relatively new tasks. Training time ranged from a few hours for relatively simple tasks to more than 100 hours for more complex composing tasks. In the only study comparing disabled learners to a nondisabled control group, training helped LD students to transfer learning, but performance was still significantly below a nondisabled control group which received no training.

How can literacy transfer best be facilitated?

As some of the studies above indicate, it is possible to teach successfully for transfer, but it takes significant, focused effort. An examination of literacy instruction studies in which transfer of learning was assessed reveals some patterns for effective transfer instruction. Again, as earlier, there are few instructional studies which address literacy transfer for low literate adults. When such studies are not available, the selection of studies reported in this section will focus upon older children, adolescent, or undergraduate readers.

Modeling, practice, and feedback

Several literacy studies have shown that when instruction (a) explains and models effective literacy practice, (b) provides sufficient practice time, and (c) provides substantial feedback, students are able to transfer freshly learned literacy strategies to new tasks. Several successful approaches to modeling, practice, and feedback emerge from research. Among these approaches are reciprocal teaching to demonstrate metacognitive strategies, think-alouds to demonstrate cognitive and metacognitive processes, and computer-guided instruction to model the use of concept mapping to help comprehend textbook chapters.

Palincsar and Brown (1986) report on a series of studies with children and early adolescents in which students successfully learned to transfer several metacognitive reading strategies (i.e., making predictions, asking questions, summarizing, and clarifying) to new situations through the use of reciprocal teaching. The instructional plan involved up to 20 training sessions from first introducing reading strategies to eventual independent transfer of those strategies to a variety of new materials.

In reciprocal teaching, teachers carefully explain and model four strategies: prediction, questioning, summarizing, and clarifying. The teacher and students then alternate roles in applying and giving feedback on each strategy. After the student understands a strategy, the student begins extensive guided practice of the strategy and receives praise or explanatory feedback on performance. Again, roles of learner and teacher alternate. In some situations, students alternate roles of student and teacher with each other. At the end of training, students in all studies demonstrated that they had learned the reading strategies and were able to independently use them with various content material. This conscious transfer of reading strategies to new situations is probably best categorized as high road transfer since it involves conscious thought and choices. Deciding whether it is near or far transfer is difficult to determine without arbitrarily deciding how different from practice materials the new materials must be to constitute far transfer.

Ehlinger (1989) taught adolescents to use a think-aloud strategy to monitor their reading comprehension. Think-alouds involve students reading and then pausing to orally practice the following components: make a prediction, make an analogy, discuss any confusion, and use fix-up strategies. Sixty-four eighth-grade students learned think-alouds over a period of three 45-minute training sessions in one of three conditions:

- *passive modeling*, in which students simply heard the teacher model thinking-aloud strategies while reading in each session;
- *active modeling*, in which students observed modeling and then practiced thinking aloud and received feedback; and
- *full range modeling*, in which students were provided with a rationale for the modeling activity and a self-efficacy "pep-talk" before observing modeling, practicing think-alouds, and receiving feedback.

Students in the final two conditions were significantly better able to monitor their own reading comprehension and reported significantly more transfer of the think-aloud strategies to school classes other than the one in which the strategy was learned. They also provided significantly more responses to the question, "How has the think-aloud helped you?" Since the strategies are mindfully chosen and applied, this would most appropriately be called high road transfer. Since students reported applying the strategy in several classes, both near and far transfer appear to have occurred.

Weisberg and Balajthy (1989) use explicit instruction, modeling, practice, and feedback to teach below average high school readers to do summary writing and develop graphic organizers. Training took place during six 40-minute training sessions over an eight-week period. All students demonstrated their abilities to summarize and develop graphic organizers. One month after training, students were asked to transfer their learning to two real-world social studies passages—nuclear power plant disasters and the death penalty. For both passages, students demonstrated their abilities to transfer what they had learned to new materials. Again, because the strategies were mindfully chosen, the study appears to be assessing high road transfer. Instruction centered on social studies text passages, so transfer appears to be near transfer to other social studies passages.

Mikulecky, Clark, and McIntyre-Adams (1989) developed three interactive computer programs to guide undergraduate students to concept map biology textbook chapters using modeling, practice, and feedback. The three 30–40 minute programs taught students to identify key ideas, compare and contrast those ideas, and graphically map how the ideas related to each other. Fifty undergraduate biology students, matched by SAT scores, were assigned to either a treatment or a control condition. In the treatment condition, students used computer programs to guide them through reading a textbook chapter on embryo development. At the end of the third session, students took a chapter examination asking them to apply the strategies they had learned. After the third session, students returned for a transfer task in which students were to read a new biology chapter on blood composition and be tested on identifying key ideas, comparing and contrasting those ideas, and graphically mapping the ideas. The control group read the embryonic development chapter and took a chapter examination. The group then returned a week later to read the blood composition chapter and take that chapter examination. The treatment group scored significantly higher on all portions of the first chapter examination, and this advantage held for the transfer chapter a week later. In each case, the students performed about a grade level better. In addition, the treatment group also outperformed the control group on a test given in a biology class that had not been designed as part of this study. A majority of students in post-experiment interviews were able to suggest ways they might apply what they had learned to other classes. The strategies learned in this study are best termed high road because they were usually mindfully applied. The transfer of strategies from one biology chapter to another is best described as near transfer, though many students expressed intention to apply strategies to other subject areas, which would be far transfer.

Cooperative/social group studies

Several literacy learning studies indicate that learning in social groups and pairs can provide enough interaction to facilitate transfer to new situations. A major area of study involves cooperative learning. Cooperative learning situations in literacy usually involve two or more students working together to improve their understanding of text or to retain material in texts.

Studies in this area have been performed by McDonald et al. (1985) and O'Donnell et al. (1985, 1987). McDonald et al. (1985) taught cooperating pairs of undergraduates to use and transfer reading strategies for summarizing important ideas by listening and correcting summary mistakes of others. O'Donnell et al. (1985, 1987) demonstrated that undergraduates, participating in cooperative editing groups to write and refine operating instructions for automobiles, could transfer their newly learned expertise to individually writing directions for operating a tape recorder. Various other techniques for using pairs or social groups to learn and transfer literacy comprehension strategies have been examined by Larson et al. (1985).

In O'Donnell et al. (1985), investigators examined whether cooperative dyad, or pair, work in a writing instruction task would transfer to new individual writing tasks. College students were randomly assigned to either a cooperative dyad or an individual condition. Students in the cooperative dyads were asked to cooperatively write instructional directions on starting a car and driving it away from the curb. No guidelines were given on how to interact or about how to cooperate. Students in the individual groups were asked to write directions to this same task. In session two, participants worked alone to complete the second writing instruction task (transfer task) on writing directions for how to operate a tape recorder and play back a conversation. Investigators found that students working in dyads outperformed the individuals on both communicativeness and completeness, and transferred this cooperative learning to independent work on the transfer task. This finding of cooperative dyads facilitating transfer in writing and editing tasks was further confirmed in a similar study, O'Donnell Larson, Dansereau, and Rocklin (1986). In a third study which involved rewriting rather than editing, O'Donnell et al. (1987) did not find the improved transfer effect for cooperative dyads. The investigators suggest that more than one experience in rewriting is necessary for internalization and subsequent transfer to independent writing tasks.

Investigators (McDonald et al., 1985) studied the effects of a systematic cooperative learning strategy on the acquisition of college text material and on transfer of strategy skills to independent learning. Two experiments were conducted of three sessions each. College students were randomly assigned to one of three groups: system group, no-system group, and individual study. The strategy system required each member of the pair to read about 500 words of a 2,500 word passage. One member of the pair acted as recaller and tried to summarize from memory what had been learned. The other member acted as facilitator/listener and tried to correct the errors in the recall and facilitate the learning by elaborating on the material learned. The partners alternated roles. Results indicate that the system pairs and the no-systems pairs significantly outperformed the individual study group. Using a systematic study strategy in pairs transferred to later individual performance. Students who study in pairs using a systematic learning strategy outperformed students who studied alone in an initial learning task, and this benefit transferred to an independent learning situation. Examiners suggest that transfer occurred because of the combination of the strategy and the pair interaction.

Larson et al. (1985) investigated the effectiveness upon transfer of metacognitive and elaborative activities in varying cooperative learning contexts. These investigators examined the importance of listener activity by assessing three types of dyads: (a) those that emphasized metacognitive activity (jointly using study strategies), (b) those that emphasized elaborative activity (jointly going beyond ideas in the text), and (c) those in which the listener remained silent. Results demonstrated that metacognitive groups outperformed the elaborative group and the control/passive group on initial acquisition of textbook information. On the independent transfer passage, the elaborative group outperformed both the metacognitive and control groups. Larson et al. conclude that the elaborative group facilitates transfer to individual learning because the elaborative strategies were internalized, whereas the metacognitive groups seemed to use each other to improve performance but did not internalize and transfer the strategies.

The studies described above outline a pattern of situations in which cooperative learning facilitates the transfer of literacy abilities and strategies. Transfer appears to occur when there is sufficient time to practice strategies, and when the cooperative activity calls for the learner to internalize what has been learned. When this does not occur (i.e., when a second person serves as a mental coach and metacognitive monitor), then transfer does not occur. Most of the studies described above instruct learners in a mindful strategy and thus seem to address high road transfer. It is unclear whether the writing and editing studies involved mindful strategies (high road) or internalized, automatic processes (low road). It may be that some of both sorts of transfer were involved. In terms of near and far transfer, the studies above are probably best described as mid-distance transfer.

Cognitive apprenticeships

Berryman and Bailey (1992), in *The Double Helix of Education and the Economy*, have examined the mismatch between most schooling and the sorts of higher level use of skills called for in the changed global economy. After reviewing the extensive body of research on transfer, they conclude: "We know now that certain practices of schools impede learning. More effective learning may not be sufficient for transfer, but poor initial learning will certainly impede it" (p. 49). These authors, drawing upon the work of Resnick (1987) and others, suggest a "cognitive apprenticeship" model for any learning which is to have application or transfer to the workplace. This model is extensive and requires teachers to play new roles and for instruction to be a good deal more organized and though-out than is currently the case. The content, methods, sequencing, and sociology of a cognitive apprenticeship model of learning, as presented by Berryman and Bailey (1992, pp. 90–96), are outlined below.

Content: Teach the background knowledge about a domain and how to perform within that domain at the same time. This means that instruction must integrate

- domain knowledge (i.e., concepts and facts),
- tricks of the trade (i.e., strategies use by experts),
- cognitive management strategies (i.e., goal setting, planning, monitoring), and
- learning strategies (i.e., finding and reorganizing knowledge).

Methods: Teach in a way that gives students a chance to observe, engage in, invent, and discover expert strategies in context. This means employing many of the following methods:

- modeling (i.e., demonstrating expert performance),
- coaching (i.e., offering hints, support; feedback, reminders),
- scaffolding and fading (i.e., starting with a scaffold of teacher support and through several practices having that support fade),
- articulation (i.e., any method to get students to articulate or explain their invisible thought processes),
- reflection (i.e., any method that allows students to compare their performance and processes to those of experts), and
- exploration (i.e., any device that forces students into new problem solving on their own).

Sequencing: Stage learning in a way that builds multiple skills and allows the learner to discover what can be generalized. This means instruction must be designed with

- increasing complexity (i.e., from simple to requiring more and more skills and concepts for performance),
- increasing diversity (i.e., choosing a wide enough variety of tasks for students to see both the possibilities and limits of transfer), and
- global before local skills (i.e., develop a strong sense of the overall terrain—how this will be used—before the details).

Sociology: The learning environment should reproduce the technological, social, chronological, and motivational character-istics of real-world situations. This means

- situated or contextualized learning (i.e., real tasks like using reading and writing in an electronic message system to communicate questions and advice),
- community of expert practice (i.e., experts and learners work

together to perform tasks so learners can progress toward expertise),

- intrinsically motivated learning (i.e., students engage in tasks that make sense to the learner and are interesting in their own right),
- cooperative learning (i.e., students of varying abilities working together to solve problems), and
- competitive learning (i.e., competing against other teams, previous performance, and expert performance; focus on strengths and weaknesses for improved performance).

Most current adult literacy instruction involves an instructor providing general practice exercises and some feedback for learners who are attempting to improve their general literacy abilities. Devising adult literacy learning experiences that incorporate the elements of a cognitive apprenticeship model would be challenging and involve the total restructuring of most adult literacy instruction. The model provides a clear, well-conceived framework for instruction, and it is based upon what research suggests is a likely pathway to transfer. It also implies a good deal more than the few weekly hours of drop-in voluntary attendance in adult literacy and workplace literacy classes that typify current practice.

Broader definitions of literacy transfer

Most of the research exploring the nature of transfer reported in this report defines transfer fairly narrowly (i.e., how well do specifically defined strategies or learnings transfer to new situations) or correlationally (how well do literacy test scores correlate with each other or with some other area of performance). Lytle (1990) has studied adult low-level literates using more long-term and ethnographic methods for detecting changes as adults improve in literacy abilities. Although her work does not directly address the issue of transfer, Lytle's observations from comments made by learners in self-reflection journals suggest an expanded definition of transfer. Lytle observes that improved literacy abilities among adults often involve lifestyle changes that precede or parallel improved literacy performance. Comments from successful learners' journals indicate incremental changes in

- beliefs about what literate behavior is and about one's own literacy ability,
- literacy practices away from the classroom,
- literacy processes and strategies deemed appropriate for different tasks, and
- plans for one's education and literacy use in the future.

It may be that such changes in lifestyle and perception of self are necessary for any meaningful transfer of literacy abilities in the everyday sense.

Mikulecky and Lloyd (1992) included interview and questionnaire items in their workplace literacy program assessments to measure changes in the areas mentioned by Lytle (1990). They found that such changes did occur in some programs, but only when instruction directly addressed improving learner beliefs, literacy practices, processes and strategies, or plans for the future. Changes in learners' beliefs about their literacy abilities and changes in literacy practices away from the classroom were almost always associated with improvement in measured literacy performance.

Bandura (1989) has examined the role of belief in relation to changed performance using the concept of *perceived self-efficacy*. Bandura and others have determined that learners who believe they can be effective tend to continue trying and learn from initial mistakes whereas those who do not hold such beliefs tend to be hampered by self-doubt and stop after an initial failure. Although tested ability is important in predicting future application performance, Bandura has found that perception of *self-efficacy* is slightly more important. For purposes of literacy transfer, it is likely that both improved ability and improved belief in one's ability are both important. This is an especially important finding for adults with low literacy abilities. Such adults have often failed regularly at literacy tasks and are hindered by both low ability and very low senses of their own abilities to be effective.

Atwell (1984) has used year-long case-study methods to describe changes in adolescent students immersed in a "literate environment" within her classes. Students read and write extensively to communicate with each other and with the teacher through response journals. Classroom activities include brief modeling of literacy strategies imbedded in long-term group projects that involve the reading and writing of literature. Over the course of the year, Atwell reports several anecdotes documenting students' changed views of themselves in terms of literacy and changes in life-style as they begin to characterize themselves as readers and writers. These changes in self-perception and life-style are likely to be very important for long-term changes in literacy abilities and subsequent transfer. Developing life-long learners with a sense of competence for continued learning and who see themselves as part of a literate community may be as important as teaching for direct transfer of learning. In one sense, choosing a literate life-style might be an extended expression of Salomon's high road notion of transfer.

Conclusions

Literacy ability does transfer to some degree. However, most studies reveal a relatively low degree of correlation between reading performance with different sorts of material requiring differing background knowledge and reading strategies. The aspects of literacy which do transfer may be attributable to the very basic, internalized aspects of reading (i.e., how to move eyes over a page, recognizing letter/sound relationships, recognizing very basic vocabulary). Practicing reading enough to internalize and make these basic processes automatic appears to transfer. Thus, for low literate adults, it seems advisable to provide several hundred hours of practice with materials within the reach of the learner to insure that this sort of low road transfer is obtained. Furthermore, research among learning-disabled adolescents indicates that learning disability does not preclude transfer, though it may make it more difficult to obtain high levels of performance.

Learning to transfer mindful, high road strategies (i.e., summarizing, problem solving, studying, writing for multiple audiences, editing, etc.) does not appear to transfer as automatically. Several studies have documented that this kind of transfer is possible—at least to tasks that highly resemble the original learning task (i.e., near transfer). Instructional methods demonstrating transfer employed a good deal of focused practice on the part of learners and were often characterized by extensive modeling and elaborated feedback. Some cooperative learning strategies (where learners are encouraged to internalize newly learned strategies) seem to facilitate transfer to new situations. The cognitive apprenticeship model offered by Berryman and Bailey (1992) incorporates modeling, feedback, cooperative learning, and realistic social contexts. It is the most fully developed outline for how to achieve transfer of learning and also the most difficult to accomplish. Having adults work cooperatively to improve literacy while involved in authentic tasks that use literacy appears to be the best context to foster high road transfer.

References

Artley, A. S. (1944). A study of certain relationships existing between general reading comprehension in a specific subject matter. *Journal of Educational Research, 37*(6), 464–473.

Atwell, N. (1984). Writing and reading literature from the inside out. *Language Arts, 61*(3), 240–252.

Au, W. K., & Leung, J. P. (1991). Problem solving, instructional methods, and logo programming. *Journal of Educational Computing Research, 7*(4), 455–467.

Bandura, A. (1989). Regulation of cognitive processes through perceived self-efficacy. *Developmental Psychology, 25*(5), 729–35.

Berryman, S. E., & Bailey, T. R. (1992). *The double helix of education & the economy*. New York: Columbia University, Teachers College, Institute on Education and the Economy.

Bigge, M. L., & Shermis, S. S. (1992). *Learning theories for teachers*. New York: Harper Collins.

Brizius, J., & Foster, S. (1987). *Enhancing adult literacy: A policy guide*. Washington, DC: Council of State Policy and Planning Agencies.

Campione, J. C., Brown, A. L., Ferrara, R. A., Jones, R. S., & Steinberg, E. (1985). Breakdowns in flexible use of information: Intelligence-related differences in transfer following equivalent learning performance. *Intelligence, 9*, 297–315.

Carroll, J. B., (1981, May). *Analyses of reading test data*. Invited research presentation, International Reading Association Convention, New Orleans.

Chase, W. G., & Simon, H. A. (1973). Perception in chess. *Cognitive Psychology, 4*, 55–81.

Chi, M. T. H., Feltovich, P. J., & Glaser, R. (1981). Categorization and representation of physics problems by experts and novices. *Cognitive Science, 5*, 121–152.

Collins, M., Carnine, D., & Gersten, R. (1987). Elaborated corrective feedback and the acquisition of reasoning skills: A study of computer-assisted instruction. *Exceptional Children, 54*(3), 254–262.

Cormier, S., & Hagman, J. (1987). *Transfer of learning: Contemporary research and applications*. San Diego, CA: Academic Press.

Dawson, V. L., & Zeitz, C. M. (1989). Expert-novice differences in person perception: Evidence of experts' sensitivities to the organization of behavior. *Social Cognition, 7*(1), 1–30.

De Corte, E., & Verschaffel, L. (1986) Effects of computer experience on children's thinking skills. *Journal of Structural Learning, 9*, 161–174.

Duffy, T. M. (1985). Literacy instruction in the military. *Armed Forces and Society, 11*, 437–467.

Ehlinger, J. (1989). *Thinking-aloud: An examination of its transfer to other learning situations*. (ERIC Document Reproduction Service No. ED 315 737)

Ferrara, R. A., Brown, A. L., & Campione, J. C. (1986). Children's learning and transfer of inductive reasoning rules: Studies of proximal development. *Child Development, 57*, 1087–1099.

Gagne, R. M. (1965). *The conditions of learning*. New York: Holt, Rinehart & Winston.

Gardner, H. (1983). *Frames of mind: The theory of multiple intelligences*. New York: Basic Books, Inc.

Gelzheiser, L. M. (1984). Generalization from categorical memory tasks to prose by learning disabled adolescents. *Journal of Educational Psychology, 76*(6), 1128–1138.

Grandgenett, N., & Thompson, A. (1991). Effects of guided programming instruction on the transfer of analogical reasoning. *Journal of Educational Computing Research, 7*(3), 293–308.

Greenan, J. P. (1982). The development of generalizable skills instruments for identifying the functional learning abilities of students in vocational education programs. *Journal of Industrial Teacher Education, 20*, 19–36.

Hunter, J., & Hunter, R. S. (1984). Validity and utility of alternative predictors of job performance. *Psychological Bulletin, 96*, 72–98.

Jensen, W. (1985). Compensatory education and the theory of intelligence. *Phi Delta Kappan, 66*(8), 654–58.

Judd, C. H. (1908). The relation of special training to general intelligence. *Educational Review, 36*, 28–42.

Keefe, D., & Meyer, V. (1988). Profiles and instructional strategies for adult disabled readers. *Journal of Reading, 31*(7), 614–619.

Kerchner, L. B., & Kistinger, B. J. (1984). Language processing/word processing:

written expression, computers and learning disabled students. *Learning Disabled Quarterly, 7,* 329–335.

Kirsch, I., & Jungblutt, A. (1986). *Literacy: Profiles of America's young adults* (Final Report No. 16-PL-02.) Princeton, NJ: National Assessment of Educational Progress.

Langer, J. (1987). A sociological perspective on literacy. In J. Langer (Ed.), *Language, literacy, and culture: Issues in society and schooling* (p. 1–20). Norwood, NJ: Ablex.

Larson, C. O., Dansereau, D. F., O'Donnell, A. M., Hythecker, V. I., Lambiotte, J. G., & Rocklin, T. R. (1985). Effects of metacognitive and elaborative activity on cooperative learning and transfer. *Contemporary Educational Psychology, 10,* 342–348.

Lederer, D., Orlando, D., & Cevoli, E. (1983). *Latin vibes curriculum: Sixth and seventh grade.* Saddle River, NJ: Saddle River Board of Education.

Lytle, S. L. (1990, April). Living literacy: The practices and beliefs of adult learners. Presented at an invited symposium of the Language Development SIG, *Adult Literacy/Child Literacy: One World or Worlds Apart* at the annual meeting of the American Educational Research Association, Boston, MA.

Mayer, R. E. (1975). Information processing variables in learning to solve problems. *Review of Educational Research, 45*(4), 525–541.

McDonald, B. A., Larson, C. O., Dansereau, D. F., & Spurlin, J. E. (1985). Cooperative dyads: Impact on text learning and transfer. *Contemporary Educational Psychology, 10,* 369–377.

Mikulecky, L. (1992, December). *Workplace literacy programs: Variations of approach and limits of impact.* A paper presented at the annual meeting of the National Reading Conference, San Antonio, TX.

Mikulecky, L., Clark, E., & McIntyre-Adams, S. (1989). Teaching concept mapping and university level study strategies using computers. *Journal of Reading, 32*(8), 694–702.

Mikulecky, L., & Ehlinger, J. (1986). The influence of metacognitive aspects of literacy on job performance of electronics technicians. *Journal of Reading Behavior, 18,* 41–62.

Mikulecky, L., & Lloyd, P. (1993). *The impact of workplace literacy programs: A new model for evaluating the impact of workplace literacy programs* (Tech. Rep. No. TR 93–2). Philadelphia, PA: University of Pennsylvania, National Center on Adult Literacy.

Mikulecky, L., & Winchester, D. (1983). Job literacy and job performance among nurses at varying employment levels. *Adult Education Quarterly, 34,* 1–15.

Morris, N. M., & Rouse, W. B. (1985). Review and evaluation of empirical research in troubleshooting. *Human Factors, 27*(5), 503–530.

O'Donnell, A. M., Dansereau, D. F., Rocklin, T. R., Lambiotte, J. G., Hythecker, V. I., & Larson, C. O. (1985). Cooperative writing: Direct effects and transfer. *Written Communications, 2*(3), 307–315.

O'Donnell, A. M., Dansereau, D. F., Rocklin, T. R., Larson, C. O., Hythecker, V. I., Young, M. D., & Lambiotte, J. G. (1987). Effects of cooperative and individual rewriting on an instruction writing task. *Written Communication, 4*(1), 90–99.

O'Donnell, A. M., Larson, C. O., Dansereau, D. F., & Rocklin, T. R. (1986).

Effects of cooperation and editing on instruction writing performance. *Journal of Experimental Education*, 54(4), 207–10.

Osgood, C. (1949). The similarity paradox in human learning. *Psychological Review*, 56, 132–43.

Palincsar, A. S., & Brown, A. L. (1986). Interactive teaching to promote independent learning from text. *The Reading Teacher*, 39(8), 771–777.

Perkins, D. N., & Salomon, G. (1989). Are cognitive skills context-bound? *Educational Researcher*, 18(1), 16–25.

Reder, S. (1994, February). What does the NALS measure? Issues of dimensionality and construct validity. Paper presented at *Addressing Society's Needs with Literacy: Third North American Conference on Adult and Adolescent Literacy* (International Reading Association), Washington, DC.

Resnick, L. B. (1987). *Education and learning to think*. Washington, DC: National Academy Press.

Ritter, B. T., & Lofland, W. T. (1924). The relationship between reading ability as measured by certain standardized tests and the ability required in the interpretation of printed matter involving reason. *Elementary School Journal*, 24, 529–46.

Royer, J. M. (1979). Theories of the transfer of learning. *Educational Psychologist*, 14, 53–69.

Salisbury, R. (1934). A study of the transfer effects of training in logical organization. *Journal of Educational Research*, 28, 119–129.

Salomon, G., & Globerson, T. (1987). Skill may not be enough: The role of mindfulness in learning and transfer. *International Journal of Educational Research*, 11(6), 623–637.

Salomon, G., & Perkins, D. N. (1987a). Rocky roads to transfer: Rethinking mechanisms of a neglected phenomenon. *Educational Psychologist*, 24(2), 113–142.

Salomon, G., & Perkins, D. N. (1987). Transfer of cognitive skills from programming: When and how? *Journal of Educational Computing Research*, 3(2), 149–169.

Schoenfeld, A. H., & Hermann, D. J. (1982). Problem perception and knowledge structure in expert and novice mathematical problem solvers. *Journal of Experimental Psychology: Learning, Memory, and Cognition*, 8(5), 484–494.

Scribner, S., & Cole, M. (1978). Literacy without schooling: Testing for intellectual effects. *Harvard Educational Review*, 48(4), 448–461.

Scribner, S., & Fahrmeir, E. (1982). *Practical and theoretical arithmetic: Some preliminary findings* (Working paper No. 3). New York: City University of New York, Graduate Center, Industrial Literacy Project.

Starch, D. (1927). *Educational psychology*. New York: Macmillan.

Sternberg, R. J. (1988). *The triarchic mind: A new theory of human intelligence*. New York: Penguin Books.

Sticht, T. G. (1982). *Basic skills in defense* (Professional Paper 3–82). Alexandria, VA: Human Resources Research Organization.

Sweller, J. (1990). On the limited evidence for the effectiveness of teaching general problem-solving strategies. *Journal for Research in Mathematics Education*, 21(5), 411–415.

Thorndike, E. L., & Wordworth, R. S. (1901). The influence of improvement is one mental function upon the efficiency of other functions. *Psychological Review*, 8, 247–261.

U. S. Department of Defense. (1984). *Counselor's manual for the armed services vocational aptitude battery, form 14.* Washington, DC: Author.

U. S. Department of Labor (1991). *What work requires of schools: A SCANS report for America 2000.* Washington, DC: Author.

Venezky, R. L. (1990). Definitions of literacy. In R. L. Venezky, D. A. Wagner, & B. S. Ciliberti (Eds.), *Toward defining literacy* (pp. 2–17). Newark, DE: International Reading Association.

Weisberg, R., & Balajthy, E. (1989, May). *The effects of topic familiarity and training in generative learning activities on poor reader's comprehension of comparison/contrast expository text structure: Transfer to real-world materials.* Paper presented at the annual meeting of the International Reading Association, New Orleans. (Eric Document Reproduction Service No. 305418)

19

LITERACY AND CULTURAL IDENTITY

Bernado M. Ferdman

Source: *Harvard Educational Review* (1990) 60(2): 181–204

We are frequently reminded by public-service announcements on television and radio that being literate can change one's life: Life is better if one can read and write, the ads tell us. At first, there seems to be little that is controversial about this message. Nevertheless, although educators share the goal of developing more literate members of society – after all, this is a primary role of the schools – they disagree about what constitutes literacy and how best to achieve it. The television ads do not analyze the nature of the personal changes brought about by literacy, nor do they suggest how *becoming* and *being* literate are processes that can vary across individuals and groups and are shaped and given meaning by society.[1] Literacy, I believe, (and in this I concur with the ads) touches us at our core in that part of ourselves that connects with the social world around us. It provides an important medium through which we interact with the human environment. For this reason, a consideration of the relationship of literacy and culture must be a fundamental component of any analysis of literacy and the individual.

While a number of writers (see, for example, Akinnaso, 1982, 1985; Goody, 1977, 1982; Goody & Watt, 1963; Ong, 1982; Said, 1983; Scribner & Cole, 1981) have debated and discussed the connections between literacy and culture and the human mind, few have directly addressed the implications of cultural diversity within a society for the processes of becoming and being literate. For example, Akinnaso (1981) and Goody (1982, 1986) discuss the cultural changes that accompany the introduction of literacy in oral societies. Similarly, Ong (1982) contrasts orality and literacy and the implication of their differences for understanding cultures based in one of the two modes. These analyses tend to use a societal frame of reference and therefore to assume a high degree of cultural homogeneity within societies. Other work (Goody, 1977) concentrates on the cognitive implications of the introduction of writing systems, thus emphasizing the individual level of analysis. Attention to intra-societal diversity, however, requires attending at once to issues on both societal and individual levels. In this paper, I discuss from a social psychological perspective the relationship between literacy and the individual in a multiethnic society such as the United States. More precisely, I explore how a person's identity as a member of an ethnocultural group is intertwined with the meaning and consequences of becoming and being literate. Each of us maintains an image of the behaviors, beliefs, values, and norms – in short, of the culture – appropriate to members of the ethnic group(s) to which we belong. This is what I call *cultural identity*. Cultural identity, I argue, both derives from and modulates the symbolic and practical significance of literacy for individuals as well as groups.

The goal of the paper is to provide a theoretical framework for thinking about the way literacy and culture influence each other at the level of the individual. After placing the issue in context, I elaborate and refine the construct of cultural identity and suggest how it can be useful in understanding the processes of literacy education.

Given great diversity in educational achievement among ethnic groups in the United States, the question of the relationship between literacy and cultural identity is driven by a desire to better understand the status of ethnic minorities and to find improved ways for schools to serve their members. At the same time, examination of this question can help to clarify literacy as a multifaceted and multilayered construct. A look at literacy education and acquisition in the context of an ethnically diverse society forces us to go beyond viewing these processes simply as the transmission and internalization of a set of cognitive functions or skills, and to consider both the symbolic aspects and the content of what is taught and learned. In doing so, we are also confronted with the need to clarify our underlying assumptions and values about the nature of such a society.

The role of values

How ethnic differences in school performance should be addressed by educators has been a source of controversy and debate.[2] "Equal opportunity" is the ultimate goal; but there is disagreement on what this means and how to achieve it. Discussion of the relationship of literacy and culture takes place amid societal concern with issues of individual and collective rights: To what extent do individuals and groups in a multiethnic society have a right to define and maintain distinctive identities? And to what extent do these rights complement or conflict with each other? The United States proclaims the value of equal access to opportunity without barriers or advantages based on ethnicity, race, or gender. In one version of this value, individual merit and accomplishment are seen as the only legitimate sources of social and economic success. The educational system is promoted in this regard as "the great equalizer" – the institution that can and should provide citizens with the tools they need to be productive members of society. In this view, which emphasizes the similarities among people, fairness means measuring each individual by the same yardstick. It also means that all individuals must be treated similarly. To do otherwise would be to perpetuate inequities.[3] Another way to think about equal opportunity, however, is to emphasize the differences among people – in particular, those differences rooted in culture and therefore in group memberships. In this alternative view of equal opportunity, fairness involves choosing a yardstick appropriate to the person and group. To ignore group membership is to deny an important part of the individual. Indeed, treating everyone the same can result in the very inequities that are to be avoided (see, for example, Ferdman, 1988; Ferdman 1989; Gordon, 1985; Thurow, 1987).

Divergent views on the proper nature of the relationship among culturally diverse ethnic groups in the society may be an underlying source of disagreement: Should each group pursue its own way and be free to maintain its own heritage, norms, and values, following a pluralist model? Or should one group's culture be emphasized and should assimilation be required? Or should some new "American" blend be developed, composed of something of each group, in line with the "melting pot" model? Debate over these alternatives has persisted throughout U.S. history (see Feagin, 1989; Gleason, 1982; Hirschman, 1983) and is characteristic of plural societies (Babad, Birnbaum, & Benne, 1983, Berry, 1983, 1986). Ultimately, the choice is a value-laden one. An assimilation perspective emphasizes the dysfunctionality of differences and the maintenance of the dominant culture, and so demands that subordinate groups acculturate. The "melting pot" view, also referred to as "amalgamation," maintains that the ideal society takes something from each of its component ethnic groups to create a new culture ultimately shared by all. In contrast, the pluralist position prizes diversity and so holds that it is preferable for the various ethnic groups in a society to co-exist in a kind of "vegetable soup" (Babad et al., 1983), such that each group maintains its own culture to the extent and in the ways that its members wish to do so.

Depending on one's position in this debate, ethnic diversity in school achievement would be dealt with differently. Views that emphasize acculturation, or the "melting pot" ideal, would consider it more fair to use the same measure for all individuals, regardless of group membership. For example, students considered at risk of dropping out of school may be encouraged with magnet schools or other special programs. Seen from strict assimilation or "melting pot" perspectives, the ethnic group to which any specific student belongs should matter little, so long as the opportunity to participate is available equally to all who are judged to need the program. It would also be unfair under these models of ethnic relations to institute special programs with different outcome goals or content for African-American, Italian-American, or Native-American students. Within these models, the fairest approach is to direct special programs to individuals, with needs defined in a global manner. Furthermore, success in the program should be defined similarly for all participants – for example, being able to read at or above a tenth-grade level.

If cultural pluralism is valued, however, individual merit needs to be defined in a culturally relativistic way that takes group membership into account. To the extent that the maintenance and development of distinctive ethnic cultures are valued, these cultures must be given consideration in the educational system. In formulating a drop-out prevention program, it would be not only practical, but also more fair, to explicitly link content and outcomes to the cultures of the participants. To the extent that groups differ, programs could be designed and implemented differently and selection criteria made group-specific. Success in this model would be conceived from a multitude of perspectives based on students' group membership and individual needs.

Literacy has become an important focus for this debate. Because schools are viewed as the institutions most responsible for literacy education in this society, these conflicting values affect the thinking and policy that shape the way children become literate.

Perspectives on individuals and groups

Beyond requiring reflection on our values regarding intergroup relations, a look at literacy in a multiethnic context demands examination of the relationship of the individual to the group. If, in shaping individual development, the educational system and society at large are to pay attention to group-based diversity – whether the goal is to strengthen it or to reduce it – then we need a more focused understanding of the psychological concomitants of ethnic differences. Certainly, in spite of commonalities within ethnic groups, a good deal of within-group variance will also be present, especially in a heterogeneous society (Ferdman & Hakuta, 1985). That is, even valid group level characterizations are not automatically applicable to all or even most group members. Consequently, from a social psychological perspective, we need to better understand the interrelationships between collective and individual experience and behavior. We must conduct such an exploration at the intersection of the group and individual levels of analysis, at once considering both between-group and within-group diversity.

At least in part, the degree of within-group diversity, both real and perceived, may be a function of the predominant values regarding the type of ethnic relations desired in the society. Each model mentioned earlier – pluralism, assimilation, or "melting pot" – carries with it particular

431

assumptions about the degree to which individual behavior and identity do or should follow from those of the group as a whole and thus may function as a filter for the interpretation of the links between the individual and the group levels. For example, a pluralist may consider it legitimate to interpret individual behavior in light of group patterns, while an assimilationist would prefer to focus on individual-level traits. In the illustration used earlier, the pluralist would be comfortable in considering a student's ethnicity in assessing the factors likely to lead to success in a drop-out prevention program, especially to the extent that specific connections could be made between cultural features of the group and the design of the program. Two students displaying the same behavior – say, speaking little in class – would be understood differently as a function of their different cultural backgrounds.[4] The assimilationist, in contrast, would prefer to stress individual characteristics – motivation, intelligence, or home environment, for example – without regard to ethnicity, and therefore with little or no thought to the differential meaning, expression, or incidence of these factors across groups. Alternatively, an assimilationist might recognize culturally based differences, but would prefer to eliminate rather than highlight them. For an advocate of assimilation, the meaning of individual behavior would either be self-evident or else construed from a mono-cultural perspective. So to understand a student who speaks little in class, his or her ethnic background would be seen as superfluous.

In turn, beliefs about the nature of the relationship of individuals and groups may affect which perspective is adopted on ethnic relations. For example, someone who sees groups simply as collections of similar individuals may be more likely to favor a "melting pot" approach, since this approach will not restrict individual freedom of choice. Such a vision of society allows plenty of room for individual differences – all the more so because such differences are not correlated with group membership. In contrast, those who view the group level as primary, as giving definition and meaning to the individual, would tend to prefer pluralism, because they will see individual freedom present only when the groups people belong to are allowed to flourish. From a pluralistic perspective, it is the denial and washing away of group boundaries that ultimately eliminates personal freedom.

Literacy and culture

Ethnic diversity, by its very nature, directs attention to the role of culture in the individual's transactions with the social world. Monica Heller (1987) provides a useful perspective on the type of culture that distinguishes an ethnic group:

> [For members of an ethnic group] shared experience forms the basis of a shared way of looking at the world; through interaction

432

they jointly construct ways of making sense of experience. These ways of making sense of experience, these beliefs, assumptions, and expectations about the world and how it works underlie what we think of as culture. However culture is not only a set of beliefs and values that constitute our normal, everyday view of the world; it also includes our normal, everyday ways of behaving.

(p. 184)

In this view, culture includes both specific behavioral characteristics typifying a group and the underlying views of social reality that guide those behaviors. This latter part is what Triandis (1972) termed "subjective culture ... a group's characteristic way of perceiving its social environment" (p. viii). These definitions of culture suggest that a person's view of social reality is mediated by collective representations of that reality.

In a society tending toward homogeneity, it is easy to think of literacy simply in terms of specific skills and activities. Given broad cultural consensus on the definition of literacy, alternative constructions are either remote or invisible, and so literacy becomes a seemingly self-evident personal attribute that is either present or absent. In such an environment, literacy is experienced as a characteristic inherent in the individual. Once a person acquires the requisite skills, she also acquires the quality of mind known as literacy, together with the right to be labeled a literate person. Judgments about a person's degree of literacy are not dependent on the situation. Rather, because there is wide agreement on what constitutes a literate individual, a person carries the label regardless of whether or not she continues to demonstrate the behaviors that first earned her the designation. A person accepted as being literate is not considered to be any less literate when she is watching television or when she is sleeping than when she is writing a novel or reading the back of a cereal box.

In a multiethnic context, however, the cultural framing of literacy becomes more obvious. De Castell and Luke (1983) argue convincingly that "being 'literate' has always referred to having mastery over the processes by means of which culturally significant information is coded" (p. 373). In this view, literacy does not simply consist of a universally defined set of skills constant across time and place. Since cultures differ in what they consider to be their "texts" and in the values they attach to these, they will also differ in what they view as literate behavior.[5] An illiterate person is someone who cannot access (or produce) texts that are seen as significant within a given culture. That same person, in another cultural context, may be classified as being quite literate. When a number of cultures co-exist within the same society, it is more likely that we will encounter variant conceptions of what constitutes being literate.

Because culture exists as a product of social interaction and organization, de Castell and Luke ask us to view literacy as meaningful only in the social context of particular communities. Purves (1987) similarly points out the ways in which being literate involves mastering conventional wisdom and common knowledge and, in so doing, entering into a kind of "textual contract." What is important is that what is "common" and what is "conventional" are defined in reference to a group, to a particular community at a given point in time. This reference point constitutes culture and determines what will be construed as literacy. As Purves (1987) explains, "[b]eing literate ... involves activities that bring various store-houses of knowledge into action when the situation calls for them" (p. 224). This knowledge base includes linguistic information, text models, and "socio-cultural norms of literacy acts" (p. 224) that all feed into defining behaviors and cognitive operations as literate. To become literate a person must master, in addition to a set of culturally defined skills, all the cultural information involved in decoding and producing texts, including the frames of reference for comprehending their contents.

In a culturally heterogenous society, literacy ceases to be a characteristic inherent solely in the individual. It becomes an interactive process that is constantly redefined and renegotiated, as the individual transacts with the socioculturally fluid surroundings. A new arrival to the United States from a small village in Malaysia, unable to read or write in English and unfamiliar with the Latin alphabet, would not immediately have all the skills required of a literate person in his new country and would in all likelihood be seen in the workplace as functionally illiterate. At home, however, he teaches his sons to read the Quran, maintains an elaborate accounting system for his lending society, and is revered as a teacher and wise person. As Scribner (1986) put it, "literacy is ... a *social* achievement.... [It] is an outcome of cultural transmission.... Literacy has neither a static nor a universal essence" (pp. 8–9). Because culture is in flux, so are the definition and consequences of literacy (see, for example, Cook-Gumperz, 1986).

Literacy, then, in large part, involves facility in manipulating the symbols that codify and represent the values, beliefs, and norms of the culture – the same symbols that incorporate the culture's representations of reality. Because the processes referred to by de Castell and Luke are themselves part of the culture, to be defined as literate this manipulation must be done in a culturally appropriate manner. To be literate it is not enough, for example, to know how to sign one's name. One must also know when and where it is appropriate to do so.[6] Reading and writing behaviors must be done in the "right" way. "The enterprise of defining literacy," Scribner (1986) reminds us, "... becomes one of assessing what counts as literacy in some given social context" (p. 9). For example, the skills necessary to be considered literate in a society that employs pictographic writing can be quite different from those necessary in a society that uses an alphabetic system. Similarly, literacy for a supermarket shopper might be defined in terms of the ability to negotiate varieties of text printed on a number of different surfaces in a multitude of type-faces, with little emphasis on handling writing instruments or proper spelling. In contrast, literacy for a secretary/clerk might well include appropriate use of spelling and punctuation and the ability to decode many types of handwritten documents. In each of these situations, food-shopping and secretarial work, the particular distribution of skills may also vary from culture to culture. That is, cultures will have particularistic definitions of the behaviors and skills a person would need to demonstrate in order for him or her to be considered a literate food-shopper or literate secretary.

In addition to being skilled in the use of methods of representation such as the alphabet, writing implements, books, and so on, the literate person must be familiar with a particular configuration of meanings in context, to comprehend appropriately the content of what is encoded and decoded. *Becoming* literate means developing mastery not only over processes, but also over the symbolic media of the culture – the ways in which cultural values, beliefs, and norms are represented. *Being* literate implies actively maintaining contact with collective symbols and the processes by which they are represented. Thus, literacy goes beyond superficial transactions with a printed or written page and extends into the ability to comprehend and manipulate its symbols – the words and concepts – and to do so in a culturally prescribed manner.

The school is a particularly important institution for mediating the process by which the individual becomes literate and for reflecting societal views of what constitutes literacy. Roth (1984) put it this way:

> Social/cultural control is tied directly to the structure of know-ledge and to the manner in which knowledge is presented in the schooling context. Schools, acting as agents for the culture, control the extent to which personal knowledge may enter into the public knowledge of school curriculum; they thus have a direct influence upon cultural continuity and change. In selecting what to teach and how it is to be taught and evaluated, schools reaffirm what the culture values as knowledge...
>
> Because literacy provides a powerful means for individuals to make a personal tie to society in general, literacy acquisition, particularly reading instruction, holds implications for cultural transmission, that is, for how knowledge is transferred, reproduced, and transformed. The prime focus of 1st grade is to establish reading literacy so that the "knowledge" our culture sees as significant may be maintained.

(p. 303)[7]

Roth's analysis certainly holds for a homogeneous society in which the schools are indeed "agents for the culture" of their constituents. To apply to a multicultural society, however, her view must be expanded to consider the relationship of the culture(s) represented by the school and those of its pupils.

In a multicultural environment, the individual who is becoming literate may be faced with an array of alternative methods and contents representing different views of literacy. The value placed on behaviors that are construed as literate in the context of one group will not be equivalent to the value given them by a different culture. For example, penmanship might be much more valued by the Chinese, who must spend long hours learning the appropriate brush-strokes for each pictogram, and who generally value the aesthetic qualities of text, than by North Americans, who might primarily emphasize the content. In a religious Christian community, it is likely that time spent reading the Bible is considered to be well spent; while among secular intellectuals, it may be considered more important to read the daily newspaper. Whereas those raised in upper-class New England may place a premium on being familiar with the classics of U.S. literature, midwestern farmers may be more concerned with their ability to read the latest commodity exchange tables and the manuals for their machinery. Educators in the United States tend to see creative writing by children as a valued activity, and this perspective is incorporated into school curricula. This may appear strange in other countries, however, where students are encouraged to learn and copy the work of great thinkers rather than to produce original work.

As part of their formal schooling, children encounter the preferences of the educational system, the school, and the teachers, regarding which behaviors to emphasize. These preferences have in turn been shaped by the sociocultural environment of the school and its agents (such as teachers, teacher assistants, principals, textbook writers, and editors). Other messages are conveyed through interactions with family and peers, the media, and even the various segments of the educational system. Whether these messages are congruent depends in part on the degree of cultural heterogeneity represented by the messengers. In educating their pupils toward literacy, schools vary in the degree to which they incorporate the cultural views of the ethnic groups to which their pupils belong. To the extent that schools tend to reflect the dominant culture, pupils from the dominant ethnic group are more likely than are ethnic minority students to find consistency between the various constructs of literacy. In either case, because literacy education tends to be left primarily to the school, children become literate in the cultural image represented by their school.

So it is that literacy education can constitute a profound form of socialization. A person who becomes literate does so in the context of a particular definition of literate behavior. She is, as Purves (1987) and others (Heath, 1986; Wallace, 1986) remind us, trained to internalize the behaviors appropriate to a functional member of a specific social community. In the case of a majority child attending majority schools, this is essentially transparent in that neither educator nor pupil need consciously attend to the ways in which they are engaged in a process of cultural transmission: In the case of minority group members, however, the process may be less smooth, depending on the extent to which their group's standards for cultural significance differ from the dominant group norms. For members of cultural minorities, the potential conflicts will be greater, as will the salience of group membership.

The meaning of the process and symbols involved in literacy education will differ depending on what reference group the individual uses to interpret them. Thus, at the individual level, whether deliberately or not, the process of becoming and being literate involves becoming and being identified with a particular culture. The relationship of the individual to the group forms the basis for cultural identity. In the following sections, I elaborate on this point.

Cultural identity

From a social psychological perspective we are most concerned with the mutual influence of the individual and his social environment. Cultural identity is a concept that can help to conceptualize these links. In this section, I delineate the related but distinct constructs of group and individual cultural identity. By its very nature, culture is meaningful only with reference to the group, yet it is enacted by individuals. This is why culture is a central concept in understanding how the person and the collective are connected.[8] We must clarify what is meant by cultural identity to understand its interaction with literacy.

The group level

An ethnic group's cultural identity involves a shared sense of the cultural features that help to define and to characterize the group. These group attributes are important not just for their functional value, but also as symbols. For example, for many Puerto Ricans in the United States, the Spanish language is not just a means of communication; it also represents their identification as Latinos and their difference from the majority culture. Even if Spanish reading and writing ability is absent, the desire to conserve some degree of Spanish speaking ability may reflect a desire to maintain distinctiveness from the surrounding society (see, for example Ball, Giles, & Hewstone, 1984; Hakuta, Ferdman, & Diaz, 1987). Group cultural identity has to do both with the particular features of the ethnic group and with the significance that is attached to these features in a societal context. A group's cultural identity will play an important role in the nature and outcome of the intergroup comparisons that it makes, and thus in the way the group comes to evaluate itself (see, for example, Ferdman, 1987; Montero, 1987; Tajfel & Turner, 1986). When a group perceives that its cultural features compare favorably with those of other groups, it should come to hold more positive images of itself. If, on the other hand, features central to the group's cultural identity are viewed negatively in the larger society, the group will probably incorporate a negative component into its self-evaluation.

Kochman (1987) makes a useful distinction between emblematic and nonemblematic ethnic indicators: "Emblematic indicators are those racial and cultural features that serve an identity function or otherwise mark and maintain social boundaries" (p. 220) between the in-group and the out-group. These are features that in-group and out-group members will tend to think of as "ethnic." Nonemblematic indicators are those cultural patterns that do not serve such functions, and of which in-group and out-group members may or may not be aware.[9] For example, anthropologists and other social scientists may identify characteristic features of the group's behavior that are not otherwise generally linked to the group.

As defined here, cultural identity at the group level involves those features of the group that are widely perceived as emblematic by the in-group. While outsiders may consider particular features as characteristic of most group members, thereby rendering them emblematic in Kochman's sense, these features would not necessarily form part of the group's collective cultural identity unless the in-group internalized this external point of view or had otherwise also incorporated these features into its self-image.

Smolicz (1981) uses the concept of core values similarly, although in a more restrictive sense than intended here. According to him, core values "generally represent the heartland of the ideological system and act as identifying values which are symbolic of the group and its membership" (p. 75). What is important in defining the centrality of a cultural feature is not the particular type of value or characteristic. Rather, "whenever people feel that there is a direct link between their identity as a group and what they regard as the most crucial and distinguishing element of their culture, the element concerned becomes a core value" (pp. 76–77). So, for example, while for some groups maintenance of the native language may function as a core value, for others, the centrality of the family or religious life may play this role. As elaborated here, then, an ethnic group's cultural identity is based on such core values, but also extends beyond them to include other features and values that the group generally perceives itself to possess and which help it to maintain its character as a group. This might nevertheless form part of the group's cultural identity,

438

because it is a characteristic that is seen as identifying and distinguishing the group.

The individual level

In conceptualizing cultural identity at the group level, I have assumed a certain degree of uniformity within the group. Nevertheless, although members of the same ethnic group will tend to demonstrate shared cultural features (this is in part what defines their common ethnicity), variation within groups will also be present. Individual members of ethnic groups will vary both in the extent of their identification with the group and in the degree to which their behavior is based on the group's cultural norms (see, for example, Boekestijn, 1988; Ferdman & Hakuta, 1985). In a multiethnic society in which members of different groups are in various degrees of contact with each other, a variety of options may be available to individuals regarding how to relate not only to other groups but also to their own. Ethnic group members will express their choices in part through the behaviors they demonstrate in different types of situations. Especially in the case of minority group members or immigrants, the extent to which an individual follows the group's typical cultural pattern may be an indication of the degree of that person's psychological assimilation or acculturation (Berry, 1986; Graves, 1967). Jones (1988) points out how such variation may also reflect minority group members' perceptions regarding the instrumentality[10] of particular behaviors in different contexts, such that an individual may behave in accordance with the group's cultural patterns in some situations but not in others. The distinction between the group and the individual level is important, in part because, as Berry (1986) puts it, "not every individual participates to the same extent in the general acculturation being experienced by his group" (p. 38; see also Berry, 1983) and conversely, because some individual group members may acculturate more rapidly than the group as a whole. Thus, over time, acculturation processes may affect both what the cultural features are at the group level (Taylor & McKirnan, 1984) and whether particular individuals demonstrate them (Berry, 1986). In addition, contextual factors may influence whether individuals are likely to behave in line with the group's cultural identity. Because of this intragroup variation, to render cultural identity useful as a psychological construct we must transpose it to the individual level. Beyond behavioral differences, we should expect within-group diversity in the degree to which particular features are seen as central to the group's identity.

At the individual level, cultural identity has to do with the person's sense of what constitutes membership in an ethnic group to which he or she belongs. Each person will have a particular image of the behaviors and values that characterize the group's culture. The term is distinguished here from the related and broader social psychological concept of *social identity*, as well as from *ethnic identity*. Tajfel and Turner (1986) define social identity as consisting "of those aspects of an individual's self-image that derive from the social categories to which he [*sic*] perceives himself as belonging" (p. 16). Their notion of social categories is quite broad, encompassing any type of group to which people perceive themselves as belonging.[11] Such categories of course include ethnicity, but can range from school sports teams to professional identifications, from social club memberships to gender or race classifications, and from nationality groups to psychological groups (for example, "jocks," "yuppies," "nerds"). Social identity incorporates both the person's knowledge of membership in particular social categories and the value and feelings attached to those memberships. Ethnic identity can be defined as the portion of an individual's social identity that is associated with membership in an ethnic group.[12] Cultural identity, while linked closely to both ethnic and social identity, is neither equivalent to them nor coterminous. While both ethnic and cultural identity help the individual to answer the question, "Who am I?", cultural identity is the component that associates particular cultural features with group membership. Social identity and ethnic identity deal with the symbolic aspects of social categorization – the boundary between the in-group and the out-group – and the associated affect. A particular individual, for example, may base her social identity primarily on gender, while her sister may focus more sharply on her Polish background. Thus, the first sister's ethnic identity as a Polish-American would be somewhat less strong than that of the second sister (see Babad, Birnbaum, & Benne, 1983).[13]

Cultural identity as defined here is a more specific construct. Cultural identity involves the perceived bases for a person's ethnic categorization – that which is inside the boundary – and the person's feelings about this content. The second sister's cultural identity includes the perception that being Polish generally implies being strongly Catholic and maintaining close family ties. It also incorporates her feelings about these features – she is somewhat ambivalent about the first, and she feels quite positive about the second. Cultural identity thus includes the individual's internalized view of the cultural features characterizing his or her group, together with the value and affect that the person attaches to those features.

Paralleling the distinction made here between cultural and ethnic identity, Keefe and Padilla (1987) discuss the difference between the processes of acculturation and ethnic identification. Acculturation involves changes in the cultural patterns shown by groups when they come into contact with one another. In ethnic identification, in contrast, "the particular assemblage of cultural traits becomes less important than the attitudes of members toward the people and culture of in-group versus out-group as well as members' self-identification" (p. 41). Thus, an individual may maintain a strong identification with a particular group while adopting new cultural traits. Similarly, Herman (1977), in studying the nature of Jewish identity, suggested that its analysis at the individual level must address both a) the nature of the individual's relationship to the Jewish group as a membership group; and b) the individual's perception of the attributes of the Jewish group, his or her feeling about them, and the extent to which its norms are adopted by him or her as a source of reference (p. 39). The first component involves aspects of the person's ethnic affiliation – in the present terms, both ethnic and social identity – while the second has to do with the ways in which that affiliation is represented – what I refer to as cultural identity.

Two people may perceive their identification as members in a particular group to be just as central to their ethnic identity, yet define its meaning quite differently. For example, for one Jew the primary features of being Jewish involve following the religious laws and becoming learned in the Bible and in the Talmud; while for another, religious observance is secondary or non-existent; more emphasis is placed on Jewish values and on supporting the State of Israel (Herman, 1977). Yet both claim an equally strong connection to the Jewish people. Similarly, Puerto Ricans living in New York and in Puerto Rico, while sharing an ethnic identification, will have divergent experiences and ways of looking at the world, with resulting differences in their cultural identities. For one, the experience of minority status and ethnic distinctiveness in an urban environment will play a relatively more central role; while for the other the Spanish language and living on the island will be relatively more important (Flores, 1985; Ginorio, 1987).

Thus, cultural identity involves those parts of the self – those behaviors, beliefs, values, and norms that a person considers to define himself or herself socially as a member of a particular ethnic group – and the value placed on those features in relation to those of other groups. Changes in those features would imply a shift in the person's way of thinking about him- or herself in a social context. Via his or her cultural identity, the individual answers the question, "What is the appropriate way for someone like me, for someone having my ethnicity, to interpret and to behave in the world?" While, at the group level, a collective set of emblematic cultural features that compose the group's cultural identity may exist, at the individual level, what is relevant is the person's particular perspective on the collective view. Individual members of an ethnic group will vary in the extent to which they perceive specific attributes as central to their cultural identity and in the value they give these attributes. In addition, they will vary in the degree to which they see themselves as representing these attributes.[14]

Status and power differentials between groups may play a role in the cultural identity individuals come to hold. In a multiethnic society, the minority group member[15] is typically identified in group terms, while members of the dominant group will be more likely to see themselves and to be seen by others in individual terms, "or at least as not belonging to any particular category" (Deschamps, 1982, p. 89; see also Tajfel, 1978). Guillaumin (1972) has suggested that minority groups tend to have complex views of the majority and not just of their own group; whereas, the majority tends to see the minority as a deindividuated mass. Thus, we might expect that members of minority groups will be more aware of their attributes as being associated with group membership and thus as forming part of their cultural identity. Members of the dominant group, in contrast, because they may be less accustomed to thinking of themselves in group terms, may be less conscious of the cultural sources for behavior. For them, identity may be construed primarily at the individual level and not be perceived as connected to the group's features. One implication of this is that minority group members are able to choose (and sometimes are forced) to adopt the dominant ("mainstream") perspective to interpret social reality.

Cultural identity and literacy

Because literacy is a culturally defined construct, it follows that it should have close links to cultural identity. At the societal level, literacy education involves not just the imparting of particular skills, but also the transmission of values (de Castell & Luke, 1983). Kádár-Fülop (1988) points to the development of "language loyalty" – the encouragement of positive attitudes toward the language – as an important function for literacy education. De Castell and Luke (1983; 1987) forcefully show how literacy campaigns are carried out in the context of particular social agendas. In an ethnically diverse society, these values are not necessarily shared across groups. Indeed, de Castell and Luke (1987) write that:

> If literacy campaigns are seen primarily as attempts to forge or to impose a common cultural tradition, and only secondarily as attempts to disseminate competence at reading and writing, then we ought to reconsider the alleged current crises not as failures in the mass transmission of reading and writing but as failures of a far more fundamental kind: failures in the mass inculcation and perpetuation of a desired sociocultural tradition.

> (p. 428)

From a social psychological perspective, the question becomes one of describing the individual, interpersonal, and intergroup processes by which such failures (or successes) may come about.

The concept of cultural identity permits such an elaboration. The idea that cultural symbols have affective significance for the individual suggests that the process of becoming and being literate will tap into these feelings. When there is a mismatch between the definition and significance of literacy as they are represented in a person's cultural identity and in the learning situation, the individual is faced with making a choice that has implications for his or her acquisition of reading and writing skills, as well as for his or her relationship to particular texts and the symbols they contain. The student must either adopt the perspective of the school, at the risk of developing a negative component to his or her cultural identity, or else resist these externally imposed activities and meanings, at the risk of becoming alienated from the school; whereas, for majority children, the school's perspective is likely to parallel whatever cultural identity they have. This is less likely for members of ethnic minorities.

Henry Giroux (1987) points out how individuals' "stories, memories, narratives, and readings of the world are inextricably related to wider social and cultural formations and categories" (p. 177). In the context of literacy education, the issue has to do with what is experienced by the student as "owned" and what is experienced as "not owned" by his or her group. Which texts and which writing tasks does the student engage in as "ours" and which as "theirs"? When a child perceives a writing task or a text and its symbolic contents as belonging to and reaffirming his or her cultural identity, it is more likely that he or she will become engaged and individual meaning will be transmitted or derived. In contrast, those tasks and symbols that serve to deny or to devalue aspects of the individual's cultural identity, or even those that are neutral in relation to it, may be approached differently and with less personal involvement. For example, reading in a group setting and analyzing texts is an important component of Jewish religious practice. An Orthodox Jewish child who perceives these activities as important components of his cultural identity may become more involved in similar tasks at school because they are linked to his sense of who he is. A child who, for cultural reasons, is accustomed to reading aloud, with a group, may approach reading assignments at school differently from a classmate who thinks of reading as something that is done alone and silently. Another student, who believes that reading books assigned at school is not "something my people do," will probably be less likely to complete such assignments. This same child may be very adept, however, at reading other materials, such as comic books.

Two personal examples are in order here. As a child, I delighted in reading anything I could get my hands on. But one of my favorite types of stories as an eight- and nine-year-old was *midrashim*, myths and legends based on the Bible. If Norse legends were given to me, I was just as likely to read them; but, they did not have the same impact on me, and I did not see them in the same light. Because of my Jewish identity, my relationship to King David or to Abraham was a more personal and significant one than my connection with Thor. The Biblical stories, because they touched on my cultural identity, had practical and symbolic meanings that went beyond the story and extended into helping me learn more about myself and my group in a social context and gave me conceptual tools with which to interact with other group members. Similarly, when I want to read a Latin American author, I will do so in Spanish, my native tongue, rather than in an English translation. My choice is based not only on a desire to read the original, but also to reaffirm my connection with Latin American symbols and texts. In spite of ostensibly similar content, I experience the images and meanings differently in the two languages.

These examples highlight the ways personal meaning is derived from broader social meanings. However, the relationship of reading and cultural identity may not be a function of only the symbolic content of the text. The significance of the text itself and the context in which it is read may be at least as relevant, if not more so. For example, therefore, if reading *The New York Times* contributes in an important way to my cultural identity, I will relate to that text differently from someone who approaches it as an outsider. Similarly, reading *The New York Times* every day will have a different meaning when I do it in New York than when I do it in Paris. While in both cases the activity may be similarly related to my cultural identity, in the latter case it may be seen as a more obvious statement of where I stand in relation to my social environment.

Relevant to this issue, Hakuta and I (Hakuta, Ferdman, & Diaz, 1987) conducted a study of Puerto Rican elementary school children and their parents in New Haven, Connecticut. We found some indication that reading Spanish newspapers reflected not only language proficiency but also degrees of identification with being Puerto Rican. At intermediate levels of English ability, twice as many of those respondents who planned to return to Puerto Rico, as compared with those planning to stay in New Haven, reported that they regularly read *El Vocero*, a Spanish-language daily newspaper flown in from the island.[16]

Matute-Bianchi's (1986) research among Mexican-descent and Japanese-American high school students and Trueba's (1984) work in the Mexican-American barrio show that for ethnic minority group members, perceptions of themselves and others in a social context and of the value of their education in relation to those social perceptions contribute significantly shaping their attitudes toward school-related activities. In the California high school that she studied, Matute-Bianchi was able to distinguish five sub-groups among students of Mexican descent on the basis of how they identified themselves ethnically and which behavior patterns they perceived to go along with these labels. For some of the groups (the "Mexicans" and the "Mexican-Americans"), success in school was not viewed as incompatible with cultural identity. As they learned the dominant culture of the school, these students did not believe that they had to give up what they considered important about their identity as Mexicans.

In contrast, for other groups (the "Chicanos"), maintaining their identity involved engaging in behaviors that ultimately reduce the chances for academic success:

> Chicanos and Cholos ... appear to resist certain features of the school culture, especially the behavioral and normative patterns required for school achievement. These norms, assumptions, and codes of conduct are associated with being white or gringo or quaddie or rich honkie. To adopt these cultural features – that is, to participate in class discussions, to carry books from class to class, to ask the teacher for help in front of others, to expend effort to do well in school – are efforts that are viewed derisively, condescendingly, and mockingly by other Chicanos. Hence, to adopt such features presents these students with a forced-choice dilemma. They must choose between doing well in school or being a Chicano.
>
> (Matute-Bianchi, 1986, pp. 253–254)

The Japanese-Americans who were interviewed by Matute-Bianchi were all successful students. They, in contrast to their peers of Mexican descent, did not see components of their ethnicity in conflict with their identities as students. Thus, they saw no need to behave differently in the school context from the ways of the dominant culture. This was the case even for students who outside of school participated in activities such as praying at a Buddhist temple, which is explicitly linked to their Japanese identity.

Trueba similarly found that the families he studied perceived a clear relationship between literacy in English and acculturation. As he put it:

> Posing as illiterate in some contexts was equivalent to keeping one's own identity as "cholo" i.e., as marginal in school and involved with peers in other activities. In the home, however, dedication to books and relative facility to deal with text signaled eagerness to make it in the Anglo world, and that had a price, because it required some adjustment in peer reference groups and in social activities.
>
> (Trueba, 1984, p. 33)

Thus, we may expect that those people who wish to become more acculturated will be more likely to engage in activities that will help them to acquire English literacy.

I have argued so far that cultural identity mediates the process of becoming literate as well as the types of literate behavior in which a person subsequently engages. At this point, it becomes possible to formulate more precise questions as a guide to future thinking and research about the ways cultural identity affects how and whether an individual becomes literate as a result of schooling:

1 How is literacy defined in the individual's group, and what is its significance? What behaviors are included in this definition?
2 What significance do particular texts have for the individual's cultural identity?
3 How do the particular pedagogical approach, the texts that are used, and the purpose of literacy as communicated by the school relate to the learner's motives and sense of identity (and more subtly, what messages does a reading and writing curriculum communicate about the value of the learner's culture)?
4 What relationship does the learner perceive between the tasks assigned in school and his or her cultural identity? Must the learner change the nature of his or her self-concept in order to do what is asked?

Attention to these questions by researchers and educators may help us to better understand how the meaning of literacy for individuals is influenced by their sense of themselves as cultural beings. In turn, such understanding should better serve members of a heterogeneous society as they acquire literacy.

Until now, the discussion has focused on the implications of cultural identity for literacy development. The relationship, however, is better seen as bi-directional. Not only will cultural identity mediate the acquisition and expression of literacy, but literacy education will also influence and mold the individual's cultural identity. Modifying the means by which the person interacts with others across time and space – that is, making the person "literate" – will eventually require the person to redefine (or reaffirm) his or her own view of the self in a social context. A clear example is that of the immigrant who seeks – or is forced – to acculturate not only by learning a new language but also by adopting a whole new set of symbols and meanings. I was struck, one recent November, by a picture in *The New York Times* showing newly arrived Vietnamese immigrant children in school dressed as Pilgrims and Indians in "celebration" of the Thanksgiving holiday. Clearly, they were being asked as a condition of citizenship to take as their own a new set of cultural icons and referents. The school was teaching the children not only to understand the images and associations evoked by Thanksgiving but to do so from the perspective of the dominant culture. In a more subtle but no less powerful way, the reading and writing activities that children are asked to engage in at school, to the extent that they are accepted, will ultimately affect not only the children's sense of who they are, but the ways in which they can figure out their cultural identity.

Literacy education, as de Castell and Luke (1987) so forcefully argue, can never be content-free. By providing the individual with the symbolic material with which to understand and transact with the social environment and by requiring him or her to do so in particular modalities, the range of possibilities for the person is channeled and narrowed. Certainly, this is a significant and indispensable part of socialization. The problem may arise for ethnic minority group members who as a result must dissociate from those aspects of themselves that would otherwise serve to provide them with a positive sense of identity in the social environment.

Linguists and psychologists (Erickson, 1984; Guiora, 1985; McEvedy, 1986) have pointed to the cognitive aspects of this channeling process as it occurs in learning a first or second language. Guiora and his colleagues (Guiora, 1985), for example, found that children who spoke languages with greater gender loadings (Hebrew) developed gender identity sooner than those speaking languages with little gender loading (English) or none (Finnish). McEvedy (1986) points out how the concept of *we* is very general in English, but much more fine-tuned among the Pitjantjatjarra of Australia, who employ different pronouns depending on exactly who is in the situation and how distant they are from the speaker. These arguments suggest that, for example, a French child who is educated in English and grows up without learning the French language will have a different experience of gender and of interpersonal relationships than a child educated in French, as a result of the use of different linguistic markers in the two languages.

The issue, however, extends beyond this, into the meanings that become attached to various symbolic representations as they relate to the person's sense of his or her integration into a cultural group and of the group's place in society, into what Erickson (1984) refers to as the "politics of social identity." Erickson summarizes Scollon and Scollon's (1981) work among Alaskan natives in this context:

> In their interpretation, Alaskan native teenagers come to see the acquisition of Western written literacy as a kind of metaphoric adoption of a new ethnic group identity. To become literate in school terms would be to disaffiliate symbolically from their parents and other members of the Alaskan native village, a few of whom are "literate" in traditional knowledge and skill, such as that involved in hunting, and many of whom are marginally literate in school-like practices of literacy. Caught in ambivalence between multiple cultural worlds, Alaskan native youth resist adopting the complete system of school-defined literacy, and then suffer the consequences of marginal acquisition. They do not belong fully to the old ways or to the new.
>
> (p. 539)

447

We might ask what happens to those Alaskan natives who do fully adopt "school-defined literacy." Their cultural identity, also, should be fundamentally altered. Indeed, in becoming and being literate in this way, the materials they now have access to, because they are mostly generated by other ethnic groups, will provide them with perspectives on their own ethnic group that are probably quite different from those originated by the Alaskans themselves.

It would appear, then, that the impact of literacy education as a socialization agent on individuals' cultural identity can be either destructive or constructive. When the person loses the capability to derive and create meaning in a culturally significant way, he or she becomes less, not more, literate. To the extent that successful learning, as defined from the school's point of view, forces the ethnic minority child to become disconnected from what is personally significant, his or her ability to construct a positive and coherent cultural identity will be weakened. I do not wish to argue, however, that children must learn only about the heritage and products of their own culture. Indeed, the opposite is true. James Banks (1977, 1981, 1987) presents a useful view of multi-ethnic education that aims towards inclusion rather than exclusion. He recommends providing all students with "cultural and ethnic alternatives" (1977, p. 8) so that they learn about both their own culture and those of others. One goal of this approach is to prevent minority group members from feeling that they must become alienated from their identity to do well. By explicitly incorporating into schooling a culture-sensitive approach, students can be allowed to discover how what they are learning relates to their ethnic identity. As they learn, they will then be able to better articulate their cultural identity. This process can occur not only as they discover what is their own; it is also facilitated through contrast, as they discover what belongs to others.

Literacy education, when it acknowledges the role of cultural identity, may serve to enhance self-esteem as it derives from a sense of self in a social context. If individuals can acquire the tools to better define their cultural identity – by, for example, comparing it with a range of possibilities – then learning about a range of cultural products[17] can be enriching. To do this, the individual who is becoming literate must be encouraged to consider the relationship of what is learned to the self and to the group, by calling attention to the ways in which alternative perspectives on the methods and contents of literacy are possible. When this is done, it may result in an environment that can more readily empower members of dominated groups (Cummins, 1986). Rather than aim for a curriculum that avoids discussions of ethnicity, the goal should be to facilitate the process by which students are permitted to discover and explore ethnic connections.

As pointed out earlier, the process by which literacy education shapes individuals' cultural identity takes place in an intergroup context. Because the definition of becoming and being literate at the societal level has to do in part with defining group boundaries and status, the debate over literacy in a multi-ethnic society reflects variant values regarding the proper place of the society's component groups. Implementing literacy education that authorizes and fosters variations in cultural identity implies realignments in groups' positions such that previously devalued groups – together with their cultures – become recognized and appreciated.[18]

The ongoing debate over cultural literacy (Hirsch, 1987) may be interpreted in this light: The controversy is about the issue of what should constitute cultural identity at the national level and what should be the nature of the relationship of minority and dominant groups in the society. In terms of the present discussion, the problem with Hirsch's recommendations is not the idea that Americans should be more familiar with a variety of terms and ideas. Rather, it is with the assumption that the meaning and significance of the terms are absolute. Hirsch's view of writing and reading skills as culture-bound makes good sense. The issue in regard to cultural identity, however, is that of the relevance of the content for the reader or writer. What does a particular concept symbolize in relation to the individual's sense of self as group member and in relation to the state of intergroup relations in the society? In literacy education, attention must be given not only to teaching lists of important facts, but to develop individual skill in exploring the relationship of these facts to the self. Students must be encouraged to discover and decide for themselves – in the context of their cultural identity – what information and what values are conveyed. What makes a particular fact important and for whom? For example, the value attached to the concept *Crusades*, and even what is described by it, will probably be quite different for a Jewish, a Christian, and a Moslem individual. Thus, in the United States, the drive to educate all students about a set of "facts" in the name of literacy education can be seen by minorities as a thinly veiled guise for the imposition of a particular type of cultural identity. This way of pushing one version of knowledge may simply serve to allow the dominant group to maintain its position while still espousing democratic and meritocratic values.

How then can teachers and other educators better acknowledge their students' cultural identity and consider it in planning and providing more effective literacy education? I suggest that the first step in this process involves turning inward. Before helping others to do so, one must initially explore one's own values and attitudes about ethnic diversity, as well as one's degree of awareness of the role culture plays in one's own formation. A teacher should feel comfortable with his or her own background before attempting to delve into that of others. After doing this, I believe that educators will be more likely to adopt a strategy that recognizes cultural differences as important, but not the only source of individual variation. Teachers and other educators can become educated about other cultural forms that literacy can take and about the different cultural influences on their students. These can be incorporated into educational plans. In doing this, it is important not to automatically apply generalizations about a group to individual students. But avoiding stereotyping and over-generalization does not mean avoiding the reality of culture. Teachers can discover ways of encouraging students to explore the implications of their ethnicities and to engage in self-definition. Explicitly and positively linking classroom activities to the students' cultural identities could also be a way of motivating students; in the recent motion picture, *Stand and Deliver*, Jaime Escalante gained his students' interest through his high expectations and by connecting math to their Mayan forebears. By providing a range of literacy experiences and explicitly linking them to their cultural sources, teachers can give students more involvement and choice in their own formation.

Conclusion

I have argued that cultural diversity plays an important role in influencing the relationship of literacy and the individual. People's perceptions of themselves in relationship to their ethnic group and the larger society, as reflected in what I have called cultural identity, can change, and in turn be changed, by the process of becoming and being literate. As the United States debates alternative visions of positive ethnic relations, those advocating the goal of extending literacy to all members of the society might well incorporate a view of all individuals as cultural beings. If this is done, perhaps more sensitive and articulated models of literacy acquisition can be developed that better take into account the social context in which literacy is defined and expressed. When everyone – minority and majority alike – is encouraged and supported in the development of a clear and strong cultural identity, we may well see a society, not of excessive uniformity and constraint at the individual level or undue divisiveness at the group level, as some might suggest, but rather, a society which would permit the full range of individual variation, choice, and flexibility, while at the same time recognizing the importance group identifications hold for individuals. In such an environment, perhaps literacy can indeed become a universal characteristic.

Acknowledgements

An earlier version of this paper was presented at the First Gutenberg Conference, *Towards A More Literate America: Perspectives on School and Society*, held at SUNY/Albany, February 27–28, 1988. I am grateful to Alan Purves and to the participants at the First Gutenberg Conference for their many helpful suggestions regarding this paper. I would also like to thank Niyi Akinnaso, Ana Mari Cauce, Débora Ferdman, and Janet Powell for carefully reading and thoughtfully commenting on prior drafts.

Notes

1 *Becoming* and *being* are emphasized to stress the dynamic aspects of literacy. Rather than conceiving of literacy primarily as a passive characteristic of the individual and so considering someone to "be" literate regardless of what he or she does, in this article I focus on the active facets of literacy and on the ways in which literacy can be thought of as "a way of carrying out social transactions" (Carraher, 1988, p. 95). In this view, being literate means engaging in particular activities that so define persons as they transact with the social environment.

2 This debate itself forms part of the interethnic relations in the society. The lines dividing various points of view often follow ethnic boundaries. Moreover, the approach that is adopted has implications not just for pedagogy, but also for ethnic stratification. An example of this can be seen in the debates over bilingualism and bilingual education (for one account, see Hakuta, 1986), in which Hispanics are more likely to favor language transition programs that include a child's native Spanish over immersion programs using solely English (for example, Hakuta, 1984). We can expect that the type of program ultimately used in a particular school district will impact not only on how children learn, but also on the status and opportunities available to Hispanics in that district. It is in this sense that the struggle is over the relative power between groups and not simply an educational issue.

3 Note, for example, the proliferation of a mainstreaming policy for special populations that were previously segregated within the educational system.

4 For a useful discussion of an attributional perspective on intercultural education in multicultural societies, see Albert and Triandis (1985).

5 In their article de Castell and Luke (1983) show how the dominant definitions of literacy in American schools have shifted historically, from 19th century views that emphasized moral, religious, and civic aspects of literacy instruction, to more current views that emphasize functionality, basic skills, and measurability.

6 Reder (1987) gives the example of Hmong immigrants, who were able to produce a signature on documents, but did not comprehend what this implicated. When someone else would explain the legal implications, however, they would sometimes refuse to sign.

   Reder also points to a number of "collaborative literacy practices" in the communities he studied, in which two or more people work together to produce or decode texts. From an individualistic conception of literacy, we might view someone who requires or prefers help in reading or writing to be less literate than someone who works alone. In a different cultural context, however, it is the failure to collaborate that may be defined as less literate.

7 It must be noted that Roth's use of the term "culture" is somewhat imprecise and is more general than my usage of the term in this paper. She seems to use "culture" as a synonym for "dominant group" or "mainstream society." In either case, her use of the first person ("our" culture) is appropriate only for those groups adequately represented by the school. For those whose culture is different than that (or those) of the school, read "their" in place of "our."

8 The present analysis focuses on cultural identity as an aspect of ethnicity in a multi-ethnic society. This emphasis is not meant to suggest that other social

451

categorizations – for example, gender, race, and class – do not play an important role in linking persons to groups and therefore in helping to form individuals' identities and world view. Indeed, it is probable that similar arguments to those presented here could be constructed linking literacy to these other components of people's social selves (Babad et al., 1983). This paper, however, is restricted to exploring the relationship of literacy to cultural diversity as it derives from ethnic differences.

9 As Kochman (1987) puts it, "outgroup members are too far removed from the context in which such distinctive ingroup cultural patterns are displayed. Ingroup members, on the other hand, are often too close to their own culture to be able to see it" (p. 224).

10 By instrumentality, Jones (1988) refers to the utility of the behavior in obtaining desired outcomes.

11 Tajfel (1977) writes: "Any society which contains power, status, prestige and social group differentials (and they all do), places each of us in a number of *social* categories which become an important part of our *self*-definition (p. 654, author's emphases).

12 Because social identity may refer to any type of social group (see Tajfel, 1981; Ferdman, 1987) the concept is too broad if we are interested in focusing specifically on the individual's relationship with ethnic groups. The notion of ethnic identity, as it is defined here, is intended to serve this purpose.

13 Of course, every individual belongs to a number of social categories and so has many influences on his or her sense of self. Each of us constructs a social identity from these various components which include, in addition to ethnicity, categories such as gender, race, or socioeconomic status. The problem of how each person answers the question, "Who am I?" is complex and multifaceted. Ultimately, each individual derives a unique identity on the basis of his or her particular combination of experiences and group memberships (see Babad et al., 1983; Taylor & Dubé, 1986). Thus, although the focus here is on the ways in which ethnicity and culture influence a person's identity, this is not meant to suggest that these are mutually exclusive with other social categories. Indeed, there are interactions between group memberships such that being African American is incorporated differently by a middle-class woman than a working-class man.

14 Within-group variation in cultural identity need not be idiosyncratic. Differences in individuals' cultural identities could be systematically associated with other factors – socioeconomic status or place of residence, for example. We might expect that, in general, wealthy members of the English nobility will not have the same conception of what it means to be English as will poor laborers in Liverpool, in spite of a shared ethnic identification. A recent immigrant from Mexico living in a poor neighborhood of Los Angeles might have a different conception of Hispanic culture than a sixth-generation landowner in New Mexico, although both identify as Latinos.

It should be noted that the construct of cultural identity is not meant to replace concepts such as social class. Although social class can interact with ethnicity in producing an individual's cultural identity, it can also operate independently to influence values, behavior, and experience. The concept of cultural identity, however, permits understanding some of the differences between members of the same social class who come from different ethnic backgrounds.

15 The term "minority group" is used here in the sociological sense to mean a group with less power than the dominant group and whose members are

treated unequally and in an inferior manner in society (Feagin, 1984; Shaefer, 1988).

16 The question on the survey reads as follows: "If you had to move again, where would you like to move?" Respondents could mark one of five answers: 1) would stay in the same neighborhood, 2) would move to a different neighborhood, 3) would move to Puerto Rico, 4) would move to a different country (specify), or 5) would move to another city or state (specify).

17 I use the term *cultural products* to signify how all that is taught in schools is culturally produced.

18 In such a context, groups previously considered "minorities," groups whose members' cultural identity is largely disparaged within the society, could cease to be so designated. Groups could be understood in terms of their specific features and their uniqueness rather than in terms of their relative dominance and subordination.

References

Akinnaso, F. N. (1981). The consequences of literacy in pragmatic and theoretical perspectives. *Anthropology and Education Quarterly, 12*, 163–200.

Akinnaso, F. N. (1982). On the differences between spoken and written language. *Language and Speech, 25*, 97–125.

Akinnaso, F. N. (1985). On the similarities between spoken and written language. *Language and Speech, 28*, 324–359.

Albert, R. D., & Triandis, H. C. (1985). Intercultural education for multicultural societies: Critical issues. *International Journal of Intercultural Relations, 9*, 319–337.

Babad, E. Y., Birnbaum, M., & Benne, K. D. (1983). *The social self: Group influences on personal identity.* Beverly Hills, CA: Sage.

Ball, P., Giles, H., & Hewstone, M. (1984). Second language acquisition: The intergroup theory with catastrophic dimensions. In H. Tajfel, C. Fraser, & J. Jaspars (Eds.), *The social dimension: European developments in social psychology* (Vol. 2). Cambridge: Cambridge University Press.

Banks, J. A. (1977). *Multiethnic education: Practices and promises.* Bloomington, IN: Phi Delta Kappa Educational Foundation.

Banks, J. A. (1981). *Multiethnic education: Theory and practice.* Boston: Allyn and Bacon.

Banks, J. A. (1987). *Teaching strategies for ethnic studies* (4th ed.). Boston: Allyn and Bacon.

Berry, J. W. (1983). Acculturation: A comparative analysis of alternative forms. In R. Samuda & S. Woods (Eds.), *Perspectives in immigrant and minority education.* New York: University Press of America.

Berry, J. W. (1986). Multiculturalism and psychology in plural societies. In L. H. Ekstrand (Ed.), *Ethnic minorities and immigrants in a cross-cultural perspective* (pp. 35–51). Berwyn, NY: Swets North America.

Boekestijn, C. (1988). Intercultural migration and the development of personal identity: The dilemma between identity maintenance and cultural adaptation. *International Journal of Intercultural Relations, 12*, 83–105.

Carraher, T. N. (1988). Illiteracy in a literate society: Understanding reading failure in Brazil. In D. A. Wagner (Ed.), *The future of literacy in a changing world* (pp. 95–110). Oxford: Pergamon Press.

Cook-Gumperz, J. (Ed.) (1986). *The social construction of literacy*. Cambridge: Cambridge University Press.

Cummins, J. (1986). Empowering minority students: A framework for intervention. *Harvard Educational Review*, 56, 18–36.

de Castell, S., & Luke, A. (1983). Defining 'literacy' in North American schools: Social and historical conditions and consequences. *Journal of Curriculum Studies*, 15, 373–389.

de Castell, S., & Luke, A. (1987). Literacy instruction: Technology and technique. *American Journal of Education*, 95, 413–440.

Deschamps, J. (1982). Social identity and relations of power between groups. In H. Tajfel (Ed.), *Social identity and intergroup relations* (pp. 85–98). Cambridge: Cambridge University Press.

Erickson, F. (1984). School literacy, reasoning, and civility: An anthropologist's perspective. *Review of Educational Research*, 54, 525–546.

Feagin, J. R. (1989). *Racial and Ethnic Relations* (3rd ed.). Englewood Cliffs, NJ: Prentice Hall.

Ferdman, B. M. (1987). *Person perception in interethnic situations*. Unpublished manuscript, Department of Psychology, Yale University, New Haven.

Ferdman, B. M. (1988, August). Values and fairness in the ethnically diverse workplace. In Faye Crosby (Chair), *Emancipation, justice and affirmative action*. Symposium conducted at the 2nd International Conference on Social Justice and Societal Problems, University of Leiden, Netherlands.

Ferdman, B. M. (1989). Affirmative action and the challenge of the color-blind perspective. In F. Blanchard & F. Crosby (Eds.), *Affirmative action in perspective* (pp. 169–176). New York: Springer-Verlag.

Ferdman, B. M., & Hakuta, K. (1985, August). Group and individual bilingualism in an ethnic minority. In K. Hakuta & B. M. Ferdman (Co-chairs), *Bilingualism: Social psychological reflections*. Symposium conducted at the meetings of the American Psychological Association, Los Angeles.

Flores, J. (1985). "Que assimilated, brother, yo soy asimilao": The structuring of Puerto Rican identity in the U.S. *Journal of Ethnic Studies*, 13, 1–16.

Ginorio, A. B. (1987). Puerto Rican ethnicity and conflict. In J. Boucher, D. Landis, & K. A. Clark (Eds.), *Ethnic conflict: International perspectives* (pp. 182–206). Newbury Park, CA: Sage.

Giroux, H. A. (1987). Critical literacy and student experience: Donald Graves' approach to literacy. *Language Arts*, 64, 175–181.

Gleason, P. (1982). American identity and Americanization. In W. Petersen, M. Novak, & P. Gleason, *Concepts of ethnicity* (pp. 57–143). Cambridge: Harvard University Press.

Goody, J. (1977). *The domestication of the savage mind*. Cambridge: Cambridge University Press.

Goody, J. (1982). Alternative paths to knowledge in oral and literate cultures. In D. Tannen (Ed.), *Spoken and written language: Exploring orality and literacy* (pp. 201–215). Norwood, NJ: Ablex.

Goody, J. (1986). *The logic of writing and the organization of society*. Cambridge: Cambridge University Press.

Goody, J., & Watt, I. (1963). The consequences of literacy. *Comparative studies in society and history*, 5, 304–345.

Gordon, M. (1985). Models of pluralism: The new American dilemma. In N. R. Yetman, *Majority and minority: The dynamics of race and ethnicity in American life*, 4th edition (pp. 523–530). Boston: Allyn and Bacon. Reprinted from M. Gordon (1981), Models of Pluralism: The new American dilemma. *The Annals of the American Academy of Political and Social Science*, 454.

Graves, T. D. (1967). Psychological acculturation in a tri-ethnic community. *Southwestern Journal of Anthropology*, *23*, 337–350.

Guiora, A. Z. (1985, August). The psychodynamic aspects of bilingualism. In K. Hakuta & B. M. Ferdman (Co-chairs), *Bilingualism: Social psychological reflections*. Symposium conducted at the meetings of the American Psychological Association, Los Angeles.

Guillaumin, C. (1972). *L'idéologie raciste: Genèse et langage actual*. Paris: Mouton.

Hakuta, K. (1984). Bilingual education in the public eye: A case study of New Haven, Connecticut. *NABE Journal*, *9*, 53–76.

Hakuta, K. (1986). *Mirror of language: The debate on bilingualism*. New York: Basic Books.

Hakuta, K., Ferdman, B. M., & Diaz, R. M. (1987). Bilingualism and cognitive development: Three perspectives. In S. Rosenberg (Ed.), *Advances in applied psycholinguistics, Volume 2: Reading, writing and language learning* (pp. 284–319). New York: Cambridge University Press.

Heath, S. B. (1986). The functions and uses of literacy. In S. de Castell, A. Luke, & K. Egan (Eds.), *Literacy, society, and schooling: A reader* (pp. 15–26). Cambridge: Cambridge University Press.

Heller, M. (1987). The role of language in the formation of ethnic identity. In J. S. Phinney & M. J. Rotheram (Eds.), *Children's ethnic socialization: Pluralism and development* (pp. 180–200). Newbury Park, CA: Sage.

Herman, S. N. (1977). *Jewish identity: A social psychological perspective*. Beverly Hills, CA: Sage.

Hirsch, E. D. (1987). *Cultural literacy: What every American needs to know*. Boston: Houghton Mifflin.

Jones, J. M. (1988). Racism in black and white: A bicultural model of reaction and evolution. In P. A. Katz & D. A. Taylor (Eds.), *Eliminating racism: Profiles in controversy* (pp. 117–135). New York: Plenum.

Kádár-Fülop, J. (1988). Culture, writing and curriculum. In A. C. Purves (Ed.), *Writing across languages and cultures: Issues in contrastive rhetoric* (pp. 25–50). Newbury Park, CA: Sage.

Keefe, S. E., & Padilla, A. M. (1987). *Chicano ethnicity*. Albuquerque: University of New Mexico Press.

Kochman, T. (1987). The ethnic component in Black language and culture. In J. S. Phinney & M. J. Rotheram (Eds.), *Children's ethnic socialization: Pluralism and development* (pp. 219–238). Newbury Park, CA: Sage.

Matute-Bianchi, M. E. (1986). Ethnic identities and patterns of school success and failure among Mexican-descent and Japanese-American students in a California high school: An ethnographic analysis. *American Journal of Education*, *95*, 233–255.

McEvedy, M. R. (1986). Some social, cultural and linguistic issues in teaching reading to children who speak English as a second language. *Australian Journal of Reading*, *9*, 139–152.

Montero, M. (1987). A través del espejo: Una aproximación teórica al estudio de la conciencia social en América Latina. In M. Montero (Ed.), *Psicologia política latino-americana* (pp. 163–202). Caracas: Editorial Panapo.

Ong, W. (1982). *Orality and literacy: The technologizing of the word*. London: Methuen.

Purves, A. C. (1987). Literacy, culture and community. In D. A. Wagner (Ed.), *The future of literacy in a changing world* (pp. 216–232). Oxford: Pergamon Press.

Reder, S. M. (1987). Comparative aspects of functional literacy development: Three ethnic American communities. In D. A. Wagner (Ed.), *The future of literacy in a changing world* (pp. 250–270). Oxford: Pergamon Press.

Roth, R. (1984). Schooling, literacy acquisition and cultural transmission. *Journal of Education, 166*, 291–308.

Said, E. W. (1983). *The world, the text, and the critic*. Cambridge: Harvard University Press.

Scollon, R., & Scollon, S. (1981). *Narrative, literacy and face in interethnic communication*. Norwood, NJ: Ablex.

Scribner, S. (1986). Literacy in three metaphors. In N. L. Stein (Ed.), *Literacy in American schools: Learning to read and write* (pp. 7–22). Chicago: University of Chicago Press.

Scribner, S., & Cole, M. (1981). *The psychology of literacy*. Cambridge: Harvard University Press.

Shaefer, R. T. (1984). *Racial and ethnic groups* (3rd ed.). Glenview, IL: Scott, Forsman.

Smolicz, J. (1981). Core values and cultural identity. *Ethnic and racial studies, 4*, 75–90.

Tajfel, H. (1978). *The social psychology of minorities*. London: Minority Rights Group.

Tajfel, H. (1981). *Human groups and social categories*. Cambridge: Cambridge University Press.

Tajfel, H., & Turner, J. C. (1986). The social identity theory of intergroup relations. In S. Worchel & W. Austin (Eds.), *Psychology of intergroup relations* (pp. 7–24). Chicago: Nelson-Hall.

Taylor, D. M., & Dubé, L. (1986). Two faces of identity: The "I" and the "we." *Journal of Social Issues, 42*, 89–98.

Taylor, D. M., & McKirnan, D. J. (1984). A five-stage model of intergroup relations. *British Journal of Social Psychology, 23*, 291–300.

Thurow, L. C. (1987). Affirmative action in a zero-sum society. In R. Takaki (Ed.), *From different shores: Perspectives on race and ethnicity in America* (pp. 225–230). New York: Oxford University Press. [Reprinted from Thurow, L. C. (1980). *The zero-sum society: Distribution and the possibilities for economic change*. New York: Basic Books.]

Triandis, H. C. (1972). *The analysis of subjective culture*. New York: Wiley.

Trueba, H. T. (1984). The forms, functions, and values of literacy: Reading for survival in a barrio as a student. *NABE Journal, 9*, 21–38.

Wallace, C. (1986). *Learning to read in a multicultural society: The social context of second language literacy*. Oxford: Pergamon Press.

456

20

(SUB)VERSIONS

Using sexist language practices to explore critical literacy

Pam Gilbert

Source: *The Australian Journal of Language and Literacy* (1993) 16(4): 323–331

In January this year, a Sydney magistrate dismissed charges of malicious damage made against four women who had added text to, or 'defaced' (as the police claimed), a lingerie billboard advertisement. In a surprising and – I suspect – unprecedented move in this country, the magistrate, Ms Pat O'Shane, was quoted in a newspaper report as saying that 'the real crime' had actually been perpetrated by the advertisers, whose advertisement featured the text 'You'll always feel good in Berlei' above the visual image of a woman in underwear cut in half by a saw wielding magician (see note). The four women had added the words 'Even if you're mutilated' above the original Berlei ad, in an attempt to make, as one of the women charged with the offence claimed in a newspaper report, 'a feminist political statement subverting the advertising text to raise the awareness of sexist advertising'.

In this paper, I want to suggest that an examination of issues associated with this particular and contemporary social incident raises a number of important considerations in any discussion of 'critical literacy', both in terms of how we might want to define critical literacy as a concept for the classroom, and in terms of how we might begin to address it at the level of practice. I want to suggest that the incident demonstrates key questions about reading and the making of textual meaning, and about what we have often fairly loosely described as 'the social context' of a particular text: the web of discourses within which any text is inextricably entwined, and within which readers and writers of texts are inextricably entwined. More importantly it can demonstrate how language practices associated with the construction of gender can often provide a powerful site for work with critical literacy.

Critical literacy in the classroom

I would argue that if critical literacy is to mean anything of significance to us as educators in the nineties, it has to address the practices by which words enact social meaning, and the practices by which we, as social subjects, make meaning. It has to address how it is that social subjects are able to make the range of meanings they are able to make – the repertoires of readings they have access to – and it is has to address how these repertoires can be broadened. If literacy in its most basic sense is about having access to the practices involved in the making and re-making of textual meaning (about being able to write and to read), then critical literacy must be about an exploration of those practices in terms of the social meanings such practices implicitly (and perhaps explicitly) authorize or silence.

But herein lies the crunch. As most educators who have worked with critical language study in the classroom know only too well, classroom practices that will engage students with the social context of literacy are difficult to construct and to enact. The social context of literacy learning has still, as work by Kress (1985), or Gee (1990), or Luke (1993) amply demonstrates, some distance to travel in classrooms, because the issues associated with a 'critical' literacy are complex. How, for instance, can students learn about the social context of language, unless they are able to experience the impact of actual language practices in contexts that are of interest and concern to them?

In his study of social linguistics and literacies, Gee draws a distinction between what he calls 'acquisition' and 'learning', arguing that a Discourse – his term for 'a socially accepted, association among ways of using language, of thinking, feeling, believing, valuing, and of acting that can be used to identify oneself as a member of a socially meaningful group or 'social network' (p. 143) – is not mastered through learning. It can only be mastered by acquisition: by experiencing it in functional settings through 'a master-apprentice relationship in a social practice' (p.154).

A grasp of 'critical' literacy – of what I would call the social contextualization of language practices – necessitates a grasp of how language operates in a social sense. And I would agree with Gee that such understandings are learnt in functional settings and can not be divorced from social practice. To work with a commitment to *critical* literacy, therefore, will inevitably necessitate an engagement with the politics of language practices, and examples from Lankshear (1989), Freebody (1992), and Walkerdine (1990) have demonstrated what this might reveal in terms of group oppression through ethnicity, socio-economic status, or gender. To explore the social context of language practices is inevitably to explore the networks of power that are sustained and brought into existence by such practices. It is to explore how language practices are used in powerful social institutions like the state, the school, the law, the family, the church, and how those practices contribute to the maintenance of inequalities and injustices. For teachers, it means engaging with issues that are often controversial, certainly contemporary, and perhaps quite volatile.

So: of what value is the Berlei ad incident in terms of exploring both the complexities of critical literacy, and the possible ways we might work with language and the social in classrooms? I suggest that it raises three key questions which are fundamental to working with critical literacy, and in the remainder of this paper I will address each one. Initially, the incident illustrates the potential of working with 'real' texts, 'real' social practice, 'real' cultural networks and groupings. In this case the text is enmeshed within a range of social attitudes, values, and assumptions about gender relationships a field of social knowledge that, I would argue, all contemporary Australians have access to, albeit in a range of ways and from a number of different positions.

Secondly, it provides a demonstration of how different 'readings' or meanings can be made from texts, dependent upon the way in which a reader is positioned in relation to a text. Consequently it offers the possibility of exploring a range of readings and how they have been made, and invites consideration of why one reading has been privileged over another. Finally, the incident also provides compelling evidence of the impossibility of reading in a social vacuum. The meanings that were made of this text were possible, because the readers drew differently upon the cultural context. The original advertising text, and its later graffiti addition, can not be made sense of in terms of just the words and images on the page, as if they had no history or context.

Language practices and social constructions of 'femininity' and 'masculinity'

Texts that address issues of gender particularly as in this example where the central issue is about male violence to women allow entry to particular social practices, if only implicitly, to at least fifty percent of students. *All* women experience the impact of violence, aggression and domination from men to women. Although they may not be able to name such actions or recognize them as oppression, they have *lived* them.

Young women almost daily encounter verbal and perhaps physical harassment in the playground, on their way to school, in casual employment, at parties. They almost daily encounter magazine and billboard images of women in humiliating poses for the male gaze; television images of women being chased, hunted, attacked, raped; news reportage of horrendous assaults, abductions, rapes and murders of women and girls by single men or groups of men. To actually name these practices and to cluster them together as part of a whole pattern, makes for such an uncomfortable picture of the future for a woman, that most of our female students, not surprisingly, choose not to speak about them. But they *know* them at the level of lived experience.

And so do young men, although in a different way. They know the taunts and jeers that both mock women, and keep young men within narrowly accepted bands of masculinity. 'Look at your man!' 'Don't be a girl'. 'You're just an old woman.' They know the physical pushing, grabbing, fondling. They know the jokes, the put-downs, the insults. They know the power that comes from being male, and the weakness that comes from being deemed non-male. They know gender relations and the construction of femininity and masculinity at the level of real language and real action.

Texts that specifically look at issues of conflict between the sexes – or look at specific representations of women and men – allow students the opportunity to work with known experience perhaps in different ways. Issues of equity and 'a fair go' are easy ones for children to latch on to and support, and there is increasing evidence that quite young children can understand more complex matters like sexist language practices and discriminatory social organisation. They may find such matters upsetting and disturbing, because they represent a challenge to much that has been taken for granted, but they are quite able to see the unfairness or narrowness of events surrounding them, if they have access to a discourse or set of language practices which names inequity and narrowness.

The construction of gender is such a dominating set of social practices in our culture that it provides a rich field of shared experiences for working with in the classroom. In addition, as most State Departments of Education move towards policies of social justice and equal employment opportunity, gender equity has become almost an authorized field of inquiry. An examination of sexist language practices in our culture could hardly today be deemed controversial or volatile. On the contrary, it would seem to be a field of investigation that would support much of the thinking behind any text-context language policies, or behind any social context language programs.

Textual meaning and textual authority

However the Berlei ad incident provides more than just an example of the potential of gender relations as a common set of social experiences to draw upon in exploring language practices. While material like this can clearly provide an entry point for many students, it also illustrates key issues about reading and textual authority in a way that makes such meanings accessible.

What does this particular billboard text 'mean'? Quite clearly it means different things to the different people involved in the incident. Its meaning depends on who reads it, for what purpose, and in what context. It has no singular, finite and static meaning. And yet as this incident demonstrates well, once a text is loosed from its authorized, legitimated meaning, the conditions of possibility for that authorized meaning become accessible for investigation.

Attempts to tie a text to a single 'reading' usually serve the interests of powerful social institutions: institutions which rely upon a tightly controlled set of social practices for their operation. The legitimacy and author-ity of many of these institutions (like the law, some religions and certain political orthodoxies) depend upon the controlling of social meaning, and the exposure of such practices is surely fair game for the critical literacy classroom. Key questions could then be: whose interests are best served by the single meaning so authorized? why is it important in particular contexts to *control* meaning, and make other readings appear 'wrong', politically motivated or just naive?

In the Berlei incident these issues become foregrounded. The 'meaning' of the ad became central to the event. A spokesperson (a woman) from the agency handling the Berlei account offered a reading which we could probably regard as a 'dominant' reading: the reading many Australians might make of such an advertisement. The spokesperson claimed that the concept used in the billboard ad was well-recognized as a 'clichéd magic trick'. It was not, she said, a violent situation.

Like a second ad in the series, in which a woman in her underwear was trapped in the hand of King Kong, the ads claim to have been intended to be harmless, rather off-beat attempts to promote Berlei products. They merely provided, the spokesperson said, images of 'women in situations they would not normally find themselves in but still feeling comfortable in Berlei'. In this authorized, yet really quite bizarre reading, an association with violence and misogyny for the near-naked woman and the saw is ruled out. Both these elements of the design of the text were to be read as incidental and irrelevant to its function of selling underwear. The graffiti artists were said to have missed the point. They had mis-read the text.

I suggest that the five women graffiti artists were well aware of the authorized reading that would be offered of the Berlei ad – the reading which had made it possible in the first place for the ad to be mounted on a billboard and displayed prominently in a busy urban area in a contemporary Australian city. But they made another reading of the text which undermined its smiling innocuousness and foregrounded instead the mutilation of a partly clothed woman. They resisted the dominant reading which read female semi-nakedness and injury as normal and acceptable in contexts aimed to sell by attracting attention. Instead they read both of those elements as dangerous and un-acceptable in a society which has high statistics for male violence to women, while claiming to promote equity, justice, and safety for all of its citizens.

Their argument was that the text could be read differently: that its linking together of a partly clothed woman smiling while she was being sawn in half made unavoidable connections with a vast sadistic pornography industry and an increasing incidence of horrendously violent and misogynist sexual attacks on women. And the surprising and extraordinary feature of this incident was that the magistrate agreed with them. She supported the women: she made a similar reading.

Rather than authorizing the legitimacy of the 'populist' or dominant reading of this advertisement – a reading which was only possible if the text was severed from other texts related to the mutilation of women – she supported a 'resistant' reading which lined the text up within discourses of violence and misogyny. She read *against* the reading argued for by the advertising agency: she read against an a-political reading. Yet this 'reader' was positioned powerfully within the institution of the law as a magistrate, within an institution which relies upon the practice of isolating and tying down a single textual meaning.

I suggest that the reading offered by the magistrate would have been a surprise to the women graffiti artists and to the ad agency.

> Account Director Belinda Fookes said she was 'a little surprised' that a judge should be condoning a crime against a paid advertiser.

And it is here that a whole range of issues to do with critical literacy can be considered. What 'readings' are commonly made by the judiciary on issues associated with women? Why? And whose interests are supported by such readings? One of the first questions the new nominee for President Bill Clinton's Attorney General post was asked by reporters was if she was a feminist. Are new male appointments to the High Court similarly asked if they are patriarchs or masculinists? The temptation here is to suggest that the history of legal readings indicates that the law has not often been able to read through the lens offered by feminism. It has not been able to read women's oppression; it has not been able to read male violence.

A feminist position provides a reading frame through which to filter various social practices in terms of how they work, and for whom they work. It offers ways through which oppressive, unjust, and violent social practices can be recognized, resisted, and perhaps reduced. There may be no single approach to feminism (and no single 'feminism'), but for classrooms, a straight-forward approach which regards gender as a social construction held largely in place by a range of social practices – many of them language practices – is a starting point.

Such an approach provides students with a reading frame through which to make other (subversive?) meanings of many of the social language practices of families, schools and the electronic and print media. Basic practices like learning how to recognize sexist road signs, electronic games, and terms of abuse, or learning how to notice inequitable representation of women and men in books, TV programs, films and magazines, are obvious and relatively easy starting points. Gender is not difficult to read, once students have appropriate reading frames. Then the possibility exists for reading subversively in other areas: for reading against a commonsense, preferred and populist set of meanings and foregrounding unfair, unjust and dangerous practices.

Intertextuality and critical literacy

Reading can then be part of a real attempt to read the social: to make sense of the texts and signs of our culture. It becomes functional, connected, integrated. Once reading is freed of the shackles of locating a singular and authoritative textual meaning, it can instead focus on how meanings are made, and how different readings can be made by different groups of people, for different purposes. This will mean recognising both the positions that readers take up in relation to texts, and the discourses that are brought into play by different readers and different readings. It will mean focussing on the intertextual experiences of readers, and the intertextual connections between social texts. In the Berlei incident, commercial discourses which justify the display of female flesh as a marketing strategy dominated in the construction of the advertising text. This is not surprising: these are recognisable conventions for that particular text-type. Female bodies have been commonly used as a marketing strategy for the sale of most things: beer, cars, holidays in sunny Queensland, classical music concerts, homes, boats ... I think it highly unlikely that students would be surprised or puzzled by the visual combination of two such disconnected images as a bikini-clad model and a can of car upholstery cleaner in a magazine advertisement. They know the reading expected: they have lived with the social reality of this construction of women through magazines, films, posters, TV shows, newspaper articles, all of their lives. And they have also lived with advertisements that constantly push that association to include discourses of violation to women's bodies. Take, for instance, the challenge recently to the 'good clean fun' beer ad which showed a woman's clothing being ripped off by a dog.

However in this particular Berlei advertising incident, the reading which legitimated the use of a partly clothed female body as a commercial marketing strategy, was subverted and challenged. A group of women wanted to provide a social warning that other discourses were implicated and given legitimacy by this particular combination: that the text had other readings, some of which were very dangerous to women. They wanted a connection seen between documented social violence to women and the prevalence of advertising texts which sold products through the display of female flesh in humiliating, demeaning, or dangerous situations.

They wanted other readings of this text freed so that they could be named and recognized. They wanted connections made between this text and other texts which harm women. They wanted to emphasize the impossibility and naivety of arguing that an image of a near-naked woman smiling while she was being sawn in half had nothing to do with social violence against women. They wanted the social context of this text restored.

Conclusions

Contemporary social texts – like this particular one reporting on the actions of a group of women – offer rich possibilities for exploring key language issues.

- How are readings or meanings made of texts?
- Why do people make different or 'subversive' readings? How is this possible?
- What is the effect of certain readings upon social action and social life?

In this paper I have suggested that texts associated with the social construction of gender relations provide useful starting points for exploring these issues. Gendered language practices are so obvious, so prevalent, and, I have suggested, so accessible to students – *if* students are introduced to a few fairly simple feminist reading frames. Then the social world starts to look a little different, as even young children are able to recognize.

The social construction of gender through language practices provides an obvious window through which to interrogate the authority of a text, and an obvious window through which to explore how social practices and language practices are entwined. It fairly simply explodes the myth that textual meanings are fixed and determined, and demonstrates how important it is to understand the discursive histories of both readers and writers in the making of textual meanings. Once students are able to read and name sexist practices to (sub)vert dominant and more obvious readings then, I suspect, they can understand the critical dimension to literacy.

References

Department of Education, Employment and Training (in press) *The construction of gender at the P-3 level of schooling: Report from a Gender Equity in Curriculum Reform Project.*

Freebody, P. *Inventing cultural-capitalist distinctions in the assessment of HSC papers: Coping with inflation in an era of 'literacy crisis'.* Paper presented at the Inaugural Australian Systemics Conference on Literacy Social Processes. January, 1990.

Gee, J. *Social linguistics and literacies.* London: Falmer. 1990

Gilbert, P. and Taylor, S. *Fashioning the feminine: Girls, popular culture and schooling*. Allen and Unwin: Sydney. 1991.

Kress, G. *Linguistic processes and socio-cultural practice*. Deakin University Press: Geelong, Vic. 1985.

Lankshear, C. Getting it right is hard: redressing the politics of literacy in the 1990's. In Australian Reading Association *Literacy: making it explicit, making it possible*. ARA Annual Conference Papers. 209–228 1991.

Luke, A. *The social construction of literacy in the primary school*. Macmillan: Sydney. 1993.

Walkerdine, W. *Schoolgirl Fictions*. Verso: London, 1990.

21

SHOW MUM YOU LOVE HER

Taking a new look at junk mail

Jennifer O'Brien

Source: *Reading* (1994) 28(1): 43–46

Pink and gold . . .

A jeweller's catalogue sits in front of me as I write. It came through my letterbox on April 19th. The cover shows a full colour photograph of a gold watch, a deep red jewellery box, a gold pen, a pink bow and a card reading *To Mum With Love*. Mothers' Day is on May 9th. There's clearly plenty of time for families to mull over the gift suggestions and decide how they'll reward Mum this year.

Last year, as the avalanche of Mothers' Day catalogues poured into my letter box and tumbled out of newspapers, I decided that they were an everyday text crying out to be approached from a new perspective. I wanted to offer my 5–7 year old students a different way of looking at a ritual as taken-for-granted as Mothers' Day and the advertising material that accompanies it.

In this article I want to show how I have taken up some of the specific insights of researchers and theorists to make changes to the reading and writing in my classroom. I want to show how the conversations I have with my students and the activities that I design around texts are framed with a different, critical edge. I want to bring together three key notions concerning literacy. First, it is important for students to learn to analyse their texts; second, children need to learn ways of dealing with texts from the world outside school and third, teachers need to show their students possibilities for looking closely at texts that are normally taken-for-granted. In short, it is crucial for students and teachers together to add to the ways in which they presently deal with texts.

Analytical readers . . .

Freebody and Luke (1990) argue that successful readers in our society operate in four different ways. They "break the code" so they can read the words on the page; they read to make sense of the text; they read to make use of the text, perhaps as a source of information; and they analyse or ask questions of the text.

Baker and Freebody (1989) also make a strong case for extending the roles that young students take on as readers; in addition to operating as hearers of stories, they can explore with their teacher ways of analysing texts. (p. 197)

It is this analytical role that my students and I are exploring in my classroom; my aim is to offer my students opportunities to ask questions about the messages they receive in things they read.

Everyday texts...

Baker and Freebody (1989) maintain that literacy instruction in the early years of schooling does more than teach children to read and write; it plays a critical role in introducing them to a version of literacy referred to by these researchers as "school-literacy". (p. xix) They point out that the reading usually practised at school, involving literature and books written for use in the classroom, is a very specific literacy which fails to take account of the many texts students come across in everyday life. Teachers need, therefore, to introduce to our students ways of tackling the myriad texts that fill the world outside school.

As I shall show in this paper, I have taken up this recommendation that reading lessons could include out-of-school texts. I have framed the Mothers' Day catalogue activities so that my students have opportunities to deal with a range of questions regarding text functions, the interests of the writers and the construction of the reader. (Baker and Freebody [1989] p. 195)

Finally, Lankshear's (1989) arguments for "a proper literacy" for young students have had a strong impact on my own classroom practice, encouraging me to draw the conclusion that it is crucial that students acquire, share, and consider their own knowledge.

Questioning commonsense understandings...

Freebody and Luke (1990) argue that an important component of being a successful reader is learning to question the commonsense understandings that allow us to take for granted texts and the way they represent the world. In the classroom, our conversations, questions and tasks are framed critically so that my students and I can explore texts in this new way.

I decided to take up the challenge of opening up to my students' inspection the whole subject of something as "natural" and unquestioned as Mothers' Day.

I want to give you a chance to think in new ways about Mothers' Day catalogues ... what happened

My overall aim was to set tasks that would give students a chance to think about the version of reality constructed by the text and to think about different possibilities for constructing reality. In other words, to consider the broad question, What sort of world is constructed in and by this text; what other possible worlds could have been constructed?

The process

- We started with piles of catalogues on the students' tables. Younger and older children sat together, as they usually did, so that they could work together.
- Each section of this activity consisted of a half page giving each student a space to draw and label in response to each critically-framed activity.
- Before students tackled each section, we talked about what I was asking them to think about and to do, and my reasons for designing the activity.
- After each page had been completed, we talked over what they had drawn and written and their reasons for what they had chosen.
- At the end everyone had a set of half pages which we stapled into booklets.

Page by page ...

- Page 1: Before you look inside these catalogues, draw and label 6 presents for mothers you expect to see in Mothers' Day catalogues.

My aim here was to find a way to bring students' **commonsense knowledge** to the fore so it could be examined.

- Page 2. Draw and label some presents you wouldn't expect to find in Mothers' Day catalogues.

Here, I made it possible for students to **examine their commonsense knowledge** through the process of putting what was expected and what was not expected side by side.

- Page 3. Look through the catalogues. Draw and label 6 kinds of presents you can find in Mothers' Day catalogues.

Children now looked at the world as represented in the catalogues.

- Page 4. What groups of people get the most out of Mothers' Day?

I made it possible to examine reality by asking the **critically framed question** rarely asked at this level. I have interrupted the taken for granted and opened up a way to start to look differently at a largely unexamined aspect of the world outside school.

- Page 5. Draw and label any presents you were surprised to find.

Here I was looking to jolt students' commonsense view of the way things are, to disrupt their expectations.

- Page 6. Make two lists: How the mothers in the catalogues are like real mothers … How the mothers in the catalogues aren't like real mothers.

Children were able to consider contradictions with the world of their own experience.

- Page 8. Make a new Mothers' Day catalogue full of fun things instead of clothes and things for the house.

This activity made it possible to consider other ways in which mothers could be represented apart from the pretty in pink/utilitarian image in most of the catalogues.

Reflecting on what happened

A positive view

All students, including the youngest, were able to respond at a level appropriate to their age and ability as a consequence of my framing of instructions (*Draw and label*), the whole-class talk throughout the entire episode, and the mixed-age seating arrangements.

In a number of ways, this activity made space for my students to engage in the range of successful reading roles (Freebody and Luke 1990) and to share and consider their own knowledge. They were able to identify and represent their own view of the world; to accept the challenge of comparing their view of the world and the view presented in the catalogues; and to imagine and represent a different reality from that of their experience and that of the text.

I was pleased because while they were having fun class members were engaged in talking about issues, such as who benefits from the commercialization of Mothers' Day and the representation of mothers in junk mail.

The episode offered my students a chance to develop critical understandings of their world; to examine the catalogues' claim to be a "natural" part of their everyday world.

Making changes

Aware of the limitations of activities which view critically only the visual representation of society, I have designed the following activities to offer older school students and adults opportunities to take a critical look at a largely unexamined part of their world. I have drawn their attention to the way language is used to construct reality, and to the critical issue of the positioning of readers in and by texts. In addition, I have framed the tasks around written rather than pictured responses.

Make lists of the following:

- The words that are used about mothers.
- The words that are placed near the word "mother".
- The sorts of shops that publish catalogues.

Put these people:
mothers ... fathers ... children ... grandmothers ... grandfathers ... aunts ... uncles ... friends **into groups** under these headings:

- MEANT TO BE READERS OF MOTHERS' DAY CATALOGUES
- PROBABLY NOT MEANT TO BE READERS OF MOTHERS'S DAY CATALOGUES

Talk about the decisions you've made.
   Talk about these questions:

- What do the women like who get these presents?
- What do they do?
- What are they interested in?
- If you only knew about mothers from these catalogues, what would you be able to say about them?

Look at this list of groups of people who have something to do with Mothers' Day:

- Mothers
- Fathers
- Children
- Shopkeepers

Write down what you think are the good things about Mothers' Day and the not-so-good things for the people in each group.

Make lists of

- The words the writer uses to make you want to buy these things
- Words the writer *wouldn't* have used with these pictures
- The words the writer uses most. What message does this give you?

References

BAKER, Carolyn and FREEBODY, Peter (1989) *Children's first school books: Introductions to the culture of literacy*. Oxford: Basil Blackwell.

FREEBODY, P. and LUKE, A. (1990) "Literacies programs: Debates and demands in cultural context" in *Prospect: Australian Journal of E.S.L.* Vol 5 No 3, 1990.

LANKSHEAR, Colin with LAWLER, Moira (1989) *Literacy, schooling and revolution*. New York: The Falmer Press.

22

CLASSROOM EXPLORATIONS IN CRITICAL LITERACY

Barbara Comber

Source: *The Australian Journal of Language and Literacy* (1993) 16(1): 73–83

> Yeah, your brain would have taken it in, like if you just read that book, another book which is the same story line or something, ah your brain will just take it in unconsciously; and you just read it like, 'Oh the mum's staying home and she cooked terrible meals and blah blah blah' that's funny, isn't it? You mightn't take it in, you know, serious; and you wouldn't know that you would and it might come up somewhere else, like you're listening to the radio and you fall asleep and the next day you remember everything that was on the radio and it's stuck in your brain.
>
> Geraldine

> The kids might not understand it then but they might kind of hang around; If kids keep getting messages like that, even if they don't really notice it, you keep reading the books ... they still get the messages. It will get stuck in their memory.
>
> John

These quotations are part of an ongoing conversation that took place in a Year 5, 6, 7 composite class over several weeks. The impetus for the discussions was the teacher's question, 'Should we read *Counting on Frank* to little people?' (Clement, 1990). Geraldine and John were part of a classroom literacy culture where their teacher, Josie McKinnon, asked students to consider the kinds of social realities constructed in texts. In this article I describe practices from two classrooms where teachers are exploring versions of critical literacy.

Critical literacy, literacy and empowerment, literacy and justice (Edelsky, 1991), explicit teaching (Delpit, 1988), Garth Boomer's epic teacher (1989), postmodern literacy pedagogy (Bigum and Green, 1992) are key descriptors to launch literacy educators into the nineties. In 1991 the AJLL included a feature issue on critical literacy and another focus issue with this title is planned for later this year. In Brisbane in July 1992 a working conference on critical literacy was held at Griffith University. Increasingly educators are writing about literacy and literacy pedagogy in critical discourses (see, for example, *Discourse* volume 12, number 2).

Tertiary educators are being challenged to develop critical social literacy in their pre-service training of teachers (Christie, 1992). Critiques of process approaches and whole language are multiple and varied as educators rush to join the new critical literacy club (see Comber, 1992). However, as the working conference on critical literacy signalled in its title, what critical literacy is or how it is to be constructed are still very much matters of contestation. That critical literacy remains problematic and changing is perhaps exactly as it should be as long as teachers are part of the debate. We need to document multiple cases of critical literacies developed in different contexts.

My interest is in the ways in which teachers construct different versions of literacy and pedagogies from competing educational discourses. I asked a number of teachers what they understood by the term critical literacy and what kinds of classroom practices they thought exemplified critical literacy. One of my colleagues responded by making obvious the multiple definitions that already exist.

That's a tricky one. I understand it as many things a deliberate attempt to position thinking about curriculum and teaching into a more political context and away from unthinking social reproduction; or a new, higher-order level of response to texts (according to some authors anyway); or a way of reading/writing, e.g. reading against the grain, etc, etc.

Another teacher explained that critical literacy involves both consciousness-raising about the discourses of dominant cultures and taking action to resist, expose, and overturn these discourses. Others recalled the active construction of political literacy among peasants in South American societies.

In this paper I explore critical literacy in two primary school classrooms. My reason for focussing on primary classrooms is twofold. Firstly, much of the most illuminating writing about postmodern and critical literacy perspectives has come from educators working in tertiary and secondary contexts (Mellor and Patterson, 1991; Lee, 1991; Luke and Gilbert, 1991; Morgan, 1992).

While there has been a number of penetrating criticisms of primary school literacy pedagogies (Baker and Freebody, 1989; Luke, 1992; Baker and Davies, 1992; Martin, 1984) there have been few classroom descriptions of possibilities for critical literacy in the early years of schooling. Secondly, I want to question any suggestion that critical literacy is a developmental attainment rather than social practice which may be excluded or deliberately included in early literacy curriculum. I hope that the National English Profile will create possibilities for critical literacy in the early years of schooling and not endorse it only for higher levels.

Critical literacy can take many forms (Comber, 1992). In a selective review of literature, I identified three different principles guiding approaches to critical literacy. In classrooms where a critical literacy position is advocated, teachers:

1   Reposition students as researchers of language;
2   Respect student resistence and explore minority culture constructions of literacy and language use;
3   Problematise classroom and public texts.

The teachers whose work is described here have initiated students into a socially critical approach to literacy by problematising texts. In exploring their practices I want to consider some of the following questions about classroom cultures of critical literacy.

What kinds of conversations will children be having about texts?
Whose voices will be heard in these classrooms?
What kinds of questions will teachers be asking?
What kinds of tasks will teachers be setting?
What kinds of knowledge and representations of reality in texts will be contested?

As a starting point for understanding how teachers can help students to become critical readers I find it useful to refer to Freebody and Luke's (1990) descriptive framework of readers' roles. They explain:

> (A) successful reader in our society needs to develop and sustain the resources to adopt four related roles: code breaker ('how do I crack this?'), text participant ('what does this mean?'), text user ('what do I do with this here and now?'), and text analyst ('what does all this do to me?')

Freebody and Luke (1990) argue that text analysis is part of what successful readers do along with other roles. In the early years of schooling students learn what it means to read and write successfully in terms of school practices. They need opportunities to take on this text-analysis role from the start, as a part of how our culture defines literacy, not as a special curriculum in the later years of schooling or in media studies.

The decisions authors make in books for children

Jenny O'Brien is a junior primary teacher in a suburban disadvantaged school in South Australia. She is constructing literacy events with her five to eight year old students which are infused with her understanding of critical literacy. In particular she works on problematising the texts which children read and the texts which she reads to the class. Here I consider the literacy events that O'Brien constructs in the classroom and what this offers these students in their first experiences of school literacy.

Drawing on insights from Freebody and Baker (1989) O'Brien changed the kinds of ways she talked about texts in her junior primary classroom and the ways in which she encouraged students to read texts. Instead of asking children what they think of a story or which characters are their favourites or what they like best O'Brien encourages the children to consider the text as a crafted piece in which authors make decisions to represent realities in certain ways. Over several terms children were asked questions such as the following:

What do writers say about girls, boys, mothers and fathers in the books you read?
What do adults think that children like to read about?

O'Brien recorded children's responses to these questions on charts as they read numerous and varied texts. After reading *Counting On Frank* (Clement, 1990) she asked the children the following questions:

If you knew about families only from reading this book what would you know about what mothers do?
What would you know about what fathers do?

Students were asked to look for the constructions of reality depicted in texts. O'Brien emphasised through her questions and tasks that writers and illustrators make decisions about what to portray. They could have depicted other kinds of mothers, teachers, fathers, foxes, boys, girls. Even though many of these children had not yet mastered their roles as codebreakers they were already being invited to participate in a critical literacy curriculum where authors' crafting was not simply admired but also disrupted in terms of the versions of reality that were represented. Children were invited to show how they understood the writers' constructions of characters. For example, across a range of tasks O'Brien asked the children to:

Draw a witch like the one in this story.
Draw a different witch.
Draw the mean characters in this story.
Draw different mean characters.
Draw a different Mrs. Fox helping to save her family. Use speech bubbles and labels to show what she could say and do to save her family.

Draw the farmer as he is shown in the text.
Draw a farmer that Michael Morpurgo could have shown in the book.
Draw and label the sort of father Diana Coles showed the king to be in the novel.
Draw and label a different kind of father the king could be.

O'Brien has developed a simple approach to text analysis with very young students. Listing the tasks here does not do justice to the kinds of talk around text O'Brien made possible, but it does show how the tasks that she set for children prevented texts being taken as neutral or natural representations of the world. It also indicates how even in the earliest days of schooling teachers might create a space for children to interrogate the worlds of books. In emphasising the decisions that writers and illustrators make about what they include and how they depict it she has changed the kinds of discussions that students have about texts.

O'Brien did not reserve this kind of scrutiny for literary works. Recently the children analysed mother's day catalogues and junk mail using the following task guidelines for their reading and recording.

Draw and label six presents for mothers you expect to see in mother's day catalogues.
Draw and label some presents you wouldn't expect to find in mother's day catalogues.
What groups of people get the most out of mother's day?
Look through the catalogues. Draw and label six kinds of presents you can find in mother's day catalogues.
Draw and label the kinds of people who are shown giving the presents to the mothers.
Draw and label any presents you were surprised to find in mother's day catalogues.
Make two lists: how the mothers in the catalogues are like real mothers; how the mothers in the catalogues aren't like real mothers.
Make a new mother's day catalogue full of fun things.

This intensive examination of the catalogues offered the children an opportunity to consider a gendered cultural event and its connection with marketing and advertising. These young children became conscious that shopkeepers make the most out of mother's day. There were labelled drawings of Myer's and other major retailers. The children realised who pays for junk mail to be put in their letter boxes and what it is intended to achieve.

In O'Brien's classroom children also have opportunities to make a personal response to stories and to construct their own texts, but they do this aware that all texts are based on decisions about ways of presenting the world. Non-fiction texts are also examined in terms of what kinds of knowledge they present and what kinds of information are missing. The children are invited to discuss the kind of information that writers and publishers believe is appropriate for children to read.

In the literate culture that O'Brien is constructing the teacher's role as a mediator between child-reader and authorial text is altered. The sanctity of author is not preserved or romanticised. Rather the teacher acts as a broker in the children's interests to scrutinise the valued portrayals made. She has changed the kinds of questions she asks, the tasks that count as early literacy, and the readings that are possible. In this classroom children become aware that texts are socially constructed artefacts and vehicles for different kinds of reality presentations. O'Brien works with them to examine the 'natural' representations in stories and the versions of know-ledge authorised in non-fiction texts.

Allowing multiple reading and negotiating critical feedback

Josie McKinnon teaches in a disadvantaged Catholic primary school in an inner suburban area. Towards the middle of the first term she began to prepare her class for critically reading and evaluating the 1992 shortlisted books for the Children's Book Council of Australia Annual Awards. She started by having them read some of the nominated picture books that were commended in the 1991 list. She also read them a newspaper article about the shortlisted books for 1992, which pointed out that none of Paul Jennings' books was included on the list. What was valued in the awards was questioned and made problematic.

Because the class operated as learning partners with a junior primary class McKinnon had her students consider the extent to which texts were suitable for reading with that age group. In one session, debate arose about whether Counting On Frank (Clement, 1990) should be available in the school. The text depicts a boy who is very knowledgeable about all kinds of mathematical trivia and calculations. His skill eventually wins him a trip to Hawaii. The book is narrated from the point of view of this char-acter. Other characters include the boy's father, a TV addict; his mother, an inconsiderate cook who needs her son to help her do the shopping; and a large dog, who is featured in a number of the illustrations. The mother is shown in only one illustration where she is put with the boring grills she cooks every night! She is missing from the final illustration where the boy, father and dog, complete with dog food, leave for their holidays in Hawaii. The book award judges reviewed this book in the following way (1991):

Rod Clement's book is a work of inventive and creative origin-ality. His use of mathematical and creative ideas opens up discus-sions of concepts of space and estimation. The thought processes of the little boy are reproduced very authentically through both text and illustration.... There is a lovely use of dead-pan humour throughout.... (p. 4)

The judges construct a narrator who develops a life of his own. We are even told that the little boy's thought processes are 'reproduced authentically'. The judges contribute to a response to literature that naturalises the world of the text as a version of reality. The only criticisms made by the judges were of a misspelling not picked up during the proof-reading, and the disadvantages of high gloss paper. No mention was made of the ways in which characters conform to stereotypes.

McKinnon decided to spend time on this text. In particular she asked the students to consider whether it was a book that they would want to share with their learning partners in the junior primary. Conscious of her influence on previous discussions she decided to remove herself from the talk and set up the discussion as a class meeting. Each speaker was nominated by the chairperson, Sarah. In describing this extended literacy event I include segments of transcript of a class meeting to illustrate the kinds of talking that went on over a period of weeks.

Sarah: The first item on the agenda is *Counting On Frank*.

John: It's a funny book ... and if the mother had been in there more and been a nicer person it'd be much better and I think much more enjoyable.

Ellie: I don't think the book should be used in the library because it's kind of s ... saying to kids like it's kind of sexist and I don't think that's how the world should look; it should be more non-sexist.

Kelly: Um I don't think this book is very good because the father's always saying, If you've got a brain use it; but then again he's never using his brain in the story or you know he's not, he's sort of making a point, and then sort of, and then not doing it himself.

Mary: It's sort of saying that um fathers just sit around and watching TV and laughing at the house, and mothers cook for them meals and make you go shopping with them and cart the trolley around. It's not very ... positive, of mothers.

John: I think that like that kid's really square and it means like if you're smart you're square. It's just putting smart people down cos I mean none of them are dressed or anything like ... respectable ... like it's a bad attitude to people ... saying like it doesn't matter, like it might upset Dad or something.

Geraldine: I think it's saying that only the ... like it is a very traditional book and I don't think that's very good, but it's also saying that if you've got a lot of time at home you could calculate it all. I mean I couldn't calculate all that like I couldn't know that

24 dogs would fit in my bedroom or anything and I think it would disappoint the little kids if they couldn't calculate it either.

Quyen: The mother doesn't go on holidays. That's just saying that the mum is just stays home to cook and do the housework.

Ellie: I think the pictures are good the kids might you know think they were really good but I think maybe that they should try and get another message across in the book. It's stupid.

Renee: I think that at the end it's really stupid because it's saying like, 'Oh leave mum home, she doesn't mean anything except for cooking and she has to look after us,' but it's like the dog is more important and it has to come everywhere and the dog food has to too.

Ann: I reckon that when you first look at the book you think it's funny and it doesn't give that impression afterwards except if you look into it a bit more then you start to see what it's actually saying about parents and their personalities.

Geraldine: Yeh, your brain would have taken it in, like if you just read the book, another book which is the same storyline or something, ah your brain will just take it in unconsciously; and you just read it like, 'Oh the Mum's staying home and she cooked terrible meals and blah blah, blah.' That's funny, isn't it? You mightn't take it in, you know, serious; and you wouldn't know that you would and it might come up somewhere else, like you're listening to the radio and you fall asleep and the next day you remember everything that was on the radio and it's stuck in your brain. . . .

Josie: Do you mean like sub-conscious messages?

Geraldine: Yeh.

Mark: Well I think um it's OK to read it to little kids because um sort of like they, they don't they wouldn't really be able to pick that kind of stuff. They just think it's meant to be funny. Because they're not adults to pick up that kind of stuff yet. It might give them sub-conscious messages but they don't really know a lot . . . about stuff yet. They're just learning how to talk, well not talk um write and stuff.

Ellie: Um well in one way I mean it is true that some people are still really traditional and I mean that's just maybe someone's life, you know the story of their life.

Mary: What Mark said about the book and how it's funny story. . . . Even though they think it's a funny story they will actually look at the pictures and say, 'My mum cooks food like that,' it's boring like in the book.

John: Um what Mark was saying and Geraldine was saying, the kids might not understand it then but they might kind of hang around and. . . . If kids keep getting messages like that, even if they don't really notice it you're still just if . . . you keep

reading the books ... they still get messages, it will get stuck in
their memory.

The students in McKinnon's classroom have been asked to make a decision
about the appropriateness of a text for their younger co-students. It is not a
hypothetical task, but constructed in the social reality of their lives. Their
teacher has created a space for different kinds of readings in previous discussions about the ways in which writers construct realities. The students
responded to the virtual absence of the mother-character in the text and the
put-downs that she receives both obliquuely and directly. John also pointed
out his problem with the main character, a brainy boy, being square. Some of
the students worried that for the younger children it might be difficult to distinguish between the view of families constructed by the narrator and their
own lived realities. Different students' readings foreground their problems
with each of the main characters. It is not only the treatment of the mother,
but the father and son represent different kinds of stereotypes, the lazy dad
and the brainy but square son. The students' collaborative re-reading of the
text begins to reveal a different kind of story than the one they first laughed at.

At the end of a lengthy series of discussions where students argued for
many different readings of the book, the class decided to write to the author
to raise some of their unresolved concerns and questions. The discussions that
followed about the most appropriate way to critique the published work of a
writer led to talk about grammar, wording, tactfulness, layout. What you can
say and what you cannot and how you say it, became central questions for a
group of volunteers who worked on a draft. The principal became the final
editor as the volunteers wanted their letter to go out with the school's name
attached, realising it might then be read more seriously than a response from a
group of unknown individuals. The principal showed them the changes that
needed to be made to their text and explained why these were necessary.

The lengthy discussions that McKinnon allowed, the numerous close re-
readings, the question about the suitability of a book for younger children
and finally the taking action by writing to the author meant that this group
of students began to realise that it was possible to read texts in multiple
ways and that it was possible to construct critical feedback. Books and
authors could be questioned. This was not always easy. Mark resisted this
new approach and argued consistently over a number of discussions that it
was taking the book too seriously to treat it in this way and that young
children wouldn't even notice anyway. Some discussions reached the point
where the teacher felt they were getting onto dangerous ground because
they were beginning to explore ethical and moral questions and she was
unsure how to proceed. This raises some questions about where teachers'
reading of texts fits in a critical literacy curriculum, and what teachers
might do with the debates and contradictions that emerge. We need more
accounts of the ways in which practitioners deal with these questions.

Creating spaces for critical literacy

Critical literacy needs to be continually redefined in practice. The sketches provided here are limited, in that they can indicate only partially how these teachers are attempting to construct classroom cultures of critical literacy. These glimpses may be useful to practitioners new to this term. The following unfinished list of questions represents my attempt to monitor my own work in terms of the spaces I create for text analysis.

Do I:

- create opportunities for critically reading the media's versions of education, schools, students, teachers and literacy?
- create opportunities for critically reading department of education and Commonwealth policy documents and profiles?
- create space for disruptive readings and multiple readings of set texts?
- demonstrate critical text analysis?
- demonstrate how to construct critically social texts?
- use metatextual tools to scrutinise the constructed nature of texts?
- research the ways in which critical readers, writers and speakers operate in different contexts?

In thinking about what critical literacy might be like in classroom practices, I keep returning to the question:

'If you only knew about literacy from being in this classroom what would you think it was for?'

The development of critical literacy for educators

Over the last year I have searched in our newspapers for articles which present a positive view of schooling, literacy achievement and the work of teachers. However such journalism is rare. Rather recent media headlines include such as the following:

'School system a certified debacle'
'Literacy problems a barrier to output'
'Education chief admits school violence growing'
'Employers slam school training'
'Literacy languishes while the cult "elitists" linger'
'Young readers, writers just make the grade'
'Literacy test attacked as a stunt anyone can pass'
'SA's school system fails the test of time'.

We need to ask how teachers are positioned in these texts and why. If we begin to practise critical literacy on texts which construct the nature and effectiveness of our work it may then follow that we will pursue similar kinds of reading in classrooms. Professional associations might become advocates for the publishing of different kinds of headlines about literacy and education. It is time to practise critical literacy about the profession in the community to present alternative readings of teachers' work in schools.

References

Baker, C.D. and Davies, B. 'Literacy and gender in early childhood', *Discourse*, volume 12, number 2, 1992.

Baker, C.D. and Freebody, P. *Children's first schoolbooks: Introductions to the culture of literacy*. Oxford: Blackwell, 1989.

Bigum, C. and Green, B. 'Technologizing literacy: the dark side of dreaming', *Discourse*, volume 12, number 2, 1992.

Boomer, G. 'Literacy: the epic challenge beyond progressivism', *English in Australia*, 89, September 1989.

The Children's Book Council of Australia Annual Awards: Judges' Report, reprinted in *Reading Time*, volume 35, number 3, 1991.

Clement, R. *Counting on Frank*, Angus and Robertson, 1990.

Christie, F. and team members, *Teaching English Literacy:* a project of national significance on the preservice preparation of teachers for teaching English Literacy, August, 1991.

Comber, B. 'Critical Literacy: a selective review and discussion of recent literature', *South Australian Educational Leader*, volume 3, number 1, 1992.

Delpit, L. 'The silenced dialogue: power and pedagogy in educating other people's children', *Harvard Educational Review*, 58, 1988.

Edelsky, C. *With literacy and justice for all: rethinking the social in language and education*, The Falmer Press, 1991.

Freebody, P. and Luke, A. 'Literacies Programs: debates and demands in cultural context', *Prospect: Australian Journal of ESL*, volume 5, number 3, 1990.

Luke, A. 'Stories of social regulation: the micropolitics of classroom narrative', in B. Green (editor), *The Insistence of the letter: Literacy and curriculum theorizing*, Falmer Press, 1992.

Luke, Allan and Pam Gilbert (guest editors), *Discourse*, special Issue: 'Australia Discourses on Literacy'.

Luke, A. and Gilbert, P. 'Reading gender in a teacher education program', *English in Australia*, 95, March, 1991.

Lee, A. 'Reading the differences', *English in Australia*, 95, March, 1991.

Martin, J. 'Types of writing in infants and primary school', in L. Unsworth (editor), *Reading, Writing and Spelling*, Proceedings of the fifth Macarthur Reading and Language Symposium.

Mellor, B. and Patterson, A. 'Reading character: reading gender', *English in Australia*, 95, March, 1991.

Morgan, W. 'Truth or dare: the challenge to literature in critical theory and textual practice', *Opinion*, volume 21, number 2, 1992.